Armeno-Turcica

Indiana University Uralic and Altaic Series
Denis Sinor, Editor
Volume 164

Armeno-Turcica

SELECTED STUDIES

Edmond Schütz

Indiana University
Research Institute for Inner Asian Studies
Bloomington, Indiana
1998

Library of Congress Catalog Card Number: 98-65446
ISBN: 0-933070-43-8

CONTENTS

PART II   Linguistic Studies

PART III   Historical Studies

This volume contains *xii* + 420 pages.

PREFACE

The selection of articles appearing in this volume as well as their grouping under three headings was made by Professor Edmond Schütz himself. However, his goodwill did not extend to include the writing of a preface to this volume; the articles should speak for themselves, he argued, though, I suspect that a certain reluctance to write anything that is not scholarship might have played a role in the decision.

Born in Hungary in 1916 and a Turcologist by training, quite early in his scholarly life, Professor Schütz developed an interest in Armenian literature, history, and linguistics and became a pioneer of Armenian studies in his native land. He was also instrumental in establishing close relations between the Hungarian and Armenian academies. He was elected to an external membership in the latter.

Close ties link him to Indiana University, which he first visited in 1962 and where, over the years, in the Department of Uralic and Altaic Studies, he taught several classes on Turcology. Since his meticulous scholarship goes hand in hand with considerable personal charm, he has remained a welcome presence on the Bloomington campus. Essays of his appeared already in volumes 3, 134, and 145 of this series. The last of these is No. XIV of this volume.

I consider it a privilege to include this selection of Professor Schütz's articles in our *Indiana University Uralic and Altaic Series,* and I express my thanks to him and to all those who gave permission for their reproduction.

Denis Sinor

PART I

ARMENO-KIPCHAK STUDIES

ON THE TRANSCRIPTION OF ARMENO-KIPCHAK

BY

E. SCHÜTZ

Nearly half a century has passed since the first publication of Kipchak literary records in Armenian script[1] yet it was only later that J. Deny stressed their fundamental importance for comanistic studies. J. Deny's paper[2] aroused the interest of scholars, and this resulted in the publication, in recent years, of several Armeno-Kipchak texts that could be found in different countries.[3]

Following this impetus, increased attention has been devoted to the significance of Armeno-Turcica, it will be, therefore, perhaps not without interest to make a cursory survey, from the Armenistic point of view, of the relevant and still up-to-date text editions and treatises.

The first report of scientific value in the Armenistic literature on our subject was written by the Venetian Mekhitarist, Minas Bzhshkiants[4] whose work has conserved fundamental and unique data concerning the scattered and assimilated Armenian colony of Podolia. M. M. Bzhshkiants wished to acquaint the dispersed Armenians with the history of the destruction of Ani[5] and the dispersion of the Armenians, and in this connection he gave a detailed description, based on investigations on the spot, of the Armenian colonies in Eastern Europe. In 1808, he visited the Armenians of Transylvania, Moldavia, Bolgaria, in 1820 he went to Galicia, Tataria Minor (Novo-Rossia) and Tauria (Crimea).

Speaking of the Armenian cultural monuments, M. Bzhshkiants describes the Armenian magistrative-judicial, ecclesiastical-administrative and religious

---

[1] The historical and linguistic background of the question was outlined by F. Kraelitz-Greifenhorst as early as 1912 who also gave the Armeno-Kipchak translation of a psalm for a sample *(WZKM XXVI*, pp. 307—324). He pointed out the close relation of Armeno-Kipchak to the Coman *(op. cit.* pp. 312—313), but the major work he planned to write on this subject has never been published.

[2] *JA* July—Sept. 1921, pp. 134—135.

[3] The works of T. I. Hrunin, J. Deny, M. Lewicki and R. Kohnowa.

[4] The vicar of Tauria.

[5] = Bagratid Armenia.

I

documents written in the "Tatar" language which he came across in Lvov and
Kamenets and even publishes excerpts from some of them. This rich Armeno-
Kipchak material has since passed, in its major part, into libraries in Poland,
to Kiev, into the libraries of the Mekhitarists of Vienna and Venice, the
Bibliothèque Nationale and other libraries. We are still far from knowing
all the documents in the public libraries all over the world and in private
possession. M. Bzhshkiants himself complaints that many codices have been
lent to readers and have never been restored.

These codices have been repeatedly mentioned in Armenistic literature,
for the most part with reference to M. Bzhshkiants, but the Armeno-Kipchak
linguistic documents have been looked upon by Armenian philologists rather
as some sort of curiosities and were considered beyond the limits of Armenistics
in the strict sense of the word.

While editing the well-known law-book of Mekhitar Gosh compiled in
the 12th century and widely used during the subsequent centuries, V. Zh.
Bastamiants was concerned also with the Paris manuscript of the Armeno-
Kipchak translation[6] but, as he writes in the preface to the critical edition,
his knowledge of Azerbaijani helped him precious little in coping with this
language, nor was the assistance of an Armenian student from Constantinople
with his knowledge of Osmanli any more useful, because of the "corrupt style"
of the text.

V. Zh. Bastamiants ignores M. Bzhshkiants' reports and believes that
the translation of the law-book was meant rather for the Crimean Armenians
living in Tatar environment.[7]

H. K. Kushnerian who in 1883 went on a pilgrimage to the famous
image of the Virgin at Kamenets, in his report on the journey mentions the
Tatar language of the Podolian Armenians (of Kamenets): "From the end of
the 16th century. . . until 1625 (sic!) they exchanged their smooth Armenian
language for the rude language of the Tatars who ravaged and destroyed their

---

[6] *Da'astanagirk' Hayoc'*, Vałaršapat 1880 pp. 48—50.

[7] Kh. Samuelian also seems to share this opinion. See Армянский судебник
Мхитара Гоша. Yerevan. 1954. p. XXXIV. note 1.

Hitherto there is but *one* Armenio-Kipchak linguistic document figuring as of
"Crimean" origin, the one obtained from Crimea by abbé François Sevin collecting
oriental manuscripts in 1728—1730 in Constantinople for the Paris royal library (Sevin's
letter of Dec. 2, 1729, to the minister Maurepas, *apud:* Fr. Macler, *Catalogue* p. XIV).
Since the codex is not included in Macler's catalogue, it cannot be ascertained whether
it was originally written in Crimea or obtained from Podolia. This question can hardly
be solved until the whole Armeno-Kipchak material is collected, the material known
so far comes at any rate from Podolia. Neither Bzhshkiants nor Kushnerian makes
mention of such records either from Crimea or from among the codices the Armenians
settled in 1778 in the Yekaterinoslav province had taken along, though both of them
visited these Armenian colonies.

I

homes".[8] Judging by these words, H. K. Kushnerian must have had rather superficial information on the Kipchak language of the Podolian Armenians which he regarded as that of the Mongol-Tatars.

One of the principal works in Armeno-Kipchak research for the Armenologists is Gh. Alishan's edition of sources.[9] This contains the annals of Kamenets-Podolsk in Armenian from 1430 to 1611, in Armeno-Kipchak from 1611 to 1624 and again in Armenian from 1649 until 1652, as well as the relevant colophons written in the Podolian Armenian colonies and the pastoral letters of the Armenian Catholicoses. It is to Alishan's credit that he took the greatest care in publishing this linguistic material which was but partly intelligible to him. He was well aware of the historical value of the text, and in one of his comments refers even to the necessity of a translation: "For those knowing Turkish this language is not unintelligible if no Polish and [other] foreign words are mixed with it ; yet if someone is versed in both [languages], he can easily translate it into our language or any known European language".[10] The Armenian material of the *Kamenits* was indeed made use of in works on the dispersion of the Armenians, yet the Armeno-Kipchak part has not yet been given a comprehensive linguistic treatment as a whole. J. Deny did make an attempt to make up for this deficiency but his above-mentioned edition relies only on the fragmentary Paris manuscript.[11]

The catalogues of Armenian manuscripts are important aids in the investigation of Kipchak texts. Owing to the abundance of Armeno-Kipchak texts in Vienna, as well as to the scientific description of the codices, foremost importance should be attributed to H. Y. Tashian (Dashian)'s catalogues covering the manuscripts of the Vienna Hofbibliothek (Vienna 1891) and of the Mekhitarist library (Vienna 1895).

For the description of Armenian manuscripts in some European libraries and private collections we are indebted to Fr. Macler. His lack of knowledge in Turkology, however, impeded him in giving a thorough description of the Kipchak material ; for his catalogue of the Armenian manuscripts kept in the Bibliothèque Nationale he borrowed the short descriptions of the Kipchak documents from abbé Martin's hand-written catalogue. Fr. Macler was the one to call attention to the only extant Armeno-Kipchak printed book known so far, a prayer book published in 1618 in Lvov, the *Alyyš bitiki*.[12]

---

[8] *Patmut'iwn gałt'akanut'ean Xrimu hayoc'* (The history of the Crimean Armenian colony). Venice 1895 p. 197.

[9] *Kamenic', Taregirk' hayoc' Lehastani ew Řumenioy* (Kamenits, the Chronicle of the Armenians of Poland and Rumania), Venice 1896.

[10] *Ibid.* p. 67.

[11] In his publication J. Deny never refers to Gh. Alishan's edition of the complete Venice manuscript.

[12] Prepared for publication by the author.

I

Macler's catalogue of Armenian manuscripts compiled in 1925 in Lvov registers a period of transition.[13] Some of the items listed can be found in the manuscript collections of different libraries in Poland.

K. Roszko has recently given a good description of the Armenian (including Armeno-Kipchak) manuscripts in Poland.[14] The list in volume XXI of the *RO* (p. 156) may be regarded as a supplement to it for the Armeno-Kipchak material.

Furthermore, the exploitation of the Armeno-Kipchak manuscripts requires a thorough study of the contemporary cultural conditions of the Podolian Armenians. In this field N. Akinian has made important contributions having written the biography of the most significant notary of the Armenians in Lvov, Minas Tokhatetsi, and having published the philological edition of the "Travels" of scribe Simeon of Poland.[15]

The study of the history of the Podolian and Moldavian Armenians has recently gathered considerable impetus in the Armenian SSR. A department for the relations with the countries of people's democracy has been organized in the Institute of History of the Armenian Academy of Sciences.[16] Quite a number of papers have already been published on the Podolian Armenians in the journals of the Academy of Sciences of the Armenian SSR.[17] Disregarding now, in compliance with the purpose of our review, the papers based on the Russian—Polish material, among the treatises in Armenology we mention L. Khachikian's paper[18] giving a good survey of the cultural life of the Podolian Armenians. He refers, among others, to the Kipchak part of the annals of Kamenets (pp. 73—74) but makes no mention of other monuments of the Kipchak language. Thus it remains an open question whether or not there are Armeno-Kipchak texts among the codices that had come from Podolia to the Matenadaran.

---

[13] *REA* VII. p. 94 *et seq.*

[14] *Catalogue des manuscrits arméniens et géorgiens*, Warszawa 1958.

[15] *Hing panduxt talasac'ner* (Five emigrant poets), Vienna 1921. — *Simēon dpri Lehac'woy ulegrut'iwn* (The travel accounts of scribe Simeon of Poland), Vienna 1936.

[16] [An important event right at the beginning of the activities of the department was the conference of Armenian and Ukrainian historians and philologists held in Yerevan (Oct. 23 to 26,1959.). Only brief reports have so far reached us on the discussions having paramount importance for our subject: Вопросы истории, 1960 no. 2. p. 220, Українский історичний журнал, 1960 no. 1. pp. 143—145, Telekagir, 1959 no. 11—12. pp. 129—133.]

[17] *Telekagir* (Известия АН Арм. ССР) and the *Patma-banasirakan Handes* (Историко-филологический журнал) started in 1958.

[18] *Haykakan galtavayrerə Ukrainayum XVI—XVII darerum* (The Armenian colonies in the Ukrain in the 16th and 17th centuries), in *Telekagir* 1954 no. 4, pp. 45—80.

I

The recently published Russian version of Hovhannes Kamenitsatsi's contemporary chronicle in a great help is studying the Kamenets chronicle.[19]

*

The rendering of a text with the characters of another language is necessarily a compromise, in which the phonetic system of the transcribed language can only be approximated to a certain degree. In case of the Kipchak texts in Armenian script the conditions of transcription are rather favourable since the differentiated system of the Armenian alphabet is more or less suitable for rendering the sounds occurring in the Kipchak language. Owing to the considerable amount and volume of the texts we may have good hopes of threshing out the problems in the orthography of the Armeno-Kipchak texts. The material published so far is in itself sufficient to permit a preliminary survey.

It is common knowledge that the Armenian orthography is particularly conservative and has changed but slightly since the 5th century to our days. Yet as a result of this conservatism the phonetical changes that have taken place during the past fifteen centuries have remained hidden, and in Armenian texts these deviations can be traced only by considering certain fluctuations in the spelling and the behaviour of the loan words.

The most important change that has taken place in the phonetic system of the Armenian language over part of the speech area is the "second Armenian Lautverschiebung". This is the most essential difference between the literary language of the Armenian SSR and the literary language of the Armenians who have fled west since the 11th century. From the standard language of the medieval Cilician Little Armenia there is an unbroken line leading to the phonetic system of the modern, so-called West Armenian literary language. Hence the Armeno-Kipchak texts of the 16th and 17th centuries represent an important stage between the two extremities of development and may prove useful in studying the development of the so-called West Armenian phonetic system.

On the other hand, viewed from the side of Turcology, the "second Lautverschiebung" (having affected the sets of explosives and affricates) as well as the phonetic system of the contemporary West Armenian literary language offer a possibility for the reconstruction of the phonetism of the Armeno-Kipchak linguistic documents. This fact was recognized at the earliest stage of research by the Turcologists studying the Armeno-Kipchak texts and was duly considered when creating the transcription systems used in text editions published so far.

---

[19] *Xot'ini paterazmi patmut'iwnə* (History of the Khotin war) in *Patma-banasirakan Handes* 1958 no. 2, pp. 258—286; for the relation of the two chronicles see E. Tryjarski's paper: *Przegląd Orient.* 1959 pp. 211—214.

I

Nevertheless, in some publications we come across phonetic values differing from the norms of "western" pronunciation. In the following we shall make an attempt at elucidating these cases.

In his fundamental publication, the only edition of texts of the spoken language so far, T. I. Hrunin adopts the above principle. In his phonetical comments of the text, however, he fails to give an unequivocal picture of some problems. He states, for instance, that ц is rendered by дца, дза, цо in the texts.[20] This should obviously be understood to mean that *j (dz)* is rendered by *š* while *g* and *š* are used for *c (ts)*. This is not very significant for the Kipchak because these sounds occur in the Ukrainian, Polish and Armenian words only. There might arise some misunderstanding from his remark that ча and че are used for denoting ч.[21] T. I. Hrunin in all probability refers to the phonetic values of *ç* and *ǯ*. In the latter case the generalization may be restricted to saying that the sound *č* is generally rendered by *ç* ; while *ǯ* might almost be regarded as a lapsus calami.[22]

Owing to the mixed use of the classical and modern western denominations of the Armenian letters, T. I. Hrunin's comments on the rendering of the sound *k* are again somewhat ambiguous as far as transcription is concerned. As he states *k*, in words with front vowels is represented by *q*.[23] This statement does not seem to be corroborated by the other linguistic documents where *q* and *p* occur both without distinction. Nor is it unimportant that in the Polish words with back vowels *k* is denoted only by *p*.[24]

As to the transcription system of the *Eph.* J. Deny inserts the sounds not reflected in the script, and omits the aspiration of *k* and *t*. — Since there is no facsimile in his edition, it seems indicated to draw attention to a few misspellings liable to suggest false conclusions. E. g. the sign of the plural: *ritşerleri* 3[4] (recte: *-lari*) ; *keçirdiler* 7[11] (r.: *-lar*) ; radical ending in voiceless consonant + initial consonant in inflectional ending: *kokda* 7[3], *ḫlïçdan* 7[10], *boluşgay* 9[12] (r.: *kokta, h[ï]lïçtan, boluşkay*) ; *χ: haçtï, haçïp* 4[13, 14] (write *ḫ* for *h*) ; verb forms: *edip şlatip* 2[19] (r.: *etip işlatip*), *edi* 9[20] (r.: *edir*), *edir* 11[16] (r.: *etip*), *etti edi* 10[5] (r.: *etip edi*), *olturur edi* 18[2] (r.: *olturup edi*), *angar* 5[3] (r.: *angdi*), *bar edi* 16[7],

[20] p. 95.

[21] Probably these Armenian denominations of letters reflecting no exact phonetic values may have prompted the editors of the *Dat.* to confound the phonetic values of the affricates.

[22] See below. — This phenomenon has been pointed out already by F. Kraelitz-Greifenhorst, *op. cit.* p. 312.

[23] T. I. Hrunin, *op. cit.* p. 95.; — Вопросы языкознания 1958 no. 6. p. 114.

[24] The above-mentioned regularity would among others make it advisable to distinguish the tenues and the tenuis aspirates in transcription which would also be useful as far as the history of Armenian orthography (and phonetical development) is concerned. Text editions in general neglect the aspiration. In the *Dat.* it is marked, though not with complete consequence.

I

20[11] (r.: *baredir*); inflectional ending, possessive personal suffix: *etkan songra* 3[6] (r.: *etkandan songra*), *pohrebda* 5[8] (r.: *-ga*), *tayfasï* 13[6] (r.: *-sïn*), *dinsizin* 15[19] (r.: *dinsizni*), *ayïna* 16[19] (r : *ayïnda*), *kunlarina* 19[12] (r.: *kunlarinda*), *babaslar* 19[13] (r.: *-larï*), *yandan* 2C[ₐ] (r.: *yanda da*), *songǧun* 20[4] (r.: *songǧusun*), *kişilar* 20[10] (r.: *-lari*), etc.

Among those who have hitherto published texts, M. Lewicki and R. Kohnowa have come up against the greatest difficulties in transcription because of all the Armeno-Kipchak documents the orthography of the *Dat.* adheres the most strictly to the classical Armenian spelling. The spelling system here adopted is not a very fortunate blend of transliteration and transcription. The reading is made rather difficult by the Armenian transcription uncommon in Turcology. Thus, for instance, the letter *ե* having the phonetic value of *j (je)*[25] is rendered by *e*, the letter *ը* by *ə*, while the sound *y*, when not reflected in the original (which is particularly frequent in this text), is not transliterated. Inadequate letters are frequent in the transcription, though of no serious consequence thanks to the excellent facsimile. The Armenian letters are tabulated alphabetically[26] for the most part with their Western Armenian phonetic values in Meillet's system. It would have been advisable to include *ֆ (f)* and *օ (o)* which have belonged to the alphabet since the Middle-Armenian period and to mark the different phonetic values some letters have in different positions. The authors ignore the "second Lautverschiebung" of the affricates. The erroneous transcription of *ծ* and *ձ* is not particularly disconcerting because the sounds *c* and *dz* do not occur in Kipchak words (but e. g. in Armenian words: *Հերձուածող* 177v[2, 9] = *herjoŭacoy*; recte: *hercvajoy*). The rendering of *ճ* by *č* is, however, somewhat misleading. The transcribed form of *ճան*, for instance, is throughout *čan* instead of *jan*. The letter *ջ* exceptionally occurring in some cases (and standing for *č*) is incorrectly rendered by *ǰ*: *Աւնունջի* (*Awnunǰi*, recte: *Onunči*) 156v[22]; *նեջիկ* (r.: *nečik*) 160v[15], 166r[6]; *օնջիկ* ('rzecznik') 190v[13]; *ջխար-* (r.: *čyҳar-*) 190v[16].

*

A peculiarity in the social-cultural life of the Podolian Armenians of the 16th and 17th centuries is that their standard language is the Kipchak. We know this from scribe Simeon's report concerning the first decades of the 17th century: "The Armenians of Lvov do not know the Armenian language but speak Polish and Kipchak, i. e. Tatar language".[27] This is supported by

---

[25] In my transcription I use K. Grønbech's symbols. — The meanings of Kipchak words are not quoted, unless they fail to figure in J. Deny's comprehensive glossary or in case of ambiguity.

[26] *Dat.* p. 253.

[27] N. Akinian, *Simèon*, p. 346.

I

Alembek's chronicle (1603—1605): „[Armeni] sacra in Ecclesia nativo ser-
mone semper peragunt, domi semper Tartarorum lingua utuntur".[28] But not
only their spoken language is Kipchak; this is the language in which their
official documents (protocols, minutes at tribunals), even the ecclesiastic ones
(marriage and birth certificates, wills *[diatʿik < διαϑήκη]*, marriage contracts
[grorenkʿ]), are drafted. Kipchak is used in ecclesiastic matters not only on
account of the population's requirements but also because the priests themselves
have but a scanty knowledge of Armenian. A satirical poem known as the
„Vipasanutʿiwn Nikolakan" says: "[The priests in Lvov] do not know
the Armenian language and do not understand what they read".[29] This is
corroborated by Vardan Hunanian (in a letter of his written to the Armenians
of Tokat in 1703): ". . .in those times the priests were very unlearned in erudi-
tion and inexperienced in the Armenian language, as the people themselves".[30]

Though this picture is characteristic of most priests of local birth, but it
cannot be generalized. However different the value of our Kipchak texts is,
they all testify to the fact that their scribes and translators mastered both
Armenian and Kipchak relatively well, and offer a fairly complete picture of
Kipchak phonetics.

In the Armeno-Kipchak texts of the 17th century that we had the opportunity to examine certain letters generally denote the same sound in whatever position they stand, a fact that indicates the standardization of the
Armeno-Kipchak orthography. On the other hand, in the script of the *Dat.*
we find several phonetic forms unusual in Armeno-Kipchak texts. Most of
these forms reveal no Kipchak linguistic properties but are rather characteristic of Armenian orthography. The discrepancies of spelling in the linguistic
documents are mainly due to the different degree in which the scribes mastered
the Armenian language, i. e. orthography.

In the following we wish to point out a few orthographical properties
deriving from the classical Armenian orthography (letters and letter groups)[31]
which will permit the exclusion of phonetic forms incongruent with the Kipchak
pronunciation, from the texts transcribed.

ւ (աւ, եւ, ոյ, իւ)

In the early days of Armenian written literature the sign ւ was presumably used to denote the semivocal *u (w)* and formed diphthongs with vowels.
At any rate there could be no great difference between the phonetic value of

[28] *RO* XXI p. 158.
[29] Gh. Alishan, *Kamenicʿ*, p. 202.
[30] *Ibid.* p. 127.
[31] The term "letter group" I apply to two characters closely linked historically.
The two letters had earlier represented a closer phonetic unit (e. g. diphthong), the
pronunciation of which was later modified, yet the letter group has survived.

I

ւ and that of *վ* because, beside the combinations *աւ, եւ (և)* and *իւ*, to *ո* the letter *վ* was joined. (The letters *ու* were used for *u* on the model of the Greek *ου*.) When not in preconsonantic position the pronunciation of *ւ* must have become the same as that of *վ* at a very early stage. In the period having now our attention the letter *ւ* in intervocalic and final position had the same value as *վ* which shows that its use is but an orthographical peculiarity.

աւ | In the Armeno-Kipchak texts the intervocalic and final *աւ* denotes av. This is the symbol for av throughout the *Dat.* (with the rare exception *Ճանաւար [ǰanavar]* 167v[3, 5, 7]). In the *Eph.* the letter group *աւ* is more frequent: beside *ալպաւուդ (alpavud)* 11[21], *ալպաւուն* 22[12]; *աւալ (aval)* 9[2]; but *Šayavat* invariably with *աւ, Սպանիաւատ (Stanislav)* 13[17]. The trend towards the standardization of the spelling shows up even in Armenian words: instead of *դաւիթ ('David')* we find *Թավիթ* 4[19]. — In the *AB* the word avaz is written *աւազ* in seven instances and *աւվազ* in one. (Since late Middle Armenian the sign *թաւ (t'aw)* ˜ has been used to stress the value v of *ւ* in manuscripts and later in print. Hence: *աւ̃ազ* 21[7]. In the Kipchak texts we have examined, the sign t'aw occurs in a few cases only.) The word *Šayavat* (the basis and in derivatives) is written nine times with *աւ*, seven times with *աւվ*.

In preconsonantic position the pronunciation of *աւ* became short open o as early as the end of the first millenium, and in Middle Armenian texts *աւ* and the new sign *o* are used alternately. In the transcription of foreign words and names, for instance: *Կաւատւ̃բրէ ('Godfried Bouillon') HChr.* 56[8, 17]; *Աւդն, Աւդոն ('Otto, German emperor') ibid.* p. 53 & passim. In words other than Armenian it occurs in initial position and in uncial writing only: *Dat. Աւլ (Ol)* 168r[17], 181r[12], 181v[4], 183v[11, 19]. (In the transcription erroneously: O; the authors were probably disconcerted by the sign ° used to stress the pronunciation of *Աւ* as o, a sign common in medieval Armenian texts.) But we have a correct transcription in *Աւշդայ (Ošta)* 159r[9], 163v[3]; *Աւհաննէս (Ohannes)* 211r[20] is missing in the transcription. — This sign in the uncial writing is maintained throughout the *AB* too: *Աւթուզ (Otuz)* 90[3], *Աւղլու (Oylu)* 113[11], *Աւթ (Ot)* 89[3], *Աւթլու (Oïtu)* 118[6] (but with a minuscule letter: *oթլու ibid.*), *ԴԱԻԳՐՈԻ (TOГRU)* 150[2].

եւ(և) | Of the letters for e only *ե* occurs in connection with *ւ* in the Armenian script (in case of minuscule letter in ligature *և*). In the Kipchak material open e + v have the sign *եւ*: evet in both *Dat.* and *AB եւեդ* passim; *Eph.* Kevorovic *բեւորովիզ* 1[19], 5[2]. The ligature *և* is used regularly in the Armenian words, in Kipchak words we find it seldom, e. g. in the *Dat.: դև (dev)* 167v[9, 11], 177r[22]. (This form of writing was probably suggested by the Armenian word *դև* of the same meaning [and origin].) In the phrase *պաշևուչու (baš-ev-učču,* erroneous transcription: *bašlovuču)* 169r[12] we have the Armenian conjunction

I

և (ew, jew) 'and'. In Kipchak hendiadyses the conjunction *ու (u)* 'and' is frequent. In our example *ու* is replaced by *և* in order to avoid cacophony. The pair *ու — և* permits the inference that in the mentioned hendiadyses we have to do with the Armenian conjunction *ու*.[32]

ով | In Kipchak texts the regular sign for *o* is *ո* though sometimes even *ո* occurs, without phonemic difference. The latter we come across most frequently in *ov*, but this is due to the close orthographical link between the elements of the letter group *ով* in Armenian orthography. In the *Dat.* it is frequent in the suffix groups *-ovuču, -ovlu* and also in *jiχov* which is always written *երխով*; further *jovuχ երյուխ, Krakov* ('Cracow') *քրաքով, Ilov* ('Lvov') *իլով, tolov թոլով*; in Kipchak morphologic pairs with *u — o : սուվ (suv* 'water') and *սով (sov), սուվ-* (suv- 'to love, like') and *սով- (sov-)* etc.

In the language of the scribes the pronunciation of *ո* in initial position was obviously *vo* (as in the New Armenian literary language) because this letter does not occur in this position. An exception to this is the case when — in compliance with the orthography of the Armenian literary language[33] — *ո* is followed by *վ*; in this case the initial *ո* is pronounced *o*. Accordingly, we find *ով* for *ov* also in initial position in the *Dat.: ով (ov), ովրանչիք (ovran-čik), ովրան- (ovran-), ովրազ-, ովրաթ- (ovrat-),* yet the sign *ov* also appears: *ովրաթ- (ovrat-)* 158r[21].

In the *Eph.* too the letter group *ով* is still frequent: *իլով (Ilov* 'Lvov') 1[11], 4[6], 20[21];[34] *երխով (jyχov)* 21[2], but: *չովրա (čovra)* 13[3], *Ֆոսքով (Moskov)* (six times).

In the *AB*, where an advanced standardization of the orthography can be observed, the letter group *ov* is used in the overwhelming majority of the cases. In initial and medial position its use is almost exclusive: *ov (ov), ովրանչիք (ovrančik), ովրազ-, ովրաթ- (ovrat-), ովուն- (ovun-), չովրա (čovra), սով- (sov-), սովակ (sovak), սովուք (sovuk), սովուն- (sovun-), սովունչլուք (sovunčluk)*; but *govda կովսա* ('body, corps') 135[15]. The same is found in the suffix groups *-ovlu, -ovsuz, -ovuči.* In final position, however, *ով* occurs still rather frequently: *ùրխով (byχov)* 93[4], but *ùրղով* 105[1], *իլով (Ilov)* frontp.[12], *juχov* ('church') is written five times with *ով* and five times with *ov*; *jyγov* ('id.') twice with *ով* and once with *ov*.

---

[32] Though in such hendiadyses even initial *ու* is generally preceded by the conjunction *ու*, this fact does not contradict the possibility of Armenian origin of this conjunction, because for the conjunction 'and' *ու* is used exclusively from Middle Armenian on. — For another interpretation see J. Deny, *Eph.* pp. 77—78.

[33] That is, without the restriction as in Polish Armenian: Hanusz, p. 22; Acharian, p. 38. Cf. Karst, p. 21, note 4.

[34] In 1[11] the transcription *Ilav* is a misspelling for *Ilov,* whence the conclusion drawn therefrom *(Eph.* p. 88) is void.

I

The alternate occurrence of the Kipchak *ov* ~ *uv* (e. g. *suv* ~ *sov*, *ovran-* ~ *uvran-*) may suggest the assumption that the use of the letter group of *ուֆ* would perhaps indicate a shift of the pronunciation toward *uv*,[35] yet on realizing that also the unequivocal *ov* is often rendered by *ուֆ*, further that this letter group occurs in any position and that the standardization of orthography entails a preference for *ոֆ*, it becomes obvious that this phenomenon should be looked upon only as an Armenian orthographic peculiarity.

Should the dialectal pronunciation of a preconsonantic *ու* happen to be something like *ov*,[36] this does not necessarily mean the decomposition of the letter group *ու*, but merely indicate that the first element in the sound group is but an inserted vowel. Thus the word *Նուիրակ Eph.* 4[19], *novirag* in the glossary should be read rather *n(ə)virag*. The correct reading of *սիմէոն ու աննայ (Simeon Ovanna) Dat.* 179v[14] is *Simeon u Anna* ('S. and A.'). *Čowap* 157r[11], *čuvap* 169v[12], *čovap* 175v[2] standing in the transcription of the *Dat.* for *ճուապ* should be corrected into *ǰuap* pronounced with a hiatus (cf. *CC joap*).

___*իւ*| The letters *իւ* in Old Armenian must have denoted originally the sound group (diphthong) *iw*. In the course of the development of the language — with the coincidence of the values of *ւ* and *ֆ* — in prevocalic and final position it has conserved its pronunciation *iv* up to our days. Before consonants (i. e. in closed syllable also at the end of the words) it turned into a rising diphthong *i̯u*.

The history of the pronunciation of *իւ* has not yet been worked up, and their value in Middle Armenian deduced by Karst[37] cannot be regarded as covering all possibilities. This sound group i. e. diphthong has generally become monophthongal *(u, e, i)*. The pronunciation *ü* beside *u* may be regarded as proven, though the example *կիւռ* is not conclusive because it may be an earlier borrowing with sound replacement, its medieval re-adoption being *կիր*, on the basis of the contemporary Greek pronunciation.[38] The picture ignores the "traditional" pronunciation *ju* which can presumably be traced as far back as this period, and it is highly probable that many *իւ* signs conceal a *ju* with sound replacement.

In modern West Armenian literary language the preconsonantic *իւ* is pronounced *ju*, *i̯u*, *jü*, *ü*.[39]

In the Armeno-Kipchak texts here investigated *իւ* (occurring only in preconsonantic position) denotes *ju*. In the *Dat.* the phonetic value *ju* is ren-

---

[35] For Middle Armenian cf. Karst, p. 21.

[36] Cirbied, *Gramm. arm.* p. 651.

[37] Op. cit. pp. 22, 66, 118.

[38] Hübschmann, *Arm. Gramm.* p. 357.

[39] F. Feydit, *Manuel de langue arm.*, Paris 1948. p. 13.; A. Abeghian, *Neuarm. Gramm.*, Berlin—Leipzig 1936, p. 21.

I

dered by *ի* in the majority of the cases. In the second syllable *ju* is invariably
written *ի*: *bujur-* 27 times *պուիւր-*, *bujurul-* twice *պուիւրուլ-* (but cf.
p. 154 *bujruχ*: *պոյրուխ*). The same applies also to the initial position in most
cases: *իւրաք* (*jurak*) 161r[8], 190v[2], *իւզլու* (*juzlu*) 170r[13]. The situation
is, however, complicated by the inclination of the copyist to use *ե* for the initial
j-. This has yielded the following variants, in which the sound *j* has a double
representation: *եիւք* (*jjuk*) 187r[17], *եիւխու* (*jjuχu*) 160v[15], *եիւկուն-* (*jju-
gun-*) 175v[20]. The frequently recurring word *juz* appears three times as *իւզ*
and four times as *եիւզ*. The fluctuation of orthography becomes obvious when
the two different kinds of spelling occur in one and the same line: *եիւզդայ իւզ*
(*jjuzda juz* 'face to face').

Beside the standardized form *ճուվ-* (*juv-*) (4th line) in Kraelitz's publication we find *իւրաք* (*jurak* lines 13 and 20), *իւզ* (*juz* line 14). In the
Eph.: *ճուզ* (*juz*) 9[13]. In the *AB* — in course of the orthographical standardization — we find almost invariably *ճու* in initial position and *յու* in medial
position for *ju* : *juban-* : *ճուպան-* 27[4], *juχla-* : *ճուխլա-* three times, *juχov*
always with *ճու*, *ճուխու* (*juχu* 'dream') 27[1], *juk* and derivative forms:
ճուք(-), *juv-* five times *ճուվ-*, *juz* 12 times *ճուզ*. In medial position: *bujur-*
invariably *պույուր-*. On the other hand, *juru-* : *ճուրու* 121[8], 135[10], but
իւրու 47[2], *jurak* 23 times plus its derivatives: *ճուրաք(-)* but *իւրաք* 146[15].[40]

It follows from our examples that in the above cases *ի* cannot be read *ü*
(which would yield *ürak*, *üzlu*, *üz*).[41] Hence this cannot be judged by the same
standard as the renderings *ի* = *ü* to be attributed to the influence of the
Armenians of Turkey.[42]

Ը

The Kipchak velar *i* (*y* in our transcription) is rendered by the closest
related *ը*. But in the first syllable, in some suffixes and inflectional endings
in writing it is often omitted. The problem of the representation of this sound
varies with the different texts. In the texts tending toward "phonetic" transcription and thus departing from the classical Armenian orthography most
of the *y* sounds are represented (by *ը*), except mostly in cases when one of the
sounds in the first or last syllable is a liquid (e. g. *իլիկ*; *-լխ*, *-ումր*). In these
cases the editors of these texts fail to give an equivalent to *y* in transcription,
except for J. Deny who marks it by *(ı)* or without brackets or, in some cases,

[40] As we have seen in other connections, the classical orthography was conserved
latest by the uncial writing.
[41] *Eph.* p. 83 sub: *yuz.* — Consequently, it is rather an orthographical feature than
a phonetic development in Armeno-Kipchak, as is assumed in *Phil. Turc. Fund.* p. 83.
[42] J. Deny does not distinguish these two phonetic values though is plausible in
supposing that also the latter should be reckoned with. *Eph.* p. 19.

I

omits it.[43] In the orthography of the *Dat. y* is often absent, nor is it rendered by any sign in the transcription of the text, in accordance with the system of transliteration of the authors.

In Armenian *ը* is a mid-vowel assuming the timbre of its environment, pronounced with different intensity in different positions yet generally weakly, whence the tradition of neglecting it in writing. Under the impression of the written form of the words in which it occurs, the descriptive grammars gener-ally treat it as being a euphonic inserted sound. In many cases it can be demon-strated to derive from the reduction of vowels having full sonority (*ի, ու*) when these find themselves in unstressed position in consequence of inflection or word composition. In Armenian the consonant groups are no real clusters since there is in most cases some sound there reduced to *ə* (*ը*) which is not re-flected in writing. This phenomenon can not always be grasped etymologically, yet can at any rate be demonstrated already in Old Armenian.[44] In syllables originally containing *ի* or *ու* having become unstressed the reduction of the vowels to *ə* (*ը*) is a phenomenon still surviving. (Reduction must be distin-guished from the cases in which the sound simply falls out at the syllabic limits. See e. g. in Middle Armenian the dropping of *ա* in the medial position.) Reduction, however, often affects other sounds as well in Middle Armenian[45] and is a frequent phenomenon in dialects. In Podolian Armenian, for instance, any of the five principal vowels may be reduced to *ə*.[46] As to the group containing consonant + *r* in final position in this dialect, H. Acharian describes it as a local peculiarity,[47] though these forms were recorded by J. Hanusz most prob-ably under the influence of the written forms, and we are inclined to think that we have to do with a sound group containing: consonant + *ə* + *r*. (Cf. Armeno-Kipchak *-տըր* (*-dyr* 'is').

Further arguments in favour of the consonant clusters being merely orthographical are as follows: at the point of separation *ը* is inserted even if originally absent in script ; in poetical works *ը* always forms a syllable even if not marked ; medieval authors often use in writing *ը* even in prose texts. For Armenian words occurring in Kipchak texts the classical orthography is used in most cases, but in the *AB* the inserted letter *ը* often appears also in Arme-nian words, e. g.: *սըրբուհի* ('The Holy Lady') 109[2], *մըկըրտանել* ('baptize') 131[11], *նըշան* ('sign') 166[9].

On the basis of spelling of CC *iarlga*, etc. *l* and *r* in these cases are supposed to be voiced consonats in Cumanian. The above quoted Armeno-

[43] The unwritten *y* was, in his opinion, "sometimes, probably" not pronounced. *Eph.* p. 19.
[44] Hübschmann, *Chronologie*, p. 157 ; *Esquisse*, p. 53.
[45] Karst, pp. 55, 39.
[46] Hanusz, p. 93.
[47] Acharian, p. 32.

I

Kipchak examples seem to be of similar nature. It must, however, be remembered that in our texts the omission of *y* occurs also with other consonants, e. g.: *alyyš* and derivates in *Dat.* always *ալղշ*, (but *sayyš* and deriv. *սաղըշ*), *jalyyz* always *եալղզ*, *χysχa* once *խրսխա*, once *խսխա*, *tynčsyzlyχ* *թնչսզլխ* 164r[20], etc. In the standardized spelling of the *AB* the *y* (*ը*) is rendered in the majority of cases. But *-lyχ* is represented by *-լխ* in some 30 per cent of the cases; further *čyχar-* 8 times *չըխար-* twice *չխար-*, *jazyχ* 10 times *եազըխ*, 4 times *եազխ*.

Most of the examples seem to point rather to an Armenian orthographical phenomenon, but on basis of a certain consistency in omission we are inclined to think that the sonority of *y* in certain clusters was perhaps reduced (*ʸ*).

յ — ǰ, ǰ

Most of the orthographical, i. e. phonetical problems are connected with the letters used for *ǰ*, *ǰ*, and the pronunciation of the letter *յ*. In Old Armenian *ǰ*, *ǰ* were usually represented by *յ*. This use, however, was discontinued as early as prior to the Middle Armenian period.

    յ- | Losing its sonority and intensity the initial *ǰ* gradually turned into *h*. In Meillet's opinion the traces of the beginning of this process have been conserved in the initial *յ* of *յիսուն* 'fifty' and the initial *h* of *հինգ* 'five'.[50] The value *h* of initial *յ* in Middle Armenian is attested by cases of double orthography.[51] This seems to be supported by the fact that in medieval texts *հ* is sometimes found as a tentative spelling of the sound *ǰ* in foreign words, e. g.: in the chronicle of Grigor Akantsi[52] *jasaχ* : *հասախ* II[21], but *յասախ* XII[25, 43] or *ասախ* IV[44], XII[4]; *jarlyχ* : *հարլախ* VII[20]; *jaryuči* : *արղուչի* XII five times. The omission of *ǰ* shows that the common nouns that had soon become loan words shared the fate of the Armenian initial *յ*, i. e. its transformation through a weak *h* into a very weak, unmarked aspiration. (Since the Middle Armenian period *յ*, and sometimes *հ*, have been used also for denoting the secondary weak aspiration occurring before the original initial *ա* and *ո*.)

We find the same result in Podolian Armenian where the initial *յ* is pronounced either *h* or *ø* (here and there secondary aspiration also appears).[53] According to Acharian, the initial *յ* = *ø* in the Podolian and neighbouring dialects, while the words with an initial *h* (written) are literary adoptions.[54]

This *յ* is often left unrepresented even in the Armenian words occurring in Kipchak texts, e. g.: *ովան(ն)ēս (Ovan[n]es) Dat.* 180v[1, 4, 20], *Ոհաննēս*

[50] *Esquisse*, p. 30.
[51] Karst, p. 34.
[52] *HJAS* XII/3—4.
[53] Hanusz, p. 69.
[54] Acharian, p. 91.

I

(Ohannes) Dat. 211r[20]. In contemporary Armenian texts too, e. g.: ապե֊ թական *(apet‘agan* 'Japhetide'), այսմաւուրք *(ajsmawurk‘* 'martyrologium').[55] That is why it may seem to be more correct to denote the initial *յ* in the Kipchak texts by *h,* or by *‘* or to omit it altogether, that is to transcribe e. g. *Eph.* յունվար, յունիս, յովանէս, յակոբ as *hunvar, hunis, (H)ovanes, (H)agop* and not with an initial *j; Dat.* յարութի 177v[15], [19] should be transcribed rather *harut‘j(un)* than *yarut‘i(v)n.*

The contemporary initial *j* is represented by *ե.* For instance, in Minas dpir's colophon of 1565 the name of the papal legate sent to Lvov is written Ֆրանցիսքուս Եօհան(էս)[56] 'Franciscus Johannes'.

_____*յ* | The final *յ* was no longer pronounced in Middle Armenian and was therefore often omitted in writing as well.[57] Yet under the influence of the classical orthography — in proportion to the scribe's knowledge of it — it was adopted as a rule of spelling that final *ա* and *ո* (often even other vowels) might not stand without a final (mute) *յ* in foreign words either. Since in Armenian there was no *j* pronounced at the end of polysyllabic words, the problem of rendering the pronounced final *j* never arose. In case of loan words ending in *j* the scribe had no other alternative than to use the letter *յ* which, however, was not pronounced. This accounts for the fluctuation in the spelling of the foreign words ending in *j*. The *յ* was now used now omitted, yet of these cases no conclusion can be drawn as to the pronunciation of the final *j* in a foreign word. For instance the Mongolian name *Čayataj* is written Չաղատա by Kirakos Gandzaketsi[58] and Չաղատայ by Grigor Akantsi.[59] The two different ways of spelling cannot be regarded as a reasonable ground for the conclusion — as F. W. Cleaves states — that the ending represents a Mongolian *-ā*,[60] because what we are up against is nothing more than a characteristic feature of medieval Armenian orthography.

The use of the final mute *յ* is rather general in our Kipchak texts so that it coincides with the use of the *j* pronounced. The editors of the texts solve this problem by not transliterating the mute *յ*. This, however, may lead to many a controversy in transcription. Thus in the *Dat.* the mute *յ* is often represented while the pronounced *յ* is omitted. This is particularly embarassing in the case of the neg. opt. *մակայ (-magaj)* and the supine *մակա (-maga).* If in the original the pronounced *յ* is not written as, e. g. the opt. *-կա* in the *Eph.*,[61] it should be put down to mere inaccurateness in spelling.

[55] Akinian, *Hing,* pp. 155—156.
[56] *Ibid.* p. 65.
[57] Karst, pp. 22, 25, 60, 62—65.
[58] Ed. Venice 1865, Name Index.
[59] *HJAS* 1949, Name Index.
[60] *Ibid.* p. 418.
[61] *Eph.* p. 21.

I

The scribe of the *Dat.* (and other monuments) sometimes compensates the muteness of the final *ɟ* by writing two *ɟ* letters, e. g.: *այդմակայյ (ajtmagaj)* 178r[17], *պոլմակայյ (bolmagaj)* 162v[10], etc. but sporadically only.

_____ *ʼɟ, oɟ* | In Old Armenian the diphthong *oį* was represented by *ʼɟ*. This situation changed when in Middle Armenian the *ʼ* became more closed.[62] The combination *ʼɟ* assumed a new phonetic value before consonants,[63] such as, for instance, in foreign words: *պաղտունʼ* ('Baldouin'), *Լʼɟս* (Louis').[64] When in the 12th century the *o* was introduced to denote the open *o*, it became possible to write the diphthong *oį* in foreign words as *oɟ*.

The *oj, oį* is represented by *oɟ* also in the Armeno-Kipchak linguistic monuments with "standardized" orthography, invariably in every position i. e. either before vowel or before consonant, e. g.: in the *AB boj* : *պoɟ*, *χoj* ('sheep') *խoɟ*. *χoj-* ('to put') *խoɟ-*, *ojan- oɟanʼ-*. In the *AB uj* and *uį* are represented by *ʼɟ* (before both vowel and consonant), e. g.: *ujat- ʼɟատ-*, *bujruχ պʼɟրʼʼխ*, *bujruχči պʼɟրʼʼխʼ*.

In the *Dat.*, however, *oj* is more often written *ʼɟ* as against *oɟ*, e. g.: *χoj-* proportionally 26 times *խʼɟ* and 7 times *խoɟ* ; *boj* four times *պoɟ* and twice *պʼɟ*, *χojči խʼɟʼ* 179v[12]. The two ways of spelling in these cases are pu rely orthographical variations, the use of *ʼɟ* showing a conservative attachment to the accustomed letter group.

On the other hand, *bujruχ* is written ten times *պʼɟրʼʼխ* in the *Dat.* which should obviously be read with *uj* (according to the modern literary pronunciation), and not with *oj*. The fact that *χoj-* is spelt now *խʼɟ-* now *խoɟ-*, seems to contradict our opinion, but — as we think — no absolute consistency may be expected from a 16th century scribe. His style is characterized by the struggle of the traditional Armenian orthography with the standardizing tendency of adaptation to a foreign phonetic system.

The reading *bujruχ* is supported by several facts: *a)* in the *Dat.* itself we find once *պʼʼɟրʼʼխ* (164v[22]), *b)* the verbal stem is *bujur-*, *c)* the *AB* is unanimous in giving the reading *bujruχ*.

_____ *-ɟ-* | The weakening of initial, but mainly of final *ɟ* was not (or but partly) shared by the *ɟ* in medial position, having conserved its value *j*, *į* up to our days.

Most of the Kipchak *j* and *į* sounds are represented medially by *ɟ*, e. g.: *այախ (ajaχ)*, *այդ- (ajt-)*, *հայպատ (hajbat)*, *խայդ- (χajt-)* ; in falling diphthongs throughout.

[62] Karst, p. 21.
[63] At the end of polysyllabic words the letter *ɟ* became mute while in monosyllabic nouns the traditional pronunciation is *oj*.
[64] Karst, p. 25.

Of the rising diphthongs the *i̯a* is, however, often written *ѣա*, e. g. *dunja* almost throughout *տունեѣա*; *eja* in the *Dat.* *էѣա* (but in the *AB* *էյա*). This is presumably due to the early diphthongization of medial *ѣա* in Armenian. The representation is not consistent: *Dat.* *օյատ-* *(ojat-)* 160v[14], but *ուեատ* *(ujat)* 175r[6].

There is a fluctuation of spelling in the sound combination *i̯a*, e. g.: *Dat.* *bijan-* is throughout *պիѣան-*, *tijar* is *դիѣար* seven times and once *թիար*. *Tijasi(dir)* 'должно, soll' is represented by *դիѣասի*, *թիѣասի* nine times, by *դիասի* once and occurs nine times as *դիասի*, *թիասի*; or *nijat* (نیت) is twice *ѣնաթ* and three times *նիաթ*. The missing of the *j* does not necessarily involve the absence of *j* or *i̯*. In Armenian orthography the glide is not marked at the limit of compounds ending in *i*, e. g.: *ձիավոր* *(ci[i̯]avor* 'horseman'), *միամիտ* *(mi[i̯]amid* 'simple-minded'). In monographs on dialects the *i̯* is usually marked. The forms *ciavor, miamid* of these words were recorded by J. Hanusz and H. Acharian from the Podolian dialect obviously under influence of the written forms.

The glides in such groups of sounds as *i̯i̯y, yi̯i*, etc. is problematical. Inconsistent orthography may perhaps be due to varying pronunciation. E. g. *Dat.* *խըյն* *(χyjn)* 178r[23], but *խիյընլը* *(χi̯i̯ynly)* 162v[3]; *AB* *խըյն* *(χyjn)* 47[7], but *խըյըն* *(χyjyn)* 50[9] and six times *խըյին* *(χyjin)*. In addition to this, it would be important to investigate the question in connection with the present ending in *-ըѣր, -ѣըր* (or *-ѣѣր, -ըѣր*). (But we find also: *բազգըѣիրպվկղ* 192r[22] 'we write'.) The frequent dissimilation of *y*, resp. *i* makes the problem even more involved.

Thus, the spelling might be regarded as Armenian orthographical peculiarity. But not always. There might be a fluctuation in pronunciation as indicated by the script in the above examples. (Further cf. CC *yar, xian*).

The double representation of *j*, *i̯* also occurs, e. g.: *Dat.* *գեթխոյѣա* *(-լըխ)* *(kɛtχoja-lyχ)* 162r[9], 170v[7], 297r[17]; *դարպիѣѣատ* *(tarbijat)* 182v[14] (but nine times — *ѣѣատ*). In these cases there is, not by all means gemination; the fluctuation is rather an orthographical one, a border case of representing the falling and rising diphthongs.

---

j-, je- | The initial *j* in our Armeno-Kipchak documents is represented invariably by *ѣ* (except for the initial *ju-*). The initial *ѣ* in preconsonantic position, however, stands for *je-*. This corresponds to the pronunciation in the modern Armenian literary language.[65]

For denoting initial *je-* the *Dat.* uses the traditional Armenian spelling, i. e. *ѣ*, e. g.: *jeng-* *ѣենկ-* *(ѣե-)*, *jengil-* *ѣենկիլ-*, *jer* *ѣեր*, *jerga* *ѣերկա*. In the other texts the standardized representation prevails, e. g.: *Eph. jer* three times *ѣր* but

---

[65] In Podolian Armenian the initial *ѣ* is pronounced *je* under stress only, i.e. in monosyllabic words, otherwise it sounds *e*.

I

three times *kէp*, *jeber-* twice *kuykէp-* but twice *kէuykէp*; in *AB je-* ('eat') is represented by the following spelling variants: *k-* once, *kէ-* twice; *jel* *hy* twice, *kէy* once; *jer* ten times *hp*, 26 times *kէp*; *jetiš-* once *hqhz-* and once *kէqhz-*.

The use of *kէ* beside the orthographical *h* is found even in Armenian words in the *AB*, e. g.: *kէpnpqnuթիւն* ('trinity') 65[6], 110[14], 168[7]; *kէpnւսաղէմ* ('Jerusalem') 67[9], 149[5].

Some remarks on palatalization

Palatalization is indicated by the frequent use of *h* or *kէ* after *k* (*q, p*) instead of the *է* that one might expect. The use of *h* was observed also by J. Deny in different texts[66] who has included three of such cases in his glossary: *keç- (keç-), kel- (kɛl-), ketχoya*. In our texts this phenomenon is quite common.

In the *Dat.* we have, for instance, *keč-* three times as *qէչ-, pէչ-* and three times as *qhչ-*; *kečmiš* *qէչմիz* 190v[14] but *kečir- qhչhp-* 163r[14]; *kel-* 17 times *qէl- (pէl-)* but 16 times *qhl- (phl-)*; *keltir-* four times *qէlqhp- (qէlթhp-)* but three times *qhlqhp-*; *kerak* is throughout (38 times) *qhpwp (qhpwp)*; *keri* is invariably (four times) *qhph (phph)*; *kez* is always written *phq* (eight times). At the same time *e* in the syllable *ken-* is consistently written *է*, e. g.: *kendi* (48 times) *pէնդի, qէնդի*; *kensi* (three times) *qէնսի*; *kengaš, -li* (six times) *pէնկաz, -լի*.

In the first part of the *AB k* (*q, p*) is followed now by *է* now by *h*. Beginning from page 63 a third spelling (*kէ*) alternates with the previous two, e.g. *keča* twelve times *qէչw (pէչw)*, but *qhչw* 163[6] and *qkէչw* 110[7]; *kečir-* six times *pէչhp- (qէչhp-)* but *phէչhp-* 163[13]; *kel-* nine times *qէl- (pէl-)* but five times *qkէl-*; *keltir-* five times *qէlqhp- (pէlqhp-)* but *phէlqhp-, qkէlqhp-* 67[3], 138[8]; *kerak* *phpwp* 5[11] and *qkէpwp* 122[4]; *keraksyz* *qkէpwpupq* 113[5]; *keri* three times *pէph*, but twice *phph* and four times *phkէph*; *kez* throughout *phq*.[67] In the *AB* even the spelling of the syllable *ken-* is fluctuating: *kendi* 33 times *pէնդի* five times *phննդի* and seven times *phկէնդի*.

The use of *kէ* can be attested even in Armenian words: *kero(v)pe* ('cherub') *phpnւpէ* 128[5], *pէpnւpէ* 157[1], but *phկէpopէ* 75[10].

It is a question open to doubt whether to regard the phonetic value *je* of the alternating spelling, i. e. the palatalization of the *k* as generally valid for all cases, or to see a fluctuation of the pronunciation in the fluctuating spelling. We are inclined to believe that the latter alternative is more probable.

Here is the conclusion J. Deny has drawn from the above phenomena of orthography, resp. pronunciation: "Cette observation est importante parce

---

[66] There is no example for this in the *Eph*.

[67] The uniform written form of *kez* may have been influenced by the spelling of the Armenian word *phq* ('to you').

I

qu'elle permet de supposer que la mouillure était tout de même plus développée en arméno-coman que ne l'indique l'orthographe générale de cette langue".[68] In this assumption of J. Deny's a considerable part must have been played by the possibility of a parallel with the palatalization in the Karaim. On the problem of velar, resp. palatal vocalism in Armeno-Kipchak I wish to comment on another occasion. All I wish to say here is that the orthography of the texts here investigated does not permit any inference as to the general validity of this phenomenon. Thus the origin of this, in our opinion peculiar, phenomenon should be investigated in itself beyond the limits of the Kipchak language.

The first obvious possibility that suggests itself is to look for some explanation in Armenian. Palatalization is a characteristic common to many an Armenian dialect (Van, Qarabaγ, Hadrut', Maraγa, Agulis, Urmia, Karčevan, Meγri, etc.). It is conspicuous that in the dialects palatalization affects in the first place the sounds *g*, *k* and *k'*. But one must not be misled by this resemblance, because other sounds are also subject to palatalization, such as *t* and *t'*, and even unvoiced affricates, not only in initial but also in medial and final position. In addition to this, palatalization occurs not only before palatal but also before velar vowels. Thus the origin of this phenomenon must be looked for somewhere else.

Considering the masses of Armenian immigrants into Podolia from territories under Ottoman Turkish rule, one might be inclined to attribute palatalization to Osmanli influence. This explanation, however, does not seem to be probable because palatalization is not restricted to *k* in Osmanli either where it occurs also before velar vowels.

This phenomenon may more probably be ascribed to Polish influence because *k* before *e* is always palatalized in Polish. This assumption seems to be supported by the fact that in the Polish sound group *k* + *ę* no palatalization occurs, as can be observed in the material of the *Dat*. in the syllable *ken-*. (In the *AB* compensation, on the one hand, and the fluctuation of the spelling, on the other, has become general.)

In a few words J. Deny mentions another kind of palatalization illustrated by five examples.[69] He quotes the plural *bilyar* from T. I. Hrunin's first sample of texts. It must, however, be remembered that such "palatalized" forms abound in T. I. Hrunin's texts. J. Deny includes into the glossary of his *Eph.* more of them, at least those in which palatalization occurs before vowel: *kla- (klya-)*, *bila (bilya)*, *Ilov (Ilyov)*. By quoting these examples J. Deny wishes to support the assumption that in Armeno-Kipchak the palatalization was more developed than is indicated by the general orthography of the

[68] *Eph*. p. 19.
[69] *Ibid*. p. 20.

I

language. It must, however, be realized that T. I. Hrunin uses the ль in order to distinguish the sound from the Slavic velar *l*, which shows that from these data no conclusion can be made concerning palatalization. Hence the form of the above mentioned *bilyar* in normal transcription would be *bilar*.[70] J. Deny's other example, *çyeyrek*[71] is transcribed in the *Eph.* as *çyeryek* (22⁶) while the manuscript has *չէրէք* which deprived this form of its conclusive value. As to the examples *otlyaş* and *bağişlyagin*, I was not in a position to check them. (The latter is not included in the glossary.) The *ъ* (?) in *dyortunçi* in all probability cannot be accounted for in the Kipchak.

At any rate, this question requires a more detailed examination with due regard to the individual data ; a few sporadic data, as we have seen, can hardly be regarded as sound basis for general inferences. In the *Dat.*, for instance, the consequently recurring *ъ* in the words *zera* and *heč* (զերայ, չէչ) seems to suggest palatalization. The only support we have in accounting for the tonality of the vowel is the ی in the original of these words (زیرا, حج). [It might be a similar orthographical phenomenon as the transcription of closed *é* by *ի* in Middle Armenian texts, e. g. *լիկաթ* oFr. légat, *սինիշեալ* sénéchal (Karst, p. 19.).] This, however, hardly entitles us draw general conclusions because at the same time the words *peša* (پشه) and *pešakar* are written with *է*: *պէշա*, *-քար*). In the *AB* both above-mentioned words occur with *է*: *զէրա*, *չէչ*.

սա, շա

The Armenian sibilant + unvoiced stop were closely linked as early as in Old Armenian. No euphonic sound could separate them but in initial position they preceded them (in pronunciation but not in spelling). That, for instance, *ստանալ* was pronounced *əstanal* can be concluded from the conjunctive aorist.[72] This property of the group sibilant + tenuis has been conserved up to our days. In the sound group *սա* and *շա* the *ա* has remained a tenuis in spite of the "second Lautverschiebung" in Middle Armenian, that is *սա* and *շա* were used to render the *st* and *št* of foreign words, respectively. Examples: *շաստէլ* (Old French *chastel*), *մայստռ* (*maistre*) ;[73] *կիլամ Պաստարտ* ('Guillaume Bastarde') HChr. 49⁴⁰ ; *տուկ Տասա որ Ռիչէ* ('duc d'Austriche') HChr. 60³¹, 63²⁶.[74]

In most of the dialects of the western type, this pronunciation has been conserved in every combination of *s, š* + *p, t, k*. This phenomenon can be

---

[70] The form *bi* of *bij* occurs in the text of the *Eph.* itself too: *anyng biliki* (— *ապիլիքի* 'his Highness') 9⁸ which J. Deny, however, transcribes into *biyliki*.

[71] *Eph.* p. 20.

[72] *Esquisse*, p. 53.

[73] Karst, p. 33.

[74] Owing to the incorrect division of the sequence of letters the denomination of rank was interpreted as a French proper name and included in the Index as *Dos de Riche*.

I

observed in the Suceava Armenian dialect as well, though _ստ_ is sometimes pronounced _sd_. H. Acharian, however, attributes this — with good reason — to the influence of the literary language.[75] This pronunciation has been conserved in Podolian Armenian too and without exception at that: _վասdàգ_ _vastàg_, աստուած _astvàdz_, Հրիշտàգ _hrištàg_, դ_ա_շ_ն_ _tašt_.[76]

Following the western Armenian literary pronunciation the editors of our Kipchak texts write _sd_, _šd_ for _ստ_, _շտ_ resp. instead of _st_, _št_, e. g.: Kraelitz line 10 _ուստումա_ (recte: _ustuma_).[77] This orthographical phenomenon (occurring also in the orthography of Turkish speaking Armenians) Kraelitz erroneously regards as a "Konsonantenwandel".[78] Examples from the _Dat._: աստիջան _(astiǰan)_ 170v[18], ուստալիխ _(-լրք)_ _(ustalyχ)_ three times, ուստ- _(ust-)_ with different possessive suffixes occurs 24 times ; քրիստան _(kristan)_ 25 times ; ֆրիշտա _(frišta)_ five times ; ստորոծ _(storož)_ 180r[15]. Nor is _սպ_ pronounced _sb_ but _sp : սպրաւոծատսա_ _(spravoṭatsa)_ 173v[5].

The use of _ստ_, _շտ_ for _st_, _št_, resp. is gaining ground with the standardization of the orthography. In the _Dat._ we already find _ուստատ (ustat)_ 173v[21] ; ֆրիշտայ _(frišta)_ 167v[10], 182v[23] ; ստոլմիստր _(stolmistr_ 'magister stabuli') 295v[19]; ստարոստա _(starosta)_ four times. In the _Eph._ the signs _ստ_, _շտ_ prevail: ժրվնոստ _(žyvnost)_ 2[21] ; ստարոստ_ա (starosta)_ 2[10] ; ուստ _(ust)_ 4[9], 13[13]. (In the forms _sdaranyesi_ 2[17] and _sdurmovat_ 3[3] the _d_ is a misspelling in the transcription since the original is _սդարանեսր_ and _շդուրմովատ_.) Besides, _st_ and _št_ were sometimes rendered by the letter group _սթ_ and _շթ_, e. g.: քաշթալան _(kaštalan_ 'castellanus') 6[3], 9[1].

The letter group _ստ_, _շտ_ in initial position represented originally _əst_ and _əšt_, respectively. It cannot be ascertained for sure whether the above examples were pronounced with or without a prosthetic sound. The chances are that both pronunciations were current. The name _Stecko_ in the _Eph._ is written _ստէցքո_ 1[8], with M. Bzhshkiants _Ստանցքըն_.[79] The readings _Sdimbol, Sdmbol_ in the _Eph._ (p. 92.) would be correctly: _Stimbol_ (or with an undistinctly pronounced prosthetic sound). In Armenian texts we find different spellings of 'Stambul', but anyway _st_ is rendered, here too, by _ստ_ ; in Abraham Ankiwratsi's and Arakel Baγishetsi's 15th century jeremiacs on the fall of Byzantium we find: _Ստամպոլ._ _Ստրմպոլ_ and _Ստրմպոլ_. In scribe Simeon's travel accounts: _Սdամպոլ, Սdրմպոլ._ Also the initial letter group _սկ_ allows of two possible readings: _Սկուդար Skudar_ or _əskudar ;_ սկէլէ, սքալա _(սկ.)_ _(ə)skele, (ə)skala._

In the _AB_ both spellings occur: _dost (dost)_ 15[10], _խաստա_, _-լրխ (χasta-lyχ)_ three times. The signs _ստ_, _շտ_ have proved most persistent in the words

[75] _Op. cit._ pp. 108—109.
[76] Hanusz, p. 41.
[77] In brackets I give the correct pronunciation only.
[78] _Studien zum Armenisch-Türkischen_, p. 20.
[79] _Op. cit._ Document A. D. 1463: p. 87.

I

kristan, ust, friśta : ․քրիստանլիք *(kristanlik)* 133[7], *ust* 16 times ուստ and 8 times ուսդ ; *friśta* eight times with շտ and five times with շդ. The conservatism of the orthography of *kristan* and *friśta* has possibly been enhanced by their resemblance to their Armenian equivalents: ․քրիստոնեայ *(k'ristonya)* and Հրեշտակ *(hreśtag ;* from the same root as *friśta).*

To sum up it may be said that *st* and *śt* could be rendered either by ստ resp. շտ or by սդ resp. շդ without difference in phonetic value.

*

The orthography of our Armeno-Kipchak texts is essentially a uniform, "phonetical" system of spelling which suggests the idea of applying a uniform system of transcription to it. In our analysis above we wished to draw attention to cases in which certain features of this spelling system mix with certain properties of the classical Armenian orthography. Since the "traditional" representation of certain sounds or sound groups is not consistent, the transcription systems employed so far have sometimes ignored these "exceptions". The transliteration of these orthographical "exceptions", however, is liable to disintegrate the general picture of the Armeno-Kipchak phonetic system and arouses doubt as to the possibility of an unequivocal interpretation of the sounds.

As to the basis of the transcription system, we would like to desist from the Armenian system of transcription because it is the phonetic system of the Kipchak that is to be represented. The Armenian script enables us in most cases to ascertain the Kipchak phonetic value of the letters. Hence the application of the Turcological transcription seems to be more adequate. J. Deny's system lies close at hand but the diacritical signs entail printing difficulties. That is why I have adopted here K. Grønbech's signs (supplemented for foreign words).

Owing to the orthographical properties of Classical Armenian, the transliteration does not give, as we have seen, an adequate picture of the Kipchak phonetic system. A compromise seems therefore to be indicated consisting in the adoption of the literal transcription with the amendment of italicizing the letters representing phonetic values differing from the usual orthography, as e. g. bu*j*ruχ, bu*j*ur-, fri*śt*a, etc. (In these examples I have italicized *two* letters because we are faced with the traditional spelling or letter groups.) This method can, unfortunately, be applied for running texts only, for quotations of single words the use of the original characters is anyway advisable.*

I

ABBREVIATIONS

Hrunin   Т. И. Грунин: *Памятники половецкого языка XVI века.* In: *Академику В. А. Гордлевскому к его семидесятипятилетию. Сборник статей.* М. 1953. pp. 90—97.

Kraelitz   F. v. Kraelitz-Greifenhorst: *Sprachprobe eines armenisch tatarischen Dialektes in Polen.* In : *WZKM* XXVI. p. 307—324.

Eph.   J. Deny: *L'Arméno-Coman et les "Ephémérides" de Kamieniec* (1604—1613), Wiesbaden 1957.

Dat.   M. Lewicki, R. Kohnowa: *La version turque-kiptchak du "Code des lois des Arméniens polonais" d'après le ms. no. 1916 de la Bibliothèque Ossolineum.* In: *RO* XXI. pp. 153—300.

AB   *Ayot'k' hasarakac' k'ristonèic'* — *Alyyš Bitiki.* Ilov 1618.

HChr.   Hethum, Seigneur of Coricos: Relation of Chronicles ... In: V. A. Hakobian, *Manr žamanakagrutyunner XIII—XVIII dd.* [Short chronicles of the XIII— XVIII centuries, vol. II. Yerevan 1956. pp. 37—80.]

Esquisse   A. Meillet: *Esquisse d'une grammaire comparée de l'arménien classique,* 2. ed. Vienne 1936.

Karst   J. Karst: *Historische Grammatik des Kilikisch-Armenischen.* Strassburg 1901.

Hanusz   J. Hanusz: *Lautlehre der polnisch-armenischen Mundart von Kuty in Galizien.* Wien 1889. (Sonderabdruck aus *WZKM* Bd I—III.)

Acharian   H. Ačarian: *K'nnut'yun Ardiali barbari.* [The dialect of Kuty, Suceava and Transylvania] Yerevan 1953.

I

AN ARMENO-KIPCHAK DOCUMENT OF 1640
FROM LVOV AND ITS BACKGROUND IN ARMENIA
AND IN THE DIASPORA

by

EDMOND SCHÜTZ (Budapest)

I THE GREAT SÜRGÜN

1,1. The Seljuk and Tatar-Mongol onslaughts are the fateful disasters that most seriously decimated the Armenian people in the late Middle Ages. At the same time, it should not be overlooked that the hostilities at the turn of the 16th century (during the 50 years from 1580 to 1630) resulted in the destruction, looting and flight of a considerable part of the Armenians living both in the Armenian mother-country and on the territory of ancient Armenia Minor.

The population driven by the Seljuk invasion to the border regions of the East-Anatolian area, was decimated by the continuous Ottoman-Persian wars of the 16th century, the Jelâli revolts of the turn of the century, the famine following the acts of war, and 1604/1605, during the "great sürgün", when half of the population of Armenia was carried away by Shah Abbas from the Ararat basin and from the area of Lake Van.

The most important question involving the survival of the Armenian people was, how far the remainder of Armenians could preserve their most essential prerequisites, their language, religion and national consciousness. Since in that historical period, the leading force of the people under foreign domination was provided by the ecclesiastic organization, the Armenian monophysite autocephalous church played an especially important role.

The present study attemps to examine how far the preservation of the Gregorian-Armenian religion, and the full adherence to it, could ensure the survival of the Armenian people in the mother-country under the given special circumstances,[1] what alternative development came about in the Persian and Turkish Mussulman surroundings, and how the campaign of conversion to Roman Catholicism carried on by the Congregatio de Propaganda Fide in Eastern Europe in the most significant Armenian settlement led to assimilation in the Armenian Diaspora in Poland. In the period concerned in the Patriarchal See of the Katholicos in Echmiadzin and in Lvov in the seat of the Armenian archbishop, two ecclesiarchs of especially long function

---

[1] *Hay zolovrdi patmut'yun*, ed. by the Historical Institute of the Academy of Sciences of the ArmSSR, vol. IV. Erevan 1972, p. 116. (Abbrev.: *Patmutyun*)

II

were active: in the mother-country at Echmiadzin the Katholicos Melkisedek (1593-1624) and in the Polish-Ukrainian Diaspora Archbishop Nikol Torosowicz (1627-1681). The importance of the religious factor from the viewpoint of the people or minority under foreign domination was reflected by the circumstance that the contemporary — mainly antiuniate — sources[2] deal with the activities of the two ecclesiarchs in considerable detail.

One of the main objectives of the first part of this research was to find an answer to certain details of the most diputed questions, i.e. to what extent the destruction and transmigration of the Armenian population was brought about by the devastations of the Jeláli revolts, and the "great sürgün", the carrying off of the Armenian population to Persia by Shah Abbas in 1604—1605. How was it possible under such circumstances of disarray to preserve their ethnic integrity in Armenia, and what role did the church play in this as a cohesive force? The answer to the negative human features of Melkisedek discussed in the sources in detail, is given by the savageness of the age itself. At the same time, it can be regarded as a positive feature that as a result of his manoeuvres and the maintenance of good relations with the governor Amirguna khan and the Persian notabilities surrounding him, something of the autonomy of Armenia could more or less be preserved, since it was in the interest of the local regime of Khan Amirguna to prevent the monarchic centralism of the Shah from taking further masses of the Armenian productive population to Persia.

During the Ottoman-Persian wars at the turn of the 17th century, a decisive change was brought about by the ascension of Shah Abbas. In the Turkish Empire, the exhaustion caused by the military expeditions, carried out on two fronts for a century, resulted in the loosening up of the military system. All this was complemented by the harem diplomacy full of intrigues, where the devširme forces or the spahis gained the upper hand, thrusting Turkish internal and external policy into complete confusion. In addition, the Jeláli revolts, broke out with much greater force. If the Western powers hostile against the Austrian emperor had not prevented the unfolding of a large-scale offensive against the Turks on the Austro-Hungarian front at the time of the s.c. Fifteen Years' War 1593-1606,[3] a warfare on the Austro-Hungarian front and at the same time on the Persian front, to be faced by the Ottoman Empire simultaneously could have shortened the duration of the Turkish occupation of Hungary and

---

[2] The most important Armenian narrative sources: Tavrižec'i, Aŕakel, *Patmut'iwn Aŕak'el vardapeti Davrižec'woy*. Vałaršapat 1896, 3. ed.; French transl.: M. Brosset, *Collection d'historiens arméniens:* vol. I, SPb 1874: *Livre d'histoires, composé par le vartabied Arakel, de Tauriz*, pp. 267–608; Russian translation: Arakel Davrižeci. *Kniga istorij*. Translated by L. A. Chanlarjan. Moscow 1973; (Abbrev.: Tavrižeci — Tavr/Bros — Tavr/Xan.). — *Žamanakagrut'iwn Grigor vardapeti Kamaxec'woy kam Daranalc'woy* (Abbrev.: Daranalci). ed. M. Nšanean. Jerusalem 1915 —; Zakarij Kanakerci, *Chronika*. Russian transl. by M. O. Darbinjan-Melikjan. Moscow 1969.

[3] The closing act of the s.c. fifteen-years war in Hungary, the peace treaty of Zsitvatorok, has recently been thoroughly analysed by G. Bayerle, *The Compromise at Zsitvatorok: Archivum Ottomanicum*, vol. VI. Leuven, 1980, pp. 5–53.; *GOR*, vol. IV., Pest 1829, pp. 390–396.

II

eventually in the Balkans by a century, and could also have brought about other far-reaching consequences on the eastern Persian front. Such a development would also have been beneficial for the Ottoman Empire. It would have curtailed the centuries-long agony of the "sick man of Europe",[4] that could have used the resources wasted in wars to concentrate its forces to establish a more or less firm, uninational and unilingual state.

1,2. The loosening up of the Ottoman military system on the Hungarian front began with the Fifteen Years' war. Despite the mobilization, a considerable part of the spahis remained at home on their estates, many turned back while on the road, and many deserted.[5] After the battle at Mezőkeresztes (Turkish: Haçova) (1596) won by the Ottoman army, Chighaloghli Sinan pasha ordered a general review, and took strict measures to control the armed forces. The 30,000 spahis missing from the battle array were simply cancelled off the *timar defter*, what meant that they not only lost their military provender, but also their *timar* estates. Some of them were punished severely, and some were executed. The number of the deserters and soldiers and officers ruled out of the ranks amounted to about 50,000.[6] These small-holder and medium landowner officers and common soldiers had no other choice than to form revolting groups or to join the already existing ones.[7]

In assessing these movements, historians have formed two contrasting evaluations. There were some researchers who extended the positive evaluation of the originally revolutionary movement of positive character also to the looting undertakings of plunderers and guerilla bands.

Since the main field of movement of the Jelâli revolts, East Anatolia had a significant Armenian population the evaluation of the Armenian historiography is therefore of major importance. One decade ago, M. Zulalyan attempted to give a comprehensive picture on the Jelâli movements between 1590 and 1628. He divided the movements of this half a century into three periods, viz.: 1) 1598–1608: the movements led by *timar* small-holders (under the leadership of Qara Yaziji and Deli Hasan, etc.); 2) 1608–1610: the revolts that broke out in the territories of East Anatolia, Syria, Lebanon and Mesopotamia, especially among the national minorities (Syrians, Libanese and Kurds); and 3) the moves of Abaza pasha in revolt against the rule of the Janissaries.

[4] See the report of an Italian envoy dated 1599: Hurmuzaki, *Documente privitoare la Istoria Românilor*. Bucureşti, vol. III, part II, p. 534: apud A. S. Tveritinova, *Vosstanie Kara Jazidži — Deli Chasana v Turcii*. Moscow–Leningrad 1946, pp. 50–51.
[5] Akdag, M., *Celâlî isyanlari* (1550–1603). Ankara 1963, p. 3.
[6] Tveritinova, *op. cit.*, 52–53; Shaw, St., *History of the Ottoman Empire and Modern Turkey*, vol. I. Cambridge Univ. Press 1976, p. 186; *GOR*, vol. IV, p. 271. H. Inalcik, *Military and Fiscal Transformation in the Ottoman Empire, 1600–1700; Arch. Ott.* VI, 1980, p. 290.
[7] *Naima Tarihi*, vol. I, p. 170; Akdag, *op. cit.*, p. 3; M. K. Zulalyan, *Jalalineri šaržumə ev hay žolovrdi vičakə Osmanyan kaysrut'yan mej*. Erevan 1966, p. 152.

II

Thus contracted, the impression could, of course, arise that these movements are handled by the author as one unit.[8] At any rate, from the reliable disclosure of the facts, it is clear that the undertakings mentioned under one common name, did in fact have heterogeneous motives and objectives. But neither movements of self-nominated pashas whose unique objective was to take over power in certain provinces, nor robbers' undertakings that tormented and destroyed the people can by any means be described as progressive movements.

The Jelâlis came from different social classes and thus their objectives differed. Their groupings included poor peasants, nomads, all kinds of declassed elements, deserters (firari), and also small and big feudals. Tveritinova concentrated her attention on the revolt led by Qara Yaziji, which she considered as a typical movement. In the judgement of the movement, it is decisive what social layer formed the bulk of the Jelâli troops. In her view, in the revolt of Qara Yaziji, the peasants compelled to leave their lots (čiftbozan) were in majority, and therefore she regarded it as a "peasant movement."[9]

In contrast to this V. Hakobyan stated with justification that even if such a movement consisted partly of peasants, they were mixed of all kind of social elements, and the leadership was in the hands of deserters (firari) from the Ottoman army and feudals; thus it could not be called a "peasant movement".[10] In the résumé of his monography, Zulalyan also states that the movements with entirely different motives and aims had at any rate a common feature, viz. that "the protection of the interests of the rayas participating in the movement was alien to them", i.e. a negative evaluation.[11]

The Qara Yaziji revolt known fairly well from the sources is equally informative from the viewpoint of the composition of the Jelâli troops, the social origin of the leader of the movement, the policy of the movement, and its activity. Opinions differ considerably in assessing the origin of the leader of the movement and the rank he gained in the local military organization or in most cases bestowed on himself. According to Qara Chelebizade and other contemporary Turkish historians, Qara Yaziji would have been some officer deprived of his rank and his emoluments. According to Kâtib Chelebi, he was a segban commander, while according to Arakel Tavrižeci, he served as a tüfenkči with different sanjak begs. According to Pechevi and others, ha was a kaymakam in the mirliva of the Sanjak of Sivas.[12] These diversified

[8] Zulalyan, op. cit. 45, sq., 57, 59; 255–56.

[9] Tveritinova, p. 59; Zulalyan, pp. 130–31, 139, 217–18; V. Hakobyan — A. Hovhannisyan, Hayeren dzeŕagreri XVII dari hišatakaranner (1601–1620 t'ŕ.), vol. I, Erevan 1974, p. VII. (Abbrev.: Hišatakaranner XVII d. I.)

[10] Hišatakaranner XVII d., I, pp. VIII, XIII–XIV.

[11] Zulalyan, pp. 217–220 (On Qara Yaziji see p. 153–157).

[12] Qara Čelebizade, Revza al-abrar. Bulak A. H. 1126. p. 487; Kâtib Čelebi, Fezleke, vol. II. p. 127: apud Tveritinova, p. 53; Tavrižeci, 632; Tavr/Bros. 577; Tavr/Xan. 486; Tarih-i Pečevi, II, p. 252: Tveritinova, p. 54.

II

definitions of rank reflect the status and titles he conferred on himself or received from his superiors during his career. With his army of 36,000 men, he gained a foothold in the fort of Urfa (Edessa). In a treacherous way he delivered Husein pasha to the *serdar*, seemingly he feigned loyalty to the Sultan, as a result of which he was appointed sanjak-beg of Amasia, and then due to an illegal collection of taxes he was transferred to Čorum.[13]

The real aim of his revolt, his mutiny became manifest, when he won a victory at Kaiseri over Ibrahim pasha who was sent against him. At that time, he already regarded himself as the lord of the region and issued sultan's edicts (*kaysariyye hükm-i šerif*).[14] Finally he was defeated by the Serdar, Hasan pasha. With the remainder of his troops he gained a foothold in the mountains on the coast of the Black Sea, where he was killed in 1602 (very probably by his satellites).

The main feature of the career of Qara Yaziji was the sacking of the cities of Edessa, Amasia, Chorum and Kaiseri coming under his rule after 1599, and the devastation of the region. After his defeat in 1601, he marched towards Sebastia (Sivas). He raided the villages, and caused terrible devastation in Sebastia. His hordes killed about 20,000 inhabitants, Armenians and Turks (*horom*) alike, and he then set fire to the city.[15]

The Chronicler of the region, priest Grigor Daranalci and many others commemorate the sad event in similarly dark colours. In his colophone, the priest (*erec*) Yakob of Tokat says that Qara Yaziji "caused more serious devastation than Lang Tamur".[16]

Deli Hasan, the younger brother of Qara Yaziji, started his Jelâli career in a similar manner. Coming from Yanik, he devastated the region, and when he took Tokat (Eudokia) from the Serdar Hasan, his hordes caused terrible devastation and sacked the city. The priest-poets who escaped from Tokat, and sought refuge in the Crimea and the Armenian colonies in Poland, commemorated the tragic events in their jeremiads.[17]

[13] Tavriżeci, 633; Tavr/Bros. 578; Tavr/Xan. 487; Kâtib Čelebi, *Fezleke*, I, pp. 127–28: apud A. X., Safrastyan, *Turkakan albyurnera Hayastani, hayeri ev Andrkovkasi myus tolovrdneri masin*, II. Erevan 1964, pp. 79–80.

[14] *Tarih-i Naima*, I, pp. 294–96: Safrastyan, I, 68–69; Tveritinova, p. 71.

[15] *Tarih-i Pečevi*, II, p. 252: apud Zulalyan, pp. 148–49; Tavriżeci, 634; Tavr/Bros. 578; Tavr/Xan. 488; *Hišatakaranner XVII d.*, I, Nos. 138, 154, 163; Cf. pp. VIII–IX.; *GOR*, IV, pp. 304–5; Zulalyan, *Arevmtyan Hayastan XVI–XVIII dd.*, Erevan 1980, p. 140. (Abbrev.: *Arevm. Hay.*) In this monograph M. Zulalyan delimited the peasantry, the victims of Jelâli devastations, from the plundering bandits.

[16] Daranalci, p. 25–26; on the basis of several editions the colophons are quoted in: *Hišatakaranner XVII d.*, I, p. 125 (No. 154.). — In the ms cited by Zulalyan (p. 150.) the comparison with Timur Lenk is missing (Matenadaran, No. 1875.) — The colophon published on p. 299/b is not marked in the Archive Catalogue (Eganyan, et alii, *C'uc'ak dzeŕagrec' Matenadarani*. Erevan I, 1965, p. 664.).

[17] Stepanos Tokateci, *Olb i veray Evdokia mec kalak'in*: Akinean, N., *Hing panduxt talasac'ner*. Vienna 1921, p. 131; Gh. Ališan, *Hayapatum*, III. Venice 1901, pp. 307–22; *Hišatakaranner XVII d.*, I, pp. 244–52; (No. 315). — Lazar episkopos Tokateci: Akinean, *Talasac'ner*, p. 215; Jakob erec Tokateci: *ibid.*, pp. 173–4; Azaria Sasneci, see note No. 25.

II

The activity of this group did not cease even after the death of Qara Yaziji (1602) and the execution of Deli Hasan (1605). It broke up into groups of 3,000 to 12,000 men, which under the leadership of different commanders, laid waste the country.[18] There was a long series of such Jelâli commanders, who destroyed the region with their troops, and ruined the population. Arakel Tavrîžeci also gives a long list of them, viz.: Kosa Safar, Injaxan, Tavul. Yola Syghmaz, Tangri Tanymaz, Gokapaxan Čyplax, Qara Sahat, and Aghaian Piri, etc.[19]

Yeremia Chelebi in his versified chronicle on the history of the Ottoman cites enumerates the Jelâli leaders one by one, whose nicknames already betray their robber-chief character, viz.: Kesekes ('strike and kill'); Kör Ghaya ('Blind Rock'), Abu Hancher ('Dagger-father'), Topuzi böyük ('Big mace'), Siki-böyük ('Big-bodied'), and Ghara Sahat ('Last Judgement').[20]

Arakel Tavrizhetsi also commemorates in detail the inhuman ravages of the Jelâlis in the Ararat region during the period, when Shah Abbas retreated in 1603. During the advance of Sinan, Jelâlis also joined him, because he promised them an amnesty, but many of them deserted to Shah Abbas in fear of retaliation.[21]

The local commanders of Jelâli troops who ravaged the Ararat basin acted like petty monarchs already before the occupation of Erivan.[22] Topal (Lame) Osman pasha took up residence in Karbi and from there sent hords of his men to requisition provisions and fodder. They resorted to inhuman torture, hanging the peasants by their feet to force them to reveal where they had hidden the remainder of their victuals. An old sick monk in the Cloister Hovhannavank was tortured to death in an effort to make him disclose the hiding-place of the church treasures and vestments.[23] They tormented the people with similar methods everywhere.[24]

Azaria Sasneci related a long series of cruel deeds committed by the Jelâlis between 1591 and 1609, in the colophone of a Kanonagirk, in a lengthy jeremiad. He was one of the most authentic contemporary witnesses, since in his village of Sasun his family was killed by the Jelâlis. He was also captured by them and he managed to escape only some years later.[25]

[18] Tavrîžeci, 86–87; Tavr/Bros, 311; Tavr/Xan. 94–5.

[19] *Ibidem;* Kâtib Celebi, I, p. 38: Zulalyan, p. 165; *Hišatakaranner XVII d.,* I, 443 sqq.

[20] Eremia Čelebi, Matenadaran ms, No. 1675, 88/a–89/a:Zulalyan, p. 165. Yeremia Keomiwrǰean, *Patmuťiwn hamaŕot 400 tarwoy Osmancʼocʼ ťagaworacʼn.* Publ. by Ž. M. Avetisyan. Erevan 1982, pp. 167–169.

[21] The Kurd Ghazi Khan and Ulama Oghli Haybat-bek: Tavrîžeci, 15–6; Tavr/Bros. 277–8; Tavr/Xan. 46–47. Cf., Zulalyan, *Arevm. Hay., 150.*

[22] Hovhannisyan, A., *Drvagner hay azatagrakan mtkʼi patmuťyan.* vol. II, Erevan 1959, pp. 81–2. (Abbrev: *Drvagner*)

[23] Tavrîžeci, 80sq; Tavr/Bros. 307sq; Tavr/Xan. 89, sqq.

[24] Daranalci, p. 44., see also p. 41, sqq.

[25] Akinean, N., *Matenagrakan hetazotuťyunner,* IV. Vienna 1938, pp. 241–308. Cf. Ačaŕyan, Hr., *Andzanunneri baŕaran,* V. Erevan 1962, pp. 264–5. New edition of the colophon: *Hišatakaranner XVII d.,* I, 341–46; the text of the jeremiad: *ibid.,* 437–50.

II

To make an evaluation of the Jelâli revolts of the half a century, it is primarily necessary to take into consideration, what was their objective. In modern literature this is first of all stressed by V. Hakobyan.[26]

1.2.1. Since the composition of the troops was very heterogeneous, it is necessary to examine this question in its details. First of all, their leaders originated from different grades of the social layers. The upper layer was represented among them only in a slight degree. Perhaps only Abaza, pasha of Erzerum, could be included here, who also originally held high posts in the army of the Sultan and in the military administration. His revolt — from the viewpoint of loyalty to the Sultan — has so to say a positive motive, viz.: it was an act of vengeance against the Janissaries for the assassination of Sultan Osman,[27] in which act, at the same time, the spahi-*devširme* hostility was expressed.

In the other Jelâli movements, it was not possible to discover any intention that could be regarded as "noble." And the leaders: Qara Yaziji, Deli Hasan, and in 1608–1609 Janpolad pasha and Kalender oghli[28] were self-made military leaders, with military organizing ability, their aim, however, was not at all to overthrow the power of the Sultan or to oppose it. And it cannot be said that they would have represented the interests of the devşirme or the spahi party. They were even less induced to revolt in order to protect the interests of the people. The only aim of the self-made pashas or begs of mostly unclarifiable origin, was to detach a domain for themselves in one or the other province (*vilayet, nahiyye*). This was the aim of Qara Yaziji, Deli Hasan, and Janpolad, and then of Janpolad-oghli or Kalender-oghli, but as soon as they were defeated by the *serdar* marching against them with an army or by some sanjak beg sent against them, they showed themselves ready to accept the governing of some administrative unit in the service of the Sultan, or they went over to the camp of the Shah.

The flocking together of the other smaller groups of troops can even less be called a revolt, in a similar way to the factions formed from the troops of Qara Yaziji or Deli Hasan, the hordes of 2,000, 3,000, 4,000 or 6,000 men ravaging in East Anatolia, and the groups consisting of a few hundred men.[29] The leaders of these hordes can rather be described as robber chiefs. Their main objective was loot. This is clearly shown, for example, by the fact that the vice-chiefs of Deli Hasan did not even accept the posts of military administration offered to them, because the loot in Sebastia (Sivas) and Tokat encouraged them to engage in further pillaging adventures.[30]

[26] *Hišatakaranner XVII d.*, I., pp. VIII, XII.

[27] Tavriženci 638–9; Tavr/Xan 491–2; Daranalci, pp. 212–234 (219–230); Zulalyan, *Arevm. Hay.* 163.

[28] Daranalci. p. 101; Carmelites, I, 93. Cf. Zulalyan, pp. 174, sqq.

[29] *A Chronicle of the Carmelites in Persia and the Papal Mission of the XVIIth and XVIIIth centuries*, I., London 1939, 98.

[30] Zulalyan, p. 167. — W. J. Griswold in his recently published monograph on the Jelâlis brings some eloquent evidence on the grave crimes of the plunderers of the peasant population, which triggered the Great Flight (*büyük kačgun*), but does not draw a sharp dividing line, to differentiate between the "regular" Jelâli revolts at the turn of the century, and the predatory bands (*The great Anatolian Rebellion, 1000–1020/1591–1611. Islamkundliche Untersuchungen*, Band 83, Berlin 1983, pp. 49, sqq.).

II

The riff-raff was reluctant to fight against the regular army, partly because the military elements (*firari*), especially the non-commissioned officers of lower ranks, deserted the army to escape from military service, while the starving peasants who joined were hardly a suitable fighting element, and the *levends*, although willing to plunder the defenceless population, were not prepared to fight against the regular army.

In most cases it is difficult to assess whether during the looting, the intentions of the leader or of the *levends* in the horde were decisive. At any rate, the *levends* forming the bulk of the troops could frequently be fuglemen, because without a rich loot they were unwilling to follow the leader. Thus, it is hardly characteristic of the movements that in certain cases they expressed the intentions and aims of different layers of the population, and that they would have displayed the character of class struggle.[31]

1,2,2. However, at a certain period, the Jelâli movements emerged as revolts of groups of nationalities. The revolts breaking out between 1608 and 1610, on the basis of the popular character of the elements directing the movement, or participating in it, are summed up by M. Zulalyan as nationality movements.[32] Undoubtedly many nationalities lived in the eastern vilayets of the Turkish Empire, but these cannot be accurately defined in the composition of those who revolted. The presence of the Kurd leaders and commanders is conspicuous, but their appearance is not confined to the given period. From among the nomad, warlike people who were accommodated to a settled way of life with difficulty, troops of robbers were frequently formed before 1608, which terrorized the regions, viz.: Gzir-oghli (1591), Mahmud (1595), Ghaya-Chaghu-oghli (1608)[33] and many others. Janpolad-oghli, who devastated the whole of Anatolia in 1608, was a Kurd. The Kurd tribal chiefs (Ghazi xan, Ulama-oghli Haybat-bek), who went over to the loyalty of the Shah in 1603, have already been mentioned.[34] However, the national descent of a leader does not make the revolt a national (nationality) movement, and essentially this was not at all decisive from the viewpoint of the revolts concerned.[35] The Kurd origin of the leader (or the troop) is mentioned by the sources, probably because their belligerent, fierce nomad character sharply distinguished them from the sedentary population. With regard to the nationality of the victims, no differentiation was made, both Christians and Turks were killed.[36]

At any rate it has to be taken into consideration that in the territory of East Anatolia under Turkish rule the Kurd element had become dominant by this time. It

[31] Zulalyan, pp. 217–8. Cf. *Hišatakaranner XVII d.* p. VII.

[32] Zulalyan, p. 181, 219–20. Cf. *Patmuťyun*, IV, p. 113.

[33] Daranalci, pp. 32–34; Tavriżeci, 632; Tavr/Bros. 576; Tavr/Xan. 486.

[34] Tavriżeci, 15–16; Tavr/Bros. 275; Tavr/Xan. 46; on other Kurd chieftains who went over to the Shah's side see *Carmelites*, I. p. 97.

[35] *Hišatakaranner XVII d.*, I., p. XII.

[36] *Ibid.*, pp. 112, 116, 125, 126; cf. *ibid.* pp. IX–X.; Daranalci, p. 143.

II

had been settled in the regions depopulated as a result of the Persian advance, or was intentionally settled there as a people ready to fight. However, this represented a danger, not so much for the central power of the Sultan, but primarily for the local sedentary population.[37]

1,2,3. This period of the Jelâli revolts between 1608 and 1610 represented the last blow for the population of the regions inhabited by Armenians, since by that time most of the population that escaped Jelâli devastations had been killed by famine; those who were not crippled or old had fled to distant regions.

The chronicles, jeremiads and colophones accurately reflect the real picture of the Jelâli movements, viz.: the Jelâlis "devastated and ruined the whole region from Constantinople to the city of Erivan, from Baghdad to Demir Kapu (Derbend), and from the White (Mediterranean) Sea to the Black Sea".[38]

The Persian–Ottoman wars raged for a century, the devastating activity of the Jelâlis, and the central moves against them, all involved disastrous consequences for the population of East Anatolia: "The Armenians were dispersed, everybody fled where they could, to find a place for themselves, where they could escape and survive (the disaster). There were people, who fled to Rumelia, Bogdan [Moldavia], Poland, Kaffa [pars pro toto — Crimea], and the coast of the Pontus".[39] Hakob Tokatetsi speaks similarly about the flight of the refugees from Tokat: "they fled to foreign countries, to Frankstan [to Western countries] and to Persia".[40] Stepanos Tokatetsi writes about this as follows: "Many went to Istanbul, Bursa, Edirne, to the country of the Franks [to Western countries], Bogdan [Moldavia] and to Poland".[41]

From Kamakh, from the surroundings of Erzinjan large masses moved to Istanbul and Rodosto.[42] In the Crimea in 1605 Daranalci met Armenians in every major city, who were new arrivals from their old Armenian homeland.[43] And when he travelled from Kaffa to Istanbul, he found the Armenian population from Erzerum and its surroundings there, who at that time had been living there for two years.[44]

---

[37] On the sway of Kurdish tribes see also: V. Hakobyan, *Manr žamanakagrut'yunner XIII–XVIII dd.*, II, Erevan 1956 (Vardan Bałišeci): p. 357; (Yakob Karneci): p. 560; Cf. *Drvagner*, II, p. 87.

[38] Tavrižeci, 87; Tavr/Bros. 311; Tavt/Xan. 95; see also *Hišatakaranner, XVII d.*, I, p. 294 (Srapion Baberdaci: No. 359).

[39] Tavrižeci, 88; Tavr/Bros. 312; Tavr/Xan. 95. Cf. *Hišatakaranner XVII d.*, I, pp. XV–XVI.

[40] Ališan, *Hayapatum*, III, p. 320.

[41] *Ibid*, p. 315; Akinean, *Hing pandukt talasac'ner*, p. 120.

[42] Daranalci, p. 108; to Rumelia, Belgrade, Boghdan and Poland, *ibid*. p. 95–96.

[43] *Ibid*. p. 51.

[44] In 1610 the Armenians, who in the previous years had fled to Istanbul, Rodosto and the Western provinces of Anatolia, have been obliged to return to their old home to East-Anatolia, but the authorities succeeded to gather altogether 7000 and send them back under the leadership of priest Grigor Daranalci to Kamakh, Erzincan and surroundings. Daranalci pp. XXXV–XXXVII; cf. Zulalyan, *Arevm. Hay*. pp. 158–59.

II

Such refugees had been met in 1608-1613 by the priest Simeon Lehatsi in Istanbul and in West Anatolia; over 40,000 such refugee families lived in Istanbul. Galata and Skutari.[45]

Among the tens of thousands fleeing from the Jelālis, Abraham Pahlavunents came to the Crimea in 1602. His grandchildren commissioned a priest to compose in 1690, a voluminous colophone to the memory of their ancestors (later known under the title "Nesvita Chronicle"), which contains the history of the Armenians escaped to the Crimea.[46]

No direct numerical data is available regarding the increase in the number of refugees in the Crimea at the turn of 1600. At any rate, this process is suggestively shown by the increase in the number of codices copied in the Crimea. While from the previous 16th century altogether 10 codices have been preserved, from the 17th century the Matenadaran possesses 103 codices.[47]

From the region of Lake Van, part of the refugees moved towards the east. A priest from Artamet writes in his colophone that those surviving after the war and the famine went to the Jezire, Bagdad, Arabia, Northern Mesopotamia (Asorestan), Tebriz, Qazvin and Khorasan.[48]

The final result was that due to the wars, the Jelāli devastations and the terrible famine, the whole territory of East Anatolia, the Armenian mountain region, the ancient area of Armenia Minor became practically uninhabited "from Salmast up to Georgia, and Istanbul, and along the southern region as far as Amida and Aleppo".[49]

1.2.4. Those who remained at home, who survived the Jelāli ravages, were decimated by famine. There were years of scarcity in each decade at the end of the 16th century (1573, 1574, 1583, 1595). Many colophones mention the excessive prices in 1604 and 1605 in Mokk, Khizan and Artamet, and in Van in 1607.[50] But as a result of the constant war conditions, the advance and retreat of the devastating armies, the constant Jelāli requisitionings and robberies, and the unsown fields following the flight of the population, a terrible famine occurred. The process culminated in 1606-1610,

---

[45] Simeon dpir Lehaci, Ulegruťiwn (ed. N. Akinean). Vienna 1936, p. 8; Russian translation by M. O. Darbinjan: Simeon Lehaci. Putevye zametki. Moscow 1965, p. 37.

[46] Bžškian, M., Canaparhorduťiwn i Lehastan. Venice 1830, pp. 340–1.

[47] Schütz, E., Armeno-kiptschakisch und die Krim: Hungaro–Turcica: Studies in honour of J. Németh (ed. J. Káldy-Nagy). Budapest 1976, pp. 190, 192–3. (Misprints in the paper should be corrected for: XIV. cent.: 13 mss, . . . XVIII. cent.: 41 mss.) The figures include only the codices kept in the Matenadaran, still they give a reliable proportion, because the codices of the Crimean settlements (transported together with the evacuated population in 1789 to Nor-Nakhichevan), during the years 1920–30 have been transferred to the Matenadaran. Eganian, O., et alii. C'uc'ak dzeŕagrac'... Matenadarani. I, Erevan 1965, pp. 160–61.

[48] Hakobyan, Hišatakaranner XVII d. I. No. 244., p. 194.

[49] Ibid.

[50] Hišatakaranner XVII d., I, No. 182; cf. p. Tavrižeci, X; 87–88; Tavr/Bros. 312; Tavr/Xan. 95; Daranalci, 30–37, 42, sqq; Zulalyan, Arevm. Hay. p. 157.

256

II

indicated by the extraordinary deprivations that had set in during the preceding years.[51]

The population fled to escape the famine "from the gate of the Huns [Derbend], from the gate of the Alans [Dar-i-Alan], from the mountains of the Caucasus as far as the Pontus and Ephesus, from Cappadocia as far as Damascus, Sis and Mesopotamia".[52]

But the disaster was also increased by the war raging between the Turkish Serdar Sinan pasha and Shah Abbas in 1604. "These two lords of the world — Tavrizhetsi complained — devastated and ruined our country, when they waged war: the *Serdar* (Sinan pasha), who came from the west and the Shah, who came from the east, both during advance and retreat. What onerous taxes they afflicted on the people and with what cruelty they collected them . . . How they destroyed the houses (of the peasants) and their gardens, looted the wheat and grain from their granaries, took everything they had, drove away their sons and daughters, and openly and secretly killed off the innocent people. We do not possess sufficient words to enumerate what they did in our country."[53]

However, the situation was even more desperate farther to the north. The population was compelled to eat all kinds of animals: horses, mules, cats, dogs: they even chewed the grass. And then the surviving population was forced by the famine to engage in even more horrible deeds. Some people dug up corpses from their graves, and even cases of cannibalism occurred. Tavrizhetsi reports such cases in the area of Erzerum and Sebastia (Sivas), and even in the Ararat basin, in Oshakan and Bejni. Packs of wolves roamed the villages and anyone who set off on a journey, risked his life.[54]

1,2,5. Thus, in conclusion, the pauperization, decimation and flight of the population of East Anatolia were caused by the war situation, first of all by the excessive taxes assessed to cover the burdens of the two-front warfare, by the multiple marches of the Turkish and Persian armies through this territory, as well as by the insurgent, revolting troops named comprehensively Jelâlis, by the self-made local monarchs usurping power in the eastern provinces, and by the predatory bands increasing in number with the pauperization.

As a whole, the Jelâli movements — as has been seen — were primarily characterized by the circumstance that short-lived provincial petty monarchs maintained themselves and their pretentious mercenaries from the exploitation of the people.

[51] Hakobyan, *Hišatakaranner XVII d.*, I, 180, 202, 278; cf. XIV–XV.

[52] Hakobyan, *Manr žamanakagrut'yunner, I*, p. 186, lines 22–25. The flight to escape starvation see also: Daranalci, p. 96, 68–69; Tavriẑeci, 92; Tavr/Bros. 314; Tavr/Xan 98–99.

[53] Tavriẑeci, 78–79; Tavr/Bros. 307; Tavr/Xan. 88.

[54] Tavriẑeci, 88–92; 635–36; Tavr/Brcs. 312–14, 580; Tavr/Xan. 96–99, 488–89. 489; Hakobyan, *Hišatakaranner XVII d.*, I, 278, 289, 194.

II

The smaller groupings, parts of the dissolved revolting troops, or the deserters, declassed elements, and *levends* formed predatory bands that ground down, exploited and murdered the local population.

But how can the role of the Jelâli troops of this period be assessed from the viewpoint of the countries of the Turkish western front? Although the Jelâli movements emerged in the rear of the Ottoman army, and thus they weakened the Ottoman military potential, the Austrian imperial power could not exploit this possibility to liberate the territory of Hungary, since the Western league, with its constant military threat to the Austrian Empire, deprived the Austrian imperial armed forces of their striking-power, and thus they had to conclude a peace treaty in 1606 (at Zsitvatorok). This, on the other hand, made it possible for the Ottoman supreme command to liquidate the Jelâli revolts in East Anatolia even with the disorganized troops. Thus the Jelâli revolts essentially provided assistance only to the Persian shah.

2.1. At the end of the 1570s — before the Jelâli revolts of a larger dimension — the Ottoman Empire had the strength to start a new offensive against the Persians for the occupation of the Transcaucasian territories. At the beginning of the reign of Shah Abbas, who ascended to the throne at the age of 14, in 1578, Persia was in a paralyzed position, because in 1588, in agreement with the Ottomans, the Uzbeks launched an attack, and at the same time, from 1588 to the 1590s the Persian provincial lords, petty monarchs of the border regions, revolted.[55] Thus, in 1590 Persia was compelled to conclude a peace treaty with Turkey, according to which East Georgia, East Armenia, Kurdistan, North and even South Azerbaijan came under Turkish rule.

The Shah, recovering from the attacks of the provincial lords, first of all had to reorganize his unmanageable army consisting of (nomad) Qizilbash tribes on a new basis,[56] and thus he could exploit neither the first ten years of the s.c. 15 years' war fought (1593–1606) on the Western front nor the renewed revolts against Turkish supremacy in Wallachia, Moldavia and in the Balkans in the 1590s.[57]

At the beginning of the century, the Shah could already take advantage of the last years of the 15 years' war raging on the territory of Hungary, and of the Jelâli revolts that flared up in East Anatolia. The reason for this is revealed in a concise form by a report forwarded by the Superior of the Carmelite mission in Persia to the Pope in 1606, viz.: "All the supplies sent [by the Ottomans] are short and insufficient, whether for the Persian front, or for the Hungarian, or against the rebels in question".[58]

[55] 1588 in Luristan, 1589 Rustam Mirza in Sistan, 1589, the Qizilbash tribes nomadising in Fars and Kerman, 1590 the Prince of Ghilan.

[56] Pigulevskaja, N. V., Jakubovskij, A. Ju., Petruševskij I. P., et alii, *Istorija Irana*, Leningrad University 1958, p. 273; *A Chronicle of the Carmelites in Persia and the Papal Mission of the XVIIth and XVIIIth Centuries*, London 1939, I, p. 160–61; Cf. Hovhannisyan, A., *Drvagner hay azatagrakan mtk'i patmut'yan*, Yerevan 1957, II, p. 90. (Abbrev.: *Drvagner)*

[57] 1594 revolt led by Voivod Michael in Wallachia; 1596–98 uprisings in Bulgaria, and at the turn of the century revolts broken out in South-Serbia, Crna-Gora, Herczegovina, Dalmacia, Albania: A. D. Novičev, *Turcija.* Moscow 1965, p. 36.

[58] Fondo Borghese, ser. IV., p. 319, apud: *Carmelites*, I, p. 97.

II

In the last three years preceding the peace treaty at Zsitvatorok in 1606 (see note 3) the Shah launched a general offensive, thus in 1603–1604 he succeeded in occupying Tebriz and East Armenia, and then gradually the other parts of Transcaucasia.

The series of exchanges of envoys with the Western great powers, aimed at starting a joint offensive against the Sultan, was in vain.[59] Finally Shah Abbas succeeded alone. The Prior of the Carmelite mission wrote in his report sent in 1608 from Isfahan to the Pope: "the King of Persia is very powerful, and *has no longer need of the Christian Princes* to help him".[60]

In 1604, Shah Abbas occupied Julfa, Nakhichevan, and then, after ten months of blockade, the Turkish garrison at Erivan also surrendered. The hostilities demanded several tens of thousands of Armenian victims on both sides. The troops of the Shah advanced to Erzerum and in the south as far as Lake Van.[61]

The provincial lords — both Moslems and Christians — afflicted with excessive taxes and other deprivations by the Turks, went over to the Shah, in Azerbaijan, in the province of the Mars [Kurds], the Kurd Ghazi Khan, Ulama-oghli Haydar bek, and the Georgians revolting against the Turks who carried away their king, Simeon to Istanbul. Several provincial lords *(melik)* went over to the Shah in the territory of the Caucasian Albania *(Alvank)* — Northern Azerbaidjan, and part of the population emigrated to the territory of Persia.[62]

According to the Persian view, the occupation of the Transcaucasian and East-Anatolian territories was essentially regarded as a recuperation, liberation.[63]

2,2,1. But did the appearance of the troops of the Persian Shah represent a redemption to the population of Armenia? The troops sent in 1603–1604 to the area of Erzerum, then to the surroundings of Lake Van, and to the region of Manazkert and Maku drove away about 23,000 Armenians from these regions to the Ararat plain, and then together with other local nationalities (Mohammedans, Jews) to Persia.[64]

Since the Shah did not have much confidence in his newly organized army and calculated that he could not measure his strength with the well trained Janissaries, outnumbering his troops by far, he resorted to the tactics of a "scorched earth" policy: when he received information about the approach of the army of the Serdar, Chighal-oghli Sinan pasha, he used brutal force to drive away the people of the southern

---

[59] Such a joint intervention was requested in 1596 from Philipp II, king of Spain by Simeon, king of Georgia: Macler, F., *Notices de manuscrits arméniens ou rélatifs aux arméniens vus dans quelques bibliothèques de la péninsule ibérique et du sud-est de la France: REA* I (1920–22), p. 9–12; Cf. *Drvagner*, II, p. 75.

[60] *Carmelites*, I, p. 98.

[61] Tavriżeci, p. 30; Tavr/Bros. 283–84; Tavr/Xan. 55–56.

[62] Tavriżeci, p. 15–17; Tavr/Bros. 275–76; Tavr/Xan. 46–47. sqq.; Cf. Danelyan L., *Aŕakel Davriżecu erka orpes Sefyan Irani XVII dari patmut'yan skzbnalbyur.* Yerevan 1978, p. 108.

[63] Muhammad Parang, *Šah Abbas Kebir*, Tehran A. D. 1902, p. 198: apud Danelyan, *op. cit.* p. 65.

[64] Tavriżeci, pp. 30, 33, 35; Tavr/Bros. 283–86; Tavr/Xan. 55–56, 58, 60.

II

Armenian provinces on this side of the Arax, and he burnt down their towns and villages in order to halt the further advance of the Ottoman army.[65]

The Persian troops sent off in all directions in the Armenian lands, situated on this side of the Arax, drove away the population from Erivan, the Ararat basin and from the neighbouring counties *(gavars)* to the Ararat plain. Their columns formed immense lines extending from the village of Garni to the river Arax.[66] The possessions that the inhabitants left behind, their houses, grain, and fodder were burnt to prevent them falling into the hands of the Ottomans. Torture was used to compel the stragglers to hurry, otherwise they were killed. Those hiding in caves in the mountains were pursued and cruelly massacred.[67]

The people were driven by sword and sabre to the river Arax. There were very few rafts, barges, and horses and horned cattle, which if not used as saddle animals, could at least be used for clinging to while crossing the river. "Who could manage, clung to the rims of barges, others held on to the edges of rafts, others clang to the tails of horses, oxen and buffaloes, again others tried to reach the opposite bank by swimming. Those, who could not swim, the weak ones: old men, old women, children, girls, and boys covered the whole river, and the stream washed them away, like a stalk of straw in the spring flood". If the patroling soldiers took a fancy to a woman, a girl or a youth, they helped them to the opposite bank only to take them away for themselves.[68]

2.2.2. Memory frequently fails about the sufferings of the Armenian people, and even history neglects the memory of the deportation of the people of East Armenia, first of all from the Ararat basin to Persia and that their ruin deprived present day Armenia of over half of its Armenian population,[69] and in their place, Azeri and Kurd tribes streamed in during the rule of Amirguna khan, placed by Shah Abbas at the head of the khanate of Erivan *(Chuqur Sa'ad)* (1605-1625).

The figure given by the Augustine missionary Antonio Gouvea for the number of Armenians deported from the vilayet/khanate of Erivan, marks 100,000 families.[70] Of course, the figure given by the Armenians of New Julfa to the Carmelite missionaries (arriving in Persia in 1608) was exaggerated, according to them 400,000 Armenian families would have been deported by Abbas to Persia. The number of

[65] Tavr. 40–41; Tavr/Bros. 288; Tavr/Xan. 63.; Tavernier, J. B., *Les six voyages de J. B. Tavernier.* Paris 1678, livre IV, chap. VI, p. 460.; cf. Zulalyan, p. 53.

[66] Tavr. 40; Tavr/Bros. 288; Tavr/Xan. 63.; *Itinéraire du très-révérend frère Augustin Badjetsi, évêque arménien de Nahidschévan* (trad. par. M. Brosset), *Journal Asiatique*, série 3, tome III, 1837, mars., p. 224.

[67] Tavrižeci, 47, 52; Tavr/Bros. 293–94; Tavr/Xan. 67, 70.

[68] Tavrižeci, 42–45; Tavr./Bros. 288–89; Tavr/Xan. 64–66. A. Badjétsi, *op. cit.* p. 225.

[69] Makveci, Hovhannes, *Olh Hayastaneayc' ašxarhi Erevanay ew Julayu*, p. 183; Karkareci, Petros, *Olh...* p. 179; in: Xačatryan, P. M., *Hay mijnadaryan patmakan volber*, XIV–XVII dd., Erevan 1969.

[70] Ezov, *Snošenija Petra velikogo s armjanskim narodom*, SPb 1898, pp. 467–471; *Drvagner*, II, p. 85; cf. Danelyan, *op. cit.*, p. 105.

II

people is, as a rule, put to 350,000.[71] Of these, 10,000 families from among the Armenians of Nakhichevan previously converted by the Dominican missionaries residing in Nakhichevan.[72] According to Georgian sources, the number of displaced Armenian families was 80,000.[73]

2.2.3. In addition to the conception of a "scorched earth" policy the inducing motive in transferring the Armenians to Persia was that with their help the Shah wanted to promote the production of raw silk in Persia and its sale abroad. Therefore, he settled the peasants first of all on the southern coasts of the Caspian Sea, in the regions rich in mulberry trees, 27,000 families in Gilan and 24,000 families in Mazanderan.[74]

These resettlements were also repeated later: Georgians, Armenians, Mohammedans and Jews were transferred to the Fahrabad region from the territory of Georgia, and in 1618 from the region of Erivan, Ganja, Tebriz and Ardebil.[75] The deported people, however, could not bear the unhealthy humid climate and the stinking air, and thus, most of them died of different diseases.[76] Estimates show wide differences of survival.[77] The other part of the rural population were settled in the counties in the vicinity of Isfahan.[78]

Shah Abbas had earnest intentions for the silk merchants of Julfa to play a significant role in Persian silk trade. At the date of the *sürgün* the population of the Julfa area consisting of about 10,000 big families were given 3 days to gather up their possessions to be carried along, which however, they could not take with them on account of the absence of carts and pack-animals.[79]

Finally the inhabitants of the town were driven out to the bank of the river Arax. There the soldiers helped them to get to the opposite bank on horses and camels. After this, the Shah issued order to burn down and demolish the town.[80]

[71] *Patmut'yun*, IV, Erevan 1972, p. 99; Zulalyan, p. 254; *Istorija armjanskogo naroda*. Erevan 1956, p. 220; cf. also Abrahamyan, A., *Hamaŕot urvagic hay galt'avayreri patmut'yan*. Erevan 1964, I, p. 253.

[72] *Carmelites*, I, pp. 100, 157.

[73] Melikset-Bek, L, *Vrac' albyurnerə Hayastani hayeri masin*. Erevan II, 1936, p. 112.

[74] *Carmelites*, I, 99–100; Cf. *Drvagner*, II, p. 99.; Tavrižeci, 67; Tavr/Bros. 301; Tavr/Xan. 80.; Tavernier, *op. cit.* I, IV, chap. VI, p. 460.; as to some European travellers 30,000 to Ghilan, see: Carswell, J., *New Julfa*. Oxford 1968, p. 3., 74.

[75] Tavrižeci, 455; Tavr/Bros; 488; Tavr/Xan. 354–55.

[76] Tavrižeci, 133, 148; Tavr/Xan. 126–27, 137. Tavr/Bros. 333, 341;

[77] Out of the 10,000 transferred families by the middle of the century hardly 400 families survived — related Tavrižeci, 456; Tavr/Bros. 488; Tavr/Xan. 355. According to Rafael du Mans, in 1660 out of the 30,000 families transferred to the South-Caspian region only 1,200 remained alive. See L. Carswell, *New Julfa*, p. 74; From the 24,000 resettled in Mazenderan only 5–6,000 survived — as to Tavernier, *op. cit.*, I, IV, chap. VI, p. 460.

[78] Tavrižeci, p. 46; Tavr/Bros. 291; Tavr/Xan. p. 67; Cf. Zakaria Kanakerci, *Chronika*. Transl. by M. O. Darbinjan-Melikjan. Moscow 1969, p. 48.

[79] Matenadaran MS No. 2381, p. 253/b: apud: *Hišatakaranner XVII d.*, p. 428

[80] Tavrižeci, 57–62; Tavr/Bros. 296–99; Tavr/Xan. 74–77; see also *Manr žamanakagrut'yunner*, I, p. 182–83; Tavernier, *op. cit.*, I, IV, chap. 6, p. 460.

II

2,2,4. The inhabitants of Julfa were settled in the new quarter established on the opposite bank of the river Zanderud in the city of Isfahan, which district received the name of the township of New Julfa. Tavrizhetsi enumerated in detail the advantages enjoyed by the rich inhabitants of New Julfa.[81] Shah Abbas endeavoured with a purposeful policy to attach the inhabitants of New Julfa to their new home. He made friends with the merchants, who very soon received commissions for the transaction of the whole raw silk trade of Persia.[82] The Shah was a regular guest of the city magistrate of the Julfans, with the family of Kalantar Safar Khoja, and he was present at ceremonies on the Armenian church holidays.[83]

All these favours brought about the picture of the "good ruler" among the Armenians of Isfahan. Tavrizhetsi relates a story about the ruler doing justice in disguise among the people.[84] Such and similar stories chanted the exuberant praises of the Shah.[85]

At any rate, the Shah expected with justification that the old people, who had been born in old Julfa and constantly longed for home, would die soon. Their descendants, however, being born in their new home, who found prosperity there, would have affection for New Julfa and regard this country as their native home.[86] After all, the Western travellers in the 17th century found a rich Armenian community in New Julfa with 30,000 inhabitants.[87]

[81] Tavriżeci, 64–65; Tavr/Bros. 300–301; Tavr/Xan. 78–78.

[82] Even Tavernier, who was not well disposed towards the Armenians, had to admit the special abilities of Armenian traders. Shah Abbas's first trial to commission Persians to sell silk in Europe failed totally, but his Armenian merchants brought him a rich gain. Tavernier, I. IV, chap. 6., pp. 466–67. The kalantars, Khoja Nazar and Safar were his confidential councillors. Matenadaran Ms No. 201. apud Baiburtyan, *Armjanskaja kolonija Novoj Dżulfy v XVII weke*. Moscow 1969, p. 19–20; see the diaries of European travellers: Carswell, *op. cit.*, pp. 78–80 and 6.

[83] Shah Sefi has often been a guest with Khoja Soutenon, *kalantar*. Carswell, *Op. cit.* p. 7.; Tavernier, I. IV, p. 517. Tavriżeci, p. 64; Tavr/Bros. 300; Tavr/Xan. 79. Carmelites I, 308 and 245. P. della Valle, *Les Voyages de — dans la Turquie etc.*, Paris 1663, III, 100–13. For other accounts see: Carswell, 78–79; Carmelites, I. 1245–46. A. Olearius, *Vermehrte Newe Beschreibung Der Muskowitischen und Persischen Reyse*. Schleszwig 1656, IV. chap. 19, 428 (same presence of the Khan of Semakha).

[84] Tavriżeci, pp. 173–76; Tavr/Bros. 352–53; Tavr/Xan. 154–56 Daranalci even carried this feeling to exaggeration, saying that the Shah was more fond of the Armenians, than his own people, *op. cit.*, pp. 38–39.

[85] E.g. Poser, H., *Tagebuch seiner Reise... durch... Armenien, Persien...* Iena 1675, p. 20, apud: Drvagner, II, p. 108. Similar praise with Tavernier, *op. cit.*, b. IV, chap. 6, 460–61. About the justness of Shah Abbas a good many anecdotes (of course according to the tradition left by the people of New Julfa) with H. Ter-Hovhaneanc', *Patmut'iwn Nor Julayu*, Aspahan I, pp. 47–48, 79. and with Srabyan, A., *Hay mijnadaryan zruyc'ner*. Erevan 1969, p. 258–59 (Nos 19–21.).

[86] Tavriżeci 67; Tavr/Bros. 301; Tavr/Xan. 80. At home they had been maltreated by the Turks and Persians... so they had no reason to regret because of leaving the homeland of their forefathers. Tavernier, *op. cit.*, pp. 460–61; the Shah did not tolerate any injustice done to them, *ibid.* p. 468; cf. Danełyan, *op. cit.*, p. 210.

[87] Chardin, J., *Voyages du chevalier Chardin en Perse et autres lieux de l'Orient*, III, Paris 1811, p. 165. *Hay żolovrdi patmut'yun*, IV, Erevan 1972, p. 100.

262

II

2,2,5. To attach the Armenian population to Isfahan, in addition to the economic advantages, the Shah also utilized the creation of religious ties for this purpose. In 1614–1615 he ordered that the most respected religious relic of the Armenians, the right hand of Saint Gregory, the Illuminator *(Lusavorich)*, and even several sanctified stones of the cathedral of Echmiadzin, an altar together with its pedestal, as well as two candelabra, be brought to Isfahan, in order to place these into a church to be built in Isfahan, and so to say to transplant the Armenian ecclesiastic centre of Echmiadzin to Persia.[88]

How well the psychological manoeuvre of the Shah worked, is shown by the fact that the new generation already considered New Julfa as their home. This is reflected by the attitude of the local people, who tried to convince the Katholicos Philippos making efforts for one and a half years in Isfahan to ensure the return of the ecclesiastic relic, with the opposite argumentation, viz.: "they are living in an alien country, among Mohammedans... and there is nothing else to strengthen them in their Christian faith than this miraculous relic." Neither the inhabitants of New Julfa, nor their *kalantar* Sarfraz Khoja wanted to deliver the right hand of Saint Gregory, the Illuminator. The Katholicos could manage to get a ferman from the Shah only with many presents and even then only by a cunning stratageme he could smuggle the relic out of the city.[89]

The European travellers and envoys were well informed about the state and position of the Armenian settlement in Persia. The reason for this is that the Armenians spoke several languages, maintaining constant contact with the missions, and having a European outlook were commissioned to provide supply for the foreign envoys in Isfahan and guide them.[90]

A considerable number of the reports conveyed by the travellers originate from the wealthy Armenians in New Julfa, who because of their distinguished position and their good connections with the Shah, mostly related favourable tidings about the system of the Shahs.

In 1628, sir Thomas Herbert was received at the city gates by the Armenian Khoja Nazar. The envoys of the Prince of Holstein were received in 1637 by the *kalantar*, Sarfraz beg and his brother Elia beg, and were accompanied to their quarters. On his arrival in Isfahan in 1633, Tavernier was entrusted to the care of the Armenian *kalantar*, etc.

This generation had already forgotten, or did not even know about the "great *sürgün*". Tavrizhetsi draws attention with justification to the deplorable past and to the

[88] The idea has been suggested by Katholicos David, living secluded in a village near Isfahan, in all likelihood, in order to wrest the supreme power out of the hands of Melkisedek: Tavriželi, p. 207; Tavr. Bros. 368; Tavr/Xan. 177. The stone architectural fragments brought from Echmiadzin are still extant in Julfa in the courtyard of the St. George Church. See Carswell, *op. cit.* Plate 21.

[89] Tavriželi, p. 318–21; Tavr/Bros. 364–72; Tavr/Xan. 256–58.

[90] Tavernier, *op. cit.* IV, 6, pp. 468. and sqq., further IV, chap. 15, p. 519; Olearius, 1. IV. cap. 39, pp. 514–15; Further travellers' relations see: Carswell, *op. cit.* pp. 81–82.

II

sad fate of the Armenians transferred to other regions, viz.: "Those who praise the Shah, saying that he is a Christian-loving, country building, peace-loving ruler, (should consider), in what his love of the Christians consists, when he destroyed the whole Christian world, Armenia and Georgia, killed them off with sword, famine and driving them away to slavery, and the remaining ones he drove over to Fahrabad and Isfahan, where they are perishing day by day in different ways."[91]

2,3. But the Armenian community in Persia was also threatened by another factor, even if not by direct annihilation, like the settlements in Gilan and Mazenderan, but through the loss of their ancient religion, the loss of their language and their national consciousness. After the punitive actions and forcible resettlement, Mohammedanization was the threatening factor that forced a considerable part of the Armenian colony in Persia to undergo assimilation.

Shah Abbas conceived the idea already at the inset of the "great *sürgün*" that the next generations of the Armenian colony will become Mohammedan for some interest or the other.[92]

The Armenian colony stuck to its faith with strong persistence. This applied to the settlers in Isfahan and Shiraz, as well as to the Armenians settled in New Julfa and in the area of Isfahan. In 1658 — when Arakel Tavrizhetsi visited Isfahan — the Georgians, who had settled there, had all given up their ancient faith, but the Armenians strictly adhered to it.[93]

However, the situation was different in the new army of the Shah. The Shah recruited his *ǧulams* from among the ranks of Caucasian youths, Georgians and Armenians, who were very soon obliged to adopt the new faith.

The shahs availed themselves of every opportunity to convert the members of the different nationalities to the Mohammedan faith. Shah Abbas feared that the Roman Catholic missions would exert a constantly strengthening influence on the Armenians and would convert many of them. The missionaries originating from various monastic orders, came to Persia on behalf of different Western kings: the Carmelites were envoys of the Italian King, the Capuchins were sent by the French King, the Augustines by the Portuguese King. Thus, the Shah regarded the converting activity of the missions as an attempt of the respective kings concerned to extend their sphere of authority over his, the Shah's Armenian subjects.

When the Augustines arrived in Isfahan in 1604, and the Armenian Katholicos David made a profession of allegiance before them addressed to the Pope; the Shah — to whom the news about this event was conveyed in a somewhat polarized form —

[91] Tavriżeci, p. 134; Tavr/Bros. 334; Tavr/Xan. 127. A more concise negative characteristics: Tavr. 25; Tavr/Bros. 280; Tavr/Xan. 53.

[92] Tavriżeci, 67; Tavr/Bros. 301-2; Tavr/Xan. 80–81; cf. *Drvagner*, II, p. 99.

[93] Tavriżeci, p. 134; Tavr/Bros. 334; Tavr/Xan. 127-28. Quite a number of stories about Armenian martyrs told by Tavernier in chapter: Exemples de la fermeté des arméniens à soutenir leur religion contre la persecution des mahométans; *op. cit.* pp. 510–18.

II

became immensely indignant, saying that the Augustines "wanted to make *his* Armenian subjects Portuguese".[94]

The relationship between the Shah and the missions representing the Western powers resulted from different components. The antipathy of the Shah towards the Portuguese (and from their union of 1580: the Spanish–Portuguese) King was of earlier standing, due to the anti-Persian attitude of the Portuguese viceroy of the island of Hormuz, and the absence of the Portuguese–Spanish military aid promised in vain for decades.

His anger against the Augustines was further increased by Antonio de Gouvea, abbot of Cyrene, when at the occasion of an official reception he referred to the Armenians of Isfahan several times as *"his* Armenians" [i.e. Christians assigned to his care by the Pope]. The Shah regarded this as Spanish–Portuguese interference and punished the Armenians of Isfahan with serious reprisals. He immediately demanded back the sum of 400 *tumans* granted to the poorer families of the community following the *sürgün*, regarded by the latter not as a loan, but as a subsidy. At that time they were told that either they refund the amount, or adopt the Mohammedan faith, or give their sons or daughters to the Shah for proportionate amounts. When the Shah, after the unconsidered statement of Gouvea, raised the subject of claiming back the "loan", immense consternation arose, and 300 families gave up their Christian faith to save their children.[95] The debts of those who apostatized, assumed the Mohammedan faith, were cancelled, while those who did not become converted, had their son or daughter taken away.

Upon the instigation of the chief mollah, in 1621 again a wave of Mohammedanization started in five villages in the vicinity of Isfahan, and then this was extended to 43 villages. The Mollah ordered that the Armenian Christians of these hamlets be circumcised. The New-Julfans became afraid that these measures would also be extended to the capital. However the Shah very soon found out what harmful economic consequence the religious persecution of the Armenians would entail. Therefore he stopped the abuses.[96]

The edict issued by Shah Abbas before his death (1629), according to which whoever of a Christian family adopted the Muslim faith should inherit the property of all his relatives up to the seventh generation, had very serious consequences for the Christian communities. The avalanche set in motion by this infamous edict is reflected by the circumstance, that by 1654, i.e. in twenty years, (according to the calculation of

[94] *Carmelites*, I, 100–101.
[95] *Carmelites*, I, p. 207; Tavrižeci, pp. 149–162; Tavr/Bros. 341–348; Tavr/Xan. 137–47.
[96] *Carmelites*, I. 255–57; Cf. *Bajburtjcn, op. cit.*, p. 21. It is very likely that this information has been mixed up with another one, according to which the Shah as an act of gratitude to Allah for granting him victory over the Turks in capturing Baghdad in 1623 gave the order that in 43 hamlets of the province the Armenians should be circumcised: *Carmelites*, I, p. 271.

II

the missionaries) more than 50,000 Christians became renegades to save themselves from beggary.[97]

This tendency became even stronger at the time of the subsequent shahs.[98] In 1658 the tyrannous Shah Abbas II ordered that the Jews living in his realm, numbering about 100,000, had to become converted to the Mohammedan religion. Thereafter, he started the conversion of the Armenians and the other Christians, so that even the younger brother of the patriarch, an archbishop himself, gave up his Christian faith. "I think — the Carmelite monk added — that this poor Armenian community will in the end have to become completely Mohammedan".[99]

About the heavy taxes and the religious persecution the Katholicos Hagop of Julfa wrote a letter to the Tsar in 1673 as follows: *"In Persia nostris ecclesiaeque nec non eius ministris vectigalia exotica imponuntur ... (Armeni) ad carceres trahuntur, vexantur, excruciantur, denique quod ultima et praecipua mahometanorum est intentio ad ritum illorum compelluntur"*.[100]

The compulsion to embrace the Mohammedan faith resulted in the assimilation of a significant part of the Armenians. The vexation and the assessment of heavy taxes was also continued during the time of the next rulers and thus continuously new masses of the colony left for foreign countries, first of all for India.[101]

2,4 But what happened in the first half of the 17th century, at the times following the "great *sürgün*" in the mother-country? The order of the Shah was extremely strict that a system of waste land zone should be maintained against the Turks. On the other hand, it was an imperative interest of Amirguna khan to restore the economic life of the province (khanate) of Armenia *(Chuqur Sa'ad)* placed under his administration. The main concern of the Khan was, of course, ensuring provisions for the Persian garrison. "Since the attack of the Ottoman armies marching on every occasion through the area of Erivan, the Shah therefore, ordered that as long as the state of war existed, the land of these regions should be left uncultivated ... But Amirguna khan asked the Shah to

---

[97] This message has been intimated in the letter of Paolo Piromalli addressed in 1632 to the Congregatio de Propaganda Fide, see: *Carmelites*, I, 288, note 3. Cf. also Tavernier, *op. cit.*, I. IV, chap. 14, p. 511.

[98] An eloquent example is related by A. Olearius. Even Shah Sefi, a constant visitor of his Armenian friends did not refrain from violence even with his favourites. At one occasion he by force had Elias Bek, the brother of the Armenian Kalantar circumcised, though he could not induce him to apostasy. Olearius, *op. cit.*, I. IV, chap. 44, p. 533.

[99] *Carmelites*, I, 364–365. At the time, when Chardin visited New Julfa, it was the Armenian kalantar who was forced to adopt the Mohammedan faith, and had his name changed to Mohammed Piri: Chardin, *op. cit.* III, pp. 165–66.

[100] *Armjano–russkie otnošenija v XVII veke*. Edited by V. A. Parsamjan. Yerevan 1953, p. 98.

[101] Cf. Seth, M., *The Armenians in India*, Calcutta 1937. The rest of the Armenian settlement returned in 1828 from Persia to the homeland: Neumann C. F., *Geschichte der Übersiedlung von 40 Tausend Armeniern, welche im Jahre 1828 aus der persischen Provinz Aserbaidschan nach Russland auswanderten*. Leipzig 1834.

266

II

allow the soldiers to carry on cultivation on the lands in the vicinity of the fort (of Erivan) for themselves and for their horses. If before the harvest, news was received that the armies of the enemy were approaching this region, then the whole crop could be destroyed, and if nothing happened, then the harvest could be completed within one day and the grain brought into the fort and thus provisions for the soldiers could be ensured. Many of the peasants of Erivan, who were hiding somewhere ... in ones, or twos, and in certain places even two or three families, started to cultivate the land."[102]

The Shah's order to maintain a "scorched earth" policy was very strictly adhered to, and thus the restoration of the economic life of the Ararat valley could take place only sluggishly, in the final result only after peace was concluded (1612, 1618, 1639).[103]

At any rate, during the country-wide scale demographic movement, the nationality picture of the province became entirely mixed up. During the 16th century, Ustajlu, Alpavut and Bayat Qizilbash tribes migrated to the vilayet of Erivan (at that time Alashkert and Bayazet also belonged to it). In the place of the Armenians carried away to Persia, Aq-qoyunlu, Qajar and other tribes were settled here.

At the time of the Jelâli revolts, the infiltrating Kurd tribes became more and more dominant in East Anatolia. With their inroads, they constantly pestered the sorrounding territories under Persian rule. Several military expeditions were led against them by Amirguna khan, and he also brought over to the Erivan Khanate contingents of several other nomad tribes. During his military expeditions against Kars, Maku, Bayazet and other regions, he also transferred many Armenian peasants to the territory of the khanate of Erivan. The biggest profit for Amirguna was represented by the Armenian peasants, not only because — as non-Mohammedans — they paid the *jizye* tribute, but because unlike the nomad nationalities in the fertile Ararat plain, they pursued the ancient branches of agriculture. At any rate, in these decades the population of East Armenia became of a mixed composition, because in addition to the Armenians, Kurds and masses of the Azeri tribes were represented in a high percentage.

After the death of Amirguna khan (1625), his son and successor Tahmaz-quli khan, also adopted military operations to replace the scanty population, directed attacks against Archesh, Khlat and Artske, and again drove many Armenian peasants to the Ararat valley.[104]

[102]Iskander Bik Turkman (Munši), *Tarih-i alem aray-i Abbasi*. II. Tehran A. H. 1335–6/A. D. 1916. pp. 787–88, in: *Hay žolovrdi patmut'yun* IV, 103.

[103] A considerable part of the population could outlive the 1604–5 campaign only in the Northern provinces. A. Badjetsi's remark, according to which Shah Abbas has been induced by the Holy Ghost to let the Armenians of Nakhichevan and Erinchagh return home (*op. cit.* pp. 226–27.), can refer only to the period following the peace-treaties with the Turks, and even so in sporadic cases. The statement is an exaggerated generalisation, not corroborated by other sources. — Echmiadzin regained its vaqufs only in 1644: Papazyan H. D., *Hrovartakner/Ukazy. II.* Erevan 1959, p. 269.

[104] Zakarij Kanakerci, *Chronika.* Moscow 1969, pp. 70, 116; Hakobyan, *Manr žamanakagrut'yunner,* I, 187.

II

The depopulation of the region was also, of course, the most serious difficulty on the Turkish side. In 1618, the retreating Halil pasha wanted to solve this problem and so he carried away 30,000 Armenians and Azeris from Marand, Khoy and Salmast and settled them in the depopulated regions of Van and Diyarbekir.

3,1,1. For the Armenian population of Armenia, the scene of operations of the Persian–Turkish wars, decimated by the Jelâli devastations, and the *"great sürgün"*, the unity of the language did not represent an absolutely firm basis of national identity, since in the Azeri and Kurd surroundings, the majority of the Armenians also spoke one or the other of these languages. The main cementing force was mainly the common ancient religion. Thus the role of the Armenian ecclesiarch was of especially major significance. In the period concerned, during the rule of Shah Abbas, and the belligerent eastern absolute monarchy, this post was held by the patriarch Melkisedek. An abundant and very negative characterization of his personality is gained from our main source, the chronicle of Arakel Tavriżeci. Melkisedek was of a violent and inconsiderate character, but he skilfully manoeuvred between the two Mohammedan powers. Maintaining good relations with the leading layers of the occupant Persian power, obliging the leaders with bribery and gifts, he still helped the Armenian continuity, with great difficulty, through one of the most serious periods of Armenian history. No effort is made here to excuse the dark sides of his character, but to examine the historical reality in the field of ecclesiastic policy.

In this disastrous period, originally there appeared at the same time, two and even three Katholicoi on the scene, viz. David Vałarshapatetsi (1590–1629), Melkisedek Garnetsi (1593–1624), and Srapion Amdetsi (1603–1606).

David coopted Melkisedek to his side in the difficult years of the Ottoman pressure of taxation, with the idea that Melkisedek as a *nvirak* (legate) would visit the Armenian inhabited regions and Diasporas and try to collect the tax demanded by the Turkish authorities.[105]

When in 1604/1605 Shah Abbas occupied Armenia and drove away the population to Persia, David complying with the order accompanied the deportees. Melkisedek, on the other hand, on his own, from half-way, from the bank of the Arax river returned to the mother-country and took up his seat in the S. Katolike cathedral in Erivan (instead of Echmiadzin, destroyed during the wars).[106]

M. Ormanean, the ecclesiastic historian, does not include Melkisedek among the Katholicoi, because Armenian ecclesiastical law does not recognise the institution of co-Katholicoi, and at the most he regards him as a co-adjutor, with a limited sphere of authority.[107] At any rate, in practice, in the turbulent centuries of Armenian history, it

[105] Tavriżeci, 6; Tavr/Bros. 271; Tavr/Xan. 40. Akinean, *Movses III*, pp. 38–39. Melkisedek set out to collect alms for the Echmiadzin See. On his round-tour he came also to Istanbul, where for a transitory period (1599/1600) he was elected even Armenian Patriarch of Constantinople: Ormanean, M., *Azgapatum*, II/2. Beyrout 1960, col. 2290.

[106] Tavriżeci, 202, 205–6; Tavr/Bros. 366, 368; Tavr/Xan. 174, 176.

[107] Ormanean, *Azgapatum*, II/2, cols. 2287–90, 2317.

268

II

frequently occurred that at the same time several Katholicoi held the title of the ecclesiarch. For 40 years in the present case, Melkisedek "under the most difficult circumstances"[108] sat more or less firmly in the chair of the Katholicos. He held the post of co-adjutor or co-patriarch since the year 1599, and from 1604, when he visited the Shah before his campaign to conquer the Ararat valley,[109] Melkisedek became the Shah's favourite. When Melkisedek at the time of the *sürgün* did not follow his compatriots to Persian soil, and returned from the bank of the Arax river, he had not been rebuked for his demeanour, but the Shah wanted to install him for Katholicos and tacitly accepted him as the leader of the See of the Armenian Christians.

There are authors who voiced the opinion that the function of the Katholicos was divided territorially, in the Persian New-Julfan Armenian colony David would have performed the function of the Katholicos.[110]

It is possible that in the beginning, after the *sürgün*, the Shah preferred David "rather", who followed his order in coming to Isfahan.[111]

There came a period, when David saw the opportunity to topple Melkisedek: when Frank (i.e. Western) monks dug out the holy relics of S. Hripsime and tried to smuggle them out of the country.[112] David Katholicos seizing the opportunity hastened to the Shah and denounced Melkisedek charging him with complicity, calling him *Smuk satan xalife* i.e. 'Patriarch selling the (holy) bones'.[113] Therefore by his Ferman dated 1610 Safar (May) the Shah demanded from Amirguna to initiate an inquest to clear up the matter whether the "Frank" fathers had any complices.[114]

The ferman does not contain any direct hint to the person of Melkisedek; we know about his negative role in this incident only from the narrative of Tavriżeci and the Ferman issued in 1629 by Shah Sefi enthroning Movses Vardapet into the seat of Armenian Katholicos.

Though the Shah — after the case of the Hripsime relics — seemed to get inclined to entrust the Echmiadzin See to David,[115] but as soon as the Shah departed from the neighbourhood, from the region of Atrpatakan, Amirguna Khan grew outrightly inimicable towards David, so he chose better to withdraw to Isfahan.[116]

[108] Akinean, N., *Movses III. Tat'evac'i Hayoc' katolikosn ew ir žamanakə*. Vienna 1936. p. 37.

[109] Tavriżeci, 27; Tavr/Bros. 281; Tavr/Xan. 54.

[110] Tadeo di S. Eliseo (A. D. 1611): Propaganda, t. 189, f. 186: Akinean, *Movses III*, p. 322.

[111] Tavriżeci, 205–6; Tavr/Bros. 367–68; Tavr/Xan. 176–77.

[112] *Ibidem*.

[113] *Ibid.* Azeri *sümük* 'bone'. The Shah, the military commanders themselves, and the army, consisting — before the reorganisation — exclusively of Azeri tribes, so the language used in the Court and the army was Azeri.

[114] The text of the Ferman see: Papazyan, op. cit., II. Persian: 482–83. Russian: 320–21. Armenian: 90–91.

[115] Tavriżeci, 207; Tavr/Bros. 368; Tavr Xan. 177.

[116] Tavriżeci, 214–15; Tavr/Bros. 373; Tavr/Xan. 183–84; Ormanean, *Azgapatum*, II/2, cols. 2425–26.

269

II

In any case, David had been instrumental in the transplantation of Armenian holy relics to Isfahan. He gave the advice to the Shah to let the right hand of Saint Gregory and a number of stone blocks, consecrated altar pedestals of the Echmiadzin cathedral transported to the Persian capital.[117] The Shah understood what significance the holy relics would mean for the sake of tying the Julfa Armenians more tightly also with religious bonds to their new home, if a new Echmiadzin was established in Isfahan.[118]

But David did not perform the function of the Katholikos in Isfahan, and did not even act as an ecclesiastic leader of the New Julfa colony, only in the beginnings, at certain limited occasions.[119] The church functions were ceded to the local Armenian churches, but the central affairs, even of ecclesiastic nature were administered by the *kalantar*, at that time Khoja Nazar, so much so that even the ecclesiastic relics brought in 1613–15 to New Julfa were not entrusted to the care of David either, but were taken to the house of Khoja Nazar.[120] David after his return to Persia, resigned his office as Katholicos, withdrew to the village of Fringikan (in the neighbourhood of Isfahan) and devoted himself to prey for the health and prosperity of the Shah.[121]

Even Ormanian, who did not acknowledge Melkisedek's right of succession to the seat of Katholicos, is of the opinion that David performed only minor ecclesiastical functions for the Armenian community in Julfa.[122] Simeon Erevantsi left David simply out the list of the Katholicoses (as exerting no function).[123] The Julfans remembered David only at the moment when Melkisedek in 1624 left his post, they called David to take the seat of Katholicos, but this had not been realized.[124]

In the final conclusion, general (ecclesiastical) opinion also acknowledged the situation developed in practice, which also became clear from the dating of the colophons of the codices copied in this period. Out of 156 codices in 130 Melkisedek has been named as Katholicos, and only 16 codices, copied in Isfahan (Šoš), mentioned David in the office of Katholicos, while 10 other codices from Isfahan both of them, jointly.[125]

---

[117] Tavrižeci, 277; Tavr/Bros. 371; Tavr/Xan. 181–82. See also note 89.

[118] Tavrižeci, 199–201; Tavr/Bros. 365; Tavr/Xan. 172–73.

[119] *Carmelites*, I, p. 101.

[120] Tavrižeci, 211–12, 320–21; Tavr/Bros. 371, 424; Tavr/Xan. 181, 258. (*Kalantar, kelonter:* Olearius/p. 514) 'gubernator'. Tavr/Bros. 468: 'leur chef, gouverneur sous l'autorité royale, leur juge'.

[121] Tavrižeci, 217; Tavr/Bros. 374; Tavr/Xan. 185.

[122] Ormanean, *Azgapatum*, II/2, cols. 2425–26. We know about his acting as Katholicos, when he was preparing myrrh in Echmiadzin in 1610, but exclusively for the Ispahan Armenian community. Cf. Papazyan, *op. cit.*, 482–83, 320–21, 90–91.

[123] Simeon Erevanci, *Džambr, pamjatnaja kniga, zercalo i sbornik vsech obstojatelstv svjatogo prestola Ečmiadzina*. Moscow 1958, p. 173.

[124] Tavrižeci, 232–33; Tavr/Bros. 381; Tavr/Xan. 195–96.

[125] *Hišatakaranner XVII d.*, II. passim

II

3.1.2. Arakel Tavrizhetsi accused Melkisedek that his appointment was gained by bribery.[126] This opinion is often referred to. But in this opinion two or three quite different kinds of pecuniary tributes, presents or fines were confounded.

Bribery — either in the form of open present, or as secret allotment — was an organic concomitant of (eastern?) secular and ecclesiastic diplomacy. And the advantages enjoyed by Melkisedek during all the reign of Amirguna khan are strikingly proved by Melkisedek's career.

The most steadfast supporters of the function of Melkisedek as Katholicos were Amirguna khan and the Persian leaders of the vilayet, and later khanate of Erivan, whom Melkisedek favoured — mainly also beyond his means — with gifts.[127] But this protection of Amirguna towards Melkisedek was respected even by Shah Abbas. Amirguna khan also played an important instrumental role in the expansion and consolidation of the power of the Shah. This is why the Shah appointed him *beglerbeg* of the vilayet of Erivan, or with the Persian nomenclature, to khan of the khanate of Erivan.[128] Amirguna supported Melkisedek almost to the end of his life (1625), even at the time of the smuggling out of the Hripsime relics by Latin (Frank) priests, which was a rather unrewarding part for the Khan, since the Shah was enraged by the case.[129] The anger of the Shah was, of course, evoked not by the sacrilege in the Christian sense, but by the fact that the offenders were Augustine priests under the aegis of the Portuguese King.[130] At this juncture, the support of Amirguna Khan really was of decisive importance for Melkisedek to remain at liberty, moreover, to keep the throne of the Katholicos.

As regards the question of gifts, this was not only a general custom in the eastern world, in the court of the Shah, but was — so to say — compulsory. When Shah Abbas marched in to Old Julfa in 1604, in the house of the merchant Khoja Khachik, his son received the Shah with a tray heaped with gold coins and the other merchants also handed over gifts worthy of the Shah.[131] The revered vardapet Movses had to expend 1000 tumans for bribery in 1629 at the court (see note 146). But the saintly Katholicos Philippos also appeared before Shah Sefi (in 1637/38) with a tray full of gold coins in order to get back the S. Lusavorich relic taken by Shah Abbas to Isfahan.[132] So bribery in oriental diplomacy is not in general regarded as a dishonest means. In addition it should not be forgotten that Shah Abbas was especially greedy, besides the taxes streaming from all directions, he continuously expected gifts from foreign delegations, as well as from his own noblemen.[133]

[126] Tavriẑeci. 185, 218–19; Tavr/Bros. 374–75; Tavr/Xan. 185–86.
[127] Tavriẑeci. 7, 215–16; Tavr/Bros. 372–73; Tavr/Xan. 41, 184.
[128] Tavriẑeci. 27; Tavr/Bros. 271; Tavr/Xan. 54.
[129] Tavriẑeci. 208–9; Tavr/Bros. 369–70; Tavr/Xan. 178–79.
[130] Tavriẑeci. 185–86; Tavr/Bros. 356–57; Tavr/Xan. 162–3.
[131] Tavriẑeci. 25; Tavr/Bros. 280; Tavr/Xan. 52.
[132] Tavriẑeci. 320; Tavr/Bros. 424; Tavr/Xan. 257.
[133] E. g., in 1618 at the audience given to the delegation of Philip III, King of Spain, 400 servants carried in a long procession the splendid gifts ornamented with precious stones, 30 camels carried precious

II

3,1,3. Permanent tax was a heavy burden. The Armenian land, devastated during the centuries-long Persian—Ottoman wars, was heavily burdened by taxes. Katholicos David could not pay the tax during the Ottoman period, since the Jelâli guerilla bands consumed even the remaining crops. Thus the unpaid taxes of the Katholicosate amounted to 50,000 *guruşes*.[134] The Katholicos David co-opted Melkisedek and then Srapion to help him settle the tax burden. Melkisedek went around all the regions inhabited by Armenians, in 1603 he visited even the rich community of Lvov. The same year the myrrh-benediction was also arranged to collect oblations from the believers. When the collecting of oblations was not as successful as it had been expected, the Katholicoi were compelled to pawn ecclesiastical treasures, devotional articles, mainly with Mohammedan usurers. This was related by the Katholicos David in tears in 1603 to the priest Grigor Daranałtsi.[135]

David and Melkisedek tried to get rid of the tax burden and transferred the office of the Katholicos to the *vardapet* Srapion of Tigranakert (Amida), originating from a rich family, in the hope that the latter with his great renown could collect a good deal of money to cover the debts.[136]

At that time, Shah Abbas occupied Tebriz and advanced towards Erivan. When he occupied Nakhichevan and Erivan, he demanded that David and Melkisedek should pay to him the large amount they already owed the Ottoman Turks. The Katholicoi had no alternative, and had to pay. Moreover, the men of the Shah also extorted additional sums from Srapion (despite the fact that Srapion was not even recognized by the Shah as Katholicos.)[137]

As to the tribute burdened on the Katholicos' See different versions were related by Tavrizhetsi. Some informants mentioned a fine in the amount of 300 or 500 tumans, levied on Melkisedek, because of his unlawful deeds.[138] But elsewhere (in the enthronement ferman of Movses) no such fine is mentioned, so it rather seems more

---

eastern spices. *Carmelites*. I, 239–240; The presents of the Holstein delegation, see Olearius, *op. cit*. I. IV, chap. 38, p. 507–8; the presents handed over by Tavernier, *op. cit*., I. IV, chap. 15, p. 520–21. — Later the Shahs have become so accustomed to the inflow of presents, that they did not even take the trouble to take a look at them: Chardin, *op. cit*. III. p. 195.

Carmelites, I, 159: On the festive reception at the occasion of Persian New Year the dignitaries paid their respects to the Shah with "gifts" of immense sums (extorted out of the provinces). The Grand Vizier presented 50,000 tumans, others 40,000 tumans, and so forth.

[134] Tavrižeci, 8; Tavr/Bros. 271–2; Tavr/Xan. 42; Daranałci, *op. cit*. p. 54.

[135] Daranałci, *ibid*. This case was not unparallelled. In 1606 because of fearing being ransacked by Jelâli robbers, Armenian pilgrims did not dare to visit Jerusalem. So the S. Jacob monastery has got into such a poverty, that they were compelled to pawn their church treasures. *Ibid*. p. XXVI.

[136] Tavrižeci, 9–13; Tavr/Bros. 272–74; Tavr/Xan. 42–45.

[137] Tavrižeci, 27–29; Tavr/Bros. 282; Tavr/Xan. 54–55. Cf. Danełyan, *op. cit*. p. 209. — Srapion has been released for a sum of 6,000 guruşes paid by the Julfans. Daranałci, *op. cit*. p. 58.

[138] Tavrižeci, 187, 218; Tavr/Bros. 374–75; Tavr/Xan. 185, 187. Cf. Ormanean, *Azgapatum*. II/2, 2337–40.

272

II

probable that these amounts were the arrears accumulated all through the years, when the Katholicos was unable to pay the yearly tribute.

It is a documented fact that Melkisedek undertook a yearly tribute, most probably after the vicissitudes suffered during the inquest about his complicity or connivance in the Hripsime relics case. Up to 1617 he held the office of the Katholicos, so his seat seems to have come in danger, that induced him to undertake the heavy burden of the tribute. But the ferman corroborating him in the Katholicos's seat allows also another suggestion. The ferman nominated him Katholicos of Üch-Kilise (i.e. Echmiadzin). But at the same time it extended his scope of authority not only on Chuqur Sa'ad vilayet (the Erivan Khanate), but also on the Armenians of the Persian metropolis, Isfahan, the *tümen* of Nakhichevan, the Gökche See (Lake–Sevan region), Khoi, Salmast, Ganja, also; which enumeration covered all regions inhabited by Armenians under Persian rule. (There is no hint in this document that this tribute should have been a fine).[139]

It is only after Melkisedek's flight from the country in 1624 that one learned from an official document about his improper deeds.

Only the installation chart of Movses Vardapet to the post of the Armenian Katholicos issued in 1629, mentioned Melkisedek's misdeeds, though characterised in a moderate tone; saying that "it has been reported that Melkisedek ... took the Seat of the Katholicos of *Üch-Kilise* unlawfully and committed" in the days of Shah Abbas I "inadmissible (*na-sawab* 'unpardonable, improper, sinful')" deeds. Therefore he has been caught and delivered to the Hight Court. In order to escape punishment he assumed the obligation to pay a yearly tribute of 100 tuman Tabrizi as *peškaš* and then continued to lead the affairs of the patriarchate ..." In the second paragraph of the ferman this direct accusation (without, however, mentioning the motives) is almost nullified by the assertion that "this sum had been burdened on the shoulder of Katholicos Melkisedek by some people who bore grudge on him". In any case this phrase is not sufficient to exempt Melkisedek of all responsibility. It may be rather an astute wording of Khoja Nazar, who motivated the assessment of the *muqata* by personal enmity, that is to say, it was qualified for a personal affair of Melkisedek. Such a tribute has never been assumed by any other Katholicos and so — Melkisedek gone — the motive of the tribute became vain and void, so Nazar requested the Shah graciously to suspend the assessment of the same.[140]

The undertaking to pay the *muqata*, however, was not quite unequivocally a simple personal matter of Melkisedek, though one of the terms in the chart *taqabbol* denoted a tribute paid for the sake to obtain a high post. Nonetheless from the 16th century on, but especially the fermans issued in the first half of the 17th century, leave no doubt, that also on the clergy and ecclesiastic institutions a lower or higher tax was

[139] Papazyan *op. cit.* II, 486–87, 323–4, 86–87.
[140] Papazyan, *op. cit.* II, 502–3, 334–5, 104–6.

II

levied. When Shah Abbas I conquered Armenia in 1604–5, his first act was to collect by force from the Katholicoi the arrears of taxes, originally exacted by the Ottoman regime.

This tax was all the heavier weighing on the population, since in the *tiul* system the amount assessed by the ferman. 1617 has been assigned to Aghurlu bek *qušči* ('[royal] falconeer') for the entertainment (feeding, *kormlenie*) of four detachments of ghulams, garrisoned in Echmiadzin.[141]

This meant a double disaster for the rural population, because above other kinds of taxes they had to supply with provision the ghulams, their servants, provide fodder for their saddle horses, and pack animals. The *ghulams* mercilessly extorted all their supplies, and consumed all victuals. Neither did they spare the priests and monks.[142]

Melkisedek had no other choice but to borrow money at a high interest. So the amount of the unpaid tax during the subsequent years accumulated to 600 *tumans*.

Melkisedek finally appeared before the Shah and cried that he was unable to collect more money, but the Shah remained merciless. Therefore, Melkisedek in 1624 transferred the office of the Katholicos to his nephew Sahak, and in 1625 one night he secretly crossed the river Arax and fled over to the Turkish side, and then via Erzerum and Istanbul he went to Lvov.[143]

In historical literature often a comparison is made: while Melkisedek could not attain to get cancelled the tribute, that afflicted the reduced and pauperized population of Armenia, the Katholicos Movses (1629–1632) achieved it at the very beginning of his accession to the throne.[144] In this matter, the contrast in unjustified, because the cancellation of the tax was attained only in 1629, after the death of Shah Abbas, and even then with great difficulty. Though Vardapet Movses appeared before the Shah in 1628, with the expectation that with regard to his merits gained in 1626, by teaching three Persian artisans the proper method of bleaching wax, he would be able to achieve success; the courtiers however, dissuaded him, saying that "the Shah is very greedy and parsimonious, and he would by no means give up such a large revenue of money".[145]

---

[141] Papazyan, *op. cit.* II, 486–7, 323, 93.

[142] Tavrižeci, 222–27; Tavr/Bros. 375–78; Tavr/Xan. 188–192.

[143] Tavrižeci, 224–28; Tavr/Bros. 377–79; Tavr/Xan 190–93. Papazyan, *op. cit.* II. 502, 335, 105.

[144] Akinean, *Movses III*, 114–123. *Hay žolovrdi patmuť yun*, IV, 119: *azatwecaw* "(the Armenians) have been freed of" the passive voice in the text avoids the answer to the personal issue. — The text of the ferman cancelling the obligation see: Papazyan, *op. cit.* II. 502–3, (401–3), 334–36, 104–6.

[145] Tavrižeci, 308; Tavr/Bros. 418; Tavr/Xan. 249. — Wax bleaching was of major importance for the Shah, fond of splendour. At festival occasions the attendants lighted a very great number of candles around a very large fishpond where the Shah was sitting, *Carmelites*, I, 187. This illumination by candles (P. *čiragāni*) at the funeral ceremonies of Shah Abbas I in 1629 lasted for three days, and cost 3,000 tumans. *Carmelites*, I. 307. — The mastership of Movses vardapet in wax bleaching was the main motive that the Shah named him sacristan *(lusarar = čirâgčigir)* of Echmiadzin. Papazyan, *op. cit.* II. 500–1, 333–4, 104. — Tavrižeci, 300–303; Tavr/Bros. 413–14; Tavr/Xan. 244–45; Oscan's colophon in the Amsterdam edition: Tavr/Bros. 596–97.

II

When Movses was informed about the death of Shah Abbas and the accession to the throne of Shah Sefi, he thought that the time had come to request the cancellation of the tax. But even so he had to go begging to the court for eight months, and could attain the granting of his request only with the support of the influential *kalantar*, Khoja Nazar. By the way, a very large amount of money — about 1,000 tumans [equal to the total of ten years' taxes!] — had to be spent on gifts distributed among the court attendants. Thus, if we examine the details of achieving this result, then it becomes clear that the cancellation of the heavy tax was not primarily due to the personal merits of the Katholicos Movses.[146]

It is hard to understand why the Shah did not cancel this comparatively small amount — 100 *tumans*[147] — for a decade. The main reason apparently could be the conception of principle, viz. why should he exempt the giaour Christians of the tax. Moreover, it must be taken into consideration that Shah Abbas completely reorganized the Persian army.[148] A considerable part of the time of the Shah's rule was spent with the fight againts the Ottoman power, which represented an immense financial burden. In fact, these fights ended only with the occupation of Baghdad in 1623. At the time of Shah Sefi, only the military expedition of Sultan Murad IV should be mentioned. As a matter of fact, the occupation of Erivan and its re-occupation by the Persians (1635–1636) were the salient military events, and then with the occupation of Baghdad by the Turks (1638) and the peace treaty of 1639 the series of the Persian–Ottoman wars came to an end.

The feeble, sickly and mistrustful Shah Sefi I was mainly interested in domestic affairs. He removed, or killed off the most talented court and military officials who remained from the time of Abbas I,[149] and the debaucherous Abbas II was an addict of liquor and harem pleasures. The shahs were unwilling to go to war against the Ottoman Turks, despite the urging of the Western delegations. Shah Sefi (1629–1642), Abbas II (1642–1666) and Sulaiman (1666–1694) rejected the proposals of the Western powers, saying that they lived in peace with the Turks and did not intend to break peace.[150]

3,1,4. Thus, in assessing the manoeuvring of Melkisedek it must be well taken into consideration that the period of his rule was separated from that of the Katholicoi who followed him by just as sharp a caesura, as the reign of Shah Abbas I from that of the shahs following him. The belligerent monarch Shah Abbas enlarged his empire by

[146] Tavrižeci, 308–11; Tavr/Bros. 419–20; Tavr/Xan. 250–52. Cf. Simeon Erevanci, *Džambr*, Moscow 1958, p. 90, 174, 201–2.

[147] 100 tuman — 100 sequin, zecchino, resp. 1350 scudi (A. D. 1608, 1615): *Carmelites*, I, 159–60, 218. — 100 tuman — 1500 écus (A. D. 1666) Chardin, *op. cit.* III, p. 395. —

[148] *Carmelites*, I, 161; *Drvagner*, II, 90–92; N. V. Pigulevskaja, A. Ju. Jakubovskij, I. P., Petrusevskij et alii, *Istorija Irana s drevnejšich vremen do konca XVIII veka*, Leningr. Univ, 1958. 272–3.

[149] Tavernier, *op. cit.*, l. V, chap. 1, 571–75; Zakarij Kanakerci, *Chronika*, Moscow 1969, 67–69.

[150] *Carmelites*, I, 355, 357 (A. D. 1646, 1657), 423 (A. D. 1684).

II

incorporating most part of the Transcaucasus, while his successors did not wage war. From the point of view of the Armenian population the reign of the Shahs must be evaluated in a way opposite to that of the Persians. While Shah Abbas I deprived Armenia at least of half of its population, having dragged them to Persia, during the rest of the Safavids the fraction of the Armenian population surviving in their mother-country enjoyed comparative peace.

And this turn of historical fate left its mark also on the ecclesiastic life of Armenia. The period of the ecclesiastic functioning of Melkisedek (1593–1624) almost coincided with the span of regime of Abbas I (1587–1629), which was mostly occupied by warfare. Melkisedek had to cope with the situation of utter misery, and in addition with a forceful monarch and the Persian local governing authority. What he was able to achieve under such a pressure, could be attained only with cunning, manoeuvring and bribery. This of course, does not absolve him of responsibility for his illegal and forcible deeds, but perhaps does provide an explanation for it.

Melkisedek had also to cope with the increased missionary activity of the Roman Catholic Church. All the Eastern Christians hoped for their liberation from under Muslim yoke by the Pope or by the Christian monarchs of the West. But very soon they had to realize that the promises were not to be taken by their face value, but — on the contrary — they had to endure severe punishments for their eventual conversion.

3,2. The antiuniate sources blame Melkisedek that he professed obedience (hnazandut'iwn) to the Pope on several occasions and submitted himself and his church to the supremacy (hpatakut'iwn) of the Pope.[151]

In 1602, Melkisedek undoubtedly wrote a letter to Pope Clement VIII, which was carried to the Pope by Hovhannes Terzntsi. The original letter has not been preserved, but the content of the letter was included by the Pope in the letter he wrote to King Philip II.[152] Melkisedek asked the Spanish King to instruct the Portuguese governor of the island of Hormuz to collect the general 10 per cent customs duty from the Armenians, equal to that paid by the other Christian merchants, and should not demand twice as much.

The explanation for this letter, dating from the Turkish era, is the fact that the Armenian merchants already before the Persian–Ottoman war of 1604, were the main buyers of the raw silk produced in the Persian province Ghilan and they transported it along the Turkish route to the seaports. However, at the turn of the century, because of the Jelâli rebels, the predatory bands, the transportation by caravans along the old

---

[151] Ališan Gh., *Kamenic', Taregirk' Hayoc' Lehastani ew Řumenioy*, Venetik 1896, 205; (F. K. Zacharyasiewicz) Wiadomość o Ormianach w Polsce: Biblioteka Naukowego Zakładu im. Ossolińskich, t. 2, Lwów, 1842, pp. 69–79. Russian translation: *Ukrainsko-armjanskie svjazi v XVII veke*, (Sbornik dokumentov). Ed. Ja. Daškevič (Abbrev: *Svjazi*), Kiev 1969, 52; Gr. Petrowicz, *L'unione degli Armeni di Polonia con la Santa Sede (1626–1686)*, Roma 1950. (Abbrev.: *L'unione*) 10–11.

[152] VaticanArchives, Arm. XLIV, vol. 46, fasc. 281, p. 264: apud Akinean, *Movses III*, 295–98.

II

route became highly endangered. Otherwise, the belligerent parties in principle did not prevent trade even during wartime.

The motive of the letters originating from the Armenian patriarchs, in addition to the idea of national liberation, was mainly the freedom of trade and exemption from duty on the Western market, even if this does not appear *expressis verbis* in the details of the documents published so far.

In 1610, again Melkisedek sent the *vardapet* Zakaria to the Pope, who proceeded from Constantinople to Rome in June 1611, joining Simeon Lehaci, the pilgrim from Zamość. The letter paid homage to the Pope with abundant oriental flowery speech and professed allegiance to him *(hpatakut'iwn)*.[153]

On March 22nd 1613, Melkisedek again sent the vardapet Zakaria to the Pope with a new letter, the content of which is known to us from the *Relatio brevis*. However, it is not disclosed what leading motive induced him to offer allegiance at that time, but the papal court, to win over the broad masses of the Armenians, had this declaration of allegiance printed in Rome and disseminated it in the regions inhabited by Armenians.[154]

When Grigor Kesaratsi, a fierce enemy of the church union, patriarch of Constantinople, learned about this declaration, he sent an infuriated reproving letter to Melkisedek (in 1614), but even he doubted that it should have been drawn up by Melkisedek, he surmised that it was falsified by the *vardapet* Zakaria.[155]

At any rate, the authorship of Melkisedek seems to be confirmed by the fact that in Echmiadzin in 1613, he received the papal envoys with solemnity, including Fr. Redemptus, who read before him the letter of Pope Paul V and asked Melkisedek to accept the dogmas. Although Melkisedek showed himself to be compliant with regard to the minor dogmatic discrepancies; the deviations in the rites, on the other hand, were held by the legate to be reconcilable with Roman Catholic Church usage. Thus, an agreement seemed to have come about and — according to the Carmelites' report — Melkisedek again made a declaration of allegiance.[156]

It is difficult to verify how far this detailed report corresponded to the facts and how earnestly this declaration was taken by Melkisedek, particularly because in later letters he always stressed the divergencies in dogmas and ceremonies separating the two churches.

[153] Abraham Bzovius, *Pontifex Romanus*, Coloniae Agrippinae 1619. pp. 202–5: Akinean, *Movses III*, 309–10. — Simeon Lehaci, *Ulegrut'iwn, Taregrut'iwn ew yiśatakarank'*. Ed. N. Akinean. Vienna 1936. p. 176; S. Lehaci, *Putevye zametki*. Translated by M. O. Darbinjan. Moscow 1965, 80.; Ormanean, *Azgapatum*, II/2, 2316–17.

[154] Sruandzteanc, G., *T'oros Albar*, II, 288–93 apud Akinean, *Movses III*, 324–325; *Drvagner*, II, 109; *Azgapatum*, II/2, col. 2316; Cf. *Svjazi*, 52. *"basma grow" T'oros Albar*, p. 289, apud Akinean, *Movses III.*, 326.

[155] Among other things, Ormanean tried to refute the authorship of Melkisedek by stating that because of the theft of the Hripsime relics at this time Melkisedek has been imprisoned. Ormanean, *Azgapatum*, II/2, 2322–23. However, the chronology of the case is still unclarified.

[156] *Carmelites*, I, 210.

II

In 1622 and 1623, presumably induced by the debts burdening him and his church, he again addressed letters to the Pope.[157] The session of the Propaganda Fide held on January 10th, 1623 had good reason to doubt the sincerity of these declarations.[158] Melkisedek's next moves were a clear proof of this. Otherwise, if he had been led by the intention to join the Pope, after his escape-like departure in 1624, he would not have gone via Constantinople to Lvov, but to Rome. His activities in the Armenian Diaspora of Poland, in Lvov — up to the time of his death in 1627 on Polish soil — were focused on collecting money.[159] For lack of documents we cannot verify, whether by these means he wanted to cover his debts.

The foregoing analysis seems to show, that these declarations of allegiance did not represent an unconditioned submission to papal supremacy. Such declarations of allegiance were frequently made by Armenian Katholicoi before and after Melkisedek, who viewed the help of the Pope as the only means to liberate the Eastern Christians from the Mohammedan oppression.[160]

This was the motivating force also for the Katholicos David who in Isfahan (immediately after the "great *sürgün*"), in the church of the Augustines took an oath for the union of the church.[161] In 1605 and 1607 he repeated his allegiance to the Pope, asking at the same time for protection of the Christian Church of the Armenians.[162]

Katholicos Movses III (1629–1632) maintained friendly relations with the Dominicans and with the Armenian–Catholic priests and bishops, Augustinus Bajents of Nakhichevan. The friendly manifestations of Movses were exaggeratedly misinterpreted by the missionaries in their reports.[163]

An exchange of letters with the Papal curia was also frequent at the time of Movses, but with the debate over dogmatic and ceremonial questions, the Katholicos evaded the urged declaration of allegiance.[164]

---

[157] According to Stepanos Roszka, *Žamanakagrut'iwn kam tarekank' ekelec'akank'*. Vienna 1964, p. 171; Dashian, J., *Mayr c'uc'ak hayeren dzeragrac' Matenadaranin Mxitareanc' i Vienna*, Vienna 1895, p. 679–81. Similar statement: *L'unione*, p. 11.; Akinean, *Movses* III., 328–29.

[158] Acta S. Congr. An. 1622–1625; t. 3.: apud Akinean, *Movses* III., 329.

[159] Ališan, *Kamenic'*, p. 203; *L'unione*, 19–20.

[160] In the middle of the 16th century, when the Turkish-Persian wars flared up, the Katholicos Stepannos Salmasteci personally visited the Pope in 1549; the Katholicos Michael Sebastaci sent a letter to the Pope in 1564, and in 1575 the Katholicos Thaddeos paid a visit to the Pope and professed allegiance to the head of the Roman Catholic Church. *Hay žolovrdi patmutyun*, IV, 92–93.; Akinean, *Movses III*. 286–7.

[161] *Carmelites*, I, 101. Cf. Akinean, *Movses* III, 300–4.

[162] P. Fr. Antoine de Gowea, *Relation des Grandes Guerres et victoires obtenues par le roi de Perse de Cha-Abbas contre les empereurs de Turquie Mohamet et Ahmet son fils*. Translated from the Portuguese. Rouen 1646. p. 412.: Akinean, *Movses* III, 303–4. *Carmelites*, I, 101.

[163] According to Vardan Hunanian Katholicos Movses III sent a confession of allegiance, signed also by 12 of his bishops, to Pope Urban VIII. (Akinean, *Movses* III, p. 350.), the copy of which has been preserved in the possession of Hunanian. The same statement is repeated by St. Roszka, *Žamanakagrut'iwn*, p. 173. Cf., Ciamcian, *Patmut'iwn Hayoc'*, III. Venice 1784, p. 610–12.

[164] Akinean, *Movses* III, 339–59; *Carmelites*, I. 319.

II

In the beginning of his function as ecclesiarch, the Katholicos Philippos of Aghbak (1633–1655) also maintained friendly relations with the Roman Catholic missions, moreover allegedly he also made a declaration of allegiance,[165] but the forcible Roman catholicisation in Poland estranged him.[166]

With the first appearance of the Roman Catholic missions, since they were at the same time also the mediators of the military alliance between the Western powers and the Persian Shah, there was a great expectation among both the Armenian priests and laymen. The Carmelite superior Fr. Paul Simon reported to Rome about 1607 that the Armenian patriarch, and many archbishops adjured him to beg His Holiness not to abandon them and indicated to him ancient prophecies of the Armenian saints, whereby the Latin (Frank) princes were to free the Armenians from the Mohammedan bondage.[167]

The friendly manifestations towards the Latin Church and the Pope, were exaggerated in the reports of the Roman Catholic missionaries. The principle of the *quid pro quo* was simply disregarded, since after all the Armenians, harassed by the two Mohammedan powers, did receive any help neither from the Pope, nor from the Western Christian monarchs. In effect the negotiations carried on with the Papal Court and the Catholic missions over several decades remained unsuccessful on both sides.[168]

3,3,1. The Katholicoi not only turned to the Pope and to the "Latin" rulers for the liberation of their people from the Mohammedan yoke, but as the representatives of their community also in financial and trade affairs. The Armenian merchants were important mediators of East—West trade already in their old home, in (Old) Julfa (Agulis, Nakhichevan, etc.). Their significance increased even more after their transfer to New Julfa, where they became the most important agents of the Persian raw silk trade to the West.

The undisturbed commerce was hindered, on the one hand, by the Persian–Turkish wars that endangered the caravans passing through Anatolia towards the Aegean Sea, or in the direction of Aleppo. On the other hand, on the route leading towards the south, the customs-boundary established on the island of Hormuz situated at the entrance to the Persian Gulf (in the possession of the Portuguese, since 1515) represented a heavy burden on them because here a double customs-duty was

[165] Oudenrijn, O, P., *Linguae Haicanae scriptores ord. prea. Coner. Fratrum Unitorum et FF. Armenorum.* Bern 1960, p. 53.

[166] *Carmelites,* I, 321, 344.

[167] *Carmelites,* I, 99. — During the epoch of the Crusades more similar apocryphal prophecies had been composed; the most renowned being the prophecy of Nerses Parthev: *Patmut'iwn S. Nersisi Part'ewi.* Venice 1853, p. 90.; *Vie de Saint Nerses,* transl. by J-R. Emine: Langlois, *Collection des historiens anciens et modernes de l'Armenie.* II. Paris 1869, p. 38. Cf. A. S. Anasyan, *Armjanskie istočniki o padenii Vizantii.* Erevan 1957, pp. 97–98, 9–10. — This prophecy has been made use of by Clemens Galanus in his work preaching church-union: *Conciliatio Ecclesiae Armenae cum Romana.* Roma 1661: cf. Anasyan, *op. cit.,* p. 329.

[168] *Carmelites,* I, 210.

II

assessed on Persian subjects, and especially on the Armenians to induce them to adopt the Roman Catholic faith.[169] However, similar difficulties also had to be faced in the Western countries, where discriminating sanctions were applied towards the "schismatics". Only the Roman Catholic Armenians received equal treatment with the other Christians. So the adoption of the Roman Catholic faith was at the same time of major importance in order to gain commercial privileges.

Catholicisation also had antecedents on Armenian soil. In Nakhichevan and its surroundings (Krna, Jahuk, Aparank) a Dominican mission *(fratres uniti)* had existed since 1330,[170] which gathered quite a number of adherents from the population of the surrounding districts.

During the "great *sürgün*" of 1604, the Armenians of Nakhichevan also shared the lot of the others, and several thousand Roman Catholic families were transferred to New Julfa.

According to the exaggerated figures given by the local Armenians to the Catholic missions, in addition to 400,000 families of Armenian–Gregorian faith, 10,000 Catholic families were driven away to Persia. Even if these figures cannot be accepted at their face value, but the proportion can perhaps be used. Accordingly the number of the Roman Catholic families at about 1604 represented about 2.5 per cent of the transferred population.[171]

The Roman Catholic Armenians had a separate church. The first (S. Mary) was built by Khoja Shevelin in Isfahan (not in New Julfa).[172] At the end of the 17th century, the Shahrimanian family had the S. Avetik church built. The churches of the Carmelites, Jesuits and other orders were erected by the financial help of the Roman Catholic Armenians.[173] However, from the number of churches, no accurate conclusions can be drawn concerning the number of the Roman Catholic believers.[174]

At first, Shah Abbas I readily received the Roman Catholic missionaries, because he hoped, that through the mediation of the Pope he could get help for his war waged against the Turks. However, he did not favour the converting activity of the missionaries, because this would have withdrawn his Armenian (and other) subjects from his supremacy. The Shah exerted his rule over the Armenians in New Julfa through the Armenian *kalantar*, and in the Armenian mother-country through the Katholicos of Echmiadzin.

[169] *Carmelites*, I, 101–103.
[170] Oudenrijn, *op. cit.*, 24, sqq.; *Carmelites*, I. 410–11.
[171] *Carmelites*, I. 100, 157.
[172] *Carmelites*, I, 191.
[173] Tavernier, *op. cit.*, 1. IV, chap. 6, p. 469. A. D. 1632: 15 churches, see Acharean, Hr., *C̣uc̣'ak hay dzeṙagrac̣' Tawrizi*, Vienna 1910, p. 33; Akinean, *Movses* III, p. 335.
[174] Ter-Yovhaneanc̣, Y., *Patmut'iwn Nor Džulayu or y Aspahan*, I, Nor Džula 1880, p. 264–67; Carswell, *op. cit.*, p. 8. Contemporary European travellers on the Armenian churches, see Carswell, *op. cit.*, pp. 84–86.

II

3.3.2. In support of the missions and in direct contact with the Pope, the head of the Gregorian-Armenian church also played an important role in trade questions. In 1602, Melkisedek asked the Pope to mediate to the Spanish King to reduce the customs-duties on the island of Hormuz imposed on Armenians or to grant them equal treatment with other Christian merchants. The Portuguese governor of the island (from 1580 Portugal was united with Spain) instead of the usual 10 per cent customs-duty collected a double duty from the "schismatic" Armenians, "the Persian traders" and forced them to buy also other goods, which they did not want, at a price of 60% above the market price.[175]

The expected result was not attained even by the protracted bargaining with the Spanish King. Thus the Shah resorted to the use of arms. In 1614 his troops took the fort of Gombrun (Bender Abbas) on the coast across Hormuz, and in 1622, with the help of the British navy, they occupied the island of Hormuz.[176]

Despite the increasing British trade influence, the major part of the export trade in Persian raw silk remained in the hands of the Armenian merchants of New Julfa because in 1617 the Julfans submitted the highest purchase offer to the Shah.[177]

3.3.3. An intercession of the Katholicos was of vital importance for the Armenian merchants. They very much needed the support of Western monarchs, as they were not readily received in the countries of the West.[178]

The French government protected the interests of the French merchants against foreign competition with duties. In 1622, the chamber of commerce of Marseilles lodged a complaint with the magistrate claiming that the activity of the Armenian merchants adversely affected French trade ("pour la décheutte qu'ils apportent au negoce et Commerce"). As a result, under the threat of a high fine, French ships were fordbidden (1622) to take Persian or Armenian merchants on board on their voyage both there or back.[179]

This prohibition seriously affected the Persian raw silk trade of the Armenians, particularly because the Dutch and English bought their supplies of raw silk on the French markets.[180]

To get this embargo removed, Khoja Nazar, the Armenian *kalantar*, organized a meeting in 1628 and 1629 with missionaries, to appeal to the Pope to use his influence with Louis XIII the King of France in this case.[181]

[175] The letter of Clement VIII to King Philip III: Vatican Archives, Arm. XLIV, vol. 46, doc. 281, p. 264.: Akinean, *Movses* III, p. 296; They rob them shamelessly: *Carmelites*, I, 102–3; I. 318; Chardin, *op. cit.*, III, p. 206., Cf. *Drvagner*, II, 103–4.

[176] Chardin, *op. cit.*, III, 206–7.; *Carmelites*, I, 142, 212, 266. Cf. Bajburtjan, V. A., *Armjanskaja kolonija Novoj Džulfy v XVII veke.* Moscow 1969., p. 46.

[177] *Carmelites*, I, 244., *Drvagner*, II, 103–4., Bajburtjan, *op. cit.*, p. 44.

[178] The Pope Urban VIII in his letter addressed to the Armenian Katholicos is surprised that Armenian monks and traders, who have come to Rome, complained of being ill received, *Carmelites*, I. 302.

[179] Macler, Fr., *Notices des manuscrits arméniens ou rélatifs aux Arméniens vus dans quelques bibliothèques ...du sud-est de la France: REA* I, 1920–22, pp. 91–96.

[180] Bajburtjan, *op. cit.*, p. 57.

[181] Akinean, *Movses* III., 384–86; Bajburtjan, *op. cit.*, p. 58.

II

The main motive for cancelling the prohibition was very likely the international political and economic situation, and the direct presence of the British and the Dutch East India Companies on the Persian market. To compensate for this competition the French government admitted the Armenians as trade mediators; Richelieu in 1629 ensured free trade ("toute liberté et sureté") for the Armenian merchants of Julfa ("Choffelins et Persians") in the French ports and cities.[182]

Later on, Louis XIV also intervened several times with the Turkish Sultan concerning the privileges of the Armenian merchants, but only for the Catholic Armenians.[183]

The Italian market was also very important for the Armenians. A similar request of the Julfan merchants was discussed by the Holy synod in 1630 and adopted a decision, on the basis of which the Armenians, in the territory under the suzerainty of the Pope, could have, at their own expense, guest houses (*domus*) built for themselves in the ports and cities where they could transport their goods and enjoy exemption from duty (*franchita*). However, these advantages only applied to the Armenians of the Roman Catholic faith or with the intention of conversion. The Holy See promised to intercede with the rulers of other countries to ensure similar advantages.[184]

3,3,4. However, in Persia the Armenians refrained from manifesting their friendship or sympathy towards the Europeans or reacting to the conversion appeals of the Roman Catholic priests. In their contacts with the missions, they had already bitter experience: the promise of conversion given to the Augustines resulted in very serious consequences for them.[185] Thus, thereafter "they appreciated the Catholics as much as the Iranian government appreciated the Europeans".[186]

Finally, in the course of the decades, the New-Julfans became accustomed to their Persian surroundings, and the new generation regarded New Julfa as its native land.[187] Essentially, they were satisfied with their economic conditions and several of them became very rich merchants. Each Shah maintained a close connection with the distinguished Khojas, first of all with the *kalantar*, the head of the Armenian colony. They were frequent guests at their houses, for example Shah Abbas I with Khoja Nazar,[188] and Shah Safi with Khoja Soultenon.[189]

---

[182] *REA* I, 1920–22, pp. 21–22, 104–105. — As the Armenians wanted to take the countervalue of the raw silk in gold and silver coins out of the country, so complaints were voiced, and prohibitive decrees brought one after the other: A. D. 1622: *REA* I, pp. 100–3/17–20; A. D. 1639–59: *REA* I, pp. 22, sqq/105, sqq. Cf. Bajburtjan, *op. cit.*, p. 58.

[183] Bajburtjan, *op. cit.*, p. 136.

[184] Prop. Persia An. 1648, incl. vol. 209, f. 29: Akinean, *Movses*, pp. 386–87; *Drvagner*, II, 108.

[185] See above notes 161, 162.

[186] Chardin, *op. cit.*, VIII, p. 110.

[187] Tavrižeci, 67; Tavr/Bros. 301; Tavr/Xan. 80.

[188] Tavrižeci, 64–65; Tavr/Bros. 300; Tavr/Xan. 79. Cf. Kiurdian H., *Džulayeci Xoja Nazar i iwr gerdastanə*, Boston 1943.

[189] Tavernier, *op. cit.*, I. IV. 517; Carswell, *op. cit.*, p. 7.

II

Thus the Armenian families were afraid to give up their Gregorian faith for the Roman Catholic; their conversion would have drawn the anger of the Shah and eventually his retaliation upon themselves and their family. As has been mentioned, as a result of the persecutions that flared up from time to time as a result of the despotism of the suspectful tyrants of incalculable mood, several families sought refuge under the protection of the Mohammedan religion in order to avoid the reprisals.[190]

In fact, there were only few people, who became converted under the influence of the missionary activity. The small number is shown by the fact that the enacted conversions were described in the missionary reports in lengthy detail.

The catholicisation of the wealthiest Shahrimanian-Sarrat family of New Julfa is regarded as an extraordinary case. In 1646 Khoja Sarrat [Sahrat?] and 11 members of his family converted to the Roman Catholic faith which they kept for generations. They supported the missions with significant donations and encouraged their teaching activities.[191]

Their wealth and influence secured them privileges and indemnity to a certain degree, but in certain cases economic sanctions were imposed upon some members of the Roman Catholic Church. Thus in 1697, such a high tax was assessed on two Shahrimanian brothers that they had to convert to the Mohammedan faith to stop persecution.[192]

As a result, the other members of the family transferred the sphere of their activity to Italy, where they enjoyed the full support of the Pope.[193]

3,4. Thus, essentially the years from 1580 to 1630 represented a new decimation of the Armenian people in East Anatolia, the peak of which were the Ottoman-Persian wars and the Jelâli revolts.

Similar destruction and depopulation was caused to the mother-country by the "great sürgün" (1604–5), when a large part of the population of the southern counties,

[190] Armenians having embraced the Roman Catholic faith were persecuted also by Armenian-Gregorian clerics. Carmelites, I, 456–461.

[191] It is characteristic to their world-wide economic activity that Khoja Sahrat Zakar Shahrimanian was the leader of the trade delegation from New Julfa which presented the "diamond throne" to Tsar Alexei Mihailovich as a gift in 1660. Gh. Alishan, Sisakan, Venice 1893, p. 446; Armjano-russkie otnošenija v XVII veke. Sbornik dokumentov. Red. V. A. Parsamjan. Erevan 1953, p. 21, sqq. — They have got as far as the Netherlands: see Sarukhan A., Hollandan ew hayera XVI-XIX darerum. Vienna 1926, p. 61.

[192] Carmelites, I, 457–58, II, 1361.

[193] In 1696, two other Shahrimanian brothers received the citizenship of Rome, and obtained exemption from customs-duty in the ports of Rome and Ancona. Khoja Markar granted a loan of 200.000 ducats to Venice to support the fight against the Turks. In acknowledgement Emperor Leopold bestowed the title of "Hungarian count" to him (Sheriman) and his family in 1699. The copy of the privilege see: Dashian, J., Cʻucʻak dzeṙagracʻ Matenadaranin Mxitareancʻi Vienna. Vienna 1895, pp. 920–21. — My relative paper read at the Conference of Safavid Art (Venice, June 5, 1978): "An Armenian Financier of New Julfa — a Hungarian Nobleman". On the Shahrimanian family consult: Carmelites, I, 376, 436–38, 457–59, 485, 500, 515; II. 1078, 1080–82. — On the Armenian-Italian relations in extenso: L. B. Zekiyan, Le colonie armene del medio evo in Italia, in: I. Simposio Intern. di Arte Armena, Venezia — S. Lazzaro 1978, pp. 803–929.

II

and a significant proportion of the population of the northern counties were dragged to Persia. In Persia, the majority of the peasants settled down in Mohammedan surroundings, then gradually losing their Gregorian religion and Armenian language they were assimilated by the Persians. The Armenian (and Georgian) youths enlisted as *ghulam*s in the guard of the Shah suffered the same fate.

In fact, only the New-Julfans, settled in the southern district of Isfahan, remained a firm unity. Although the wave of Mohammedanization, that flared up several times, reached this city too, but because of the economic significance of the Armenians, the shahs refrained from forcible conversion. At the same time, the closer connections of Armenian families with the Roman Catholics turned the shahs against them. The closer links of the wealthier families with the Roman Catholic missions was justified by several important reasons, viz.: their sons could get European-like higher education only in the missionary schools, which was essential for the young men who later got engaged in international trade. A knowledge of Western languages got all the more important when the export of Persian raw silk was mostly handled by Armenian merchants. Their trading activity in France and Italy, and their settlements there, involved irrevocable consequences. For the benefit of a European home, they had to pay by losing their Gregorian-Armenian faith, which meant a gradual assimilation into the adoptive nation.

With regard to the mother-country, after the "great *sürgün*" the Armenian language and culture were maintained by the decimated Armenian population and the escapee-resettlers. Their tenacious adherence to their religion and language, the carriers of Armenian national consciousness, helped to preserve ancient Armenian culture, and national identity.

II THE ARMENIAN CHURCH

To preserve Armenian-Gregorian religion, language and culture was even more difficult in the Diaspora, in the Armenian settlement formed in the West-Ukrainian border region of Poland by the emigrants, who gradually settled there from the 13th century. The region developed into a very important economic emporium (in the voivodships: Województwo Ruskie, and Województwo Podolskie), with the centres of Lvov and Kamenets-Podolsk.

The Armenian church, as the organization holding together the community, was in the centre of interest in the 17th century sources. In that period this interest was shown in the church, and especially in its leader, the archbishop of Lvov, because in 1630 archbishop Nikol Torosowicz became converted to the Roman Catholic faith, and thus started the process, during which, under the pressure of the Jesuits, the population was finally compelled to accept the church union. Contemporary antiuniate sources fully placed the odium for the uniation on archbishop Nikol.

II

4.1.1. There is considerable literature on the uniation of Nikol Torosowicz (Thorosenc), archbishop of Lvov, on his conversion from the Armenian-Gregorian to the Roman Catholic faith. The antecedents and the direct consequences of this step are in general reproduced both by the Gregorian and Roman Catholic authors unanimously on the basis of the information acquired from the delegates sent from Lvov to Echmiadzin and from the letters of the Lvov community to the Katholicos, contained in the chronicle of Arakel of Tabriz. Two other very detailed and important demonstrative groups of sources were recently added to this detailed descriptive source: the documents of the Armenian common jury of Lvov, the documents of the Polish magistrate of Lvov, as well as the recently disclosed and published material from the archives of the Congregation de Propaganda Fide and from the archives of the Vatican.[194]

The direct antecedents of the consecration of Nikol to archbishop are narrated by Tavriẓeci as follows: "A few days after Melkisedek arrived in Lvov, a 23 years old monk sent to him mediators and intercessors (*midžnords ew barexoss*), who asked that he should consecrate Nikol to the bishop of the Armenian nation (*azg*). And the mediators brought to him many gold coins and promised even more".[195]

The report of Tavriẓeci is accurately confirmed by the municipality documents of Lvov. According to these, Torosowicz gave 300 thalers to the patriarch, and the sister of Nikol sent to him another 100 (*levkovy*) thalers.[196] The *"Vipasanutiwn Nikolakan"* attributed to Simeon of Poland (Lehatsi) also narrates in detail the act and its preparations.[197] According to this, Torosowicz gave 150 *guruses* to Melkisedek.[198]

Nikol was the son of an Armenian merchant named Jakob *"ex magna familia et nobilissimi viri filius"*[199] (*mecazgi ew p'art'amac' zarmi*).[200] As a seminarist Nikol was

---

[194] The source material recently detected by Ukrainian and Armenian researchers in the Central'nyj Gosudarstvennyj Istoričeskij Archiv and the Lvov Archives I quote from the volume-series *Istoričeskie svjazi i družba ukrainskogo i armjanskogo narodov* (Abbrev.: *ISDUAN*), being the Proceedings of the Armenian-Ukrainian Conferences held in turns in Erevan and Kiev (Erevan 1961, Kiev 1965, Erevan 1971) and from the papers of the historians Ya. Daškevič, G. Pingirian, N. K. Krivonos, V. Grigorian, V. Voskanian, and others. The rich source material of the Congregazio di Propaganda Fide and the Vatican Archives has been presented to the public by Gregorio Petrowicz: *L'unione degli Armeni di Polonia con la Santa Sede (1626–1686)*. Roma 1950, (Abbrev.: *L'unione*).

[195] Tavriẓeci, 364; Tavr/Bros. 445; Tavr/Xan. 288. On the solemn reception of the Patriarch see: Pingirian: *Banber Hayastani Arxivneri*, 1974. No. 3, pp. 99–102.

[196] Pingirian: *ISDUAN* 1971, p. 362. ("Istorija" Arakela Davriẓeci i ee istočniki ob antiuniatskom dviženii v armjanskich kolonijach na Ukraine v 20–50-ch gg. XVII v.) In French: *Le chapitre 28 du "Livre des Histoires" d'Arakel Dawriẓeci et ses sources concernant le mouvement des colonies arméniennes d'Ukraine durant les années 20–50 du 17e s.* in: *REArm* XIV, p. 451.

[197] *Simeon dpri Lehac'woy Ulegrut'iwn*, ed. N. Akinean. Vienna 1936. pp. 399–405.

[198] Ališan, *Kamenic'*, p. 203. Cf. Akinean, *Movses III.*, p. 250.

[199] Congr. Gen. v. 291, f. 167: apud Petrowicz: *L'unione*, p. 14.

[200] Simeon Lehaci, *Ulegrutwin* (Ed. N. Akinean): Colophon, IX., p. 410; Echm. Ms. 1004 (i.e. Matenadaran Erevan), 190/b; Akinean, *Movses III.*, 250; *Ukrainsko-armjanskie svjazi v XVII veke. Sbornik dokumentov.* Ed. Y. R. Daškevič. Kiev 1969, p. 83;.

II

the pupil of patriarch Hovhannes Khul in Istanbul, the latter consecrated him to *abela* and regarded him as his disciple.[201] Despite the clear protest of the Armenian community, Melkisedek consecrated the priest Nikol bishop on January 3rd, 1627 at night in the suburban monastery Khachkatar. At the ceremony, archbishop Hovhannes Khul was one of the officiators.[202] The vehement protest against the raising of Nikol to this dignity was made because of his young age and his inappropriate moral life. The protestors asserted that they had another candidate for this office, a "worthy candidate".[203]

There were, of course, many self-appointed candidates. According to the *Vipasanutiwn Nikolakan*, when the priests heard that Melkisedek made traffic of this high spiritual dignity for money, they arrived one after the other, bringing gifts of money.[204]

According to the Latin text of the "Relatio Brevis", on his arrival Melkisedek wanted to consecrate first Hovhannes Khul and then Zakharia Bernatowicz archbishop, and only when they refused (*his detrectantibus*) to accept this dignity,[205] Der Nicolas Torosowicz, a monk of the S. Antonius monastery was considered.[206]

The candidation of Hovhannes Khul as archbishop is not mentioned in any other source. According to the papal nuncio in Warsaw, Zakharia Bernatowicz doctor of divinity, was highly appreciated (*in molto credito*) by the Armenians. He was the son of Toros Bernatowicz, a senior.[207] His alleged reluctance to accept the archiepiscopal chair demands an explanation from the historians, since Zakharia actively participated in Armenian ecclesiastical life. In a similar manner to his father, he must have been a firm antiuniate, since he was one of the co-authors of the antiuniate pamphlet of Holubowicz. Simultaneously with the letter of the Armenian seniors written to the Katholicos Movses III on July 25th, 1631, he also sent a separate letter to the Katholicos.[208]

It is surprising that the famous and rich Bernatowicz family would not have endeavoured to ensure this high ecclesiastical dignity for itself. At that time, the family was already at its full strength, since Toros Bernatowicz, "the true protector of the

[201] Alishan, *Kamenic'*, p. 211.

[202] Tavrižeci, 364–65; Tavr/Bros. 445–46; Tavr/Xan. 289. — According to *L'unione*, p. 19: January 8. The date corrected by Y. Daškevič: Daškevič-E. Tryjarski, *Dogovor N. Torosoviča s l'vovskimi i kameneckimi armjanami 1627 g. kak pamjatnik armjano-kipčakskogo jazyka: Rocznik Orientalisticzny* XXXIII/1., Warsaw 1969, p. 85. Cf. Pingirian: *ISDUAN* 1971, p. 362; Idem, *REArm* XIV, p. 451.

[203] Tavrižeci, 364; Tavr/Bros. 445; Tavr/Xan. 289; Alishan, *Kamenic'*, p. 211; Ciamcian, *Patmut'iwn Hayoc'*, III. Venice 1786, p. 630. — Protest of the seniors against the illegal consecretion: Pingirian: *Banber Hay. Arxiv.* 1974, no. 3. Doc. no. 3.

[204] Alishan, *Kamenic'*, p. 203.

[205] Cong. Gen. v. 293. f. 183 v, seq.: *L'unione*, p. 16.

[206] Echm. MS. № 1004 (= Matenadaran Erevan), 190/b. Akinean, *Movses III*. 249–250.

[207] Congr. Gen. (Prop. Fide), II, f. 113v: *L'unione*, p. 52.

[208] F. K. Zacharyasiewicz, *Wiadomość o Ormianach w Polsce: Bibl. Nauk. Zakladu im. Ossolinskich,* vol. 2. Lwów 1842, p. 78: apud *Svjazi*, p. 54.

II

sacred Armenian faith" stood at the head of the community as a leading personage for a quarter of a century.[209]

Several members of the Torosowicz family are also mentioned in the documents. Ivaszko Torosowicz was a fellow senior of Toros Bernatowicz in 1600.[210]

It is conspicuous that in a document in which the community protested in 1647 against the dissension and quarrels prevailing in the board of seniors, several members of the Torosowicz and Bernatowicz families also appear as signatories.[211]

On the basis of the considerable material in the archives of the municipality of Lvov, and on the basis of 3 manuscript volumes of testaments and marriage contracts,[212] it would be very useful to gain a more detailed picture of the leading Armenian families of this period, that would complete the frequently quoted book of S. Barącz "On the lives of famous Armenians", and perhaps it would provide an answer to the background concerning the election of archbishop Torosowicz, which for the time being still holds many secrets.

Presumably, it also played a role in the seeming unconcern of the Bernatowicz family that the archbishops of Lvov did not play a leading role in the life of the Armenian community. Financially they were entirely dependent on the board of seniors and were obedient executors of their decisions.

In the literature on Nikol, in the main, the authors state as an undoubted fact that Melkisedek deliberately sought a priest of Roman Catholic disposition for the archiepiscopal post, although this question is still far from being elucidated.

In their letter addressed to the Katholicos Movses (July 25, 1631), the Armenian seniors enumerated the personalities who, involved in the ecclesiastic legal status of the Armenians, upset prevailing order.[213] First they mentioned the Katholicos Melkisedek and placed their main odium on him. Undoubtedly with the forcible consecration of Nikol, he started the dissension. However, in connection with the appointed person, Nikol, they only disapproved of his young age and his way of life, unworthy of an archbishop.[214] At the same time, they did not mention any possible candidate in his place but merely stressed that they had another "worthy candidate". The absence of a

---

[209] Toros Bernatowicz is undersigned among other seniors in two decrees of Sigismund III dated April 7, 1600. See Bischoff, F., *Urkunden zur Geschichte der Armenier in Lemberg*, pp. 92–97. He figures as *erespoxan* on the document containing the vow made by Torosowicz on May 6/April 26, 1627: *Rocznik Orient.*, XXXIII/1. 1969, p. 79. and on its confirmation in Latin: Congres. II, f. 101v: *L'unione*, p. 22; *Svjazi*, p. 54. The partisanship to either creed (true or feigned) cannot be sharply delineated even in the Bernatowicz family. Cf. Pingirian: *Banber Hay. Arxiv.*, 1974. no. 3, Doc. no. 5.

[210] In a colophon dated after 1611 among the seniors three Torosowiczes appear at the same time: V. Hakobyan, (A. Hovhannisyan), *Hayeren dzeḫagreri hišatakaranner*, *XVII dar*. I, 1974, pp. 435–46.

[211] CGIA USSR, Lvov, f. 9, op. 1, t. 397, pp. 521–23. Russian translation in *Svjazi*, pp. 96–97.

[212] Bibliotheca Mechit., Vienna, Nos 441, 447; Bibl. Mech. Venice No. 1788, Cf. *Acta Orient. Hung.*, XXIV, 1971, p. 267–69.

[213] Zacharyasiewicz, p. 75–78: *Svjazi* pp. 52–54.

[214] Tavrižeci, 364; Tavr/Bros. 445; Tavr/Xan. 289.; *Kamenic'*, p. 211.

II

counter-candidate is even more incomprehensible, since the major part of the main sources originate from persons of antiuniate affiliation. This is especially inconceivable, when according to the letter addressed to the Katholicos Movses, the seniors prior to his arrival to Lvov knew that Melkisedek was a "true and real Uniate", who had already professed allegiance to Pope Paul V in 1610, and moreover on his arrival in Lvov he had shown the letter of Pope Gregory XIII to the seniors according to which, Melkisedek himself recognized the supremacy of the Pope. They also sent copies of these documents to the Katholicos Movses. Moreover — according to the letter — Melkisedek also called on the representatives of the community to recognize the Roman Church.

The true catholicisation of Melkisedek — as discussed earlier — is in all events questionable. The sincerity of the statement of allegiance had been doubted even in the Congregation and Papal court. At any rate they used this letter of allegiance (dated 1613) in order to encourage the Armenian Diasporas to accept the church-union, and distributed the printed copies all around in Armenian settlements. Such a copy also came into the hands of the Armenian seniors, who attached it to the letter sent to Movses.

For a historical analysis, it would be good to know whether a copy of this document was in the possession of the seniors (or of certain persons among them) before the arrival of Melkisedek. It is striking that they even had a copy of the letter of the Katholicos Movses addressed to Pope Urban VIII, in which the officiating Katholicos recognized the papal supremacy and expressed a desire for a renewal of the love and unity that had existed between S. Gregory, the Illuminator, and Pope Sylvester. In a strange way the seniors also sent a copy of this letter to the Katholicos himself.[215]

On the other hand, from the correspondence of the papal nuncio in Warsaw and the Congregatio (1626) — after the arrival of Melkisedek in Lvov — it becomes clear that the parties concerned did not seem to have known about the statement of allegiance of Melkisedek. The nuncio promised that as soon as it was possible to negotiate with the aged and decrepit Katholicos Melkisedek, the nuncio would endeavour to win him over for the church-union.[216]

From the antiuniate sources regarding the year 1626 it does not become unambiguously clear that Melkisedek would by any means have sought a priest of strongly Catholic faith (fermo della fede cattolica).[217]

In fact, the precise fear of the Polish secular and ecclesiastical authorities was that "the patriarch would consecrate [antiuniate — E. Sch.] bishops and would engage in other acts pernicious (pernicioso) for the Roman Catholic religion". In order to

---

[215] Zacharyasiewicz, p. 77: Svjazi, p. 54.
[216] L'unione, pp. 9–10.
[217] Ibid. 11–12, 23.

288

II

avoid eventual official action against Melkisedek, the seniors of Lvov stressed that there was no reason for anxiety, since the Katholicos Melkisedek uniated with the Holy See.[218] The Armenian seniors — at that time? — presumably ventured to refer to the Uniate disposition of Melkisedek, because they believed that even Melkisedek himself did not take his former declarations of allegiance earnestly (see above), and, in addition, the Polish royal edicts of privileges continued to ensure the free election of bishops for the Armenian community.

According to Gregorio Petrowicz, however, the patriarch did not immediately embark on the consecration of the new Armenian archbishop, because first he wanted to carry out a "psychological preconditioning" in interest of the uniation.[219]

The question of catholicisation was not at all raised at the occasion of the consecration. When the Armenians learned that Melkisedek — in spite of their protest — consecrated Nikol Torosowicz, Melkisedek took the wind out of their sails by saying that at any rate "he would take" the newly consecrated bishop "along with himself",[220] which assertion is completed by M. Pidou in the *Relatio Brevis* that Melkisedek would place Nikol at the head of a diocese *(nahang)* in Armenia.[221]

When a few days later, Melkisedek set off for Kamenets,[222] he did take Nikol along with him, but he sent him back from Jazlowiec to Lvov. Nikol — aware of the feelings of the Armenians of Lvov towards him, did not want to return and insisted that Melkisedek should issue a pastoral letter in which he anathemized everybody who did not recognize Nikol as their archbishop.[223]

It is characteristic of the Armenian community that despite the fact that Melkisedek resigned his post as Katholicos in favour of Sahak in 1624, the Armenians of Lvov did not even think of challenging the authority or competence of the patriarch of Echmiadzin.[224]

It is surprising that Tavrižeci does not report on the next turn of the events, viz. that the seniors asserted their right which they acquired from the Armenian patriarchs and the Polish King, and entitled them to elect the bishop of the Armenian *natio* themselves *(ius eligendi)*.[225]

4,1,2. This legal right of the seniors, however, was not discredited by Nikol. Knowing that the financial basis of his post depended on the seniors, he realised that it

[218] *Ibid.* 9.

[219] *Ibid.* 12, 23.

[220] *Kamenic'*, p. 204; Akinean, *Movses III.*, p. 251.

[221] *Bini miut'iwn*, p. 21.

[222] According to Petrowicz in early February: *L'unione*, p. 19.

[223] Tavrižeci, pp. 365–66; Tavr/Bros. 446; Tavr/Xan. 289. The original document see: P. Daian, *L'archivio dei PP. Mechitaristi di Venezia*, S. Lazzaro 1707-73, Venice 1930, p. 3.: *L'unione*, p. 20. This document bears the same date as the document of consecration of the archbishop: January 8, 1627. Corrected by Y. Daškevič to: February 25/15, 1627.: *RO* XXXIII, p. 85.

[224] Tavrižeci, 366; Tavr/Bros. 446; Tavr/Xan. 290.

[225] *L'unione*, pp. 22, 61, 91. This privilege has always been respected also by the Roman Papal Court, ibid. 238, 248, 261, 296, 300.; Zaharyasiewicz, p. 76: *Svjazi*, p. 49.

II

was worth coming to terms with them, and subjecting himself to the legal customs of the Lvov community. He, therefore, considered his episcopal consecration by Melkisedek as void, because "this contradicted the law and order *(jergalik)* in force in Lvov and Kamenets, received by them from the patriarchs of sacred memory and from the kings and which ... has been approved by the Polish King Sigismund III ruling at present". Nikol made a vow in the same 1627 year to the Council of Seniors that he would firmly adhere to his faith, would remain loyal to the church of S. Echmiadzin, of S. Gregory, the Illuminator, and would adhere to all ecclesiastic ceremonies and rites to the old customs: *"ant ičipmen sp dajarda / ki kendi inamimda hasdad bolgajmen hem poslušni / sp ečmiadzinga. A toruna sp Lusaworičning da / barča ixov ceremonialarin hem jergalikni eski adadka / kora zaxovat etgajmen"*.[226] If he did not keep to the law of S. Gregory, the Illuminator, he should be removed from the archiepiscopal chair, and lose his archiepiscopal authority over the Armenian clergy, the board of the seniors and the whole Armenian community.

It seemed that with this vow, a compromise was reached between the archbishop and the community. Since Nikol "made a vow in writing which was confirmed by an oath, se we (the seniors) feel reconciled with him" and he now has been elected archbishop by the Armenian community: *"Ill-mum Dominum Nicolaum Torosowicz pro Cathedrali Archepiscopo elegimus ..."* The signatories included Toros Bernatowicz *erespoxan* (provisor), representing the board of seniors and the election was confirmed by King Sigismund III of Poland.[227]

The question is unanswerable, whether archbishop Nikol would have adhered to this vow made to the Armenian community if disturbing circumstances had not come about later.

At any rate, according to the evidence of the sources, the compromise was upset by a secondary circumstance. Nikol, who was not scrupulous in ceremonial and liturgical affairs, failed to observe the 40 days' fasting term after the consecration of a priest, and he received a strict admonishment from *vardapet* Grigor Kesaratsi ('of Caesarea–Kaisarea'– the former Armenian patriarch of Constantinople 1623–1626) who had just arrived in Kamenets. A clash occurred between the two ecclesiarchs and as a result archbishop Nikol wanted to get rid of Grigor Kesaratsi. He turned to the *vojt* of Kamenec, who expelled Grigor from the country as a Turkish spy *(čašut)*.[228]

---

[226] CGIA fond 9., op. 1. t. 381, pp. 1901–1906. The original text of the vow has been published by J. Daškevič and E. Tryjarski: *RO* XXXIII/1, 1969, 77–92 + IV. The Armeno-Kipchak, Latin, Polish texts have been inserted into the Protocols of Nov. 20, 1630 of the Lvov Polish Magistrate in connection with the subsequent lawsuits. The Latin text has been published by Z. Obertyński, *Die Florentiner Union der polnischen Armenier und ihr Bischofskatalog.* Roma 1934, pp. 61–63.

[227] Congr. Gen. v. 293, f. 184v: *l'unione,* pp. 21–22. In their letter (July 25, 1631) addressed to Katholicos Movses the seniors refer to this vow, see *Svjazi,* p. 53. It is surprising Tavrižeci's silence about this very important document, though he made good use of the Echmiadzin Archives. G. Pingirian, in her thorough paper *(ISDUAN* 1971, *REArm* XIV) about the trustworthiness of Tavrižeci's Chronicle does not enlarge on this missing link. Y. Daškevič *(RO* XXXIII/1.) does not touch on this problem either.

[228] Tavrižeci, 366–69; Tavr/Bros. 447; Tavr/Xan. 290–92; *Kamenic;* p. 25; Akinean, *Movses III.,* p. 255; *L'unione,* pp. 25–26.

II

The case can be judged from two points of view: on the one hand, Nikol did not observe the ecclesiastic prescriptions in the given case, while from the other point of view, Grigor Kesaratsi did not have the right to interfere in the affairs of the diocese of Lvov. Tacitly the patriarch of Constantinople exerted patronage over the archbishopric of Lvov, but this was mainly based on the personal relationship of Hovhannes Khul to Melkisedek and his former pupil Nikol.

It must not be overlooked that Grigor Kesaratsi was a strict and firm follower of the Armenian–Gregorian faith, and was regarded as one of the most eminent theologists of this faith. In the period concerned, he enjoyed an especially high authority by the circumstance that he consecrated the priest Movses doctor of theology *(vardapet)*. The universally respected Movses, also favoured by the Persian Shah, ascended the throne of the Katholicos of Echmiadzin in 1629.[229]

At the same time, it must also be taken into consideration that Grigor was of a "violent, stubborn and rigid" nature.[230] He was somewhat hostile to Nikol, the student of Hovhannes Khul, a constant antagonist of Grigor in the patriarchal chair of Constantinople, who very likely played an important role in urging Nikol's consecration. After all, Khul was one of the officiating witnesses. Grigor's animosity against Nikol could have been much stronger, since during his decades-long conflict with Khul, in 1626, he was evicted from the patriarchal throne by Zakaria Vanetsi (patriarch of Constantinople, 1626–1631, 1636–1639), again a pupil of Khul.[231]

After his expulsion from Kamenets, as soon as he arrived in Moldavia, Grigor immediately anathematized Nikol. Since the ecclesiastic consequences of the anathematization also afflicted the community of Lvov, the seniors voted to give 3,000 *guru\u0161e*s to Nikol for travelling expenses to enable him to travel to Grigor's seat Kaisarea (Kayseri) and ask for his absolution. Nikol, however, in the course of his journey, met Grigor's fierce enemy, Aristakes of Harberd in Brussa, who convinced him that Grigor had no right to anathematize the archbishop of Lvov.[232] At any rate, Nikol, following a cunning policy, chose an intermediate solution. Under the pretext of sickness, he asked for the absolution of the anathema by letter. However, the trick did not work; on the contrary, when Grigor found out about the deception, he repeated the anathema.[233]

[229] See the characterisation of Grigor Kesaraci from the Gregorian-Armenian viewpoint: *imastut'eamb partam* 'opulent in wisdom', *kari parke\u0161t* 'very chaste' Tavri\u017eeci, 366; Tavr/Bros. 446; Tavr/Xan. 290.

[230] *b\u012bnakan, kamapa\u0161t* 'wilful, stubborn'; *xstapahanj* 'rigid, stringent': Akinean, *Movses III.*, p. 255. Quoted by Ormanean, *Azgapatum*, II/2, col 2353 (this is the Armeno-Catholic viewpoint).

[231] The sharp personal fight of the church notables is reflected by the frequent periodic change of their governing era in the Armenian patriarchal seat of Constantinople: Hovhannes Xul: 1600–1601, 1610–11, 1621–23, 1631–36 († 1636). Grigor Kesaraci: 1601–8, 1611–21, 1623–26. († 1632). *Azgapatum* III/3, L–LI; *ibid.*, II/2, cols 2357–58; 2382–83.

[232] *Kamenic'*, p. 206.

[233] Tavri\u017eeci, 366—370; Tavr/Bros. 445–9; Tavr/Xan. 290–93. — The documents recently discovered by G. Pingirian in the Lvov Archives, containing Torosowicz's confession, corroborate Arakel's narrative: Pingirian, *ISDUAN* 1971, p. 363

II

4,1,3. The antiuniate Armenians previously believed that Nikol would adhere to the obligation assumed in 1627 to remain loyal to Echmiadzin, and they did not blame him so much for violating it but rather the Katholicos Melkisedek. In fact they considered that the direct cause prompting the uniation of Nikol lay exactly in the inconsiderate anathema of Grigor, and this was expressed in their complaint addressed to Katholicos Movses on July 25th, 1631; "Grigor in a similar degree (to Melkisedek) was the cause of the chaos that has befallen us ... without any administration of justice, without a legal procedure, without the observation of the ecclesiastical laws and the rules of jurisdiction, even without being the legate of the Katholicos and not being invested with any other right of a sublegate ... he sentenced" Nikol.[234]

Curiously enough, the strongly antiuniate minded Simeon Lehaci in his satiric poem: *Vipasanutiwn Nikolakan* mocking and ridiculing the archbishop Nikol, judged Grigor's behaviour in the same tone "This was the first cause that became the beginning of all troubles".[235]

The next motive, which induced Nikol to the uniation, was the decision of the legate Khachatur Kesaratsi. The legate sent by the Katholicos to Lvov, met Grigor Kesaratsi on the way, who informed him in detail about the events, and enraged him in advance against Nikol.[236] Despite this, Khachatur and archbishop Nikol could have reached a peaceful solution. Khachatur "spoke with the Armenian priests and seniors *(išxan)* that they should make peace, but they did not want to come to a compromise". Khachatur's warning foreshadows the disastrous events, the definitive rupture between the community and the archbishop: "My suspicion is that our stubbornness will finally perhaps shower a disastrous trouble upon us" — the legate Khachatur said.[237]

The same tone is also apparent from the letter of the seniors from 1631.[238] They enumerate those who were guilty in the occurrence of the evil and all the disastrous consequences that took place up to 1631. From several passages of the letter, the conviction becomes clear that the writers would finally have preferred a peaceful solution. According to the letter, the irreversible step was finally brought about by the stubbornness of Grigor Kesaraci and this was completed by the fact that Khachatur allowed himself to be persuaded to maintain the anathema.

[234] *Svjazi,* p. 53. (Zacharyasiewicz, p. 77.).

[235] *Kamenic',* p. 206. — Has it not been the consonance of this and similar text details which induced G. Pingirian to conjecture the identity of Simeon Lehaci, the author of the *Vipasanut'iwn Nikolakan,* with priest Simeon Mikolajovič, the envoy of the seniors in 1631 to Katholicos Movses ? A number of other unknown features of Simeon Lehaci's biography, the solution of his identity and his identification with Simeon Muratovič see: Y. Daškevič, *Simeon Lehaci, kto on* ? *Księga pamiątkowa ku czci E. Słuszkiewicza.* Warsaw 1974, pp. 65–77; idem, *Siméon Dpir Lehaci. Qui est-il?* *REArm,* XII, 1977, 347–64.

[236] Tavrižeci, 372; Tavr/Bros. 449; Tavr/Xan. 294. Akinean, *Movses III.,* p. 260.

[237] Tavrižeci, 375; Tavr/Bros. 450; Tavr/Xan. 296. — On the intrusion of Toros Torosowicz and others to frustrate the negotiations of the seniors and the Legate Xachatur see: Pingirian: *Banber Hay. Arxiv,* 1974, p. 105, Doc. no. 4.

[238] *Svjazi,* p. 53.

II

The step taken by the legate Khachatur is judged similarly by the author of the *Vipasanutiwn Nikolakan:*

> "Ter Khachatur what did you do,
> What trouble you brought upon our heads,
> You came perhaps to us,
> To let our churches be taken away,
> Why did you listen to the advice of evil men ...[239]

By this assertion they also disapproved with those priests and their fellow seniors who uncompromisingly wanted to subdue Nikol.

To a certain degree they accused even the Katholicos Movses, because after the tone of his letter adressed to Urban VIII it could hardly be expected that Nikol would yield to the will of Grigor Kesaratsi or the antiuniate seniors, since the Katholicos in his letter praised the Holy See and recognized its supremacy.[240]

Thus the irreversible step came, "when *vardapet* Khachatur wanted to sentence him ... Nikol Torosowicz became frightened of the sentence and of being removed from his episcopal office, he, therefore refused to defer to the legate and to Your Holiness [i.e. to the Katholicos Movses]".[241]

The *Vipasanutiwn Nikolakan* describes the event as follows:

> "Nikol went to the Jesuits, weeping,
> Upon what they told him: confess allegiance to the Pope,
> If you submit to the Pope
> and take the oath with us,
> we shall be of help to you
> we shall protect you from all dangers."[242]

According to the chronicle of Tavrizhetsi: "Nikol did not see any other way out, he went to the 'Frank' priests [in this case: to the Dominicans] ... first of all the Jesuits, he came to an agreement with them and gave them the following statement: I, the Armenian bishop Nikol, from my free will, join the Roman Catholic Church and I accept the supremacy of the Pope together with all its consequences, and I solemnly promise to perform all his orders."[243]

All this information taken from antiuniate minded sources show to the effect that Nikol Torosowicz would have wanted to attain a certain *modus vivendi* with the seniors, but the arrival of Grigor Kesaratsi upset the state of affairs. Torosowicz being a light-minded prodigal person did not keep the rigid prescriptions of the Church, and

---

[239] *Vipasanut'iwn Nikolakan: Kamerc'*, p. 210.

[240] *Svjazi*, p. 54.

[241] *Ibid.*, 53.

[242] *Kamenic'*, 209.

[243] Tavrižeci, 375–6; Tavr/Bros. 45C–51; Tavr/Xan. 296–97.

II

so the clash between him and the scrupulous bishop Grigor became inevitable. In his distress, being such an unstable personage, it was easy for the Jesuits to persuade Torosowicz to take refuge with them.

The estrangement between the archbishop and the community could have — after all — also a financial background: the archbishop was greedy and prodigal, who loved splendour and opulence, and the seniors, Armenian merchants, as a rule, were parsimonious, moreover avaricious. But this does not give sufficient motivation for his ruthless deeds against the members of the community. There must have been a much stronger force behind him, the Jesuits, who instigated him to the atrocities, and gave him also helpers for the execution, and these were the seminarists of the Jesuit college.

In my opinion it was highly instructive to enlarge upon this issue at length, because it showed, what minute events evoked fatal consequences, in this case an antagonism and rupture between the head of the Polish Armenian clergy and the Patriarchate of the mother-country.

4,1,4. What happened in the ecclesiastic life of the Armenian colony in Lvov in the following years, is characterised by the veritable terrorism of the archbishop. Nikol "defied (his priests) to hold divine service, to administer the Sacraments, and to bury the dead".[244] This report is accurately confirmed by the documents discovered by G. Pingirian in the State Archives of Lvov; the report of the royal examining judge L. Krassuski from February 27th, 1631. When L. Krassuski, upon the request of the seniors, walked round the houses of the antiuniate Armenians, as a result of Nikol's prohibition he found unburied dead in almost every house. The families protected their health by pouring tar on the corpses to prevent the diffusion of the epidemic.[245] The body of the *erespoxan* Bernat Bernatowicz, who died in 1632, was clandestinely smuggled out to the cemetery of Jazlowiec by his relatives,[246] to get buried in compliance with the traditional Armenian–Gregorian rites.

Nikol Torosowicz ordered that those antiuniate priests who did not obey his prohibitive instructions should be beaten by his servants, monks and the seminarists of the Jesuit college and be put into his (own) prison. The documents of three more similar cases (1631, 1633, 1636) have been published recently.[247]

The situation is characterized in a summarized form by the letter of the seniors dated from July 25th, 1631 (quoted above several times), as follows: Nikol "has those

[244] *Svjazi*, p. 50; Tavrižeci, 379–80; Tavr/Bros. 453; Tavr/Xan. 299; Simeon Lehaci, ed. Akinean, p. 413; *Svjazi*, p. 84.

[245] CGIA USSR, Lvov, f. 9, op. 1, t. 381, pp. 258–59: See *Naukovo informacijnij Bjuletenj Archivnogo Upravl. URSR*, Kiev 1963, No. 5, p. 48; Pingirian: *ISDUAN* 1971, p. 365, idem, *REArm* XIV, p. 454.

[246] *Nauk.-inform. Bjul. Archivn. Upravl. URSR*, 1963 *ibid.*; Pingirian: *ISDUAN* 1971, p. 365; Idem: *REArm* XIV, p. 454.

[247] CGIA USSR, Lvov f. 9, op. 1, t. 382, pp. 1117–20; *Svjazi*, p. 42–44. (Arrested the priest Simeon Mihajlowicz, who in 1631 took the letter of the seniors to the Katholicos in Echmiadzin.) — Ibid., t. 48, pp. 446–451: *Svjazi*, pp. 58–62. Pingirian: *Nauk-inform. Bjul.*, Kiev 1963, pp. 48–49. (About the personality of Zakaria Bernatowicz see above: notes 205, 207.) — CGIA USSR, Lvov, f. 52, op. 3, t. 51, pp. 327–33: *Svjazi*, p. 72–76.

294

II

priests, who do not obey him, arrested and beaten, he throws them into a stinking prison, and has irons put on their necks. He tortures them until they declare they will accept (the Roman Catholic faith). He does, what he deems to be good, because he is supported by the church authorities, especially by the Jesuits, and by the secular authorities."[248]

Over the next two decades, only a few documents relate similar incidents or they may not have been discovered or published so far. However, the circumstance that the antiuniate Armenians were compelled to convene clandestinely in private houses for a ceremony or divine service, is also confirmed by data from 1647. Nikol also acknowledged in a letter written to the secretary of the Propaganda Fide, the prelate Ingoli, that with his clerics he had attacked such congregations, punished their participants and put them in prison [249]

4,1,5. In all his activities, Torosowicz primarily relied on the Jesuits. Although he formally made the papal declaration of allegiance in the church of the Carmelites on October 24th, 1630, he did so at the instigation of the Jesuits. At every stage, the Jesuit priests and the students of the Jesuit college were of decisive character, as well as in the forcible acts also committing assaults.

The main supporters of this course of archbishop Nikol were the local magistrates, who since the establishment of the Armenian colony under the Polish administration endeavoured to curtail their legal privileges, to withdraw their exemption from taxes and customs duties and to curb their religious line to bring them under the aegis of the Roman Catholic Church, by which their canonical autonomy would have also ceased.

From the very beginning, the Armenian seniors had been in favour with the Polish kings. In the 17th century, however, they no longer enjoyed such an exceptional legal state as they had in the past in exchange for the promotion of commerce, carried on by the East-West trade operators, and for the large lowns given to the Polish kings, in return to which their original privileges were repeatedly renewed.

From the religious point of view, Wladislas IV (1632–1648), the successor of Sigismund III, though a pupil of the Jesuits, was a tolerant and even liberal ruler. He also wanted to solve the Armenian ecclesiastic question. He returned by decree (1633) all the Armenian churches.[250] He himself arrived to Lvov to return the main church to the community, but because of the Jesuit power he had to yield.[251] King Wladislas started investigations in the case of the conflicts between the community and Torosowicz. In 1635, in connection with the destruction of devotional objects by Nikol, he personally came to Lvov.[252] In 1647 he again convened a committee to

---

[248] *Svjazi*, pp. 50–51.
[249] "cum clericis meis intercepi, incarceravi et poenis arbitrariis punivi" (April 8, 1647): Cong. Gen. v. 64, f. 148: *L'unione*, p. 123.
[250] Cong. Gen. v. 298, f. 151: *L'unione*, p. 61.
[251] Tavrižeci, 381–82; Tavr/Bros. 453–54; Tavr/Xan. 301.
[252] Simeon Lehaci (ed. Akinean), colophon, IX. pp. 415–16; *Svjazi*, pp. 86–87; *L'unione*, pp. 79–80.

II

investigate the discord. The further work of the committee was halted by the death of King Wladislas in 1648.[253]

During the reign of King John Casimir (1648–1668), who was a Jesuit cardinal before his accession to the throne, the case of the church-union was decided definitively.

4.2.1. In the 1630s the antiuniate Armenians — gaining confidence from the conciliatory attitude of King Wladislas, who was ready to promote a *modus vivendi* in the intricate church affairs — at first were unwilling to come to any agreement.

And it was at this juncture, that Paolo Piromalli, a Dominican monk, stepped in. Pater Paulus, the mediation of whom the attached Armeno–Kipchak document refers to, was used as mediator to bring about an agreement between the Armenian community and the archbishop, and to achieve the peaceful uniation of the Armenian community. Between 1631 and 1637, P. Piromalli taught Latin in Armenia in the seminary of Echmiadzin. Thus, as a result of his knowledge of the Armenian language and his acquaintance with the mother-country he seemed to be most suitable for this mediating role. Therefore, Piromalli was sent by the Congregatio to Lvov in 1638 to settle the discord. Then in January 1639, together with archbishop Nikol, they went to Warsaw to be received at audience by the king. Piromalli at all events wanted to persuade the people (first of all the notables, the seniors) of Lvov to eliminate the dogmatic and liturgical "errors" and the ceremonial differences between the Roman Catholic and the Armenian–Gregorian creed.[254] In a letter to the Congregation (1639), Piromalli reported that he succeeded in inducing the Armenians to eliminate the dogmatic faults and the liturgical aberrations *(errores)*.[255]

Presumably, the note in the Files of the Armenian Council of Lvov *(Acta— oragrut'iwn)* dated from July 12th, 1639, reported on this: *"Pater Pawel Dominikan mnixbila tawanut'iwn večindan kendina pokazat ettix. xajsi tawanut'iwnumuz usna bijanyp. da podpisaccada boldu čeznatetipki jaxši katoliklardyr. da jazdi padšhga da A[nyng] B[ijlik]-ina. Hem legatka anglatyp, ki bizim anidzac Nikol axpaš bizni jamanda nejcnotlivej anglatyl edi. ki biz heretiklar bolgaj biz. ol večtan ki bizni kozdan čxargaj."* "In the discussion with the Dominican monk Pater Paulus, we showed him our Credo, and he rejoiced very much at our Credo, and it has been signed to acknowledge that we were good Catholics, and he wrote [to his effect] to His Majesty the king. He informed the [Papal] legate that our cursed archbishop Nikol spread

[253] Cf. the letter of Torosowicz addressed to the Congregazio, Cong. Gen. v. 65, f. 169: *L'unione*, pp. 127–29.

[254] *L'unione*, pp. 99–102. — On the relation between Torosowicz and Piromalli see: *Azgapatum*, II/2, cols. 2437–40: Piromalli was of a forceful character, his methods had been violent: During his first stay in Armenia in 1632 he wrought much turbulence in the Nakhichevan community (Akinean, *Movses III.*, pp. 376, sqq.). — After his return to missionary activity in the East, in Isfahan (1647) he caused embarrassment and alarm preaching in the streets on the errors of the Armenians (*Carmelites*, I, 376–77.).

[255] Cong. Gen. v. 81, f. 426: *L'unione*, pp. 101-2.

II

about us (the insinuation) that we were bad and immoral, that we were heretics, in order to denigrate us."[256]

Presumably, the Credo mentioned here was the one confessed in Lvov by the archbishops of Lvov at their consecration. (See note 323.)

In August 1639, the Congregation summoned Piromalli to Rome to report in connection with the questions regarding the correction of the Armenian liturgy. At that time (in addition to the letter of recommendation written by King Wladislas IV to Pope Urban VIII) Piromalli took along with him the declaration of the Armenians, in which they categorically rejected the acceptance of the union as long as archbishop Nikol was not removed from Lvov and they did not get at least temporarily *(ad saltem)* one church for their own use, and as long as their delegates together with Piromalli did not consult the Katholicos Philippos in connection with these questions.[257]

On April 20th 1640, before the special session of the Congregatio, Piromalli reported on the situation of the Armenians in Poland and Armenia. According to him, the minimal requests of the Armenians — the removal of Nikol and the return of at least *one* church to the antiuniates — should be granted. According to him this was the "sine qua non" of the agreement.[258] Despite this the Congregation decided that it would not comply with these conditions.

On his return to Poland, Piromalli brought letters from the Pope to the King, from the Congregation to the Polish archbishop in Lvov, to the Roman Catholic chapter in Lvov and to Nikol, but these essentially spoke about the questions of the union and did not contain anything positive for the antiuniate Armenians.

As soon as the Armenians of Lvov were informed about the return of Piromalli from Rome,[259] they hurried to Warsaw. Attached to this paper is the text of the instructions given to the Armenian delegation by the council of seniors, dated December 19, 1640, a valuable social and church document of the Armenian community of Lvov and a precious linguistic record in their Armeno-Kipchak vernacular.

The essence of the instruction was as follows: the delegates should by no means agree to the union, it was out of question that they would accept alterations in the Armenian-Gregorian dogmas and liturgy qualified by the Roman Catholics as "errors". They should do everything they could in order to ensure that the "cursed bishop" was relieved of his offices and removed from Lvov. At that time, the seniors still hoped that the King (in accordance with his decision of the year 1633) would

[256] Bžškian, M., Čanaparhordut'iwn i Lehastan. Venice 1830, p. 114.

[257] Cong. Gen. v. 293, f. 256: L'unione, p. 102.

[258] Cong. Gen. v. 293, f. 247, sq: L'unione, p. 104. Cf. Tavrižeci, 383; Tavr/Bros. 454–55; Tavr/Xan. 302.

[259] Piromalli started on his journey back to Poland by the middle of 1640, but because of illness he arrived to Warsaw only on the 15th December, see: L'unione, p. 105.

II

return *all* the churches and the documents of the community, which Nikol illegally took into his possession.

However when they learned that Piromalli did not bring any favourable concession in their interest, they raised more moderate claims: they requested only the removal of Torosowicz and the return of *one* of the four churches.

Based on the report of Piromalli, the Congregatio was not at all sure that if a church was handed over, the Armenians of Lvov would come closer to the union, in fact it doubted that they sincerely wanted the uniation at all. They considered that the question could be solved only if they sent a legate to the Katholicos Philippos to bring about the universal church-union of the Armenians, and they assigned this task to Piromalli. The starting of this undertaking was considerably promoted by the fact that on January 20th, 1642 the Katholicos Philippos sent a "credo" to the Pope, and also sent a copy of it to the Armenians of Lvov.[260] Hereafter, Piromalli, together with four delegates of the community of Lvov, set out for Echmiadzin at the end of September 1642.

Torosowicz clearly saw that Piromalli was a *persona grata* in the Roman curia, and that he was recommended for the attention of the Polish court and ecclesiastic circles. This raised Nikol's suspicion that eventually Piromalli would be selected as a possible candidate in his place. Piromalli's chances would increase considerably, if he could succeed in bringing about the church-union, not only of the Armenians of Lvov, but also of those of Armenia. He therefore used all his guile and intrigue to ensure that Piromalli was unsuccessful. For this purpose, he hurried to Rome and at the general assembly of the Congregation on April 20th, 1643 he specially stressed the merits he had achieved so far to bring about the church-union and that, despite the stubborn opposition of the schismatics for 10 years, he held all the four Armenian churches in his hands. He underlined that Piromalli hindered his work by promising the Armenians that they will get back their churches and receive another archbishop in Nikol's place. The Congregation decided in favour of the maintenance of the archbishopric of Lvov at all costs and voted for him even a biennial subsidy of 200 scudi. This decision was apparently influenced by the fact that the "declaration of allegiance" of Philippos did not completely contain the liturgical demands of the Roman Catholic Church *(credo imperfecta).*[261]

However, since the Congregation was aware of the general aversion against Torosowicz and the justification of the accusations brought against him, they intended to detain Nikol in Rome until Piromalli returned from Armenia. However, Nikol organized a good counter-action, viz. the well timed letter of his brother, in which he informed the Secretary of the Congregatio that the Armenians of Lvov were ready for

[260] Congr. Part. v. 3, f. 235: L'unione, pp. 104, 108; St. Roszka, *Żamanakagrut'iwn kam tarekank' ekelec'akank'*. Vienna 1964, p. 176 Alishan, *Kamenic'*, pp. 139–40.

[261] *L'unione*, pp. 109–111.

II

the union, while the Katholicos of Armenia rejected Piromalli's appeal for the union. Torosowicz won a complete victory over Piromalli.[262]

4,3,1. The archiepiscopal rule of Nikol Torosowicz for half a century (1627–1681) weighed heavily on the Armenian colony of Lvov (of Poland) throughout the 17th century. The antiuniate Armenians considered him the depraver of the community and the enforcer of the union with the Roman Holy See. Roman Catholic intellectual literature endeavours to obscure the serious moral faults of the archbishop, with the consideration that in final conclusion he brought about the ecclesiastic uniation of the Armenians of Lvov with Rome. Already before his consecration the Armenians of Lvov protested to patriarch Melkisedek. They did not consider Nikol Torosowicz suitable for this high office, on the one hand because of his young age (23 years), and on the other hand because of his moral attitude. "He openly and boldly led a loose and immoral way of life" — Tavrizhetsi reported.[263]

The accusation against his moral life (in the published literature) was explicitly expressed in the letter of Zakaria Agam, pupil of the Congregation sent to Lvov, in 1647:.: "vivet cum meretrice", or elsewhere "vitam agit sordidissimam, cum mulier manet et eam tenet publice et fovet, cum qua prolem suscepit..trinam".[264] He lived together with a woman and had 2 (here 3) sons from her.[265]

In 1652 Torosowicz vowed to Katholicos Philippos that he would give up this "loose" way of life, but in this respect hardly any change occurred, because in 1673 he made the same vow to the Congregatio, when he was nearly 70 years of age.[266]

In addition to the question of the church-union, the main conflict between the seniors, the community and the archbishop, and the long series of law-suits before the royal chancellery and the city magistrate of Lvov were mainly the result of Nikol's unscrupulous financial extortions.

In competing for the archiepiscopal power Nikol was attracted "rather by the attire (the *pallium*) than by the soul"[267] — a point mentioned by the Papal nuncio in Warsaw in 1637. According to Simeon Lehaci, King Wladislas said: "He became

---

[262] The Dominican priest was driven out of Echmiadzin by the antiuniate Armenians. He never again returned to Lvov, but retired to the Armenian Dominican mission of Nakhichevan, where he was elected archbishop from 1655 to 1664: *L'Unione*. pp. 113–15; Oudenrijn, O. P., *Linguae Haicanae scriptores ord. pred. Congr. Fratrum Unitorum et FF. Armenorum*. Bern 1960, p. 50, etc.

[263] Tavrižeci, 364–5, 384; Tavr. Bros. 445, 455; Tavr/Xan. 289, 302–3. Simeon Lehaci gave a similar characterisation of him: "He is still young and ignorant, he is of hazy thinking and lacks judgement; morally he does not follow the correct path. He is bad and false *(apirat)* in every matter and case. He is impudent and has no proper sense and consideration." Akinean: *Simeon*, (Colophon, IX.) p. 410. *Svjazi*, p. 83. — About the intention of Nikol to take a wife the Congregation has been informed by the Legate of Warsaw already before Nikol's conversion: *L'unione*, p. 14, note 6.

[264] Cong. Gen. v. 65. f. 60.: *L'unione*, pp. 123, 131.

[265] At the time of arrival of Galanus to Lvov the majority of the Armenian priests was married: *L'unione*, pp. 195–96.

[266] Tavrižeci, 387; Tavr/Bros. 457; Tavr/Xan. 305; Congr. Part. v. 22, f. 5, and 277: *L'unione*, p. 266.

[267] *L'unione*, p. 89.

II

converted to our faith, because of the property and the ecclasiastical treasures." Nikol was captivated by the splendour and glitter of archiepiscopal power. To display his dignity, he wore precious cloaks and kept a coach and horses: "20–30 beautiful (saddle?)-horses, precious carriages with Arab *(tajik)* horses, he dressed in batiste *(behez)*, scarlet robe *(cirani)*, velvet *(maxmur)*, and atlas, and wore cloaks lined with sable *(samur)* and beech-marten fur *(vašax)*."[268]

In addition to lavish spending at home, his journeys involved especially high expenditure. When he travelled to Rome in 1634, he was accompanied by a retinue of 30 people.[269] On the occasion of his visit to Rome in 1668, he was accompanied by 22 persons, who needed carriages drawn by 14 horses.[270] On these occasions his expenses were subsequently borne by the Congregatio.[271]

The expenses of his journey to the Katholicos Philippos in 1652, amounted to 2,000 *gurušes.*[272]

But his expensive way of life could not be covered by his archiepiscopal benefice or his family property. He was forced to resort to illegal and immoral forcible methods. In 1630 he took possession of the church and the sacristy, together with the devotional articles and over 1,000 precious codices. He then broke into the premise *(xuc)* of the corporation of seniors, and took the ecclesiastic and private deposits.[273]

"The archbishop sold the books, the devotional articles and the ecclesiastic treasure, and partly used them for bribery. He had certain objects crushed, and handed them over to Jews, who sold them as broken silver. Thus scattered and squandered, he wasted everything, the infinite richness of properties and treasures".[274]

In his famous colophone IX, Simeon Lehatsi enumerated in detail the precious devotional articles, "which were collected in the course of 500 years by the pious" believers, specially stressing the 200–300 precious codices, partly originating from Sis and Kaffa, from the royal treasury and from the libraries of the *vardapets*. The author complained that all of these were sold, squandered and destroyed by Nikol.[275]

[268] Simeon Lehaci (ed. Akinean), Col. IX. pp. 417, 415; *Svjazi*, pp. 87. 85. He sold his horses only in 1673, as an expression of submission to the severe stipulation of the Congregatio: *L'unione*, p. 247. (The saddle horse: *bedäwi* 'Bedouin' or *bedä'i*)

[269] Congres, II, f. 108v: *L'unione*, p. 66; or in 1642: "accompagnato da un numeroso seguito": *L'unione*, p. 109.

[270] Acta v. 58, f. 4: *L'unione*, p. 236.

[271] In 1635 he was granted 50 scudi, in 1643 200 scudi for his travel expenditures: *L'unione*, p. 76, 111–112; in 1629 his travel expenses were covered by the seniors: 3.000 guruš-es, Tavrižeci, 370; Tavr/Bros. 448; Tavr/Xan. 292. For comparison: a 2–3 storied house built of stone in the town cost 2–3, or 4.000 guruš-es: Simeon Lehaci (ed. Akinean), p. 377; Simeon L., *Putevye zametki*, p. 243.

[272] Tavrižeci, 385; Tavr/Bros. 456; Tavr/Xan. 303–4; cf. *L'unione*, p. 136.

[273] Tavrižeci, 376–77; Tavr/Bros. 451; Tavr/Xan. 297–98. Cf. Bileckij: *ISDUAN* 1965, p. 90; CGIA USSR Lvov, f. 9, op. 1, t. 381, 383, etc.; Pingirian, *ISDUAN* 1971, p. 364; CGIA USSR Lvov, f. 52, t. 48, 446–51; *Svjazi*, p. 61. Pingirian: *Banber Hay. Arxiv*. 1974. no. 3. p. 108–110 Doc. 6–7.

[274] Tavrižeci, 384; Tavr/Bros. 455; Tavr/Xan. 302. The squandering of the ecclesiastic treasures has been related similarly in the letter addressed in 1631 to Movses Katholicos: *Svjazi*, p. 50.

[275] Simeon Lehaci (ed. Akinean), Col. IX., pp. 411–13; *Svjazi*, p. 84.

II

The seniors sued the archbishop for the return of the appropriated valuables. However, during the reign of Sigismund III they did not achieve any result, since he enjoyed the full support of the King[276] standing under Jesuit influence, of the Papal nuncio, the Polish archbishop of Lvov, the magistrate of Lvov and primarily of the Jesuits. With his liberal character, King Wladislas became a protector of the seniors. In 1634 — when Torosowicz was staying in Rome — royal instructions were given to officials to open the treasure-chest standing in the council-chamber but they found it completely empty.[277] The damage and loss has been estimated to 100,000 gold coins by the seniors, and 300,000 scudi by the Warsaw nuntio.[278]

Fortunately, many of the silver vessels and precious books sold by the archbishop came to Armenia, from where they were bought back by Armenian merchants.[279]

4,3,2. Torosowicz did not tolerate any contradiction or independent action on part of the priests belonging to his diocese. The written pleadings in general suggest that the archbishop took action against the priests concerned, applied force against them and imprisoned them because of their antiuniate creed. The archbishop, however, was not such an intransigent Uniate, or such an unselfish fighter for the Roman Catholic faith.

The attacks against certain Armenian private houses by the archbishop and his satellites primarily did not serve as a punishment of the believers of Gregorian–Armenian faith and the priests present, but were rather an intimidating action, such as for example the surprise attacks of 1633 or 1636 often referred to.[280]

A similar case was reported by Tavrižeci, when a young couple wanted to get married "secretly, without the knowledge of the archbishop." The archbishop's armed men burst into the house and dragged the priests — bound, bare-headed and bare footed — before the archbishop, who imprisoned the priests and the parents of the

[276] In 1631 the King instructed the Polish wojt and the magistrates to support the catholicized Armenian bishop: Gromnicki, T., *Ormjanie w Polsce. Ich historja, prawa i przywileje.* Warsaw 1889, pp. 26–27; Macler, Fr., *Rapport sur une mission scientifique en Galicie en Bukovine (juillet-août 1925): REA* VII, 1927, 23–24; *L'unione*, pp. 50–54.

[277] Congr. Gen. v. 59, f. 178v: *L'unione*, p. 79; *Svjazi*, p. 87; Simeon Lehaci (ed. Akinean), Col. IX., p. 417.

[278] Pingirian: *ISDUAN* 1971, 364 (CGIA USSR, Lvov, f. 9, op. 1, t. 382, pp. 59–61); Nunz. Pol. v. 47, f. 57: *L'unione*, p. 79. — According to Mgr. Ingoli's statement Torosowicz deposited the treasures in a safe place: Nunz. Pol. v. 47, f. 58: *L'unione*, 80–81; but Torosowicz was unwilling to disclose it: Congr. Part. v. 22, f. 144: *L'unione*, 91–92. Pingirian: *Benber Hay. Arxiv.*, 1974, no. 3. Doc. 8. (1636)

[279] Tavrižeci, 384; Tavr./Bros. 455; Tavr/Xan. 303. Silver articles pawned with a Lvov silversmith: CGIA USSR, f. 9, op. 1, t. 384, pp. 38–40: *Svjazi*, pp. 57–58. Cf. *REArm*, IV, pp. 281–82.

[280] Pingirian: *Naukovo-inform. Bjul. Archivn. Upravl. URSR*, Kiev 1963, No. 5., pp. 48–49: *Svjazi*, pp. 58–62 and 72–76.

301

II

bridegroom, and only released them for a fine of 400 *guruŝes* per person, and when the fine was paid, the wedding could take place.[281]

Although some documents do not mention the imposition of fines, it was a permanent practice of the archbishop, to collect it from priests, as stated by Simeon Lehaci: "Torosowicz arrested the priests for the slightest offence, put them in prison, and imposed a fine on them of 300–400 *guruŝes*. He similarly fined the seniors, who were the consuls *(datawork')* of the Armenian community".[282] It was primarily considered to be an offence, if the sacraments were administered without notification, i.e. without the share postulated by the archbishop.

In the prevention of baptism, marriage and burial ceremonies, it was not the antiuniate character of the ceremonies, but the neglection of the archbishop's share which played the main role. This is confirmed by a series of data: "He permitted the dead to be buried only for money *(gandz)* — stated Arakel Tavriżeci — . . . when after the burial they wanted to erect a tomb-stone on the grave, he again demanded money *(gandz)*, and only after the payment did he grant the permit for erecting the grave-stone".[283]

In order to prevent priests from other towns to be invited to perform the ceremonies, he posted special sentries at the town gates.[284]

At one occasion for such an "offence" he imprisoned also the priest-writer Simeon Lehaci and he could "hardly *(haziw)*" been redeemed by Armenian merchants (certainly for a high ransom).[285]

With regard to the later period, only one or two cases of such encroachments are known (at least in the documents of the magistrate of Lvov published so far). This does not mean that Torosowicz gave up the ransoming.[286] This is also attested by the report of the priest Zaccaria Agam sent to the Congregation in 1647: *"est ipsius (i.e. of Torosowicz) spoliare sacerdotes armenos"*, thus he collected the emoluments due to the priests and did not distribute them according to the ecclesiastic prescriptions.[287]

Because of the numerous complaints made in connection with the unjust fines and abuses against the Armenian priests, the Papal nuncio in Warsaw, a major patron of Torosowicz, was finally obliged to institute an investigation in 1647.[288] But neither

---

[281] Tavriżeci, 380; Tavr/Bros. 453; Tavr/Xan. 300. Y. Daŝkevič doubts, whether the two cases would refer to the same event, because in the latter the priests had been released from prison only in October: *Svjazi.* pp. 151-2.

[282] Simeon Lehaci (ed. Akinean), Col. IX, p. 413; *Svjazi,* 84-5.

[283] Tavriżeci, 379–380; Tavr./Bros. 452–53; Tavr/Xan. 299–300.

[284] Simeon Lehaci (ed. Akinean) p. 413; *Svjazi,* p. 84–85.

[285] Simeon Lehaci, p. 413; *Svjazi,* p. 85. Cf. Daŝkevič, *Simeon Lehaci, kto on ? (E. Sluszkiewicz Memorial Volume),* pp. 75–76; ide, *Siméon Dpir Lehaci, qui est-il ? REArm,* XII, 1977, p. 355.

[286] About the occasional alm spending of the believers, the different smaller donations, the momentous foundations and generally the church incomes a precise information is given by Simeon Lehaci: (ed. Akinean), pp. 339–343; Simeon L., *Putevye zametki,* pp. 244–47.

[287] Cong. Gen. v. 65, f. 165: *L'unione,* p. 124.

[288] Cong. Gen. v. 64, f. 150, sq.: *L'unione,* p. 123.

II

did Torosowicz later stop to demand illegally contributions for himself, this becomes clear from several reports from the periods preceding the arrival of Galanus in Lvov (1664) and following it. Torosowicz was willing to administer the sacraments only for excessive fees *(spesa intolerabile)* and he placed extra charges *(tasse insolite)* on baptism, burial and wedding, so that the young men from poor families were compelled to abandon their intention of getting married. In his letter (1662) the nuncio explained this by saying that the alms and other grants received from the believers were insufficient to enable Torosowicz to maintain the standard worthy of an archbishop, and cover the expenses connected with his life-partner *(concubina)* and his two sons.[289]

It is characteristic that these abuses of Torosowicz were mentioned in the reports only here and there, and even then with muted strings. However, even with the grave sin of simony he was accused in the report of Galanus, viz.: Torosowicz sold the sacerdotal offices for heavy sums *(prezzi exorbitanti)*, and what is more, to the "most ignorant" *(ignorantissimi)*.[290]

Due to all these complaints, the Congregatio had for a long time been considering the removal of Torosowicz, but because of his earlier "merits" they kept delaying the decision, and Torosowicz, with his astute manoeuvring and compromising policy, always succeeded in eliminating his possible rivals. It is characteristic that the interest of the Armenian believers in Poland played a minor role in the eyes of the Congregatio. The financial abuses of the archbishop were included in the solemn promise only as the 12th, last paragraph viz.: that he should not demand a higher charge for the administration of the sacraments than was fixed by the nuncio.[291]

4,3,3. The reprisals of archbishop Nikol against the priests sent by the seniors to the Katholicos of Echmiadzin come in another category. Since he did not tolerate any separate negotiations he afflicted them with the most serious maltreatment.

He had Simeon Mikolajowicz cruelly beaten and put into prison in 1631, before Simeon set off for Echmiadzin.[292] Simeon was also molested by Torosowicz on several other occasions. His persecution is confirmed also by other documents in the archives of Lvov.[293]

The same fate awaited those two priests who in 1646 went to visit the Katholicos. They were put in jail by Torosowicz, and released only for a ransom of 1500 gold coins.[294]

4,4,1. From the letters of the nuncios in Warsaw, the Congregatio was well aware of the personal way of life of Torosowicz and his relations with the Armenian

[289] Cong. Gen. v. 225, f. 100: *L'unione*, p. 151.
[290] Cong. Gen. v. 224, f. 101v: *L'unione*, pp. 216–17.
[291] Congr. Part. v. 22, f. 5, and 277: *L'unione*, p. 266.
[292] CGIA USSR Lvov, f. 9, op. 1, t. 382, pp. 1117–1120: *Svjazi*, pp. 42–44.
[293] Pingirian: *ISDUAN* 1971, p. 358.
[294] Tavriżeci, 382–83; Tavr/Bros. 454; Tavr/Xan. 301–2; CGIA USSR, Lvov, f. 9, op. 1, t. 396. pp. 1540–41: *Svjazi*, pp. 94–95; Pingirian, *ISDUAN* 1971, p. 359.

303

II

community. But because of his personal confession of allegiance and his activity to bring about the church-union of the community, the Congregatio was prepared to shut its eyes to his private life, the crimes he committed against the anti-uniate priests and believers were regarded by the Congregatio, so to say, as his merits.

However, it soon became clear from the reports that nothing was happening concerning the church-union,[295] and in 1638 the Congregatio sent its legate, Piromalli, to Lvov. However, Torosowicz considered every delegate from Rome to be a denouncer and even a possible personal rival. He therefore used all his guile to remove them from Lvov. The failure of Piromalli's visit to Echmiadzin was a complete success for Nikol.

When in 1647, the Papal nuncio in Warsaw was finally compelled to start an investigation, Torosowicz in a very clever way, instead of defending himself, launched an attack, to present his use of illegal force as a justified act, carried out in interest of the Roman Catholic Church.[296]

When his position was threatened from the east, i.e. the initiative started by the seniors with Katholicos Philippos, it was frustrated by Nikol in 1652 when he signed allegiance to the Katholicos. As a result, in his pastoral letter Philippos admonished the community and called for their obedience towards the bishop and their reconciliation with the archbishop.[297]

Following this move, there was silence both in the community of Lvov and in the Congregatio for about ten years, but then the question, if not of the replacement of Torosowicz, but of the appointment of a coadjutor, was raised with regard to his advanced age.[298]

The only possible candidate was Hovhannes Kieremowicz, titular bishop of Moldavia, who was, of course, persona non grata in the eyes of Torosowicz, because he reprimanded Nikol's "scandalous life" on several occasions. The manoeuvring ability of Torosowicz is confirmed by the fact that in this particular case he did not refrain from referring — of course, with a reversed indication — to the right of *ius eligendi* of the Armenian seniors, naturally in his own best interests.[299]

The main rival for Torosowicz was the Theatine monk Clemens Galanus (1610–1666). For a long time, the Congregatio had planned to establish a college to promote the Catholic education of the Armenian youths of Lvov, and Pater Galanus was selected to lead it.[300]

[295] L'unione, p. 100.
[296] Cong. Gen. v. 64, f. 148: L'unione, p. 123.
[297] Alishan, Kamenic', pp. 250, sqq: cf. L'unione, pp. 131–37.
[298] Cong. Gen. v. 225, f. 37, sqq: L'unione, p. 145.
[299] Cong. Gen. v. 120, f. 322: L'unione, p. 248. In final result, Kieremowicz did not receive the authority even of a coadjutor, but only a suffragan bishop. And after his death (1677) his post remained vacant.
[300] Galanus spent more than a decade in Armenia and Georgia, and three years he was teacher in the seminary of the Armenian patriarchate in Constantinople. Azgapatum, II/2, cols. 2533–38; Soukias Somal.

II

In a latent form, of course, Galanus was also commissioned to observe the religious life of the whole Armenian community. Archbishop Nikol immediately expounded his misgivings to the Congregatio about the status, they intended to give to Galanus — in addition to teaching in the college — and he also announced his own right of supremacy over education: *"se subjacere, omniaque nonnisi nutu et arbitrio meo facere"*.[301]

In interest of the definitive removal, Torosowicz was called to Rome in 1668, with the intention that he would not be permitted to return to his diocese. After a protracted debate, finally the choice for the post of the coadjutor fell on Vartan Hunanian, an Armenian disciple of the Congregatio. The incredible persistence and organizing ability of Torosowicz is reflected by the fact that with his letters he stirred up the ecclesiastic and secular leaders of Lvov and Warsaw. Even the Polish King sent a letter to Pope Clement X asking permission for Nikol to return home. The majority of the seniors also asked for the return of the archbishop, because even though they were dissatisfied with him at least he was a native of Lvov.[302]

At last, to ensure his return home, archbishop Nikol accepted all the conditions of the Congregatio, and in 1675 he returned to Lvov, accompanied by Vartan Hunanian.[303]

But soon after his arrival home once again he gained the upperhand. It became clear that he had inaugurated Hunanian as his coadjutor only under coercion. Neither the Armenian community did accept Hunanian that time.[304] In order to prevent further conflicts, Hunanian asked to be sent to the Armenian communities living in Turkish-Tatar missionary territory. Thus Torosowicz, having got rid of his last rival, spent his last years undisturbed until his death on October 24, 1681.

As was pointed out earlier, during his more than half a century long archiepiscopal activity, Torosowicz strictly ensured that no legate should interfere in the life of his diocese. He was able to prevent all the possible successor candidates and coadjutors from remaining in Lvov, and did not tolerate anybody who may have eventually had the inclination or desire to get ahead of him. Autocracy was always his leading principle, as later, with the arrival of Galanus, he definitely and sharply expressed to the Congregatio, viz.: *"persuadeat . . . sibi ill-ma Dominatio me nullo modo pati posse quempiam qui, ad latus meum existens, velit audeatque mihi praeesse . . ."*[305]

Torosowicz resorted to all types of cunning and forcible means and methods, and the fact that he was able to assert his will in such a masterly manner towards those

---

Quadro della Storia Letteraria di Armenia. Venice, 1829, pp. 203–5; Neumann, *Versuch einer Geschichte der armenischen Literatur,* Leipzig 1836, pp. 242–45.

[301] Cong. Gen. v. 225, f. 122; *L'unione,* p. 165. Galanus function lasted altogether two years; he died 1666.

[302] *L'unione,* pp. 225–29, 235, 246–51, 255–56, 266–70.

[303] Cong. Part. v. 22, f. 7, and 277; *L'unione,* p. 266; Congres, II, f. 413; *L'unione,* p. 297.

[304] *L'unione,* pp. 300–1; *Svjazi,* p. 126.

[305] Cong. Gen. v. 225, 1. 132; *L'unione,* p. 165.

II

who opposed him, amazed even his opponents. It appears that some admiration was concealed in Arakel Tavrižeci's characterization though intended to be ignominious, viz.: 'ingenious mystifier' (hančarel xorhrdakan).[306]

However, Torosowicz applied admirable tricks not only toward his rivals, but also in his manoeuvering between the Armenian-Gregorian and the Roman Catholic Church over half a century.

4.4.2. When he first took office he showed his two main characteristics: his stubbornness (est pertinax) and, in cases of emergency, his readiness to engage in any kind of compromise.[307]

Although after his consecration by Melkisedek, he enjoyed the support of the Roman Catholic high clergy and especially the personal aid of the Jesuits, still he did not venture to challenge the ancient right of the seniors of the community of Lvov, their right to freely elect their bishop (ius eligendi); in particular, he was compelled to do so because of his financial circumstances. After all, the archiepiscopal incomes were ensured for him by the council of the seniors.[308] This is how the election of the archbishop on part of the Armenian ecclesiastic people and the community of Lvov took place as a result of his profession of allegiance to the church of Echmiadzin.[309]

When there was the threat that he would be removed from office, because of the anathema of Grigor Kesaratsi, in his despairing situation — upon the encouragement of the Jesuits — he fled to the Roman Catholic Church, and made a vow of allegiance in Rome in 1635.[310]

When, after their twenty five years long quarrel, the seniors, with the aid of their declaration of church-union, were able to proceed against the hated archbishop ("anicac axpaš") from the Roman Catholic position, he concluded an agreement with the Katholicos Philippos who was then staying in Constantinople in 1653: "archbishop Nikolayos turned to us with deep humbleness and showed full obedience towards us."[311]

The Katholicos thought that this vow would ensure the preservation of the Armenian-Gregorian faith, and the ecclesiastic customs and rites of the Armenian settlement in Poland. On the other hand, for Nikol the agreement meant the confirmation of his archiepiscopal authority by the Katholicos of Echmiadzin.[312]

Torosowicz was compelled to make another turnaround in 1673, when after being detained in Rome for five years, he signed a vow to the Congregation containing strict stipulations.[313]

[306] Tavrižeci, 385; Tavr/Bros. 455 ("doué de perspicacité"); Tavr/Xan. 303 ("genialnyj plut").
[307] L'unione, p. 96.
[308] Biblioteka Ossolińska, Wrocław. Ms. Collection, No. 1646, II. pp. 47-9; Svjazi, p. 106-7.
[309] Daškevič, Y., E. Tryjarski: RO XXXIII, 1, 1969, 77, sqq.
[310] L'unione, pp. 45, 66, 81.
[311] Ališan, Kamenic', p. 255.
[312] Tavrižeci, 386; Tavr/Bros. 456; Tavr/Xan. 304; Gromnicki, op. cit. p. 30; Macler; REA VII, 1927, p. 27.
[313] L'unione, pp. 265–66, 247.

II

In our opinion, he undertook all these steps in order to ensure his financial position and the undisturbed exertion of his power. The priority of financial reasons was reflected both by the serious financial aspect of the reprisals against the priests (discussed earlier) and his dependence on the seniors, and such details are revealed only by the 1654 agreement.

Essentially the confrontation between Torosowicz and the council of seniors did not have religious motives. The community did not see a threat to the Armenian-Gregorian faith even after the catholicisation of Torosowicz (1630, 1635), since he did not introduce the "corrections" desired by the Roman Catholic Church either in the liturgy or in the rites, a fact experienced by the Theatines who arrived in Lvov in 1664. However, as the ecclesiastic revenues have been collected by the seniors, and Torosowicz could not freely dispose of it, he tried to hold them to ransom over the administration of the sacraments and thus compel them to comply with his will.

The autonomy of the Armenian community in Lvov — gained from and repeatedly renewed by the Polish Kings — was curtailed during the course of time. From 1469, the Armenian institution of the *vojt* (wojt, 'Vogt') was abolished, and from 1510 criminal cases and real estate cases were taken away from the authority of the council of seniors.[314]

However, this did not affect the customary law of Armenian inner autonomy. After this, the council of seniors was — tacitly — deprived of its leadership (with gradual changes in the number), but continued to manage the inner affairs of the Armenian community under the leadership of one or more *erespoxans*. The *erespoxan* "deputy, representative", allows for several interpretations. It was in fact a deputy — arbitrarily elected by the Armenian community — of the cancelled post of the *vojt*, or the continuer of his curtailed functions. Since his sphere of authority also covered ecclesiastic possessions, he was regarded as the secular superviser (provisor) of the Church. (This is the background of the folk-etymological form: *erecpoxan*.).

The most important thesis of customary law of this privilege was that the church properties and thus the devotional articles were all in the possession of the community, and the council of seniors headed by the *erespoxan* disposed of them. The disposition of the ecclesiastic properties was of such a degree that even the collection of offerings of money at the time of divine service, and the collecting of the fees paid for the bell-ringing on the occasion of weddings and burials belonged to the tasks of the seniors. And this not only applied to the cathedral of the Blessed Virgin Church, but also to the S. Cross (*Surb Xač*) and S. Anne churches in the suburb, and to the convent, as well as to the (not functioning) monastery [315]

[314] Bischoff, F., *Das alte Recht der Armenier in Polen: Oesterreichische Blätter für Literatur und Kunst*. Vienna 1857. No. 33, p. 218; Petrowicz, G., *L'organisation juridique des Arméniens sous les monarques polonaises: REArm*, IV, 1967, pp. 340, 344–45; Dachkevitch, Y., *Sur la question des rélations arméno–ukrainiennes au XVII᷐ siècle:* REArm, IV, 1967, pp. 264–5; Bischoff, F., *Das alte Recht der Armenier in Lemberg*. Wien 1862, pp. 39–42.

[315] Bibl. Ossolińska, Wroclaw. Ms No. 1646, II, 47–49. Translated by Y. Daškevič: *Svjazi*, pp. 106–7.

II

At the same time, this meant that the priests of the Armenian colony were entirely dependent on the community, which through the council of seniors managed the ecclesiastic real estates, and decided on the utilization of the ecclesiastic foundations. The community paid the priests and at the same time it looked after the repair of the ecclesiastic buildings and covered all other expenses. In brief, this meant that the priests and bishops in financial respect were fully dependent on the board of seniors and all of them deferred to this customary law.

In the text of the vow given by archbishop Nikol on April 26, 1627, the financial aspect of the rules of customary law was not expounded. The major part of the vow was of religious character and emphasis was placed on allegiance towards the Katholicos of Echmiadzin. The financial subordination was so self-evident that only point 3 made a short reference to it, inasmuch as "the archbishop observes the old agreement (*eski pakta*) made with his predecessors, both in respect of affairs and receipts, and will not demand more either from the community of Lvov or from that of Kamenets, and they will not demand more from him either" (lines 54–57).[310]

Over the next quarter of a century, the seniors experienced the fact that the financial rights and obligations had to be rigorously laid down with regard to Nikol. After the agreement made with Katholicos Philippos in 1653, the council of seniors concluded a thorough and detailed agreement with the archbishop on November 11, 1654. From this agreement it becomes clear that all the ecclesiastic possessions were the property of the community and only the council of seniors could decide on the allocation of the income originating from them. According to the agreement, the archbishop received the income of the S. Cross (*Sp. Xač*) church in the suburb named Krakow and the interest due on the legacies donated to the church. But at the same time — (emphatically) in accordance with the old rights — the seniors "manage all the premises and stone houses belonging to the church".

This document throws some light on the background of the reprisals exerted by Nikol against the priests, viz.: "His Excellency the archbishop should not collect a quarter-yearly percentage from the incomes of the priests" (based on the benefits and legacies directly due to them), and should not seize other incomes, but only what is due to him". The last stipulation illustrates the illegal claims made by the ecclesiastic people on the community: "Neither His Excellency the archbishop, nor the priests should gain any kind of extraordinary benefit from the community, they must be satisfied with what is due to them according to the customs of the (Armenian) church (of Lvov.)"[317]

The prohibitions included in the agreement clearly indicate that the privileges of the community or the council of seniors were infringed by the archbishop and that he extorted illegal percentile shares from the priests. The fact that Nikol did not refrain

---

[310] Daškevič–Tryjarski: *RO* XXXIII/1, 1969, pp. 82–3. Cf. above, p. note 226.
[317] Bibl. Ossolińska. Wrocław, Ms. Collection. No. 1646, II, pp. 47–9: *Svjazi*, 106–7.

II

from ransoming the community even later on, is illustrated by point 12 of the vow given to the Congregatio in 1673.[318]

The community had experienced Nikol's financial unreliability from the period when, after his catholicisation in 1630, he appropriated the valuables and devotional articles from the council cabinet (*xuc*), and many of these were sold or pawned by him.[319] Therefore, in the agreement of 1654 there was a separate passage, according to which the devotional articles should be handed over to the sacristan, who — in accordance with the (repeated) royal decree — was obliged to return them to the seniors.[320]

4.4.3. However, the seniors not only wanted to hold the financial reins in their hands, they also wanted to control the actions of the archbishop in his efforts to gain power, and thus, on the ecclesiastic level, they fought against the archbishop with his own weapon.

The most effective means was the handing in of a *confessio fidei* that was equally acceptable to both the Roman Catholic Church and the Armenian-Gregorian Church. They signed such a confession in 1641 and presented it to King Wladislas IV, in which they declared allegiance both to S. Peter and S. Gregory, and accepted the decisions of the first seven councils.[321]

They handed over a confession with a similar text to the new Polish king John Casimir in 1652. However, before accepting it, the king set the condition that it should also be countersigned by Katholicos Philippos.[322] There was no obstacle to this, since it was based on an old Pontificale (*dzeřnadrut'iwn*), and the bishops of Lvov were also consecrated on the basis of this confession in the past, a fact confirmed by Philippos in his pastoral letter addressed to the community of Lvov on February 12, 1653.[323]

These two confessions were of considerable assistance to the seniors, when they requested that the Polish kings, ascending the throne one after the other, should confirm their privileges. The Armenians of Lvov frequently had dissensions with the Roman Catholic patricians of the city, who again and again disputed the primary rights of the Armenians, and declared them aliens, settled after the incorporation of the city into the Polish state (1340), who were not entitled to the rights due to the Roman Catholic inhabitants of the city.

To counter this disadvantageous discrimination, in 1578 the Armenians presented to King Stephen Báthory the privilege document allegedly received from a certain Ruthenian king Daniel Fedorovich in 1062. On the basis of this, Báthory

[318] Cong. Gen. v. 22, f. 5, p. 277; *L'unione*, p. 266.
[319] See above notes 273–278; Tavriżeci, 376–77; Tavr/Bros. 451; Tavr/Xan. 297–98; Pingirian: *ISDUAN* 1971, p. 364; *Svjazi*, p. 61.
[320] *Svjazi*, p. 107.
[321] *L'unione*, p. 134.
[322] *Bŕni miut'iwn*, p. 26.
[323] *Kamenic'*, p. 253.

II

verified their primary rights and from that time on, the text of this document from 1062 was included in the further renewals (renovatio) on several occasions.[324]

Here it is important to underline the significant circumstance that the renewal dates coincide with the dates of the confessions (confessio fidei) given by the seniors. The Polish kings considered these confessions to be so significant in the process leading to the catholicisation of the Armenians that subsequently they confirmed all their former privileges.

When the Armenian delegation sent to Warsaw in 1640 to negotiate with Piromalli could not achieve any result, the Armenians realized that without making concessions they would not attain any result, so they submitted the confession of faith to Wladislas in 1641. As a result, Wladislas renewed their rights in 1641, based on the main evidence of their primary chart, the text of the allegedly original privilege document from 1062.

4,4,4. The literature of Roman Catholic orientation considers the church-union of the Armenians of Lvov and Poland to be a merit of Torosowicz. Gr. Petrowicz does not find the agreement of archbishop Nikol with Katholicos Philippos in 1653 to be objectionable, because in fact the main aspect was that with his personal uniation he brought the Armenian community nearer to the religious union, and thus despite the whole ambiguity of the action, he paved the path along which Galanus could thereafter proceed further.[328]

In our opinion the entire career of Torosowicz indicates that he was not at all a devoted hero of the Roman Catholic faith, but was compelled to catholicize "in his desperate position" because of the anathema of Grigor Kesaratsi.[329] Moreover, the seniors themselves were also definitely guilty of straining the situation because, trusting in their financial omnipotence, in their arrogance, they even encouraged Khachatur Kesaratsi, legate of Echmiadzin, to maintain the anathema.[330] It can be presumed that without being driven into a tight corner Torosowicz would not have adopted the Roman Catholic faith. However, it is difficult to imagine that Torosowicz,

---

[324] That this alleged privilege was a falsification, it has been demonstrated in a thorough study by Y. Daškevič. and newly corroborated the doubt as to the authenticity of the document voiced by several historians since more than a century (1844): Daškevič, J.: Naukovo-informacijnij Bjuletenj Archivn. Upravl. URSR. Kiev 1962. pp. 9–21; idem, Les Arméniens à Kiev (jusqu'à 1240) I, REArm, X, 1973–4, pp. 341—356. There are historians, who regard the fragment of the alleged 1062 document incorporated into the renovation as authentic: V. K. Voskanian, ISDUAN 1961, 64; V. Mikaelian, Ġrimi haykakan gaľuti patmuťiwn, 1964, 53–63, and others.

[325] Kamenic', p. 253.

[326] Bischoff, F., Urkunden zur Geschichte der Armenier in Lemberg, pp. 118–124; CGIA USSR Lvov, f. 52, op. 3, t. 619, pp. 725–34; Svjazi, pp. 99–106.

[327] Kamenic', pp. 255–56.

[328] L'unione, pp. 157–9.

[329] L'unione, p. 45.

[330] Tavrižeci, 372; Tavr/Bros. 449; Tavr/Xan. 294.

310

II

with his greed for power and his expensive way of life, would not have had a sharp clash in the course of this career with the thrifty council of seniors, who also claimed to exert full power over the archbishop.

The relations of Torosowicz with the Papal curia, were always tense. Torosowicz advocated the Ruthenian form *(iuxta formam Ruthenorum)* of uniation, while the Congregatio adhered to the preservation of the union according to the council of Florence.[331]

Several decisions were adopted at the assemblies of the Congregatio for "corrections" to be made in the Armenian liturgy and rites.[332] Eloquent confirmation of the retarding activity of Torosowicz is shown by the fact that in 30 years, until the arrival of Galanus in 1664 insignificant changes ensued in this question.

On the basis of the immense material of the Congregatio so far not explored, Gr. Petrowicz elaborately documented the relationship between Torosowicz and the Congregatio.[333] The Congregatio was fairly well informed about the negative features of Torosowicz. It also repeatedly considered the question of removing the archbishop, but this conception has never been carried out, attributing to his credit that the archbishop himself adopted the Roman Catholic creed and the inclusion of the community into the church-union seemed to be achievable only by his mediation. He enjoyed the full support of the "Latin" clergy of Lvov, especially of the Jesuits, and he was also favoured in the royal court of the king Sigismund III and John Casimir, who received a Jesuit education, and even with King Wladislas IV (originally of liberal attitude), after his shift to the side of the Hapsburgs (1637), and especially through the good offices of Queen Cecily Renata of the Hapsburg family. There was in fact no other possible person in sight, who would have been acceptable to the seniors of Lvov.

The reports of Galanus make it clear that no essential change took place in the religious life of the Armenians in Poland up to 1664. According to Galanus, Torosowicz did not care for one or the other faith, but was solely interested in his own glory and financial interests. Although he himself took the Roman Catholic faith, he tacitly condoned the people to remain loyal to the Katholicos. In this way, he achieved the purpose of resting upon two pillars, of obliging both the Pope and the Armenian Katholicos, viz.: he received archiepiscopal governing authority from the Pope, and with the help of the Katholicos he retained the obedience of the Armenian clergy, while on the other hand, through this he also received (or extorted) emoluments from the Armenians.[334]

Archbishop Nikol "could have corrected the errors *(errores)* found in the Armenian ecclesiastic books, liturgy, mass and in the rites merely with the wink of an eye, but he did not do so because he feared that if a perfect union did come about, he

[331] *L'unione*, p. 66–69.
[332] *Ibid.*
[333] Petrowicz, *L'unione*. Recension by Daškevič see: *REArm*, I, 1964, 462–66.
[334] Cong. Gen. v. 225, f. 167: *L'unione*, p. 172.

II

would find himself confronted by two difficulties: he could be removed by the Pope in order to grant the request of the Uniates and Torosowicz's personal enemies and, moreover, he would lose the income he gained" from the non-uniates.[335]

The fact that Torosowicz did not want to compel the priests to accept the spirit of the Roman Catholic dogmas, is shown by the circumstance that in 1664, out of 20 priests only two were monks, while the remainder were ministers, and as it was the custom in the Armenian Church, they were married, and only two of them were Roman Catholic.[336] It is perhaps most characteristic of the traditionalist standpoint of Torosowicz that his right hand, vicar Brocki, the archpriest (avagerec) of the cathedral, was a firm adversary of the church-union. Torosowicz sent Brocki away from the diocese only after the stringent threats of Galanus.[337]

Torosowicz was compelled to agree to the correction of the "errors" (errores) in the Armenian liturgy in order to avoid further harassment from Galanus. Reluctantly, he issued orders to the Armenian priests for the transformation of the liturgy and rites in the Roman Catholic spirit and for the holding of mass according to the Latin liturgy.[338] However, the lower clergy preached against the innovation of the liturgy for the sake of preserving traditions. Of course, another significant motive was that they feared they would lose the parochial emoluments received from the non-uniate Armenians.[339]

With the forcible implementation of the formal elements of catholicisation, in two years Galanus had carried out every "correction" in the Armenian liturgy and rites. Some of these — also in the judgement of the Roman Catholic historian, and of course from the tactical point of view — were unnecessary, and even harmful, for they estranged even the elements inclined to Roman catholicism, since they forced them to give up the ecclesiastic traditions they had become accustomed to through the generations.[340]

Torosowicz endeavoured to delay the liquidation of the old Armenian traditions under the pretext of catholicisation, also after the death of Galanus (1666). The forced Latinization was received in an especially hostile manner by the Armenians of Zamość, Jazlowiec and Kamenets-Podolsk.

The sharp opposition of the seniors to Latinization was expressed in the way they hindered the activity of the Theatines. They did their utmost to remove them from the premises, which at the time were assigned to them temporarily in the neighbourhood of the S. Cross church (cf. jury pleadings dated January 22 and 29, 1671).[341]

[335] Ibid.
[336] Cong. Gen. v. 225, f. 166v et f. 76, sq.: L'unione, p. 173.
[337] L'unione, 179–80. The characteristics given by M. Pidou: Bīni miut'iwn, p. 18.
[338] L'unione, pp. 177–190.
[339] L'unione, pp. 182, 193.
[340] Cf. L'unione, pp. 206–7.
[341] Gos. Naučn. Bibl. Lvov. f. Ossoliński, Ms Archives, No. 1723, II. 1. 18: Svjazi, pp. 118–9. Cf. Daškevič: Banber Matenadarani, t. 9, 1969, p. 235. — (The buildings burned down the next year.)

II

Despite the "corrections", the Theatines could not make an end to the exertion of the Gregorian faith until the death of Torosowicz (1681). Torosowicz continued his activity in the old way even after his return from Rome. He permitted the sacraments to be administered in the ancient Gregorian way, and did not care about the old "heretic" customs and the errors in the liturgy — nuncio Martelli wrote in his report.[342] Changes occurred only when the old priests had died out and the generation educated in the Theatine school, under "Latin" priests of Italian origin, in the spirit of the Roman Catholic dogmas, took over the ecclesiastic functions.

4,4,5. The process of catholicisation among the Gregorian–Armenians of Poland in fact did not start in the 17th century, but practically at the same time as the conversion of the orthodox Ukrainians.

The Armenian community, i.e the Armenians who had settled down in the 14th and 15th centuries, as a result of given loans and different services rendered to the Polish kings, have received a number of privileges from them. At the same time, the immigrants who continuously arrived in the 16th century, received permission to settle only if they asked for their admission under the authority of the law of Magdeburg, which at the same time also meant their catholicisation. From the Acts of the magistrate dating from the 15th and 16th centuries, it can be seen how the magistrate stood on the defensive against the new immigrants. In this attitude, it received the full support of the Armenian community that had settled down in the foregoing centuries, which was afraid the new wave of immigrants would endanger their financial interests. Therefore, the community itself also urged that new immigrants should be prevented from settling down in the towns, and thus in 1561, King Sigismund Augustus of Poland suspended the new admissions into the framework of the law of Magdeburg.[343]

In the 17th century, with regard to catholicisation, the Armenian community of Lvov was in the most exposed position. Lvov was the seat of the Armenian archbishop. The pressure on the part of the Catholic magistrate was strongest here, in the economic emporium of East–West trade.

The disclosure of the details of the process of catholicisation is the task of future historical research because direct figures concerning the number of the Uniates are rather scant. For example, according to M. Sielski, general of the Jesuits, there were only 2 Catholics in the Armenian council of seniors in 1636. In most cases, it is difficult to define the religious affiliation of the seniors. According to a document from 1633, the number of Catholics among the people or notables (?) was "more than ten", or "several tens", which apparently refers to the number of heads of families.[344] The partisanship to one or the other side was not unequivocal, whatever faith they confessed, first of all they felt themselves Armenians.

[342] Acta, v. 47, f. 225, sqq.: L'unione p. 307.
[343] Bischoff, F., Das alte Recht der Armenier in Lemberg. Vienna 1862, pp. 61-2; (e.g. A.D. 1427; pp. 14-15; 1436: 16-17; 1440: pp. 17-8; 1455: 20; 1512: pp. 42-3.)
[344] Svjazi, p. 46; REArm, IV, 1967, p. 263; REArm, V, 1968, p. 347.

II

In 1647, 52 members of the community lodged a report and asked for the remedy of the evil conditions prevailing in the council of seniors of the dissension and even hostility.[345]

Galanus and his companions were of the opinion even in 1664 that the church-union of the Armenians with Rome was "simulated and superficial" (kelceok ew i verin eress). When Galanus threatened he would lay information with the king against Nikol and this might involve the withdrawal of privileges, in order to counterbalance this step the seniors signed a proforma (arerewuyt) agreement on December 25th, 1664.[346] Although this meant that they jointly adopted the Roman Catholic creed, it cannot be established who and how many were those, who actually confessed it. However, this was indifferent from the viewpoint of the legal status.

Undoubtedly the process of catholicisation started out from the upper layers of society. Therefore, the elucidation of this question is considerably assisted by the protocols (Acta) of the council of seniors of Lvov, especially by the volume comprising the material of the years 1668–1686, written in Polish,[347] whose sociological message was thoroughly analysed by Y. Dashkevich.[348] In addition to the seniors forming the leading layer of the community, from the rate of the contributions paid on festive occasions, the whole layer of the nobility of the city is in fact revealed. This is of major importance from the viewpoint of the question discussed here, because first of all these layers would gain the most from the catholicisation, i.e. they would enjoy the financial advantages originating from the old privileges.[349] Individual catholicisations also occurred before the arrival of Galanus, for example, the senior Bernatowicz was catholicised in 1661.[350] There were also many, who as a result of their antipathy towards Torosowicz, attended divine service in the Roman Catholic churches.

The situation began to change with the activity of the school established by the Theatine monks, especially after the death of Torosowicz (1681), when the alumni of the Theatine school raised in the spirit of the Roman Catholic Church had already grown up. They became the propagators of Polonization and of Latinization, in church service not only in Lvov, but also in the provincial cities, where they were sent as parsons.

[345] The background of this discord does not become clear from the documents. Most probably the main reason for the complaint was the unjustified use of the contributions (jasax) collected from the members of the community. CGIA USSR, Lvov, f. 9, op. 1, t. 397, pp. 521–23: Svjazi, pp. 95–97.

[346] Bîni miut'iwn, pp. 31, 38, 164; Azgapatum, II/2, col. 2537.

[347] Daškevič, J., Administrativni, sudovi i finansovi knigi na Ukraini v XIII—XVIII st.: Istorični džerely ta ich vikoristania, vol. IV, 1969, p. 144.

[348] Daškevič, J., Armjanskoe samoupravlenie vo L'vove v 60–80-ch gg. XVII v.: Banber Matenadarani, vol. 9, 1969, 217. sqq.

[349] Ibid, p. 233; Petrowicz: REArm, IV, 1967, p. 352.

[350] Barącz, S., Żyvoty slavnych ormjan w Polsce. Lvov 1864, p. 75.

II

One frequently mentioned reason for the disintegration of the Armenian colony is that the Armenians of Armenian–Gregorian faith left their homeland because of the religious despotism under the archiepiscopal rule of Torosowicz.[351] By the thorough analysis of the demographic data also Y. Dashkevich came to the conclusion that the decline of the Armenian population in the Lvov area was the consequence of the religious iniquities.[352] The elucidation of the background of the fluctuation in the number of the Armenian families requires still further research.

In the country-wide context, a major change appeared in the number of the Armenians after 1672, when the Turks occupied Podolia, devastated Kamenec Podolsk and the neighbouring towns of Jazłowiec, Snyatyn, Żwaniec and Horodenka. The Armenian inhabitants fled from here to Tyśmenica, Bereżany and other small towns.[353]

Although in 1664–1665, Kamenets Podolsk, and Zamość, etc. were still the citadels of the Gregorian faith, after the scattering of the inhabitants to the different towns under the influence of the parsons, coming from the theological college of Lvov, the catholicisation was gradually accomplished. However, it should be noted that while in 1664 the total number of Armenians on Polish-Ukranian territory was 3,000,[354] in 1678, according to the report of nuncio Martelli, it was only 600.[355] The quoted figures are not exact statistical records, but rather biased estimates, so one cannot draw decisive conclusions from them as to the demographic movements of the Armenians of Poland.

5,1. In the Middle Ages, the church was the cementing force of the peoples living under foreign rule and in foreign religious surroundings. The ancient religion and the language of the preaching was the main support in the preservation of their national individuality. The comparison of the fate of the Armenian mother-country and the Armenian colony living in the Polish–Ukrainian border region in the 17th century reflects the different development of the two segments of the people living in entirely different political and religious surroudings.

5,2. The colony formed in the Polish–Ukrainian border region by the Armenian population who fled in masses to the west after the Mongol invasion (1236), had a different fate among the Christian states. The Armenian settlement of Monophysite faith came within the range of the forcible counter-reformational conversion campaign of the Congregatio headed by the Jesuits. The counter-reformation in Poland developed its full strength in the middle of the 16th century. The forced conversion

[351] Tavriżeci 384; Tavr/Bros. 455; Tavr/Xan. 303.

[352] CGIA Lvov f. 9, op. 1, t. 384, p. 1790: Dachkevitch, Y., Sur la question des relations arméno–ukrainiennes au XVIIᵉ siècle, REArm, IV, 1967, p. 263; idem, L'établissement des arméniens en Ukraine pendant les XIᵉ—XVIIIᵉ siècles: REArm, V, 1968, p. 347.

[353] Daškevič; REArm, V, 1968, 346–7, 338, 339, 341 sqq; V. R. Grigorjan, Istorija armjanskich kolonij Ukrainy i Pol'ši (Armjane v Podolii). Erevan 1980, pp. 46–47.

[354] L'unione, p. 169; Bṙni miut'iwn (Compendiosa Relatio) p. 153.

[355] Cong. Gen. v. 471, f. 314: L'unione, p. 306; Daškevič: REArm, V, p. 363.

II

carried out with the efficient co-operation of the Jesuits very soon had its result. The church union of Brest in 1596 placed the believers of the East European Slav Orthodox Church under the rule of Poland, under the aegis of the Pope.[356]

In the preservation of the national identity of the Armenian community, the Church played an especially important role in Poland, because prior to their arrival to the new adoptive country the Armenian community had lost the other most important feature of their national character, their Armenian vernacular, already in the Crimea, and adopted a Crimean Kipchak dialect.[357]

In the Jeláli period, at the time of the "great *sürgün*" and in the decade of the great famine, the Armenians who fled to the Polish–Ukrainian territory could have played an especially important role in the re-Armenization (as the re-Armenization process has been triggered by the new-comers in the 1600-s in Crimea). But in Lvov the late newcomers, could only settle in the suburbs and in the small towns of the border region. Thus they did not have a re-Armenizating influence on the old inhabitants, but together with them they also became Polonized soon. The same fate befell the Armenians in the neighbouring small towns with the difference that the linguistic influence of the Polish population affected them directly and their Polonization took place only a few decades later.[358]

The decline of the Armenian settlement in Poland has to be examined in its full complexity.[359] Some people regard the ecclesiastic despotism of Torosowicz as the main reason for the decrease of the Armenian colony in the 17th century. This, however, would mean the exaggeration of the role of the archbishop. According to a number of sources and opinions, the forced catholicisation was predominant. However, it must be considered that the economically consolidated families, who became incorporated into Polish economic life, did not leave the country. As a result of the change in the international trading routes, the Armenian colony of Lvov lost its old dominant role in the transit trade by the middle of the 17th century, but that time the economic potentates had already amalgamated with Polish trading circles, and many of them were raised to the rank of Polish noblemen. On the other hand, the next commercial middle layer, became an important link in trade with Istanbul, Moldavia, and Transylvania, and to a smaller degree with the Crimea,[360] while many of them

---

[356] *The Cambridge History of Poland,* from the origins to Sobieski (to 1696). Cambridge 1950, pp. 399, sqq: 413–14.

[357] Schütz, E., *Armeno–kiptschakisch und die Krim: Hungaro–Turcica: Studies in Honour of J. Németh.* Budapest 1976, pp. 185–205.

[358] Schütz, E., *Re-armenisation and Lexicon; From Armeno–Kipchak back to Armenian: Acta Orient. Hung.,* XIX, 1966, pp. 99–105.

[359] Cf. Daškevič: *REArm.* V, 1968, pp. 364, 366.

[360] Nistor J., *Die auswärtigen Handelsbeziehungen der Moldau im XIV., XV. und XVI. Jh.* Gotha. 1911, pp. 18–88; idem, *Handel und Wandel in der Moldau bis zum Ende des 16. Jahrhunderts.* Czernowitz 1912, pp. 13, sqq., 56, 67 and passim.; Pach Zs. P., *A Levante-kereskedelem erdélyi útvonala, Századok,* 1975, No. 1. pp. 21–31. idem, *The Shifting of International Trade Routes in the 15th–17th Centuries: Acta Historica Ac. Sc. Hung.,* vol. XIV, 1968.

II

found their place in the local retail trade. This indicates that the main factor in the dissolution of the Armenian colony in Poland was the complete change in economic conditions.

And this applies first of all to Lvov. The dissolution of the other largest centre, Kamenets Podolsk, was brought about by the Turkish invasion of 1672. From Kamenets Podolsk, most of the inhabitants and primarily the Armenians, fled to the towns situated farther to the north. This was the time when new Diasporas were formed and the Armenian inhabitants in other towns increased, viz. in Bereżany, Brody, Horodenka, Tyśmienica and Zamość, etc. These small settlements, however, did not play any role in the economic life of the colony, and within one or two generations they were absorbed into the Polish–Ukrainian population.[361]

The example of one of the most considerable Armenian settlements of the late middle ages shows that the loss of their ancient religion was an important factor in losing their national identity. But in this case two other major motives largely contributed to the acceleration of the process. First of all, the loss of their mother tongue, already in their previous station of exile, in the Crimea. The rest of this colony, because of the fundamental change in world trade routes, having lost its former importance, became morselled to pieces, the transit traders continued their route of peregrination to further countries to the South and the West. The already Polonized families amalgamated with the surrounding Polish population. Their memory has been preserved only by their family names.

[1978, 1980]

III THE DOCUMENT
The Instructions

The text of the Instructions given to the Delegation sent by the Council of Armenian Seniors in 1640 from Lvov to Warsaw has been preserved in Ms No. 1788 of the Mekhitarist Archives of Venice, S. Lazzaro Island. The Manuscript, during my stay in Venice, has been placed at my disposal by the Mekhitarist Fathers, for which courtesy I express my deep gratitude.

---

[361] *REArm. V.*, pp. 337–359; V. R. Grigorian, *Istorija armjanskich kolonij Ukrainy i Pol'ši (Armjane v Podolii)*. Erevan 1980. pp. 41, sqq.

II

Text

[135/v25] *Anno: 1640 Anun a[stuco]j Die 19: Decembris:* /

Instruk'c'ia Varšovga K'ètk'anlarga Pat'(e)r /
Pavlus bila:

Bij T'engrining al̦yšin da Blogoslavènstvosun Berijirbiz / *Alarnyng B̄k̄'laryna B̄r̄
Aɣalarymyzga Spravaga k'ètk'anlarga* / *Varšov* [136/r] *ga hali xutlu jolga K'èlganyna
pat'er pavlusnung: B̄r̄ erecp'o/xan p̄n̄ Awedik'k'a. B̄r̄ Bernat'ovic' p̄n̄ ivašk'oga B̄r̄ pan
Sahak'k'a Agop/ša Oɣluna B̄r̄ p̄n̄ Misk'oga B̄r̄ Aw·[e]dik' erec'p'oxan Oɣluna. Da
pospo/lityjdan p̄n̄ Gresk'oga B̄r̄ Holub Oɣluna:*

•

(5) *Bij T'engri B̄k̄'[y]n[y]znyng jolunuznu Ač'yx etk'aj Da Bahaban xač'i bi/la
saxlagaj Barča jamandan. esk'i Dušmannyng felindan Da ja/man k'išilarnyng
Aldamaxyndan. Bahaban frištasy bila saxlagaj ra/fajjel Da mik'ajel uzatk'aj Da Barč'a
sovunč'luk'lar bila jan* / *u t'en Bizga k'èltirgaj Amen èyici:*

(10) *Biz Duxovnyjlar Da Andyč'k'an xardašlar Da barč'a pospoli/tyj Ašaɣa
podpysanyj. xajsilary natenč'as ilov šaharynda tapul/dux: Berijirbiz naprud. B[ij]
T'[engri] Al̦yšin Da bu instruk'c'ijany* / *Bizim Andyč'k'an xardašlarymyzga joɣari
mjanovanyj Varšovga iš k'orma* / *pat'er pavlus bila. xajsi hali taža k'èldi roma šaharindan*
(15) *sek'izin/či urban paptan:*

*Bij T'engri B̄k̄'[y]n[y]zny jaxši sahl[y]xta k'èltir. Da varšovda k'orušup pa/ter
pavlus bila sezip ne k'èltirdi romadan Da bizim išimyz ne t'er/minlar usna turdu. Bizga
ilovga Dostateč'nyj xabar jazgajsiz/da tez:* /

Egar jazovumuz Bizim k'èndi jerinda turdu esa neturlu (20) *pod/pislarymyz Da
mohurumuz bila podanyj Boldu k'èndina Da Anyng* / *xol bitik'i bila bizga bergan
k'onfrontovac'c'a bolyjer xabulumuz:* /

Egarki nema sprec'ivnyj punk'tlar k'èltirip esa ja unijagaj k'lagaj / *bizni k'èltirma.
xolarbiz. T'[engri] joluna Bir nemagaj xajil bolmagajsiz . .* / *Dane bizda xajil Digulbiz:* /

(25) *Egar k'lasa Disput'ovat etma. Ol erorlar uč'un xajsilaryn ilovda* / *etk'an galaji
etijjedi. neturlu igi sviadomyjsiz. Na Ol barsar bar/ča Gt'ȳḡosk'a Any ozga turlu etmanyz
tek' barsyn Gt'ȳḡšk'a:* /

Anicac' Axpašni egar klasalar xaryštyrma. ja zhodalar birga/- [136/v] *syna.
neč'ik' Aval boluredi etma. Na Anar birturlu xajil Di/gulbiz Dani k'larbiz k'i k'èndin bu
išlarga xaryštyrgajsiz:* /

K'i barča ixovlarny bizga Obètnic'asyna kora usnyj bunda / *bolgan. Bizga barč'any
ODdat ettirgaj Aktalary bila birga:* / (5) *Da Barč'a Dobrolary bila Alarga naležonc'yj:* /

*Xajrat etk'ajsiz k'onječ'nje Axpašni Bundan Algajlar. A/-laj k'èndin neč'ik
Ašagèrdlaryn Birga. romaga ja k'laštorga ja* / *Ozga jary k'ètargajlar k'i Aty birga
xalmagaj:* /

318

II

Egar Axpaš bila k'ontroversialar k'lagaj bolma ja Dek'ret/-(10)lar. T'engri joluna xolarbiz k'i Ostrožnje birgasyna postupo/vat etk'ajsiz Da saxyngajsiz ki bir nema ič'ina Aldanma/gajsiz. xajsik'i Bizim Dinimyzga Da Gt'ỹğšumuzga - xata / k'ėltirgaj Bunu barč'any igi k'ozlanyz: /

Egar Gt'ỹğōska k'ėtmaxuč'un Anda k'lasalar galaji etma na / (15) rozumit etijirbiz k'i bunda ilovga almijin Anda konec'in etk'ajsiz: /

Korolnu A[nyng] B[ijliki] Vitat etk'ajsiz Da xolgajsiz k'i bu Sprava/da šaγavat'ly bolgaj Da spravamyzny tez ODpravit et'kaj: /

Egar xolaj tušsa. Da Ol spravalarny zač'entyj rajc'alarbila / zat'on Ok'azyjon Hem bir k'ošt Artyndan bolsanyz ODpravit etma Da/ (20) xolaj bolsa. T[engri] Atyna ODpravit etk'ajsiz. Alajk'i igi bolgaj / Da Dušmanlarymyz Sovunmagaj: /

Pan Svižinsk'ijga t'olagajsiz šahat nema bošatk'aj. zera ek'i / jyl nema xulux etmady Da xajrat etk'ajsiz jarym jurgėlt bila / tutma. Da jangi interc'iza birgasyna etma egark'i boluresa bolma:

(25) Pan kaprusnu Vyk'upit' etip Ovga k'ėltirgajsiz zera provent/larymyz t'engri bergaj k'i Dvorda Ajentlar saxlagajbiz: / Berijir biz skladk'a šösyndan xajsin zobratettix šm̄ā f. / [137/r] Dayyn Berijirbiz ixov šösyn Bu spravaga Algan Zadik' TorosOγlu / rabič'k'adan. Da Anyng Ovundan šm̄ā f. t'oxuzjuz: Bu eki šm̄ā / bila iš k'orgajsiz. Neturlu sizni t'engri O/vratyptyr jak'o naj skromnyj: /

A xajdak'i. T'[engri] Sovundursa Bizni Šp jyxovlar bila. Da potreba / (5) šö k'orguzsa. Na ek'i Min flŕwgadeg Obėtnic'a etk'ajsiz Artyxk'a / xajil Digul biz: /

Barč'a spravalarymyzda Bizim pospolityjimyzdan bašxa. Bijlk[y]n[y]z bila / jebergan bir nema etmagajsiz Alaj radada neč'ik' barč'a sprava/larda Alarnyng bilmaxy bila bolgaj: /

(10) Dotego Beryjyr biz Ariberi. Bal(y)x Vanėnka limon suvu Butarda / č'amič': /

Xalgan išlarda. B[ij] T'[engri]ga Da Blk'[y]n[y]znyng najvyššij Axylynyzga Beri/jirbiz. ki znesitsa bolup pospoluyj xardašimyz bila Ortamyzdan Bij/likin[y]zbila Vyslanyz. neturlu Dayyn xolaj Da oxšašli bolgajsiz Blk[yn]yz / (15) joγari jazylgan išlarny k'ormaga nega barč'aga unama Da xab/ul etma k'larbiz: /

Berijir biz Buturlu joγari mjanovanyj. ek'i šm̄ā šöny šafova/njega. Bŕ p̄ñ ivašk'o Bernat'ovick'a Da p̄ñ gresk'oga Holub Oγluna. / k'i Alar bu turlu šölar bila Disponovat etk'ajlar Da jaxši sah/ (20) l[y]xta k'ėlip Hesepin bergajlar: /

<table>
<tr><td>Bu Aktta bolganlar</td><td>Ašaγa jazylgan budur</td></tr>
</table>

Ulu mohurnun jeri:

<table>
<tr><td>+ Jovanes erec':</td><td>+ Bij Kšnung Arzanisiz xulu simon erec'</td></tr>
<tr><td>+ Daniel Holub Oγlu: —</td><td>+ Men pet're Kirkoša Oγlu Vank / erec'p'oxany:</td></tr>
<tr><td>(25) + Gresk'o Dŕ luk'aš Oγlu:</td><td>+ Men ivašk'o Jakub Oγlu Ste/p'anovic' andyč'k'an aγa:</td></tr>
</table>

319

II

+ Men Xač'k'o Pet're Oɣlu andyč'k'an aɣa:
+ Jakub Zadik Oɣlu: —
(30)
+ Zadik' Avedik' Oɣlu: —

[137/v]
+ Andrij lazar Oɣlu stcp'ano/vic' vlasnyj xolum bila:
+ Men Toros Holub Oɣlu jašk'ovic':
+ Men xač'k'o Domažirsk'ij
(5) vlš xol[u]m [bila]:
+ Men lazar Mat'iašovic' nenk'i me/nim pajima tušar žoɣovurtbla t'l:
+ Men gresk'o Bƒ misk'o Oɣlu Dƒ/Vask'ovic': —

+ 2 Min ƒga. Obětnica etma xač'an/ ixovlar berilsa. Ol zaman sk'ladk'a/ baryˇ pospolityj bila berilgaj Ja/kub šimk'o Oɣlu vlasnyj̱ xolumbla:
+ Gabriel bartasovic vlasnon renkon:
+ Men murad emin Oɣlu bilinijirmen andrij
+ Jask'o Tuman Oɣlu juxnovic':

+ Men Avedik' polibovsk'ij: —
+ Men Ovanes Boydan —/ Oɣlu vlasnyj̱ xolumbila —
+
— —
+

(10) xajsi instruk'cijany K'jetxojal[y]x Aktalarga Duxovnyj̱ Toranyng/inserovat etma Simařladylar: —

Translation

[135/v25] Anno D(omini) 1640 December 19
Instruction to those going to Warsaw (to have
discussion with, or to meet) Pater Paulus (cf. notes 254–262).

We give the blessing and benediction of the Lord to the honourables, the Seniors, to those going on business to Warsaw [136/r] and to the coming of Pater Paulus now on a beneficial journey. To Pan Avedik erecpoxan, to Pan Ivaško Bernatovic, to Pan Sahak son of Agopša, to Pan Misko son of erecpoxan Avedik, and on part of the community to Pan Gresko son of Pan Holub.

*

(5) May the Lord make the journey of your lordships open (give you a cloudless time (?)) and may the guardian angel with his cross protect you from all evils, from the intrigue of the primordial enemy and from the fraudulence of the wicked people. May the guardian angels Raphael and Michael protect and accompany them (on their journey) and (full) of all happiness in body and soul bring them back to us. Amen, so be it!

(10) We ecclesiastic people and juror brothers and the members of the community (all) who have signed below, who at present stayed in Lvov, give first of all the blessing of the Lord, as well as this instruction to our above mentioned juror

320

II

brothers, who go to Warsaw to arrange the case with Pater Paulus, who has just arrived from the city of Rome. (15) from Pope Urban VIII.

May the Lord bring back your lordships in good health, and meeting (negotiating) with Pater Paulus you may get to know, what he has brought from Rome and in what conditions our case stands. And to us in Lvov you may write sufficient news and urgently.

If our document remained in its own (original) condition, as (20) we handed it over (presented) to him [furnished] with our signatures and seal, and it tallies with his manuscript given to us (with authentication), we accept it.

If he brought points [paragraphs] contradictory to this or he wanted to persuade us to [church] union, we ask, for God's sake, you should not agree to anything, just as we do not agree to it either.

(25) If he would like to discuss those "errors" (error), about which he spoke during his stay in Lvov, about which you have good knowledge, if he wanted to go to the Katholicos of all [Armenians], you should not do anything, let him go to the Katholicos.

If they wanted to involve the cursed bishop or the agreement with him into it (136/v) as they had done before, we shall by no means agree to it, and we do not want him to be included into these affairs.

That — in accordance with his promise given to us about this — he should have all the churches given back to us, together with the Files, (5) and together with all movables belonging to them.

Make all efforts [to ensure] that the bishop be definitively (by all means) removed, both he and his pupils together with him, they should take them to Rome, or to a monastery or elsewhere, that even his name (memory) should not subsist.

If in connection with the bishop controversies would arise or decrees [be brought], (10) for God's sake we ask you to proceed cautiously, and take heed, lest you be deceived in anything that could do harm to our religion and to our Katholicos, you should take good care of this.

If they would like to carry on discussions in the issue of going to the Katholicos, (15) we take cognizace of that, not to bring [him] to Lvov, you may finish it (arrange it) there.

You greet His Majesty the King and request him to be gracious also in this case and to settle our case quickly.

If it would go easily that you could settle this case with the stubborn councillors on this occasion and at the same cost and this (20) would go easily, then — in the name of God — you may do it, so that it should be good and our enemies should not rejoice.

To Pan Swiżinski you should pay, perhaps he would give some reduction, because for [the past] two years he has not rendered any service, and try to keep him with half remuneration, and to conclude with him a new agreement, if it is possible.

(25) You should ransom Pan Kaprus and bring him home, because God may grant financial means that we could keep commissioners in the court. We have given

II

from the reserve money, what we have collected, altogether X (?) florins, (137/r) besides this we give from the money of the church, what we have raised for this purpose from Zadik Rabička, son of Toros, and from his household a sum of 900 florins. With these two amounts you should settle the matter, as God has taught you, as most moderately.

Oh, if God would cheer us with the sacred churches, and if necessity (5) should arise for money, then you may assume liability up to 2,000 florins, we are not willing to give more.

In all our affairs without the community, besides the (comission) sent with your lordships, you should not do anything, both in the council, and in all cases everything should be with their knowledge.

(10) To this, there and back (for the journey) we give fish, a small can of lemon juice, butter and raisins.

The other affairs we entrust to God, to the excellent minds of your lordships that agreeing with our brothers from the community, who from among us has been sent out with your lordships, as your lordships find easy and proper (15) to arrange the affairs described above, we agree to everything and desire to accept.

We give thus the above mentioned two sums of money as per account rendered to Pan Ivaško Bernatovic, and to Pan Gresko the son of Holub in order that they may dispose of this money this way and returning in good (20) health they may render account.

Persons present in this act   undersigned

Place of the great seal

+ priest Yovanes (erec)

+ Daniel, Holub's son

(25) + Gresko, son of Der Lukas

+ I, Xačko, Petre's son sworn agha
+ Yakub, Zadik's son —

(30)
+ Zadik, Avedik's son. —

+ Ohan, Xačko's son. —
(137/v) + Andrij Stepanovic, Lazar's son with my own hand
+ Toros Yaškovic, Holub's son

+ the unworthy servant of our Lord Christ, priest Simon (erec)
+ I, Petre, Kirkoša's son, secular supervisor of the monastery *(erecpoxan)*
+ I, Yakub's son, Ivaško Stepanovic sworn agha
+ two thousand florin's bond (for the case, if the churches were delivered, then the reserves of the whole community may be given) Yakub Šimko's son, with my own hand
+ Gabriel Bartošovic, with my own hand
+ I, Murad, Emin's son acknowledge?
+ Yasko Yuxnovic, Tuman's son. —

+ I, Avedik Polibovski. —

322

II

(5) + I Xačko Domažirski
with my own hand
+ I Lazar Matiašovic, what share fal's
on my part with the community (I pay)
+ I, Gresko, Der Vaskovic Baron
Misko's son.

+ I, Ovanes, Bogdan's son with my
own hand

+

— — —

+

(10) The deputies *(kětxojalyx)* order that these instructions should be included in the Files of the ecclesiastic court of justice.

Vocabulary

ačyx 136r5 open, clear, cloudless (weather); successful
aya senior
ajent (P.) 136v26 agent, commissioner
aktalar 136v4 Acts, Files (of the Jury)
aldamax 136r7 fraudulence, falsity
aldan- 136v11 to be deceived
andyčkan 136r10, 13 juror; — *aya* 137r/26, 27 juror senior
anicac (Arm.) 136r28 cursed, damned
uriberi 137r10 here and there, to and fro
arzanysyz 137r22 unworthy
artyx 137r5 more
ašaya 136r11 below; — *jazylyan* 137r21 uncersigned
ašagerd (Arm.) 136v7 pupil, disciple
bahaban (Arm.) 136r5 guardian; — *frištasi* 136r7 his guardian angel
barča gatuyigos (Arm. amenayn hayoc'katuñikos) 136r27 patriarch (katholicos) of all (Armenians)
baron (Arm.) *bř* (Abbrev.) Mr.
bašxa (cum -*dan*) 137r7 without, besides
bij tengri God Lord
bijlik Abbrev.: *bīk* lord; honourables; *bijlīkiniz* your lordship; (Korol) *A(nyng) B(ijliki)* 136v16 His Majesty (the King)
bilmax 137r9 knowledge
bitik 136r21 (written) document
bir; — *nema* (negat.) 136v11 nothing; —*turłu* (negat.) noways
blogoslavenstvo (P. blogosławienstwo) blessing; *alyyš da* — 135r4 blessing
bošat- 136v22 to release, to give reduction
butar (P.) 137r10 butter
čamič (Arm.) 137r11 raisin
dekret (P.) 136v9 decree
digul 136r24, 136v1, 137r6 not
disponovat (P.) *et-* 137r19 to dispose
disputovat (P.) *et-* 136r25 to dispute, discuss
dobro(lar) (P.) 136v5 goods
dostatečny (P.) 136r18 sufficient
duxovnyj (P.) 136r10 ecclesiastic, clerical, churchman; — *tora* 137r10 church court
dušman 136v21 enemy
ėgici (Arm.) 136r9 so be it!

II

erecpoxan (Arm. folksetym. instead of: *eresp'oxan*) 136r1, 3 provisor, supervisor, councillor (secular) of the community

eror (Lat.) 136r25 (religious) error

eski old; — *dušman* 136r6 archenemy, primordial enemy

fel (P.) 136r6 intrigue

florin (P.) Abbrev: *fl* 137r2,5 etc. florin

galaji 136r26, 136v14 talk

gatuyigos (Arm.) Abbrev.: *ğlŷ ǧš* Armenian patriarch

xajil bol- (cum Dat.) 136r23, 24, 137r6 to consent, agree

xajrat et- 136v6, 23 to make efforts, try

xaryštyr- 136r28, 136v2 to mix, involve, include

xata 136v12 damage, harm

xol hand, — *bitiki* 136r21 hand-writing

xul 137r22 serviceman of the guards, Janissary

xulux 136v23 service

xutlu 136r1 lucky, auspicious, beneficial

ixov 136v3, 137r1, 28 church; cf. *jyxov*

inserovat (P.) *et-* 137v11 to insert

instrukcia (P.) 135v2, 136r12 instruction

interciza (P.) 136v24 contract; — *et-* to conclude an agreement

iš 136r17, 136v2 case, affair; — *kor-* 136r1, 137r3, 15 to settle a matter, arrange a case

jaxši good; — *sahlyxta* 137r19 in good health

jaman 136r6 bad; misfortune, evil

jazov 136r19 document

jyxov 137r1, 28 church; cf. *ixov*

joyary above; — *jazylgan* 137r15 above written; — *mjanovanyj* 137r17 above mentioned

jol road, journey; *tengri joluna* 136r23, 136v10 for God's sake ˉ

jurgêlt (P.) 136v23 remuneration, a year's wage (<Jahrgeld, see A. Brückner, *Slownik etym. języka polskiego*, Warszawa 1957, p. 209.)

kêltir- 136r9, 16, 22, 136v26 to bring; 136r23 to induce, persuade

kêt- to go; *kêtkan* 135v2, 5 going; *kêtmax* 136v14 the going

kêtar- 136v8 to take away

kêtxoja (<Pers. kethuda) deputy; — *kêtxojalyx* 137v10 deputies, Armenian court officials

kla- 136r22, 25, 137v2, 9 to wish

konfrontovaccja (P.) *bol-* 136r21 to be confronted, to tally

konječnje (P.) 136v9 by all means, definitively

      kontroversija (P.) 136v9 controversy, divergency

kor- to see; *iš* — 136r13, 137r3 to settle a matter

korguz- 136r5 to show

korol (P.) king; here 136v16: Władysław IV, Polish king, 1632–48.

koruš- 136r16 to meet, negotiate, have an interview

košt (P.) 136v19 costs

kozla- 136v13 to watch, keep an eye on, take care of

men 137r23 I

min 137r5, 27 thousand

mjanovanyj (P.) called; *joyari* — above called

mohur 136r20 seal

na 136v1, 14, 137r5 then

na ten čas (P. na tą czas) 136r11 at present

najskromnyj (P.) 137r3 most modest, moderate

324

II

najvyšŝij (P. najwysszy) 137r12 highest, excellent
naleźončyj (P. należący) 136v5 pertaining, belonging(s)
naprud (P. naprzód) 136r12 first of all
ne 137r17 what; *neturlu* 136r19, 137r3, 14 what kind
nečik 136v1 as
nema 136r22 something; (+ neg.) 136v22, 23 nothing
nenki 137v6 how much
obětnica (P.) promise; — *et-* 137r5 to assume liability
oddat ettir- 136v4 to let hand over
odpravit (P. odprawić) et- 136v17, 19, 20 to settle a case
oxŝašli 137r14 convenient, suitable
orta middle; *ortamyzdan* 137r13 of us
ostrožnje (P. ostrożnie) 136v10 cautiously
ov house; *ovga keltir-* 136v25 to bring home
ovrat- 137r3 to teach
ozga different; — *jary* 136v8 elsewhere; — *turlu* 136r27 other
paj 137r7, 13 share
pap (P.) 136r15 pope see *sekizinči*
pater pavlus 136r1, 14, 16 P. Paulus Piromall see n. 254–262
podanyj (P.) 136r20 handed over
podpysānyj (P.); *ašaya —* 136r11 undersigned
pospolityj (P.) 136r3, 137r7, 13 community
postupovāt (P. postupować) *et-* 136v10 to do a business, to proceed
potreba (P. potrzeba) 137r4 need, necessity
provent (P. prowiant) 136v25 provender(s), (financial) means
rada (P.) 137r8 council
rajca (P.) 136v18 alderman, member of council
rozumit (P.) et- 136v15 to understand, take cognizance of
saxyn- 136v11 to take heed of
saxla- 136r6 to protect; 136v26 to keep
sahlx; jaxši — 136r16 good health
šб — serebro 136v27, 137r1, 17, 19 money, (silver) coin
sekizinči eight; — *Urban* 136r14 Pope Urban VIII (1623–44)
sez- 137r17 to get to know
sklad (P.) 137r28 stock
skladka (P.) 136v27 reserve (money)
sm̄ā — suma (P.) 137r2, 17 sum, amount
sovun- 136v21 to rejoice; *sovundur-* 137r4 to make rejoice, cheer up
sovunčlux 136r8 joy, happiness
šp̄ — surp (Arm.) 137r4 sacred
sprava (P.) 135v5, 136v16, 17, 18, 137r7, 8 case
sprecivnyj (P. sprzeciwny) 136r22 contradictory
suv water; *limon suvu* 137r10 lemon juice, lemonade
svjadomyj (P.) 136r26 informed, having knowledge about sth
šafovanje (P. szafowanie) 137r17 account (giving)
šayavatly 136v16 gracious
šahat 136v22 perhaps
tapul- 136r11 to be found
taźa kėl- 136r14 to come instantaneously, just arrive
ten body; *jan u —* 136r8 in body and soul

325

II

tek 136r27 only

termin (P.) 136r17 term, condition

tez 136r18, 136v17 quickly, urgently

toxuzjuz 137r2 ninehundred

tola- 136v22 to pay

tora 137v10 court

una- 137r15 to consent, agree

uzat- 136r8 to accompany

vanènka (P.) 137r10 *wanna, wanienka* Germ. Wanne, see Brückner, *Slownik etym.* p. 600–1.) pot, small can

vlasnyj (P.) own; — *xolumbla* 137r30, 137v 2, 4, 5 manu proprio

vlasnoñ renkon (P. wlasną ręką) 137r31 m.p.

vykupit (P.) *et-* 136v25 to ransom

za ten okazyjon (P. za tą okazją) 136v19 on this occasion

zaćentyj (P. zacięty) 136v18 obstinate, stubborn

zhoda (Ukr. zgoda) 136r28 agreement, accord

zobrat (P.) *et-* 136v27 to collect

žoγovurt (Arm.) 137v7 people, community = *pospolityj*

326

II

1. F. 135v

2. F. 136r, 1—15

327

II

3. F. 136r, 16—28

1640

4. F. 136v, 1—15

5. F. 136v, 16—27

6. F. 137v, 1—16

II

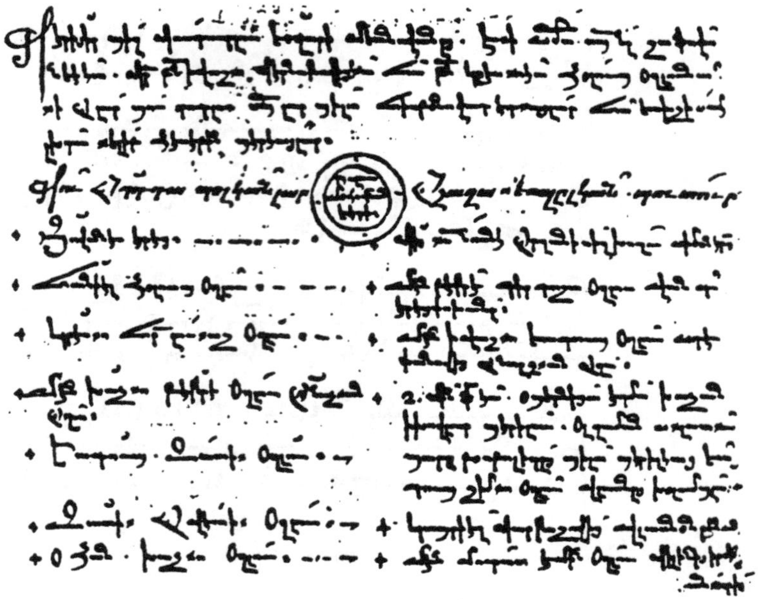

7. F. 137v, 17—32

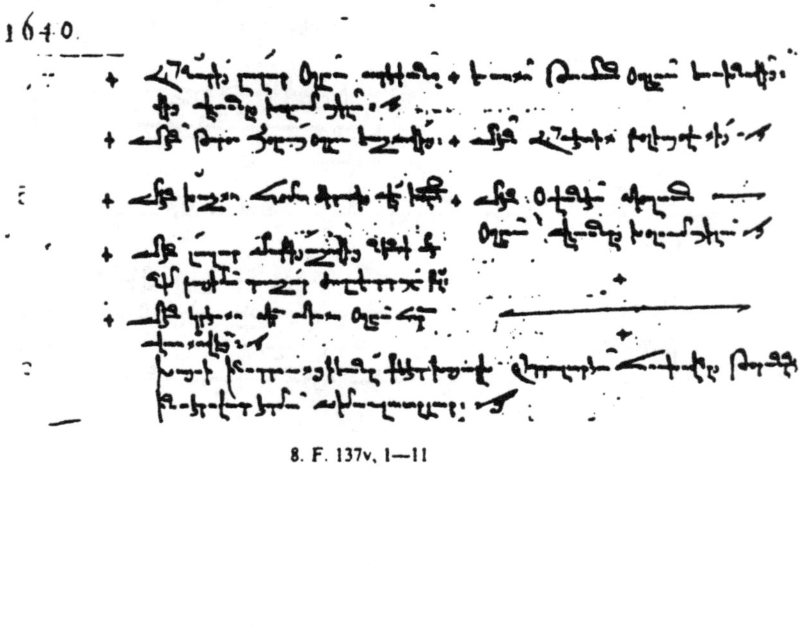

8. F. 137v, 1—11

AN ARMENO-KIPCHAK PRINT FROM LVOV

BY

E. SCHÜTZ

The knowledge we have in Armenistic literature about the short lived venture of a printing house which began to operate in 1616 in Lvov, is based on the data of M. Bzhshkiants' work[1] and the colophon of the Armenian Psalter of 1616.[2]

Priest Hovhannes Karmatanents (Karmadanients), son of Murad K. of Baγes (Bitlis) and Anna, set up on the side of the Armenian monastery of Lvov "with great exertion and at large expense, in the course of one year", a printing press and "first, in the way of an experiment", printed the psalms of David (*Սաղմոս ի Դաւիթ*) the 15th of December, 1616.[3]

According to M. Bzhshkiants, Karmatanents, in addition to the Armenian Psalter, also published medical and *aytark* (Zauberbuch) works. According to St. Aconts Kiwer (Kövér), on the other hand, "beside the psalter an *aytark* book was found in that area, including *bžškaran* (medical recipes), set up in even cruder type and coarsly printed; we believe that this also issued from the same press".[4] Unfortunately neither author tell us where he received his information from. It would appear from the words of M. Bzhshkiants that

---

[1] *Čanaparhordutiwn i Lehastan* [Travel into Poland]. Venice, 1830, pp. 99—100. — The data of M. Bzhshkiants are not known to G. Zarbhanalian in: *Patmutiwn hayerèn dprutean* [The History of Armenian Literature] II. Venice 1905², pp. 234—235 and idem: *Patmutiwn haykakan tpagrutean* [The History of Armenian Printing]. Venice 1895, pp. 64—67. therefore he takes the Psalter for the single product of the Lvov press.

[2] See G. Zarbhalanian: *Haykakan matenagitutiwn* [Bibliographie Arménienne]. Venice 1883. p. 598; idem: *Tpagrutiwn*, loc. cit.; Gh. Alishan: *Kamenic*, pp. 171—172.; N. Akinian: *Simèon dpir*, p. 345.

[3] The booklet, which has 478 unnumbered pages (towards the end a few pages are missing) and is decorated with pictures and marginal figures, also contains, after the psalms, several prayers. — This copy was found by the vardapet H. Hovhannes Zohrapian — as an inscription in his own hand tells us — in the course of his journey in Poland in Sniatyn (Zarbhanalian: *Tpagrutiwn*, p. 64). — According to St. Aconts Kiwer, the place was Stanislawów (*Ašxarhagrutiwn č'oric' masanc' ašxarhi* [Geography of the Four Parts of the World], Part II, vol. 2. Venice 1802. p. 136).

[4] ,,. . .girk' mi aytarac' handerj bžškaranaw", loc. cit.

III

he did not see the book(s?) in question. A. Kiwer's specific statement about the quality of the printing, however, would imply that it came from an eyewitness. Thus, it is safer to assume as more probable that we have to hold only one *aytark*-book in evidence.

Of these only the Psalter has so far been found and even this is extant in a unique copy in the Mekhitarist library in Venice.

Beyond these facts literature knows little about the life and work of H. Karmatanents. It is for his use that Siméon dpir (scribe) in Lvov, in 1618—19, copied the translation of a collection of sermons by Gregorius Theologus (Gregory of Nazianzus: *Aŕ ors* = Πρὸς τούς) and its expositions *(lucmunk).*[5]

According to J. Dashian (Tashian), a missal copied by Marutha dpir in 1645 was also made for him.[6] But the Ter (Der) Hovhannes mentioned here can hardly be identified with our Karmatanents for the owner of this missal is called in the colophon a "newly ordained priest", whereas Karmatanents, already in 1616 figures as *ereč* and in 1618 as *ḱahanay*.

The information we have about the last years of Karmatanents is in St. Roszka's Chronology: "1671. Hovhannes Karmatanents of Leopolis, suffragan bishop (i.e. auxiliary b. or vicar) administered our churches when archbishop Nicholas was in Rome. He instituted many reforms, ordered the mass-book and the ritual properly orthodox, he was in Rome and after many exertions died in Christ in the year of the Lord 1678."[7]

However, the output of the printing house in Lvov was not limited to Armenian books; it also included an Armeno-Kipchak print aswell.

The existence of this Armeno-Kipchak print has hitherto escaped the attention of the Turcologists. In a note to his article on the Armenian books in the Amsterdam library, Fr. Macler mentions a "pièce rarissime", a "mi-arménien, mi-tatar" prayer book which was printed in Lvov in 1618.[9]

---

[5] See the colophons in *op. cit.* of N. Akinian, pp. 393—394. — The dating of the colophon of the *Aŕ ors* is partly blurred. J. Dashian does not concern himself with the question of the date; he assigns it to before 1700 on the basis of Karmatanents' bibliographical data *(Cat. Mechit.* Wien, p. 365). — Gh. Alishan publishes it to be read, first as 1618 and, in the second instance, as 1659 [*op. cit.* pp. 174, resp. 193). The second reconstruction (1659) is unwarranted, especially in view of the data of the *"Lucmunk'"*. Cf. N. Akinian: *op. cit.* pp. XXX—XXXI.

[6] *Cat. Mechit.,* p. 366. — See the colophon: *Cat. Hofbibl.,* Wien, p. 22.

[7] Alishan: *op. cit.* p. 143. — To the problems concerning the personality of Karmatanents I shall revert an other time.

[9] *REA* VII. p. 83. — Following him A. Sarukhan: *Hollandan ew hayerə žz. — žf. darerum.* [The Netherlands and the Armenians in the 16th to 19th centuries.] Vienna 1926. p. 191. (= *Handes Amsorya* 1928. col. 453.) and H. S. Anasyan: *Haykakan matenagitu!yun e—žə dd.* |Armenian Bibliology of the 5th to 18th centuries.] Yerevan, vol. I. 1959. col. 628.

III

After having found access, with the zealous mediation of the Interlibrary Loan Service of the Széchényi Library and by the courtesy of the University Library of Leyden, to the microfilm of the booklet, it became clear that the work is an Armeno-Kipchak prayer book, which has only the title of the

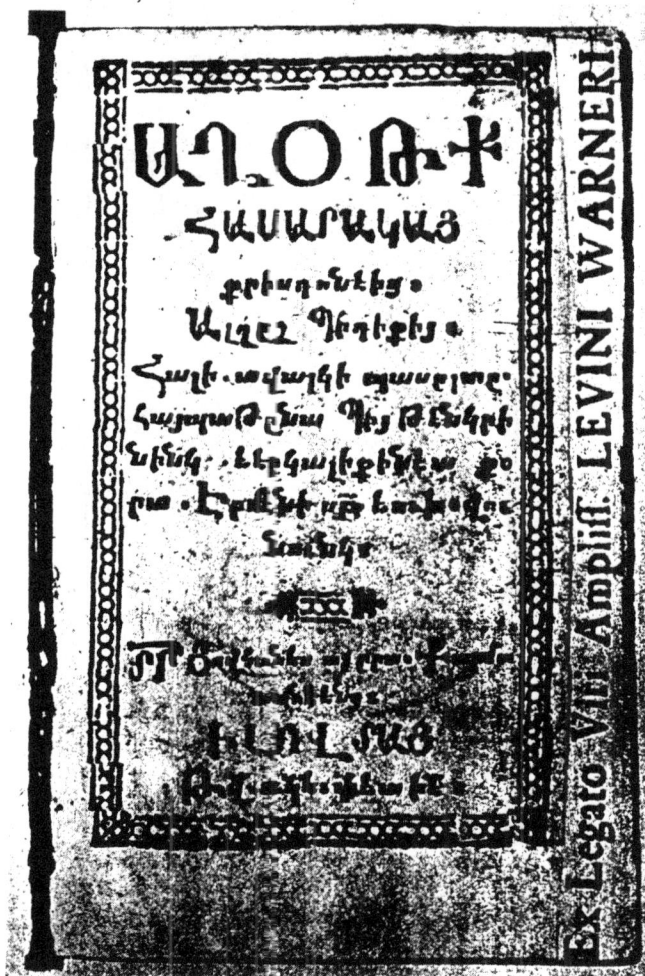

book and, in some instances, the title or opening words of psalms in the Armenian language.

Without doubt, the booklet is a translation from Armenian. Already the title page tells us that the breviary was made for the followers of the Armenian rite. Although I have not succeeded by correspondance in identifying the original of the book, it is obvious that the booklet, both as regards

III

its structure and the major part of its contents, agrees with the accepted breviary of the Armeno-Catholics.[10]

The Armenian origin is also borne out by the language of the translation which follows with servile accuracy the Armenian original. (This is also be-

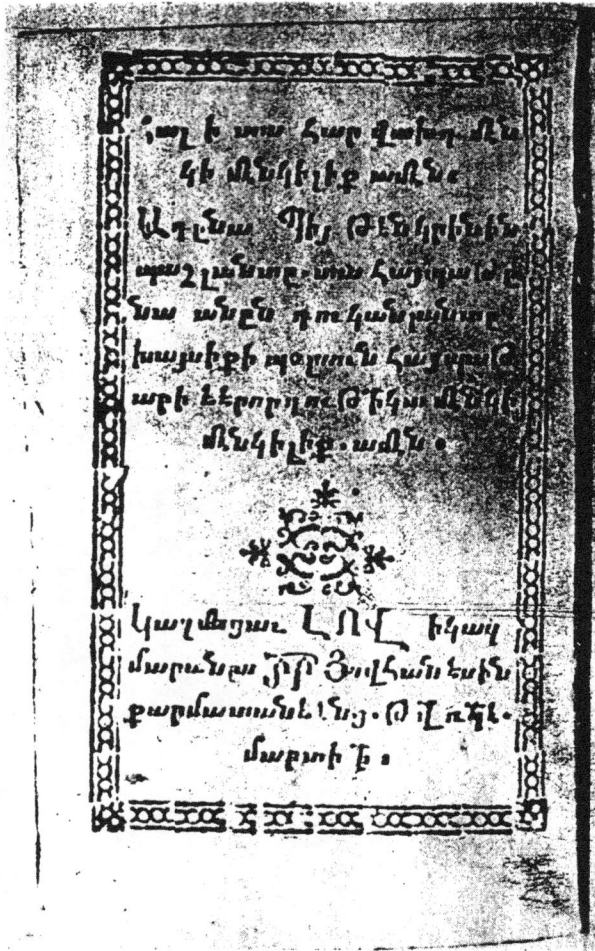

trayed also by the translators errors, resp. the calque-s.) The liturgical terms and the biblical proper names are left in their Armenian forms.

[10] *Kargaworutiwn hasarakac' alotic' hayastaneayc' ekelec'woy arareal S. Sahakay hayrapeti, Yovhannu Mandakunwoy ew ayloc' srboc' harc'n meroc'*. Venice 1934. (Abbrev.: Karg.) = *Breviarium Armenium sive dispositio communium armeniacae ecclesiae precum (a Sanctis Isaaco patriarcha, Mesrobio doctore, Kiudo atque a Joanne Mantagunensi habita nunc primum in latinam linguam translatus)*. [J. Aucher]. Venice 1908. (Abbrev.: Brev.).

III

The Description of the Booklet

Armeno-Kipchak Prayer Book, printed in Lvov, 27th of February to the 20th of March, 1618. In-32, 168 pages. "Reliure orientale gaufrée avec deux (4) lanières de cuir en guise de fermoirs . . . Relié *ibidem* la même année."[11] Leyden, University Library, B. U. 878. G. 9. (Ex Legato Viri Ampliss. Levini Warneri).[12]

Contents

Title page: *ΑΓΟΤʳ Kᶜ | hasaragacᶜ | k̃ristonèicᶜ. | Alγyš Bitiki. | Hali, avalgi basyldy, | hajbatyna Bij tengri|ning, jergalikinja ko|ra, Ermeni s[ur]p juχovu- nung. | — D[E]R Hovhanes ašy̆ra, Karma|daneenc (sic!). | ILOVDA | tv[aganin] r̄kè[= 1067] pᶜed[rvar] r̄è[= 27].*

Preces communium[13] christianorum. Prayer Book. Now printed for the first time to the glory of the Lord God according to the rite of the Armenian Holy Church. — Der Hovhanes . . . Karmatanents. In Lvov. The 27th of February, 1618.

[11] Fr. Macler obviously stresses this because he understands the word *kazmaran* in the colophon in the modern, general sense 'bindery', whereas as used by Karmatanents it means 'printing press'.

[12] L. Warner was Dutch ambassador to Constantinople around 1662. See Sarukhan: *op. cit.* p. 95. Cf. *Levini Warneri De rebus Turcicis, epistolae ineditae.* Lugd. Bat. 1883.

[13] catholicorum.

[14] This ancient Christian religious emblem appears also in the Lvov court where decisions were confirmed by a special seal which "bore the image of the lamb carrying the banner and above it a circular legend in Armenian". A. B. Karinyan: *Aknarkner hay parberakan mamuli patmutyan* [Survey of the history of the Armenian periodical press] I. Yerevan 1956. p. 66.

III

52— 59 Ps. 101.
59   Reference to Psalm 50.
60— 61 Ps. 129 (Karg. 206, Brev. 142).
62   Reference to Psalm 142 (Karg. 206—207, Brev. 142—143).
63— 64 Repleti sumus mane misericordia (Karg. 123, Brev. 91).
64— 65 Introduction to the Benedictio trium puerorum.
66— 80 Benedictio trium puerorum (ex proph. Danielis, cap. III, v. 26—45,
         52—88; Karg. 124—129, Brev. 92—96).
80— 82 Canticum Mariae Dei genetricis (Luc. I, v. 46—55; Karg. 132,
         Brev. 98).
82— 86 Benedictio Zachariae (Luc. I, v. 68—79; Karg. 133—134, Brev.
         98—99).
86— 87 Oratio Simeonis Senis (Luc. II, v. 29—32; Karg. 134, Brev. 99).
87   Reference to Psalm 50 (Karg. 152—154, Brev. 106—107).
87— 91 Ps. 148 (Karg. 156—158, Brev. 109—110).
91— 93 Ps. 149 (Karg. 158—159, Brev. 110—111).
93— 94 Ps. 150 (Karg. 159, Brev. 111).
95—100 Gloria in excelsis Deo (Karg. 160—161, Brev. 111—112).
100   Praecatio (Karg. 162, Brev. 112).
101—110 Oratio Manassae regis (Karg. 198—202, Brev. 143—146).
110—128 Preces Sancti Narsetis Clajensis (Karg. 403—409, Brev. 283—288.)
128—143 The Creed before Confession (Tawanuti[un], χostovanutiwn alnyna).
144—149 Ps. 50 (Karg. 245—247, Brev. 174—175).
150—152 Prayer at Sunset (Alγyš tum zamanyna).
152—156 Supplication towards Sunset (Xoltχa tumga χarši).
155   Reference to the prayer of Nerses Clajensis and the Pater noster.
155—156 Ave Maria.
156—160 Hymnus Ambrosianus (Supplication towards Sunset).
160   Reference to Psalm 6.
160—163 Bearing the Body of Our Lord (Koturganda Bijimyznyn tenin).
163   Reference to p. 112.
163—167 Gloria tibi, Domine (Karg. 397—398, Brev. 289—290).
167—168 Oratio.
168   Colophon (in Armenian): Made in Lvov in the printing house
         (կաղկարան) of Der Hovhanes Karmadanjenc. The 20th of March,
         1067 [= A. D. 1618].

*

But we can find references to Armeno-Kipchak prints in Armenian literature also.

In his standard work (in the chapter:. . . on the printing of Armenian books) M. Chamchian says the following: "In that time, as well as earlier,

III

other Armenian books had been printed at various places, among them in Poland, where a prayer book was printed in the Tatar language in Armenian characters for those who had come from the country of the Tatars and had been brought up in that language."[15] Although M. Chamchian fails to give the exact date and place of the publication in question, it would appear that this prayer book was identical with the one discussed above.

Further M. Bzhshkiants informs us that the printing house of Lvov produced also a Tatar Psalter in 1705.[16] One must be, however, cautious in assessing this information, because 1705 is too late a date as compared with the ascertained age of the Armeno-Kipchak texts known to us. I think we are entitled to suppose that M. Bzhshkiants misunderstood his source, in all probability M. Chamchian's words. In the lines immediately preceding the part quoted above Chamchian speaks of the bible published in Constantinople in 1705. It may be assumed that Bzhshkiants identified the adverbial "in that time" with 1705 (the date of the appearance of the Constantinople bible) and disregarded the appended "as well as earlier" phrase of the rather vague and loose indication of time. Thus, I think we are right to infer that his laconic reference concerns the same book, the Armeno-Kipchak prayer book of 1618.

Very noteworthy is the remark made about Armeno-Kipchak books by Christophorus Lukácsi, parochus Armenopolitanus: "Armenopoli in Bibliotheca Parochiali ostenduntur libri, armenicis characteribus sed Tatarico idiomate scripti, continentes preces quotidianas; manifesto Argumento linguam Tataricam Armenis nostris fuisse olim admodum familiarem."[17] The reference is rather problematic. Although in the 16th and 17th centuries as also in later Armenian literature, it is "Tatar" the common denomination for Armeno-Kipchak, doubt may still arise as to the above mentioned Tatar books, if they were undoubtedly Armeno-Kipchak linguistic records. That we think in the first place of Armeno-Kipchak texts, is justifiable on the grounds that we possess no information about other kind of Tatar texts written in Armenian characters in this area. At all events, it still remains a question whether Lukácsi did not use "liber" in the sense of 'liber manuscriptus, codex'; such an interpretation would seem to be suggested by "scriptus".[18] Up to now I have failed

---

[15] *Patmutiwn Hayoc'* [History of Armenia] Venice. vol. III. 1786. p. 664.

[16] *Op. cit.* p. 100. The dates 1705 and 1618, even in Armenian lettering, can hardly be confounded.

[17] *Historia Armenorum Transsilvaniae*, Viennae 1859. p. 15.

[18] The Szamosujvár—Gherla MSS were catalogued decades ago. (Cf. Fr. Macler: *Rapport sur une mission scientifique en Transylvanie, Sept.—Oct. 1934. Manuscrits arméniens de Transylvanie.* Paris 1935. p. 20.). As I have been kindly informed by Dr. V. Inglisian, the catalogue comprising 51 Armenian MSS, which will appear shortly in the Vienna Mechitarist T.pography, contains no Tatar MS in Armenian script.

III

in my efforts to trace down by correspondence the "Tatar" books in question. The organ of the Transylvanian Armenians[19] also made mention (on Lukácsi's authority) of a Tatar book in the parochial library at Szamosujvár (Gherla—Armenopolis), but when I had access to the microfilm of this book, it appeared that it was a synoptic catechism in Polish and Tatar,[20] which cannot be identical with any of the books mentioned by Lukácsi, because the catechism was printed in Latin characters. I could only hope to throw some light on this problem by a personal visit to Transylvania.

*

The question arises as to how to account for the remarkably short life (1616—1618?) of the printing press of Lvov whereas the demand for books in the region would have justified its further operation. This refers also to a potential market for books in the Armeno-Kipchak language for Kipchak (Tatar) continued to be the vernacular of that province for a long time after 1618.

The circumstance that Armenians who gave votive commissions for the copying of books gave their preference to hand-written works can hardly explain the early termination of the Armenian printing venture in Lvov, for the products of the printing press, through the activity of Armenian merchants, could have reached far-away places with Armenian inhabitants, as we see this through many centuries in the history of Armenian printing.

One might find some explanation in the low aesthetic standard of the printing house's products. The equipment must have been quite simple, and the types were even more primitive[21] than those of the first Armenian prints that had been made a century ago.

Still we have to seek an explanation rather in the situation of the local church: the vigorous opposition of the Armenians of Gregorian creed against the tendency for a union with Rome; the long-wearing era of the Armenian archbishop Nicol Thorossowicz, not very favourable to cultural endeavours[22], — and last but not least the personal career of Karmatanents and eventual economic difficulties which still waite for an elucidation.

Our Armeno-Kipchak print — the hitherto only extant product of this kind — is at any rate an interesting document of cultural history. We shall publish a few specimens of it in one the next numbers of our periodical.

[19] "Armenia" I/1. (1887) p. 9. and, mostly on basis of this information, also other weeklies edited by Transylvanian Armenians.

[20] Katechizm z Okazyi Tatarzyna.... Lemberg 1728.

[21] Karmatanents seems to have had a flair for rapid work. The printing of the "Alɣyš Bitiki" took less than a month. It may be assumed that he had his primitive characters made in Lvov. Cf. Aconts Kiwer: loc. cit.

[22] Arakel Tavrizhetsi, cap. XXVIII., etc.

III

ARMENO-KIPCHAK TEXTS FROM LVOV (A. D. 1618)

BY

E. SCHÜTZ

We present here a few selections from the Armeno-Kipchak prayer-book *(Alyyš bitiki)* printed in Lvov in 1618.[1]

1. The 6th Psalm (pp. 37—40).

2. *Uč igitning χoltχasy* = Benedictio trium puerorum (Preceded by the prayer of Azarias) (pp. 66—80. Ex proph. Danielis cap. III. v. 26—45, 52—88).

3) *Inam bila χostovanel bol·ıp* = Fide confiteor (pp. 111—128). 24 short prayers written by Nerses Clajensis, one for each hour of the solar day, a manuel of devotion which has enjoyed great popularity among the Armenians and has many a times and oft been published in print.[2]

Nerses, with the by-name Šnorhali (= Gracious), 1102--1173, a famous ecclesiastical author, was from 1166 the Patriarch (Catholikos) of the Armenians, residing in Hromkla.

The 6th Psalm

37[6] *Saymosu tavitnyng.* | *BIJ JURAK|lanmaχyng bilaj* | *sening χar-šila|magin meni da ne očašma|χŋng bila sening ogut|lamagin meni.|*

Jarlyya manga bijim, | *zera χasta men [.] ongalt* | *bojumnu menim zera muš|38χulandylar sovaklar|ym menim.* |

Janym menim bek mušχ|ullandy, da sen bij | *nega dingraj.* |

Λajt bij da χutχar | *bojurnu menim, tirgiz* | *meni bij jarlyyamaχyn|ga kora sening.* |

---

[1] See *Acta Orient. Hung.* XIII, pp. 123—130. — For the transcription of the text, see *Acta Orient. Hung.* XII, pp. 143—160. — The texts are obsequious translations, yet some minor omissions also occur. No reference is made to these obvious omissions. In the glossary, however, I note the places where the translator misunderstood the original Armenian text.

[2] The Mechitarists of Venice alone published it as a separate booklet nine times between 1810 and 1882, in an increasing number of languages: in 1810 in 6, in 1837 in 24, and in 1882 in 36 languages.

19*

*Zera kimsa bolmas ki | olumda angaj seni. ja | tamuχta tapunmaχ | etkajlar
sanga. |*

*Xazγandym men kus|tunmaχymda menim juv|39dum barča kečany or|num-
nu menim da jašlar|ym bila menim tošakimni | čylattym. |*

*Mušχulandy jurak|lanmaχtan kozum menim | oprandym men ustuna |
barča dušmanlarymnyn | menim. |*

Kjeri turunuz barča|nyz, χajsilaryngyz ki e|tiirsiz torasizlikni. |

*Išiti [sic!] bij avazyma jyγ|lamaχymnyng menim išiti | bij alγyšima
menim da | 40 bij χoltχamny menim jop|sundu. |*

*Ujalgajlar da mušχu|langajlar asry barčaj | dušmanlarym menim, χaj|tkaj-
lar kjeri da ujal|gajlar asry tezindan, | da mušχullangajlar. |*

Uč igitning χoltχasy

(Benedictio trium puerorum)

*[Dan. cap. III. 26—45.] 66 ALΓYŠLI | sen bij tengri, | atalarymyzdan
bizim, | alγyšli hajbatlan|gan atyn senin mengilik.|*

*Konuluk bila kečir|ding bu barčany da | bizim bila toγru sen|sen bij, da
barča išla|ryn senin toγrudur.|*

Jolung sening toγru|67dur, da barča toran | senin konudur.|

*Toγru tora kjeltir|din ustumuzga bizim | barčaga kora, neninki | jeberdin
ustumuzga | bizim, da šaharina ari | atalarymyznyng bizim | jerusaγemnyng. |*

*Toγruluχ bila da ko|nuluk bila jeberding | bunu barča ustumuz|ga bizim,
jazyχlarymyz | učun bizim. |*

*Torasizlandyχ ašyn|68dyχ baštaχ bolup sen|dan jazyχly bolduχ | barčada,
da bujru|χungnu sening saχ|lamadyχ.|*

*Saχlamadyχ, nečik si|marladyn sen bizga, ki | jaχšini tapkajbiz biz |
sendan.|*

*Hali barčany χajsin|ki etting, da neniki je|berdin ustumuzga | bizim,
toγru jarγu bi|la etting.|*

*Čyχara berding bizni | 69 χoluna dušmanlarymᵛz|nyng bizim torasiz-
lar|nyng beklarga da baš|taχlarga.|*

*Xoluna χannyng tora|sizning da jamannyng, | barča jerda čyχaraj | ber-
ding bizni. |*

*Da hali joχtur bizga | vaχt ačma aγzymyzny | bizim ki ujatly da ta|ba
bolduχ χullaryna | sening χul[l]uχ etkan. |*

*Joχsa čyχara berma | bizni sonγuga dingra, | 70 atyn učun sening, ta|γytma
niatynny senin | da kjeri etma jarlyγa|maχyngny seni[n]g bizdan. |*

*Apraham sovukung u|čung [sic!] sening, da sahag | χulung da ari israje|-
ling učun senin. |*

*Atadyn alarga da ajt|ting, arttyrijim zurja|tynyzny sizin nečik jol|duzlaryn
koknung, da | nečik χumnu χyrγγy|na tengizning. |*

IV

Da hali bij eksildiχ | 71 biz neki barča ĵynslar | da zabunluχta biz | har jerda bugun jazᵸχ|larymyz učun bizim. |

Joχtur bu zaman buj|ruχči markare, da jol | korguzuči, ne butov | χurban, ne temjan ore|nkka, ne jer χurban|larny sunma alnyna se|ning, jarlyγamaχ tap|ma sendan. |

Joχsa bojumuz bilaj a|šaχlaryp, da ĵanymyzn|yn mušχuluχu bila jop|-72sunovlu bolyjiχ biz | nečik butov χurban | χojlarnyng da tuvar|larnyng, da nečik tu|man tuman semiz χozu|lar. |

Bu turluj jopsunov|lu bolsun χurbanymyz | bizim, bugun alnynga | senin ki tugal tapul|gajbiz a[r]tyndan sening | da dugul ujat umsan|ganlarga sanga. |

Da hali kjelirbiz ar|tyndan sening barčaj | 73 jurakymyz bilaj bizim | χorχarbiz sendan χol|arbiz juzunna senin | bij ujatly etma bizni.|

Joχsa etkin bizga se|kinlikina kora sening. | da kopluχuna jarly|γamaχynnyn senin χut|χar bizni tamašalaryn | učun senin, da haj|batly bolsun atyng se|nin mengilik. |

Ujatly bolgajlar bar|časy χajsilaryki χyjn|arlar χullaryngny sen|74ing, ujatly bolgajlar | zulumlary alarnym, da | barča χuvatlary a|larnyng syngajlar. |

Da tanygajlar ki sen|sen bij tengri jalγyz | hajbatlanypsen usna | barča dunjanyng. |

[Cap. III. 52—88.] *Alγyšli sensen bij ten|gri atalarymyzdan bi|zim, ogovlu da ajruχ|su bijiklangan atyn | sening mengilik. |*

Da alγyšlidir atyng | ari hajbatynyng senin | 75 ogovlu da ajruχsu [. . .].*

Alγyšli sen daĵaryn|da hajbatly arilikin|ning sening, ogovlu [. . .]. |

Alγyšli sen ustuna | olturγučungnung | padšahlyχynnyn senin | ogovlu [. . .]. |

Alγyšli sen ki oltu|rupsen kjeropelarda, | da baχyjirsen tibsiz|likka, ogov[. . .]. |

Alγyšli sen usna toχ|talmaχᵸna koknun, og[. . .]. |

Alγyšlangyz barča iš|76laryᵸ ejamyznyng, bijni | alγyšlangyz da bijik|latyngyz any mengilik.|

Alγyšlangyz kok bijni | alγᵸš[. . .]. |

Alγyšlanyz frištala|ry ejamyznyn, suvlar ki | ustuna koknung, bij|ni alγᵸš[. . .].|

Alγyšlangyz χuvat|lary ejamyznyng, gunaš | da aj bijni, al[. . .].|

Alγyšlanyz jolduzlar | koktagi jaymurlar da | jayγš bijni, alγᵸš[. . .].|

77 Alγyšlangyz barča jel|lar ot da isi bijni, al[. . .].|

Alγyšlanyz sovuχlar |da χurγaχ jayγš da | χarlar tuškan bijni, | alγᵸš[. . .].|

Alγyšlanyz buzlar da | ačyχlyχlar da χar, | alγᵸš[. . .].|

Alγyšlangyz kunduz | kečalar, jaryχ da χar|amγu bijni, alγᵸš[. . .].|

Alγyšlangyz bulut|lar da jašramaχlar da | jer bijni, alγᵸš[. . .].|

---

* The refrains are abbreviated in the original.

IV

78 *Alγyšlangyz taγlar | da orlar, barča bitiš|lari jerning, bijni al*[. . .].| *Alγyšlangyz čovraχ|lar tengiz da ozanlar | bijni, alγyš*[. . .].| *Alγyšlanyz ulu ba|lyχlar da barčaj χaj|naškanlar χajsikij | suvda učar χušlary | koknun bijni, al*[. . .].| *Alγyšlanyz kazanlar | da hajvanlar oγlanla|ry adamlarnyng, bijni | alγyš*[. . .].| **79** *Alγyšlagaj israjel bij|ni, alγyš*[. . .].| *Alγyšlangyz kahana|lar bijni, alγyš*[. . .].| *Alγyšlangyz χullary | ejamyznyng, bijni al*[. . .].| *Alγyšlanyz ǰanlar da | tynyχlary toγrular|nyn, alγyš*[. . .].| *Alγyšlanyz arilar da | ašaχ juraklilar bijni | alγyš*[. . .].| *Alγyšlangyz anania | azaria da misajėl, bij|ni alγyšlangyz da bij|***80***iklatyngyz any, mengi | mengilik.*

[Fide confiteor]

(Preces Narsetis Clajensis)

111 *INAM BILA XOs*|tovanėl *bolup da | jerni oparmen sana, a|ta oγul ari ǰan etilma|gan da olumsuz tarbi|at jaratučisi friš|talarnyn da adamlar|nyn da barča bolganlar|nyng, jarlyγa sening | jaratkanlarynga da | manga kop jazyχlyga.*|

*Inam bila χ*ostovanėl *| bolup da* jerni *oparmen | sana, ajirylmagan ja|***112***ryχ, ata oγul ari ǰan | da bir tengrilik, ja|ratuči jaryχny da | tas etuči χaranγulu|χnu tas et menim ǰanym|dan χaranγulu jazyχ|ny da biliksizlikni,|da jaryχlat esimni | menim bu sahat al|γyš etmaga sana bijan|čina kora, da jopsun|ijim sendan χoltχamny | menim, da jarlyγa* [. . .].|

Ata koktagi konu ten|gri, ki jeberding *sovuk|***113***lu oγlunnu χoltχasy|na bulargan adamlar|nyng, mėγa senin alnyn|ga jerdan kokka dira | jopsun meni nečik kje|raksyz oγulnu da kij|dir mana burungi ja|ryχly tonnu χajsiki|jalanačlandym jazyχ | bila, da jarlyγa* [. . .].|

Oγ*lu tengrinin konu | tengri, ki ašaχlandyn | atanyn χojnundan da | aldyng ten ari* gujs *ma|riamdan χutχarylma|***114***χymyz učun bizim χač|landyng da komuldung | da turdun oludan* [sic!] *da | aγyndyn hajbat bilaj |kokka, mėγa senin alny|na jerdan kokka dira, | an meni nečik χaraχči |ni, χačan kelsang χan|lyχyn bila, da jarlyγ*[. . .].|

J̌any tengrining konu | tengri, ki endin *horta|nanda da vėrnadunda | da jaryχlattyn meni, | juvmaχy bila s*[*ur*]*p* avaz|*annyn, mėγa* jerdan *kok|***115***ka dira senin alnynga | aryt meni ekinči teng|rilik ot bila, nečik s*[*ur*]*p | arakėllarny ari vėrna|dunda, da jarlyγa* [. . .].|

Zadasyz tarbijat mė|γa sana aχylym bila me|nim, ǰanym da tenim bi|la, anma ilgarigi jazyχ|larymny menim, ari atyn | učun senin, da jar[. . .].|

*Baχuči barčasyn méya | sanga sayyšim bila so|zum bila*j *da χylynga|nym bila, buzgin χol bi|*116*tikin jazyχlarymnyn me|nim, da jazgin atymny | menim mengilik duftar|da, da jar[. . .]. |*

Tergovuči japuχlar|ny méya sana erkli u | erksiz bilganym da bil|maganym bila bošatlyχ | ber jazyχly χuluna | χajsiki sp *avazandan | toyganymdan, čaχ bu | kunga dinra jazyχly | men tengrilikingnin al|nyna sezikliklarym bila | menim da barča boyun|*117*larym bila tenimning, | da jar[. . .]. |*

*Barčany ajovuči bij, | χojgin kozat kozlaryma | menim ari χorχunnu se|nin ki artyχsy baχma|gajmen da χulaχym bila | jazyχ išitmagajmen da | ayzym bila jalyan soz|lamagajmen da jurakym | bila jaman sayyš etma|gajmen da χollarym bila | jaman χylynmagajmen, | da ajaχlarym bila ja|man jollarga barmagaj|*118*men joχsa kuzat barča | tepranišlaryn tenim|nin menim, ki bar|čada | bujruχuna kora senin | bolgajlar, da jar[. . .]. |*

Otlu tiri ks *otlu so|vukunnu senin χajsi|ki saldyn dun[j]ada pa|lajlat bojuma menim, ki | kujdurgaj aruvsuz|luχun janymnyn menim, | da arytkaj χijasyn e|simnin menim, da aryt kaj jazyχyn tenimnin | menim, da jandyrgaj ja|*119*ryχ bilmaχyn bila jura|kyma menim, da jar[. . .]. |*

A χylly [sic!] *atanyn* hs *ber | mana aχyl, jaχšini sa|γyšlama da sozlama da | etmaga alnynga sening | har sahat, da jaman sa|γyštan da χylynmaχ|tan χutχar meni, da [. . .]. |*

Klavuči jaχšylⁿχny | bij jaχšy etuči χojma|gin meni erkima kora me|nim barmaga, joχsa jol | korguz manga har vaχt | sening erkina kora, da [. . .]. |

120 *Koktagi χan ber mana | učmaχynny senin χajsi|ki χyrer etting so|vuk|lularyna senin, da ku|čajt jurakimni menim ki | koralmagaj jazyχny da | sovgaj senin ari toran|ny. da jar[. . .]. |*

Ajovuči jaratkan|larny saχla janymny da |tenimni menim senin ari | χačin bila, aldovuči | jazyχtan, synamaχyn|dan eski dušmannyn da |jaman kišilarnyng,| 121 *aldamaχyndan da bar|ča tynsyzlyχtan janym|ny u tenimni, da jar[. . .]. |*

Kozatuči barčadan | ks *ongun sening kolga | bolgaj ustuma menim | kunduz u keča, ovda | olturganda jolda ju|ruganda juχlaganda | turganda ki heč ses|kan|magajmen, jar[. . .]. |*

*Tengrim menim χajsiki | čšarsen χolunnu senin | da toldurursen barča | jaratkanlaryngny jar|*122*lyyamaχyn bila sening | sana simarlarmen janym|ny menim, sen χajyur da | hadirla jan u ten kje|rakymny. bu kundan | čaχ mengilikka diraj, | da jarly[. . .]. |*

*Xajtaruči bulargan|laryny, χajtar meni ja|man ovrančiklarymdan | menim, jaχšy χylynmaχ|ka da berkirt janym | da menim χorχulu olar | kunumnu da χorχu|sun tamuχnun, da so|*123*tukun učmaχnyng. ki | χajtkajmen jazzχtan* [sic!] *| da χylyngajmen toyru|luχnu, jar[. . .]. |*

Čovraχy olumsuzluk|nun aχtyrgin jurakim|dan menim pošmanlyχ ja|šin, nečik bornigning, | ki juvgaj jazyχyn boj|umnung menim dunja|dan kječkanym|dan ilga|ri jar[. . .]. |

IV

Baɣɣǐlovuči jarlyɣa|maχny, baɣɣǐla manga | konu inam bila, da jaχ|124ǐi
amal bila, uluǐlu | bolup ari tenindan | da ari χanyngdan kel|maga senin alnynga
j[. . .].|

Jaχǐi etuči bij jaχǐi | frǐtaga simarlagaj | sen tatlylyχ bila si|marlamaga
ǰanymny me|nim, da uruǐsuz kečir|maga, eski duǐmannyn | jamanyngdan
[sic !], χajsiki | kok tibina dyrlar, ja[. . .].|

Jaryχ konu k̄s arzani | et ǰanymny menim sovunč|luk bila kormaga jary|-
125χyn hajbatyngnyng se|ning undalgan kunda | tynmaga jaχǐy umsa bi|la, čaχ
senin hajbatly | ekinči kelganyna dira.|

Jaryuči konu χačan | kelsan hajbaty bila a|tanyng, jaryu etmaga | tirilarga
da olularga | kirmagin jaryuga χu|lung bila senin, joχsa | χutχar meni mengilik
| ottan, da iǐittirgin | manga sanly undovun | artarlarnyng kokdagi | 126 χanly-
χynga sening, ja[. . .].

Baryna jarlyɣovuči | bij jarlyɣa barča in|anganlarga sana menim|gilaryna
da jatlarga, | tanyganlarga da tany|maganlarga tirilarga | da olularga boǐat
du|ǐmanlaryma menim da me|ni koralmaganlarga da | χajtar alarny jaman|lyχ-
laryndan, χajsiki | bardyr juraklarynaj | menim učun da jarlyɣa | alarga da
manga kop | 127 jazyχlyga, da jarly[. . .].

Hajbatly bij jopsun | χoltχasyn χulunnung | senin, da tugalla jaχ|ǐylyχka
jalbarmaχym|ny menim, parėχoslu̇χu | bila s̄p a[stua]dzadzinning da | s̄p
hovanes garabėdnyn | da s̄p stėpanos burun|gi tanyχynnyng, da bi|zim atamyznyn
s̄p lusav|oričnin, da s̄p arakėl|larnyng da markarelar|nyn da s̄p hajrabėdlar|-
nyn da s̄p mardiroslar|128nyn da s̄p gusanklarnyn | da barča friǐtalar|nyn
mikajėlnin da kap|rielnin sėrovpelarnyng | da kėrovpelarnyng da | barča arila-
ryngnyn se|nin kokdagilarnyng da | jerdagilarnyn, da sana | hajbat da jerni opmaχ |
ajirylmagan s̄p jerrortu|tj[un]ga hali da har kjez|da mengi mengilik amen.

Glossary

The order of letters as in K. Grønbech's *Komanisches Wörterbuch*, except: *ǰ* follows *d ; y (= ı, ı̄)* follows *i.*

The Coman and Kamaim parallels are indicated in J. Deny's ,,*Ephémérides*" *de
Kamieniec (Ural-Alt. Bibl.* IV.).

ač- 69[10], 121[13] etc. 'aperio — to open'
ačyχlyχ 77[8] 'tempus serenus — clear weather'
adam passim 'homo — man'
aɣyn- 114[4], 132[7] 'ascendo — to ascend'
aɣyz (aɣz-) passim, *ahz-* 4[10] 'os — mouth'
aɣotk̈ (Arm. աղօթք) Title p.[1] 'preces — prayers'
aχyl 115[7], 119[4] etc. 'mens, sapientia — mind, wisdom' *(aχylly* 119[3] mistake
  for *aχyly* 'his mind'.)
aχtyr- 123[6] 'effluere facio — to cause to flow'

IV

aj 76¹², 88² 'luna — moon'

ajaχ passim 'pes — foot'

ajirylmagan 111¹⁴, 128¹⁰ etc. 'indivisibilis — indivisible'

ajovuči 117³, 120⁹ 'provisor — guardian'

ajruχsu 144¹⁰ 'amplius — thoroughly'. ∼ *bijiklangan* 74¹¹, 75¹ 'superexaltatus'

ajt- passim 'loquor — to speak'

al- passim 'sumo — to take' (See also *koralma-*)

aldamaχ 121¹ 'fraus — fraud'

aldovuči 120¹² 'illecebrosus — deceitful'

alγyš passim 'benedictio, oratio — benediction, prayer'

alγyšla- passim 'benedico — to bless'

alγyšli passim 'benedictus — blessed'

aln- (+ poss. suff. ∼ *-yma, -nġa, -na*) passim 'coram — before' *(alnyna senin(g)* more frequently than *alnynga senin(g)* 'coram te — before thee')

amal 124¹ (عۥا Pl. ڄاڶ) 'opus — work, deed'

an-, ang- passim 'memini, recordor — to remember'

Anania (Arm. ԱՆԱՆԻԱ) 79¹³ 'Ananias'

Apraham (Arm. ԱԲՐԱՀԱՄ) passim 'Abraham'

arakēl (Arm. ԱՌԱՔԵԼ) passim 'apostolus — apostle'

ari passim, *ary* 16¹, 'sanctus — holy' (With biblical personal names and Armenian clerical expressions we find Arm. $\overline{sp}$ = *surp*.)

arilik 29², 75³ etc. 'puritas, sanctitas — purity, holiness'

aryt- 115², 118¹²·¹³ etc. 'purifico — to purify'

art. artyndan bar- 51¹⁰, ∼ *kjel-* 72¹⁴ 'sequor — to follow'

artar (Arm. ԱՐԴԱՐ) 125¹⁵ etc. 'iustus — just'

artyχ passim 'plus — more'; *artyχsy baχ-* 117⁶: In the original Armenian text we find ՀԱՅԵԼ ՅԱՐԱՏ 'to regard indecently'. The translator misread ՅԱՐԱՏ 'unchaste' for the homonymous ԱՌԱՏ 'abundant, copious'.

arttyr- 70¹⁰, 105⁷ 'multiplico — to multiply'

aruvsuzluχ 118¹⁰ 'sordes — impurity'

arzani 30⁶, 97¹⁰ etc. 'dignus — worthy'

asry 40⁴·⁷, 47¹·⁸ 'valde — very much'

a[stua]dzadzin (Arm. ԱՍՁՈՐՁԻՆ) 127⁷ 'dei genetrix — mother of God'

ašaχ 79¹¹, 81¹⁴ etc. 'humilis — low, humble'

ašaχlan- 56⁹, 71¹³ etc. 'inclinor, humilior — to descend, to be humble'

ašyn- 67¹⁵ 'inique ago, pecco — to commit a fault, sin'; *ašyngan* 29⁶, 31⁶, 41ᴸ 'peccatum — transgression'. (Calque modelled on the Arm. homonyms: ԱՆՑԱՆԵՄ 'to pass, surpass' × ՅԱՆՑԱՆԵՄ 'to transgress, trespass, commit a fault, a crime')

ašyra title p.¹⁰ 4¹⁴, 5⁹ 'by, above'

at passim 'nomen — name'

ata passim 'pater — father'

IV

ata- 30[8], 70[9] 'polliceor, promitto — to promise'

avalgi title p.[5] 'pristinus — primari(ly)'

avaz passim 'vox — voice'

avazan (Arm. ԱՒԱԶԱՆ) 114[14], 116[10] 'lavacrum, baptisterium — font, basin'

Azaria (Arm. ԱԶԱՐԻԱ) 79[14] 'Azarias'

baɣyšla- 35[6], 123[14] etc. 'largior — to grant, bestow'

baɣyšlovuči 123[13] 'largitor — donor'

baχ- passim 'intueor, aspicio — to regard, look'

baχuči 115[12] 'speculator — onlooker'

balyχ 'piscis — fish'; *ulu* ∼ 78[7] 'cetus — whale'

bar- 84[15], 117[15] etc. 'vado, pergo — to go, walk'

bar- ; ∼ *-dyr* 55[4], 126[13] etc. 'est — (there) is'

barča passim 'omnis — all'

bary 'omnis — all'; *baryny tutuči* 96[3], 101[7] 'omnipotens — omnipotent';
    baryna jarlyɣovuči 126[2] 'misericors omnium — all-merciful'

basyl- title p.[5] 'to be printed'

baštaχ 69[3] 'praevaricator — prevaricator'; ∼ *bol-* 68[1] 'rebello — to revolt,
    rebel' (Cf. Kazan Tatar: باش ایشتاق 'безначальный, своевольный' Budagov
    L., Сравн. словарь I. p. 226.)

bek 69[3] 'firmus — firm' (The translator took the adjective ԻԽՈՒԿ 'hard,
    severe' for a noun); 38[3] 'valde — very much' (used independently, not as
    a complement of an adjective.)

ber- passim 'largior — to give, grant' (See also *čyχara ber-)*

berkirt- 122[12] 'infigo — to fasten'

bij passim 'dominus — lord'

bijanč 112[10] 'beneplacitum — pleasure'

bijiklan- 'exaltor — to be elevated, exalted' (See *ajruχsu)*

bijiklat- 76[2], 79[15] etc. 'elevo, exalto — to elevate'

bil- passim 'scio — to know'

bila passim '(instr.) — with, by'

biliksizlik 112[7] 'ignorantia — ignorance'

bilmaχ 119[1] 'sapientia — wisdom'

bitik title p.[4], 83[15] 'scriptum, liber — writing, book'; *χol bitiki* 115[15] 'chirogra-
    phum — hand-writing'

bitiš 78[2] 'germinantia — growth'

biz (∼ *-ni, -im, -ga)* 'nos — we'

boyun 116[15], 135[15], 140[8] 'membrum — member' .

boj passim 'persona, animus — person, self (Arm. ԱՆՁՆ)'

bol- passim 'sum, fio — to be, become'

bornig (Arm. ՊՈՌՆԻԿ) 123[8] 'peccatrix, fornicatrix — sinful woman'

bošat- 42[7], 126[8] etc. 'veniam concedo — to forgive'

bošatlyχ 85⁵, 116⁸ etc. 'venia — forgiveness'
bu 'this' *(bunung* 8⁷, *bunun* 42¹⁰, *bunu* 67¹², —, *bundan* 80¹² but *mundan* 28¹²; —, *bularnyng* 86¹).
bugun passim 'hodie — to-day'; *bugungi kunnu* 163¹⁰ 'id.'
bujruχ 68³, 118⁴ etc. 'praeceptum — commandment, precept'
bujruχči 71⁵ etc. 'princeps — prince, chief (Arm. իշխան)'
bulargan 113², 122⁸ 'errans (perditus) — erring (person)'
bulut 77¹³ 'nubes — cloud'
burungi 113⁷ 'primus — first'; ~ *tanyχ* 127⁹ 'protomartyr'
butov χurban 71⁷, 72², 148¹¹ 'holocaustum — burnt-offering'
buz 77⁷, 89⁴ 'glacies — frost, ice'
buz- 115¹⁵, 144⁹ 'deleo — to destroy'

čaχ ... anča 5⁵, *čaχ ... dinra* 61⁴, 116¹¹, *čaχ ... dira* 122⁶, 125⁴ 'usque ad — until'
čyχara ber- 68¹⁵, 69⁷⁻¹⁴, 137⁴ 'trado — to hand over' (Cf. kar. T. *čyγara ber-* 'ausliefern').
čylat- 39⁴ 'madefacio, rigo — to moisten. irrigate' (Cf. *Kāšy. čilä-* 'befeuchten')
čovraχ 78⁴, 99¹⁰, 123⁵ 'fons — fountain'

da passim 'et — and'
dajar (Arm. տաճար) 75² 'templum — temple, church'
dr̄ = der (Arm. տէր) title p.¹⁰, 168¹⁰ 'dominus, pater' (Title of priests)
dingra 38⁵, 69¹⁵ etc. 'usque ad — until' (See *čaχ)*
duftar 116³ 'catalogus — (note)book'
dugul 18¹, ³, ⁵, 72¹² etc. 'non — not' (Cf. *Dat*. 14 times *dugul*, 14 times *tugul)*
dunja passim *(duna* 118⁸, 164¹³; *dujna* 162¹⁴, 163³) 'terra, mundus — earth, world'
dušman passim 'inimicus — enemy'

ǰan passim 'spiritus, anima, animus — ghost, spirit, soul'
ǰyns passim 'gens — generation'

eja passim 'dominus — lord'
ekinči 125⁵, 115² 'secundus — second'
eksil- 24³, 70¹⁵ 'imminuor — to diminish (intr.)' (In 70¹⁵ the translator misread *նուազիլ* 'to diminish' instead of *նուաղիլ* 'to grow weak'.)
en- 24⁷, 114¹¹ etc. 'descendo — to descend'
erk 99⁷, 119¹² etc. 'voluntas — will'
erkli 116⁶, 135⁵ 'volens, ultro — willing(ly)'
erksiz 116⁷, 135⁶ 'nolens, invitus — involuntary(ly)'
ermeni title p.⁸, 62⁹ 'Armenus — Armenian'
es 112⁸, 118¹² etc. 'mens — mind'

IV

eski dušman 120[14], 124[10] 'arch-enemy' (In Arm. *dew* 'daemonus — devil')
et- passim 'facio — do, make' (In composite verbs it also serves as an auxiliary.)
etilmagan 111[4] 'increatus — increate'
etuči 112[4], 119[11] 'faciens — doer'

frišta 76[6], 111[6] etc. 'angelus — angel'

garabėd (Arm. 4*արապետ*) 127[8] '(Johannes) Baptista — Baptist'
gujs (Arm. *կոյս*) 113[14] etc. 'virgo — virgin'
gunaš 76[11], 85[11], 88[1] 'sol — sun'
gusank (Arm. *կուսանք*) 128[1] 'virgines — virgins'

hadirla- 86[13], 122[4] etc. 'paro — to prepare'
hajbat passim 'gloria — glory'
hajbatlan- 66[4], 74[7] 'glorificatus sum — to be glorified'
hajbatly 65[1], 73[10] 'gloriosus — glorious'
hajrabėd (Arm. *Հայրապետ*) 127[14] etc. 'patriarcha — patriarch'
hajvan 78[13] 'pecus — animal'
hali passim 'nunc — now'
har passim 'omnis — all, every'
hasarag (Arm. *Հասարակ*) title p.[2] 'communis, καθολικός — common'
(This adjective originally may have belonged to the preceding word [cf.
e. g. Acta Orient. Hung. XIII, p. 126, note 10.], and in this case the translation would be 'common prayers'.)
heč 133[1], 148[12, 15] (a word intensifying a negation); *heč nema* 43[1], 44[4] 'nihil —
nothing'; *heč* 121[10] 'nunquam — never'
hortanan (Arm. *յորդանան*) 114[11] 'fluvius Jordan'
Hovanes (Arm. *յովանէս*) 127[8] 'Johannes — John'
hs = *hisus* (Arm. *յս̄*) passim 'Jesus'
χač (< Pers. < Arm. *խաչ*) 110[2], 120[12] etc. 'crux — cross'
χačan 125[6] etc. 'quando — when'
χačlan- 114[1] etc. 'crucifior — to be crucified'
χajγur- 122[3] 'curam habeo — to care' (Cf. kar. T. *kaiγyr-* 'Sorgen haben'.)
χajnaš- 'scatet aliqua re — to swarm'; *χajnaškanlar* 78[8] 'quae moventur (in
aquis)'
χajsi (ki) passim 'qui — who'
χajt- passim 'revertor — to return (intr.)'
χajtar- 122[9] etc. 'reduco — to lead (turn) back'
χajtaruči 122[8], 150[8] 'reductor — who leads sy back'
χan 124[3] 'sanguis — blood'
χan passim 'rex — king'
χanlyχ 110[11], 114[8] etc. 'regnum — kingdom'

IV

χar 77⁵ etc. 'nix — snow'
χaraχči 114⁷ 'latro — thief'
χaramγu 33², 77¹¹ 'tenebrosus, tenebrae — dark(ness)'
χaranγulu 112⁶ 'tenebrosus — dark'
χaranγuluχ 112⁴ (χaramγuluχ 85¹³, 86² etc.) 'tenebrae — darkness, obscurity'
χaršila- 37⁹, 45⁵ 'arguo — to reproach'
χasta 37¹⁴, 141² 'infirmus — ill'
χazyan- 38¹⁴ 'acquiro — to acquire. gain' (Arm. վաստակեմ. The translator used here the meaning of the passive instead of the active voice 'laboro — to labour')
χyjas 28¹⁴, χijas esimnin 118¹² 'conscientia — conscience' (Cf. قِياس, Kar. T. kyịas 'measuring. comparing')
χyjna- 73¹⁴ 'tormento, torturo — to torment, torture'
χylyn- 117¹³, 123³ etc. 'opero — to make, do' (Cf. CC killin-); χylyngan 115¹⁴ 'opus — deed'; χylynmaχ 119³, 122¹¹ 'id.' (28¹⁵ written: χlynmaχ)
χyrer et- 120³ 'promitto — to promise'
χyryγ 70¹³, 133⁶ 'litus — coast, shore' (Cf. Kar. T. kyryị)
χoj 72³ 'aries — ram'
χoj- passim 'pono; (con)cedo — to place; to leave'; see also χulaχ
χojun 113¹³ 'sinus — bosom'
χol passim 'manus — hand'
χol- passim 'quaero. peto — to demand. implore'
χoltχa 40¹, 112¹² etc. 'oratio. deprecatio — petition, supplication' (Arm. խնդիր. In 113¹ the translator misunderstood the expression ի խնդիր which means 'in search of'.)
χorχ- passim 'timeo — to fear'
χorχu 117⁵, 122¹⁴ etc. 'timor, metus — fear, dread'
χorχulu 122¹³ etc. 'formidabilis — dreadful'
χostovanél (Arm. խոստովանեմ) bol- 29⁸, 111¹· ¹² 'confiteor — to confess'
χostovanutjun (Arm. խոստովանութիւն) 128¹³ 'confessio — confession (of sins)'
χozu 72⁵ etc. 'agnus — lamb'
χul passim 'famulus, servus — servant'
χulaχ passim 'auris — ear'; χulaχ χoj- 54², 137¹· ⁶ 'auribus percipio. exaudio — to give ear to, listen' (Calque of Arm. ունկն դնեմ)
χuluχ (sic!) 57¹³, 69¹³ 'servitium — service'
χum 70¹³, 104⁶ 'arena — sand'
χurban 71⁹, 72⁸ etc. 'sacrificium — offering. sacrifice'. See also butov
χurγaχ 77⁴ 'ariditas — aridity'
χuš passim 'avis — bird'. See also: uč-
χutχar- passim 'libero — to deliver'
χutχarylmaχ 82¹³, 113¹⁵ etc. 'salus — salvation'
χuvat passim 'robur — power, force'

IV

ilgari (with Abl.) 123¹¹, 129¹⁰ 'prius quam — before'
ilgarigi 115⁹ etc. 'antiquus — former'
Ilov title p.¹² 'Lvov, Lemberg'
inam 123¹⁵ etc. 'fides — faith'
inangan 6¹⁰, 126³ 'credens — believer'
isi 77² 'aestus — heat'
Israjel (Arm. *իսրայէլ*) 79¹ etc. 'Israel'
iš passim 'opus — work, deed'
išit- passim 'audio — to hear'
išittir- 24⁹, 125¹³ 'auditum facio — to make hear'

jaɣyš 76¹⁵, 77⁴ 'ros, pruina — dew, white frost'
jaɣmur 76¹⁴ 'imber — rain'
jaχši, jaχšy 119⁴, ¹¹ etc. 'bonus — good'; ~ *etuči* 124⁵ 'beneficus — beneficient'
jaχšilᵘχ, jaχšylᵘχ 16¹⁴, 119¹⁰ 'bonitas — goodness'
jalanačlan- 113⁹ 'exuo — to undress, to get denuded'
jalbarmaχ 127⁵ etc. 'petitio — petition'
jalɣan 117⁹, 137¹³ 'mendax, mendacium — false, lie'
jalɣyz 74⁶ etc. 'solus — alone'
jaman 122⁹ etc. 'malus, pravus, iniquus — evil'
jamanlyχ, (-lᵘχ) 106¹⁰, ¹⁴ 'improbitas — malice'
jandyr- 118¹⁵ 'accendo — to kindle'
japuχ 116⁵ etc. 'occultus, secretum — secret'
jaratkan 111¹⁰, 120⁹ etc. 'creatura — creature'
jaratuči 111⁶ etc. 'creatrix, creator'
jarɣu 125¹⁰ etc. 'iudicium — judgment'; ~ *et-* 125⁸ etc. 'iudico — judge'
jarɣuči 125⁶ 'iudex — judge'
jarɣyχ passim 'lux, lumen — light, splendor'
jarɣyχlat- 112⁶, 114¹³ 'illumino — to enlighten'
jarɣyχly 85¹², 113⁷ 'lucidus — luminous'
jarlyɣa- passim 'misereor — to have mercy on'
jarlyɣamaχ passim 'misericordia — compassion, mercy'
jarlyɣovuči 126² etc. 'misericors — merciful'
jaš 123⁷ etc. 'lacryma — tear'
jašnamaχ 77¹⁴ 'fulgur — lightning'
jat 126⁵ 'alienus — stranger'
jaz- 116² 'scribo — to write'
jazyχ (jazᵘχ) passim 'peccatum, delictum — sin'
jazyχly passim 'sceleratus, peccator — sinful, sinner'
jeber- 110⁴, 112¹⁵ etc. 'mitto, dimitto, induco — to send, dismiss, take along'
jel 77¹ etc. 'ventus — wind'

IV

jer passim 'locus, terra — place, earth'

jerdagi 128⁸ 'terrestris — earthly'

jergalik title p.⁷ etc. 'ritus — rite'

jerrortuljun (Arm. *երրորդութիւն* and corrupt orthogr.: *եէր(ր)որդ-*) 65⁶, 110¹⁴, 129², 168⁷ 'trinitas — trinity'

Jerusayem (Arm. *Երուսաղէմ*, and corrupt orthogr.: *եէր-*) 57¹⁰, 67⁹, 149⁵ 'Jerusalem'

jyγlamaχ 39¹³ 'fletus — weeping'

joχsa passim *(joχesa* 104³) 'sed, autem — but'

joχtur passim 'non est — there is not'

jol passim 'via — way'; ∼ *korguzuči* 25⁹, 71⁶ 'dux — guide'

jolduz 70¹¹, 76¹³ 'stella — star'

jopsun- 112¹¹, 126² etc. 'suscipio, accipio — to receive, accept'

jopsunovlu 71¹⁵, 72⁷ 'acceptabilis — acceptable'

juχla- 121⁹ etc. 'dormio — to sleep'

juχov title p.⁸ etc. 'templum, ecclesia — church'

jurak passim 'cor — heart'

juraklanmaχ (sic!) 37⁷, 39⁵ etc. 'indignatio, furor — indignation, anger'

jurakli ; ašaχ ∼ 79¹¹ 'humilis corde — of humble heart'

juru- 121⁸ etc. 'eo — to walk'

juv- 38¹⁵, 123⁹ etc. 'lavo, abluo — to wash'

juvmaχ 114¹⁴ 'lotio — baptism'

juz passim 'facies — face'

kahana (Arm. *քահանա(յ)* 79³ 'sacerdos — priest'

Kapriel (Arm. *Գաբրիէլ*) 128³ 'Gabriel'

kazan (Arm. *գազան*) 78¹², 89⁹ 'bestia — wild animal, beast'

ke- : On the orthography and pronunciation of words beginning with the syllable *ke-* see: Acta Orient. Hung. XII, pp. 156.

keča passim 'nox — night, evening'

kečir- 66⁶, 124⁹ etc. 'transigo — to transmit' ·

kečkan 123¹¹ 'egressus — departure (from the world)'; *kečkanlar* 35⁶ 'defuncti — deceased'

kel- passim 'venio — to come'

kelgan 125⁵ 'adventus — arrival'

keltir- 67³ etc. 'apporto — to bring'

kerak 122⁴ 'necessarius, necessaria — necessary, necessity'

keraksyz 113⁵ 'indignus — unworthy'

keri et- 14¹⁰, 70³ 'repello — to reject'; *keri tur-* 39¹⁰ 'discedo — to withdraw (intr.)'; *keri χajt-* 40⁶ 'revertor — to turn back (intr.)'

kéro(v)pe (Arm. *քերովբէ*) 75¹⁰, 128⁵ 'cherubim'

kez passim 'mal, fois, times'; *har* ∼ 128¹¹ 'semper — every time'

IV

ki passim 'qui; ut, quod, quia — which; that'

kijdir- 113⁶, 141⁷ 'induo alicui — to put sy on (a dress)'

kimsa + neg. 38¹⁰ 'nemo — nobody'

kir- 125¹⁰ etc. 'intro — to enter'

kiši 120¹⁵, 139¹⁴ 'homo — man'

kje- : All words beginning with this syllable are listed as beginning with *ke-*.

klavuči ; jaχšy ~, ~ *jaχšylᵘχny* 48⁶, 119¹⁰ (Calque of Arm. բարեկամ 'bene + volent = friend') 'benevolens — benevolent'

kok passim 'coelum — heaven'

koktagi 76¹⁴ etc. *(kokdagi* 125¹⁵, 128⁷) 'coelestis — heavenly'

kolga passim 'umbra — shadow' (Arm. հովանի 'shadow, shade, shelter'. In 121⁵ the translator chose the meaning which does not fit into the text.)

komul- 114², 132⁴ 'sepelior — to be buried'

konu passim 'verus, iustus — true, just'

konuluk 66⁶, 67¹⁰ etc. 'veritas, iustitia, iudicium — uprightness, equity, justice'

kop passim 'multus — much, many'

kopluχ (sic!) 73⁷ etc. 'multitudo — multitude, great number'

kor- passim 'video — to see, behold'

kora passim 'secundum, propter, iuxta — according to, conformably with'

koralma- 120⁶, 126¹⁰ 'odi — to hate'

korguz- passim 'ostendo — to show'; *jol korguz-* 64¹, 119¹⁴ 'viam ostendo, perduco — to show the way, guide, lead'

korguzuči see: *jol*

kotur- passim 'levo, expando, fero — to raise, lift, bear'

koz passim 'oculus — eye'

kozat (sic!) 31², 117⁴ 'custos — guard'

kozatuči 121⁴ 'custos — guard'

k'ristonèic' (Pl. Gen. of Arm. քրիստոնէեայ) title p.³ 'Christianorum — of the Christians'

k̄s = *k'ristos* (Arm. քս) 'Christus — Christ'

kučajt- 120⁴ 'corroboro — to strengthen'

kujdur- 118¹⁰ 'uro — to burn (trans.)'

kun passim 'dies — day'

kunduz 77¹⁰ 'dies — day'; ~ *u keča* 110⁶, 121⁷ etc. 'die ac nocte — day and night'

kustunmaχ 38¹⁴ etc. 'gemitus — groaning'

kuzat- 118¹ 'dirigo — to direct' (See also *kozat)*

lusaworič (Arm. լուսաւորիչ) 127¹¹, 143¹ [S. Gregorius] 'Illuminator [ecclesiae Armenorum]. *(Eph.* p. 89. *Lusarovič* laps. cal.)

mardiros (Arm. մարտիրոս) 127¹⁵, 157¹² 'martyr' (See also *tanyχ)*

Mariam (Arm. Մարիամ) 113¹⁴ etc. 'Maria — Mary'

IV

markare (Arm. Մարքարէ) 71[6], 127[13] etc. 'propheta — prophet'

méʏa (Arm. Մեղա(յ)) 113[3], 114[5] etc. 'peccavi — I (have) sinned'

men (menim, manga [mana 151[6], 162[10]], *meni, menda, mendan)* 'ego — I'

mengi 128[12] etc. 'aeternus; saeculum — eternal; eternity'

mengilik 122[6], 125[12] etc. 'saeculum; aeternus — eternity; eternal'

menimgi 126[1] 'meus — my, mine'

Mikajél (Arm. Միքայէլ) 128[3] 'Michael'

Misajél (Arm. Միսայէլ) 79[14] 'Misael'

mušχullan-, mušχulan- 37[15], 38[3] etc. '(con-)turbor — to be vexed'

mušχuluχ (sic!) 71[15] 'conturbatio — distress, misery'

ne passim 'quid — what'

ne . . . ne 71[7] etc. 'neque . . . neque — neither . . . nor'

nečik passim 'sicut — like, as'

neki 71[1], 88[7] etc. 'sicut, velut — as, like'

niᶦat (written: Նիաթ) 70[2], 149[8] 'resolutio, testamentum — intention. resolution. testament'

očašmaχ 37[10] etc. 'ira — anger, wrath' (Cf. *oč* 18[2], 109[10] 'id.')

ogovlu 74[11], 75[1] etc. 'laudabilis — praiseworthy' (Cf. *og-* 97[7] 'laudo — to praise')

ogutla- 37[11], 45[7] 'castigo — to chasten'

oʏlan passim 'iunior — youth'; *oʏlanlar* 78[13] 'filii — sons, offsprings'

oʏul passim 'filius — son'

ol (anyng [anyn 28[4], 55[10]], *any, angar [anar* 91[5]], *anda, andan)* passim 'is, ille — he, that'; *ol turlu* passim 'ita — so'

olar kunu 122[13], 133[11] 'dies mortis — day of death'

oltur- 75[9] etc. 'sedeo — to sit'

olturʏuč 75[6] etc. 'sedes, thronus — chair, seat, throne' (ẓ and ż are frequently confounded in Arm. orthography: *Eph.* Gloss. *olturğuş*)

olu 114[3], 125[9] etc. 'mortuus — dead'

olum 38[11] etc. 'mors — death'

olumsuz 111[5] etc. 'immortalis — immortal'

olumsuzluk 123[5] 'immortalitas — immortality'

ong 121[5] etc. 'dextera (manus) — right hand'

ongalt- 16[7], 37[11] *(onalt-* 98[10]) 'sano — to heal'

op- 'osculor — to kiss'; *jerni op-* (Calque of Arm. Երկիր պագանեմ) 111[3, 13] etc. 'terram osculor, prosterner > adoro — to adore'; *jerni opmaχ* 128[9]. *jer* ~ 100[2] 'adoratio, prostratio'

opran- 39[7], 41[6], 59[1] 'invetero, veterasco — to consume (intr.), grow thin'

or 78[2] 'collis — hill'

orenk (Arm. Որէնք) 71[8] 'sacramentum, eucharistia — sacrament, etc.'

IV

orun 39¹ here: 'lectus — bedstead'
ot passim 'ignis — fire'
otlu 118⁶ 'igneus — fiery, ardent' (The first *otlu* in line 118⁶ is a misunderstanding instead of *ot.)*
ov 121⁷ etc. 'domus — house'
ovrančik 122¹⁰ 'consuetudo — habit'
ozan 78⁵ 'flumen — river'

padšahlyχ 21¹, 75⁷ 'regnum — reign'
palajlat- 118⁸ 'accendo — to inflame'
paréχosluχ (Arm. բարեխօս + suff.) 29¹⁴, 127⁶ 'intercessio — intercession'
péd[rvar] (Arm. փետրվար) title p.¹³ 'Februarius — February'
pošmanlyχ 104³, 123⁷ 'poenitentia — repentance'

saγyš 115¹³ etc. 'cogitatio — thought'
saγyšla- 119⁴ etc. 'cogito — to think'
Sahag (Arm. սահակ) 70⁶ 'Isaac'
sahat 112⁹ etc. 'hora — hour'
saχla- 68⁴‧⁶ etc. 'observo, custodio — to observe, preserve'
sal- 118⁸, 153⁴‧⁸ 'iacio — to cast, throw'
sanly 125¹⁴ 'beatus — blessed'
sarnauči 3² 'lector — reader'
sekinlik 73⁵ 'mansuetudo — gentleness' (Cf. *sekin* [սէկին] 92³ 'mansuetus — gentle, soft')
sen (senin[g], sanga [sana 42¹¹, 52¹¹], *seni, senda, sendan)* 'tu — you, thou'
semiz 72⁵ 'pinguis — fat'
sérovpe (Arm. սէրովբէ) 128⁴, 156¹⁴ 'Seraphim'
seskan- 121¹⁰ etc. 'commoveor, pertimesco — to be shaken, to get frightened'
seziklik 116¹⁴ etc. 'sensus — sense'
simarla- 122² etc. 'commendo, committo, praecipio — to commend, commit, order'
siz passim 'vos — you'
syn- 74⁴ 'conteror, rumpor — to break, crush (intr.)'
synamaχ 120¹³ etc. 'tentatio — temptation'
sonγ 'finis — end'; *sonγuga dingra (dijin)* 17¹⁴, 69¹⁵ 'in perpetuum — for ever'
sov- 33¹³, 120⁷ 'amo, diligo — to like, love'
sovak 38¹, 41⁷ etc. 'os — bone'
sovuχlar 77³ 'frigus — cold'
sovuk 118⁶ etc. 'amor — love'
sovuklu 112¹⁵ etc. 'dilectus — beloved'
sovunčluk 124¹⁴ etc. 'laetitia, exultatio — joy'

IV

soz 115[13] etc. 'verbum — word'

sozla- 117[9], 119[5] etc. 'loquor — to speak'

$\overline{sp}$ = *surp* (Arm. սուրբ) passim 'sanctus — holy' (Cf. *ari)*

Stépanos (Arm. ստեփաննս) 127[9] 'Stephanus — Stephen'

sun- 71[10] etc. 'extendo, praebeo — to present, offer'

suv 76[7], 78[10] etc. 'aqua — water'

šahar 67[7] 'civitas — city'

tšukurlu 32[10] etc. 'gratus — thankful, grateful'

ᵃba 69[11] 'opprobrium — blame, reproach' *(tabala-* 54[4] 'exprobro — to reproach')*

tay 78[1] etc. 'mons — mountain'

tayyt- 70[1] (طاغتق) 'dissipo — to scatter, disperse'

tamaša 73[9] here: 'mirabilium — miracle, wonder'. Arm.-Kipchak texts generally use the Armenian terminus: սքանչելիք *(əskančélik)* 13[8], 14[3].

tamuχ 38[12], 122[15] etc. 'infernum — hell'

tany- 74[5], 126[8] etc. 'cognosco, novi, scio — to recognise, know'

tanyχ ; burungi tanyχ 127[10] 'protomartyr' (Cf. μάρτυρος 'witness'; Arm. վկայ 'witness, martyr')

tap- 68[8], 71[11] etc. 'invenio — to find'

tapul- 72[10] 'invenior — to be found'

tapunmaχ et- 13[10], 38[12] here: 'confiteor — to confess' (Cf. χostovanél)

tarbijat, tarbiiat 111[5], 115[6], 130[13] 'natura — nature, essence'

tas et- 112[5] etc. 'disperdo, dissipo — to dispel, dissipate'

tatlylyχ 124[7] etc. 'suavitas — sweetness, suavity'

tavanutjun (Arm. դաւանութիւն) 128[13] 'confessio — confession (declaration of faith)'

temjan 71[8] (Pol. tymian, Russ. тимян) 'tus — incense'

ten 113[14], 115[8] etc. 'corpus, caro — body, flesh'

tengiz 78[5] etc. 'mare — sea'

tengri passim 'deus — god'

tengrilik 112[2] etc. 'divinitas, deitas — divinity, deity'; 115[2] 'divinus — divine'

tepraniš 118[2], 135[14] 'motus — motion'

tergovuči 116[5] 'scrutator — examiner'

tezindan 40[7] etc. 'velociter — suddenly'

tib ; tibina 124[12] etc. 'sub — under, beneath'

tibsizlik 75[11] 'abyssus — abyss'

tirgiz- 38[7] etc. 'vivifico, salvum facio — to revive, save'

tiri passim 'vivus — living'

tyn- 125[3], 165[10] 'requiesco — to rest'; *tyngan* 35[11] 'defunctus'

tynyχ 79[8] 'anima — soul, spirit'

tynsyzlyχ (sic !) 121[2] 'calamitas — calamity'

20*

IV

toγgan 116[11] 'ortus — birth'

toγru 66[8], 67[3], 68[13] etc. 'rectus, verus, iustus — right, true, just'

toγruluχ 67[10], 123[3] etc. 'iustitia, veritas — justice, rightousness'

toχtalmaχy koknun 75[13] 'firmamentum — firmament (of heaven)'

toldur- 121[11] etc. 'impleo — to fill (tr.)'

ton 59[1], 113[8] 'vestimentum, stola — garment'

tora 67[1, 3] etc. 'iudicium, lex — judgement, law'

torasiz 69[2, 5] etc. 'iniustus — unjust'

torasizlan- 67[15] (= Arm. Pass. *ախորժեցաւ*, Act.—*եաց*) 'legem perfringo, pecco — to break the law, sin'

torasizlik 39[12] etc. 'iniquitas, iniustitia — iniquity, injustice'

tošak 39[3] 'stratus — couch'

tugal 72[10] etc. 'perfectus, completus — perfect, complete'

tugalla- 127[4] 'perficio, impleo — to fulfill'

tum 150[1], 152[11] etc. 'crepusculum, vesper — sunset'. The word probably reflects a case of phonetic and semantic contamination. 1) Of the four parts of the day, *tum* denotes, in church usage: 'vesper, eventide'. It seems probable that here we have the instance of the Turkish word *tun, tün* 'evening, the time of rest' being mixed with the word *tuman* 'darkness'. (J. Deny regards *tum* as an archaism preserved in ecclesiastical usage, and he does not exclude its possible connection with the word *tuman*. *Eph.* pp. 76, 77.) 2) It can be assumed that *tum* with the meaning 'sacramentum' has a different origin. It probably originates from the Armenian word *թիւմ (tjum, tüm)* 'thymus'.

tuman tuman 72[4, 5] etc. 'innumerabilis — innumerable'

tur- 114[3], 121[10] etc. 'sto, (ex)surgo — to stay, rise'

turlu ; bu ∼ 'sic — thus'; *ol ∼* 'ita — so'; *har ∼* 36[13] 'omnis generis — of all kinds'

tuš- 77[5] etc. 'cado — to fall'

tuvar 72[3] 'pecus — cattle'

tv[aganin] (Arm. *թվականին*) title p.[13], 168[11] 'anno'

u passim (conjunction with hendiadyses, Cf. Acta Orient. Hung. XII, p. 148.) 'et — and' (Otherwise: *da*)

uč- ; učar χuš 78[10], 89[11] 'volucris — wild fowl'

učmaχ 120[2], 123[1] 'paradisus — paradise'

učun passim 'pro, propter — for, for the sake of'

ujal- 40[3, 6] 'erubesco — to be ashamed'

ujat 72[12], 140[3] 'confusio, pudor — confusion, shame'

ujatly ; ∼ et- 73[4] 'confundo — to confound, ashame sy'; *∼ bol-* 69[11], 73[13], 74[1] 'confundor — to be confounded, get ashamed'

ulu passim 'magnus — big, great'; see also *balyχ*

ulušlu bol- 124[1] etc. 'particeps fio, communio — participate, to get a share'

IV

umsa 34[7], 125[3] 'spes — hope'

umsangan 72[12] 'sperans, confidens — who trusts, hopes'

undal- 84[14], 125[2] 'vocor — to be called'

undov 125[14] 'vocatio — invitation'

urušsuz 124[9] 'incolumis — uninjured'

usna = *ustuna*

ust- ; + poss. suff.: ∼-*uma, -una* 'super (adversus) me, illum — upon (against) me, him'; *senin ustuna* or *ustuna senin(g)* 'super te — upon thee'

vaχt 69[10] 'tempus — time'; *har* ∼ 119[14] 'semper — always'

vérnadun (Arm. *վերխանութ*) 114[12], 115[4] 'caenaculum — upper room (where the last supper of Jesus was held)'

zabunluχ (زبونلق) 71[2] etc. 'infirmitas, miseria — weakness, debility'

zadasyz 30[3], 160[14] 'immaculatus — immaculate, spotless' (Arm. *անստեղ*; 115[6] the translator misread *ստեղ* 'increatus' for *անստեղ* 'immaculatus')

zaman passim 'tempus — time'

zera passim 'quoniam — because'

zulum 74[2] 'violentia — violence, force'

zurjat (ذرت Pl. ذریات) 70[10] etc. 'semina — descendants'

IV

RE-ARMENISATION AND LEXICON
FROM ARMENO-KIPCHAK BACK TO ARMENIAN

BY

E. SCHÜTZ

The language of the Podolian[1] Armenians underwent fundamental changes in the second half of the 17th century: the spoken Armeno-Kipchak gave place partly to Polish, and partly to Armenian. This process was the outcome of the general historical situation.

The basic reason of this shift lay in the change of the routes of the world trade. The discovery of America, on one side, and the circumnavigation of the African continent, on the other, from the 16th century on deprived the caravan transit trade of its importance. One part of the Armenian traders living in the south-eastern provinces of Poland (Województwo Ruskie and W. Podolskie) was compelled to migrate further to the West, the remainder took the recent and shorter trading route to Constantinople, or joined the cattle trade with a starting point in East-European countries. A considerable number of them carried on his former occupation in local retail trade and the handicraft industries (currying, tannery, goldsmith's work). Thus the route leading to the Crimea had lost its commercial significance; there was no more need for Armeno-Kipchak. In local trade the language of the state, Polish, or the language of the great part of the local population, Western Ukranian, began to assume unrivalled importance.

The second principal factor promoting the process of adopting the Polish tongue was the Church union. Under the pressure of the papal Curia and the Polish Catholic hierarchy, and the aid of the pro-Habsburg policy of the Polish king the Armenian archbishop of Lvov, Nicholas Thorossowicz during his more than half a century long rule (1623—1678) accomplished the union of the Gregorian Armenians of Podolia with the Roman Catholic Church. (Regarding the language of the liturgical literature this event brought no momentous change, since the liturgical texts had been composed only to a modest part in Kipchak, most of it was classical Armenian.)

The military situation also contributed to the diminishing use of Kipchak: Ottoman Turcs took the province of Podolia with Kamenec, the citadel of the

---

[1] As to the designation of the dialect see note 30.

V

Armeno-Kipchak language, but a great many people fled even from Lvov on
receiving the news of the advancing Turkish army.

Beside Polonisation, the other main trend of this period was the re-
Armenisation in this colony. On the Eastern borderland Polish magnates
received large feudal estates, on which they founded towns, and by promises
of granting privileges allured Armenian immigrants. In the opening phrase
of a charter translated from Polish into Armenian in 1751 we can read the following: "As I wish welfare and lustre to my inherited town Raszków, I well-
come all kinds of people, especially traders of Armenian nationality."[2]

The Ottoman Empire embarked upon its expansionist policy towards
Persia during the 16th century and the area of the renewing clashes was just
the territory of Armenia. From the country economically ruined already by
the previous conquerors, but also from the eastern provinces of Anatolia
inhabited by Armenians a steady flow of people were going towards the West,
first of all to the eastern provinces of Poland. The waves of emigration were
given added impetus especially in the first decade of the 17th century by the
jeláli wars, Shah Abbas' policy of depopulation, then the years of famine
induced thousands and thousands of Armenian families to flee towards the
West.

Of the Armenians of Tokat escaping from the *jeláli* wars, we read in the
jeremiads of two poets, fugitives themselves. Hakob Tokateci (Jacob of
Eudocia) writes:

> "They have fled to foreign countries,
> To the land of Franks and Persia."[3]

Or Stepannos Tokateci (Stephen of Eudocia) who fled also from Tokat
and finally settled down in the Crimea:

> „They were dispersed just like dust,
> All of them departed to different places.
> Some went to Istanbul,
> Some to Bursa, Adrana,
> Many of them to Urumeli,
> To the land of Franks, to Bughdan, Leh."[4]

The newcomers settled down first of all in the newly founded Polish
towns; in the two big cities Lvov and Kamenec they could gain a foothold at
best in the suburbs and had to fight against their compatriots, the previous
settlers to get a place inside the city. This process cannot be attested in its

---

[2] M. Bžškeanc', *Čanaparhordut'iwn i Lehastan*, Venice 1830. p. 165.
[3] Gh. Ališan, *Hayapatum* vol. III. p. 320. (the land of the Franks = Europe).
[4] *Ibidem* p. 315. and N. Akinean, *Hing panduxt talasac'ner*, Vienna 1921. p. 120.

V

details by documentary material; the linguistic situation must have been in the state of transition as in the same period in certain towns in Anatolia, about which we are informed by the sharp eyed Simeon Lehaci who crossed in the 1610-s as a pilgrim through Anatolia. E. g. in Kayseri, Konia "and other towns" the population living in the inner town or in the fortress *(nrsec'i, brtac'i)* did not know Armenian, only Turkish, the people in the suburbs, outskirts *(drsec'i)* did.[5]

The primary stage of the adoption of another language is bilingualism. We can hardly distinguish this phenomenon in the old texts, because anyone who masters two languages, writes equally well either in one or the other language. In consequence of their international trading activity and the unceasing historical vicissitudes, there had been very many polyglots and this faculty of theirs were made good use of by the Polish state in the 16th—17th centuries, because they were often employed as interpreters in diplomatic missions.[6]

In the following I propose to determine the extent of the period during which Polish words can be regarded as loanwords in Kipchak texts, also I examine the question how Polish got the upper hand and when it replaced Kipchak in general use. Further I shall examine in what circumstances and to what extent Armenian still survived in the Podolian area.

The sources of this change in the 17th century can be traced back to the 16th century. I refer in this connection to Minas Tokateci's literary activity. The polyglot Minas was the author of several poems in Armenian, but the main part of his life-work belongs into the sphere of ecclesiastical writings in Kipchak. To him we owe the most valuable cultural record in Kipchak of the 16th century, the translation of the Introduction of the Armenian code of laws by Mechitar Goš.[7] In the Kipchak text translated excellently from Armenian we can hardly find Armenian words, at most some ecclesiastical expressions. On the contrary, the legal, juridical terms are Polish, *e.g.*: *očizna* 'inheritance', *pokuta* 'punishment, penitence', *storož* 'ward', etc. Altogether there are only 26 Polish words to be found in the text comprising 76 manuscript pages, and even these are technical terms, so they must be considered loanwords.

The process of transition from one spoken language to the other in Podolia can be best observed through the language-use of a family the subsequent

---

[5] *Simèon dpri Lehac'woy ułegrutiwn.* Edited by N. Akinean, Vienna 1936. p. 326, 333.

[6] Reychman J., *Znajomość i nauczanie języków orientalnych w Polsce XVIII wieku.* Wrocław 1950. p. 15. Concerning gift of tongues of the alumni of the college of Theatin monks we get a vivid picture from E. Tryjarski, *Ze studiów nad rękopisami i dialektem kipczackim Ormian polskich,* Rocznik Orient. XXIII/2. p. 39. sqq.

[7] *Hing panduxt,* p. 84 — The photocopy of the manuscript text see RO XXI. (1957) p. 166—240.

V

generations of which composed the Kamenec Chronicle. The Chronicle had been begun in Armenian by Der Hovhannes, an archpriest, who continued it until his death (1611). The continuer of the Chronicle, priest Axent, was a man who new several languages, and so he had been often sent on Polish diplomatic missions to negotiate with the Turks between the years 1613—1621.[8] Though the part of the Chronicle composed by him is in Kipchak, but the proportion of foreign words allows us to conclude that bilingualism attained already an advanced stage. The 43 manuscript pages (the chapters of the Chronicle relating the events of the Cecora and Khotin war) contain 534 Kipchak word items, and already 310 Polish ones, i.e. the proportion is 60 : 34%.[9]

Bilingualism is well characterised by the rate of words belonging to the different grammatical categories (in round figures): nouns 130, composite verb forms 90, adverbs, conjunctions 50, adjectives 40. Especially characteristic is the high proportion of verbs. The verbs are composed of Polish infinitives and the Turkish auxiliary verb *et-*, or reflexive infinitives (in two cases Polish past Participle + Polish *się* or Ukranian-Russian *-cя*) + Turkish auxiliary *bol-*.

If priest Axent's brother, archpriest Hagop (Jacob) had made some entries in the Annals of Kamenec, these must have been done in Polish. The characterisation given by Axent shows that Hagop was mixing a great deal with Polish ecclesiastical people.[10]

Such phenomena permit the inference that bilingualism with some social circles of the Armenian community tended towards the adoption of the Polish language. The dates of the official documents provide us with a foothold concerning the culmination point of this process.

The marriage contracts and the wills of the members of the Armenian community of Lvov have come down to us in 3 volumes. The first volume contains the records of the period 1572—1630, the second from 1630 to 1642, both in Kipchak, but the end of the third (A. D. 1643—1667) already in Polish.[11]

---

[8] In 1613 interpreter and intendant of the mission of Adam Górski. See Kamenec Chronicle Venice MS 88[8—10]; in 1619 member of the escort accompanying the family of Simeon, the Prince of Moldavia, ibid. 106[21—22]; in 1620 attendant of Turkish Chawshes to Warsaw, ibid. 107[5—6].

[9] Kamenec Chronicle MS 107—115, 122—157. The occurring Turkish words totalling 4% are military, administrative technical terms. Considering that the text deals with the war of Osman II., the use of Turkish words is minimal. There is only one Rumanian word: *pyrkalab* 'intendant' 2% of the words are Armenian.

[10] See Schütz E., *An Armeno-Kipchak Chronicle on the Polish—Turkish Wars* in 1620/21. (in the press) Series: BOH MS p. 13 sqq.

[11] Mechitarist Library in Vienna, MS No. 441. — Mechitarist Library in Venice, MS No. 1788. — Mech. Lib. in Vienna, No. 447. — See Dashian J., *Catalog der armenischen Handschriften in der Mechitaristen Bibliothek zu Wien*, Vienna. 1895. p. 919.

V

A paschal table of the years 1654—1671 has been preserved in Kipchak.[12] The last ecclesiastical texts in Kipchak that have come down to us are the homilies of Anton vardapet.[13]

One of the most important group of records are the protocols of the jury of Kamenec from the years 1559—1664.

The sequence of dates provided by these documents will serve as a very important piece of evidence in determining the date of transition to the adoption of a new language. From the comments of V. R. Grigorian we infer that entries in Polish occur only towards the end of these records.[14]

Concerning our topic we possess the most substantial evidence in the entries of the birth-register of Lvov. Births are entered into the register from 1681 on in Polish, and the register of deaths is written in Polish from 1671 on.[15]

All these data testify that in the Podolian colony of Armenians Kipchak as a commonly used language yielded its place to Polish.[16] As a result of the historical-economical motives outlined above the Kipchak speaking group became all the more reduced in members, and most of the priests of local birth gradually took up the use of Polish, as a second mother tongue.[17]

Naturally, this process was not complete and absolute, and older people continued to use their traditional speech. We find interesting evidence of this e.g. in the protocols of council elections and the court protocols of the town Stanisławów. On the margin of the protocols of the municipality elections in the years 1681—1689 some dozen pages contain Kipchak glosses, and the same is the case with the court protocols of the years 1692—1702. On the other

---

[12] Bibliothèque Nationale, Paris MS Arm. No. 170. Here the final date does not serve as a definite basis as the table must have been drawn up before-hand, i.e. in 1653.

[13] Mech. Libr. in Vienna MS No. 479, 480, 481.

[14] From the 32 volumes originally known there remained only 27 (15.254 pages). From these texts only a fraction has been published up to now. I. I. Hrunin published four of the earliest entries (1559) composed in Kipchak. Академику В. А. Гордлевскому к его 75-летию. Moscow 1953. pp. 90—97. His book containing 280 additional entries is to appear shortly. V. Ř. Grigoryan was the first to draw up a list of the volumes according to the subsequent years: *Kamenec'-Podolsk kayaki haykakan datarani ardzanagru'yunnera (XVI d.)* (Tribunal acts of the town Kamenec Podolsk, XVI. cent.) Yerevan 1963. — As to the language of their composition it is necessary to observe that most of the entries are in Kipchak, some volumes are in Armenian and only the end is composed in Polish. See V. Ř. Grigoryan, *op. cit.* 45—46.

[15] Mechitarist Library in Vienna MS No. 440. 31/a—46/b; 47/a—51/b.

[16] Polish documents in Armenian script have recently been published by V. Grigoryan and A. Pisovich who point out their value for the history of the Polish language: *Hayatar leheren vaveragrera* (Polish documents in Armenian Script) In: *Banber Matenadarani* No. 7. 225—236.

[17] Bžškeanc' refers to a Prayer Book in Kipchak printed in 1705. I hope I have succeeded in proving that this dating was due to a misunderstanding. *AOH* XIII. p. 129.

V

hand, in the electoral protocols of 1736—1742 the marginal entries are only in Armenian.[18]

With the Armenians of Podolia another parallel linguistic trend can be observed: the re-Armenisation of the colony. The historical background to this process — as exposed above — was the waves of immigrant groups.

As a matter of fact, "re-Armenisation" sounds a paradox since the official language of the church of the colony had always been Armenian. But we should not forget that the Armenian manuscripts written in the 16th century in this area are for the most part copies, as the majority of the priests of local origin could not even understand Armenian liturgical texts.

The authors of the original literary works composed during this period in this area were not of local origin, but were mostly immigrants from Tokat (or the Crimea), and the language of their works was almost unmixed Grabar.

Minas, the most prolific Armenian writer of the 16th century of this area, composed official documents of the Armenian parish of Lvov in Kipchak, but wrote his poems in Armenian. Minas came from Tokat but his Grabar language contained only a sprinkling of foreign words; so e.g. in his droll poem "Panegyric on the *herissa*" (1562) there are but a few Turkish (including Arabic) words: *xabar* 'message', *yaldel* (غلط + Armenian Inf. ending -b_l) 'to commit an error', *yabul anel* 'receive', *yarib* 'wanderer', *armayan* 'gift'.[19]

In his Jeremiad about the 1551 events in Wallachia (= Moldavia) there appear the almost international terms *vojvoda, vojt* (Vogt), *byrgar* (Bürger) (lines 131, 179) and a few special Rumanian terms: *armaş* 'Rumanian nobleman' (lines 71, 133, 313), *vister* 'the vestiary of the church' (lines 62, 70, 84, etc. *Mintank* 'Muntenia' (+ Arm. Plural ending -p, line 293.)[20]

Hakob of Tokat (from 1604 priest of Zamość) relates in his Jeremiad the events which occurred in the years 1593—1595. Nonetheless, there are no Rumanian words in his poems; the category of foreign words only include a few Ottoman Turkish military expressions: *top* 'canon', *tifang* 'gun, rifle', *vazir* 'vizier', *sanjax* 'banner' (lines 41, 117, 215.).[21] In his Jeremiad on the ruin of Tokat the vocabulary is similar to this, except that some words of daily use are to be found in it: *yumaš* (قیمش) 'cloth', *bezastan (bezestan)* 'bazaar', *šadyrvan* 'fountain (for ablutions)', *bazirgjan* 'dealer', etc.[22]

In the "Jeremiad on the fall of Tokat" composed by Stepannos also from Tokat the elements of vocabulary are similar: *tazi* 'greyhound', *čadyr* 'tent', *čardyx* 'trellis', *araxjeni* 'cloth', *tapsi* 'pan'.[23]

[18] *Katalog rękopisów ormiańskich i gruzińskich.* By K. Roszko and J. Braun. Warshaw 1958. Nos. I. 23, 25 and 24. pp. 24—25.

[19] N. Akinean, *Hing panduxt*, p. 103—111. lines 12, 27, 28, 170, 191.

[20] *Ibid.* 85—102.

[21] Akinean N., *Matenagrakan hetazotutiwnner*, IV. Vienna 1938. p. 4. sqq.

[22] Ališan Gh., *Hayapatum* III. 317—322.

[23] *Ibid.* 307—316.

V

Lazar Tokateci belonged also to this wave of immigrants who fled to the land of "Ruz" (Województwo Ruskie) in the first decade of the 17th century. In 1606 he was conferred upon the office of priest in Jazlowiec, and later Kamenec. His poems also deal with the loss of Tokat. ("The praise of Tokat", "The ruin of Tokat").

Besides the immigrants from East-Anatolia there also came from the Crimea immigrants who had been allured by the advantegeous privileges.

One of the most outstanding prose writing of the Podolian area at the beginning of the 17th century was the Travel Account of Simeon Lehaci (of Poland) of his pilgrimage in the Turkish Empire, Italy, Egypt, Jerusalem in the years 1608—1619. Simeon's parents had migrated some time in the 16th century from Caffa to Zamość, where Simeon attained the grade of an ecclesiastical scribe *(dpir)*. The language of the Travel Accounts is pure Grabar in the religious passages, but otherwise a common spoken language of a literary standard. The major part of his itinerary took him across Turkish territory and so it is not surprising that we find several hundred Turkish words in his Accounts of literary value. Aside from these, foreign words are rather rare in the Accounts; Polish words e.g. *altembas* 'brocart', *pivnica* 'cellar', *čamlit* 'camlot', and some more.[24]

These Armenian immigrants from Anatolia and the Crimea maintained Armenian as a spoken language in the Podolian and Russian provinces of Poland. The language of everyday life and that of literature were sharply separated in grammar aswell as in vocabulary, but the somewhat loose Grabar of Minas and Simeon's language full of foreign words and grammatical forms of the vulgar tongue were the resuscitating factors of the Armenian tongue which was already on the verge of submerging in the Podolian area.

An important role was played in the maintenance of Armenian by the continuing use of Grabar in the Church.[25] We must, however, point out that at the commencement of the 17th century most of the local clergy did not understand it, and so Armenian would have remained but a dead letter, had it not been for the Armenians arriving from the East *(panduxt — yarib)*. The literary works of the new immigrants are not copies of religious texts incomprehensible for them, but a living literature, and the priests and notaries who wrote them contributed by their spoken language to the maintenance of Armenian also in these districts.

The newcomers were welcomed by the whole network of newly founded Polish towns (Zamość, Jazlowiec, Stanislawów, etc.). The Armenian and other

[24] *Simèon dpri Lehac'woy Utegrutiwn*, pp. XIII and passim. With the Ottoman-Turkish loanwords we shall deal in a separate paper: *Turkish Loanwords in Simeon Lehaci's Travel Accounts.*

[25] *Banber Matenadarani* No. 7. p. 225.

Acta Orient. Hung. Tomus XIX. 1966

V

merchants of Lvov and Kamenec no doubt tried to prevent the business competitors from settling down, and at most they were tolerated in the suburbs.[26] The linguistic revival, the re-Armenisation of the business centres should be conceived of as taking place in a centripetal way. The language of the new settlers in the country or in the suburbs served as a regenerative force in the use of Armenian in daily speech. It is a noteworthy fact that from Zamość Simeon found his way to Lvov, and Lazar Tokateci from Jazlowiec to Kamenec, i.e. their carreers show this centripetal trend.[27]

Unfortunately the texts published up to now hardly reflect the everyday language of this period of linguistic revival, that of re-Armenisation. Still, we possess a fairly good proof of it, in the text of the privilege granted by Joseph Liubomirski to the Armenians in Raszków in 1751.[28] The *Prawa*, the privilege was translated from Polish into Armenian by Oxentios Nikoleanc, son of Khosrow and was commissioned by Augustinowicz, the Armenian archbishop of Lvov. The language of the document is the spoken idiom sprinkled with graber expressions, and besides there are to be found some grammatical forms being the peculiarities of the -*um* branch of dialects.[29] But the official grabar is every now and then pushed aside by forms of Polish-Armenian, so it must be inferred that the translator fully aquired aswell the spokem idiom of this area. The lexical structure of it gives a characteristic picture of the spoken language of that period. There are in it some 60 Polish, and some 60 Turkish words. There is only one Kipchak word: *kora* 'according to'. The Polish words are exclusively juridical terms: *privileg, artikul, dekret, protokul, kontribucia, ržečpospolita* (= rzecz pospolita) 'state', *urend* (= urząd) 'office', *činš* (= czynsz) 'tax', *probošč* (= proboszcz) 'priest', *strona* 'party', *pčatel* 'to seal', *pozov anel* 'to summon'. The Turkish words occurring in it are common expressions: *bazirgan* 'merchant', *gelur* 'income', *xarǰ* 'expenditure', *ǰurum* 'crime (cürüm)', *sunčlux* 'guilt (suçluk)', *γavγa* 'strife (qavγa)'. It is interesting that Christian (canonical) law is denoted by an expression of Mohammedan law: *šariat*. Adjectives: *tamam* 'complete', *bašxa* 'separate'; verbs: *tamamel* 'to complete', *xarǰel* 'to expend', *ǰurumel* 'to commit a crime' (with Armenian verbal ending). All in all we get the general view that expressions referring to the state-apparatus were rendered in the official state language, while the Ottoman Turkish expressions already formed part of the basic vocabulary of the spoken language of the settlers.

As can be seen, even a single document composed in the common language can furnish us with a helpful detail about the evolution of Armenian

---

[26] Armenian speaking new-comers were allowed to settle down only in the outskirts; the same can be seen in several towns of Anatolia: Kayseri, Sivas, etc. See above.

[27] *Ułegruťiwn*, p. 355. — *Hing panduxt*, p. 211.

[28] Bžškeanc῾ M., *Čanaparhorduťiwn i Lehastan*, pp. 165—175.

[29] Ačaryan, *K῾nnuťyun Ardiali barbaři*, Ycrevan 1953. p. 201.

V

from the 17th century onwards. It is to be hoped that records of this kind will enable us to see more clearly the trend of the history of Podolian Armenian.

Information by travellers can generally provide but scanty aid to drawing conclusions concerning language history; at most we can find out which of the three languages (Armenian, Kipchak or Polish) people spoke. But even this information is useful, because the church registers give us only the number of the members of the parish, but no evidence which language they spoke. The notes of Minas Bžškeanc made at the time of his visit in 1820 are useful comments, when e.g., he remarks that in Tysmienica the population speaks a "very pure" Armenian, the situation is the same in Śniatyn, or what is even more "there are many old people who do not know any other language". At the same time in Stanisławów Bžškeanc states disapprovingly, that there are "many people who have forgotten Armenian".[30] This also testifies to the fact that there were many who still did speak their mother tongue. Bžškeanc was a learned Mechitarist and so his comment on the linguistic situation is of great value.

The question is: can we speak of a linguistical continuity in these provinces between the 17th and 20th centuries? To answer this question we must examine the so-called Polish-Armenian of the end of the 19th century.[31]

The designation "Polish-Armenian" is of course very wide, because it is, as a matter of fact, the language of just a single small town, Kuty. It is questionable if we are justified to generalize about the language of the town, or rather, if the dialect of Kuty was the organic successor of that of the population of the 16—17th centuries speaking Armeno-Kipchak, or if we have to deal with a "re-Armenisation" process.

Ačarian in his grammar connects the parlers of Kuty, Suceava and Transylvania into one under the denomination the "dialect of Ardial". The linguistic criteria make the connection fully justified, these three parlers are branches springing from the same root.

Historical fact testifies to the fact that these three parlers were also locally of the same origin. Kuty had been founded at the end of the 17th century by immigrants from Moldavia, in fact, by four Armenian families under the leadership of Krisztof Szadbey. The descendants of these families

---

[30] Bžškeanc'. *Čanapahrordut'iwn*, pp. 124, 125, 121.

[31] The dialect is generally called Polish-Armenian in the literature. This term is used by Hanusz *O języku Ormian polskich. I. Wyrazy zebrane w Kutach nad Czeremoszem.* Cracow 1886. and *Lautlehre der Polnisch-Armenischen Mundart von Kuty.* Wien 1889. — Y. Daškevič in his historiographical guide: Армянские колонии на Украине в источниках и литературе XV—XIX веков. Yerevan 1962. and other papers calls the dialect "(West) Ukrainian". I myself have chosen for convenience's sake a *pars pro toto* denomination, "dialect of the Podolian area", including. of course, the "Russian voyvodship" as well.

V

were called "osadcy" also in the later times.[32] One part of the population originated from Kamenec. In consequence of the royal privileges (the first dated 18th July 1715) more and more families settled. In about 1820 Bžškeanc found here 175 Armenian families.[33]

The third branch, the Armenians of Transylvania, also come in the 70's of the 17th century in large groups to Transylvania. Still I do not find adequate the denomination "of Ardial", because the settlers of Kuty aswell as those of Transylvania came from Moldavia.

The historical factors can be seen reflected also in the vocabulary. The lexical material collected by J. Hanusz in Kuty can be divided into the following groups: the main part (two 3rds) of the 1500 words is Armenian, $^1/_3$ part of it are Turkish, Rumanian and Slavic loanwords, i.e. one 10th each of the total vocabulary.[34] But it is worthwhile to take a closer look at the proportion of each group of foreign words. The latest (Slavic) stock came partly from the West-Ukranian local population and partly from the Polish (state) language, cca 90 words. These words can be considered as belonging to the basic vocabulary. The number of Polish and Ukranian words used on occasion is considerably greater. Hanusz entered into his word list only those for which the speakers did not know the Armenian equivalent.

Next to Slavic words in number follow the Ottoman Turkish words, cca 80—90. The exact number of these cannot be ascertained, because we cannot tell in each case to which language a certain word belongs, whether to Turkish or Kipchak. One part of the Turkish words the Armenians possibly brought with them from their previous home in Turkey, the other part probably entered their daily speech from the *lingua franca* of eastern trade. This process could take place the more readily as in the beginning of modern times Istanbul became one terminus of the trading routes of Armenian merchants.

How deeply these Turkish words were rooted in the basic stock of the vocabulary of Kuty Armenians is shown by the fact that about two generations after Hanusz's visit to Kuty we can still find these words in their language, as e.g. in texts of an ethnographical and folklore nature published recently by K. Roszko we find some 30 of them.[35]

Considering that the common language *(bizim til)* of Podolian Armenians in the 16—17th centuries was Kipchak, there can be found relatively few

---

[32] Baracz S., *Rys dziejów ormianskich.* Ternopol 1869. p. 100. — Bžškeanc`, *Čanaparhordu`iwn,* p. 127. — C. Roszko, *Les Arméniens de Kuty,* In: *REA NS* t. I. (1964) p. 379. It must be mentioned that a family named Szadbey is known also from Kamenec.

[33] At the end of the 19th century these Armenians too gradually coalesce with the local population. Of the 1400 Armenians belonging to the Armenian parish there are only 500 who speak Armenian. Hanusz, *O języku,* pp. 129, 130, 132.

[34] Hanusz, *Lautlehre,* pp. 5—6.

[35] *Folia Orientalia,* Cracow I/2. pp. 274—295. and IV. pp. 171—187.

V

Kipchak words in the Kuty dialect. Ačarian gives a "List of Tatar loanwords in the Polish Armenian dialect",[36] but this designation is misleading, as there are at most 5 words of Kipchak character among them, the rest, cca 18, are Ottoman Turkish. Probably Ačarian meant modern Crimean Tatar, which during the long rule of the Turks in the Crimea, and in the 19th century through the Panturkist currents, adopted a considerable number of Ottoman Turkish words.

Neither is it probable that the Suceava dialect — a monograph of which was made by Ačarian[37] — would have no Turkish and just one Kipchak word (čebar).[38] This can be hardly true, because according to Bittner the Rumano-Armenian dialect had adopted, or at least kept, "anscheinend" more old Turkish-Tatar elements than her sister dialect in Poland.[39] So we are compelled to assume that Ačarian's speaker, a priest having come for ordination to Ejmiacin, did not find it necessary to make mention of Turkish words in an Armenian grammar.

J. Hanusz in his word-list of the Kuty dialect "O języku Ormian polskich"[40] gives in each case the etymology of the word, and points also to its Kipchak origin. The correction of his errors and the rectifying of the defects was undertaken by T. Kowalski in his article "Wyrazy kipczackie w języku Ormian polskich".[41] In the following we wish to make some comments on Kowalski's views.

The most solid layer of Kipchak etymologies is constituted by the loanwords in which there is a phonetic criterion testifying the Kipchak origin of the word. Such words are but few: avalgu 'ancien, antique', kozlukh 'lunettes' (Kowalski includes it in the row of Ottoman Turkish words), kora 'according to'.[42]

Kowalski points out only a few general characteristics of the loanwords. The aspiration of unvoiced stops and affricates is considered by him an Armenian "innovation". But if we examine the question a little closer, we see that there is no sound-shift at all involved. Hanusz is not always consistent in the denoting of sounds, several times — especially finally — he writes unvoiced

---

[36] Ačaṙyan, Aṙdial, p. 191.

[37] Pazmaveb, Venice 1899. Discussing only phonetics, the rest is unpublished. (See Adjarian, Classification des dial. arm. Paris 1909. p. 79.)

[38] This seems all the less probable since — according to Şaineanu — the Rumanian language alone contains cca 1500 Ottoman—Turkish and cca 150 Tatar loanwords. Influenţa orientala asupra limbei şi culturei Romăne. I—III. Bucureşti. 1900.

[39] Einige Kuriosa aus dem armenischen Dialekte der Walachei und der Moldau. In: Huschardzan, Vienna 1911. p. 362.

[40] Cracow 1886. We always give the meanings after this work, in French.

[41] In: Księga pamiątkowa ku czci J. E. Hachana H. Seraji Szapaszała. Wilno 1938. and resume in: Sprawozd. PAU XLII. 1938. No. 6.

[42] Bittner, op. cit. p. 367.

V

stops instead of aspirates.[43] The description of this sound is not so simple, as we can see from Ačarian's characterisation. Ačarian calls them "aspirated voiced stops" *(šnč̣ey t̔rt̔run,* transcribed: *p̣', ṭ', ḳ'),* but mentions at the same time that the corresponding Armenian sound (of the dialects of Suceava and of Kuty) is not voiced, but is pronounced as French or Slavic *p, t, k.* The characterisation of the sound is uncertain, as, in all probability, the sound itself was unstable. The unstableness between aspirate and unvoiced stop was a common feature of some western dialects; in western literary language the two kinds of sound coincided and the antecedents of the process can be well observed also in the Armeno-Kipchak script in the 16th—17th centuries.

The existence of voiced and unvoiced stops is one of the surest criteria whether the word belongs to the Kipchak or to the Ottoman group. Initially the correlation is unambigous. But in final position we can find alternations: *-k, -g, -γ.* Common Turkish *-k* in some cases correlates with *-k : kobulak* 'papillon',[44] (Arm. of Transylvania *kobulak ;* cf. CC *kobelek,* Ott-T. *kebelek) ; došak* 'lit de dessus' (Cf. CC *dosak,* etc. Ott-T. *döşek).* But we find *-g : churug* 'mauvais' (Cf. CC *curumac* 'marcedo', Ott-T. *çürük* 'rotten, spoilt') and *orog* 'quenouille' (Cf. Arm. of Nor Nakhichevan *orokʿ,* Ott-T. *öräkä).* We find *-γ* e.g. in *čičaγ* 'fleur' (Cf. CC *zizac,* etc. Ott-T. *çiçek).* A correlation of this kind is to be found also in a word of velar tone: *xazuγ* 'pieu, échalas'. The final *-g* is not a Kipchak characteristic, but appears in East-Anatolian dialects, as well as in the borrowings of Armenian dialects; in Akn it is a common phenomenon: e.g. *ēt̔eg* 'pan d'un habit', *ēkʿsüg* 'défectueux', *ēmēg* 'effort', *ip̔ēg* 'soie', etc.[45]

On a semantical basis only a few Kipchak words can be separated from the Turkish ones. So e.g. *xonax* 'hôte'[46] (Cf. Houtsma Gl. *kânak* 'idem', Karaim of Luck-Halicz *konak* 'idem'). Contrarily, the first meaning of Turkish *qonaq* is 'station, inn'. We find a similar case with *baška.*[47] The phonetic form is some what peculiar, instead of *k* we would expect *x,* which in Kipchak generally corresponds to *q.* So we must assume this to be a pronunciation peculiar to the speaker. The expected form *bašxa* is all the more justifiable as this form was, in all probability, connected by the speakers with the Armenian verb *bašx(el)* 'séparer'. In such a form and meaning it is to be found also in Armeno-Kipchak records, e.g. the Kamenec Chronicle (Venice MS 133[14]) *bašxa* 'apart, separatedly'.

Kowalski regards velar articulation as an essential criterion of Kipchak. E.g. *čičaγ* 'fleur', *čhebar* 'propre, net'. The tendency towards velarization in the second and third syllables *(ä, ȧ)* is, by all means, a characteristic feature

[43] Ačaryan, *Aṙdial,* p. 16.

[44] *Handes Amsorya* 1897. p. 249. apud Ačaryan, *Aṙdial,* p. 196. Bittner, *op. cit.* p. 367.

[45] Maxudianz M., *Le parler Arménien d'Akn.* Paris, 1912. p. 109.

[46] To be found also in Roszko's texts: *FO* I. p. 293.

[47] *Ibid.* p. 291, 275[6], but see 276[23]: *bašxa.*

V

of Kipchak, but it can also be found in other Turkish languages, so, among others, in the dialects of Eastern Anatolia. Therefore other criteria must also be considered, e.g. the vocalism of the word *burjak* "exactly corresponds" to the Troki Karaim form,[48] but the medial *j* does not hint to Kipchak.

If a Turkic word has no peculiar phonetical characteristics Kowalski considers its occurrence in old Kipchak texts decisive in favour of Kipchak origin even when the word is to be found in Ottoman Turkish. So e.g. *čočxa* 'cochon de lait' (Cf. Houtsma Gl. *čučka*, Kowalski reads: *čočka*) ; *ozga* 'autre' (Cf. CC *oxga*, Ott-T. *özge*) ; *bikha* 'madame'[49] is absent from Ott-T. vocabulary.

In this matter, of course, absolute consistency cannot be achieved. E.g. Kowalski assigns the word *ǰigar* 'foie'[50] to the category of Ottoman-Turkish borrowings, though the word is found as early as the Codex Cumanicus in the special meaning 'figatus, Leber' *(gigar)*.

Kowalski applies the right method with Persian and Arabic loanwords in investigating the channel through which the given word entered the Kuty dialect. Here we hardly possess any phonetic criterion, and in the majority of the cases one has to accept Kipchak origin if the word appears in early Kipchak texts. So e.g. *xɔjar* 'concombre' (Cf. CC *chear*), or *mɔskhin* 'pauvre diable' (Cf. CC *miskin*). *Bazyrgan* Kowalski ranks among Turkish borrowings, though here one should take into account that this word occurs already in the Codex Cumanicus: *baxargan* 'mercator'. Though the possibility cannot be excluded that the same word entered by several channels.

In the case of Arabian-Persian words there is also a third possibility, the word may belong also to the Armenian basic vocabulary. So *e.g.* Kowalski classes the word *prindz* 'riz' with Ottoman-Turkish loanwords, although *princ* (բրինձ) is a Persian loanword in Armenian from the pre-Turkish period.[51] *Nišan* 'signe' may also be suspected to be of Armenian origin, the Armenian *n'šan* (նշան) belonging to the earliest Iranian loanword stock,[52] but because of the full *i* (instead of a shwa) we have to drop our supposition of Armenian origin. In classifying the word *nijath* we have an overwhelming argument in favour of Kipchak, the word often occurring in Armeno-Kipchak texts, in the *Alyyš Bitiki* and the *Tora Bitiki* in the meaning of 'intention, resolution, testament'.[53] In all probability on the basis of velarity we have to rank *mušxul* 'triste'[54] *(mušxulutⁱin* 'tristesse') among the Kipchak words. Kowalski derived the word together with the Karaim *muzyul* 'betrübt' from

[48] Kowalski, *Wyrazy*, p. 34.
[49] Ačaryan, *Ařdial*, p. 225. *FO* I. 291.
[50] Kowalski, *Wyrazy*, p. 39.
[51] Hübschmann, *Arm. Gramm.* I. 124.
[52] *Ibid.* p. 205—206.
[53] *AOH* XV. (1962) p. 305. *AOH* XII. (1961) p. 155.
[54] See also *FO* I/2. p. 294.

V

the Arabic *maḥzūn* with reference to a *hz* > *zh* metathesis and a sound-shift from *n* to *l*. But against this vague supposition it seems more probable that the origin of the word goes back to the Arabic جـ. The Ottoman-Turkish has a palatal timbre against which in Armeno-Kipchak we find the common velar form, e.g. in the *Alyyš Bitiki mušxullan-*, *mušxulan-* 'conturbor, to be vexed', *mušxulux* 'conturbatio, distress, misery'.[55]

The originally Persian *xodža* could have been borrowed by Armenian either from Kipchak, or from Ottoman-Turkish, at any rate, it existed also in Armenian dialects of Turkey. Scribe Simeon Lehaci characterises the upper class of Armenian population of Caesarea (Kayseri) in 1616—1618 in such terms: "rich merchants, famous *hodjas* of geat wealth".[56] The special meaning of the word 'rich' seems to be specially Armenian, and I think that the same meaning in Karaim was borrowed from Armenian. — A similar loanword seems to be in Kuty Armenian the word *galadži*. It appears in Houtsma's Glossary as *külāči* (Kowalski reads: *güladži*),[57] and *keleci* in Ottoman-Turkish dialects. The word is familiar in the Armenian dialects of Arabkir, Nicomedia, the Crimea, Nor Nakhičevan, Ozmi and Van.[58] Thus it may be supposed that the settlers of Kuty had brought it with them originally from their native land.

Kowalski does not accept as proved some Armenian etymologies presented by Hanusz. His doubt was possibly aroused by the phonetic features of the given equivalent: Hanusz quoted only the classical form, without mentioning that the pronunciation in Kuty was just the opposite, the Western one.

The word *jerga* 'ordre, soin', *anjerga* 'desordonné' Hanusz derives from classical Armenian *erk* 'fatigue, peine'.[59] Thomson accepts the etymology.[60] E. Słuszkiewicz tries to find a combined solution, but thinks that form and meaning have changed under Turkish influence. Kowalski is rather for Turkish origin, because of the form and meaning "deviating from the classical".[61] It must be remarked that the Western form *jerg* would not have been so deviating, but the Armenian origin is out of question, and the word has a sound Kipchak etymology. We can add, moreover, the derived form from Armeno-Kipchak *jergalik* 'rite'.[62]

According to Hanusz *korkoralu* originates of the Armenian *grgřel* 'provocare, incitare'. Kowalski finds neither the phonetic form, nor the meaning satisfactory, and connects it rather with the Turkish verb *kökre-*. Indisputably

[55] *Wyrazy*, p. 37. *AOH* XV. p. 305.
[56] *Simeon*, p. 326.
[57] See also *FO* I. 292. — *Wyrazy*, p. 35.
[58] Ačarean, *Hayerèn gawaṙakan baṙaran*. Tiflis 1913. p. 536.
[59] Hanusz, *O języku*, p. 75.
[60] А. И. Томсон, К фонетике говора польских (галицких) армян. p. 16—17.
[61] *Wyrazy*, p. 36.
[62] *AOH* XV. p. 303.

V

the origin of the word is not the word given by Hanusz, but the onomatopoetic *gorgoŕal*, Western Armenian *korkoŕal* which can be found in the dialects of Yerevan, Shirak, Van and Tilflis in the meaning 'to emit a sound like that of thunder'.[63]

Kowalski's suspicion as regards the Armenian etymology of *dzara* 'le domestique, servant' might have been aroused also by the classical form which deviates from the Kuty pronunciation. In the case of *caŕaj* the divergence was stressed by the error of the diacritical sign ˇ having been shifted to the next consonant and so there resulted a word *čaraj*, a form strongly reminiscent of the Kipchak word *čora*. Kowalski puts the question what connection there could be between the Armenian word of Kuty and the word in Troki Karaim *čora*.[64] The Karaim word is undoubtedly connected with the Polish *ciura, ciora* 'idem'. Słerski quotes also the equivalents of several Slavic languages,[65] but "because of the diversity of phonetic forms and meanings" he, at last, accepts Kowalski's solution, deriving the Polish word from the Kipchak *čora, ciora*.[66] But to return to our main problem. We must observe that the word *dzara* of the Armenians has no connection with the Polish and Kipchak words, having since the earliest written records belonged to the basic word stock of Armenian. We have tried to disentangle the coil of problem around these homonymous words, because the Polish word *ćura, ciura* often appears in Armeno-Kipchak texts,[67] as a denomination of 'horsegroom' in service of the Polish army.

In the case of *amunčnalu* 'être honteux' Kowalski (and also E. Słuszkiewicz) accepted the solution given by Hanusz, but queried if the Turkish *imenč* 'idem' had not influenced the phonetic picture of the Armenian word.[68] The epenthetic consonant *n* is also to be found in other words in the Armenian dialect of Kuty, e.g. *sunč* < Turkish *suč* 'coulpe'.[69] Of this phonetic peculiarity we can find more examples also in neighbouring Armenian dialects, as e.g. արտասունք (*artasuk'*) 'tear', Suceava dialect *ardasunk'*, Kuty *ardusunkh*,[70] or կանաչ *kanač'*, Suceava, Kuty *gananč'* 'green, verdant', in texts noted by K. Roszko: *gananč'nier* 'légumes vertes'.[71] The word in question sounds similarly in the dialect of Suceava: *amənč'nal*. This phenomenon is not a

---

[63] *Hayerèn gawaŕakan baŕaran*, p. 250 and *kəŕkəŕal* 256.

[64] Kowalski, *Karaimische Texte ... von Troki*, p. 178.: 'Knecht, Pferdeknecht', Radloff *Wb.* III. 2019 'Arbeiter'.

[65] The etymologies given by Brückner are acceptable neither from a phonetic, nor from a semantic point of view. *Słownik etym. języka polskiego*. Warshaw 1957. p. 65.

[66] *Symbolae gramm. in honorem I. Rozwadowski*, II. 1928. pp. 350—351. apud Sławski, *Słownik etym. języka polskiego*. Cracow I. 1952—1956. p. 105. It could hardly be a Slavic word, anyhow, as it has only existed in Polish since the 17th century.

[67] Kamenec Chronicle MS 133[11], 152[9].

[68] *Wyrazy*, p. 33.

[69] Hanusz, *O języku*, p. 112.

[70] Ačaryan, *Aŕdial*, p. 124.

[71] *FO* IV. p. 182.

V

peculiarity of the Western dialects, but appears also in the East, so e. g. in Tiflis: *amančil*.[72]

Against Hanusz's etymology *xayran* 'vestibule', class. Arm. *xałaran* Kowalski compares the word with Karaim *kaxra* 'idem'. As we have not more examples either of the Kuty Armenian dialect or the Karaim, the relation between the two words is rather dim. The classical form given by Hanusz perfectly fits dialectal *xayran* (*a* in medial position, as a rule, drops) and the difference in the meanings can be the result of a calque, but the difficulty can be removed within Armenian itself, *xayran* meaning 'the place (-(a)ran) where time is spent', or perhaps the radical meaning of the *xay-* root 'to move, to march' had been the starting point.

Summing up we can say that in the Armenian dialect of Kuty there are approximately 30 Kipchak loan words. On the basis of the number of loan-words we can hardly come to the conclusion that the Armenian settlers were the direct descendants of the Armenian population speaking Armeno-Kipchak. But in the light of the historical facts we may rightly infer that the Armenian immigrants from Moldavia during their stay of some one and a half centuries in Poland acquired the Kipchak words from the language of the previously settled Armenians or possibly from the refugees of Kamenec or might even have adopted some Kipchak words during their stay in Moldavia, their previous station.

The weightiest argument in favour of their Moldavian origin is the third most numerous group of words of the Kuty dialect, the group of about 60 Rumanian words. Rumanian loanwords seldom occur in Podolian Armenian. In Armenian records of Podolia dating back to the 16th—17th centuries they rarely appear even in texts relating to Rumanian historical events.[73] The privilege granted to the Armenians of Raszków in 1751, composed of the mixed, loose spoken Armenian contains no Rumanian words. The great amount of Rumanian words in the Kuty dialect cannot be explained by commercial contact, though Kuty is situated near the river Czeremosz, a border river of Pokutia and Bukovina, because the main trading routes led in the direction of Kassa (Košice).

So the lexical evidence corroborates the close kinship between the parlers of Kuty and Suceava, and moreover, testifies to the fact that the Kuty settlers had spent a long period of time in the country of Moldavia before they went on to Poland.

Summarizing what had been said above we must draw the conclusion that the main body of the Armenian population of the Podolian area speaking Armeno-Kipchak during the 16th—17th centuries either adopted Polish,

[72] Karst, *Kilik. Arm. Gramm.* p. 104.
[73] See above p. 104.

V

or — in the consequence of commercial and political reasons, war events — continued wandering further. Though Armenian remained mostly a liturgical language, still we are not entitled to speak of direct continuity of language. If it had not been for the continuous influx of Armenians from the 17th century on, there could hardly have come about a "re-Armenisation" of the colony. The settlers of Kuty, as shown, among others, by the word stock of their language, were in their majority immigrants from Moldavia, and each stage of their wanderings have left traces on their language.

V

Acta Orientalia Academiae Scientiarum Hungaricae, Tomus XXIV (3), pp. 265—300 (1971)

ARMENO-KIPTSCHAKISCHE EHEKONTRAKTE UND TESTAMENTE

VON

E. SCHÜTZ

Seit ihrer Einwanderung ins polnisch—ukrainische Grenzgebiet genossen die armenischen Ansiedler allerlei Privilegien, die von den polnischen Königen im Laufe der Jahrhunderte immer wieder erneuert wurden. Die nationalen Minderheiten wurden in Lemberg (Lwow) ursprünglich in den Rahmen des polnischen bzw. des später eingeführten Magdeburger Rechts nicht aufgenommen. Demzufolge erfreuten sie sich einer gewissen Autonomie; auch die Armenier behielten weiterhin ihre Selbstverwaltung mit ihrem Vogt (*wójt*) an der Spitze. Die Stadt sah den privilegierten Stand der Armenier nicht gerne und setzte alle Kräfte und Machenschaften ein, um sie der Gerichtsbarkeit der Stadtbehörde zu unterstellen. 1469 endete die Zwietracht zwischen der Stadt und dem armenischen Selbstverwaltungsorgan damit, daß die Amtsbefugnis des armenischen Gerichts bzw. Rates eingeschränkt, das Amt des armenischen Vogtes abgeschafft und die größeren Kriminalfälle der Kompetenz des armenischen Gerichts enthoben wurden. Später, 1510, ist es zur weiteren Begrenzung der Rechte gekommen, und auch die Angelegenheiten bezüglich der Immobilien wurden in die Amtssphäre der Statsbehörde einbezogen. Somit gerieten die wichtigsten Rechtssachen teilweise gänzlich in die Kompetenz der Stadtbehörde, teilweise in die Hände eines gemischten Gerichts, dessen Vorstand der Stadtvogt, die Mitglieder aber die armenischen Senioren (Geschworenen) waren.[1]

---

[1] Die Sammlung der Privilegien and anderer Amtsschriften: F. Bischoff, *Urkunden zur Geschichte der Armenier in Lemberg*, Wien 1864. In: *Archiv f. Kunde österreichischer Geschichtsquellen*, Bd. XXXII. und Sonderdruck. Über Entwicklung und Organisation des armenischen Rats von Lemberg s. die älteste und neueste beste Zusammenfassung: F. Bischoff, *Das alte Recht der Armenier in Lemberg*, Wien 1862; O. Balzer, *Sądownictwo ormiańskie w średniowiecznym Lwowie* [Das armenische Gerichtsverfahren im mittelalterlichen Lemberg], Lwow 1909; Analyse in: *Bulletin de la Société polonaise pour l'avancement des sciences* IX, S. 138—147; G. Petrowicz, *L'organisation juridique des Arméniens*: *REArm* IV, S. 321—354. Da das Aktenmaterial des armenischen Rates nur teilweise erhalten geblieben ist, muß das Gerichtsverfahren auf Grund der aus den 60—80er Jahren des 17. Jhs stammenden Urkunden festgestellt bzw. erschlossen werden: J. R. Daškevič,

1

VI

Doch blieben gänzlich im Kompetenzbereich des armenischen Gerichts
(*datastan*) bzw. Rates (*collegium seniorum*) die privaten Angelegenheiten (Immobilien ausgenommen). An der Spitze des Rates standen zwei Vorstände,
sog. Gemeindekuratoren (*érespoxan*). Dieses Amt war die weltliche Fortsetzung
des laischen Kuratoramts im alten Kirchengemeindegericht.[2]   Die ursprüngliche Form der Benennung ist *érespoxan* (*yérespoxan*) «Vertreter (des Antlitzes,
d. h. der Person), Kurator, russ. ктитор», die häufig belegte Form *éréc'poxan*
ist eine Volksetymologie, die vom Wort *éréc'* «Priester» beeinflußt wurde, da
es hier ursprünglich von der Vertretung eines geistlichen Vorstandes die Rede
war. Die Anrede der *Érespoxane* und Senioren war armenisch *baron*, oder
kumanisch *bij*, dem Namen wurde meistens das polnische *pan* vorgesetzt (den
Priestern gebührende Ansprache war *der* oder *baronder*). Die Mitglieder des
Gerichts bzw. Rates waren die Senioren (Geschworenen), ihre Zahl schwankte
zwischen 6 und 12, früher sogar 40. In den armeno-kiptschakischen Schriften
hießen sie *ketxoja* (< *kethüda*) oder *aya* (~ *aha*).

Das mit eingeschränkter Kompetenz ausgestattete autonome Organ
hielt seine Sitzungen in der Residenz des armenischen Bischofs bzw. Erzbischofs, in einem kleinen Saale ($\chi u c'$) ab, die Beschlüsse wurden in Proto-
kollen (Akten, *diftar*) niedergelegt.

Ein wichtiger Zweig der Tätigkeit des armenischen Rates war die Abfassung der Ehekontrakte (contractus nuptialis, arm. *krorenk'*, *grorenk'* < *gir-
orenk'* «schriftlicher Vertrag») und Testamente (testamentum, arm. *diat'ik*,
griech. $\delta\iota\alpha\vartheta\dot\eta\varkappa\eta$), die in Sonderprotokolle eingeführt wurden. Wenn diesen
Schriften auch Vereinbarungen bzw. Schenkungen bezüglich Immobilien ein-

---

Армянское самоуправление во Львове в 60—80-х гг. XVII в. (Протоколы армянского
совета старейшин как исторический источник). Die armenische Selbstverwaltung in
Lemberg in den 60—80er Jahren des 17. Jhs. (Das Protokoll des armenischen Ältesten-
rats als historische Quelle)]: *Banber Matenadarani*, No. 9, 1969, S. 213—240. Zum vergleich wird das Material von Kamenets Podolsk herangezogen: V. Grigorian, *K'amenec
Podolsk' kalak'i haykakan datarani   ardzanagrut'yunnera*. [Die Aktenstücke des armenischen Gerichts von K. P.], Jerewan 1963; T. I. Hrunin, Документы на половецком
языке XVI в. (Судебные акты каменец-подольской армянской общины). [Dokumente
in kumanischer Sprache aus dem 16. Jh. (Gerichtsakte der armenischen Gemeinde von
K. P.)], Moskau 1967. [Seit Jahren erwähnte ich öfters meinen Kollegen J. Daschke-
witsch und E. Tryjarski über meine Arbeit an den Lemberger armenischen Ehekontrakten und Testamenten der Archive der Mechitaristen zu Wien und Venedig. Unlängst veröffentlichten sie drei solche Ehekontrakte (*Rocznik Orientalistyczny*, XXXIII/ 2,
S. 67—107.), deren armeno-kiptschakischer Text und polnische Übersetzung späteren
Prozeßakten einverleibt in Lemberg aufbewahrt sind. Mein Aufsatz war bereits im Druck,
so konnte ich ihre wertvolle Publikation schon nicht in Betracht nehmen.]

   [2] Über die veränderte Lage des armenischen Gemeinderates s. noch Y. Dachkévytch
Sur la question des relations arméno-ukrainiennes au XVIe siècle: REArm, Bd. IV, S.
264—65. (Die Jahreszahl zu verbessern von 1496 zu 1469.)

VI

verleibt wurden, galten diese rechtsgültig erst nach dem sie auch in die städtischen Grundbücher eingeführt worden waren.³

Die Sammlungen der Ehekontrakte und Testamente der armenischen Gemeinde von Lemberg sind in 3 Bänden auf uns gekommen. Zwei Kodizes die in der Mechitaristenbibliothek zu Wien aufbewahrt wurden, sind 1895 aus Tyśmienica von P. V. Bartholomäus dem Archiv zugeschickt worden. Die Handschrift No. 441, die 212 Blätter umfaßt (S. 203—212 sind leer), enthält Eintragungen für das Jahr 1572—1630, und die andere, No. 447., auf 470 Blättern für die Periode 1643—1667; alles in Armeno-Kiptschakisch, «nur der letzte Teil [des MS-s No. 447.] in polnischer Sprache, immer aber in armenischer Schrift».⁴

Obwohl der Katalog Daschians keinen Hinweis auf das Material der Zwischenzeit macht, muß infolge der Übereinstimmung der Zeitpunkte für wahrscheinlich gehalten werden, laß die Handschrift der Bibliothek der Venediger Mechitaristen No. 1788., die auf 178 Seiten ähnliche Eintragungen für die Jahre 1630—1642 enthält, das mittlere Kettenglied in dieser Reihe darstellt.

Der Schreiber der Akten No. 441. ist Minas aus Tokat, wie dies am Anfang der Handschrift in mehreren Kolophonen kundgegeben, ja sogar mit doppelstelliger Kryptographie niedergeschrieben wird.⁵

Auf den ersten Seiten der Ehekontrakte berichtet ein Kolophon armeno-kiptschakisch, ein anderer armenisch (aber ganz kurz) über die Umstände der Entstehung bzw. der Redaktion der Akten (defter), ja sogar erzählt der Dichter-Notar in einer aus 18 Distichen (tun) bestehenden Dichtung über die Tätigkeit des armenischen Rates.⁶

Minas Tokateci wurde laut Beweis eines Kolophons 1510 in Eudokia (Tokat) geboren.⁷ In seinem 30 Lebensjahr griff er zum Wanderstab, und man findet ihn bald im Kreise der armenischen Ansiedler in Polen, wo er Notar des armenischen Selbstverwaltungsorgans, des neben der Kirche Dormitio Sanctae Mariae fungierenden Gerichts bzw. Gemeinderates angestellt wird. Hier wird es sein Amt die Abfassung der Amtsschriften des armenischen Sprengels bzw. der armenischen Gemeinde. Minas war einer der bemerkenswertesten Schrift-

³ Siehe z. B. den Schlußsatz eines Ehekontrakts: *any ratušta bizim toramyzga belgili etix da jazdyrdyx* «dies verlaut arten wir im Rathaus vor unserer Rechtsbehörde und ließen es einschreiben», *Krorenk'*, MS No. 441. 19v28—29. Vgl. Petrowicz, a. a. O., S. 343.

⁴ J. Dashian, *Katalog der armenischen Handschriften in der Mechitaristen-Bibliothek zu Wien*. 1895. S. 210, bzw. 909, und 213, bzw. 919.

⁵ Krorenk' No. 441. MS S. 1v, 2r—3r, 3r, 3v, 4v. S. noch Akinean: *Hing panduxt taγasac'ner* [Fünf ausgewanderte Dichter]. Wien 1921. S. 83.

⁶ S. die Zitate unten, S. 1v, 2r—3r, 4v, bzw. 3v, 4r.

⁷ D. h. er war i. J. 1565 55 Jahre alt, vgl. seine Lebengeschichte in Akinean: *Taγasac'ner*, S. 57—68.

1*

VI

steller der armenischen Diaspora in Polen, der nebst seiner Tätigkeit als Notar
auch mehrere Handschriften abschrieb und einige Schriftwerke bzw. Gedichte hinterließ. Von diesen soll besonders ein aus 440 Zeilen bestehendes
Poem, «Die Verfolgung der Armenier in der Moldau vom Jahre 1551»,[8] ferner
ein Scherzgedicht «Lob der Herisa» (einer armenischen Speise) hervorgehoben
werden.[9]

Im Laufe seines Notaramtes führte Minas mehrere offizielle Schrift-
kopienbücher. Darunter gehören zu den wichtigsten die Ehekontrakte (*Krorenk'*) und Testamente (*Diatik*) enthaltenden Bücher.

In der Beschreibung der Handschrift No. 441 bemerkt J. Daschian, daß
Blätter 5r – 149r, also die Eintragungen für die Jahre 1572 – 1618 von Minas,
und die darauf folgenden Blätter 149v – 203v (für die Jahre 1618 – 1630) von
«einer anderen Hand» herrühren. Bei einer anderen Handschrift derselben
Bibliothek (No. 452, Liste der Geldsammlungen) erwähnt er, daß die Blätter
1r – 53r (für die Jahre 1598 – 1619) und «vielleicht auch» Bl. 59r – 69r (für die
Jahre 1621 – 1623) von Minas geschrieben wurden.[10]

N. Akinean übernimmt diese, genauer nicht begründeten, und auch schon
in Daschians Fassung nicht allzu überzeugend klingenden («vielleicht auch»)
Behauptungen, und zieht daraus weitgehende Folgerungen, und zwar, daß
Minas demgemäß ein Lebensalter von 110 Jahren erreicht hätte.[11]

Hierzu muß angemerkt werden, daß von den zwei Handschriften nur
die erste einen Kolophon enthält. Die zweite (No. 452) sollte Minas aus dem
Grunde zugeschrieben werden, daß zu jener Zeit eben er der Notar war, es ist
also höchst wahrscheinlich, daß alle Akten der Gemeinde von ihm herrührten.
Es gibt zwar zahlreiche Kolophone in MS 441, aber alle stehen — wie oben
erwähnt — auf den ersten Seiten (1v – 4r), auf die Verfasserschaft der übrigen
Teile der Handschrift No. 441 bzw. der Handschrift No. 452 ist also nur durch
die Schrift zu schließen.

Daschians verallgemeinernde Ansicht ist — unseres Erachtens — nicht
stichhältig, da die Schrift in den erwähnten Handschriften überaus kein ein-
heitliches Bild darstellt. Es wäre allerdings annehmbar, daß der Notar in einzelnen Fällen aus verschiedenen Gründen durch eine andere Person vertreten
wurde, doch kann die Kontinuität der Hand Minas auch so nicht genau verfolgt werden. Daschians Behauptungen sind umso weniger annehmbar, da
die Schrift in den genannten Handschriften auch in den «vorgeschrittenen
Jahren» 'zitterlos' (*antoyloč*) ist, welchen Umstand auch schon Akinean wahr-
genommen hat.

---

[8] *Tayasac'ner*, S. 85—102. Die deutsche Übersetzung von D. Dan erschien in
Tschernowitz 1894.
[9] *Tayasac'ner*, S. 102—111.
[10] Dashian, *a. a. O.*, S. 210/909 bzw. 214/923.
[11] *Tayasac'ner*, S. 62—3.

VI

So schließen wir unsere Erwägungen für diesmal damit ab, daß die Manuskripte No. 441 und No. 452 (und andere Autographen) einer genaueren Schriftprobe zu unterziehen wären, um festzustellen, welche Teile der Handschrift No. 441 bzw. No. 452 Minas zuzuschreiben sind.

Der Grundtext der Amtsstücke hat sich im Laufe der Zeit im Gebrauch verallgemeinert. Da im Mutterland Armenien solche alte privatrechtliche Schriftstücke nicht erhalten blieben, bietet sich nur die spätere Praxis zu Vergleichungen an. Im polnischen Königreich zeigte sich bald der Einfluß der polnischen Rechtsübung bzw. Schriftabfassung, der in erster Linie selbstverständlich in den Einführungs- und den Schlußformeln und im Gebrauch polnischer Rechtsausdrücke zum Vorschein kam. Es ist interessant, daß die alten Klauseln auch in den in Ungarn (Siebenbürgen) im 18. Jh. verfaßten Schriftstücken belegt sind.

Die Textaufbau der Ehekontrakte ist folgender: Zuerst kommt die Berufung auf die göttliche Macht. Diese Invokationsformel bleibt aber in unserem Defter No. 441 bald (schon nach 1580) weg. Danach kommt die Angabe des Orts der Abfassung, die Aufzählung der höchsten Würdenträger, unter deren Herrschaft der Rechtsakt zustande kam: der regierende polnische König, der Patriarch Armeniens, der Bischof bzw. Erzbischof von Lemberg, der Pfarrer der zuständigen Parochialkirche, ferner die Mitglieder des armenischen Kommunalrates, der anwesende *Erespoxan*, und die anwesenden Senioren. In der Narration werben die Eltern des Bräutigams um die Hand der künftigen Braut, der lobwürdigen Tochter (*oyovlu xyz*) ihrer Eltern. Der allgemeine Ausdruck hierfür ist *orenkli alyšmakka* 21v12, bzw. einmal *syngarlyxka* 17v17 also «zur gesetzmäßigen Ehe, zur Frau». Hiernach folgt die Aufzählung der Aussteuer (*majja*, *vyprava*), zu allererst Gottes Segen und danach die weltlichen, leiblichen Bedürfnisse (*aval burun berirmen tengrining alyšyn, da ten jergasyndan* ... 17v19, oder *ten kerakyndan* 28v24, oder *dunjalik tirlikymyzdan* 18v16): zuerst die Gold- und Silbersachen, Juwelen, dann die Frauenkleider und das Bettzeug, an letzter Stelle die Brautgabe für den Bräutigam, der Goldring und das goldene Hemd. Zum Schluß folgt das Brautgeschenk (*bašxš*, *érésčur*), das vom Bräutigam der Braut dargebracht wird: das Festkleid (*xalat*) bzw. andere Kleider, je ein Juwel und/oder Bargeld. Der Handelscharakter des Vertrags wird in einem Ehekontrakt ausdrücklich beim Namen genannt: *bu alyš berišťan songra* 'nach diesem Ankauf-Verkaufakt' 21v22.

Nach 1580 (MS S. 26v) verändert sich der Grundtext, die Invokationsformel bleibt weg, und die einfache Formel polnischer Art verallgemeinert sich: *turup oblične brü érespoxanurnyng da ketxojalyxnyng alnyna* «persönlich vorstellig vor den Erespoxanen und Senioren». Dieselbe Formel, ohne Invokation, finden wir in einem gleichzeitigen Ehekontrakt von Kamenez Podolsk in armenischer Fassung (1574): *tadastanin arčéien ganknélov* «vorstellig vor

VI

dem Gericht».[12] Im weiteren erklärt der Vater, daß sie die Familie der Braut
kennengelernt und mit ihr Freundschaft geschlossen hatten (*dostlux ettix*),
und der Schwiegervater die Tochter seinem Sohn zu geben versprach. Schon
aus den polnischen Ausdrücken geht es hervor, daß hier der polnische Gebrauch überhandnahm. Auch die Schlußformel, wo man die Eintragung der
Vereinbarung in die Akten verlangt, wird allgemein.

Der Aufbau des Testaments ist folgender: Der Erblasser begründet seine
Handlung damit, daß er das Herannahen seines Todes (*tynszlyx*) spürt, aber
betont zur selben Zeit, daß er bei vollem Sinn und Verstand ist (*tugal fikirimda
da sayyšimda* 25v38; *nega dingra jaxši esda edim* 13v27 «solange ich bei vollem
Sinne war»; *teni bila xasta evet axylynda igi sah* 35v20 «obwohl körperlich krank,
aber was den Verstand betrifft, wohl gesund», usw.), er besinn sich der Worte
des Apostels Paul, wonach das Testament nach dem Tode gültig bleibt: *ol-
gandan songra berklixta xalyr* 12v12; *olumdan songra kerak berklikta xalgaj*
18r8;[13] «nach dem Tode in Kraft bleibe»; *olumdan songra bunjatlydyr* 13v29.
Dann läßt er den Priester und einige Amtsleute rufen und verfügt über seine
mobilen und immobilen Güter. In Fällen folgt danach eine Schlußformel. Ausnahmsweise wird die Familie gesegnet: *da algajlar tengrining da menim atalyx
alyyšimny, ki tengri alarny artlyrgaj da šayavatyn har kez ustlaryndan eksik
etmagaj* 26r24 «sie sollen den Segen Gottes und meinen Segen entgegennehmen.
Gott vermehre sie, und keiner von ihnen soll Gottes Gnaden vermissen». Es
kommt aber auch eine Fluchformel vor: *Budur menim dastymentim. Da kim
bungar xarši bolsa, bošatlxy bolmagaj, ne ol jihanda da ne bu jihanda* 12v28
«Das ist mein letzter Wille. Wer aber dagegen wäre, dem soll keine Vergebung
zuteil werden, weder in der anderen Welt, noch in dieser Welt».

Wie zäh sich die ursprünglichen Formeln in den amtlichen Schriften
lange Jahrhunderte hindurch behaupteten, läßt sich mit den verschiedenen
Ehekontrakten aus den Jahren 1492—1572—1725 veranschaulichen. Der
Grundtext eines von Bžškian mitgeteilten Ehekontraktes[14] ist mit den Texten
der armeno-kiptschakischen Ehekontrakte aus den 1570er Jahren im Grunde
genommen identisch. Der Text wird im Manuskript No. 441 zweimal armenisch
mitgeteilt (7v und 11v), und ist im wesentlichen jenem des 80 Jahre früher
verfaßten gleich. Aber denselben Grundtext finden wir auch in einigen, 150
Jahre später, in Ungarn verfaßten Ehekontrakten. Chr. Szongott teilt mehrere
Ehekontrakte vom Anfang des 18. Jhs mit, und zwar einen vom Jahre 1725
in Armenisch.[15]

---

[12] Grigorian, a. a. O., S. 289.

[13] Brief an die Juden, 9/17. «Testamentum enim in mortuis confirmatum est».
Es hätte eher für «in Kraft tritt» übersetzt werden sollen.

[14] *Čanaparhordut'iwn i Lehastan* [Reise nach Polen], Venedig 1830, S. 117.

[15] *Szamosújvár szab. kir. város monográfiája* IV. *A magyarországi örmények ethnog-
raphiája* [Monographie der königl. Freistadt Armenierstadt. Bd. IV. Ethnographie der
ungarländischen Armenier], Szamosújvár 1903, S. 243—269, 63—64.

VI

Zum Vergleich zum von Bēskian mitgeteilten Text von 1492 geben wir
die stereotypen Formel des Kontrakts aus dem Jahre 1572 (MS Bl. 7v) und
die entsprechenden Sätze aus dem Kontrakt von 1725.[16]

Nachstehend der Text des Kontrakts von 1572 (in westarmenischer
Transkription):

(1572) *Gamaw aménagalin aménagaroγin. naxaxnamoγin. hamaynic̕.
Hor ēw ortoy ēw hok̕oyn srpoy: Zor ēγēw ays šnahawor harsanik̕s. Ǎnt hovanéaw
sp haǰatgadur adzadzinnyng*[17]. *i yadzašen K̕aγak̕s ilov: i tkrut̕é parébašt ar-
k̕ayin . . ., i hayrabédut̕é . . . ēw yaŕačnortut̕é . . . avakiric̕ut̕é . . . ēréspoxa-
nut̕é . . . Zor ēgn aŕači orinac̕ k̕ahic̕ . . . ēw xntréc̕ . . .-en ziwr kovéli zt̕oŕn
(zkoyrn) . . . i yorinawor amusnut̕i. zor dr adz šnahawor aŕne. amen . . . nax
gudam zay ahui. ēw marmnawor bidoγic̕n zor drne badrasdér . . .*[18]

Im wesentlichen ist der Grundtext des Ehekontraktes mit dem eines
150 Jahre später, 1725 in Siebenbürgen verfaßten Kontraktes völlig identisch:

(1725) *Gamavən Asdudzo grimec̕oγin p̕arecac̕ Dearən meroh . . . yeγev
ays šnorhavor harsanik̕əs i hergrin Transilvanoh i K̕aγak̕ən Gherlan ənt ho-
vaneav sərpoh yeγeγec̕oh . . . i Layrabedut̕ean . . . avak yerecut̕ean . . . yev
takavorut̕ean . . .*

*Zor yeγən aŕači orinac̕ k̕ahanayic̕ . . . yer xntrec̕ . . .-en zyureanc̕ koveli
tusdrən . . . i halal amusnut̕ean. zor Der-Asdudz šnorhavor arasc̕e. Amen.
Tarc̕eal yes . . . gudamk̕ . . . nax arač̕ Asdudzo orhnut̕iwnə yer aba . . .*[19]

Also, sind die Texte wie offensichtlich im Grunde genommen identisch,
nur infolge der verschiedenen örtlichen und zeitlichen Umstände gewissen Veränderungen, Vereinfachungen unterworfen, den lokalen Gebrauchen angepaßt.

Aber nicht nur der Text der Verträge sondern auch der Gegenstand der
Staffierung behielt die alten Züge bei. Es ist ein allgemeiner Zug, daß die Aufzählung der Aussteuer mit den Gold- und Silbersachen (Juwelen) anfängt.
Aber auch in den Kleidungsstücken, Kopfputzen (Hauben), den Leibchen und
den Stoffen herrschen die mit Goldfaden gestickten und mit Perlen gezierten
vor, ja sogar das Hemd des Bräutigams ist mit Goldfaden durchwoben (*altun
kolmak*). Ein Teil der weiblichen Kleidungsstücke hat -- infolge der Mode --
die lokale Bezeichnung angenommen, in den Prunkkleidern lebten aber meistens die ererbten Kleidungsstücke weiter, aber wenn es nötig war, neue zu
verfertigen, so konnten die armenischen Kaufleute auch dafür die kostspieligen

---

[16] Ebda, S. 244—245.

[17] Suffix kiptschakisch. (Die Abbreviaturzeichen *(Pativ)* sind aus technischen
Gründen weggelassen worden.)

[18] Wiener Mechitaristenarchiv, MS No. 441, S. 7v. Derselbe armenische Grundtext
auch 11v.

[19] Szongott, a. a. O., S. 244—245. Der Text ist von Verfasser nicht der Aussprache
nach transkribiert, sondern ziemlich grob transliteriert.

VI

Stoffe erwerben. Die Ehekontrakte zeugen im allgemeinen über Wohlstand; auf bescheidene materielle Lage des Schwiegervaters findet man nur selten einen Hinweis: 1581: *miskinlikimyzga kora* 30v1, *miskin kučuma kora* 29r31. Meistens kann man schon aus der Aufzählung auf den Reichtum des Schwiegervaters schließen: viele Hochzeitsfeste armenischer Kaufleute standen denen der polnischen Edelleute kaum nach, ja sogar, wie es allbekannt ist, haben sich einige armenische Kaufleute eine legendäre Habe angehäuft.

Es ist interessant, die polnischen und die siebenbürgischen Ehekontrakte zu vergleichen. Die in der zweiten Hälfte des 17. Jhs und im 18. Jh teils aus der Moldau, teils aus Polen nach Siebenbürgen eingewanderten Armenier mußten in ihrer neuen Heimat wieder alles von neuem anfangen, doch aus den mitgebrachten Mobilgütern, aus den Einkünften, die sie sich durch Nah- und Fernhandel, oder aus Gewerbe angeeignet hatten, konnten sie bald emporklettern, ja manchmal sogar einen beträchtlichen Reichtum ansammeln.

Obwohl die Siebenbürger Armenier mit den armenischen Handelsdynastien Lembergs nicht wetteifern konnten, ist doch der Ehekontrakt strukturell gleich: auch hier kommen die Gold- und Silbersachen an der Spitze, und die Prunkkleider ererbten sich von einer Generation zur anderen in der Familie. Obwohl man in Ungarn die ungarische Mode allmählich übernahm, sind die traditionellen Kleidungsstücke erhalten geblieben, und ihre Benennungen haben sich gehalten (armenisch, polnisch, rumänisch). Auch in den Ehekontrakten begegnet man diesen Benennungen, obwohl der Kommunalrat in Armenierstadt (Szamosújvár, lat. Armenopolis, rumänisch: Gherla) und Elisabethstadt (Erzsébetváros, Heghisapetubolis, rum.: Dumbraveni) die Aneignung der örtlichen Gebräuche anempfahl: «Da wir in anderen Zeiten leben ... — lautet die Verordnung vom Jahre 1718 —, sind wir gezwungen, einige nationale Gebräuche aufzugeben und uns den Umständen anpassen».[20] Die Vorschriften betonen, daß man unter den veränderten Umständen zu sparen, und den überflüssigen Luxus zu meiden habe. Die Wiederholung der Dekrete war deshalb nötig, da man sie auch trotz der Geldstrafe nicht hielt, obwohl die übermäßige Verschwendung die materielle Grundlage mancher Familien erschütterte, «sogar Armut verursachte».[21]

In den Verordnungen des armenischen Kommunalrates offenbarte sich doch auch die Eifersucht der oberen Schichten. Die Siebenbürger Armenier waren in drei Klassen gegliedert, und es wurde einer jeden genau vorgeschrieben, was für Kleidungsstücke aus welchem Stoff man tragen, was für Eßzeuge man sich bedienen durfte, usw. Wer der höheren Klasse gebührende Kleidungsstücke trug, wurde mit Geldstrafe belegt. Den Putz hielten die Räte

---

[20] Szongott, *a. a. O.*, 272—275. Armenisch: *Handes Amsorya.*

[21] Szongott, *a. a. O.*, S. 73 ff.; Kr. Kovrigean, *Hayk' Heyisapetubolis Transiluanioy, 1680—1779* [Die Armenier von Elisabethstadt in Siebenbürgen], Wien 1893, S. 43.

VI

schon deshalb für schädlich, weil die Armenier sich mit der Zurschaustellung ihres Reichtums die Mißbilligung der anderen Völker des Landes zuziehen konnten.

Das Verbot erstreckte sich auch auf die Dekorierung der Kleidungsstücke. Eine Verordnung des armenischen Rates von Elisabethstadt (16. Juni 1750.) zählt die verbotenen Verzierungen auf: «1. Überhaupt keine aus Goldstoff, d. h. aus Goldfaden hergestellten Anzüge bzw. Kleider, sollen von unseren Mitbürgern getragen werden . . . 2. Auf keinem Kleidungsstück darf Silber- oder Goldverzierung gefunden werden, weder Schnurbesatz noch Spitze, noch Portspan, noch Tresse, noch irgendwelche Gold-, oder Silberzierde . . . 3. Es is den Bräutigamen verboten, mit Gold- oder Silber gestickte Handtücher und Halsbinden zu tragen . . .» usw[22].

Also haben die Verordnungen alle Prunkkleider und Verzierungen verbannt, die in den Ehekontrakten der armenischen Familien sowohl in Lemberg als auch in Siebenbürgen so reich vertreten sind. Die Verordnungen stellten eine Schonfrist fest, d. h. die schon längst gebrauchten Kleider und Anzüge durften ausgetragen werden. Die aus orientalischen Gold- und Silberstoffen verfertigten kostbaren Kleider und Anzüge sind teils den zuständigen Kirchengemeinden geschenkt worden, wo daraus Meßgewänder genäht wurden, so daß die Festkleider aus dem Nachlaß der reichen Familien nicht nur unmittelbar in die Museen gelangten, sondern man kann solche heute noch als Meßgewänder antreffen.

Die Ehekontrakte bieten ein sehr wertvolles Quellenmaterial zur Trachtforschung der Armenier, ihre Auswertung für solche Zwecke sollte gründlicher in Angriff genommen werden.

*

Und nun sollen einige Musterbeispiele die flüchtige Inhaltsübersicht der Ehekontrakte und Testamente veranschaulichen und über ihre armenischkiptschakischen Grundtexte Aufschluß geben.

Der einführende Kolophon des MS No. 441 (1v) lautet forgendermaßen: «Dieser Defter wurde im Jahre 1021 nach armenischer Zeitrechnung, 1572 nach lateinischer Zeitrechnung, unter der Regierung von Sigismund August für Ehekontrakte und Testamente zusammengestellt, damit alles hier [in diesem Buch] beschrieben werde. Es ist in der Stadt Lemberg, auf Verordnung der geschworenen Senioren zustande gekommen. [Es bleibe] gute Erinnerung, und dem Gericht Einheit.»

Der Gerichtsnotar Minas war aber gleichzeitig auch ein Dichter, er besang also die Bestimmung des Defters in einem aus 18 Distichen (*tun* «beyt») bestehenden armenischen Poem (je Zeilen 16 Silben mit Paarreim) (MS 3v):

---

[22] Szongott, *a. a. O.*, S. 70 ff., Kovrigean, *a. a. O.*, S. 44.

VI

«Hier in Polen, in der Lemberg genannten Stadt,
Hier wohnt die armenische Nation aus Noahs Sippe.
Auf Verordnung des Königs wird das Volk hier
    auf Grund der Gesetze gerichtet,
Die Richter nehmen überhaupt kein Bestechungsgeld an,
    sie sind nicht voreingenommen und treffen keine
    falsche Entscheidung....
Es wurde vorgeschrieben, daß die Ehekontrakte und
    Testamente hier eingeschrieben werden,
Wer dagegen verfährt, dem wird große Schande zuteil
    auf Erden,
Die 12 Senioren und die 2 großen Gerichtsvorsitzenden,
    deren Namen wir oben verzeichneten, legten einen Eid ab.»

Der armenische Kolophon, der auf die älteren Schriften hinweist, lautet (4v): «Oh, Leser, die vor unserer Zeit geschlossenen Ehekontrakte und Testamente wurden in diesen Defter nicht eingetragen. Wer jene nötig hätte, suche sie im Archiv (*xazna*) und bitte zeihe dessen nicht uns. Vom Jahre 1021 an können sie hier gefunden werden. Nach armenischer Zeitrechnung 1021 — A. D. 1572, den 1/10 Januar, in der Stadt Lemberg, unter der Ägide der Kirche Dormitio Sanctae Mariae. Mit Händen des unwürdigen Schreibers JJ. ŽŽ. MM. CC. ṘṘ. ŽŽ»[23]

Text[24]

Anno 1572

1. [5v36] *Krorenk Baron Donawak oɣlunung. | bohdannyng.   Da pan xačkonung | xznyng. nasduxnanyng: tvin. 1021: | hunvarnyng. 12: |*

[40] *Erkibila dunjani tutučinyng. da barčadan xuvatlynyng. | da baryny ajovučinin. Ataj. oɣul. arijannyng: xajsiki | boldu bu xutlu toj` tengridan tuzulgan` ilov šaharinaj. [6r] Kolgasina sp adzadzinnyng` nnčumnung. Padšahlxynaj kristan xannyng | ziɣmund Awgustosnung. Hajrabedlxynaj dn. dr. mikajel gatuɣigosnung. | Aračnortluxuna br dr krikor arhiaxbašnyng` vanly. Awakereclxyna` | dr vasko kahanajnyng: Érespoxanlxynaj` br hrihornung. da br ivaškonung: [5] Xajsiki keldi orenkning alnyna` da kahlxnyng. br donawak. da žadat | etdi br xačkodan. Učmaxly janly br awedikning oɣlundan. da anyng*

---

[23] Die Auflösung des doppelstelligen Kryptogrammes: *Minasi* also «von Minas». — Facsimile s. S. 297. A. G. Abrahamyan: *Hay gri ev grčut'yun patmut'yun* [Geschichte der armenischen Schrift und des armenischen Schrifttums]. Jerewan 1959, S. 211.
[24] Die Abbreviaturzeichen *(Patiw)* sind aus technischen Gründen weggelassen worden.

VI

| *nogarindan. pani hanuxnadan. alurnyng ogovlu xzyn' panna nasduxnany.* |
*kendining oylunaj' pan bohdanga, orenkli alyšmaxkaj: Xajsiki bij tengri | xutlu
sahatta etkaj. amen: Da men xačko pan awedik oylu' menim noga-[10]-rim bila'
hanuxnaj bila. berijirbiz' bizim oylenymyzga' pannaj nasdux|nagaj. Awal tengri-
ning alyšyn. da munung artyndan neki tengri beripdyr | dunjalik igilikimyzdan
bu — — —du — — — r: | Bašta bašbay. inǰisi altunybla:* 58. *mtxal: Mazgab' altuny
inǰisi | bila.* 27. *mtxal: Jegdanaj altunu inǰisi bila.* 48. *mtxal: Xušlar* [15] *altunu
inǰisi bila.* 26. *mtxal: Altun haǰimuk.* 9. *mtxal: Altun | bojunčax.* 24. *mtl: Altun
zynǰyl.* 30. *xzyl flori ayyry: Bir inǰi jayaj' |* 50. *mtl: Inǰi brižlar.* 20. *mtl: Ekinči
inǰi brižlar.* 10. *mtl: Inǰi zalohaj | fartuxkaj.* 10. *mtl: Inǰi bramkaj.* 18. *mtl: Inǰi
boymaj.* 6. *mtl:* 1 *sirma | jayaj.* 1 *sirma briž. Eki kumuš belbay.* 4. *somtašy gs:
Kumuš racok'* [20] *da kumuš xynlar. eksi.* 40. *florigaj.* 1. *altun kolmak.* 1. *altun
far|tux.* 1. *adamaška ton:* 2. *ton siroka' kitajka:* 1. *ton xzyl zuf: |* 1. *ton muxajar.
Br kijorgaj altun kolmak: Jana nšan juzuku' | kok jayut: Jana kijorga'* 2. *kumuš
kobok:* 2. *somtašy jarym: |* 3. *jas-yx.* 3 *ar juzlukbila. kuft cvelex' da ipakli.* 2.
*perinaj' [*25*] kamxaj juzluklar bila:* 2. *mindar' cvel'x juzluklar bila:* 1 *xad|ufaj
juvuryan.* 1. *xali. Ax oprax nečik har jaršilarnyng: | Dayynda' men xačko'
br awedik oylu. berijirmen menin oylanym nasdu|xnaj artyndan. menim kijo-
vumaj bohdangaj. majja jerinda'* 1. *taš kebit: | učmaxly ǰanly atamdan xalgan:*
1 *janyna juxov kebiti dyr.* 1 *si [*30*] janyna' rasil oylu pan pilibning: Dayyda
men xačko' bu kebitka kora' | menim turgan ovumdan vydilit etdim.* 1. *kesak
jer' menim xzymaj nasdu|xnagaj. majja jerinda' da berdim menim kijovumaj
bohdangaj. xajsiki | jerning uzunlaxu' azbarnyng uzunluxudur:* 1. *taš duvardan*
[6v] 1 *si taš duvarga dingra.* 1 *kenliki aran sartyn' čax tutup | arannyng taš
duvarindan.* 19. *lokot krakovnuny. da joyari xabax | sartyn ol taš duvarnyng'
pilip xatunnung turgan ovnungki azba|rynaj čxypdyr. andan kengliki.* 10. *lokot
gs. dyr' krakovnung lokotu.* [5] *munung kibik mulklarny men xačko berijjermen.
da berdim menim | kijovumaj bohdanga. Na rječnyj časy' da anyng potomkala-
ryna. | erkli bolgaj menim kijovumaj. bu mulklarni uživat etma. nečik | vlasny
kendining. Zera men xačko bu mulklarni berdim. menim | kijovumaj bohdanga.
majja jerinda. menim jaxši erkindan. da* [10] *konglumdan: Aj kijov kelinga
keltrijer xalat.* 1. *ǰuft | bilazuk.* 32. *mtxal: Da.* 1. *šubalx adamaškaj: Aj men | do-
navak' menim oylum bohdanbla' tutunijirbiz. pan xačko | sratymaj. ki ol jerda
xajsinki bizgaj udilit ettij kendi | turgan ovinaj' ki neča pan xačko tiridir. ki
anda nemada [*15*] budovat etmagujbiz: Evet uživat etkajbiz' neda klasax | anda
xojmaj. ja saxlamaj. munung usza dyr eki jandan da' | bizim jaxši erkimyz:
A men xačko br awedik oylu. tutunijir|men menim sratymaj pan donavakgaj.
da kijovumaj bohdangaj. ki ne e xtda klasa' bu mulklarny men bergan jazma'
xajda [*20*] ki jeridyr. povinen avyar baryp jazdyrma: Jazyldy bu krovenk tv.*
1021: *hunvari* 12:

Acta Orient. Hung. XXIV. 1971

VI

Anno 1588

2. [48r] *Krorenk. panna martanyng. pan kaspar. xzyj. da. | pan kosta-nyng. pan andryj oγlunung. tr.* 1037 *pedr|rarnyng* 12. *padyšahlxyna. stepanos-nung:* verbessert zu: *ziγmuntnung*

*Turup obličnjej. ketxojjalyxnyng alnyna*j. *pan kaspar br. zadik oγlu* [5] *bir jandan. da pan Andrij. kosta oγlu. birsi jandan. Da bu turlu | Ajttilar. Br. éréspoxanlar. Bijlar ketxojjalar. kelganymyznyng. Bijlik|ingyznyng alnyna. Sabapyj budur. Xačanki dostlux ettix. pan Andrij. | bila. br dr ning. da bijlikin-gyznyng dasturu bila*j. *Bu dur kendi. | xzymnyj. panna. martany*j. *oγluna. pan kostaga*j. *orenkbila*j. *oddat etma. pryj*-[10]-*obicat ettim. Na anda. zaraz kendi xzymnyng. artyndan. bunungki. | ryjprawa. xajsinki. bu bitik usna. jazyp. bij-likingyzga*j. *podawat et|ijirmen. pryjobicat ettim. ne učun. xolarmen ki sarnal-ga*j. *Na žadanjejsi usna. | pan kasparnyng. ketxojjalx. dastur berdilar. Anyngki bitikni sarnama*j. *| Xajsiki bu turlu. opivat etijiredi. men kaspar. berijirmen. bizim oγlanym*-[15]-*yzga. panna martaga. Aval. tengrining alγšin. Andan song-ra*j. *ten kerakindan. | Neki tengrining. šaγawatyndan. hadirlanyptyr. bu dur. Bašta.* 1. *altun | zynĵyl.* 60. *xzyl fli.* 2. *kumuš belbaγ. altynlagan.* 1. i. 3. *somtaši. da birsi. |* 2. *somtaši. da* 1. *kumuš vacok. da* 1. *kumuš xn.* 1. *juft manella. |* 1. *inĵi bramka.* 2. *altun čepec.* 4. *jezdi ton. xadifalar bila*j. 1. *kanafaca.* [20] *šuba. susar bila. podbity*j. *ax oprax. tošak orun. nečik har jaxšilarnyng. | da.* 1. *ju-vurγan. mundan songra*j. *pan kaspar prinjat etijir. pan kostany*j. *| kijovun. kensina. oγul jerinda. Da prijpustit etijir. kendi. majentnost|una. ortaxlxka*j. *Xajsiki men kaspar xojijirmen ortaga*j. 2000. *fli. da. kijov|um xojijir.* 1000. *fli. ki kun vaxt bolsa. ki potreba bolga*j. *ajyrylmaga*j. *men kaspar* [25] *Aval algaj-men.* 2000. *fli umnu. Da kijovumda. alga*j. 1000. *fli. sun. Andan | songra. neki tengri bersa. pryjrobica bolgan. sb dan. jarymda jarym algajbiz. | Nečik men. alaj ol. da menim xatyma*j. *turga*j. 15. *jylga dira. Sarnalgan|dan songra bu bitik. xoldu pan kaspar. ketxojjalyxtan.. ki sorov etkajlar. | pan kostadan kijovdan. ki bu jazovga kora*j. *barča nema. Angar. dosyt* [30] *boldumi. Na sorovu usna. ketxojjalyxnyng. juvap etti. pan kosta. Ajtip | bu turlu. ki manga. xajinatam-dan. Da xajinanamdanda. Dosyt bol|du. Nedan. kendilaryn. da potomstvojla-rynda. rječnej. kvitovat etijirmen. | Na xoldu pan kaspar. ki munungki zeznan-jejsi. kijovunung. Aktaga*j *| jazylga*j. *da pamjentnyjda. berdi. Munda zaraz. zeznat etti. pan kijov.* [35] *ki jazdyrijir. Mungar xarši. kendi syngaryna*j. *panna. martaga*j. 500. *fli. sb. nahd. |*

1572

3. [7v26] *Diatik. Miklaš oγlunung. šmečkonung. | tvin.* 1021. *hunvar-nyng.* 27. *sina. |*

VI

Men šimko miklaš oylu: men m jaxši pamjatimda ' Aldym tengrini | jura-kimaj. Da sayyndym sozun sp a-ukelnyng boγosnung: [30] xajsiki bujurijir. ki olumdan songra ' vosiat beklikt- xalyr toxtalgan: [8r] Menda nečik olumlu kiši. etijirmen jerga. menim igili-imda. xajsiki | xaldyrijirmen menim xatunumaj ' da oylanlarymaj. mendan songra budur: | Bašta bardyr menim bir taš ovum. xajsi ičinaj ki hali turijirmǝn: | xajsiki menimdyr vylasnyj. Budurki menim xardašym bila ' pan ivaško [5] bla ' pajlašypmen. mulkta ol xalypdyr ' kendi turgan ovunda. da men | xaldym ke-ısi pajymda. xajsynda ki turijjermen: Artyx ortamyzgaj | soz xalmijir: Ne anyn, mendaj bar. ne menim anda. ataj pajynda. | alaj mulktaj. nečik ozgaj majjentnostta. dosit etipbiz ' biri birim|yzgaj: Dayyda menim bu orumaj kora. bardyr bi, taš kebitim. [10] xajsyki mangaj ' učmaxly ǰanly pan krikoršadan xaldy: Bud,.r | menim mulklarim: Dayyda bardyr menim tengridan bergan igilikim. alaj | bo-čdaj ' nečik axčadaj. alaj tirlikda. kebitdaj. da ovdaj. yskylep|imaj. hysebimaj koraj: 9.600. flori: az artyx. az eksik: bu xadar | nema bar: Xajsyki majen'nosttan: Men jaxši erkim bila. čxarijir-[15]-men šahyr juxovunaj. 20. fli: Vonkdaki juxovgaj. 10. fl: Axbašgaj ' | 10. fl: Xosdovanatamaj. 10. fl: Babaslargaj. 3. ar fl: Dayyda | menim barčaj igilikimaj ' da mulklarymaj. da oylanlarymaj. Etijjermen | hokeparc menim anamny. da xatunumnu. da xardašymny ' pan ivaš|kony. Da kijovumuzny br avedik oγlu ' pan xačkonu: ki bu menim [20] te-gri bergan igilikimdan. Bašta bergajlar menim xzoylanlarymaj. | olxadar altun inǰi. vypravaj ' alaj nečik men berdim avalgi xzlarymaj: | Alarnyng krorenkinaj kora ' berilgaj. Da majja nayd ayčaj. 3 ar | 100. fl bergajlar: har birina: Da bundan songra neki xalsa | ruxomyj igilik bolgaj ' ǰarymy menim xatunumnung. da ǰ-rymy [25] bolgaj ' menim oylumnung ysteckonung: Aj stojjoncyj mulklar učua ' | budur menim erkim. ki menim xatunum tirklikinaj dijin kensining. | vladnu,t etkaj. alaj ' ne turlu ki mendaj. tirlikimdaj menim ettim: | Aj olumundan songra menim xatunumnung. bolgaj menim oy-lumnung | steckonung: barčaj stojo-icyj ' imenjalar: Dayyda men buxadar [30] nemany. simarlijirmen tengrigaj. da hokeparclarymaj. ki algajlar tengrini | juraklarinaj. da etkajlar alaj ' nečik igi bolgaj. nečikki tengri kendi|larinaj. sovukludyr. ki bermagajlar menim oylanlarymaj egirlik etmagaj: | Boldu bu. tvin. 1021. ina. Hunvarnyng. 27. sina:

[8v] Da bunuda simarlijirmen menim potomoklarymaj. ki ol hišad|aglarny ' xajsiki xalypdyr menim protkajlarymdan. ki any | etkajlar har jyl. alaj nečik men etaredim. egar juxovdaj. egar ozga jerda. opatrovat etkajlar. budur menim erkim: ki alar [5] da alarnyng potomoklaryda bunu etkajlar:

1572

4. *[10v9] Diatik. toros oylar-ung. br hagopnung. tv. 1021: hulisning. 17: [10v11] Men Hagop ' toros oγlu: Xačan keldi tengridan menim usnumaj| tynszlx. da nega dingra igi esimdı edim. angdym boγos ar|akelnyng bujruxun.*

VI

ki jazijir bu turlu. ki diatik oludan | songra bunjatlydyr: Anyng učun undadym . .
[18] *da etijirmen | menim osiatymny. bu turlu. ki menim olumumdan songra* `
[20] *menim oylanlarym.* 1 *adz aney ajtargajlar. da.* 7. *xoj bla. ma|tay etkajlar.*
atamnyng ` *da anamnyng janlaryn angajlar* . . .

1572

5. [11r1] *Diatik. Bijata*j *xatunnung' bilkanyng. | trin.* 1021. *nojpémpér-
ning.* 7 *sinda:* |
[11r8] . . . *da belgili etdim menim jaxši erkimni. | nekimda baresa teng-
rining berganindan. Aval burun čxardym* [10] *xosdovanatama*j. 2. *fl. da axbaška.*
1. *fl. da.* 5. *kh.* 5. *fl:* | *da kebitni.* 2. *oyluma*j. *dr krikorga* ` *da hovaneska* ` *eksina.* |
*čxardym kumuš xynlarym. da duxnicam. da zufumny drga*j. | *kolmaklar ortax.*
muxajir šubam hovaneska. tibi tijin: | *kitlik. da jenglar. da xalgan ax oprax. bu
barča*j *hovaneska.* [15] *Xalgan kebit čerti eksina ortax. Budur menim erkim.
kimsaga | borčum jox.*

1574

6. [16r17] *tv.* 1023. *sna. majisning.* 2. *sna. xankun:*
*Keldi bijataxatuny bilenka*j. *br jerespoxanlarnyng. da ketxojalar*[*n*]*yng
alnyna | say vaxtna kensi ajaxy bla. da ajtdy ki bijlar* ` *tv.* 1021. *ina. nojémpér-
nyng.* [20] 7. *sina* ` *xastalanypedim. da diatik etipedim nečik orenkimyzdyr: Hali
tengri | jarlyady manga*j. *da saylxymny artdrdy. ol joyary jazgan diatikimni ki
etepedim. | buzarmen. da buzdum. tora*j *alnyna. da jazdrdym bu diftarda beklik-
učun.| ki ol burungi diatikim hečga boldu: da hečdyr bilgajsz:*

1574

7. [16v20] *Diatik xačko xznyng bilkanyng: tv.* 1023. *sna. | okostosnung.*
12. *sna:* |
[16v27] . . . *ol ayač kebitimni. xajsiki xardašim | pan zaxno beripedi manga*j.
xazar xardašimning paji učun. Na men [30] *ol kebitni satdym.* 200 *floriga. Da bu.*
200. *florunu. xardaš|im zaxno* ` *oylanlary bila* ` *aldylar xollaryna bu več bila* ` 100.
flori|dan. har jyl 20. *šar flori bergajlar xarflxka* ` *nečik tutundular* ` [17r] *menim
olum kunuma*j *dingra: Aj xačan tengrining bujruxun tugallasam. | povinen bolga*j
menim xardašym zaxno ` *oylanlary bila* ` *bu axčany ber|maga*j *dijatikima*j *kora* `
*nečik simarlijirmen: Bašta sp juxovga*j. *da | vankga.* 40. *fl: Dinatama*j *dr mgr-
dičga.* 2. *fl: Xalgan kahlarga* ` 1 *ar fl:* [5] 2. *oyluma*j. 20. *šar fl.* ` *torunlaryma*j `
učmaxly janly zadigning oylanlaryna ` | 50. *fl: Budur menim osijatym. da si-
marlaganym: Br zaxno. da oylu | xačko. zyznat etdilar. joyari jazgan ketxojalar*

VI

alnyna' ki pani | bilkanyng. 200. *fi. axčasy bar xatlaryna' da klijirlar olumun|dan*
songra. dosyt etma har birina. ba dijatikka kora: [10] *Jazyldy bu dijatik. tv.*
1023. *sna: okostosnung.* 12. *sinc=*

Übersetzung

1. [5v36] Ehekontrakt von Bogdan, Sohn des Herrn Donawak und Nasduchna, Tochter des Herrn Chačko, 12/22 Januar (Arm. Zeitrechn. 1021)
A. D. 1572.

[40] Durch den Willen des welterhaltenden, des allmächtigsten und
alle Wesen schonenden Vaters, Sohnes und Heiligen Geistes kam diese gesegnete Hochzeitsfeier zustande, in der von Gott erbauten Stadt Lemberg [6r]
unter der Ägide der [Kirche] Dormitio Sanctae Mariae, unter der Regierung
des christlichen Königs Sigismund August, dem Patriarchat des Vaters Katholikos Der Michael, dem Vikariat des Erzbischofs des geistigen Vaters, Krikor von Van, und der parochialen Tätigkeit des Vaters Waško. Unter den
Ratsvorsitzenden Herrn Krikor und Iwaško. [5] Es erschien vor dem Gericht
und den Kirchenvorständen Herr Donawak und bat Herrn Chačko, den Sohn
des verewigten Herrn Awedik und seine Gattin, Frau Chanuchna, um ihre
lobwürdige Tochter, Nasduchna, für ihren Sohn, Herrn Bogdan, für eine gesetzmäßige Ehe. Es sei vom Herrgott in eine glückliche Stunde verlegt, Amen.
Ich, Chačko, Sohn des Herrn Awedik, [10] mitsamt meiner Frau, Chanuchna,
wir geben unserem Kind, Fräulein Nasduchna, vorerst Gottes Segen, und
demfolgend aus dem von Gott bescherten irdischen Vermögen folgendes: Zuerst eine Kopfbinde mit Perlen und Goldzierden, 58 Mitqal; einen Haarband
mit Perlen und Goldzierden, 27 Mitqal; ein Collier mitsamt Gold und Perlen,
48 Mitqal; Umhängsel [15] mit Gold und Perlen, 26 Mitqal, 1 goldenen Halsschmuck, 9 Mitqal, 1 goldene Halskette, 24 Mitqal; 1 goldene Handschelle,
im Gewicht von 30 Goldgulden, einen Kragen mit Perlen, 50 Mitqal, eine Perlenbrosche 20 Mitqal, abermal eine Perlenbrosche 10 Mitqal, einen Brustlatz
mit Perlen für eine Schürze 10 Mitqal, eine Stirnspange mit Perlen, 18 Mitqal,
einen Halsring aus Perlen, 6 Mitqal, einen gestickten Kragen, einen Besatz
mit Perlen, zwei silberne Gürtel 4-einhalb Griwna; ein Beutel aus Silberfaden
[20] mit silbernen Etuis, beide 40 Gulden wert, 1 goldenes Hemd, 1 goldene
Schürze, 1 Samtkleid, 2 breite Kleider aus Taft, 1 rotes wollenes Kleid, 1
Kleid aus Mohär. Dem Herrn Bräutigam ein goldenes Hemd, außerdem
einen Verlobungsring mit Zaphrstein. Abermal dem Bräutigam 2 silberne
Pokale 2 1/2 Griwna; 3 Kissen mit je 3 Überzügen aus gesticktem Zwillich
und Seide, 2 Bettpfühle [25] mit seidenen Überzügen, 2 Sitzkissen mit Über-
zügen aus Zwillich, 1 wollene Bettdecke, 1 Teppich, Weißwäsche mit allem
Zubehör. Außerdem gebe ich, Chačko, Herrn Awediks Sohn, mit meiner
Tochter Nasduchna als Mitgift meinem Schwiegersohn Bohdan 1 aus Stein

VI

(gebautes) Gewölbe, das von meinem verewigten Vater auf mich kam. Auf
der einen Seite ist der Kaufladen der Kirche, auf der anderen [30] Seite
der Geschäftsladen des Herrn Philipp, Wasils Sohn. Weiterhin habe ich zu
diesem Geschäft aus dem von mir bewohnten Haus ein Grundstück meiner
Tochter, Nasduchma, als Mitgift zugeteilt, und gab es meinem Schwiegersohn Bohdan. Die Länge dieses Grundstücks beträgt die Länge des Hofs
von der einen Steinmauer [6v] bis zur anderen. Die Breite erstreckt sich von
der Seite des Vorhauses von der Steinmauer des Vorhauses 19 Krakauer Ellen
und oben von der Seite des Steinmauertors bis zum Hof des Hauses, in dem
die Frau Philipps wohnt. Die Breite von dort beträgt 10 1/2 Ellen, Krakauer
Ellen. [5] Diese Güter gebe ich, Chačko bzw. habe schon meinem Schwiegersohn Bohdan und seinen Nachkommen für ewige Zeiten gegeben. Mein
Schwiegersohn darf diese Güter als sein Eigentum benützen, da ich, Chačko
diese Güter meinem Schwiegersohn, Bohdan aus gutem Willen und [10]
Herzen als Mitgift gegeben hatte. Dagegen bringt der Bräutigam ein Braut-
kleid, 1 Paar Armbänder, 32 Mitqal, und Damaststoff für 1 Rock. Und ich
Donawak, mitsamt meinem Sohn Bohdan, wir versprechen meinem Gevatter,
Herrn Chačko, daß wir auf dem Teil, den er uns auf seinem bewohnten Grundstück zuwies, solange er, Herr Chačko, am Leben ist, nichts [15] bauen werden.
Aber wir werden es gebrauchen, und was wir dorthin legen und aufbewahren
wollen, das hängt von unserem beiderseitigen guten Willen ab. Und ich, Chačko,
Awediks Sohn, ich verspreche es meinem Gevatter, Herrn Donawak, und meinem Schwiegersohn Bohdan, zu welcher Zeit er es verlangt, eine Schrift über
die von mir gegebenen Güter, wenn [20] es nötig ist, bin ich verpflichtet ihn
das [in die Akten] einschreiben zu lassen. Dies ist geschrieben worden [nach
armen. Zeitrech. 1021] A.D. 1572, den 12/22 Januar.

   2. [48r] Ehekontrakt der Tochter des Herrn Kaspar, Fräulein Martha
und Herrn Kosta, des Herrn Andryjs Sohn, im Jahre [Arm. Zeitr. 1037] 12/22
Februar 1588, unter der Regierung Stephans.*
   Es sind persönlich erschienen vor dem Gremium der Senioren von der
einen Partei Herr Kaspar, Herrn Zadiks Sohn, [5] und von der anderen Partei
Kostas Sohn, Herr Andryj (sic!), und trugen folgendes vor: Herren Vorstände,
Herren Senioren die Ursache dessen, daß wir vor Euer Gnaden erschienen
sind, ist folgendes: Als wir mit Herrn Andryj Freundschaft geschlossen hatten, versprach ich ihm mit dem Erlaubnis des Herrn Bischofs und Euer Gnaden meine Tochter, Fräulein Martha, seinem Sohn, Herrn Kosta, gesätzmäßig
zur Frau zu geben. [10] Und dann sofort versprach ich mit meiner Tochter folgende Aussteuer zu geben, wie es in dieser Schrift geschrieben steht, die ich
Euer Gnaden überreiche. Deshalb bitte ich, daß sie vorgelesen werde. Auf die

---

   * darunter verbessert: Sigismunds.

VI

Bitte des Herrn Kaspar gaben die Senioren Erlaubnis, die Schrift zu verlesen.
Sie lautete solcherweise: Ich Kaspar, ich gebe unserem Kind, [15] Fräulein
Martha, in erster Linie Gottes Segen, und danach von den Leibesbedürfnissen, die von Gottes Ganden erwirkt sind, und zwar zuerst 1 goldene Kette
60 Goldgulden, 2 silberne Gürtel vergoldet, der erste 3 Griwna, der andere
2 Griwna [wert], 1 silbernen Beutel und 1 silbernes Etui, 1 Paar Armspangen,
1 Stirnspange mit Perlen, 2 goldene Hauben, 4 Kleider aus Jezdi-Stoff mit
Stolen, 1 Mantel aus Kannevas [20] mit Marderfell gefuttert; Weißwäsche,
eine Bettstelle mit allem Zubehör und 1 Bettdecke. Außerdem nimmt Herr
Kaspar den Herrn Kosta an Sohnes Statt an und gewährt ihm als Partner
Beitritt zu seinem Eigentum. Ich Kaspar lege in der Gemeinwirtschaft 2000
Gulden und mein Schwiegersohn 1000 Gulden an. Käme eine Zeit, wo es nötig
wäre, sich zu trennen, so würde ich, Kaspar zuerst [25] meine 2000 Gulden
herausnehmen, und so nehme auch mein Schwiegersohn seine 1000 Gulden.
Und danach — so Gott es gäbe — aus dem verdienten Geld je zur Hälfte sowohl ich als auch er. An meiner Seite soll er für 15 Jahre bleiben. Nachdem
diese Schrift verlesen worden war, bat Herr Kaspar die Senioren, um den
Bräutigam, Herrn Kosta, zu fragen, ob es ihm alles in der Schrift Stehende,
zusagt. [30] Auf die Frage der Senioren antwortete Herr Kosta und sprach
solchermaßen: Ich bin von seiten meines Schwiegervaters und meiner Schwiegermutter zufriedengestellt, so daß ich sowohl sie als auch ihre Nachkommen
für immer entlaste. Danach bat Herr Kaspar, daß diese Äußerung seines Schwie-
gersohnes in die Akten eingetragen werde und zur Erinnerung diene. Da erklärte sofort der Herr Bräutigam, [35] daß er hiegegen seiner Gattin, Fräulein
Martha, 500 Gulden Bargeld verschreiben läßt.

*

3. [7v26] Testament von Šmečko, des Miklaš Sohn, im Jahre (Arm.
Zeitr. 1021) 1572, 27 Januar/7 Februar.
    Ich Šimko, des Miklaš Sohn, im Besitz meiner geistigen Kräfte, nahm
Gott ins Herz und erinnerte mich des Wortes Pauls, des heiligen Apostels,
[30] der verordnet hat, das Testament nach dem Tode in Geltung bekräftigt
zu belassen. [8r] Ich also, als sterblicher Mensch, verfüge der Reihe nach über
mein Hab und Gut, das ich nach meinem Tode meiner Frau und meinen Kindern hinterlasse, und zwar: Erstens habe ich ein Haus aus Stein gebaut, darin
ich jetzt wohne, das mein Eigentum ist, d. h. das ich und mein Bruder, Herr
Iwasko unter uns [5] aufgeteilt hatten. Er ist im Eigentum geblieben, in dem
von ihm bewohnten Hause, ich dagegen blieb in meinem Anteil, in dem ich
wohne. Zwischen uns blieb kein Streit, weder von seiner Seite bei mir, noch
von meiner Seite bei ihm im väterlichen Anteil, weder in den Gütern, noch
im sonstigen Besitz; wir haben einander zufrieden gestellt. Weiters habe ich

VI

hinsichtlich dieses Hauses ein Geschäftslokal aus Stein, [10] das mir vom seligen Herrn Krikorsa hinterlassen wurde. Dies sind meine Güter. Außerdem habe ich als von Gott gegebene Güter sowohl in Schulden, wie in [Bar-] Geld, als in Naturalien, in Laden·und Haus, im Geschäft, nach meiner Berechnung 9.600 Gulden, etwas mehr oder weniger. Soviel gibt es. Aus diesen meinen Gütern scheide ich aus gutem·Willen aus: [15] für die Stadtkirche 20 Gulden, für die Klosterkirche 10 Gulden, für den Bischof 10 Gulden, für meinen Beichtvater 10, die Priester je 3 Gulden. Weiter für all meine Habe, Güter und Kinder bestätige ich meine Mutter, meine Frau, meinen Bruder, Herrn Ivaško, unseren Schwiegersohn, Herrn Chačko, des Avediks Sohn, als Vormund. Sie sollen aus meiner [20] gottgegebenen Habe zuerst meinen Tochtern solche Aussteuer von Gold und Perlen geben, wie ich meinen früheren Tochtern gegeben hatte. Laut ihres Ehekontraktes soll einer jeden von ihnen auch ein Brautschatz, je 300 Gulden Bargeld gegeben werden. Und was nachdem von den Mobilgütern übrig bleibt, soll die Hälfte meiner Frau, und die [andere] Hälfte [25] meinem·Sohn gegeben werden. Was die·Immobilien betrifft, ist mein Wille der folgende: meine Frau soll bis zu ihrem Tode über sie verfügen, wie ich in meinem Leben getan habe. Und·nach dem Tode meiner Frau all meine stehende Habe soll meinem Sohn Stecko gehören. Weiters [30] empfehle ich all dies der Fürsorge Gottes an, und [empfehle] den Vormunden, damit sie Gott ins Herz schließen und handeln in der Weise, daß es gut sei, so wie Gott ihnen lieb ist, erlauben sie es meinen Kindern·nicht, etwas Falsches zu tun. Es ist·verfaßt worden [Arm. Zeitr. 1021] A. D.·1572, 27 Januar/7 Februar.

[8v] Ich verordne meinen Nachkommen, daß sie die Gedenkfeier, wie es auf uns gekommen ist, so sollen sie jedes Jahr·feiern, wie ich es getan habe, entweder in der Kirche oder an anderem Ort sollen sie hierfür Sorge tragen. Es ist mein Wille, daß sie [5] und ihre Nachkommen ebenso handeln.

4. [10v9] Testament des· Herrn Hagop, Sohn des Thoros (Arm. Zeitr. 1021) A.D. 1572, 17/27 Juli.

[10v11] Ich Jakob, des Thoros Sohn, als mich auf Gottes [Gebot] die Unruhe überkam, und solange ich beim guten Verstand war, erinnerte ich mich des Gebots des Apostels Paul, darin es heißt, das Testament sei nach den Tode gültig. Deshalb ließ ich rufen . . . [18] und ich tat meinen letzten Willen in der Weise, daß meine Kinder nach meinem Tode ein Gebet «Deus increatus» [armenisch] sagen lassen und mit 7 Schafen ein Madagh-Opfer verrichten und der Seelen meines Vaters und meiner Mutter gedenken.

5. [11r1] Testament der Bilka, Frau des Bijata, (Arm. Zeitr. 1021) A. D. 1572, den 7/17 November.

[11r8] . . . und ich gab ihnen meinen guten Willen bekannt über meine ganze von Gott gegebene Habe. Erstens nahm ich heraus [10] für meinen

VI

Beichtvater 2 Gulden, den Bischof 1 Gulden, und für die 5 Priester 5 Gulden. Das Geschäftslokal hinterlasse ich meinen beiden Söhnen, Der-Krikor und Hovanes. Meine silbernen Behälter, meinen Kissen und den Wollstoff dem Vater [Der-Krikor]. Die Hemden je zur Hälfte, meinen mit Grauwerk gefutterten Mohärmantel gebe ich Hovanes, die Schürze und die Leibchen und die übrige Weißwäsche, das alles dem Hovanes. [15] Weiters eine Marktbude ihnen beiden je zur Hälfte. Das ist mein Wille. Niemandem bin ich schuldig.

6. [16r17] Mittwoch, 2/12 Mai (1023=) A. D. 1574.

Es kam vor die Ratsvorstände und die Senioren Bilenka, Bijatas Frau, gesund auf eigenen Füßen, und erklärte Folgendes: Meine Herren, am 7/17 November (1021=) A. D. 1572 [20] war ich erkrankt und hatte ein Testament gemacht, wie es bei uns Gebrauch ist. Jetzt hat sich Gott meiner erbarmt und meine Gesundheit verbessert. Jenes oben aufgezeichnete Testament, das ich damals gemacht hatte, erklärte ich vor dem Gericht als ungültig, also getilgt, und ließ in das Protokoll zur Bekräftigung eintragen, daß mein erstes Testament nichtig geworden ist, also nehmet zur Kenntnis, daß es nichtig ist.

7. [16v20] Testament der Bilka, Chačkos Tochter, (1023=) A. D. 1574, am 12/22 August.

[16v27] ... Jene Marktbude aus Holz, die mir von meinem Bruder, Herr Zachno, [dereinst] gegeben wurde als Anteil meines Bruders, Lazar, also [30] jene Bude habe ich für 200 Gulden verkauft. Und jene 200 Gulden nahmen mein Bruder Zachno und seine Söhne in die Hände, und zwar mit der Verordnung, mir von 100 Gulden jedes Jahr bis zu meinem Tode 20 Gulden als Taschengeld zu geben, wie sie es auch versprachen. [17r] Und als ich durch Gottes Fügung [mein Leben] beende, so werden mein Bruder Zachno, und seine Söhne verpflichtet sein, das Geld laut meines Testaments, wie ich verfüge [folgenden Personen] zu geben: Erstens der heiligen Kirche [gestrichen: und], dem Kloster 40 Gulden, meinem Beichtvater Der Megerdič 2 Gulden, den übrigen Priestern je 1 Gulden, [5] meinen 2 Söhnen je 20 Gulden, meinen Enkeln, den Söhnen des verschiedenen Zadig je 50 Gulden. Das ist mein [letzter] Wille und Verfügung. Herr Zachno, und sein Sohn Chačko haben vor den oben genannten Senioren anerkannt, daß die 200 Gulden der Frau Bilka bei ihnen ist, und daß sie nach ihrem Tode alle, nach diesem Testament, zufrieden stellen wollen. [10] Dieses Testament ist niedergeschrieben worden im Jahre (1023=) A. D. 1574, am 12/22 August.

*

VI

Wörterverzeichnis

Zitierte Literatur

Ačarian, Hr., *Haycrèn gawaṙakan baṙaran* [Armenisches Dialektenwörterbuch]: *Emin-skij Etnografičeskij Sbornik* No. IX (Tiflis 1913).

Alγγš Bitiki (AB): Schütz, E., *Armeno-Kipchak Texts from Lvov (A. D. 1618): AOH* XV (1962), 291—309.

Brückner, A., *Słownik Etymologyczny*, Warszawa 1957.

Bžškian, M., *Čanaparhordut'iwn i Lehastan* [Reise nach Polen], Venedig 1830.

Eph. = Deny, J., *L'Arméno-Coman et les «Ephémérides» de Kamieniec (1604—1613)*: *Ural-Altaische Bibliothek*, No. IV, Wiesbaden 1957.

Hübschmann, H., *Armenische Grammatik*, I. *Armenische Etymologie*, Leipzig 1895.

Linde, S. M., *Słownik języka polskiego*, I—VI, Lwów 1854—1860.

Tar. Söz. = *Tarama Sözlüğü*, I—IV, Ankara 1963—1969.

Steingass, F., *A Comprehensive Persian—English Dictionary*, London 1900.

Tryjarski, E., *Dictionnaire Arméno-kiptchak d'après trois des collections viennoises*, t. I/1—3, A—K, 1968—69.

S. noch Fußnoten 1, 15.

adamaška (< Lat. *adamascus* «Samt, usw. aus Damaskus», S. Brückner, 2.) 6r21, 6v11 «Damast» z. B. 1 *šubalx* ∼ 6v11 «Damaststoff für einen Rock»; 1. *xzyl* ∼ *letnik* 30r5 «ein Sommerkleid aus rotem Damast».

adz (= *asdvadz*, Arm. աստուած) 10v20 «Gott»

adzadzin (= *asdvadzadzin*, Arm. աստուածածին) 6r1 «Gottgebarerin, die Heilige Maria»

ayač 16v28 «Baum, Holz»

ayča 8r22 «Geld». S. auch *axča*

ayγr 6r16 «schwer; Gewicht»

ax 6r26 «weiß»

axbaš 8r15, 11r10 «Bischof»

axča 8r12 «Geld». S. auch *ayča*, *nayd*, *sb*

a (geschrieben: *aj*) (Pol. a) 6v10, 6v11, 8r25 «aber, dagegen, und»

ajax 16r19 «Fuß»

ajyryl- 48r24 «sich trennen»

ajovuči 5v41 «Beschützer» (AB «provisor»); *baryny* ∼ Lehnübersetzung vom Arm. *naxaχnamoy hamaynic'* 7v4, 9r9

ajt- 16r19, 48r6, 48r30 «sagen»

akta 48r33 «Protokoll». Oft auch *diftar* genannt

al- 48r25 «nehmen»

alaj . . . nečik 8r8 «sowohl . . . als auch»

alar 8v4, *alarnyng* 6r7, 8v5, 8r22 Pl. Nom und Gen von *ol*

alγγš, *alyš* 6r11, 48r15 «Segen»

alyn «Vorderseite»; *alnyna* 6r5, 48r4, 48r7 «vor»

alyšmax «das (gegenseitige) Nehmen, Heiraten, Heirat»; *orenkli* ∼ 6r8, 8v21,

9r18, 9v21, 10r23, 12r3, 12r26 usw. «gesetzmäßige Heirat», vgl. Arm.
orinawor amusnut'iwn 7v13, 11v10 (Grigorian, S. 289, Zeile 5 von unten:
orinawor genagc'ut'iwn). Die Heirat als «Kauf-Verkauf» aufgefaßt: *alyš
beryš* 21v22. S. noch S. 269

altynla- 48r17 «vergolden»

altun 6r13, 14, 15, 16 «Gold»

ana 8r18 «Mutter»

anéy անեղ; *adz* ∼ 10v20 «unerschaffener Gott, Deus increatus»

ang- 10v12, *an-* 10v21 (in der Con. Form: *angaj*) «sich erinnern, sich ins Gedächtnis rufen (AB memini, recordor)»

any 8v2, *anyng* 6v6, *angar* 6v20, *anda* anda 6v14, 16, *andan* 48r25 Sing. Kasusformen von *ol*

anyngki 48r13 «solcher»

aračnortlux (Arm. առաջնորդ-) 6r3 «Rang, Stand eines Prälats»

aran 6v1, 2 «Vorhaus, Vordach; (Wagenschuppen»?)

arhiaxbaš 6r3 «Erzbischof»

arijan 5v41 «der heilige Geist»

art «Hinterteil»; *munung* ∼*-yndan* 6r11 «nachher»

artyx 8r6 «mehr»

arttyr- 16r21, 26r25 «vermehren»

ata 5v41, 6r29 «Vater»

atalyx «väterlich»; ∼*alyyš* 26r24 «väterlicher Segen»

awakéreclx (Arm. աւագերեց-) 6r3 «Rang, Stand eines Hohepriesters»

aval 6r11, 48r15 «zuerst, erstens»; ∼ *burun* 11r8 «zu allererst»

avalgi 8r21 «voriger»

az 8r13 «wenig»

azbar 6r33, 6v3 «Hof»

babas 8r16 «Geistlicher, Priester»

bar 8r7, 8r14 «es ist, es gibt»; ∼*-dyr* 8r3, 9 «ds»

bar- 6v20 «gehen»

barča 5v40 «alle»; ∼ *nema* 48r29 «alles»

bary 5v41 «alles»

baron 5v36 (Arm. պարոն) «Herr»; *baronder* 6r3 «Benennung eines Geistlichen
höheren Standes» (S. noch S. 266)

bašbay passim «Kopfbinde, Kopftuch»; ∼ *injisi altuny bla* 58 *mtxal* 6r13 «Kopfbinde mit Perlen und Goldzierden 58 Mitqal»

bašta 6r13, 8r3, 17r3 «zuerst, in erster Linie»

beklik 16r22 «Gültigkeit, Geltung»; ∼*-ta xalyr* 7v30 «in Kraft bleiben» S. *berklik*

belbay 6r19 «Gürtel»; *kumuš* ∼ *altynlagan* ... 3 *somtaši* 48r17 «silberner ver-
goldeter Gürtel 3 Griwna»

belgili 11r8 «offenbar»; ∼ *et-* 19r29 «bekannt machen»

ber- 6r10, 27 «geben»

VI

beril- 8r22 «gegeben werden»

berklik 12v12 «Kraft, Bekräftigung» ~-*ta xulyr* 11r5, 12v12, 18r9 «in Kraft bleibt, gültig bleibt» S. *beklik, bunjatly* und Einleitung S. 270

berma-: ~-*gajlar . . . egirlik etmaga* 8r32 «sie sollen ihnen nicht nicht erlauben etwas zu Falsches tun»

bij 16r19, 48r6 «Herr»; ~ *tengri* 6r8 «Herrgott»

bijlik 48r6 «Herrschaft»; ~-*yngyz,* ~-*ingyz* «Eure Herrschaft»

bil- «wissen, verstehen», ~-*gajsz* 16r23 «ihr sollt zur Kenntnis nehmen»

bila 6r10, 6r24 «mit(samt)»; s. *bla*

bilazuk 6v11 «Armband»

bir «ein», ~-*i* «der eine» 8r8; ~-*si* 6r29, 6v1, 48r17 «der andere»

bitik 48r11, 13, 28 «Schrift, Schreiben, Schriftstück»

biz 6v13 «wir»; ~-*im* 6v16 «unser»

bla 8r5, 10r20 «mit»; s. noch *bila*

boyma 6r18 «Schlinge, Halsring, Collier»; *inji* ~ 6 *mtxal* 25r18 «Halsschlinge mit Perlen 6 Mitqal»

bojunčax 6r16 «Halskette»; *altun* ~ 20 *mtxal xušlar učun* «goldgestickter Halskragen 20 Mitqal für Hängeschmuck»; Vgl. *boyuncak = boyunduruk, Derleme Sözlüğü* II. 747.; *mojyndyrik* (nogaisch) «gestickter Halsschmuck für Frauen aus Silber, Korall oder anderer Kostbarkeit»; entspricht arm. *vznoc'* «Kragen, Collier». S. noch Szongott, *Ethnographie,* S. 244, 245

bol- 5v42, 6v7 «sein; werden»

borč 8r12, 11r16 «Schuld»

bošatlx 12v29 «Verzeihung, Vergebung»

br «Herr»; *br dr = baronder,* s. *baron*

bramka 6r18 «Stirnspange, ein veralteter Weiberkopfputz; frontale mulierum ex gemmis, lunae corniculatae figura, ad auriculas pertingens», Linde I/162—3; aus dem Deutschen *Bram (verbrämen)* Brückner, S. 38. *sirma bramka* 16v11 «gestickte Stirnspange»; *inji* ~ 17r30, 48r19 «Stirnspange aus/mit Perlen»

briž (Poln bryź, vgl. Ukr. Russ. *брыжи*) 6r19 «1. bunte Stickereien, bunter krauser Besatz an den Frauenkleidern, Linde I/180., 2. Brosche» *inji* ~-*lar* 17r28, «Besatz mit Perlen», *sirma* ~ 17r29 «gestickter Besatz»

bu «dieser»; Kasus s. unter *bunu*

budovat (Poln. budować, Ukr. *буgovamu) et-* 6v15 «bauen»

bujrux 10v12, 17r1 «Gebot»

bujur- 7v30 «verordnen, gebieten»

bunu 8v1, 8v5; *bunungki* 48r10 «solcher»; *bungar* 12v29; *bundan* 8r23; *buxadar* 8r29 «so viel». S. noch *munung*

bunjatly 10v14, 16v25 «kräftig, in Kraft, gültig»; 13v29, 25v40 *diatik olumdan songra* ~-*dyr* «testamentum enim in mortuis confirmatum est». Vgl. *berklik.* S. Einleitung 270

VI

burun 11r9 «zuerst, erstens»; *aral* ~ 11r8 «zu allererst»

burungi 16r23 «erster, voriger»

buz- «verderben, tilgen»; *diatikimni . . . buzarmen* 16r22 «ich erkläre mein Testament als ungültig»

cvelex, cvelix (Poln. cwelich < D. Zwillich, S. Linde I/332; Brückner, 68) *kuft* ~ 6r24 «gestickter Zwillich»; *mindar* ~ *juzluklar bila* 6r25 «Polster mit Überzug aus Zwillich»

čax 6v1 «bis»

časy; na vječnyj ~ (Pol. na wieczny czasy) 6v6 «auf ewige Zeit, zur Ewigkeit, für immer»

čepec (Pol. czepiec) «Haube, Mütze»: *altun* ~ 48r19; 1 *altyn ipindan* ~ 32v22 «eine Haube aus Goldfadei.»: 1 *ipak* ~ 33v22 «eine Haube aus Seide»

čert 11r15

č(y)x- 6v4 «herausgehen, herauskommen»

čxar- 8r14, 11r9, 11r12 «herausziehen. herausnehmen. herausbringen; absondern»

da 5v40 «und» (nur teilweise enklitisch)

dayy 8r9, 6r30 *dayyn* 6r27 «auch, mehr. noch»

dastyment 12v28 «Testament» S. noch *diatik*

dastur 48r8, 13 «Erlaubnis»

diatik (Arm. < Griech. διαθήκη, Hübschmann, *Arm. Etym.*, 346) 7v26, 10v13, 11r1, 16r19, 21, 23, 17r3, 9, 10 «Testament» S. noch *dastyment, osiat, vosiat*

diftar 16r22 «Heft, Verzeichnis, Register, Akten». S. noch *akta*

dijin 8r26 «bis»

dingra 6v1, 10v12, 17r1 «bis zu»

dira «bis zu»; 15 *jylga* ~ 48r27 «für 15 Jahre»

dn (Arm. dearn, Gen. von der, Abk. dr) 6r2 «des Herrn»

dosyt (Pol. dosyć) *bol-* 48r29, 31 «genügend werden, genügen»; ~ *et-* 17r9 (*dosit*) 8r8 «zufrieden stellen»

dostlux 48r7 «Freundschaft»

dr Abk. von *der* (Arm. *տէր*) 6r2, 11r12 «Gott; Vater (als Vorname eines Geistlichen): Herr»

duxnica (Pol. Ukr.) 11r12 «eine mit Daunen gefütterte Schlafmütze, Federmütze; ein kleines Kopfkissen» (Linde, I/553)

dunja «Welt»; ~*-ni(ny) tutuči* 5r4, 38, 5v40 «allmächtig». Entspricht Arm. *amenagal* 7v4, 9r9, 11v4

dunjalik «irdisch, weltlich»: ~ *igilikimiz* 6r12, ~ *tirlikimiz* 9v24, 12r28, 15r23, 18v16, 19r17, 21v14 «unsere irdischen Güter»

jan 10v21 «Seele»; ~ *aši* 14r18 «Leichenschmaus, Totenmahl». Im Armenischen *hokuhac'*, s. Szongott, *Ethnogr.* S. 190.

jihan «Welt»; *bu* ~*-da, ol* ~*-da* 12v29 «auf dieser Welt, auf der anderen Welt»

VI

juft (հութ) 6v10, 48r18 «ein Paar»

juvap et- 48r30 «antworten»

egirlik 8r33 «Krummheit, Falschheit, Bosheit, Ungerechtigkeit»

eki 6v16 «zwei»; ∼-*si* 11r11 «beide»; ∼-*nči* 6r17 «zweiter»

eksik 8r13, 26r25 «weniger, mangelnd, mangelhaft»

éréspoxan (Arm. Լրևափոխան) 48r6 «Vorstand des Rates». S. Einleitung 266

éréspoxanlx 6r4 «Würde, Stand des Vorsitzenden des Rates»

erk 6v17, 8r26 «Wille»; *menim jaxši* ∼-*imdan*, ∼-*im bila* 6v9, 8r14 «aus meinem guten Willen»; ;∼-*i bila dunjani tutučinyng* 5v40 «durch den Willen
 des Allmächtigen». Im Arm. entspricht *gamaw amenagalin* 7v4, 9r9,
 11v4

erkli 6v7 «ermächtigt; freiwillig»

es «Verstand, geistige Kräfte» *nega dingra jaxši (igi)* ∼-*imda* (∼-*da*) *edim* 10v12,
 13v27 «solange ich bei guten Sinnen war». S. noch *fikir*, *sayyš*

evet 6v15 «aber»

fartux (Pol. fartuch, Russ. фартук <d. Vortuch, Linde 645, Brückner 118.)
 6r18, 20 «Schürze»

fikir «Gedanke»; *bolup men tugal* ∼-*imda da sayyšimda* 25v38 «bei (vollen)
 Sinnen und Verstand seiend»

flori, Abk. *fl* 16v32 «Gulden»; *xzyl* ∼ 5r20 «Goldgulden»

galaji (Arm. կալաճի in arm. Mundarten, Ačarian, *Gawar. Bar.* 536. < Türk.
 keleci, geleci «söz, lakırdı» (*Tar. Söz.* IV. 2398.) «Gespräch»; *bir soz* ∼
 bolmagaj 7r30 «es soll kein Wort Streit sein»

gaduyigos (Arm. կատուղիկոս) 6r2 «Katholikos, arm. Patriarch»

gs Abk. von *ges* (Arm. կէս) 6r19 «halb, Hälfte»

hadirlan- 48r16 «vorbereitet werden»

hajimuk «Halsschmuck?»; *altun* ∼ 8 *mtxal* 9v29, 10r29, 13v13 «goldener Halsschmuck 8 Mitqal»

hajrabedlx (Arm. hayrabéd հայրապետ «Patriarch») 6r2 «Patriarchat»

hali 8r3, 16r20 «jetzt»

har 6r26 «alle»; ∼ *biri* 8r23, 17r9 «jeder einzelne von ihnen»

heč 16r23 «nichts, nichtig»; ∼-*ga bol-* 16r23 «nichtig werden»

hišadag (Arm. յիշատակ) 8v1 «Erinnerung»

hyseb 8r13 «Rechnung, Berechnung»

hoképarc (Arm. հոքեբարձ) 8r18, 30 «Vormund»; ∼ *da opekun* 13v32 «ds»

hunvar (Arm. յունվար) 5v36, 6v20 «Januar»

xabax 6v2 «s Tor»

xačan 10v11 «wann»

xadar; *bu* ∼ 8r13, *ol* ∼ 8r21 «soviel»

xadufa, *xadifa* «Barchent, Sammet, Velvet, Plüsch, Satin; wollenes Bettzeug»;
 ∼ *jovuryan* 6r25, 15r6 «wollene Bettdecke»; ∼ *kitlik* 16v12 «. . . Leibchen»; ∼ *bork* 18r15 . . . Kappe; 2 *ton* (*keng*) *jezdi* ∼-*lar bila* 15r5, 16v12

VI

5 *ton hadir tikilgan* ~-*lar bila* 19r18 «Kleider aus breitem Jezdi Stoff,
6 Kleider mit fertig genähten ... Stolen»

xajda 6v19 «wo»

xajin; ~ *ata* 48r31 «Schwiegervater», ~ *ana* «Schwiegermutter»

xajsi 5v41, 48r11 «welcher»

xal- 6r29, 7v30 «bleiben»

xalat 6v10 «Ehrenkleid, Prunkkleid» (das vom Bräutigam als Brautgeschenk
überreicht wird)

xaldyr- 8r2 «lassen»

xali 6r26 «Teppich»

xan; *kristan* ~ 6r1 «der christliche (hier: der polnische) König»

xankun 16r17 «Mittwoch»

xardaš 8r4 «Bruder»

xarjlx 16v32 «Taschengeld»

xarši 48r35 «gegen»; ; ~ *bol-* 12v29 «gegen etw. sein»

xastalan- 16r20 «krank sein»

xat «Seite»; *menim* ~-*yma turgaj* 48r17 «er soll bei mir bleiben»; ~-*laryna*
17r8 «bei ihnen»

xatun 8r2, 18 «Frau»; *menim* ~-*um* 8r24 «meine Frau». S. noch *syngar*

xyn, xn «Scheide»; *kumuš* ~-*lar* 10r12, 48r18 «silberne Etuis, Behälter»

xyz 5v38, *xz* 6r31, 8r21, 16v20 «Tochter»; ~-*oγlan* 8r20 «Tochter»

xyzyl s. *xzyl*

xoj 10v20 «Schaf» (hier: als Opfertier, s. *madaγ*)

xoj- 6v16, 48r23 «legen»

xol 16v31 «Hand»

xol- 48r28 «bitten»

xosdovanata (Arm. խոստովանան.) 8r16, 11r9 «Beichtvater»

xuš «Vogel; Angehänge»; *altun* ~-*lar injisiz* 9r24 «goldenes Gehänge ohne
Perlen»; *altun znjyl* 32 *xzyl jiori*̀ ~ *jerina* 12r32 «goldene Kette 32 Goldgulden anstatt/für Gehänge»; *altun bojunčax* 20 *mtl* ~-*laručun* 13v12
«goldener Halsschmuck 20 Mitqal für Gehänge»; ~-*lar altyny injisi bila*
26 (36)*mytxal* 6r14, 29v25 «Gehänge mitsamt Gold und Perlen 26 (36)
Mitqal» (S. auch Grigorian: *a. a. O.* S. 435.)

xutlu 5v42, 6r9 «glücklich». Arm. *šnahawor* շնահաւոր 7v8

xuvatly «kräftig»; *barčadan* ~ 5v40 «allmächtigster» = Arm. *aménagaroγ*
ամենակարող 7v4, 9r9, 11v4

xz s. *xyz*

xzyl «rot, goldener»; 1 *ton* ~ *zuf* 6r21 «ein Kleid aus roter Wolle»; ~ *fli* 6r16,
48r17 «Goldgulden»

ič «s Innere»; ~-*ina* 8r3 «darin»

igi 8r31, 10v12 «gut, wohl»

igilik 8r1, 11, 17 «Habe, Gut»; *duxjalik* ~-*imyz* 6r12 «unsere irdischen Güter»;

VI

ruxomyj ~ 8r24 «Mobilgüter» S. noch *mulklar, imenja(lar)*; *(jaxšilx* [Hrunin, No. 288.] «Güter»)

imenja(lar) (Ukr. *именис*) 8r29 «Vermögen. Besitztum»

inǰi 6r13, 17, 18, 48r19 «Perle»

ipakli 6r24 «seiden»

yskylep (Pol. sklep) 8r12 «Laden, Kaufmannsgewölbe»

ja 6v16 «oder»

jaγa «Kragen»; *inǰi* ~ 6r16 «Kragen mit Perlen»; *sirma* ~ 6r19 «gestickter Kragen»

jaγut «Rubin»; *nšan juzuku kok* ~ 6r23 «Verlobungsring mit Zaphirstein» (Bei den Armeniern war es üblich in den Verlobungsring ein Zaphirstein einfassen zu lassen)

jaxši 6v9, 11r8 «gut»; ~-*lar* 6r26, 48r20 «Zubehör» S. noch *igilik*

jan 6r29, 30, 48r5 «Seite»

jana 6r22, 23 «wieder»

jarym 8r24 «ein Halb, Hälfte»; 2 *somtašy* ~ 6r23 «2 1/2 Griwna» ~ *da* ~ *algajbiz* 48r26 «wir sollen je die Hälfte nehmen»

jarlγa- 16r21 «sich erbarmen»

jastyx 6r24 «Kissen, Polster»

jaz- 6v19, 20 «schreiben»

jazdyr-, jazdr- 6v20, 16r22 «schreiben lassen»

jazyl- 48r34 «geschrieben werden»

jazov 48r29 «Schrift». Vgl. *bitik*

jegdana (Steingass, 1533: «an incomparable gem, a string of pearls, a necklace») hier: «Halskette»; *altyn inǰisi bila* ... 9r23, 25r17 «goldene Halskette mit Perlen»; *bir somtašy* ~ *inǰisi altunybla* 14v19 «eine Halskette ein Griwna mit Perlen und Gold»; *altun* ~ 1. *somtašy* 13v12 «goldene Kette ein Griwna»

jeng 11r14, 18r16 «Ärmel». Vgl. CC «manicha»

jer 6r31 «Platz»; *jerinda* «für, anstatt»: *majja* ~ 6r28, 6v9 «als, für Mitgift»; *oγul* ~ 48r22 «für einen Sohn»

jerga «Reihe, Rang, Ordnung, Reihenfolge, Einreihung»; *etijirmen* ~ *menim igilikimda* 8r1 «ich mache Einreihung in meine Güter»; *ten* ~-*sindan* 7r6, 15v19, 17v19 «aus der Reihe des Leibes: von Leibesbedürfnissen»

jezdi 48r19 «Jezder Kleiderstoff»

jyl 48r17 «Jahr»

joγari 6v2 «oben»; ~ *jazgan* 16r21, 17r7 «obenerwähnt»

jox 11r16 «ist nicht»

jovurγan 15r6 s. *juvurγan*

juxov 6r29, 8r15 «Kirche»

jurak 7v29, 8r31 «Herz»

juvurγan 6r26, 48r21 «Bettdecke, Steppdecke»

juzluk 6r24, 25 «Kissenbezug, Polsterüberzug»

juzuk «Ring»; *nšan* ~-*u* 6r22 «Verlobungsring»; ~ 6 *xzyl fli* 9v5 «Ring 6 Goldgulden»; ~ 4 *xzyl floriluk* «Ring 4 Goldgulden wert»

kahanaj (Arm. քահանայ) 6r4 «Priester», Abk.: *kah*, *kh*

kahlx Abk. für *kahanalx* 6r5 «Priesterschaft, Gremium der Priester»

kamxa (Pol. kamcha) 6r25, «Seidenzeug» (pannus damascenus, Linde II/296.)

kanafaca (Pol. kanawac, kanawas, kanafas < canabacium, < canabis. Vgl. Fr. canevas, Engl. canvass, Russ. канафас) 48r19 «Rockstoff, Kanevas»

kebit 6r30 «Kaufladen»; *ayač* ~ 16v28 «Laden aus Holz»; *taš* ~ 6r28 «Laden aus Stein gebaut»

kel- 6r5, 10v11 «kommen»: ~-*ganymyz* 48r6 «unser Kommen, Ankunft»

kelin 6v10 «Braut»

keltir- 6v10 «bringen»

kendi 6r8, 6v8 «selbst»; 48r22 «eigen»

kenlik 6v1, *kenglik* 6v4 «Breite»

kensi 8r26, 48r22 «selbst»; 16r19 «eigen»

kerak «nötig, Notwendigkeit»: *ten* ~-*i* 28v24, 48r15 «Leibesbedürfnisse». S. noch *ten*

kesak 6r31 «Stück»

ketxojja 48r6 «Vorstand, Senior»: *ant ičkan* ~-*lar* «die geschworenen Senioren»

ketxojjalyx 48r4, 13, 28, 30 «Gremium der Senioren»

kibik; *munung* ~ 6v5 «solcher»

kijov 6r22, 23, 32 «Bräutigam, Schwiegersohn»

kimsa (+ Neg) 11r15 «niemand»

kiši 8r1 «Mensch»

kitajka (Ukr. Pol. Linde II/360, Brückner, 231) «Taffet, Samtstoff, Nanking»; 2 *ton široka* ~ 6r21 «2 breite Kleider aus Nankingstoff»

kitlik (Pol. kitlik, kitel, kitliczek Linde, II/360.) 11r14 «Weiberkittel»; 1 ~ *zlotohlav forbotlu* 25r20, 30r2 «ein brokater Weiberkittel mit Fransen»

kla- 6v15, 19 «wünschen, wollen»

kobok (Ukr., Pol.) 6r23 «Pokal, Becher»

kok 6r23 «blau»

kolga «Schatten»; ~-*sina* 6r1 «unter der Ägide» (Arm. *ant hovaneaw* 7v6)

kolmak 11r13 «Hemd»; *altun* ~ 6r20, 22 «Goldhemd» (für den Bräutigam)

kongul 6v10 «Herz, Wille»

kora 6r30 «in Anbetracht, wegen»

kristan 6r1 «christlich»

krorenk (Arm. գրորէնք, գրաւրէնք) 5v36, 8r22, 48r1 «Heiratsvertrag, contractus antenuptialis»

kuč «Kraft»; ~-*uma kora* 29r31 «nach Vermögen»

kuft 6r24 «gestickt»

VI

kumuš 6r19 «Silber, silberner»

kvitovat (Pol. kwitować) *et-* 48r32 «quittieren, jn (für eine Summe) entlasten»

lokot (Ukr. локоть) «Elle»; *krakovnung* ~-*u* 6v2, 4 «Krakauer Elle»

maday (Arm. *Մատաղ*) 10v20 «Tieropfer, Opfertier»

maxtovlu xz 8v20, 12r25 «löbliche Tochter». S. noch *ogovlu*

majja (Pol. majątek «Vermögen, Habe, Gut») 6r28, 32, 6v9, 8r22 «Mitgift, Aussteuer, Brautschatz»

majentnost (Pol. majętność) 48r22, 8r8, 14 «Gut, Landgut, Eigentum»

majis (Arm. *Մայիս*) 16r17 «Mai»

manella (Pol. manela, manelka < Ital. maniglia, Linde III/39, Brückner, 321) 48r18 «Armband, Armspange»

manga 16r21, 48r31 Dat. von *men*

mazgab (Arm. *Մազկապ*) 6r13 «Haarband»; *altun* ~ 60 *čičak usna* 9v27 (... *altyny* 20 *mtxal* 38v25) «goldener Haarband 60 Blumen (Rosen) darauf (Goldgewicht 20 Mitqal)» Vgl. Arm. 7v17

men 6r9, 27 «ich»; *menim* 7v28, 8r1; *manga* 16r21, *menda* 8r7, *mendan* 8r2

mindar 6r25 «Sitzkissen, Matratze»

miskin 29r31 «arm»

miskinlik 30v1 «Armut»

mtxal, mtxl 6v11 «Mitqal, Gewicht 4.46 Gramm» (*Handb. Orient.* Erg. Bd. 1. H. 1. W. Hinz., *Islamische Maße u. Gewichte*, p. 7.)

muxajar, muxajir «Mohärstoff»; *ton muxajar* 6r22 «Mohärkleid»; *muxajir šuba* 11r13 «Mohärmantel»

mulk 8r5, 8, 17 «Besitz, Güter»; ~-*lar* 6v5, 7, 8, 19, 8r11 «Güter»

munung 6r11, 6v5, 16, *munungki* 48r33, *mungar xarši* 48r35, *munda* 48r34, *mundan songra* 48r21 Kasusformen von *bu*, vgl. *bunu*

na (Pol. na) 48r12, 16v29 «dann»

nayd, nahd; *nayd ayča* 8r22 «Bargeld»; *sb nahd* 48r35 «Silbergeld»

ne 6r11 «welcher; was»

neča 6v14 «solange»

nečik 6r26, 6v7, 48r20 «wie, als, wiewohl auch»; ~ ... *alaj* 48r27 «sowohl ... als auch»

nema 6v14, 8r14 «etwas»

nnčum (Arm. *Ննջում*) 6r1 «dormitio»; ~ *sp adzadzinnyng* 6r1 «Dormitio S. Mariae» (Mutterkirche der Armenier von Lemberg. S. Bžškian, *Čanaparhordut'iwn*, S. 102. ff.)

nogar 6r7, 9 «Gefährte, Ehefrau, Gattin»

nojémpér (Arm. *Նոյեմբեր*) 11r2 «November»

nšan (Arm. *Նշան*) «Zeichen; Verlobung»; ~ *juzuku* 6r22 «Verlobungsring». S. auch *jayut*

obličnje (Pol. oblycznie) 26v24, 48r4 «persönlich»

oddat (Ukr. оддати Pol. oddać) *et-* 48r9 «übergeben, hingeben»

VI

ogovlu «lobenswert, lobwürdig, löblich»; ~ *xzy* 6r7 «die wohlgeborene Tochter von . . .», s. *maxtovlu* «ds». Arm. *koveli* զովելի 7v12, 11v9

oylan 6r10, 27, 48r14 «Kind» (hier: Tochter); ~-*lar* 8r2, 33 «Kinder»

oyul 5v36 «Sohn»

okostos (Arm. օգոստոս) 16v21 «August»

ol 6v3, 8r5, 16r21, 23 «jener»; *any* 8v2, *anyng* 6v6, *angar* 6v20, *anda* 6v14, 16, *andan* 6v4

olum 7v30, 8r28 «Tod»; ~ *kunu* 17r1 «Todestag»; *olu* 10v13 für *olum*

olumlu; ~ *kiši* 8r1 «r sterbliche Mensch»

opatrovat (Pol. opatrywać) *et-* 8v4 «(ver)sorgen»

opivat (Pol. opiewać) *et-* 48r14 «lauten»

oprax «Kleidungsstück»; *ax* ~ 8r26, 11r14, 49r20 «Weißwäsche»

orenk (Arm. օրէնք «Gesetz») «Gericht (= tora)» (Im arm. Text 7v11); ~ *bila* 48r9 «gesetzmäßig» ~-*ymyz* 16r20 «unser Gebrauch»

orenkli (Arm. օրէնք + li) 6r8 «gesetzmäßig, rechtsmäßig»

orun 48r20 «Platz, Stelle; Bett» S. noch *tošak*

orta «Mitte;s Gemeinsame (Geschäft)» ~-*myzga* 8r6, «zwischen uns, unter uns»

ortax 11r13, 15 «gemeinsam, zusammen»

ortaxlx 48r23 «Partnerschaft, gemeinschaftlicher Besitz»

osiat 10v19, 16v28, 17r6 «Testament». S. noch *vosiat, diatik, dastyment*

ov 6r31 «Haus»

ovnungki 6v3 «zum Haus gehörend»

ozga 8r8, 8v4 «anderer»

padšahlx 6r1, 48r3 «königliche Herrschaft, Regierung(szeit) des Königs»

paj 8r6, 16v29, «Teil, Anteil»; *ata* ~-*y* 8r7 «väterlicher Teil»

pajlaš- 8r5 «unter sich verteilen»

pamjat (Ukr. память) 7v28, 12v11 «Gedächtnis, Sinn». S. noch *es*

pamjentnyj (Pol. pamiętny) 48r34 «denkwürdig, unvergeßlich»

pan (Pol. pan) 5v37 «Herr»

pani (Pol. pani) 6r7 «Frau»

panna (Pol. panna) 6r7 «Fräulein»

pedrvar (Arm. փետրվար) 48r2 «Februar»

perina (Ukr. перина) 6r24 «Bettpfühl»

podavat (Pol. podawać) *et-* 48r11 «einreichen»

podbityj (Part. Perf. von podbyć; syn. von podszyć «Kleidungsstück futtern»); *šuba susar bila* ~ 48r20 «Mantel, mit Marderfell gefuttert»; *šuba susar bila urgan* 22v37 «ds»; (1592) 1 *šuba kanafaca hornostaj bila potšityj* 59v9 «ein Kanvasmantel, mit Hermelin gefuttert»; Arm. 1 *zuf susar zargac' halaw* «1 Wollenmantel, mit Marderfell gefuttert» (Grigorian, S. 287.); (1592) *atlas mentlik susar boyozlary bila* ~ 62r28 «eine Atlasmantille, mit Marderkehle gefuttert»; *šuba kanafaca kiš xarnyj tibina* 40r22 «Kanvasmantel mit Zobelbauchfell gefuttert»

VI

potomok 8v1, 5, *potomka* 6v6 (Ukr. *потомок*, *-мка*; Pol. potomek, -mka) «Nachkomme, Abkömmling»

potomstvo (Ukr. Pol. potomstwo) 48r32 «Nachkommenschaft»

potreba (Ukr. *потреб̃*, Pol. potrzeba) 48r24 «Bedarf, Bedürfnis»

povinen (Pol. powinien) 6v20, 17r2 «er sollte»

prinjat (Ukr. *приняти*) *et-* 48r21 «annehmen, empfangen»

pripustit (Ukr. *припустити*) *et-* 48r22 «zulassen»

pryobicat (Pol. przyobicać) *et-* 48r9, 12 «versprechen»

pryjrobica (Pol. przyrobić się) *bol-* 48r26 «sich machen»

protka (Ukr. *предок*, *-ōки*) 8v2 «Vorfahren, Ahnen»

ratuš (Pol. ratusz) 19v28 «Rathaus»

ruxomyj (Pol. ruchomy) 8r24 «beweglich, mobil»

sabap 48r7 «Ursache»

say 16r19 «gesund»

sayyn- 7v29 «denken, über etw. nachdenken»

sayyš 25v38 «Gedächtnis, Sinn, Verstand». S. noch *fikir*

saylx 16r21 «Gesundheit»

sah 35v20 «gesund». S. noch *say*

saxla- 6v16 «aufbewahren»

sarna- 48r13 «lesen»

sarnal- 48r27 «gelesen werden»

sartyn 6v1, 3 «von der Seite, seitens»

sat- 16v30 «verkaufen»

sb (Abk. von Arm. *sbidag* սպիտակ «weiß»; vgl. Gr. ἄσπερ, Türk. *axče*) 48r25, 35 «Silbergeld». S. noch *axča, nayd*

simarla- 8r30, 8v1 «befehlen»; ~ *-gan* 17r6 «Verfügung»

sirma 6r18; 19 «gestickt»; ~ *jaya, briž* «gestickter Kragen, Besatz»

syngar 7r29, 48r35 «Ehefrau, Gattin».* S. noch *xatun, nogar*

syngarlx 17v17 «Heirat». S. noch *alyšmax*

somtašy 6r19, 48r17, 18 «Griwna»; *som* «Rubel» + *taš* + *y* oder *i* «Stein», vgl. 11v18, 20 *somkʼar* (Arm. *kʼar* «Stein»). Im poln. Text eines Lemberger Testaments (Stadtarchiv Lemberg, Fond 52, op. 3, od. zb. 545, S. 360.) steht dafür *srebni grewien* (Gen.) also «Silbergriwna». 1 grzywna = 48 grosz. S. Hoszowski, *Les prix à Lwow (XVI—XVII siècles)*, Paris 1954. S. 31. (Zu *som* = Rubel, s. *CAJ* I, 292—294)

songra 48r15, 26 «nach»

sorov 48r30 «Frage»; ~ *et-* (Abl.) 48r28 «an jn eine Frage stellen»

sovuklu 8r32 «geliebt»

* *Eph* 49a19—20: *kečti bu (19) dunyadan y. kevorovits sin (20) gardovaržovska* — «Y. K. fils a trépassé à Gardowarzowsk (?)» Hier sollte die Buchstabenreihe anders geteilt und *sīngar towaržovska* gelesen werden. Demgemäß würde sich die Bedeutung ändern: «Die Ehegeführtin Frau von Y. K. ist aus dieser Welt geschieden.»

soz 7v29 «Wort»; 8r7 vgl. *galaji*

sp (Abk. von Arm. surp * unupp*) 6r1, 7v29 «sankt, heilig»

stepanos 48r3, ~ *batorij majardan kelgan* 34v19 «Stephan Bathory polnischer König (1576—1586) 'aus Ungarn gekommen'»

stojoncyj (Pol. stojący) «immobil»; ~ *mulklar* 8r25, ~ *imenjalar* 8r29 «Immobilien»

susar 48r20 «Marderfell» (als Unterfutter, Innenmantel). S. noch *podbity*

svat (Ukr. *сват*, Pol. swat) 6v13, 18 «Schwiegervater; Brautwerber»

šayavat 26r25, 48r16 «Huld»

šahar 5v42, *šahyr* 8r15 «Stadt»

široka (Ukr. *широка*) 6r21 «breit»

šuba (Ukr. *шуба*, Pol. szuba) 11r13, 48r20 «Mantel, Pelzmantel». S. noch *podbity*

šubalx 6v11 «Stoff für einen Mantel»

taš 6r28 «Stein»; ~ *duvar* 6r33, 6v1, 3 «Steinwand»; ~ *ov* 8r3 «Steinhaus»; ~ *kebit* 8r9 «Kaufladen aus Stein»

ten «Leib»; ~-*i bila xasta* 34v20 «körperlich krank», ~ *keraki* 28v24, 48r15 «Leibesbedürfnisse, Lebensbedürfnisse»; ~ *jergasi* 7r6, 17v19, 15v19 «ds». Armenisch *marmnawcr arteanc', bidoyic'n* 7v15, 11v12 «ds». Vgl. *dunjalik tirliklar*

tengri 7v28, 48r15, 16 «Gott»

tib 11r13 «Boden, Unterteil». S. noch *podbity*

tijin 11r13 «Eichhörnchen; Feh, Grauwerk»; 1 *zuf šuba* ~ *bila podšity* 23r18 «ein Wollmantel, mit Grauwerk gefuttert» S. noch *podbity*

tiri 6v14 «lebendig»

tirlik 1. Leben, Lebensdauer 8r26, 27; 2. Vieh; *dunjanyng* ~-*i* 9r20, 19v17 «die irdischen Güter»; *dunjalik tirlikimyz* 9v14, 12r28, 15r23, 18v16, 19r17 «unsere irdischen Güter»

tynszlx 25v37 «Unruhe»; *xačan keldi tengridan menim usnuma* ~ 10v11; *xačan ki tengrining bujruxundan ustuma keldi* ~ 13v26 «als auf Gottes Gebot mich die Unruhe überkam». Vgl. Kas. *tynsyz* «ohne Atem»; KaraimT *tyn-* «verscheiden», *tynmax* «Tod»

toxtal- 7v30 «befestigt werden»

toj; *xutlu* ~ 5v42 «gesegnete Hochzeitsfeier»; Arm. *šna havor harsanik'* 7v5

ton «Kleid»; 1 *adamaška* ~, 2 ~ *široka kitajka*, 1 ~ *xzyl zuf*, 1 ~ *muxajar* 6r21—22 «ein Damastkleid, 2 Kleider aus breitem Nankingstoff, 1 Kleid aus roter Wolle, 1 Mohärkleid»

tora 19v29 «Gericht»; ~ *alnyna* 16r22 «vor dem Gericht»

torun 17r5 «Enkel»

tošak «Matraze»; ~ *orun* 8v29, 13r27, 48r20 «Lagerstatt, Bettstatt»

tugal 25v38 «voll, vollkommen»

tugalla- «beendigen, zu Ende führen»; *bujruxun* ~ 17r1 «Befehl ausführen»

VI

tur- 8r3, 48r4, 27 «stehen, bleiben, wohnen»; *menim* ∼-*gan ovum* 6r31 «das Haus, in dem ich wohne»

turlu «Weise»; *bu* ∼ 48r5, 14 «so»

tut- 6v1 «halten»; *tutuči* 5v40 s. *dunja*

tutun- 6v12, 17, 16v32 «versprechen»

tuzul-; *tengridan*∼-*gan ilov šahri* 5v42 «die von Gott errichtete Stadt Lemberg; Arm. *asduadzašen* 7v6

3-ar (= *učar*) 6r24 «je drei»

učmaxly janly 6r6, 29, 8r10 «verewigt, verschieden, verstorben»

učun 48r12 «für, wegen»

udilit (Ukr. уделити, Pol. udzielić) *et-* 6v13 «herrichten, gewähren»

unda- 10v14 «rufen»

usna 48r11, 12, 30 «auf»; *munung* ∼ 6v16 «darüber»; *menim usnuma* 10v11 «auf mich». S. noch *ust-*

ust-; ∼-*uma* 13v26 «auf mich»

uzunlux 6r33 «Länge»

uživat (Ukr. уживати, Pol. używać) *et-* 6v15 «gebrauchen, anwenden, benützen»

vacok (Pol. wacek < D. Wattsack) 6r19, 48r18 «Beutel, Säckchen, Tasche»

vaxt 6v19 «Zeit»

vank (Arm. վանք) 8r15 «Kloster»

vanly 6r3 «aus Van»

več (< väch); *bu* ∼ *bila* 16v31 «auf diese Weise»

vydilit (Ukr. виделити) *et-* 6r31 «zuteilen, absondern»

vylasnyj 8r4 «eigen». S. *vlasny*

vyprava (Pol. wyprawa) 8r21, 48r11 «Mitgift, Austeuer» S. noch *majja*

rječny (Ukr. вечный, Pol. wieczny) 6v6 «ewig»; *rječnjej* 48r32 «auf immer»

vladnut (Pol. wladać) *et-* 8r27 «beherrschen, handhaben»

vlasny (Pol. własny, Ukr. власный) 6v7 «eigen»

vosiat (Arab-Türk. vasiyet) 7v30 «Testament». S. *osiat*

*zalohа*j (Ukr. залога, Pol. zaloga, Linde VI/807) 6r17 «Brustlatz, Wämmschen, Brusttuch, Brustfleck»

zaraz (Ukr. зараз) 48r10, 34 «sofort»

zeznanje (Pol. zeznanie) 48r33 «Äußerung, Bekenntnis»

zeznat (Pol. zeznać) *et-* 48r34, (*zyznat*) 17r7 «erklären, aussagen»

ziymunt 48r3 «Sigismund III polnischer König, 1587—1632»

ziymund augustos 6r2 «Sigismund August polnischer König, 1548—1572»

zynĵyl 6r16, 48r17 «Kette, Handschelle»

zuf (Arab. sūf) 6r21, 11r12 «Wollenstoff»

žadanje (Pol. żądanie) 48r12 «Bitte, Verlangen, Aufforderung, Wunsch»

žadat (Pol. żądać) *et-* 6r5 «bitten um, fordern, verlangen»

VI

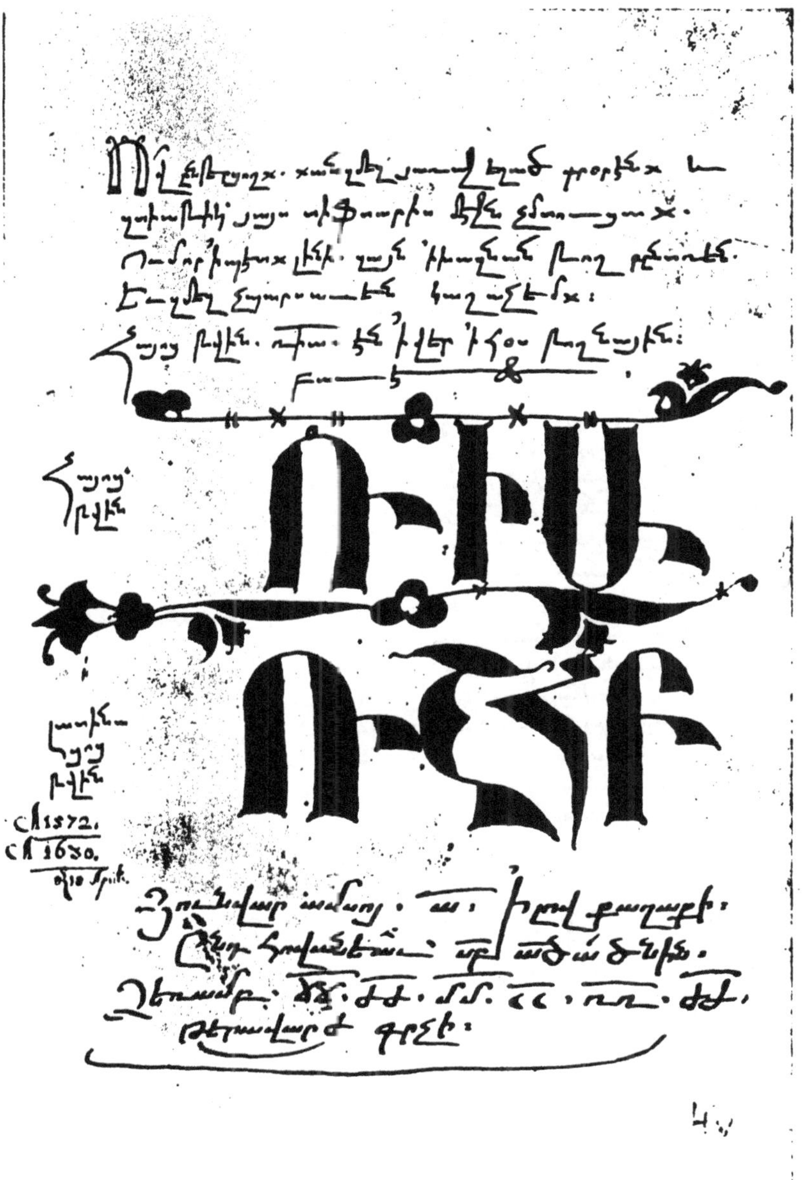

Abb. 1. Mechitaristenbibliothek Wien, MS 441, Fol 4/v

VI

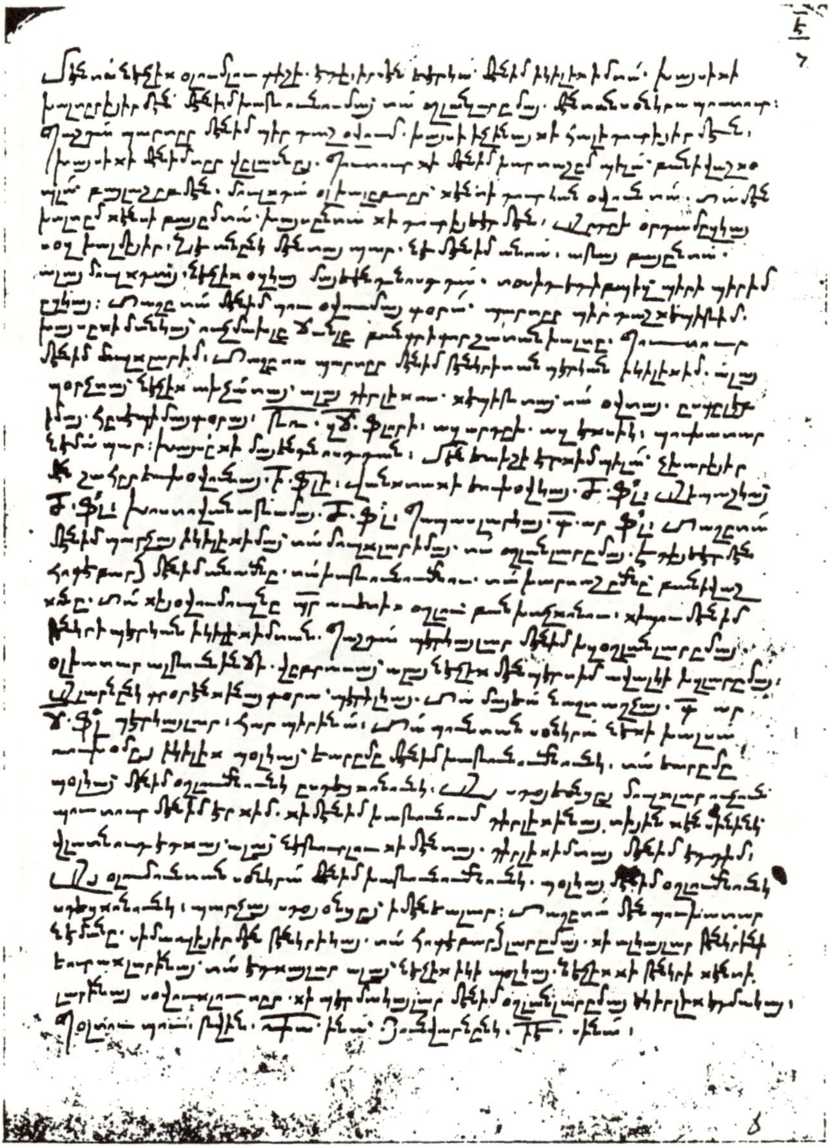

Abb. 2. Fol 8/r

VI

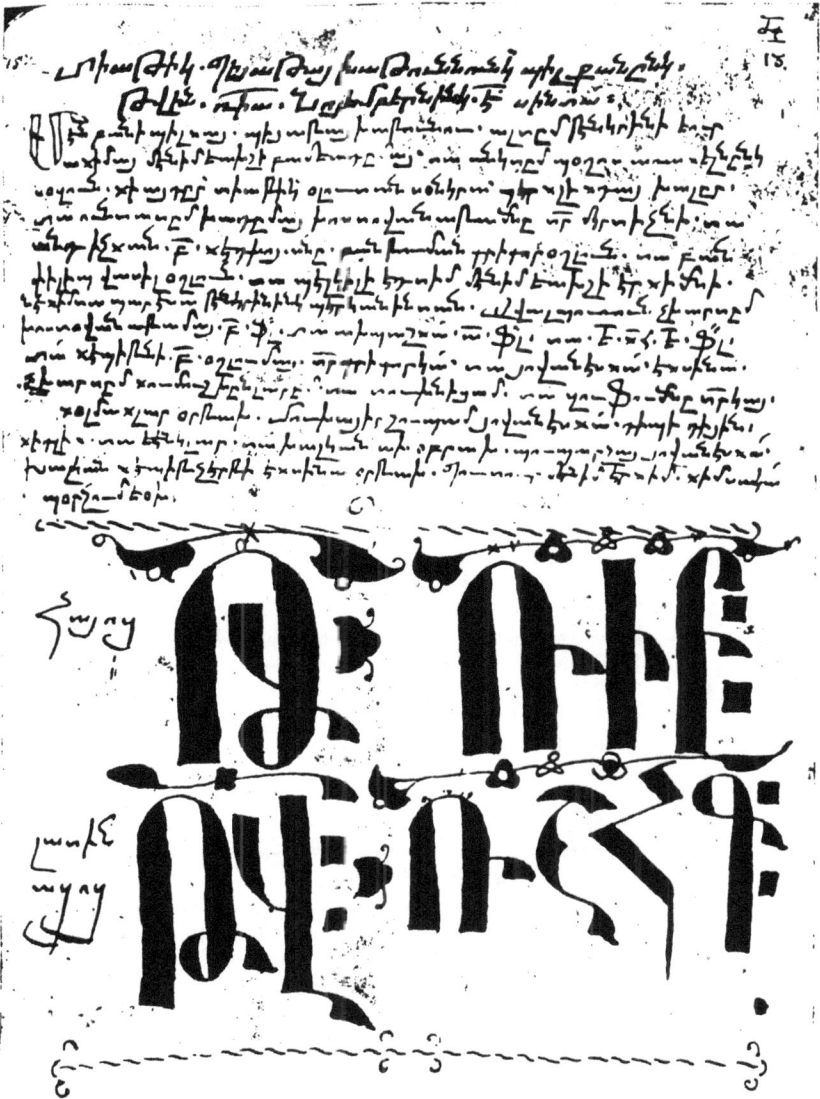

Abb. 3. Fol 11/r

VI

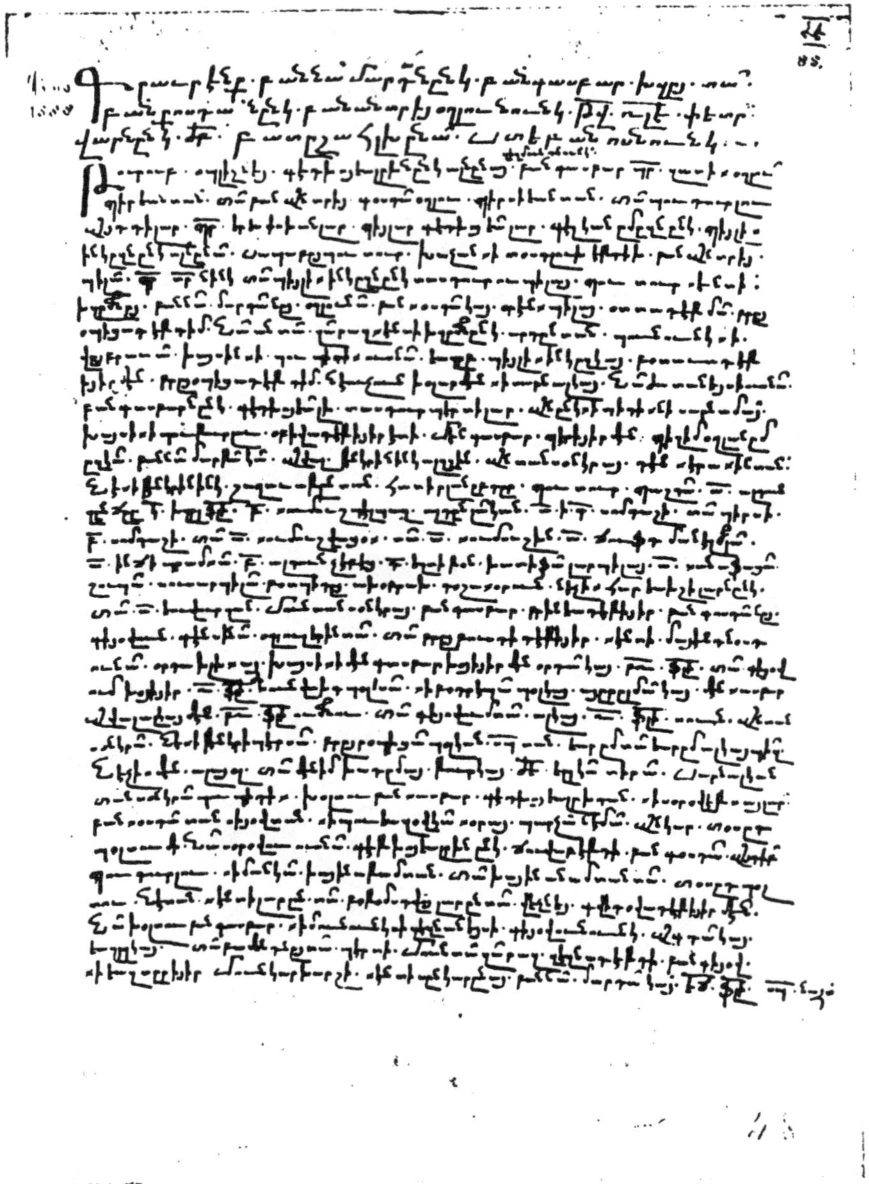

Abb. 4. Fol 48/r

VI

Armeno-kiptschakisch und die Krim

Edmond Schütz, Budapest

In der ziemlich reichen Literatur über die Armeno-Kiptschakische Sprache ist das Grundproblem der unmittelbaren Herkunft der Armenier, die in den XVI—XVII. Jahrhunderten das Armeno-Kiptschakische in Lwow und Kamenets Podolsk als Umgangsprache gebrauchten, endgültig noch immer nicht gelöst.

Die Mehrheit der Sprachforscher nimmt die Hypothese an, daß diese Armenier nach 1475, der Eroberung Kaffas nach Podolien übersiedelten. Diese Auffassung beruht im Grunde genommen auf den ähnlichen Zügen des Armeno-Kiptschakischen mit dem Krimkaraimischen und einer Variante des Komanischen.[1]

Betreffend diese Wanderung bzw. Übersiedlung nach Podolien breiter armenischer Volksmassen verfügt man aber (außer einigen Dokumenten über die Erscheinung einzelner Advenae-Familien) über keine unmittelbaren erzählenden Quellen. Die westlichen Berichterstatter bieten ausführliche Berichte über die Vorgeschichte und Verlauf der Kämpfe, aber keine über die massenhafte Abwanderung armenischer Emigranten in die Richtung von Polen.

Die unmittelbar, oder meistens aus zweiter Hand öftestens zitierte Quelle ist die Erzählung des Kolophons von 1690, einer in der Krim kopierten Menologie, der sog. Neswitaer Chronik von Kaffa.[2] Dieser Kolophon berichtet, daß die Türken nach der Eroberung der Stadt „ihr Gelübde und Versprechen brachen, und unsere Vornehmen und Adeligen Herren mit allen Mitteln zwangen, den mohammedanischen Glauben anzunehmen". Doch jene weigerten sich. Bald danach als sie beim Pascha zum Abendmahl eingeladen waren „beym Abschied entließ (der Pascha) sie einen nach dem anderen über eine enge Stiege, an deren Ausgange ihrer der Henker harrte. und ihnen die Köpfe abschlug".[3] Das letztzitierte Geschehnis ist beinahe in demselben Wortlaut in der Neswitaer Chronik erzählt;[4] Hammers Erzählung soll (wern auch aus zweiter Hand) von der Chronik herrühren.

„Und dann erlässt der Pascha den Befehl an Türken und Tataren, alle Armenier in der Stadt auszurotten. Und jene machten am selben Tage die dicht-

---

1 Auf die verschiedenen Meinungsnüancer werde ich in einer späteren Erörterung zurück-
  kommen.
2 ·Bžškian, 335—342; Ališan, II/3, 244—250.
3 Hammer, GOR, II, 139; Zinkeisen, II. 386.
4 Bžškian, 339.

bewohnte Stadt Theodosia dünnbevölkert". ... Das Gemeinvolk wurde teilweise niedergemetzelt, teilweise in Gefangenschaft geraten. Viele Knaben und Mädchen zum Sultan nach Istanbul geschleppt.[5]

In der Geschichtswissenschaft wird allgemein angenommen, daß die Bevölkerung sich nach der türkischen Eroberung auf ein Bruchstück verminderte.[6] Von einer Emigration ist weder bei Hammer noch bei Zinkeisen keine Rede. Hammer unterrichtet uns von einer massenhaften Verschleppung. Nach der Eroberung Kaffas wurden „vierzigtausend Einwohner als Anpflanzer Konstantinopels, fünfzehnhundert edle Jünglinge als Recruten der Janitscharen abgeführt".[7]

Wie bekannt, gab Mehmed Fatih den Kaymakamen eine Verordnung demgemäß der Verlust an Kaufleuten und Handwerkern aus den Ostprovinzen Anatoliens ersetzt werden sollte.[8] Für die XV—XVI. Jahrhunderte besitzt man kein allzu reiches Belegmaterial für die Wirksamkeit des erwähnten Ansiedlungsprogramms.

Die Angabe über die 40 000 gefangen genommenen und nach Istanbul übersiedelten Bewohner Kaffas, bzw. der Krim ist auf verschiedenen Wegen in den Kreislauf der Literatur eingedrungen, da hiemit die Wiederbelebung der Hauptstadt leicht erklärt werden könnte.[9]

Im allgemeinen herrschte früher in der sprachwissenschaftlichen Literatur jene Auffassung vor, daß die armenische Bevölkerung Istanbuls aus der Bevölkerung Anatoliens ergänzt worden ist.[10]

Für Hr. Atscharian kam dieselbe Angabe zur Begründung mancher linguistischer Eigenheiten der Istanbuler armenischen Mundart höchst willkommen. Wenn aus den erwähnten 40 000 Übersiedlern nur die Hälfte, also 20 000 Leute Armenier gewesen waren, so würden sie eine entscheidende Rolle bei der Gestaltung der lokalen Mundart gespielt haben.[11]

Eine der auffälligsten phonetischen Merkmale des Istanbuler und des Krimer armenischen Dialekts war die Erscheinung eines χ-Lautes anstelle des türkischen Qaf in allen türkischen Wörtern der Mundart. Die Bedeutung dieser Übereinstimmung ist desto schwerwiegender, da der Qaf in Anatolien meistens γ lautet, und so auch in der Umgangsprache der Zuzügler in Istanbul. Hiemit hat Hr. Atscha-

5 *Ibid.* 339—340.
6 Hr. Atscharian nimmt an, daß die armenische Bevölkerung der Krim auf 5—6 000 Familien herabgesunken wäre. Diese Zahl ist gegen die — von ihm — für die Vorkriegszeit angenommenen 100 000 Familien ein sehr niedriger Prozentsatz: 5—6%. [Ačarian, *Die armenischen Kolonien* (arm. in MS)]. Die Vorkriegszahl scheint, ohne Bedenken aus Ter-Abrahamians Buch (*Patmutᶜ iwn Xrimu*, I, 103.) übernommen zu sein (sieh Mikaelian, 277.) — Die Zahl ist auch von A. Abrahamian in seiner Besprechung Mikaelians Werk (*Patma-banasirakan Handes*, 1965, No 3. 283.) für übertrieben gehalten. A. Abrahamian hält 150 000—200 000 Seelen für die Vorkriegsperiode annehmbar.
7 Hammer, *GOR*, II, 139.
8 Berbérian, 8, sqq.
9 *Ibid*, und 43.; Uzunçarşili, II., 128, Fußnote 4.
10 Für die geschichtlich handgreifliche Lösung wird von sprachwissenschaftlicher Seite die anatolische Herkunft schon von den Venediger Mechitaristen (meistens Konstantinopler Abstammung) besonders betont. S. Ačemian, 39, sqq.
11 Ačarian, 8—9. (Hier bezieht sich Atscharian auf Hammers Angabe über die Verschleppung 40 000 Bewohner aus Kaffa. *GOR*, II, 139; *GOR*, 2. Ausg. I. 524.)

VII

rian also einen triftigen Beweis für eine genetische Verbindung zwischen den zwei Dialekten gefunden.[12]

Diese hohe Zahl, 40 000 Gefangene ist aber von anderen Quellen nicht bekräftigt, und dieser Umstand veranlasste H. Berbérian in seinen Forschungen über die armenische Bevölkerung Istanbuls diese Angabe in Zweifel zu ziehen.[13] In der Volkszählung vom Jahre 1478 (also gerade nach den Kriegsoperationen in der Krim) steht eine separate Rubrik für Kaffanenser und da sind bloß 267 Familien (portae) verzeichnet.[14]

Bei einem so großen Verluste an Bevölkerung ist zu erwarten, daß bei den betroffenen Landsleuten ein derartiger Schicksalschlag einen entsprechenden Widerhall auslöst. Unter dem unmittelbaren Eindruck der grausamen Kriegsereignisse können sich auch die Schreiber-Mönche sich diesbezüglicher Bemerkungen nicht enthalten, doch diese ungeheure Menge von 40 000 Gefangenen wird nicht erwähnt.

In einem Kolophon von Kaffa steht, z. B. daß die Türken „viele Armenier gefangen nahmen und große Verwüstungen machten".[15] Priester Nerses berichtet in seiner Jeremiade über den Fall von Kaffa, daß „soviel Franken es in Kaffa gegeben hat, die sind alle nach Konstantinopel geführt und verurteilt worden".[16]

In nicht-armenischen Quellen werden die Armenier oft nicht separat erwähnt. Für die Entführung der „Franken" ist natürlich die am meisten authentische Quelle der Ragusaner Berichterstatter: „Quingentas Januensium et aliorum latinorum familias Capha Constantinopolim migrare jussit truculentus drago"[17] — wo es nicht klar ist ob die Armenier in den „Lateinern" inbegriffen sind.

G. Sphrantzes berichtet zusammenfassend über die Gefangenen; nach der Eroberung der Küstenlandschaft des Schwarzen Meeres brachte der Sultan „Ansiedler, die man in ihrer Sprache Surgunen nennt, aus Kaffa (im Trapezuntischen), aus Sinope und Asprokastron"[18] nach Konstantinopel.

Was — in der Neswitaer Chronik — die Übersiedlung betrifft, so steht es da bloß, daß manche von den Adeligen, und manche vom Gemeinvolk ... als Gefangene entführt worden sind. Ungenaue Angaben gibt der Kolophon auch die Jugend betreffend; undzwar daß „unzählige Mädchen und Jungen, und junge Knaben nahmen (die Türken) gefangen, und schickten sie nach Konstantinopel zum Sultan".[19]

Dieser Bericht, also die Verschiffung zahlreicher Jungen (und Mädchen), 1500 (bzw. 500, 3000—5000) junger Genueser und anderer „Lateiner", kommt

---

12 Ibid.

13 Berbérian, 34, sqq.

14 Ibid, 50—52. Vgl. A. M. Schneider, Die Bevölkerung Konstantinopels im XV. Jh. Nachrichten Akad. Wiss. Göttingen Phil.-hist. Kl. Jg. No. 9. 233—244; R. Mantran, Istanbul dans la seconde moitié du XVIIᵉ siècle. Paris 1962. 44—53.

15 Xačikian, Hišatakaran, II, 390.

16 Archiv Jerusalem, S. Jakob Kloster, MS No. 1455. bei Berbérian, 38; Jerewaner MS No. 7 709. bei Mikaelian, 275. (Es werden verschiedene Stellen zitiert.)

17 Atti, VII/2, 488. Doc. XXV, bei Vasiliev, 246.

18 Sphrantzes/Phrantzes, III, 11, Deutsche Übers. Ivánka, 88; etwas verschiedene engl. Übersetzung bei Vasiliev, 265.

19 Bžškian, 340. Dieser Bericht wird bei Argutinskij mit jenem über die 40 000 Gefangenen verschmolzen, s. Zeitschr. Etschmiadzin, Jg. 1962. 36.

VII

in vielen Berichten vor.[19a] Über die Zahl der gefangen genommenen adulten Bevölkerung stehen uns keine genaue Angaben zur Verfügung. Allerdings scheint die Zahl der nach Konstantinopel verschleppten 40 000 Einwohner übertrieben zu sein.

Auch bei anderen großen Kriegsoperationen, schweren Verlusten, Massenübersiedlungen, Sürgüns, kommt diese hohe Zahl vor. Dieser Umstand macht uns aufsichtig, damit wir sie nicht als absolute Zahl betrachten sollen.

Die Zahl 40 000 wurde besonders durch Dschachkecis vielgelesenes Lehrbuch,, Draxt cankali" in der ganzen armenischen Literatur verbreitet. Laut ihm wanderten 40 000 Familien aus Ani nach Polen aus.[20]

Bei Kuschnerian wird 1330 die Einwanderung von 40 000 Seelen (also hier nicht Familien) nach der Krim erwähnt.[21] Der Kreislauf der beiden Zahlangaben ist in der Literatur kaum zu verfolgen.

Auch in einem anderen Zusammenhange hören wir über 40 000 Familien Armenier. Als der Priester Simeon Lehaci auf seiner Wallfahrtsreise 1608 in Konstantinopel anlangte, und sich — wie gewöhnlich — um die Zahl der einheimischen Armenier der Stadt erkundigte, erhielt er die Antwort daß da 80 ansässige Familien *(tun—portae)* und mehr als 40 000 Flüchtlingsfamilien wohnten.[22]

Aber die Zahl kommt auch bezüglich die türkische Armee vor. Bei der Belagerung der Stadt Kaffa sollten die Janitscharentruppen von Ahmed Gedig Pascha 40 000 Soldaten belaufen.[23]

Im Lichte dieser und ähnlicher disparaten Angaben wäre die Zahl der Kaffaer 40 000 Gefangenen kaum für das Nennwert zu nehmen. Es ist wohl bekannt, daß eine große Menge im Türkischen oft mit der Zahl 40 *(qïrq)* ausgedrückt wird, so kann die Zahl letzten Endes in diesem Falle auf türkische Gewährsmänner zurückgehen, die hiemit allgemein eine große Menge ausdrücken wollten.[24]

Die 40 000 Gefangenen 1475 von der Krim und die 40 000 Familien Zuzügler in Konstantinopel bei Simeon kann auf landläufige mündliche oder literarische Überlieferung zurückgehen.

Doch darf man auch nicht ins andere Extrem verfallen, und die Zahl der Gefangenen, der Flüchtlinge, der Abzügler allzu sehr unterschätzen. Aus den genuesischen Berichten ist es zu entnehmen, daß 1439 in Kaffa cca 30 000 Armenier lebten, und 1475 vor der türkischen Eroberung machte die Gesamtzahl der Armenier in Kaffa zwei Drittel der 70 000 starken Bevölkerung aus, was also ungefähr 46 000 Armenier ergeben würde.[25]

Der Prozentsatz der in Kaffa residierenden Genueser war in Vergleich ver-

---

19/a Hammer, II, 139; Heyd, II, 403.

20 Džaxkeci, *Draxt cankali*, Konstantinopel, 1735. übern. von Bžškian, 85; Zarbhanalian, II, 289.

21 Kušnerian, 189. Auch bei Glinka, S., *Obozrenje istorii armjanskogo naroda*, 11.

22 Simeon dpir Lehaci, 8; Russ. Übers. Darbinian, 37; Vgl. *AOH XX*, 311.

23 Hammer, *GOR* II, 139.

24 *qïrq ayaq* ‚Tausendfüßler'; *Qïrq bulaq* Ortsname ‚Mit hundert Quellen'; *Qïrq yašar* Personenname ‚Hundert Jahre soll er leben'.

25 *Atti*, VII/2, 480, 482 bei Heyd, II, 402; *Atti*, V, 415, VII/2, 343, bei Heyd, II, 392, s. Jakobson, 117. Małowist, 40.

VII

schwindend gering, kaum 1,5—2%, also in 1475 etwa 1 000 Leute, was die Un-
haltbarkeit der Burg bzw. der Stadt Kaffa in 1475 leicht verständlich macht, und
ungefähr mit der Zahl der von den Türken gefangen genommenen Genuesern
übereinstimmt.[26] Wenn man die Nachkriegslage in Kaffa beurteilt, muß man mit einem sehr
hohen Prozent Abwanderer bzw. Gefangener rechnen. Allerdings ist es unmöglich,
daß 40 000 Familien Armenier nach Lwow emigriert, und 40 000 Seelen mit den
„Lateinern" mitsamt in Gefangenschaft geraten hätten. Die Vermengung der
„Familien" *(tun — portae)* mit „Seelen" bedeutet ohnedies einen riesigen fünf-
fachen Unterschied.

Laut den Aufzeichnungen Martin Broniewskis war die Stadt Kaffa vor 1579
nur mehr ein Schatten ihres vorigen Standes. Die meisten Häuser und Kirchen
standen in Trümmern; es blieben mehr nur zwei katholische und armenische Kirchen wohlerhalten.[27]

Der Verfall im XVI. Jahrhundert war aber nicht bloß die Folge der Verwüstungen des Krieges. Der genuesische Handel, vormalig das Westen und Osten
zusammenkettende Zwischenglied ist aus diesem Gebiete verdrängt worden,
und dazu hatte die extensive türkisch-tatarische Produktionsweise, und der arm-
selige Lokalmarkt für die armenischen Kaufleute keine große Anziehungskraft,
sich in der Krim niederzulassen.

Doch im Hintergrund dieses steilen Rückganges stand als entscheidender
Faktor die Veränderung der Welthandelswege. Die alte Route des west-östlichen
Transithandels, dessen Emporium auch Kaffa war, hat ihre Bedeutung verloren.
Eine ähnliche Entwicklung ist auch in Lwow zu beobachten, kaum nach einigen
Jahrzehnten nach der Entdeckung Amerikas beginnt auch in Lwow die Regression.
Viele armenische Großkaufleute wandern weiter, und bei den an Stelle bleibenden
kleinen Kaufleuten beginnt eine allmähliche Assimilation.[28]

Doch mit Recht weist W. Mikaelian auf die Kontinuität der armenischen
Bevölkerung in Kaffa hin; er betont wiederholt, daß die Armenier auch nach dem
Drangsal des Kriegsjahres 1475 im gesellschaftlich-wirtschaftlichen Leben der
Halbinsel auch weiter tatkräftig teilnahmen.[29] Die spärlichen Angaben über ihre
diesbezügliche Tätigkeit läßt uns aber vermuten, daß ihre Bedeutung mit der
Abnahme ihrer Zahl und der wirtschaftlichen Notwendigkeit auch wesentlich
zusammenschrumpfte.

Dagegen kündigen die historischen und kulturellen Angaben im XVII. und
Anfang XVIII. Jahrhundert einen wesentlichen Aufschwung an.

Der Prefekt der Krimer Katholiken, der Dominikaner Dortelli d'Ascoli
zählt die Städte mit einer ansehnlichen Seelenszahl von Armeniern auf,[30] wo die
meisten früher von Armeniern bewohnten Städte erwähnt werden.

In der zweiten Hälfte des Jahrhunderts gibt der Handelsbeauftragte Chardin
auf seiner Durchreise durch Kaffa (1673) ein handgreifliches Bild über die Lage
der vormalig blühenden Hafenstadt. Unter den 4 000 Familien der Stadt seien

---

26 Jakobson, *Viz. Vrem.* VIII, 166.
27 Broniewski: *ZOOID*, VI, 348; Schwandtner, III, 271.
28 Schütz, *Rearmenisation: AOH*, XIX, 99, sqq.
29 Mikaelian, 110, 112, 117, 278, usw.
30 D'Ascoli: *ZOOID*, XXIV/2, 117.

VII

nach ihm 3 200 Mohammedaner, und 800 armenische und griechische Familien, betonend daß es mehr Armenier gebe als Griechen.[31]

Die Zahl scheint hier aber wesentlich unterschätzt zu sein, wenn man die Zuwanderung an der XVI—XVII. Jahrhundertewende und die statistischen Angaben von 1778 in Betracht zieht.

Die massenhafte Einwanderung von Armeniern in die Krim, nach Podolien und der Moldau ist aber keineswegs die Folge der wirtschaftlichen Anziehungskraft, sondern die Folge der Periode einer der schwersten Heimsuchungen für das armenische Volk.

Im Laufe des XVI. Jahrhunderts, infolge der ununterbrochenen Kriege zwischen der Türkei und Persien wurden die ohnedies schon verwüsteten armenischen Gebiete ganz zugrunde gerichtet.

Aus der Provinz Ostarmenien ließ Schah Abbas am Anfang des XVII. Jahrhunderts das ganze Volk wegschleppen, der ganze Südteil der Provinz wurde so entvölkert, in der Absicht den zurückkehrenden türkischen Kriegskräften ein verödetes Land zurückzulassen.[32]

Zu diesem Elend kam noch der Aufstand der Dschelalis zu, die 1598—1605 sich gegen den Sultan empörten, und obwohl sie am Anfang von progressiven Ideen geführt wurden, doch im Laufe der Zeit eine Plage der Bevölkerung ganz Anatoliens geworden sind.[33]

Und die darauffolgende Hungersnot und das Elend dauerte noch jahrelang von 1606 bis 1609, von Konstantinopel bis Täbriz, von Baghdad bis Derbend. Und die Armenier flüchteten nach allen Seiten, so auch nach der Krim.[34]

Die Erscheinung der armenischen Emigranten an der Wende der XVI—XVII. Jahrhunderte konnte tatsächlich einen gewissen Aufschwung in den Blutkreislauf des wirtschaftlichen und gesellschaftlichen Lebens in der Krim und in Lwow bringen, aber weder die Handelsmöglichkeiten, noch der politische Hintergrund bot einen gesicherten Lebensunterhalt für eine ungestörte wirtschaftliche Tätigkeit. Seit 1584 riß der Sultan das Recht der Ernennung der Krimkhane in die Hände, und wechselte sie nach Gutdünken. Es entbrannten ständige Fehden zwischen den Selbstkandidaten, die sich manchmal sogar gegen die Sultans Macht aufzulehnen erdreisteten. Das politische Gewirr wird vom einheimischen armenischen Chronisten der ersten Hälfte des XVII. Jahrhunderts, Chatschatur Kafajeci farbreich geschildert.[35]

Über die zahlenmässige Entwicklung und der wirtschaftlichen Rolle der armenischen Bevölkerung von Kaffa besitzen wir keine genaue Angaben in den XVII—XVIII. Jahrhunderten, doch konnte der Aufschwung nicht dauerhaft sein; die schweren Steuerbürden veranlassten die Armenier vom Sitz des Beglerbegs ins Gebiet unter unmittelbarer tatarischer Herrschaft zu übersiedeln. So war eine

---

31 Chardin, I, 125—126.
32 *Patmutᶜywn*, Bd. IV, 95—102.
33 Tavriženi, Kap. VII: Arm. 79—92; russ.: 89—99; franz.: 307—314. — Zu den verschiedenen Wertungen der Bewegung der Dschelalis s. A. S. Tveritinova, A. Akdağ, M. K. Zulalian, H. Anassian, und neulichst: V. Hakobian, *Hišatakaran*, I. pp. XII—XIII.
34 Tavriženi, Arm. 87—88, 92; Russ.: 95, 98—99; Franz.: 312, 314.
35 Hakobian, *Manr Žam.* I, 205—236. Deutsch: Schütz, *Eine armenische Chronik... AOH*, XXIX, No. 2. (1975) 133—186.

VII

Transmigration eines Teiles der Bevölkerung Kaffanenser Armenier nach Qarasu[36] bemerkbar, und es gab auch andere die die Halbinsel verließen.

Nachdem im türkisch-russischen Krieg von 1769—1774 die russische Armee den Sieg davontrug, ist im Friedensvertrag von Kütschük-Kainardschi der tatarische Khanat für unabhängig erklärt worden. Aber um das Endziel, die endgültige Annektierung des Khanats zu erreichen, um die wirtschaftliche Kraft des Khans zu schwächen, ist die christliche Bevölkerung aus der Halbinsel in die südliche Steppenlandschaft übersiedelt worden, um auch gleichzeitig den russischen Süden zu stärken.[37]

Über das Ergebnis der demographischen Bewegungen sind wir mittels der statistischen Daten von 1778 genau unterrichtet. In der für General A. W. Suworow verfertigten statistischen Tabelle sind die genauen Zahlangaben der zur Übersiedlung angeregten armenischen Bevölkerung für die einzelnen Städte separat angegeben worden.[38]

Die Gesamtzahl, 12 598 Seelen für die Krimarmenier bezeugt, daß der Aufschwung der XVII—XVIII. Jahrhunderte in der Krim nur übergänglich war, da die Bevölkerung eigentlich seit 1475, der Eroberung der Krim durch die Türken, kaum eine wesentliche Erhöhung erfahren hat.

Die Armenier sind am Don-Fluß unweit von Rostow in neu errichteten Städten: Nor-Nachitschewan, 3 weiteren Städten und 9 Ortschaften angesiedelt worden.[39] In den neuen Wohnsitz brachten sie ihren Dialekt aus der Krim mit, der nach dem Zentrum der Kolonie Nor-Nachitschewaner Dialekt benannt wird. Wieweit der Dialekt bezüglich der Fremdwörter den früheren Zustand widerspiegelt, wird unten besprochen.

* * *

Die Veränderungen der politischen Zustände der Krim und in erster Reihe von Kaffa kann auch in der Produktion des lokalen Schrifttums beobachtet werden.

Die durch die türkische Eroberung hervorgerufenen politischen und wirtschaftlichen Zustände weisen einen scharfen Bruch im Leben der Halbinsel auf. Im Maße die Bevölkerung sich durch die Kriegsatrozitäten, Gefangenschaft und Emigration zu einem Bruchteil verminderte, hörte das literarische Leben, und auch der Anspruch an literarische Werke auf, das XVI. Jahrhundert wird nur durch eine minimale literarische Tätigkeit charakterisiert.[40]

Die durch den großen Sürgün des Schah Abbas 1605 und die Dschelali-Periode an der XVI—XVII. Jahrhundertewende hervorgerufene massenhafte Flucht aus dem Mutterland und ganz Anatolien bringt einen Aufschwung ins literarischen Leben ihrer neuen Heimat.

36 D'Ascoli: *ZOOID*, XXIV/2. 120.

37 *Patmut‘yun*, IV, 415—416; Barxudarian, Kap. 1, 2.

38 Kaffa: 5 511, Baxčisaraj: 1 375, Qarasubazar: 2 809, Gözleve: 1 304, Akmečit: 259, Eski-Krim: 160, 9 Ortschaften: 1 180. Mikaelian, 369; Barxudarian, 39.

39 Barxudarian, 44, sqq.

40 Das Martirologium: *Baron Lujs*. Die niedrige Zahl des Codex-Schrifttums, s. unten.

VII

Es sind aus dieser Periode manche Dichter in Kaffa und auch Podolien[41] bekannt, die aus Tokat, der 1602 von den Dschelalis geplünderten Stadt flüchteten. Der berühmteste unter ihnen in der Krim ist Stepanos Tokateci der eine rege Lehrtätigkeit ausübte, und auch manche Gedichte hinterließ.[42] Die Träger der Literatur sind aber nicht allein die eingewanderten Armenier. Es gibt mehrere Schriftsteller von Kaffa gebürtig, die auch aus einer einheimischen Familie zu entstammen scheinen. Wenn ihre Familien Neusiedler wären, so würde dieser Umstand in ihren Schriftwerken in irgendeiner Weise zum Vorschein kommen. So verrät z. B. ein hervorragender Lwower armenischer Schriftsteller des Beginns des XVII. Jahrhunderts, Simeon Lehaci, daß seine Älter aus Kaffa stammen.[43] Beziehungen persönlicher Art kommen oft als Thema in den Gedichten vor, wie z. B. Stepanos eben seinen Lehrmeister von Tokat lobt, und sich seiner Ordensbrüder erinnert.[44]

In der aufblühenden Literatur sind mehrere einheimische Dichter bekannt, die den Beinamen Kafajeci (also Kaffanenser) tragen. So ist Simeon Kafajeci von seinen in 1683—1686 geschriebenen Versen bekannt. Seine lokale Abstammung ist auch durch den Namen seines Vaters gekennzeichnet: Chrimbej. Der Priester (Erec) Chasbeg (bzw. Chatschatur) stammt auch aus Kaffa (cca. 1610—1686), usw. dann Vardan ist 1615 in Kaffa geboren und 1680 Bischof der Chrimarmenier vom Katholikos eingeweiht worden (†1712).[45]

Die einzigartige führende Rolle von Kaffa ist schon durch diese Liste gekennzeichnet, von anderen Städten der Krim sind uns nur einige Scribae bekannt. Die meistberühmten: Martiros Chrimeci (bzw. Kafaci, Kefeci), Chatschatur Kafajeci, — derer literarische Tätigkeit unten separat erörtert wird — waren auch Kaffanenser.

Der Aufschwung der Literatur, die Erhöhung des Interesse für Literatur (wenn auch für kirchliche Zwecke) wird eklatanterweise durch die sprungartige Vermehrung der Codex-Schreiber gekennzeichnet. Viele der in der Krim geschriebenen Codices sind auf uns erhalten geblieben, da sie beim Auszug aus der Krim 1778 von den Armeniern in ihre neue Heimat mitgebracht wurden, und von dort nach der Zentralisation des Archivmaterials nach Etschmiadzin und später ins Jerewaner Matenadaran geraten sind.[46]

Die Verhältniszahlen der in Kaffa geschriebenen Codices sind beredsame Zeugen der Entwickelung der literarischen Tätigkeit (nach Jahrhunderten aufgeteilt): XVI. Jh.: 13 MSS; XV. Jh.: 23; XVI. Jh.: 10; XVII. Jh.: 103; XVII. Jh.: 41 MSS.[47]

41 Schütz: *Rearmenisation*, AOH XIX, 104—105.
42 Akinean, 115—137.
43 Simeon Lehaci, 1; Russ: Darbinian 33. Vgl. AOH XX, 311.
44 Akinean, 121—122, 128, 132—134; Ališan, 307—316.
45 Mikaelian, 304—312.
46 S. die Abhandlung von Jeganian, O., *Die MS Archivfonds des Matenadaran, Cucak*, I. 160—161.
47 Die Zusammenstellung enthält nur die in dem Jerewaner Matenadaran aufbewahrten Manuscripte aus Kaffa. Eine vollständigere Liste könnte auf Grund der Kolophonsammlungen zusammengestellt werden, doch die Herausgabe der grundlegenden Serie ist noch nicht beendet. L. Xačikians 3 Bände enthalten den 15. Jahrhundert, und V. Hakobians (und A. Hovhannissians) bisher erschienener Band die Jahrzehnte 1601—1620.

VII

Natürlich widerspiegeln diese Zahlen kein Absolutwert, vorerst da aus den früheren Jahrhunderten viele Codices verloren gegangen, oder verschollen sind. 1475 haben die Janitscharen viele Handschrifte mitgenommen, um sie für hohe Preise an armenische Bücherfreunde zu verkaufen. Auch in der besprochenen Sammlung treffen wir derartige Eintragungen über Rückankauf. Z. B. eine 1475 in Kaffa erbeutete Handschrift ist in Istanbul von Herrn Avetik angekauft worden.[48]

Diese wechselvollen obigen Zahlwerte veranschaulichen bei erster Betrachtung die in Kaffa in den XVI—XVIII. Jahrhunderten eingetretenen Umwälzungen in der Literatur.

Man muß doch die obigen absoluten Ziffern der XVII—XVIII. Jahrhundertewende aus einem anderen Grunde nicht überschätzen, da es in Kaffa damals einige außerordentlich schrifttüchtige Kopisten gegeben hat, die einzeln je ein (oder mehrere) Dutzend Codices geschrieben hatten. Dies muß desto eher in Betracht gezogen werden, sonst würde die Zahl einen allzu steilen Emporstieg und Absturz in der Literatur suggerieren, der durch den historischen Hintergrund nicht genügend begründet wäre.

Solche begabte Kopisten waren: Zakaria Abegha („Neupriester'), zwischen 1617—1643 kopierte 10 (bzw. 13) Handschrifte, Nikolos Melanawor („Tintenfreund') zwischen 1650 und 1693 21 Manuscripte, an der Jahrhundertwende Kristophor Kahanay („Priester') 11 Hschr. und Georg Erec („Altpriester') 32 MSS.[49]

Die oben angeführten historischen und kulturhistorischen Angaben beweisen die Kontinuität der armenischen Bevölkerung und Literatur vom Zeitalter der Genueser bis zur Auswanderung 1778, trotz der großen Umwälzung die die türkische Okkupation im Leben der Krimarmenier hervorgerufen hat.

Die Sprache der Literaturwerke ist ausschließlich Armenisch, undzwar Klassisch-Armenisch (Grabar), nur in den Kolphonen ist der Einfluß der Umgangsprache bemerkbar. Doch aus diesen spärlichen Resten kann die alte Umgangsprache der Krim kaum je rekonstruiert werden.

Die Nor-Nachitschewaner Mundart ist ein direkter Nachläufer des Dialekts (oder der Dialekte) der Krim. In erster Reihe vertretet sie gewiss die Mundart von der Hauptstadt Kaffa, da die Kaffanenser (5511 Seelen) in der Bevölkerung von Nor-Nachitschewan mit 44% vertreten sind. In zweiter Reihe konnte Qarasubazar mit einer Bevölkerungszahl von 2809, also 22% in betracht kommen. Doch ist Qarasubazar, was die Armenier anbelangt, eine Neusiedlung, deren armenische Population um die Mitte des XVII. Jahrhunderts aus Übersiedlern von Kaffa sich ausbildete. Auch die aus Qarasubazar stammenden Codices fallen eben auf das XVII. Jahrhundert.[50]

In unserer Suche um die Frage der fremdsprachigen Umwelt der Armenier

---

48 Xačikian, *Hišatakaran*, II, 389; Sanjian, 313. — Die Plünderung und Verkauf wird auch in Chatschatur Kafajecis Chronik erwähnt, Hakobian, *Manr Žam*, I, 210,10; Deutsch: *AOH*, XXIX, No. 2, 141.

49 Die Identität des in den Kolophonen erscheinenden: Georg erec, Georg dpir, und einfach Georg sollte durch Schriftmuster identifiziert werden. — Auch Mikaelian hielt die Beweiskraft dieser Zahlenangaben für wichtig: er stellte in einer ähnlichen Zusammenstellung die Gesamtzahl der in der Krim kopierten Codices 238 denen der in den 17—18. Jh. geschriebenen 170 MSS entgegen, Mikaelian, 302.

50 *Cucak*, II, col. 1 237.

13

von Kaffa müssen in erster Reihe die Fremdwörter, Lehnwörter in Rechenschaft
gezogen werden.

Bei den gut geschulten, höhere Bewertung bestrebenden armenischen Dich-
tern und sogar in Kolophonen sind kaum einige Fremdwörter (Türkisch, Arabisch,
Persisch) zu finden, die das Gemeingut der levantinischen türkischen *lingua
franca* sind.

In dieser Frage wollen wir die umfangreichere Literaturwerke des XVII.
Jahrhunderts von Kaffa einer Musterung unterziehen.

Die Sammlung der weltlichen Gedichte von Martiros Chrimeci bieten ein
ziemlich reiches Material.[51] Martiros, „der Stolz"[52] der Krimarmenier ist um 1620
in der Krim geboren worden. Er hat seine Schuljahre im Kloster Surb Xač (25
Km. von Kaffa, 6 Km. von Surxat) verbracht, erhielt seine weitere Schulung
aber in Tokat — also in Anatolien — vom Priester Stepanos; und Astuacatur
Taronaci, der Patriarch von Jerusalem (1645—1671) ist für seinen Patron und
Lehrmeister genannt.[53] M. Chrimeci nahm als Diplomat des Klerus in den kirchen-
politischen Kämpfen in Konstantinopel und Jerusalem lebhaft teil.

Er ist zwar vom Katholikos 1661 Bischof der Krimarmenier ernannt worden,
aber in dieser Funktion ist er nur bis 1664 benannt.[54] Er ist immer ein Patriot
von der Krim bzw. Kaffa geblieben, sich selber Ghrimeci, Kafaci, Kefeci genannt.
Auch die Geschichte der Krim hat er in Versform geschrieben, in der er sich
derselben Quelle bediente wie die Neswitaer Chronik.[55]

Sein Leben verbrachte er aber in Tokat, Jerusalem, Konstantinopel; scheint
aber im ganzen türkischen Reich herumgekommen zu sein. Schon die Thematik
seiner heiteren, häkeligen Lieder weisen auf die Umwelt hin, wo er herumkam:
Er schrieb über den Priester Hakob in Edirne (83), Ter Hunan von Sofia (89),
Priester David in Istanbul (93), Ter Simeon in Warna (97).[56]

Er erhielt den Beinamen „Tatar", aber daraus kann man weder auf sein
ständiges Aufenthaltsort, noch auf seine Abstammung Schlüße ziehen. Er ist eben
nach seiner Krimer Geburt so benannt worden.[57]

Seine religiösen Gedichte sind alle in Grabar geschrieben, aber sobald er
sich den weltlichen Themen zuwandte, ging er in die Volksprache und den Volk-
styl über, er dichtete Verse sogar im Türkischen.

Die in seinen āšïq-artigen Liedern gebrauchten türkischen Wörter und die
Sprache seiner türkischen Lieder entsprechen nicht der Krimer Aussprache,
sondern eher dem anatolischen. Das bezeichnendste phonetische Merkmal ist
die Aussprache des Qaf-s. Sie ist im Krimarmenischen und in der Konstantinopler

51 Martirossian, *op. cit.*
52 Martirossian, 8; Hakobian, *Manr Žam*, I, 228,17—20. Vgl. *AOH* XXIX, No. 2, 162.
53 Ein kleiner Bruchstück eines Lobgedichtes bei Xačatur Kafajeci, *ibid.*
54 Martirossian, 17, 25.
55 *Ibid.* 46—47.
56 Die Zahlen beziehen sich auf die Seiten bei Martirossian.
57 Er selber gebraucht diesen Beinamen im Titel seines berühmten „Fluch"-es, Martirossian,
116—125. — Martirossian ist der Meinung er konnte auch wegen seiner unbändingen Natur
„Tatar" geheißen haben, *ibid*, 8.

VII

Mundart stets χ.[58] Sonst in ganz Anatolien, und auch im türkischen Volksmund in Konstantinopel wird es γ ausgesprochen. Bei Chrimeci findet sich überall ein γ, auch seinen Namen schreibt er: Ghrimeci.

Also sowohl der türkische Wortschatz, wie die Aussprache der Fremdwörter zeigen, daß sie aus dem anatolischen Boden entsprießen, sind also für das Krim-armenische nicht charakteristisch.

Der längste Prosatext von der Krim ist die sog. Neswitaer Chronik, der Kolophon einer in der Krim geschriebenen Menologie *(Haysmawurkᶜ)*.[59] Der Kolophon, einer der wertvollsten Quellen der Frühgeschichte der Krimarmenier, bzw. von Kaffa ist von einem Priester David in 1690 in Grabarsprache verfasst, bzw. aus früheren Texten zusammengestellt worden, enthält keine Elemente der Umgangsprache, und auch keine Fremdwörter der Umwelt, so kann er hier für Fremdwortforschung nicht in Betracht gezogen werden.

Der einzige umfangreiche und an volkstümlichen Sprachelementen reicher Text ist die Chronik von Chatschatur Kafajeci, der auf 24 Blättern die Geschichte der Krim, bzw. Kaffa in der ersten Hälfte des XVII. Jahrhunderts als Augen-zeuge aufzeichnete. Die Chronik trägt Eintragungen über die Frau, und Kinder des Verfassers, aber keine über die Eltern, bzw. Vorfahren, doch ist es anzunehmen, daß sie auch Krimenser gewesen sind, sonst hätte ein Chronist darüber Erwähnung getan. Chatschatur ist allerdings 1592 in Kaffa geboren worden.[60]

Eigentlich ist das Grundgewebe der Chronik in Grabar abgefasst, aber auf Schritt und Tritt schimmert die Umgangsprache, bzw. Dialekt durch.[61]

Die in der Chronik enthaltenen etwa 150 türkischen Fremdwörter deuten auf eine türkische Umgebung in Kaffa.[62]

Kaffa war der Sitz des Beglerbegs, die Ausdrücke der Staatsverwaltung sind demgemäß alle Türkisch, so auch jene des Justizwesens. In Kaffa stationierte eine starke türkische Garnison und sie war auch ein fester Stützpunkt für Kriegs-operationen an der Nordküste des Schwarzen Meeres, die Ausdrücke für Militär und Marinenwesen sind also auch türkisch. Merkwürdigerweise sind alle Kaufla-den, und Händler mit einem türkischen Namen benannt, was nicht für die Her-kunft der Verkäufer, sondern eher der Käufer bezeichnend ist.

Tatarische Wörter kommen in der Chronik nur in einem Absatz vor, wo es über die Noghaier gesprochen wird.

In der Nor-Nachitschewaner Mundart sind die tatarischen Lehnwörter reicher vertreten, und es ist vorauszusetzen, daß auch in die Umgangssprache von Kaffa auch mehrere solche Eintritt fanden, als in die Literatursprache des Chatschatur Kafajeci. Bei der Ausbildung der Nor-Nachitschewaner Mundart kann auch jener Umstand eine Rolle gespielt haben, daß die Bevölkerung der übersiedelten Ort-schaften (1180), und auch von Qarasubazar (2809 Seelen) aus einer tatarischen

---

58 Ačarian, 8—9.
59 Matenadaran MS 7 442; Bžškian, 335—342; Ališan, 244—250.
60 Hakobian, *Manr Žam*, I, 205—206.
61 *Ibid.* 207.
62 Das enthaltene türkisch-tatarische Wortmaterial wird separat analysiert und publiziert.

13*

VII

Umgebung stammten.[63] Im letzten Falle ist also auch mit einer jüngeren Schicht tatarischer Lehnwörter zu rechnen.[64]

In jedem Falle bieten die Fremdwörter in den Sprachdenkmälern bzw. Mundarten ein wertvolles Beweismaterial. Zum Vergleich konnte die „Jeremiade über die Verfolgung der Armenier in der Moldau" herangezogen werden, wo einige rumänische Fremdwörter die moldauische Umgebung verraten.[65]

Auch im Falle eines Bevölkerungswechsels gibt es oft einige Sprachreste in der Sprache der Nachfolger, die für eine gewisse Kontinuität zeugen. Z. B. ist das Armeno-Kiptschakische in der Lwower Gegend und Podolien schon längst ausgestorben, und doch gibt es einige armeno-kiptschakische Wörter in der Sprache der späteren Nachzügler, der Armenier in Kuty zu finden.[66]

Diese, auf Grund sehr spärlicher Sprachdenkmäler dargelegten Erwägungen können für kein endgültiges Ergebnis betrachtet werden, es soll also versucht ein historisch-demographisches Beweismaterial für andere Ortschaften der Krim für Rechenschaft zu dieser Frage herangezogen zu werden.

*

Bedeutende, mit den komanisch-kiptschakischen Stämmen in enger Verbindung stehende, bzw. ihnen nahe wohnende armenische Kolonien gab es in den an die Heidenlandschaft angrenzenden größeren Städten, die Zahlangaben von 1778 betrachtend: Baxči Sarai, Kirkor (Čufut Kale), Qarasubazar, und früher Gazarat und Solxat.

Die armenische Umgansprache dieser Gegend im 15. Jahrhundert kennen wir nicht, frühere lokale Aufzeichnungen gibt es keine, die Handschriften kirchlicher Texte geben (außer der manchmal mangelhaften Orthographie) wenige Anhaltspunkte für die frühere lokale Umgangsprache, noch weniger für eventuelle Fremdwörter. So ist es auf linguistischem Wege kaum zu erhoffen feststellen zu können, ob in diesen Siedlungen das Armeno-Kiptschakische gebraucht worden ist. Nur aus den Angaben der politischen und Wirtschaftsgeschichte kann durch Wahrscheinlichkeits-Approximation Folgerungen gezogen werden, in welchen Siedlungen eine längere Kohabitation mit Komanen erfolgen konnte.

Aus diesem Standpunkt muß Baxči Sarai außer acht gelassen werden, da sie nur später das Zentrum des Krimchanats wurde; im 15. Jahrhundert versetzte Hadži Girei den Sitz der Dynastie eigentlich nach Kirkor. Der Palastkomplex, ein Lustschloß für den Chan ist am Anfang des 16. Jahrhunderts von Mengli Girei erbaut worden,[67] aber Kirkor blieb das Verwaltungszentrum auch in den nach-

---

63 S. oben.

64 Zurzeit steht mir die Grundliteratur zur Vergleichung nicht zur Verfügung. (Hr. Ačaṙean, *Turkerènè poxaṙealbaṙer hayereni meǰ*, und idem, *Knnutᶜyun Nor-Naxiᶜevani (Xrimi) baṙbari*. Allerdings bieten die im Nor-Naxiᶜevaner Dialekt abgefaßten 20 Erzählungen von R. Patkanean eine entsprechende Übersicht auch über die Fremdwörter der Mundart. *Erkeri žoghovacu*, Bd. IV, (Yerevan, 1966), 592—615.

65 Akinean, 85—102; Vgl. *AOH*, XIX, 104.

66 T. Kowalski, *Wyrazy kipczackie w języku Ormian polskich*. Vgl. *AOH*, XIX, 109.

67 Die ersten in Kirkor geprägten Münzen tragen das Datum 1454. — Die Inschrift am Hauptportal berichtet über die Erbauung des Palastes in 1503—1504. *EI* I, 584.

VII

folgenden 16—17. Jahrhunderten: hier sind Gesandte empfangen worden, die wichtigen Staatshäftlinge in Gefängnis gehalten.

Kirkor war eine alte Stadtfestung; aus der griechischen Periode blieben die gemeißelten Steine, aus denen die Stadt wieder hergestellt wurde. Die Kontinuität der Bevölkerung kann aber nicht unmittelbar nachgewiesen werden. Im Laufe der 15—16. Jahrhunderte ließen sich große Volksmassen der Karaiten nieder, so daß die Höhlenstadt *(peščernij gorod)* allmählich heilige Stadt der Karaiten wurde und deshalb die Benennung Čufut Kale (Judenburg, castellum Judeorum) erhielt.[68]

Da die armeno-kiptschakische Sprache mit dem Karaimischen wesentliche Charakterzüge gemein hat, so wäre es verlockend den Ausgangspunkt des Armeno-Kiptschakischen in die Gegend von Čufut Kale zurückzuführen, wo ein unmittelbarer komanisch—karaimisch—armenischer Sprachkontakt leicht erklärt werden könnte.

Jakobson behauptet, daß hier armenische Bewohner auch früher gelebt hätten, manche Baudenkmäler weisen genetische Beziehungen mit der armenischen Architektur auf;[69] doch konnte die Kontinuität einer armenischen Bevölkerung nicht nachgewiesen werden.

Was aber einen armenisch—(komanisch)—karaimischen Sprachkontakt betrifft, dies muß überhaupt nicht auf eine Kohabitation aller drei Völkerschaften zurückgehen, der Kontakt einzelner zwei konnte separat (also komanisch—karaimisch, und komanisch—armenisch) stattgefunden haben.[70]

Qarasubazar war einer der bedeutendsten Marktplätze der Krim, in dessen Handel und Industrie die Armener eine bedeutende Rolle spielten. Dies gilt allerdings für die späteren Jahrhunderte, als nach der Verlegung der Hauptstadt, und der Verschiebung der internationalen Handelswege Solxat (Surxat, d.h. Eski Krim) ihre führende Rolle einbüßte.[71]

Wir besitzen Berichte über das alte armenische Stadtviertel: *Xaraghač*.[72] Es gab eine große Zunahme in der armenischen Kolonie zurzeit der Dschelali Periode, als mehrere zehntausende armenischer Flüchtlinge nach der Krim gelangten. Diese Persarmenier bildeten in Qarasu ein selbständiges Stadtviertel: „Adžem mahallesi".[73] Infolge der Steuerschraubpolitik der türkischen Behörden entfernten sich — laut eines Berichts aus den 1630-er Jahren — viele Armenier aus Kaffa nach Qarasubazar.[74]

Diese Zunahme an Seelenszahl am Anfang des 17. Jahrhunderts wird auch von der sprunghaften Vermehrung der Codexabschriften bezeugt.

---

68 Keppen, 308—18; Jakobson, 128—129; Kondaraki, XV, 195. ff.; IX. 6. ff.; *Istorija i arxeologija srednevekovogo Kryma.* Moskau 1958, 51—53.
69 Jakobson, 129.
70 Karaimische Stadtviertel gab es allerdings auch in Kaffa und Solxat, usw. S. Kondaraki, IX, 7; Bžškian, 334, 323.
71 Kondaraki, XIV, 53. ff.
72 Bžškian, 244. — Die Schriftform *Giuraxač* bei Mikaelian (S. 113.) scheint darauf zu deuten, daß er die Herkunft der Benennung auf armenischen „Schwarzen Kreuz" zurückführt; m. E. wäre eher an das tatarische Wort ‚Ulme' zu denken. S. noch *AOH*, XXIX, 152.
73 Bžškian, 244; 340—41.
74 *ZOOID*, XXIV/2, 120.

VII

Es wäre also eine antihistorische Rückdatierung die große armenische Kolonie in Qarasubazar der massenhaften Einwanderung der Armenier in 1330 zuzuschreiben, wie es in der Literatur oft geschieht. Wahrscheinlich stammt diese Verallgemeinerung letzten Endes aus der Neswitaer Chronik, wo es steht, daß „die armenischen Prinzen und Adeligen von Qarasubazar bis nach Surxat und Theodosia Ortschaften und Landkreise *(gawar)* errichteten."[75] Beim Gebrauch dieser Geschichtsquelle ist es oft außer acht gelassen, daß die endgültige Abfassung des Kolophons auf 1690 fällt, und die Angaben oder die allgemeinen Behauptungen manchmal manchmal die Lage dieses letzten Zeitalters widerspiegeln.

Also, was die massenhafte Emigration Armenier im 15. Jahrhundert nach Polen betrifft, kann Qarasubazar keineswegs in Betracht gezogen werden.

Die Frage der Ortschaft Gazarat *(Gazarat/Kazarat awan)* ist höchst enigmatisch.

Mikaelian behauptet, es sei keine Spur von diesem Ort zu finden;[76] Bžškian dagegen beschreibt die Lage des Ortes: „am Fuße des großen Berges Surb Xač, am gleichnamigen Fluße, von den Tataren *Mughal özen* genannt, sind nur Spuren alter Bauten zu finden, so wie auch an dem naheliegenden *Quzgun Burun*..."[77] Der Gegensatz beider Berichte ist nur scheinbar, da in der weiten Umgebung von Solxat zu Bžškians Zeit Überreste von alten Bauten vorhanden gewesen sein könnten, ob sie aber zu einer separaten Ortschaft, oder zur Vorstadt gehörten, ist eine schwer entschiedliche Frage.

In dem Neswitaer Kolophon ist die Erinnerung an die Vorfahren der Familie Pahlavunenc, mütterlicherseits Mughalenc bewahrt, sie sollten aus Gazarat stammen.

Der Familientradition gemäß sollte der Urahn vom genuesischen Prinzen Širin zum Hypathos, bzw. Statthalter *(kusakal)* mit seiner Heeresgruppe zur Verteidigung der zuführenden Wege Kaffas ernannt werden.[78] Die bezüglichen Stellen sind in der Chronik ziemlich unklar, und die Zitate hiervon in der Literatur irreführend.[79]

Wenn Gazarat hier wirklich eine Ortschaft *(awan)* in der Umgebung oder ein Vorort von Solxat bedeuten würde, so stellt sich sofort die Frage, wie konnte die genuesische Verwaltung im Vorgelände der tatarischen Hauptstadt, der Residenz des Statthalters, eine Verteidigungstruppe gegen die Tataren in Garnizon halten?

Die zweite Unmöglichkeit ist die Existenz eines genuesischen Prinzen *(išxan jinevizac)* namens Širin. Širin ist kein Genueser, sondern die zweitgrößte Sippe in der tatarischen Hierarchie, deren Domäne sich eben an den östlichen Teil der Halbinsel, von Qarasu bis Kerč, ausdehnten. .

Die Verwechslung eines genuesischen Hochadeligen mit einem tatarischen Prinzen ist wahrscheinlich daraus hervorgegangen, daß jenem Absatz der Neswitaer Chronik, wo es sich über die Geschehnisse der Ehe der Tochter des Begs

---

75 Bžškian, 338, §. 505.
76 Mikaelian, 276, 108.
77 Bžškian, 328.
78 Mikaelian, 108. (< Bžškian, 328, 341.)
79 Auch Jakobson verlangt eine Kritik der oft zitierten Stellen, *Viz. Vrem.* VIII, 168. Fn. 4.

VII

der Širin-Sippe mit dem Sohn des Chans handelt, ein Satz über die Beziehung zwischen dem Chan und dem genuesischen Consul *(išxan)* vorangeht.[80]

Dazu waren die Širins eben die Lehnsherren eines großen Teiles des Gebietes, die im byzantinischen Sprachgebrauch die Benennung Ghazarien trug, ein Teil wovon unter genuesischer Verwaltung stand.

Was die Auslegungen anbelangt, steht im Texte kein *awan*, also ‚Ortschaft‘, sondern einfach: Gazarat.[81] In einem Falle gibt der Chronist die Stelle genauer an: daß Theodor Mughalenc, der Ahn, sich mit seinen Truppen *(zorkᶜ)* an dem Fluße Gazarats ansiedelte. Das Wort *jur* konnte auch in weiteren Sinne aufgefaßt werden, nur eben wegen der Identifizierung mit dem Fluß Mughal *(Mughal özen)* ist die Ortsbezeichnung für einen selbständigen Ort aufgefaßt worden. Bei einer derartigen Deutung der Stelle ist es aber überhaupt nicht angebracht den Vorfahren, Theodor Mughalenc, Statthalter *(kusakal)* zu nennen; für eine Ortschaft werden keine Statthalter ernannt.

Das Wort Gazarat kann nicht aus dem armenischen stammen. ‚Chazare‘ heißt im Armenischen *xazir*, Plur. Nom. *xazirkᶜ* (kann auch für Ortsname stehen), Gen. *xazracᶜ* der Buchstabe „kem“ kann aber niemals für einen *x* stehen. Der Ausdruck scheint aus dem Italienischen übernommen sein: Gazaria, was ihrerseits auf die byzantinische Provinzbezeichnung zurückgeht, die auch auf die ganze Halbinsel übertragen wurde.[82]

Die Benennung der Ortschaft kommt in der armenischen Literatur als Zitat aus der Neswitaer Chronik (aus Bžškians Buch) sehr oft vor. In der europäischen Literatur erscheint sie seltener, da für sie Siestrzencewicz's Buch als Quelle diente, und er Gazarat für eine Benennung der Stadt (Eski) Krim hält.[83]

Ein interessantes Gegenstück für Gazarat ist der Ausdruck *ašxarh honacᶜ* ‚Land der Hunnen‘, was in Kolophonen oft vorkommt, z. B. „in unserem Land der Hunnen und der Provinz Gazaria, Sawlhat von Ghrim, und unserer Hauptstadt Kafa“ *(i honacᶜ ašxarhin i Gazariay nahangis, Sawlxat Ghrimi ew Kafajis mayrakᶜalakᶜis)*.[84] Der Gebrauch scheint eine archaisierende Buchtradition zu widergeben.

Auch der Name „Mughalenc“ birgt ein Rätsel. Est ist höchst wahrscheinlich, daß die Familientradition Pahlavunenc—Mughalenc infolge des Flußnamens *Mughal özen* eben an diesen Flecken gekettet wurde. Der Name des Vorfahren ist auch problematisch, da *Mughal* ‚Mongole‘ bedeutet. Der Prozentsatz der echten Mongolen war in der Armee des großen Tatarensturmes ziemlich gering, und auch in Batus Reich bildeten sie nur die obere Schicht. Im Rahmen eines Stammesverbandes blieben nur Kereiten, die Vorfahren der Gireis, und Mangiten, die spätere Mansur Sippe, zurück. Ob der Name Mughal mit einem der zwei

---

80 Bžškian, 338.

81 ds. 328, 340, 341. (Bei Bžškian: *giwlakᶜalakᶜ*).

82 Wie später die Benennung der Hauptstadt „Krim" auf die ganze Halbinsel übertragen wurde. S. den wechselvollen Gebrauch z. B. in der Chronik von Kaffa. *AOH*, XXIX, 184.

83 Siestrzencewicz de Bohusz, *Histoire du royaume de la Chersonèse Taurique*. Spb. 1824, 320. Er schöpft seine Information aus den Aufzeichnungen des armenischen Metropoliten J. Argutinskij (H. Argutean) (*Ečmiadzin*, Jg. 1962.), die aber letzten Endes auch auf die Neswitaer Chronik zurückgehen.

84 Z. B. Xačikian, I, 502, und weiter 19, 190, 207, 244, 390, 395, 414, 511; Sanjian, 97, 98, 101.

VII

Stämme zusammenhängt, oder ob er von einem, im mongolischen Dienst stehenden Armenier herrührt, ist nicht zu sagen.

Solxat (Surxat, Krim, später Eski Krim) war schon zurzeit der Chazaren der Sitz des Statthalters der Halbinsel Krim, blieb der Mittelpunkt auch weiter unter den Komanen, und bildete die Hauptstadt der tatarischen Verwaltung auch während des Zeitalters der Goldenen Horde, bis die Dynastie der Gireis um die Mitte des 15. Jahrhunderts ihren Sitz nach Kirkor verlegte. Sie war auch der Knotenpunkt des west-östlichen Karavanenverkehrs, lag bloß je 25 Km von den beiden Seehafen-Emporien Kaffa und Sudaq entfernt.

Sie lag in der südöstlichen Ecke der Steppenlandschaft, eben an der Scheidelinie der nomaden und sedentären Völkerschaften, und hatte deshalb eine ziemlich bunte Bevölkerung: außer den Resten der Griechen, der grezisierten Urbevölkerung, Alanen, Karaiten machten den Hauptteil die früheren Nomaden, die Komanen, und die Kiptschaken der Goldenen Horde, aus.

Auch die Armenier spielten eine bedeutende Rolle im Handelsleben dieser „nomaden" Hauptstadt der Krim. Es ist möglich, daß Armenier auch schon vor der Tatarenwirtschaft der Goldenen Horde, unter den Komanen hier lebten, allerdings übersiedelten sie in Massen um 1330, aus Aqsarai.

Die imposante Ausdehnung der Stadt wird durch den, vom Ende des 18. Jahrhundertes stammenden Planaufriß bezeugt.[85] Die Ruinen der im 15—16. Jahrhundert zusammenschrumpfenden Stadt wird 1578 von Broniewski mit begeisterten Worten beschrieben.[86]

Ein farbenreiches Bild von Solxat steht bevor uns in der Beschreibung des Mechitaristen Minas Bžškian, der seine Diozöse 1820 besuchte: Gleich am Haupttor lagen die Ruinen zweier armenischer Kuppelkirchen, und in verschiedenen Vierteln der alten Stadt sind noch die Überreste sieben armenischer Kirchen erhalten geblieben. Es gab ein kompakt armenisches Stadtviertel, „Verin Hoghatner" (Oberes Hausquartal?),[87] woher farbreiche Bilder des begabten Codexilluminators, Nader, auf uns erhalten blieben.[88] All diese Angaben sind Beweise einer dichten armenischen Bevölkerung.

Welches Zentrum für die Armenier Solxat und Umgebung bedeutete, zeugt das 1338 gegründete, berühmte Kloster, Surb Xač (‚Heiliger Kreuz'), fünf Km von der Stadt entfernt, am gleichnamigen Hügel (tatarisch Agharmiš), an dessen Fuß Bžškian die „Ortschaft Gazarat" zu erkennen glaubte.

Der Vergleich der komanisch-tatarischen Bevölkerungsdichte der beiden Nachbarstädte Kaffa und Solxat ist auch besonders lehrreich.

Als die Genueser um 1266 vom tatarischen Feudalherrn die Genehmigung zur Niederlassung erhielten, war Kaffa eine unbedeutende Ortschaft.[89] Schon aus dem Charakter der Siedlung — Meeresufer, in der Umgebung Gartenkultur — ist es ersichtlich, daß der Ort kaum von Nomaden bewohnt gewesen ist. Später, als er zum Handelszentrum des Schwarzen Meeres wurde, haben die Genueser

85 In der Gos. Publičnaja Biblioteka, apud Jakobson, 106.
86 Schwandtner, III, 268; *ZOOID*, VI, 346.
87 Bžškian, 321—322; Xačikian, *XIV dari hayeren dzeragreri hišatakaranner*, 370, 419, 456, 460, 467, 518. (Mikaelian 103—104.)
88 Xorxmazian: *Banber Matenadarani*, No. 9. 201—211.
89 Heyd, II, 157—158; 163—164; Vasiliev, 171.

VII

alle Maßnahmen getroffen, um besonders die Amtsleute und überhaupt die Bewohner der Stadt von jewelcher freundschaftlichen Beziehung mit den Tataren
fernzuhalten.[90]

Also wenn man die Möglichkeiten der Beziehungen zwischen Armenier und
Komanen-Kiptschaken durchmustert, so stellt es sich heraus, daß in erster Reihe
Solxat (Eski-Krim) in Betracht gezogen werden muß. Solxat war eine der geeigne-
testen Gegende, wo die zwei Völkerschaften in enge und dauernde Beziehung treten
könnten, und wo das Komanisch-Kiptschakische die Umgangsprache war.

Die zweite Frage bezüglich der Abstammung der Lwower armeno-kiptschakisch sprechender Armenier besteht darin, woher eine Abwanderung großer
Volksmassen (nach Polen) voraussetzbar ist. In dieser Hinsicht geht wieder Solxat
voran.

Nach der Machtergreifung der Gireis, entfaltete sich eine ununterbrochene
Feindseligkeit zwischen Solxat und Kaffa, die nach dem unglücklichen Ausgang
der Lomellino Expedition 1434 zur völligen Zerrüttung der Beziehungen entartete.
Die Gegend zwischen Solxat und Kaffa ist jahrzehnte lang Schlachtfeld geworden.
In dieser Lage hatten die Fremden, und so in erster Reihe die dichte Volksschicht
der Armenier, zu leiden.

Und es kam noch ein noch schwerwiegenderer Beweggrund dazu, daß
Tausende von Armeniern aus Solxat und Umgebung abwanderten um eine neue
Heimat zu suchen. Die unmittelbare Nachbarschaft zur Residenz des türkischen Beglerbegs in Kaffa machte die Stadt für eine „selbständige" Dynastie
unbequem. Deshalb versetzte die Girei Dynastie den Sitz nach Kirkor, hiemit
verlor aber Solxat ihre frühere Bedeutung als Verwaltungszentrum und Handels-
emporium. Die Armenier von Solxat standen auf dem Scheidewege: nach Kirkor
zu übersiedeln verhieß nicht viel Existenzmöglichkeit; der internationale Handels-
weg über Solxat — Kaffa war zugrunde gerichtet. Handel durch das Schlacht-
gebiet der Erzfeinde — Türken und Perser — zu führen, war kaum möglich,
lokalen Handel in Kirkor zu treiben, hatte überhaupt keinen Sinn, desto weniger, da sich in der Stadtfestung schon Karaimen eingebürgert hatten.

In der völligen Umwälzung der politischen, und wirtschaftlichen Umstände
sehen wir die Grundursachen für die Weiterwanderung der Armenier aus dem
früheren „Lande der Hunnen", der späteren Gazaria (Gazarat), aus den Handels-
städten mit dichter armenischer Bevölkerung: Kaffa, und in erster Reihe Solxat
(Surxat — die spätere (Eski) Krim).

Es sei noch auf eine wichtige linguistische Parallele hingewiesen.

Das wichtigste Sprachdenkmal der Komanischen Sprache, der Codex
Cumanicus, birgt unter anderen ein Kolophon, auf Grund dessen festgestellt
werden konnte, daß er 1303 in einem Kloster S. Johannes unweit von Sarai ab-
geschrieben wurde (S. Johannes.. tribus a Saray civitate milliaribus disiunctus).[91]
Im Lichte dieser Angabe wäre es von höchstem Interesse zu erforschen in welcher
Beziehung die armeno-kiptschakische Sprache zum Sprachmaterial des Codex
Cumanicus steht, da in Sarai Tausende von Armeniern lebten; schon Batu Chan

---

90 Heyd, II, 371—372.
91 W. Bang, *Über die Herkunft des Codex Cumanicus*, SPAW Phil.-hist. Kl. 1913, 244—245;
    Györffy, *Autour du CC: Bibl. Orient. Hung.* V, 16.; PhTF, II, 243—244.

VII

hat sie günstig empfangen.[92] Auch die Tradition der Krimarmenier berichtet, dass die 1330 nach Kaffa, Surxat, Gazarat übersiedelten Armenier zuvor in Aqsarai lebten.[93] So konnte eventuell die Hypothese aufgestellt werden, daß diese Armenier das Armeno-Kiptschakische vielleicht schon in Aqsarai angeeignet hätten.

Gegen eine solche Hypothese sollte man einwenden, daß nur der zweite, von deutschsprachigen Mönchen geschriebene, Teil des Codex aus der Gegend von Sarai stammte, das Armeno-kiptschakische aber zum Sprachmaterial des ersten, wenn auch ebenfalls Dialektunterschiede aufweisenden, Teiles engere sprachliche Beziehungen hat. Der Urtext des ersten Teiles ist aber in einem italienisch—komanischen Sprachkreise zustande gekommen, von im westöstlichen Handel betätigten Geschäftsleuten, oder für sie aufgezeichnet worden.

Italienische Handelsstädte gibt es mehrere an den Küsten des Schwarzen oder auch des Azovschen Meeres.

Nur 10—13 Tagesreise ist Tana von Sarai entfernt. Den Venedigern ist es in den 1330-er Jahren gelungen von den Tataren ein Stadtviertel in Tana auszubedingen und sich hier einen Handelsstützpunkt auszubauen, der aber nach der Eroberung Konstantinopels (1453) nur noch einige Jahrzehnte aufrecht erhalten werden konnte. Für die anderthalb Jahrhunderte diente jedoch Tana als Umladeplatz für die Venediger gegen Osten, und eben nach der Hauptstadt der Goldenen Horde, Sarai.[94]

So kann die Vermutung nicht aus der Hand gewiesen werden, daß das in Venedig erhaltene Exemplar des Codex Cumanicus eben in diesem Handelszentrum der Venediger, in Tana, abgeschrieben wurde.

Um aber die sprachlichen Berührungspunkte des ersten Teiles, der Grammatik, des dreisprachigen Glossars (1r—55v) und des Armeno-Kiptschakischen annähern zu können, muß man einen solchen Sprachkreis finden, wo nebst dem komanisch—italienischen Sprachkontakte auch eine wesentliche armenische Kolonie lebte.

Was die Komanen betrifft, sie sind schon von Sübötei 1222/1223 zersprengt worden. Die auf dem Aufmarschfeld des großen Mongolensturmes 1236 gebliebenen Überreste sind teilweise in die tatarischen Stoßtruppen eingegliedert worden, ein anderer Teil zog sich in die Randlandschaft zurück. Die Einverleibten nahmen die Sprache des regierenden Stammverbandes, oder im Falle der Goldenen Horde, der kiptschakischen Mehrheit an, die in unserem Falle dem, im Codex Cumanicus verkörperten zweiten kiptschakischen Sprachtyp am nächsten stehen sollte.

Wenn man die Bezeichnung „Komanisch" eher für die erste Variante vorbehalten möchte, so sollte dies im Randgebiet, eher erhalten geblieben. Dies ist die Meinung mehrerer Forscher, die wegen der Merkmale des ersten Teiles — italienische Varianten in den lateinischen Worten, stellenweise italienische Orthographie, die Wortliste für laische Zwecke, viele Wortgruppen für Handelszwecke *(spetiaria; mercimonia que pertinent ad mercatorem)*[95] — auf eine mit den

92　Kirakos de Gandsak, trad. E. Dulaurier, *JA* série V, Bd. XI. (1858) 458—459.

93　Bžškian, 338, §. 504.

94　*Barbaro i Contarini o Rossii.* Publ. E. Č. Skržinskaja. Leningrad 1971, 32. ff.

95　*Codex Cumanicus.* Facsimile Ausg. K. Grønbech. 40/v, 46/r.

VII

Italienern in enger Beziehung stehenden Handelsstadt auf der Krim denken. Jireček meint das Glossar sollte in Kaffa oder in einer anderen Stadt der Krim aufgezeichnet werden, Rasovskij und Györffy geben ihre Stimmen für Solxat ab.[96] Solchat war das Marktzentrum der südöstlichen Weidenlandschaft, die schlechthin Gazarien, Gazarat genannt wurde. Nach dem Zusammenbruch des Khasarenreiches sind die Reste des Machtbereichs, bzw. der Benennung auf diesen südöstlichen Teil der Halbinsel Krim zusammengeschrumpft, und von hieraus wieder auf die ganze Halbinsel übergangen. Bei Rubruk kommen die zwei Bedeutungen — wegen der Schwankung im Sprachgebrauch seiner Informatoren — im selben Absatz zu Vorschein: I, 12. „Post illa montana (die taurische Gebirgskette)... et post illam silvam est planicies maxima que durat per V dietas usque ad extremitatem illius provincie ad aquilonem... In illa planicie solebant esse Comani antequam venirent Tartari, ...et quando venerunt Tartari tanta multitudo Comanorum intravit provinciam illam, qui omnes fugerunt usque ad ripam maris..."[97] Wie gesagt, lebten die Komanen schon vor der Ankunft der Tataren in dieser Ebene (planicies maxima), und als jene ankamen flüchteten sie in die südöstliche Gegend (provincia illa), die kat'exokhén Gasarien, woselbst die Armenier mit ihnen in Berührung kamen, und ihre Mundart übernahmen, nur sollte eben diese Mundart in den komanischen Sprachdenkmälern aufgefunden werden.

Wie es aus obigen Ausführungen hervorgeht, gibt es schwerwiegende politische und wirtschaftliche Voraussetzungen, die der letzten Auffassung beistimmen. Allerdings wird den wichtigen Beweis für die Feststellung des Ursitzes der in den 15—16. Jahrhunderten nach Polen ausgewanderten Armenier die Vergleichung der kiptschakischen Sprachen, in erster Reihe des Armeno-Kiptschakischen mit dem Material des Codex Cumanicus, und der komanischen Lehnwörter in den Nachbarsprachen bieten.

LITERATUR

Ačarian, H., K^cnnut^cyun Polsahay barɒari [Untersuchung der Konstantinopler Mundart], Jerewan 1941.

Ačemian, V. L., Grakan arevmtahayereni dzevavoruma [Die Ausbildung der westarmenischen Literatursprache], Jerewan 1971.

Akdağ, M., Celālī isyanlarī (1550—1603), Ankara 1963.

Akinean, N., Hing panduxt talasac'ner [Fünf emigrante Dichter], Wien 1921.

Ališan, Gh., Hayapatum, II/3. Venedig 1901.

Anassian H., XVII dari azatagrakan šaržumnern arevmtyan Hayastanum [Freiheitsbewegungen in Westarmenien im 17. Jh.], Jerewan 1961.

Atti della Società Ligure di Storia Patric. bei Vasiliev und Mikaelian.

---

96 D. Rašovskij, K voprosu o proisxoždenii CC. Seminarium Kondakovianum. III, 210—213; Györffy, 30.
97 A. Wyngaert, Sinica franciscana, I, 170—171.

VII

Barxudarian, V. B., *Nor Naxičevani haykakan galut^c i patmut^c yun (1779—1861 tt.)* [Geschichte der armenischen Kolonie von Nor-Nachitschewan, 1779—1861], Jerewan 1967.

Berbérian, H., *Niwt^c er K. Polsoy Hayoc^c patmut^c ean hamar.* [Materialen zur Geschichte der Armenier in Konstantinopel]. Wien 1965.

Broniewski, M., *Opisanie Kryma, ZOOID,* VI.

Broniewski/Schwandtner: *Martini Broniovii de Biezdzfedea Stephani I. Poloniae regis nomine bis in Tartariam legati „Descriptio Tartariae".* *Ad primam editionem coloniensem anni MDXCV denuo recognita & emendata:* Schwandtner, *Scriptorum Rerum Hungaricarum veteres, ac genuini,* pars III, 247—298.|

Bžškian, M., *Čanaparhordut^c iwn i Lehastan* [Reise nach Polen]. Venedig 1830.

Voyages du Chevalier Chardin en Perse, et autres lieux¦ de l'Orient. Ed. L. Langlès, Paris, Bd. I. 1811.

C^c uc^c ak dzeragrac^c Maštoc^c i anvan Matenadarani [Handschriftenkatalog des Maštoc-Archivs]. Jerewan, Bd. I. 1965, Bd. II. 1970.

Dortelli d'Ascoli E., *Opisanie Černogo morja i Tatarii: ZOOID* XXIV/2.

Györffy, G., *Autour du Codex Cumanicus, BOH* V., Budapest, 1942.

GOR — Hammer, *Geschichte.*

Xačikian, L., *XV dari hayeren dzeragreri hišatakaranner,* [Kolophone der armenischen Handschriften des 15. Jh's], Bd. II. (1451—1480) 1958; Bd. III. (1481—1500), Jerewan 1967.

Hakobian, V., *Hayeren dzeragreri XVII dari hišatakaranner* [Kolophone der armenischen Handschriften, 17. Jh.], Bd. I. (1601—1620). Jerewan 1974.

Hakobian, V., *Manr žamanakagrut^c yunner XIII—XVIII dd.,* [Kleine Chronika der 13—18. Jahrhunderte], Jerewan, Bd. I. 1951.

Hammer, J., *Geschichte des Osmanischen Reiches,* Pest, Bd. II, 1828.

Hay žolovrdi patmut^c yun. [Geschichte des armenischen Volkes], Herasugegeben von der Akad. Wiss. der ArmSSR. Bd. IV. 1972.

Heyd W., *Histoire du commerce du Levant au moyen-âge,* Bd. I—II. Leipzig, 1885—1886.

Jakobson, A. L., *Srednevekovyj Krym.* Moskau—Leningrad 1964.

Jakobson, A. L., *Armjanskaja srednevekovaja arxitektura v Krymu. Vizantijskij Vremennik* VIII, 166—191.

Keppen, P., *Krymskij Sbornik,* Spb, 1837.

Kušnerean, K. V., *Patmut^c iwn galtakanut^c ean Xrimu hayoc^c.* [Geschichte der armenischen Kolonie in der Krim], Venedig, 1895.

Małowist, M., *Kaffa w drugiej polowie XV-ego wieku,* Warszawa, 1939.

Martirossian, A. A., *Martiros Ghrimec^c i,* Jerewan 1958.

Mikaelian, V. A., *Ghrimi haykakan galuti patmut^c yun* [Geschichte der armenischen Kolonie in der Krim], Jerewan 1964.

Patmut^c yun — Hay žolovrdi patmut^c yun

Sanjian, A. K., *Colophons of Armenian Manuscripts, 1301—1480. A Source for Middle Eastern History,* Cambridge, Mass. 1969.

Schütz, E., *Rearmenisation and Lexicon (From Armeno-Kipchak back to Armenian); AOH* XIX 99—115.

Schütz, E., *Eine armenische Chronik von Kaffa aus der ersten Hälfte des 17. Jahrhunderts: AOH* XXIX/2, 133—186.

Schwandtner s. Broniewski

Siestrzencewicz de Bohusz, *Histoire du royaume de la Chersonèse Taurique,* Spb, 1824.

Simeon dpri Lehac^c woy Uleworut^c iwn [Des Armeniers Simeon aus Polen Reisebeschreibung] Wien 1936.

Simeon Lehaci, *Putevye¦ zametki* (Perevod M. O. Darbiniana): *Pamjatniki pis'mennosti Vostoka* IX., Moskau 1965. ˙

Sphrantzes/Ivánka s. *Die letzten Tage von Konstantinopel.* (Der auf den Fall Konstantinopel 1453 bezügliche Teil des dem̲ Georgios Sphrantzes zugeschriebenen „Chronikon Maius"

VII

Übersetzt von E. Ivánka: *(Byzantinische Geschichtsschreiber*, Bd. I.), Graz—Wien—Köln 1954.

Tavrižeci s. *Patmut^ciwn Arak^cel vardapeti Dawrižec^cwoy* [Geschichte (der Armenier) von Archimandrit Arakel von Tabriz], Vagharšapat 1896; russ. Übers.: A. Davrižeci, *Kniga istorij*, Moskau 1973; franz.: Übers. A. de Tauriz, *Livre d'histoires:* Brosset, *Collection d'historiens arméniens*, I. S-Péterbourg, 1874.

Ter-Abrahamian, H., *Patmut^ciwn Xrim* [Geschichte der Krim], Theodosia 1865.

Tveritinova, A. S., *Vosstanie Kara Jazyji — Deli Xasana v Turcii*, Moskau—Leningrad 1946.

Uzunçarşılı, I. H., *Osmanlı tarihi*, Bd. II, Ankara 1964.

Vasiliev, A. A., *The Goths in the Crimea* Cambridge, Mass. 1936.

Zinkeisen, J. W., *Geschichte des Osmanischen Reiches in Europa*, Gotha, Bd. II, 1854.

(Zarbhanalian, G.,) *Patmut^ciwn hayerèn dprut^cean* [Geschichte der armenischen Literatur], Bd. II, Venedig 1905.

Zulalian, M. K., *Džalalineri šaržumə ew hay zolovrdi vičakə Osmanyan Kaysrut^cyan mej* [Die Bewegung und das Schicksal des armenischen Volkes im Osmanischen Reich], Jerewan 1966.

VII

PART II

LINGUISTIC STUDIES

TANGSUX IN ARMENIA

BY

E. SCHÜTZ

It is at a very early time, indeed, already from the Vth century, *i.e.* practically from the first written records, that Turkic words begin to appear in Armenian chronicles and, from the XIIIth century onward there are also occurrences of Mongolian names and even of common nouns. Although these words, by means of dating the compositions in which they occur, can mostly be linked with certain ethnic elements, they resist at present a really systematic treatment, which can only be successfully undertaken when the clarification of the inner (textual) problems of the chronicles concerned will have been accomplished.

The incursions in the times prior to the Seljuqs hardly left any linguistic traces in the Armenian language; and the relevant words occurring in the chronicles and colophons are, without exception, the Turkic names or dignitarial designations of the invaders.

The task of identifying various strata in the Turkic stock of words appearing in the Armenian dialects will, at any rate, meet with the special difficulty that, in this case, we have to do with cognate languages or dialects of the Turkic group, let alone the additional snags that, on the one hand, with the later predominance of Ottoman-Turkish, the shades of difference become obliterated, while, on the other hand, we have no exact means of ascertaining wether an Arabo-Persian word directly or indirectly found its way into the Armenian language.

We are in a somewhat different situation as regards the linguistic remains of the Mongolian conquest. The linguistic influence of the hundred years long Il-Khan period can be separated, to a certain extent, from the Turkic material originating from the preceding and subsequent periods. Only to a certain extent, to be sure, as the linguistic influence of the Mongolian period does not necessarily mean a Mongolian linguistic influence. It is to be taken into consideration that the Mongol-Tatars constituted but a rather small part of the conquering army.[1] The troops consisted to a large part of Turkish nomads

---

[1] At any rate A. J. Jakubovskij rightly warns us (Очерки по истории русского востоковедения, Moscow 1953, p. 76), in connection with the Golden Horde: we

who joined in the hope of a rich booty or were compelled to join, and moreover (in this region) of Persians. After 1256 Armenia became "officially" subject to the rule of the Il-Khans, and in the bureaucratic machinery the main role was played by Persians. This linguistically mixed aspect of the Mongolian military and administrative apparatus remained unchanged throughout all the phases of the history of the Il-Khan empire.

This is well attested by an important, although brief, literary document: a rather slender Mongolian glossary which is embedded in the chronicle written by the Armenian monk Kirakos of Gandsak.[2] In 1236 Kiriakos, with some of his fellow-monks, had been hiding in a cave near the fortress Tavuš north of the Sevan lake when the Tatars discovered and captured them. It is to be noted that the guards who then escorted the prisoners were Persians. Kirakos and some of his companions were pressed into service as scribes to "write and read letter(s)" *(Ibid.,* p. 249[5—6]). They were presumably commanded to write proclamations in order to lure back the population to their deserted homes, or letters designed to persuade the garrisons of certain fortresses to surrender, etc. That the priests were ignorant of the Mongolian (or Turkic) language is told by themselves: ,,We do not know your language" (p. 246[5]).

Their unfamiliarity with that language is also borne out by the glossary which contains only the most elementary words (the terms of kinship, the words for the parts of the body, domestic animals, etc.) in Mongolian, that is, in some cases in Turkic, or the Arabo-Persian word, or both. Persian was undoubtedly the language by means of which they maintained their contact with the conquering troups.

During the century of Il-Khan rule only a few technical terms of military organisation and civil administration (taxation) passed from the Mongolian language — presumably by Persian mediation — into Armenian usage, and even these disappeared after the fall of the Il-Khan empire. For example, *duman, kesiktoyk, bahatur — soyuryal, χurutay, yarliχ, (y)asaχ, yam — mal, yp̌čur, tayar, tzyu,*[3] etc. The linguistic problem is somewhat simpler when we deal with purely Mongolian words, yet in most cases the Mongolian or Turkic origin cannot be sharply distinguished.

---

should not suppose that only the commanders were Mongols. (Cf. Schütz, *A mongol hódítás néhány problémájához* [= Notes on Some Problems of the Mongol Conquest]: *Századok,* 1959, p. 218).

[2] Kirakos Gandzakec'i, *Patmut'iwn Hayoc'* (Yerevan 1961), p. 248[9]; Brosset, M.: *Deux historiens arméniens, Kiracos de Gantzac, XIIIe s., Histoire d'Arménie* (SPb. 1870), pp. 135—136.

[3] F. W. Cleaves, *The Mongolian Names and Terms in the "History of the Nation of the Archers"* : *HJAS* XII (1949), 167 sqq. — Concerning the various kinds of taxes see the recent study of I. P. Petruševskij, Земледелие и аграрные отношения в Иране XIII—XIV веков (Moscow—Leningrad 1960), pp. 340—402.

VIII

It is presumably to this period, that is, to the stock of words which passed by Persian mediation into Armenian usage, that we must assign the word *tansux* (*թանսուխ*) which means 'dear, expensive, valuable, exquisite, costly, rare, extraordinary, remarkable, wonderful, exceptional'.[4]

We have data which show that the word *tansux*, as a female name, acquired quite a popularity in the Armenian language.

In the following exposition we wish to give an illustration of the intricate problem concerning the borrowing of personal names in the age of the Il-Khans, by the word *tansux*, copiously attested as a monomial personal name (*i.e.*, without the frequently used compound *xatun*, *melek*, *beki*, etc.).

In discussing the phonetic problems of this loanword, we have tried to give a glance to the difficulties which arise when the same phonetic development (or trend) is noticeable both in the language of origin and in the adopting language.

We have tried to touch upon some problems which bear on the history of personal names in Armenian: the historic factors accounting for the intricate nature of the borrowing of personal names, the explanation in folk etymology for the peculiar preference for certain frequently used names, etc. We believe that, beyond the mechanical process of setting up the types of personal names, it will be such problems of cultural history that will later call for our close attention.

Our investigations into the foreign or borrowed names occurring in the Armenian language are at present yet in the phase of collecting the necessary data. But it can already be stated in the way of a general characterisation that names of foreign origin were more frequently borne by women than men, and, in most cases, contemporary fashion seems to give a better explanation for this fact than marriages with women of foreign origin.

In collecting the personal names, our primary source lies in the colophons in which the copying monk, in the way of rewarding himself for his great work, lists the names of his relatives in order to secure their eternal salvation. So most of the women in the following enumeration are related by blood, respectively marriage, to monastics and priests as mothers, sisters or wives:

1. *T'ansuxχ* (*թանսուղխ*), the mother of a vardapet called Mkrtič who, in the Mecopa monastery in 1418, completed the copying of a volume of homilies.[5]

[4] Malxassiants, St.: *Hayerēn bac'atrakan bararan* [= Armenian Explanatory Dictionary], vol II (Yerevan 1944), p. 84.

[5] Khachikian, L. S., *ŽE dari hayeren dzeṙagreri hišatakaranner* [= Colophons of XVth Century Armenian MSS], vol. I (1401—1450), vol. II (1451—1480) (Yerevan 1955—1958). Further on abbreviated: *Hiš* : — I, p. 178.

VIII

2. *Tᶜangsoy, Tᶜangsux, Tᶜangsuy* (*Թանգսոզ, Թանկսուխ, Թանկսուզ*), the mother of bishop Sargis. She died in 1418.[6]

3. *Tᶜansu χatun*, the wife of priest Karapet who copied the New Testament in 1421 at Van.[7]

4. *Tᶜangsuχ, Tᶜangsuy* a relative of bishop Sargis who was copying in 1427 in the monastery Kotiporo.[8]

We believe that an enumeration of further names would be superfluous. The afore-quoted two-volume collection of colophons lists 12 women by this name from the period 1401—1480, and, in addition to these cases, Acharian's *Dictionary of Personal Names* contains yet 6 cases from the XVth century and 5 from the XVIth century.[9]

It can be assumed that it was by the mediation of the Persian *tansūχ* that the word passed into Armenian:[10] تنسوخ *tansūḫ* unde ar. تنسوق *tansūq* 'res quaevis pretiosissima, incomparabilis et difficilis impetratu' (Vullers, I, 467b); تنسخ *tansuḫ* 'curious, precious, rare', تنسوق *tansūq* 'anything rare, precious; present' (Steingass, 328b).[11]

The meaning 'gift, present' is clearly expressed, for instance, in a passage of Juvaini when the Qa'an says this to Edgü Temür: "Why didst not thou and thy father make *tangsuqs* (that is, novelties or rarities) like this?"[12] In this instance the Qa'an's reference is precisely to the gifts of Körgüz which are listed on the foregoing page, and hence the adequate translation of *tangsuq* should be "present".

[6] *Hiš.* I, pp. 223, 229, 363, 364. — The terminal -*z* (*զ*) in one of the examples is obviously a misprint for *γ* (*ղ*). — In the transliteration I do not distinguish *Նգ* from *Նկ* since, from Middle Armenian onward, both combinations of characters are used to denote *ng*. Cf.: Karst, *Hist. Gramm. d. Kil. Arm.*, p. 82. — This is the pronunciation in today's literary language also.

[7] *Hiš.* I, p. 260; Hr. Acharian: *Hayoc' andznanunneri baṙaran* [= Dictionary of Armenian Personal Names] vols. I—V, 1942—1962. [Further on abbreviated: *Andzn*] II. p. 279. — It was apparently because of the initial letter of the following word *χatun* that the terminal -*χ* was left out.

[8] *Andzn*, II, p. 279.

[9] It is essentially to the end of the XVth century that this dictionary comprises the stock of Armenian names. See: vol. I, p. XIII.

[10] Hr. Acharian: *Hayerèn armatakan baṙaran* [Armenian Etymological Dictionary, further on abbreviated: *Arm. bar.*] p. 1131. — *Andzn*, II, p. 279. — In neither of the dictionaries are there references to the Mongol equivalents.

[11] For the most important Turkish and Mongolian equivalents of the word cf. L. Ligeti, *Az 'ajándék' két török-perzsa neve* [Two Turko-Persian Words for 'Gift']: *Magyar Nyelv* LIII (1957) p. 158—159. Cf. also A. Mostaert — F. W. Cleaves, *Les Lettres de 1289 et 1305 des ilkhan Aryun et Öljeitü à Philippe le Bel* (Cambridge, Mass. 1962), pp. 44—45.

[12] Juvaini, *The History of the World-Conqueror*. Translated by J. A. Boyle (Manchester University Press 1958), vol. II, p. 497.

VIII

The Turkic equivalents of the word are as follows: Uighur: *tangsuq* 'köstlich' (Bang-Gabain, *AnalInd.* 43), 'köstlich, wunderbar' (Gabain, *Alttürk. Gramm.* 337); Kāšɣarī: *tangsuq* 'wunderbar', *tangsuq aš* 'Lieblingsgericht' (Brockelmann, 195; Atalay 571); Abū Hayyān: *tangsïq* 'taaccüp olunacak şey' (Caferoğlu 98); Kumanian: *tansic*, read: *tansïq* 'rarus' *(CodCum.* 160); Jagatai: *tansuy* 'wunderbar; Geschenk' (Šejχ Sul., ed. Kunos 182), *tansuy*, *tangsuq* 'chose merveilleuse; introuvable' (PdC 206); Kazan Tatar: *tansïq* 'selten'; *tansïq aš* 'eine Speise, die man nicht alle Tage zu essen bekommt' (Radl. III, 834); Balkar: *tansïq, tansïx, tansïy* ['Sehnsucht, Verlangen; sehnsüchtig . . .'] (Pröhle: *KSz* VI, 256); Turki: *tansuq* 1. 'ein wunderbares Ding, das Wunder'; 2. 'der Wunsch' (Radl. III, 835); Kazakh: *tangsïq* 'sich wundernd, vor Freude erregt, wunderbar, merkwürdig, selten' (Radl. III, 813).[13]

We can find the word frequently in the Ottoman-Turkish literature in which *tañsuq* is the commonly occurring form (less frequently with the initial *d*); 'acayip, tuhaf, şaşılacak, garip, şayanı hayret; garip, acip şey' *(Tarama Sözl.* I, 179; II, 260; IV, 738). The word belonged to the poetic vocabulary, to the grand style. Since the afore-quoted works *(Camaspname, Şehname, Süheyl ü Nevbehar,* etc.) are mostly translations from the Persian, we may even allow for the possibility of a „Rückentlehnung".

The Mongolian equivalents are as follows: Lit. Mong. *tangsuy* 1. 'plaisir, agrément, joie; agréable, délicat, exquis, joyeu'; 2. 'merveille, merveilleux' (Kow III, 1567a); Kalmuck *tanₑvg, tamsvg* 1. 'Süssigkeiten; Feinschmecker, wählerisch (beim Essen)'; 2. 'freundlich, lieblich' (Ramstedt, 377b, 379b); Ordos *tansyg, tamsyg* 'agréable au goût, savoreux, exquis, excellent' (Mostaert, 643b).[14] Furthermore, Lit. Mong. (Lessing, 778): *tangsuy* adj. and n. 'delicious, tastely; pleasant, joyous, agreeable; delicate, exquisite, marvelous, remarkable; pleasure, joy'.

It is from the Mongolian antiquity, from a letter written by Il-Khan Arɣun to the French king Philip the Fair as early as in 1289 that L. Ligeti — in his above cited article — quotes a case in which the word carries the meaning 'gift' and three such instances from the second half of the XVIIth century.[15]

As to the origin of the Turkic word *tangsuq*, it obviously comes from the root *taŋ*. This word exists in most of the Turkic languages, and, in the final analysis, it presumably goes back to the word *taŋ* which expresses 'wonderment or doubt' (Radl. III, 803).

In order to fix the period in which the word passed into Armenian, we must consider its earliest occurrences as furnishing the *terminus ante quem.*

[13] L. Ligeti, *loc. cit.*
[14] *Ibid.*
[15] *HJAS* XVIII (1955), p. 215.

VIII

If we assume that the first two of the aforesaid Armenian women called *T'angsuχ* were born approximately in the decade 1370—1380, then the borrowing of the name must have taken place before that date.

Considering merely the phonetic analogies, the Armenian word cannot be linked separately with one or the other language of the Il-Khan empire. In Turkic languages generally we find initial *t-*, the only exception being Ottoman-Turkish *d-* occurring sporadically. The dropping out of the laryngal element from -*ng*- (*η*) might have taken place even in the Turkic languages themselves, or in Persian; while the persistence of the -*ng*- in Armenian can also be regarded as a secondary phenomenon, the result of Armenian folk etymology. As to the problem of the final sound, there are several solutions which commend themselves. The terminal *χ* is the regular Armenian equivalent of the Turkish *q*, yet the *χ* might have already developed in the respective language of origin, Turkish or Persian. As to the termination of the word, Bang calls our attention to the necessity of distinguishing the suffix -*suq* from -*sïy*.[16] However, in this case we are not dealing with different formative syllables, and a voiced final sound can be found in the Eastern Turkic languages, in the Mongolian language; it appears at any rate in the Persian, and, as we shall show below, it might even represent an indigenous development of the Armenian language.

It would be rash to conclude from the appearance of the word *tansuχ* in a number of Armenian dictionaries that the word was widely used in Armenian. Our suspicion might be aroused by the fact that the great Venetian *New Dictionary of the Armenian Language* (*Ն․Հ․Բ*) does not list the word. The clue to the problem is furnished by Acharian's *Etymological Dictionary*. Acharian found but one occurrence of the word: in a medieval collection of Armenian fables.[17] Acharian applies the designation „new" to this word, but in his usage this simply means that the word was not listed before in a dictionary. However, medieval Armenian folk tales contain a great number of Arabo-Perso-Turkish words, and it is only by the frequency of occurrences that we can in each case decide wether we have a loanword or a foreign word before us. It is clear in our case that *tansuχ* is not a deeply rooted foreign word, since the dictionaries simply repeat Acharian's single instance. So it is clear that the name was not formed in Armenian from a common noun, but it was taken over as a personal name by the Armenians.

We do not have a Persian dictionary of names that would comprise the Mongolian era and the subsequent period, and, to a certain extent, just an Armenian collection of names might be a useful contribution to the material

---

[16] *Ung. Jb.* XIV, p. 212. But Gabain, *Alttürk. Gr.*, pp. 62, 75, 80.

[17] *Arm. bar.* p. 1131. Acharian made a collection of such „new" words which fill two slender brochures: *Hayerèn nor baṙer hin matenagruťean meǰ* [= New Armenian Words in the Ancient Literature], Venice 1913—1926.

VIII

of such a dictionary. Yet we have some Turkic data which attest the use of the word as a personal name. L. Rásonyi kindly informed me that in his manuscript collection of personal names he has 8 XVIIIth century occurrences of the name in the form *Tansïq* (Тансык) and *Tansïq bay* in the Kazakh language. Although in the cases listed the bearers of the name are men, the semantic category makes it obvious that women too could have borne this name. In view of the meaning ,,Schönes, Wertvolles, oder Kleines" ascribed to group V in Rásonyi's classification,[18] the inbred sense of European gallantry would make us inclined to think of women as bearers of a name with this meaning. But the consideration of the social order and cultural circumstances of the Turkic people in Asia Interior calls for a different approach. Moreover, a nomad of Inner Asia would hardly boast of a beautiful child of his and thus arouse the envy of the gods. But there is also another meaning of the word, e.g., ,,gourmand" that might possibly account for the custom of giving this name to males. And, as we have seen above, there is still another meaning, that is, ,,gift", ,,present", which makes the word an appropriate personal name to be given both to male and female infants.

However, the popularity of the name in Armenian hardly reflects Turkish tradition; it is obviously due to Armenian folk etymology.

The first part of the word was most likely identified by the Armenians with the Armenian word *tang* (*Թանգ*) which is of Persian origin. *Թանգ (tang)* as a common word means: 'dear, costly, expensive, high priced'; its derivatives: *Թանգութիւն (tʿangutiwn)* 'dearness, costliness, high price'; *Թանգարան (tangaran)* : 'treasury', today: 'museum' etc. The suffix, that is, the second part of the word, chimes with the Armenian word *suy* (with terminal unvoicing: *suχ*). The initial meaning of the word *սուղ (suy)* seems to be 'brief, short, succint, very little' ('pusillus, paulus, paululus, brevis, parvus'). Yet already the Venetian great dictionary indicates the meaning 'precious' in popular usage, and it is this meaning that progressively predominates in the modern dictionaries as 'dear, costly, high priced, expensive; brief, short, compact, scanty', while in no few cases only the initial meaning is given.[19]

It seems that the word *suy* by and by became a synonym of the word *tang*. In the dialects the two words show an interesting proportion: we find *suy* in 6 dialects and *tang* in 8 dialects.[20] Linguistic psychology might

---

[18] *Ural-Alt. Jb.* XXXIV (1962), p. 231. — Unfortunately, the stock of female names is rather thin, and this may be due either to Mohammedan religious reasons or to the fact that in official censuses the names of the male heads of families predominated.

[19] Aucher, *Arm.-English Dict.*, p. 547; *Nor baṙgirkʿ haykazean lezui* [=New Dictionary of the Armenian Language], Venice II. 1837, p. 731; M. G. Kouyoumdjian, *A Comprehensive Dictionary Armenian—English*, Cairo 1950, p. 738; *Baṙgirkʿ hašxarhabaṙ i grabaṙ* [= Dictionary of Modern and Classical Literary Language], Venice 1869, p. 489.

[20] Hr. Ačarian: *Hayerèn gawaṙakan baṙaran* [= Dictionary of Armenian Dialects], Tiflis 1913, p. 349, 979. (On the territory of Turkey the usage of *suy* predominated.)

VIII

account for this change in the meaning of the word *suy* : 'little > dear'. Neither can we rule out the possibility that it was even the name *T'angsuy* that gave an impetus to the semantic development in this direction.

The influence of folk etymology seems to be indicated and stressed by the names which take their origin from the Armenian common noun *tang* 'dear'. The *Dictionary of Armenian Personal Names* quotes 4 female *T'ang* names from the XIII—XVth centuries. It also lists 3 examples of the name with the diminutive suffix as *T'angik*. Still more frequent is the composite name *T'angxatun* of which we have 13 recorded occurrences from the XIV—XVIth centuries.[21]

In summing up it can be stated that, although the word *tansuχ*, as a common noun, cannot be regarded a real loanword in Armenian, *T'ansuχ~ T'angsuy*, as a personal name, enjoyed all the more popularity in that language.

---

[21] *Andzn*, II, 274—277. — It is, of course, rather difficult to assess the value of these occurences. Even their proportion of frequency is no full evidence, for the female names considered today typically Armenian are, in fact, often new names, and when they seem to be ancient, then, on closer scrutiny, they often turn out to be the results of literary repristinations which began in the second half of the last century. Thus, for instance, let us be careful not to be misled by the word *Թանկագին* *t'angagin* the meaning of which is identical with that of the word *t'ansuχ*. On close inspection it appears that, even as a common noun, it does not belong to the old vocabulary, and, as regards its use as a personal name, the Dictionary of Personal Names enters but one occurrence of it from 1935 (!) with the note that it is an "unusual" name. It was probably fabricated in analogy to the Turkish *Bahalu* 'pahali'. *Andzn.* II, 275; V, 352.

VIII

THE TURKISH LOANWORDS
IN SIMEON LEHACI'S TRAVEL ACCOUNTS

BY

E. SCHÜTZ

In recent years there has been an increased interest in Turkic linguistic records written in Armenian letters. The interest concentrated mainly on the extensive Armeno-Kipchak material which is of great value for the history of the Turkic languages.

We have even more (though less important) Turkish records written in Armenian characters. A large part of these documents is 19th and 18th century printed material, and so it is useful rather as comparative material for research in the phonological development of Armeno-Kipchak and also for the research in the history of Armenian orthography.

Kraelitz-Greifenhorst was the first to introduce this material into the research of linguistic history.[1] Kraelitz's basic material consisted of three Turkish periodicals printed in Armenian letters published in Istanbul at the end of the last century, the *Ceride-i Şarkiye*, started in 1885, the *Mecmua-i Ahbar* daily papers, and the *Awedaper* (*Angeliaphoros*) published by the American Bible Society (52 volumes).[2] Kraelitz also used several 19th century French novels translated into Turkish (Eugène Sue, Xavier de Montepin, Alexander Dumas, etc.) in their Armenian-spelt versions. Kraelitz did not use the Bible published by the British and Foreign Bible Society in 1875 in Armenian letters for he saw that is was a transliteration of the text written in Arabic characters.[3] To a lesser extent he used the missionary material of the Trieste (and later Vienna) Mechitarists from the turn of the 18th century. Occasionally he took a few examples from Armenian spoken in Russia on the basis of information by P. Ferhadian, a Viennese Mechitarist.

---

[1] *Studien zum Armenisch-Türkischen*: *SBAW* 168/3 (Wien 1912).
[2] From the 100 Armenian periodicals published in Constantinople during the century from the 1840-ies on cca 40 had been Armeno-Turkish (of these 32 in the fifty years between 1850—1900). See G. Stepanian: *Hayataŕ turk'eren hay mamulə*. In: *Hay parberakan mamuli patmut'yunic'* [From the History of Armenian Periodicals I,] ed. by A. B. Karinian (Yerevan 1963), pp. 239—274.
[3] Kraelitz, *op. cit.*, p. 3, footnote 1.

Acta Orient. Hung. Tomus XX, 1967

Kraelitz's main mistake was that he considered this material as a separate Armeno-Turkish language which in fact never existed.[4] Kraelitz quotes many phonetic phenomena as peculiar to Armeno-Turkish which are simply features of colloquial Turkish: for example metathesis *bajrak > barjak* or palatalization: *efkjar*, etc. This means that even if his arguments do not prove the existence of a separate Armeno-Turkish, his material can be regarded useful for the study of the contemporary Turkish. However, his statements must be treated with caution even here, for he is seeking to establish phonetic laws, where there are only foreign orthographical or linguistic phenomena to be found. For example, he supposes that the change *st > sd* etc. is a phonetic development whereas it derives only from Armenian spelling.[5] The *č ∼ c* correlation in *kralica ∼* Turkish *kyraliča, polica ∼* Turkish *poliča* he treats as a phonetic change, though these words were obviously not borrowed from Turkish.[6]

The other main error of Kraelitz is that though he realizes in some cases that the given text is only a transliteration of the Arabic script, in a separate chapter he himself discusses the Armenian spelling of *'ain, hemze* and *izâfet* and does not notice that these Arabic or Persian features appear in Armenian writing only to the extent as they appear in colloquial Turkish.[7]

This way the duality of the spelling of this linguistic material remains hidden, that is, the same texts which represent colloquial Istanbul language also reflect the Arabic spelling in many cases.[8]

Turkish material in Armenian letters has been quoted in the literature even before him, in Radloff's dictionary. The list of abbreviations of this dictionary refers to only one source of this kind, the dictionary of Turkish—Armenian—French by A. Küpelean.[9] Considering that Küpelean's dictionary was compiled from those by Meninski, Bianchi-Kieffer, Kazimirski-Biberstein, Vullers, Zenker, Barbier de Meynard, and also from the *Lugat-i Osmaniyye* and *Lehçe-i Osmani* dictionaries it seems clear that here there is no special material but only what Radloff had already used from the original dictionaries.

The transcription system used in Küpelean's dictionary reflects the western dialect, in so far as it marks the tenuis consistently with the letters

---

[4] For criticism of Kraelitz's work, see H. Acharian, *BSL* No. 61, p. 219 sqq and idem, *Hayoc' lezvi patmut'iwn* [The history of the Armenian language] II, pp. 270—271.

[5] *AOH* XII, pp. 158—160.

[6] This means that he includes a few words from Slavic languages without mentioning their provenience.

[7] Kraelitz might have had misleading examples before him such as the above mentioned *Awedaper* or Küpelean's dictionary, which mark the *'ain* with an apostrophe.

[8] For example the above mentioned novels which would normally follow the pronunciation, spell the word *etti* 'did' as ի/Ꝑṃ/ that is *itdi* اِتدی

[9] *Erek'lezuean baragirk' tadžkerèn — hayerèn — gayyerèn* (Vienna 1883).

for Armenian tenuis spirants (p՛ t՛ — փ, թ). In transcribing the sound k it differentiates between k before a palatal or q before a velar vowel, writing the first as ք and the latter as գ.

We must state, however, that the dictionary does not follow the pronunciation in every detail, it often follows the Arabic spelling especially with regard to the consonants. This is why the phenomenon of devoicing at the end of words cannot be studied from the material contained in this dictionary. On the other hand, it gives reliable information for the study of the pronunciation of vowels in the everyday language, for example, for the pronunciation of o, u : ō—ü.

Radloff does not repeat Küpelean's material literally, sometimes he gives more, sometimes less. The Arabic—Persian words of exclusively literary usage are omitted from his work, on the other hand, more derivatives, and also more stem words, are included in Armenian spelling. From Radloff's remark «die armenische [Transscription bezieht sich] auf die Schriften der osmanisch sprechenden Armenier»[10] it is not clear whether he himself collected words from the texts in the Armenian spelling or he merely transcribed into Armenian letters the words which were not included in Küpelean's dictionary. It is certain that Radloff treated Küpelean's entries with caution, and if the data reflected Arabic spelling Radloff left them out, as for example he did with Küpelean's գալբպճր (p. 59) in the case of qalypčy 'Giesser' (II, 247); and instead of Küpelean's ašjy աշճր (p. 35) he writes correctly աշճր aščy (I, 604).

There are not only these Turkish documents spelt in Armenian dating from as late as the 19th or 20th century at the disposal of the researcher. Besides the documents printed at the end of the 18th and beginning of the 19th centuries by the Mechitarists of Trieste and Vienna[11], there are records from earlier periods as well.

In the 18th century several Armenian printing-houses were founded in Istanbul and more than two hundred Armenian books came out in a century, published by about eight families of publishers. Turkish texts can be found also in these Armenian prints. I myself only had the chance to see one or two of these and I found some songs, poems and prayers in Turkish amidst the Armenian text. It seems that such texts are to be looked for in songbooks and prayerbooks in the first place. This surmise of mine was proved by the contents of some manuscripts. For example in 10 MSS of the Mechitarists in Vienna there are among other texts Turkish poems, songs, proverbs, gospels

---

[10] *Ibid.*, p. VII of Introduction.

[11] Their bibliography can be found in the catalogue of the Vienna Mechitarists: *Endhanur grac'uc'ak Mxit'arean graṙčaṙanoc'i i T'riest, i Vienna ew i Plovdiw (Filipe)* 1776—1936. (Vienna 1936), pp 69—74.

and psalms. This material would in any case deserve a more thorough examination. The dating of the manuscripts is rather uncertain. According to J. Dashian, the editor of the Catalogue most of the manuscripts date from the 17th—18th century and some (with a questionmark) from the 16th.[12]

Recently H. Berbérian has published a thorough treatise on the Turkish literature in Armenian characters.[13] He deals in detail with the most interesting chapter of the Armeno-Turkish literature, the *ašuy*-songs. The clan of these wandering minstrels was rather numerous everywhere in Armenia and in the adjoining countries, in Persia, Turkey as well as Georgia. From the 17th century up to the forties of the 19th literary history has registered as many as 400 *ašuy*s.[14] These minstrels sang their songs not only in their Armenian mother tongue, but also in Turkish, Azerbaidshani, Persian and Georgian.

But we must be very careful in the linguistic evaluation of this most interesting material. As H. Berbérian pointed out, a serious difficulty arises from the fact that these minstrels were a wandering people, and the different regions left their mark on their idiom, furthermore they themselves made efforts to adapt the text to the dialectal exigencies of their audience. Still the different versions surviving in script obviously reflect also the idiomatic peculiarities of the scribe.[15]

Outstanding among the authors of the Armeno-Turkish literature in the 17th century is a prolific personality, Yeremiah Chelebi Koemuerdshian (1637—1695), who among others translated the legend of Alexander the Great, the story of Paris and Vienne, the History of Armenia in Horenaci's version into Turkish.[16]

The book of poems by an eminent poet of the next century, Balthasar Dpir (1683—1768) includes among the Armenian songs a great many Turkish songs and «macaronic» (mixed Armenian and Turkish) poems in Armenian letters.

*

For present, till this rather rich material of Turkish manuscripts in Armenian letters becomes accessible and can be thoroughly studied from the linguistic points of view the more than 800 Turkish loanwords (included Ara-

[12] Similar material of considerable amount has recently been listed in the rich collection of the Matenadaran, 82 MSS from the 17th—19th century contain Turkish texts in Armenian letters. *C'uc'ak dzeṙagrac' Maštoc'i anvan Matenadarani* [Catalogue of Manuscripts in the Matenadaran bearing the name of Mashtoc] Yerevan I, col. 1412. As to the Catalogue, see *AOH* XIX, pp. 368—371.

[13] *PhTF* II, pp. 809—819.

[14] *Ibid.*, p. 811.

[15] *Ibid.*, p. 810.

[16] Akinian N., *Yeremia Čelebi Kömürǰean keank'n ew grakan gorcunēut'iwnə.* [Y. Ch. K.'s life and literary activity]. Vienna 1933, pp. 131—135.

bian and Persian words) in an early Armenian record, Simeon Lehaci's «Travel Accounts» may offer a rewarding study.[17]

Simeon in his Itinerary describes his pilgrimages, in the course of which he visited the main Christian places of worship between 1608—1619. His journey took him to distant places, his main destinations were Rome, Muš (near Lake Van), with the alledged tomb of John the Baptist, and Jerusalem. For our linguistic studies the most important point is that he always set out on his journeys from Istanbul. It was in Istanbul that he raised the money for his journeys by copying manuscripts, and he stayed in this city for many years.

The «Travel Accounts» is a very interesting document of cultural history, for it contains many original observations, not only about the conditions of the church in local Armenian colonies but also about the life of the villages and cities Simeon visited, about their customs and social-economic conditions.[18] Simeon intended his Accounts to pilgrims and travellers. He already recorded his impressions while on his way, «sometimes on board of a ship, sometimes on back of a mule, sometimes in inns and in xans».[19]

The everyday experiences left a mark on the style of the Armenian text for which it was rather unfavourably criticised: «he uses everyday language mixed with grabar ... it can be felt throughout how the grabar and ašxarabar [the literary and the spoken language] are competing as he is writing».[20] Simeon wrote the final version of his Accounts in 1619 after having arrived back in Lvov. He evidently polished it, replacing Turkish words by Armenian, but still most of the Turkish terms remained in the text. Naturally Simeon used Turkish words mainly when he was describing events in Turkey. So it is obvious that in the description of the sultan's visit to the mosque on Friday the units of the escort and the names of their clothes are named in Turkish (jengičari, solax, zorvaji, jajabaši, čavuš etc. or mujavaza, keča, tulux, soryuj, dolband etc.)[21].

---

[17] Akinian N., Simèon dpri Lehce'woy Utegrut'iwn [The Travel Accounts of Simeon the Scribe of Poland] Vienna 1936.

[18] There is an increasing interest in this valuable document of cultural history and translations appear one after the other: The passage on Egypt was printed by M. P. D. Roncaglia: Itinerario in Egitto di Simeone, viagiattore polacco (1615—1616): Oriens XV (1962), 130—159. The Turkish translation of the «Accounts» was edited by H. D. Andreasyan, Polonyali Simeon'un Seyahatnâmesi 1608—1619 (Istanbul 1964). The Russian edition is shortly to appear, translated by M. O. Darbinian. A part of the translation has already been published: Симеон Лехаци о странах Юго-восточной Европы. In: Восточные источники по истории народов Юго-восточной и Центральной Европы. Под. ред. А.С. Тверитиновой (Moscow 1964), pp. 253—275.

[19] Akinian, op. cit., p. 175, lines 71—72, 66—68.

[20] Ibid., XLI.

[21] Ibid., 30[601]—33[661].

Besides these, plenty of other everyday words from Turkish crept into Simeon's language. It is not surprising, for a great majority of the Istanbul Armenians used plenty of Turkish words in their speech.[22]

That the Turkish words formed a comparatively stable part of Simeon's language is proved by the fact that he uses them in connection with other countries as well, for example he calls the Pope's palace a *saraj*, his summer palace at Monte-Cavallo a *jajla*, and his rooms *oda*.[23]

The everyday use of Turkish elements is also proved by other grammatical criteria. On the lexical level it is a characteristic feature that besides nouns a smaller number of adjectives, adverbs, and even conjunctions appear *(zera, hem-hem, bila*, etc.).[24]

The combination of Turkish and Armenian grammatical elements is of great interest. There appear mixed compounds of Turkish words with Armenian suffixes. Such hybrids can be found in Simeon's language in the same forms (but not to the same extent) as in the language of the Armenians in Turkey at the beginning of this century.

There are some Turkish nouns with Armenian suffixes, for example *eskijutiwn* (Arm. suffix *-ուβիւն*) 170[42] meaning 'second-hand dealing' *haramutiwn* 87[266] 'highway robbery'. There are also some 'cross-bred' compounds, e.g. *martaboj* (Arm. *մարդ* 'man') 15[211], 16[224], 55[25], 129[101], etc. 'of a man's height'; *inčxadar* (Arm. *ինչ* 'what') 144[135] 'as much as'.

The compound verbs made up from a Turkish (Arabic) noun and an Armenian verb are very common, e.g. *hajran linel* (Arm. *լինել* 'to be') 158[270], 162[86] 'to wonder'; *xajil linel* 102[130], 287[95] 'to be inclined to'. The most frequent is the use of verbs with a *-miš* participial ending, just as it is the most frequent in the Turkish verbs of the modern Armenian dialect in Turkey. *xurmiš aṙnel* (*առնել* 'to do, to make') 212[67], 268[143] 'to erect', *donanmiš linel* 238[114], 241[24] 'to have sg decorated', *donatmiš aṙnel* 237[101] 'to decorate'. We can also find some verbs with an Armenian infinitive ending: *talnel* 197[53] 'to robe', *naxšel* 42[243], 80[78] 'to paint', *xarjel* 100[86], 284[21] 'to spend'. Also Ar-

[22] At the beginning of the 20th century H. Acharian collected 4200 Turkish words from the language of the Istanbul Armenians. (*T'urk'erēnê p'oxaṙeal baṙer hayerēni mēj* [Turkish loanwords in Armenian] Tiflis 1902) — In an other work of his Acharian relates a characteristic story about the effusion of Turkish words in the vocabulary of one part of these Armenians, in whose language all that remained Armenian were the case endings and the auxiliary verbs: An Armenian buys *halva* from a sweets vendor when a friend is passing by, to whom he tells ‹in Armenian› that he gave a false coin to the vendor: ‹*Helvaji-in xalb bešlix-ə jutturmiš əri.*› Needless to say the Turkish vendor readily understood the sentence and gave back the false 5 gurush piece. (*Hayoc' lezvi patmut'yun* [History of the Armenian language] Yerevan II, 1951, p. 273).

[23] Akinian, *op. çit.*, 149[1,2], 150 [21,22], etc.

[24] *Ibid.*

menian participles formed of such verbs occur: *tesnifaḏs* 138[138], 151[75] 'made with skill', *zyndanaḏs* 147[215] 'imprisoned'.

The fact that Simeon uses both Turkish and Armenian words for the same idea, would suggest that Turkish and Armenian was equally familiar to him, e.g. 'building' *šinuadsk'* (*շինուած֊ք*) 34[27], *šenk* (*շէն֊ք*) 174[31], but *japu* 34[28], 36[85], *japu šinel* (*շինել*) 174[37], 180[82] 'to build a building'. Or 'island' *gyzi* (*կղզի*) 37[99], 39[165], but *ada* 34[37], 43[270]. On the other hand, we must not forget that Simeon was a man of literary accomplishement and he consciously aimed at colourful style. This may be the reason why he mixed Turkish and Armenian words. The above quoted *japu šinel* construction supports this view. Simeon wanted to avoid, by using this half Turkish, half Armenian construction, the less colourful *figura etymologica*.

This conscious striving for literary style is revealed in his characteristic stylistic technique of using synonymous pairs made up from Armenian and Turkish words: *kancn* (*գանձն*) ew *xazinan* 57[71] 'treasure and hoard', *yaray ew zen* (*զէն*) 67[199] 'arms and weapons', *barkew* (*պարգեւ*) ew *armayan* 84[205] 'gift and present', *došak ew angoyin* (*անկողին*) 103[171] 'bed and couch', *šyta* (*շղթայ*) ew *zinǰil* 126[9] 'chains and fetters', *zulum ew anirawutiwn* (*անիրաւութիւն*) 87[263] 'injury and injustice', *merg* (*մերկ*) ew *čblax* 72[324] 'naked and bare', *dked* (*տգէտ*) ew *himar* 112[170] 'ignorant and fool'.

Partly because of the amount of Turkish words and partly because of their grammatical embedding, the question arises whether these elements in Simeon's language are still foreign or they are already naturalized. Although Simeon visited mainly Armenian colonies, it can be supposed that he had to speak Turkish even to Armenians in many places (*drsec'i*), and these Turkish elements were also frequent in the language of the other (Istanbul) Armenians.[25]

In judging the character of the Turkish elements in his language we should first consider the question whether Simeon could learn Turkish from his parents, for his parents had moved «from the country of the Huns, from the... town of Kaffa which overlooks the sea»[26] to Zamość where their son was born. This theory does not seem a very likely one as we cannot find a single Kipchak word in Simeon's language. The fact that after his return in 1619 from his pilgrimage to Lvov Turkish words almost completely disappeared from his language, proves that he learnt his Turkish thoroughly in Istanbul, even if he may have had some knowledge of it earlier too. In his diary, written after his Accounts there are very few Turkish words even in those parts when he is writing about Turkish events, as for example, in the parts about the Khotin War (1621) or about Abaza pasha and about the slaying of the janis-

---

[25] *AOH* XIX, p. 101.
[26] Akinian, *op. cit.*, p. XIII.

saries. In the 26 columns of the *Vipasanutiv·n Nikolakan* verses, ascribed to him, there are only five or six Turkish words altogether.[27]

From all this we may draw the conclusion that the glossary reflects the Turkish language of its time, that is of the beginning of the 17th century, and this is also proved by the phonetic state of the word-material.

*

The Ottoman-Turkish consonant system is as clearly reflected in the Armenian spelling as Armeno-Kipchak. However, here too, problems arise about the phonetical interpretation of the individual letters or letter combinations. These problems originate from the mixing of the classical Armenian orthography, Middle-Armenian phonetics and certain 15—17th century Turkish phonetic phenomena. We shall try to distinguish between the individual occurrences of these characteristics.

The orthography of fricatives and liquids needs no explanation. The spelling of the mediae among the plosives is almost unambiguous. The following two sound-combinations can be explained by Armenian phonetical development or by the history of Armenian orthography.

The spelling of *n*+media is generally inconsistent in Armenian also. This is because in this sound-combination the media did not shift towards the tenuis in the course of Middle Armenian.[28] Simeon's orthography corresponds to this when in place of mediae we sometimes find letters representing sounds that became tenuis in the course of Middle Armenian. E.g. *kändmänd* 'ruins' is spelt *խնդմանդ* (*xndmand*) 232[141]; *jängi* 'warlike' is spelt *ճինգի* (*jingi*) 233[180], but *jangči* 'warrior' is spelt *ճանկչի* 77[108]. (Though the spelling *ճէնքճի* *jenkji* 175[50] also appears.) However the spelling with *նկ* is more frequent see: 'janissary' *jengičeri* *ննկիչէրի* 215[151], 368[187] or *jengičari* *ննկիչարի* 72[329] 369[8, 12]. This «inconsistency of spelling» can also be found with some Armenian, words, for example in the same text the word *gank* 'stoppage, halt' appears as *կանկ* 200[146] instead of the standard *կանգ*.

In Middle Armenian the fricative + tenuis did not change and in this case we often find the traditional spelling, that is with the letters agreeing with the classical ortography. For example the word 'scarlet or purple' is spelt (*ə*)*skerlet*, (*ə*)*skarlat* *սկէրլէթ* 20[338], 70[279], *սկարլաթ* 71[305]. *Asker* 'soldier' is written as *էսկէր* (*esker*) 32[634], *էշկէր* (*ešker*) 241[29], 416[1]. At this point it could be asked whether these examples should not be pronounced as -*sg*-, a pro-

---

[27] Akinian, *op. cit.*, pp. 356—368, 368—370. *Ibid.*, pp. 399—405. Ališan, *Kamenic'*, pp. 202—214.

[28] Karst, *Kil. Gramm.* p. 82.

IX

nunciation which is also frequent in dialects of Anatolia.[29] The -*sk*- pronunciation of these words is supported by the alternative spelling of these words with -*sk*-, e.g. *սքէլէ* (*sk'ele*) 41[213], 53[274], *սքալա* (*sk'ala*) 25[455], 332[17]; or *սքէրլէթ* (*sk'erlet*) 148[248], *սքարխաթ* (*sk'arkat'*) 234[182].

This peculiarity of pronunciation is not restricted to the consonant cluster beginning with *š* or *s*, for we also find it sporadically with the combination of other fricatives, for example: *f*+*t*, in *diftik* 'angora goat's wool' *տիֆտիկ* 86[239], *տիֆտիք* 86[240], *müfti* *մֆթի* 36[634], 284[3], 356[13]; *köfte* 'minced mutton' *քուֆտա* 219[81] (*k'ufta*). *Deftar* 'register, list', on the other hand, occurs with etymological spelling in the form of *տէֆթար* 68[233], 149[275], 217[21].

The *p* > *v* > *f* phonetic change should be treated here, though besides a question of Armenian orthography it is also a Turkish phonetical phenomenon. For example *zabt-zapt* 'holding firmly' is *zaft* in Simeon *զաֆտ* 170[46], 205[83], *zaftči* 'a sheriff's officer, gendarme' *զաֆտչի* 305[86]. The reading of the word is secured by the alternative spelling *zaft'* *զաֆթ* 81[118]. Similarly *sabz* 'vegetable' appears in spelling as *sav(ĕ)z* *սավ(ը)զ* 68[235], 141[61], or *čorbaži* as *šorvaži* *շորվաժի* 173[20].

The combination of *x* + *t* (or an affricate) has a variety of spellings. The word *bayča* often appears with the etymological spelling *պաղչա* 21[358], 305[81], but with *x* 46[68]. This spelling is either etymological or it follows the Arabic spelling of the word باغچه. But أخته 'renegate' = *axtarma*, with the spelling -*խթ*-(*xt'*) it occurs once, 411[8], with -*ղթ*- (*γt'*) it can be found five times 54[12·16], 83[160], 266[93], 420[4]: *աղթարմայ*.

This letter combination cannot be explained from Turkish, as a spelling with *xt'* would be expected in any case. Similarly the Armenian spelling of *axtark* 'dream-book' *աղթարք* is rather unexpected as it derives from the Persian word اختر (*axtar*) 'constellation'.[30]

The uniformity of spelling in these words can be explained by a peculiarity of Armenian orthography according to which, even in modern spelling, only in 17 cases is the combination of *xt* spelt with *խտ*, in other words it is always spelt with *ղթ*.[31]

The spelling of ج in Armenian is an interesting orthographical feature and poses a phonetic problem. In Armeno-Turkish the *ǰ* is either *ղ* or *խ* initially. In the Turkish loan-words of the Istanbul Armenian dialect (as in

[29] I have dealt with this question in connection with Armeno-Kipchak: *AOH* XII (1961), 158—160.
[30] The name of the Aytamar church on the island of Lake Van can hardly be connected with this name. See: *Haykakan Matenagitut'yun* [Armenian Bibliology] Yerevan 1959, I, col. 425.
[31] Fariban A., Paris G., *Hayoc' lezvi k'erakanut'yan, uγγagrut'yan ev ketadrut'yan uγec'uyc'* [Guide to the grammar, orthography and punctuation of the Armenian language], Yerevan 1957, p. 15.

Armeno-Kipchak) it is *ļu* (*x*) which always corresponds to ج. In the Eastern Armenian dialects ج is mostly pronounced as *γ*.

In Simeon we can find both *ļu* and *η* in spelling as well as in pronunciation. For example ـۍ 'value' *ļuɾɟ́ʃɾ̣̃ʃ xyjmet'* 57[77], *xyjmat'* 18[274]; *ηļɟ́ʃ́ụɾ̣ γijmat'* 32[646]. قادری 'galley' *ļuɯɯ̣ɾ̣ɟ́ụɯ xadrya* 77[107], but *ηɯɯ̣ɾ̣ɟ́ụɯ γadrya* 36[95], 40[194], 53[277], 67[195,'196], 72[326,' 328], 77[108]. But there is also a word in which this sound is realised in three different ways: قماش 'silk stuff' with *ļu xumaš* 217[26], 312[20], 321[89], with *η* in *γumaš* 20[342], 52[240], and with *ɾ̣* in *gumaš* 17[266], 157[240], 318[22].

Medially and finally ج is always represented by *x*, e.g. 'vaquf' written as *ɟ́ụ́ɟụɾ̣β vaxyf* 69[246], 336[26]; 'street' = *uoļụụļụ soxax* 224[204], 'cutler' = *ɟ́ụļụnɯ̣́β̣ɾ̣ čaxuji* 204[68].

The documents written in Roman alphabet can throw some light upon the pronunciation of the words with *x*. In these ج is often represented by *ch*, e.g. in Argenti: *chouattlj* 'kuvvetli' (p. 43), *jochari* 'yokari' (p. 39), *dodách* 'dudak' (ibid.).[32] As Argenti is an Italian author we are entitled to suppose that he used *ch* to denote the velar plosive (*q*). On the basis of his consistent usage of the *ch* it seems, however, possible that he was aiming at representing a sound similar to a velar fricative, otherwise he could have used *c* itself in velar words. The fact that Georgievits uses *ch* very often also in the place of *q*, would seem to support this theory, for example in the word *chara* «niger» (p. 22) or *facher* «inops» (21) or in *parmach* «digitus» (21).[33] However Heffening refutes Dmitriev's view, according to which we are here faced with a case of a *q* > *ch* phonetic change. Heffening's argument is that in these texts words are frequently spelt with *k*, besides the spelling with *ch*, and this suggests a *q* or a *k*, as palatal *k* is also often spelt with *ch*, e.g. *erkech* (p. 21) *ekmech* (p. 24).[34]

To my mind ج, because of its guttural pronunciation, does not form a complete stop and thus it can impress European and even Armenian ears as a spirant. The fact that this pronunciation occurs, in certain positions, in palatal words also, does not contradict the theory of the spirantized pronunciation but in fact supports this view. In the case of -*k* it can be connected with the velarization of the finals. This can often be seen in Armeno-Kipchak, and the same tendency is present in Armeno-Turkish.

---

[32] Bombaci A., *La «Regola del parlare turcho» di Filippo Argenti*. Naples 1938.

[33] Heffening W., *Die türkischen Transkriptionstexte des Bartholomaeus Georgievits*: *Abh. DMG* XXVII.

[34] Heffening says that this spirantization is quite unknown in Turkish. (See *op. cit.*, pp. 66—67) His reasoning is not clear enough, for the spirantization of the final *q* is a characteristic feature of Azeri and of the Eastern-Anatolian Turkish dialects too. Cf. Kowalski, *EI* IV, 1001—1002.

The Armenian spelling in the case of *ty* (ﻁ) reflects a phonetic change of plosives in Turkish. In Simeon there are plenty of examples for the pronunciation of *d*, for example طبـﻪ 'layer, sheet' *ṇшщшղшj dabaya* 10[75, 77], 26[479]; طابﻦ 'sole' *ṇшщшﬡ daban* 264[54]; طوار 'beast, cattle' *ṇшﬡшр davar* 246[167]. The pronunciation is varying in دكطاﻦ 'stone pillar' *ṇḥṗṃштṇш dikmadaš* 26[495], 22[380, 384], *ṇḥṗṃшṇш tikmataš* 41[223].

This phonetic phenomenon is reflected also in early Ottoman records in Roman letters; Georgievits: *dernæc* 'unguis' (p. 21), *daraf* 'pars' (p. 26); Argenti: *datt* 'tat', *daniich* 'tanik' (p. 59), etc. and also in various dialects.

The change of the initial *t > d*, or a vulgar pronunciation, is present to the same extent in the Ottoman loan-words of the Istanbul Armenian, e.g. *dabanĵa, dayytmiš*, etc.[35]

It is unusual in our text to find -*ḳ* instead of the letters -*ṇ* and -*ṗ* for the final -*k*. Does this mean that we should pronounce these words with a -*g*?

ɀβḥḥḳ	*čftlik* 8[17]	'çiftlik, farm'
ɀорwḳ	*čorak* 207[145]	'çörek, sweetened cake'
щоᲮḥḳ	*boĵik* 317[144]	'böcek, worm'
ḥṃшḳ	*emak* 251[96]	'emək, work, labour'

Instead of the final -*k* of the everyday language -*y* appears rather often in the Anatolian dialects and also in the uneducated language of Istanbul. However the problem is not all that simple; -*ak*, -*ik*, -*uk* (-*шḳ*, -*ḥḳ*, -* nιḳ*) are frequent diminutive suffixes in Armenian and they very often remain unchanged in Western dialects also, so that these endings are often spelt -*ḳ*, even in foreign words.[36]

Also the alternative orthography shows that in most cases (and so with Simeon) this is a feature of Armenian spelling and not of a Turkish dialect. So we find that *diftik* 'goat's wool' occurs once with a final -*ḳ* 86[239], once with a final -*ṗ* 86[240]; or the word *gomruk* 'duty' appears written with -*ḳ* in *ḳoṃрṇḳ* 6[69], 25[453], 170[44], but -*ṗ* in 224[217].[37]

The development of the *g > i* change has most recently been treated by Suzanne Kakuk.[38] On the basis of the records in Roman letters and on the evidence of the Hungarian and Balkan loanwords she arrives at the conclusion that this change had not reached the Hungarian and Balkan territories. In

[35] Acharian, *Tʿurkʿerēnè poxareal barer*, p. 331.

[36] Karst, *Kil. Gramm.*, p. 33.

[37] As long as the history of the orthography of Armenian word-endings is not made clear, we cannot have a comprehensive picture of how Turkish final mediae appear in Armenian spelling.

[38] *Les mots d'emprunt turcs-osmanlis dans le hongrois et les recherches d'histoire phonétique de la langue turque-osmanlie: AOH* V, pp. 186—187.

IX

documents reflecting the 17th—18th-century Istanbul language -g- is also frequent. We find in Argenti: *chegbê* 'bisacce' (p. 55), in the letters of Süleiman: *beg, gondermege, -degin*; in Dernschwamm: *begler, dugun*. In Balassa we find: *chiczhegi, degil*, etc.[39]

In Simeon's Itinerary there are only two instances of this phenomenon: ՀԷգպէ *hegbe* 315[110] 'saddle bag'; տէգմէ *degme* 227[13], *degma* 194[102], 234[184] 'slight, small'. We can find this sound also intervocalically in the word *beg* with possessive suffix: սանճախպէկի *sanjaxbegi* 374[16], պէկլէրպէկի *beglerbegi* 75[59] '(Bosnia's) beglerbeg', պէկլէրպէկութիւն *beglerbeg* + *ut'iwn* (Armenian suffix '-ship') 370[34] 'the beglerbeg's office'.

According to the documents in Greek letters the η became *n* in the 15th century. It is always *v* in Gennadios.[40] This phenomenon, however, cannot be regarded as general. In Argenti we find the sound marked in most cases: *sanghá, jenghi, degnis* 'deniz', *ghionghullj* 'uolonteroso'.[41] In Georgievits we find: *ssenungh* 'tuus' (p. 29), *karnungh* 'ventris' (p. 30). In Simeon the original η in root words[42] appears in most cases as *ng*: յՍ՝ 'volunteer' կոնկուլու *gongulu* 374[17]; 'Janissary' ՝ ճէնկիճարի *jengičari* 31[614], 72[329], ճէնկիճէրի *jengičeri* 215[151], but also the phonetical variety -*n*- can be found: ճանճար *jančar* 369[16].

The varieties of the original *nk/ng* clusters reflect the state of Turkish pronunciation; تفنك (*tüfeng*) 'firearm' occurs only in its colloquial pronunciation: *tufak* դուֆաք 215[150], ֆուֆաք 137[125], *tyfak* ֆըֆաք 167[78], ֆֆաք 67[200], 215[156]; դֆաք 155[182].[43]

The vocalization of the final -*s* occurs sporadically in the Ottoman dialects and also in the Istanbul everyday language. We can also find it in the Turkish loanwords of Istanbul Armenian, for instance: instead of *horos* 'cock', we find *horoz* and instead of *Tiflis* it is *Tifliz*.[44]

In Simeon's Itinerary we find the following instances of this change: آطلاس 'satin' occurs in it in both forms, *atlas* 320[64], 321[89] and աֆլազ *atlaz* 18[271], 72[340], 381[41]; قونسول 'consul' *balios* 318[23], 321[88], and also պալիոզ *balioz* 25[473]; ՝ 'head, chief' րէյիզ *rejiz* 173[21].

There are some phonetic characteristics which cannot be certainly ascribed to any one of the languages, so e.g. the *č* > *c* change. The *č* retains

[39] Apud Kakuk, *Ibid*.

[40] Halasi Kun, T. *Gennadios török hitvallása: KCsA* suppl. vol. I. p. 214.

[41] Bombaci, *op. cit.*, p. 53.

[42] As we have only glosses in our text, words with possessive suffix or genetive case ending are not to be found.

[43] We have no other instance of this sound in the text. The similarly pronounced فشنك 'cartridge' in the Istanbul Armenian dialect reflects not the colloquial *fišek*, but *fišeng* where the final -*ng*, to my mind, is not a case of an Armenian phonetic change. (Cf. *RO* XIV, p. 140.)

[44] Kraelitz-Greifenhorst treats these mistakenly as examples of an Armenian-Turkish phonetic change: *op. cit.*, p. 21.

its pronunciation in Simeon's language; it is only occàsionally replaced by c, and in some of the words the two sounds alternate, e.g. *ѣшшшрцр* (*jasaxči*) 'guard, officer' 30[585], 231[120], 268[147], but with c in *jasaxci* (-*gh*) 224[219]; 'kalafatci, caulker' in the form of *կալաֆաթցի* (*galafatci*), that is with a c (ɔ: *ts*) 211[52]; *աթլազ-քամխացի atlaz-kamxaci* 'dealer in satin goods' 381[41] also with c; أچى *fuči* vulgar *fiči* occurs in Simeon once with the spelling *ֆուչի* (*fuči*) 211[56], once as *ֆուցի* (*fuci*) 82[146]; 'papuçci' occurs with -*ci* ending: 204[69] *բաբուցցի*.

The $ǰ > \underline{ds}$ ($\underline{dz}$) change is very similar: the word مجوز *mucavaza* 'a sort of turban' appears also as *մուձավազա mudsavaza* 31[618]; 'zincir, chain' occurs twice with $ǰ$ 97[9], 126[9] and once like *զրնձըլ* (*zyndsyl*) 74[22].

As Simeon comes from an Armenian colony in Poland we may suspect these to be Halich Karaim characteristics in his language, similar characteristics being found in the Armeno-Kipchak language of the Armenians of Podolia. In the Kamenec Chronicle we find proper nouns ending -*ic* instead of -*icz*, e.g. *Kevorovic* *Քէվորովիչ* 51a(5)[2], 57a(17)[16].[45] The name Hrickowicz occurs in the form of *Հրիչքովիչ Hrickovic* 57a(17)[15]; another name with -*ic*: *Tiškjevic* Kam. Chron. Ven. MS 113[8]. But this peculiarity appears in the Itinerary in common words and this seems to contradict the theory of the Podolian origin of the forms with a c; moreover there are no special Armeno-Kipchak or even to a lesser extent Karaim features in Simeon's language. So we must take in account also an alternative solution: that the $č > c$ change originates probably from a North-Eastern dialect of Anatolia.[46]

As far as the vowel-system is concerned the distinction in the marking of palatal and velar vowels is a basic question. The most intricate problem we have to face, that is the case of the labials. Originally there was no labio-palatal sound in Armenian and consequently there was no letter to represent it.

In Turkey labio-palatals were also introduced into the sound system of the Armenians living there and two compound letters were formed to mark them. These were originally the letters for the sounds *jo* and *ju* *ֆօ*(*ֆօ*), *ֆու*. In the Turkish loan-words of Istanbul Armenians the labio-palatal sounds create a stable pair of phonemes. On the basis of the records that have so far been accessible we cannot decide when these sounds were first formed and how this pair of compound letters became established.

In Simeon there are no *ֆօ*(*ֆօ*) letters and there are only two instances of the *ֆու* before a vowel: *ֆուզ* (*jjuz*) 'hundred' 20[339], (*բուզ* 193[144]) and *ֆուկ* (*jjuk*) 'burden' 215[162]. On the basis of these two instances we cannot suppose the existence of *ü* in the system of Armenian articulation, and thus we pronounce *ֆու* as *ju* in these words and regard this as an instance of double spelling of *j*.

---

[45] Deny, *L'Armeno-Coman*, pp. 28—29. In this edition the first name is spelt erroneously: *Kevoroviy, Kevorovy*.

[46] Räsänen, *Materialen*, p. 173.

When there were two ways of spelling *ju*, the archaic *ju* and the standard *ju*, it seems most likely that the two possibilities came into the author's mind simultaneously. Such double spelling occurs in careless writing in Armenian as well, so for example in the Accounts the Armenian word *juγ* 'oil' can be found spelt as *հիւղ* instead of *իւղ* 214[140].

There are several instances of the double spelling of the initial *j* in Armeno-Kipchak.[47] The spelling of the word 'dream' *ջիւխու* (*jjuxu*) TB 160v[15] supports the view that the letter combination * հիւ* representing a *jju* here and not *jü*. Otherwise the double spelling of *j* is even more frequent in the middle or words. In Armeno-Kipchak texts dating from Simeon's time the spelling *վէլիյեատ* (*velijjat*) 'vilayet, country' is rather frequent, KamChron Ven MS 109[11,13], 114[16], 146[8], etc.[48]

For the late development of labio-palatals in the language of the Armenians in Turkey we must remember that the Armenians who were settled in Istanbul after Kaffa had been conquered, came from a Kipchak area where sounds tending towards velars prevailed (*ó*, *ú*); and we should also keep in mind that the Anatolian dialect is also characterized by the back *ọ* and *ụ* which sound more like *o* and *u*.[49]

The spelling of the *e* sounds of various degrees of opening is somewhat clearer. In Armeno-Kipchak we can find the letter *է* only in first syllables which indicates that in the second and third syllables we are faced with an opener *e* sound (*ä*, *a*) and this is spelt with the letter *ա*.[50]

In Simeon in the third syllable of Arabic words we find in most cases a letter *ա*, e.g. *թէսքէրա* (*teskera*) 254[51]; *մէդրասա* (*medrasa*) 26[501], 263[9]. We find an *ա* in most cases in the ending *-at*: *խըյամաթ* *xyjamat* 212[68]; *զանահաթ* *zanahat* 141[46], 144[152], 170[39], 326[42] 'handicraft'.

There are but a few exceptions, e.g. *մէրէմէթ* *meremet* 12[133] 'repairing', further *նազարէթ* *nazaret* 'quarantaine' 50[179, 191], 52[244], 53[271]. (It seems most likely that the *e* of the third syllable is due to the influence of the word *lazaret* 'lazzaretto').

The spelling of the sound is inconsistent in Turkish words, e.g. *փէնճէրայ* *penjera* 72[341] 'window', *թէնճէրայ* *tenjera* 220[91] 'furnace', but *թէրլէթմէ* *terletme* 183[18] 'sweating'.

We can see an *ա* very often in an open or in a closed second syllable, e.g. *պիլա* *bila* 146[185], 251[74] 'still'; *չլա(յ)* *čla* 71[305,306] 'weft thread'; *չօրակ* *čorak* 207[145] 'çörek'; *նօքար* *nokar* 157[237] 'nöker'.

A velar second syllable occurs in an otherwise palatal word rather often in the records in Roman letters of this period, e.g. in Argenti: *sewmachtán*

[47] *AOH* XII, p. 150.
[48] Cf. *Ibid.*, p. 155.
[49] Kowalski, *Osmanisch-türkische Dialekte: EI* IV, p. 998.
[50] *Aspects of Altaic Civilization*, (Bloomington 1963), ed. D. Sinor, pp. 151—152.

IX

(but also *sewméch*), *bilsam*, but *eichsé* (p. 46). In these and in similar examples in Roman letters this is a case of the dissimilation of suffixes, which is different from the tendency of velarization found in stem words. In Simeon's text — because of the nature of the Turkish word material — there are no words with suffixes and consequently we have no material for comparison of the tendency of velar dissimilation (and for the opposite tendency of palatal dissimilation).

In the second syllable there is an uncertainty about the usage of *ա* or *է*, which indicates that Simeon was either aiming at marking a sound between these two, or he wished to show the uncertainty of the pronunciation; thus 'sail' *ելքէն jelken* 73[348], but *էլքա̈ն elkan* 61[26], 175[50], *ելքան jelkan* 211[50]. *սքօրլէթ, սքարլաթ skerlet, skarlat*, etc.

We can see a similar uncertainty of the orthography or pronunciation in first syllables as well: *այճար aj(j)ar* 321[106], *էճէր ejer* 215[163] 'saddle'; *քամար kamar* 215[174], *քէմէր kemer* 215[123], 309[94] 'belt'.

The velar form in Arabic words can be attributed to an educated pronunciation, but its frequent occurrence in original Turkish words shows that in these cases Simeon wanted to reproduce an *ā* sound tending towards velarity.

The *ei* dipthong often appears without the semivocal element in writing: *մէհանա (mehana)* 25[477] 'pub, inn', but *մէխանաճի mejxanaǰi* 171[80] 'innkeeper'; a '*šejx*, Musulman head preacher' as *շէխ šex* 9[42], 108[84], 110[125], 253[31], *չէխ šex* 261[44]; *չարէկ čarjek* 'çeyrek, quart' 146[193], 216[189].

This phenomenon is not limited to Turkish words only, we can find even the Polish word *sejm* as *սէյմ* 418[8] 'great divan, called sejm'.

This pronunciation is also known from the contemporary Istanbul dialect.[51] But we have examples of it from the 15th century onwards from records in Roman or Greek characters, e.g. Gennadios μπεγαμπερ,[52] Argenti: *peghamber, scéch* 'ṣayḫ',[53] Georgievits: *beth* 'beyt, carmen' (p. 31), *pegamber* (p. 32).[54] As loanword in Hungarian: *sek-iszlâm* (pron. *šek*) 'ṣaih-ul-islâm'.[55] The glides are realized here too in various ways. Where the *i* element belongs to the following syllable the spelling and pronunciation are uncertain, e.g. *սէյիս sejis* 358[64] 'stableman', but *seyr* 'to view' appears once as *սէիր seir* 160[17], and twice as *սէյիր sejir* 32[657], 237[96]. In other texts, especially when there is an *i + a* diphthong or a triple sound the spelling and the pronunciation is uncertain: *ziade — zijade; ziaret — zijaret.*[56]

---

[51] *ZDMG* LXXII, p. 244.
[52] Halasi Kun, *op. cit.*, p. 185.
[53] Bombaci, *op. cit.*, p. 43.
[54] Heffening, *op. cit.*, p. 53.
[55] Kakuk, *op. cit.*, p. 191.
[56] Kraelitz-Greifenshort, *op. cit.* p. 17. See also for Armeno-Kipchak: *AOH* XII, 155.

Velar ı is spelt with է (e) only in one word in our text: լայեխ *lajéx*
23⁴²⁴, 96¹⁰⁹, 242³⁷ 'fitting, suitable'. This spelling (and pronunciation) can
generally be found in the 16th-century documents in Roman writing, e.g. in
Argenti: *ches* 'kız, girl'; *chesrách* 'kısrak, mare'; *chesél* 'kızıl, red'⁵⁷ and also
in Süleiman's letter: *hazer* 'hazır, ready'; *kalderup* 'kaldırıp, lifting'.⁵⁸ In
Georgievits: *namazkelmak* 'oratio' (p. 24); *chater* 'katır, mulus' (p. 22); *tseger*
'sığır, vacca' (22); In Balassa: *szandeg* 'sandık'; *koiaszen* 'koyasın'.⁵⁹

This spelling can also be met with in Roman written records of other
Turkish languages, e.g. in Cumanian: 'qylyqly, einen gewissen Character
habend' is spelt either *killiHli* or *chelecli*; 'karin, Bauch' also appears as *caren*
(CC).

The editors of the above cited records, on the basis of this extensive
orthographic phenomenon arrived at the conclusion that these examples must
reflect some specially articulated velar sound which appeared mainly beside
liquids. This phenomenon is not limited to the 16th—19th century only, but
it can also be evidenced from present-day colloquial Turkish.⁶⁰

The palatal *i* sound appears in palatal and velar words alike, so it very
rarely follows the rules of vowel-harmony: խայսի *xajsi* 220¹¹⁵ 'apricot', խայիխ
xajix 39¹⁶⁹ 'boat'; զընճիլ *zynǰil* 97⁹, *zinǰil* 126⁹ 'chain'.

Some of the suffixes occur only in palatal words, for example the suffix
of the nomen actoris -*ǰi*, -*či*, e.g. չուխաճի *čuxaǰi* 381⁴⁷, *čuxači* 381⁴¹ 'woolen
draper'; ճոլճի *jolči* 211⁵⁷ 'traveller'; սոֆճի *sofči* 381⁴², 332⁶ 'wool trader'.
It is the same with the participial ending -*miš*: տոնանմիշ *donanmiš* 238¹¹⁴,
241²⁴ 'adorned'; սըխըլմիշ *syxlmiš* 235⁴⁰ 'jammed'.⁶¹

The gradual development of the labial-illabial vowel-harmony is revealed
in the records: In the 15th—16th century documents, in Gennadios, in Argenti,
in Georgievits and also in Balassa the lack of the vowel-harmony is prevailing. Suzanne Kakuk who summed this question up most recently on the
basis of confronting these examples with Herbinius' material, drew the conclusion that labial-illabial vowel-harmony became wide-spread in the 17th
century.⁶² There are various examples of the labial-illabial vowel-harmony in
Simeon. As Turkish words appear in his text only as loanwords or glosses, we
have no opportunity to examine the behaviour of suffixes from the point of

---

⁵⁷ Bombaci, *op. cit.*, 40.
⁵⁸ *RO* XII, 107.
⁵⁹ *AOH* II, 52.
⁶⁰ Bergsträsser: *ZDMG* LXXII, p. 242.
⁶¹ The sound *i* is frequent in velar words, and similarly the *y—y* < *y—i* dissimilation can often be observed in Armeno-Kipchak.
⁶² *AOH* V (1955), p. 183—185.

view of vowel-harmony. In stem-words of his text the lack of illabial vowel-harmony is prevailing:

բարու	*japu* 23[420], 1[0][80,91]	'building'
բալու	*jalu* 35[66], 36[2]	'villa'
խապլուճա	*xapluǰa* 35[44], 18[145]	'spring, fountain'
չախու	*čaxu* 83[179]	'pocket-knife'
չարշու	*čaršu* 27[510]	'market'
չարուխ	*čarux* 272[61]	'sandal'
Օսմանճուխ	*Osmančux* 185[87]	'Osmancık' (placename)

On the other hand, we can find examples of vowel-harmony, too.

ղապի	*γapi* 48[126], 3[8]8[3], 414[20]	'the (Sublime) Porte, Istanbul'
Ղուցուշէրիֆ	*Γucušerif* 241[5]	'Jerusalem the Holy'

There are also instances of the vacillating usage in the everyday language:

օյուն	*ojun* 238[103] — *օյին* *ojin* 160[11]	'play'
ֆընդըխ	*fndyx* 175[54] — *ֆընդուխ* *fndux* 67[200]	'bullet'
ուզանկու	*uzangu* 311[128] — *իզանկի* *izangi* 310[116]	'stirrup'
խապուճի	*xapuǰi* 254[57] — *խապիճի* *xapiǰi* 250[45]	'door-keeper'

As far as suffixes are concerned, apart from the above mentioned -*ǰi* and -*miš*, the case of -*lik* and -*siz* also show illabial vowel-harmony in our text., e.g.

-*lik*	*čiftlik* (varieties of script see above)	
բաղլըխ	*jaylx* 315[106]	'handkerchief'
խարճլըխ	*xarǰlx* 144[140], 235[20]	'expenditure'
բաղմուրլուխ	*jaymurlux* 18[273], 332[10]	'capote'
-*siz* *տինսիզ*	*dinsiz* 27[127]	'infidel'
սուչսուզ	*sučsuz* 147[216]	'innocent'
խութսուզ	*xutsuz* (*hači*) 295[48]	'(haji) who has not been on pilgrimage to Jerusalem'.

For -*li* we can mainly quote instances of dissimilation:

կօնկուլու	*gongulu* 374[17]	'volunteer' is regular,
but *թավանլու*	*tavanlu* 21[366], 418[ult]	'covered'
ուսքուլի	*uskuli* 222[160]	'linen cloth' not.

In the Turkish words in Simeon's text we mainly find phonetic charac-teristics that were part of the Istanbul everyday language at the beginning of the 17th century. Those forms which deviate from everyday language can

Acta Orient. Hung. Tomus XX, 1967

IX

be ascribed to the uneducated Istanbul pronunciation, or in some cases they may reflect (Eastern-)Anatolian peculiarities.

The circumstances of Simeon's stay in Turkey support the linguistic evidence. Simeon spent years in Istanbul raising the money for his pilgrimages by copying manuscripts. The presence of certain words which reflect Anatolian characteristics in his language, can be explained by the fact that Simeon crossed Anatolia three times, on his way from Istanbul to Mush and back, and later on his way from Jerusalem to Istanbul.

Simeon's Turkish glosses could provide useful evidence for the history of Turkish phonological development, and we hope that the examination of the other early Turkish records in Armenian spelling will make this linguistic picture more complete[63].

---

[63] A rather hard task is the dating and territorial delineation of such popular books as the valuable and voluminous texts published by E. Littmann and O. Spies.

KÖNIGE UND EIDECHSEN
(Bemerkungen zum Fortleben des ungarischen Wortes *király* 'König' in kiptschakischen Sprachen)

Edmond Schütz

In den mongolischen, persischen, arabischen Quellen des Tatareneinfalles nach Europa gab es ein Wort in der Form von *kerel, keler* das den Orientalisten im vorigen Jahrhundert viel Kopfzerbrechen bereitete, bis Pelliot die Frage endgültig klarstellte und festsetzte das dieses Wort nicht aus dem slavischen *korol'* sondern aus dem ungarischen Wort *király* stammt, und den 'ungarischen König, bzw. seine Land, oder Volk' bedeute[1].

Neulichst unterzog Ludwig Ligeti die mongolischen und persischen Angaben einer nochmaligen systematischen Prüfung und gab dazu den ungarischen Hintergrund[2].

In dem Bereiche der Bedeutungserweiterungen ist ein öfters vorkommender Fall, dass ein Personenname sich zu einem Ortsnamen entwickle, ein höchst seltenes Ereignis ist es aber, dass der Gattungsname « König » als Benennung eines speziellen Landes gebraucht wird. Zu diesem Fall sei es mir erlaubt ein armenisch-persisches Beispiel aus dem Jahrzehnt des Tatareneinfalles zu nennen.

In der Chronik des Dschuvaini « Tarich-i-Dschahan-Guscha » ist an einer Stelle zu lesen, dass zum Feste der Thronbesteigung von Güjük aus Rum der Sultan Rukn-ed-Din und der Sultan von Takavor (*TKWR*) kam. Schon Mohammad Qazvini hat es richtig bemerkt (III. 484-490), dass es sich hier um den armeni-

---

[1] Pelliot, *Notes sur l'histoire de la Horde d'Or.* Paris 1949, p. 115 ff.
[2] A magyar nép mongol kori nevei [Die Benennungen des ungarischen Volkes im Zeitalter des Tatareneinfalles]. Magyar Nyelv LX. [1964] 402-404.

X

schen König des sogenannten Klein-Armeniens von Kilikien handle. Der seltsame Name des Landes ist so entstanden, dass Dschuvaini den armenischen Gattungsnamen für « König » = [Ӏ*ɯʠɯɯɩɴ* *t'akawor* « aus Versehen » für die Benennung des Landes gebraucht hat[3].

Aber wie wäre es möglich, dass der Name des ungarischen Königs so geläufig geworden wäre, dass solch ein Bedeutungswandel entstanden könnte. Wenn wir aber in den russischen Annalen blättern, so wird es klar, welch eine bedeutende Rolle die ungarischen Könige vor dem Tatareneinfall in dieser Gegend gespielt hatten. In erster Reihe sei erwähnt, dass Ehen zwischen der ungarischen königlichen Dynastie und den russischen Fürstenhäusern geschlossen worden sind, aber die höchste Ursache ihrer Bekanntheit ging daraus hervor, dass sie in den letzten Jahrzehnten des 12. Jahrhunderts und in der ersten Hälfte des 13. Jahrhunderts mehrere Feldzüge nach dem Fürstentum Halitsch führten, anfangs um den ungarischen Kronprinzen zum Fürsten einzusetzen, und später zur Unterstützung der russischen Fürsten von Halitsch. So ist es nicht zu staunen, dass die russischen Annalen, so die Kiever, wie die Halitscher Annalen, auf jeder Seite von dem ungarischen König Erwähnung tun, und zwar sprechen sie nur selten vom « ungarischen König », sie nennen ihn schlechthin nur « König » (король)[4].

Aber auch in dem Leben der in der Gegend des unteren Laufes der Donau nomadiesierenden Komanen spielte der ungarische König eine wichtige Rolle, besonders nach der Ehe

---

[3] Juvaini, *The History of the World Conqueror, translated by J. A. Boyle.* Manchester I. 1958. S. 250. Um der Tatsache in diesem Falle gänzlich gerecht zu werden, muss es bemerkt werden, dass dieser Vorfall möglicherweise durch die arabische Benennung تَكْفُورِيّة *takfūrijje* (S. z. B. V. Langlois, *Le Trésor des Chartes d'Arménie,* Venise 1863. S. 224.) gefördert worden ist. Die so genannte Münze trug an einer Seite die Abbildung des armenischen Königs, und die Aufschrift: *X t'akawor Hayoc'*, also 'X. König von Armenien'. Aus der vulgären Aussprache von *t'akawor: takfur* entstand die arabische Benennung für die Münze *takfūrijje.*
[4] Die Ungarn bezüglichen Stellen aus den russischen Annalen sind von A. Hodinka gesammelt worden: *Az orosz évkönyvek magyar vonatkozásai* [Die Ungarn bezüglichen Stellen der russischen Annalen]. Budapest 1916. Siehe die gleichnamige Abhandlung hierüber von J. Perényi in: *Tanulmányok az orosz-magyar irodalmi kapcsolatok köréből* [Abhandlugen aus dem Bereiche der russisch-ungarischen literarischen Beziehungen]. Budapest, Bd. I. 1961. S. 44-45.

Stephans V. mit einer komanischen Prinzessin, und unter der
Herrschaft Ladislaus IV. der « Komanen ». So ist es verständlich,
dass auch die verschiedenen tatarischen Stämme den ungarischen König als den König par excellence betrachteten. So ist
der Name des ungarischen Königs durch die Vermittelung der
Komanen, der verschiedenen Tatarenstämme nach Osten, in die
persischen, arabischen, mongolischen, chinesischen Quellen geraten [5], zur Benennung des ungarischen Königs, ja sogar des
Landes von Ungarn, und des Volkes.

Wie es schon Pelliot nachdrücklich betonte, bedeutete *kerel*
/*keler* ausschliesslich den ungarischen und niemals den polnischen König. Dieser Umstand soll deshalb besonders hervorgehoben werden, da das russisch-ukrainische Wort король (*korol'*)
eben den '*polnischen König*' bedeutete.

Auch nach Pelliots Beweisführungen blieb noch eine in
dieser Hinsicht zweideutige Stelle in der Literatur. Die Stelle, die
für Pelliot den Ausgangspunkt bietete, stammt aus der Chronik
von Rukn-ed-Din Baibars (bzw. Nuwairi). Als Tochtu, der Chan
der Goldenen Horde, in 1299/1300 den mächtigen Nebenbuhler
Nogai besiegte, blieb Nogai tot am Schlachtfeld und seine Nachkommen entflohen in die Nachbarländer, zu den Vasallen-Dyna-
stien auf der Balkan Halbinsel. Einer seiner Enkel Qara Kösäk
begab sich ins Land von *Sešimān* (emendiert zu شِشمن *Šišman*),
in die Ortschaft بُوذُول, *Budul*, die in der Nachbarschaft von كرل
Kiräl lag [6].

Pelliot behauptete, dass *kiräl* an dieser Stelle das ungarische
Königreich bedeute, scheint aber kein triftiges Argument dagegen gefunden zu haben, dass « *Budul* » von mehreren Forschern
für 'Podolien' gehalten worden ist [7].

Diese Auffassung schien gewissersmassen dadurch unterstützt
gewesen zu sein, dass bei Nuwairi an der parallelen Stelle كورك
stand, was durch Tiesenhausen und auch von nachfolgenden Forschern zu كرك *käräk/karak* emendiert, und für 'Krakau' gehal-

---

[5] Ligeti: op. cit. p. 403.
[6] Tiesenhausen, Sbornik materialov otnosjaščichsja k istorii zolotoj ordy
[Sammlungen von Materialien zur Geschichte der Goldenen Horde]. St.
Petersburg 1884. (Baibars S. 94/119, Nuwairi: S. 140/162). Siehe Pelliot,
op. cit. S. 116.
[7] « ...même à supposer que son pouvoir [de Šišman] s'étendit jusqu'en
Podolie », op. cit. S. 117.

X

ten worden ist. Die Ortsbezeichnungen « Budul » und « Krakau » hätten sich also gegenseitig unterstützt [8].

Schon Pelliot stellte aber fest, dass jene Stelle bei Nuwairi auch orthographisch keineswegs für 'Krakau' gedeutet werden kann, und ohnedies ist der Text von Baibars der ausschlaggebende, also كوك muss zu كرل emendiert werden [9].

Da blieb aber noch immer die Deutung von « Budul ». Was die Geschichte betrifft, führte die Dynastie der Schischmaniden, Vasallen Nogais, Feldzüge meistens gegen Serbien, ist aber nicht in die Nähe von Podolien gekommen. Die Lösung des Problems ist, dass die Ortsbezeichnung, die unter « Budul » gemeint wird, der Sitz der Schischmaniden, Wid(d)in ist.

Der Name der Stadt und der Gegend stammt noch aus griechischer, lateinischer Zeit, benannt Βονωνία, *Bononia*. In den bulgarischen, serbischen Quellen des 13. und nachfolgender Jahrhunderte erscheint er in der Form *Bъdyn, Bъdon*, etc. Das ungarische Königtum hat auch enge Beziehungen zu dieser Grenzgegend gehabt, und Widdin ist im 13. Jahrhundert und auch später öfters von ungarischen Truppen besetzt worden. Die Gegend ist in der ungarischen Chronikenliteratur unter dem Namen *Bodon, Bodony* bekannt, und es gibt viele Orte in Ungarn in den Komitaten Torda, Zala, Somogy, Baranya, Heves, Nógrád etc. mit demselben Namen [10].

So ist es augenscheinlich, dass im erwähnten Namen بودول (« Budul ») der letzte Buchstabe ل zu ن emendiert werden muss, und so ist das Wort بودون als *Bodon* zu lesen. Damit ist also der letzte Anhaltspunkt aus dem Wege geschafft, was darauf hinweisen würde, dass das Wort كرل *Kiräl* an dieser Stelle etwas mit Polen zu tun hätte.

Wie es wohl bekannt ist, geht nach dem Tatareneinfall dieser orientalische Name der Ungaren in Vergessenheit. In der Geschichte erhält nach dem 14. Jahrhundert in dieser Gegend der polnische König eine führende Rolle und in der russischen/ ukrainischen Sprache wird der polnische König, der König par excellence. Man würde glauben, dass das Wort *korol'* in dieser

---

[8] S. Spuler, Goldene Horde, S. 297.
[9] Pelliot, op. cit. 117-118.
[10] Gombocz-Melich, *Lexicon critico-etymologicum linguae Hungaricae.* Budapest I. cols. 434-435.

Bedeutung auch im Krimtürkischen an Stelle des *kerels* treten
wird.

Wenn wir in den bei Veljaminov-Zernov veröffentlichten
Jarliken blättern, so fällt es auf, dass nach dem 17. Jahrhundert
wohl nur die Bezeichnung قرال also eine velare Variante als
Name des polnischen Königs erscheint, aber in den Dokumenten
früheren Datums (1520 bis Ende 16. Jh.) dieser Gattungsname
in der Form كورال vorkommt, was mit Pelliot als *köräl* gelesen
werden muss [11].

Im folgenden möchte ich eine bisher unbeachtete Beweisgrup-
pe — armenische Quellen — heranziehen. Die Bezeichnung
Կորէլ *Korel* kommt in mehreren, aus der Krim stammenden,
oder auf die Geschichte der Umgebung bezüglichen Quellen vor.

So lesen wir in der Fortsetzung der Chronik des Archiman-
driten Andreas Tokateci (aus Eudokia) folgendes: « Im Jahre
1616 Juli 20., Sonntag, 3 Stunden nach Mitternacht, kamen
die Kosaken aus *Korel* mit 100 Nachen und drangen in Kaffa
[Feodosia] ein, plünderten die Häuser und die Markt und
stifteten Brände » [12].

In der Chronik von Chatschatur Kafajeci aus dem 17.
Jahrhundert begegnen wir ziemlich oft der Benennung einer
Gegend, wohin die Tataren aus der Krim auf Raubfeldzüge
gerne ausziehen. So führt Devlet Girei in 1621 [richtig 1620]
einen Feldzug gegen *Korel* (S. 210[8]); in 1621 nimmt Dschanbek
Girei Chan an dem Feldzuge Sultan Osmans II. gegen *Korel*
teil (210[29]); Feldzüge in diese Gegend werden auch bei den
Jahren 1628, 1629, 1631, 1649 erwähnt [13].

Schon der Herausgeber der Chronik hat aus den Angaben
bemerkt, dass es hier aller Wahrscheinlichkeit nach über Süd-
west-Ukraine die Rede sei [14].

Aus den verschiedenen Stellen geht wirklich die geographi-
sche Lage der genannten Gegend hervor. An einer Stelle ist
die Rede über die Stadt Bar in Korel (225[14]), an einer anderen

---

[11] Veljaminov-Zernov, *Materialy dlja istorii Krymskago chanstva...* St.
Petersburg 1864.
[12] Hakobian, Manr Žamanakagrutjunner 13-18 dd. [Kleine Chroniken
der 13-18. Jahrhunderte]. Jerevan I. 1951. 161[14-17].
[13] Hakobian, op. cit. 215[34], 216[11], 220[2], 225[13, 21].
[14] Op. cit. S. 230, Note 12.

sollte es um den Sitz der Saporoger Kosaken handeln (Sitsch) 161[14-17], (also diese Gegend ist allerdings einbegriffen), die dritte Stelle bezieht sich auf den Feldzug Osmans II. von 1621 d.h. auf den Chotiner Krieg (210[28-37]). Kein Zweifel also, dass der Ausdruck *Korel* — ganz wie in den Jarliken — das damalige Polen meint.

Aber auch die Entwicklung des Wortes kann in den armenischen Quellen verfolgt werden. In den Jeremiaden von Hakob Tokateci (Jacob aus Eudokea), wo er das traurige Schicksal der Armenier der Wallachei (= Moldau) in den Jahren 1593-1595 beklagt, wird der polnische König einmal ꞩꞫꞩ also *kṙal* (18[138]), an anderen Stellen als ꞩꞩꞫꞩ *koṙel* (18[147], 20[213]) erwähnt. Hieraus entwickelte sich dann die Bezeichnung des Landes [15].

Das Wort *korel* für 'polnischen König, Polen' kommt in den armenischen Wörterbüchern nicht vor, sein Gebrauch ist also ganz eng stellenbedingt. Da die genannten Quellen die sogenannte westliche Aussprache widerspiegeln, muss also der erste Buchstabe als *k-* gelesen werden, dass *e* weist auf ein palatales Wort hin, und da es im Armenischen keinen *ö* Laut gibt, so pflegt ein fremder *ö* Laut mit *o* wiedergegeben zu sein. So kommen wir ganz genau zur Originalaussprache *körel*. Das Wort scheint also ein Lehnwort aus dem Krimtatarischen zu sein.

Mit der Deutung des *köräl* gibt noch ein Problem, ob das Wort nur 'polnischen König' bedeutet. Auf Grund der Angaben bei Abu-l-Ghazi: *Nämäč köräl* ist Pelliot geneigt die Benennung auch auf den 'deutschen König' auszubreiten [16], aber das ist nicht nötig, da der Ausdruck *nämäč* im Kiptschakischen eben 'Pole' bedeutet. *Nämič* ist die einzige Benennung für 'Pole' in den armeno-kiptschakischen Quellen [17].

Pelliot hält *köräl* eine Lautvariante des Wortes *käräl/kälär*, und gibt dabei Beispiele für die Lautentwicklung: *ä>ö*. Was

---

[15] Akinean N., *Matenagrakan hetazotutjunner* [Untersuchungen zur Geschichte der armenischen Literatur] IV. Wien 1938.

[16] Op. cit., 160, 120, 134, 135, 136.

[17] Z. B. Chronik von Kamenec, Ven-MS 108[24], 110[11], usw. [Deutsch heisst da: *alaman*.] M. Lewicki, Le terme *nemič* 'polonais, latin, européen' dans la langue des Arméniens polonais. Onomastica II/2. pp. 249-257. [Habe nicht gesehen].

aber den Anlass [18] zu einem solchen Wandel gegeben hat, dazu
dient Pelliot wieder mit einer geistreichen Idee, und zwar dass
dieses Wort « se retrouve » in dem Wort der Krimtürken: *köräl*
was 'Truthahn' bedeutet. Also würde das Wort etymologisch
einerseits 'la Hongroise', oder eher 'la royale' bedeutet zu
haben [19].

Ich möchte dabei erwähnen, dass das Wort *koral* in der
Bedeutung von Truthahn auch im Armenischen bekannt ist.
Es kommt in mehreren grösseren Wörterbüchern vor [20], ist aber
letzten Endes ein entlehntes Wort aus dem Krimtatarischen. Die
Krimarmenier sind am Ende der 1770-er Jahren nach der Gegend
des Unteren Dons, nach Nor-Nachitschewan und Umgebung
übersiedelt worden, ihre Sprache bewarte aber die krimischen
Elemente [21].

Der Gebrauch der Form *köräl* anstatt *kerel* scheint letzten
Endes eine Volksetymologie zu widerspiegeln, und zwar es kann
neben der ähnlichen Lautgestalt des Wortes auch die « Aufblähung » des Truthahnes, also die maliziöse Färbung des Ausdruckes
beigetragen haben. Es darf nicht vergessen werden, dass unter
köräl der polnische König - also der meistens feindliche Widersa-
cher - gemeint wird.

Als ich den Zusammenhang der Formen *köräl - käräl/kälär*
weiter verfolgte, hätte ich kaum daran gedacht, dass in diesem
Zusammenhang auch die Eidechsen in Betracht kommen könnten.
Aber die Bedeutung des persischen Wortes بوقلمون *būqalamūn*
hat mich belehrt, dass bei der Benennung des Truthahns die
Aufblähung, oder eher die Farbveränderung eine höchst wichtige
Rolle spielt. Diese Grundbedeutung hat unbedingt dabei beige-

---

[18] Op. cit., S. 160, Note 1.
[19] Ibid p. 162.
[20] Malchassiants, Hajeren bacatrakan bararan [Arm. erläuterndes Wb.]
I. S. 460; Kapamadjian, Nor bargirk hajeren lezui, Constantinopel. 1910.
S. 337, 825. Ačarian, Hajeren gawarakan bararan [Armenisches Dialektwör-
terbuch]. Tiflis 1913. S. 250.
[21] S. Ačarian, Hajeren armatakan bararan [Arm. Etym. Wb.] II. S. 275.
R. Patkanian, Žoghovacojk otarazgi bareri Nor Naxicevancoc lezui
medž metac. [Sammlung von fremden Wörtern, die in die Sprache der
Nor-Nakhitschewaner Armenier eingedrungen sind]. St. Petersburg 1870.
S. 15 - Apud N. Buzandaci, Dictionnaire Français-Arménien. Konstantinopel
p. 403. - Liebenswürdige Mitteilung des Herrn Dr. D. Mesrop Krikorian
aus Wien.

X

tragen, dass das persische Wort sowohl 'Truthahn' als 'Chameleon' bedeutet.

Und so gelangen wir zum türkischen *Eidechsen,* die in
mehreren Türksprachen (Tschagataisch, Tarantschi, Osmanli)
kälär, und 'Chameleon' *kaja käläri* lautet [22].

Ich bin also auf diesem verwickelten Wege zur Identität
der Könige und Chameleone gekommen, allerdings wird es aber
noch nötig sein auch die entgegengesetzte Richtung zu untersu-
chen, ob es ausser dem Zusammenklingen der zwei Worte auch
türkischer Sprachgebrauch mitspielt, also *kälär/käräl* als Spott-
name dienen sollte.

Um zu unserem Ausgangspunkt zurückzukehren, ist es
wichtig zu betonen, dass das Wort *köräl* wegen seiner Palatalität
allerdings nicht aus dem russisch-ukrainischen *korol'* stammt,
sondern ursprünglich aus dem ungarischen Wort herrührt, nur
die Bedeutung ist auf den polnischen König bzw. Land übergangen.

Aber m. E. hat der Gattungsname des ungarischen Königs,
oder dessen südslavisches Stammwort *kralj* ' [23] auch am anderen
Wege weitergelebt. Wie schon erwähnt, nahm in den Jarliken der
Krimchane vom 17. Jh. den Platz des كورال *köräl* die Benennung قرال *qral,* oder *qïral* für den ' (polnischen) König' ein.
Man könnte auch an das ungarische Wort *király* (*kerál, királ*)
denken, aber wahrscheinlich stammt das Wort eher aus dem
türkischen, wohin es von der Balkanhalbinsel gekommen ist [24].

Es lebt aber in den kiptschakischen Sprachen der Küsten-
gegend des Schwarzen Meeres ein Wort *qïral* in der Bedeutung
'Land' [25].

Das karatschaische und balkarische Wort deuten Hasan
Eren und Omeljan Pritsak aus der Zusammenziehung des Aus-
drucks *qara el* [26].

[22] Radlov II. col. 114, Scheich Suleiman, Houtsma G1.
[23] Kniezsa I., A magyar nyelv szláv jövevényszavai [Die slavischen
Lehnwörter der ungarischen Sprache]. I/1. Budapest, S. 268-69.
[24] Radlov, II. cols. 738, 1052.
[25] Baskakov, Nogaisko-russkij slovar', 1965. S. 201; Ch. I. Sujuntschewa,
I. Ch. Urusbiewa, Russko-karatschaiewo-balkarskij slovar', M. 1965. S. 609.
[26] H. Eren, A török magánhangzóváltozások [Die türkischen Vokal-
wechsel]. Sonderdruck aus der Zeitschrift Nyelvtudományi Közlemények
Bpest. LI. [1942] p. 6. - Pritsak: PhTF I. 366, 347.

Diese Erklärung ist sowohl von der Seite der Bedeutung, wie des Lautwandels schön unterstützt. Ich denke aber den Gedanken vorzulegen dürfen, dass es m. E. auch eine andere Lösung nicht von der Hand gewiesen werden sollte, und zwar, dass das Wort ein altes Erbe des ungarischen Wortes *királ*[27] wäre, nur hätte sich die Lautgestalt (unter der Einfluss ev. des osmanisch-türkischen *qïral-*) velarisiert. Es soll nämlich in Acht genommen, dass das Wort nur im Karatschaischen mit *a* in der ersten Silbe vorkommt, und für Bedeutung in erster Reihe (oder nur) 'Land' angegeben wird. Und diesen Gedanken halte ich deshalb beachtenswert, da das Wort eben in den südkiptschakischen Sprachen vorkommt, die wir für die Fortpflanzung des ungarischen Wortes *király-kälär* verantwortlich machen.

---

[27] Vgl. oben S. 261.

X

Edmond Schütz (Budapest)

BOLGARO-TURKIC TERM — HUNGARIAN HORSEMANSHIP

1. In the stock of loanwords borrowed from Turkic languages by
Hungarians the differentiation as to the period of the loan, or the type
of the pertinent Turkic language is based mainly on phonetic principles.
Phonetic criteria enabled linguists to separate the main class, the Chuwash
type of loanwords. The case of the Kipchak languages (Coman, Pecheneg) is
much more ambiguous, as neither the periods, areas nor linguistic peculiarities of the components of the group could be definitely ascertained
as yet. The third group of old Turkic loanwords in Hungarian have no special phonetic mark, by virtue of which the Turkic ancestor could not pre-
cizely be defined.

The background to the linguistic contact is given by the historical surroundings of Hungarian people in the 5th-9th centuries. The
Chuwash type (Bulgaro-Turkic, Onogur) word stock might have issued from
the close contact either in the Volga-Kama region (the ancient site of
the later Bolghar Khanate), or in the neighbourhood of the estuary, or
the middle course of the Don river, or both in subsequent epochs.

Nomadic confederations were always a variegated unity, where
dialectical or linguistic differences did not hinder the cohabitation or
cooperation of the different tribes.

In the 6th century with the advance of the Western Turks towards
the steppeland of the Atil-Don-Caucasus triangle the motley crowd of Tur-
cic tribes became politically united under the scepter of the Western
Turks, under the name of Khazaria, the later Khazar Khaghanate, which com-
prised different language units: Common Turks, Bolgaro-Turks, Kipchaks.

In our case — due to the absence of a special phonetical criteria
— the loanword tart- cannot be attributed to any special turkic language.

Because old Hungarian records date from late centuries so the
first appearance of a word (the terminus ante quem) is no firm landmark
for linguistic inferences, so in such cases one must take recource to
semantic deliberations having ascertained the social-economic level of
the people, or tribal confederation at a given epoch.

2. The Hungarian verb tart- ' to hold, keep, etc.' has been de-

rived from the Turkic verb tart- ('to pull, draw, ect.') already 187o by Arminius Vámbéry in his treatize Magyarés török-tatár szóegyezések [Hungarian and Turkic-Tatar word equations][1], a number of which have been quoted also in his book A magyarok eredete [The Origin of the Hungarian people][2], meant an answer - 'a counter-criticizm' - to Budenz's Comments, and again in his posthumus work A magyarság bölcsőjénél [At the Cradle of Hungarian People][3].

Vámbéry in his above mentioned treatize and books advanced his theory of the Turkic origin of Hungarians, and this did let loose a lively discussion or rather embittered polemics in Hungarian linguistic circles, called the "Turkic-Ugric Battle".

Vámbéry's theory and also the Turkic etymology of the Hungarian verb tart- was rejected by J.Budenz in his Jelentés Vámbéry Ármin magyar-török-tatár szóegyezéseiről [Report on A. Vámbéry's Hungarian-Turkic-Tatar word-equations], and by J.Szinnyei in his Eszrevételek V.Á. 'A magyarok eredete' c. művének nyelvészeti részére [Comments of the linguistic part of Á.V.'s book 'The Origin of the Hungarian People'].[4]

Budenz's authority and the rigid application of the notion and term "basic meaning" to loanwords resulted in the total disregarding of Vámbéry's conjecture by Hungarian linguists.

Budenz in his Report (and subsequent treatizes) proposed a Finno-Ugric solution instead, taking the final -t for a suffix of moment-aneity.[5] G.Bárczy took the tentative of Budenz "unconvincing",[6] and both G.Bárczy and J.Berrár labelled the verb tart- of "uncertain origin", though Berrár did not totally exclude the Finno-Ugric issue: "probably a heritage from the Finno-Ugric age".[7]

Another Turkic solution has been put forward by K.M.Palló, de-riving the verb from an Old Turkic root tïd- 'verhindern'.[8] The Turkic conjectures, at large, have been earmarked for "erroneous" by the TESz.

2.1. As to my opinion, Vámbéry's equation is acceptable. Phone-tically the Hungarian and Turkic words are identical. In linguistic train-ing the axiome is current: in etymologies not the complete identity is the real proof of common origin of the words, but the regular similarity. I wonder, if this precize phonetical identity deterred linguists from the re-evaluation of Vámbéry's etymology.

The phonetic structure of the Turkic word has always been iden-tical through all ages, from the Uighur period up to the present (Uighur, Kashghari, Qutadgu Bilig, Chaghatai, Codex Cumanicus, etc.)[9]

Each sound corresponds also in almost all modern Turkic lan-

XI

guages, with some exceptions. In Oghuz languages the initial sound is d-;
Turcoman: dart-, tart-. Modern Turkish dictionaries list tart- only in
the meaning 'weigh'[10], in Anatolian dialects the initial is d-; dart-.[11]
As a matter of fact, tart- is not an Oghuz word, in Oghuz languages the
common term for 'to pull' is: ček-.

Sound varieties show up in the vowel: The verb sounds tirt- in
Tuva Turkic, in Chuwash turt-.[12] Räsänen is of the opinion that Chuwash
tit- is not related to Turkic tut-, but to tart-[13]. He adds also a Finn
correspondency: tarttu-, which in Hungarian literature has been equated
to the Hungarian tart-.[14]

Even on Altaic field a correspondency was put forward by Ramstedt: Mongol tata-.[15] An antagonist to Altaic genetic affinity would
expect rather a loanword from tart-, because the cluster -rt- (liquid +
explosive) is generally preserved in Turkic languages: e.g. art 'back',
ört- 'cover', qart 'old man', qurt 'wolf', yurt 'territory', etc. — and
the -r- is not missing in Turkic languages bordering Mongol territory.
And in Mongolian -rt- cluster is retained, or altered to -rč- before an
-i, e.g.: T. arit- 'reinigen' ~ Mo. *arti > arči; T kert- 'Einschnitte
machen' ~ Mo. *kerti- > kerči-; T ärk 'Kraft' ~ Mo erke.[16] The final
vowel -a of the root tata- is by no means an obstacle to the equation,
because such cases are the frequent occurrences of a Systemzwang, so e.g.
T kök ~ Mo. köke; T ärk ~ Mo erke; T bärk ~ Mo berke.[17]

2.1. The difficulty in Vámbéry's equation arises in the field
of semantics. Vámbéry presents two varieties, in the first he gives two
semantic correspondencies, in the second case he concentrates his equation on the time concept: tartani 'durare' (tartozni vmitől 'sich enthalten') Chaghatai tartmak 'tartani, eltartani, húzni (to hold, keep,
pull)' ... tartinmak 'tartózkodni vmitől (to abstain)'...[18] In his
book A magyarok eredete his comments are meant for an answer to Budenz's
critical remarks. Essentially he does not refute Budenz's criticism, he
merely repeats his former equation, emphasizing that the meaning 'to
pull, draw, lead, etc.' were the secondary ones.[19] In his posthumus work
A magyarság bölcsőjénél the examples refer only to the time concept: tart
'halten', or rather 'anhalten, dauern, in die Länge ziehen' e.g. napokig
eltart 'es dauert lang', tartós 'dauerhaft' — Turkic tart- 'huzni, tartani
(ziehen, anhalten'), e.g. jillargaje tartanir 'évekig tart (es dauert Jahrelang'), tartik 'tartós (dauerhaft)'.[20]

3. In connection with Budenz's critical comments on Vámbéry's
equation we should like to enlarge on two issues: the lack of "bona fide"

XI

demonstration of evidences, as a charge against Vámbéry, and secondly the
linguistic concept of the "basic meaning" of a word in the case of a loanword.

3.1. Vámbéry's method to elucidate or to prove linguistic problems cannot be called blameless. As a matter of fact he did not explain
his arguments, did not even argue at all, he merely enumerated the Turkic-
Hungarian equations collected, and let the correspondencies speak in his
favour. Still it was not only his unprofessional way for which he was
blamed, but even more for the minor "corrections, adjustments" of the evidences, sometimes in their phonetic shape, sometimes in the meanings of
the word, in order to fit closer, and so to prove better the equation proposed.

Vámbéry had an alert ear and with a number of the old Turkic
loanwords the few centuries, or at most one millenium did not cause such
a considerable phonetic change that a connoisseur of Turkic languages
could not have detected correspondencies. So further researches proved
that a number of his equations were acceptable even by a high critical
standard. The major deficiency in his "method" was, that he did not present arguments of phonetic history, of general linguistical parallels,
and semantic correspondencies in favour of his proposition, and did not
explain or refute neither phonetic, nor semantic discrepancies.

3.2. Another issue in Budenz's and Szinnyei's (and others')
comment touch on a principal issue of general linguistics, i.e. the "basic meaning". The critics do not differentiate the concept of "basic meaning" in the case of the fundamental word stock and the borrowings. In case
of the Finno-Ugrian (or Uralic) word stock it is a justified requirement
to find out the basic meaning and take it for a starting point. The requirement is quite different in the case of loanwords because, as a rule,
special terms are taken over, the meaning of which does not always coincide with the basic meaning.

In the epoch after the disunion of Finno-Ugric people in Hungarian already all the verbs existed by the aid of which most of the vari-
ties of basic activities or happenings could be expressed, and they have
already attained a level of general sense, so that newly emerged, or in-
vented actions or happenings could be derived from them, or expressed by
their aid. So there could hardly have been an urgent necessity to adopt
a Turkic word tart- for the denotation of an action "to pull, to draw"
for which terms already existed in the Finno-Ugrian stock: "huz, von".

XI

At the stage of their social-economic evolution there was no more need for such an enrichment of the vocabulary, and this is shown by Budenz himself quoting the Turkic verb tut- 'to hold,to catch'.[21] This verb had not been taken over from Turkic, as verb in this wide sense of action already existed in Hungarian: (meg) fog,(meg) ragad, etc.

The problem concerning the "basic meaning" was viewed at from the angle of formal logic also by J. Szinnyei in his critical paper.[22] Still his theoretical remark on the development of meanings is of fundamental importance. Undoubtedly, originally nouns and verbs were closely connected with concrete objects, or activities. On the stage of the disunion of Finno-Ugric languages the verbs could already denote abstract actions, or happenings, i.e. their semantic realm expanded,the characteristic features diminished proportionally. E.g.the Hungarian verb fon 'to weave' (of Finno-Ugrian origin) originally could have denoted either the weaving of a sedge-matting, or of lattice partition walls (cf. winden - Wand), the weaving of a basket, or eventually the weaving of a net[23], but soon it was applied to any similar activity, so its signifying capacity was considerably extended.

But there is another way of denotation new processes. With the adoption of new productive procedures the new procedure can be also expressed by the aid of a loanword taken over from the people they have learned it from. So e.g. the Turkic word szür- 'to filter' surely was not taken over in a general sense, but originally it served for a special activity of wine manipulation.

From the period of the old Turkic contacts mostly technical terms had been taken over[24]. In the case of seemingly general meanings, it is probable,that the professional origin of the term is hiding in the background, and was not detected yet. Of course, in the course of linguistic consciousness convergent variants may issue forth independently, similar general physic factors being instrumental in their evocation.

A similar conglomerate process must have been at work in the case of the loanword tart- the stages of which were: a) adoption of a professional skill, and the relevant term, b) the extension of the range of meanings independently from the Turkic ancestor, c) a (partly) divergent evolution in the semantic area.

4. The stages of this semantic evolution can be traced back only by minutuous analysis of the semantic variants both of the Turkic and Hungarian verb, to detect the contacting points.

4.1. The basic meaning of the Turkic verb tart- beginning from the old Turkic languages (Uighur, Middle Turkic, Comanic, etc.) up to the

XI

present common Turkic dialects was 'to pull, to draw, to stretch',etc[25]

The basic meaning is corroborated by its general synonym: ček-. In the expressions with the verb component tart- in Common Turkic in Oghuz languages one encounters correspondingly ček-: e.g. CommonT yük tart- 'to pull a load', yay tart- 'to draw a bow', un tart- 'to grind flour', uzaqqa tart- 'to last long', etc.. Oghuz languages have ček instead of tart- : yük ček, un ček-, uzaqqa ček-, etc.

This correspondence is present also in the figurative sense: därd tart- 'to be afflicted by pain', ziyan tart- 'to suffer a loss', qïyïn tart- 'to suffer a pain'; in Oghuz languages därd ček, ziyan ček-, qïyïn ček-. This compound construction might have been primordially not Turkic, but modelled on a Persian pattern: dard kašidan, ziyan kašidan, so the Turkic expression was a Persian calque (Lehnübersetzung).[26]

The second next meaning "to stretch, to draw": CT yay tart-, Kir. jay t. (Jud.7o8) 'to draw a bow', Alt. jänï t. (R III, 857.); ayl tart- 'Gürtel schnallen' (CC, 236). Intransitive use of the same: Kir. boy tartqan qïz 'grown-up girl' (Jud. 7o9.).

tart- is often used to denote work, productive activity: Kir. čalyi tart- 'to mow', Tel. qamčï t. 'to weave a whip' (R III, 859); Kir. tuzaq t. 'to set a trap' (Jud.7o8), Alt. un tart- 'to grind flour'-(R III, 858), Kir. arïš t. 'grind barley'.

The notion "to pull down" underlies the expression signifying weighing. The expression is valid since the earliest records on (QB, Chaghatai, Chwar., Ott. see Clauson, 534.): tarazaga tart- 'to weigh', though also in this case a Persian model might be instrumental (with kašidan) as taraza 'balance, scales' is also a Persian word. A noun derived from it: tartïy, tartïq, tartuq, tartu, tartï 'weight'.[27]

An adjoining meaning of a figurative sense: sözi tart- 'seine Worte bedenken (R III, 86o.), to ponder'; Ott. tartï 'Maaß in Worten, Überlegung' (R III, 861.), though this shade of meaning could also be motivated with the basic meaning 'to hold back', as shown in the explanation given by Radloff: 'langsam reden'; cf.: tiliŋ tart! 'hold your tongue!'(see below).

Tart- is also a perfect counterpart to the English verb 'to draw' (a picture). The modern extension of the meaning in Common Turkic: surat tart- 'describe, to draw, to portrait', or even 'to take a photography of sb.'.

A whole set of meanings pointing in both directions; towards ahead or backwards: 'to breathe, to exhale, to blow - to inhale, to

XI

hold one's breath' (Clauson, p.534.). This meaning makes it most fitting
to describe playing activity on wind instruments - but also in case of
stringed instruments we encounter this verb component; in the latter case
it denotes: 'to draw the cords'. E.g. Kir. čor tart- 'to blow a pipe',
surnay t. 'to play zurna', Alt. sïbïzga t. 'Flöte spielen', Kazakh dombra
t. 'to play tamburine' (R III. 857.).

A contiguous meaning with "inhale, exhale" is 'to smoke': Kir.
tameki t.; tämäkä t. (R III, 857.).

'To coat, to overlay', e.g.: Kir. kö t. 'to soot', in the figurative: Kir. quba t. 'to become white', qubaljïn t. 'to grow pale', but
this meaning might be derived from the semantic change pointing towards
forward: to move ahead > to become > to turn, to grow sth.

In the expressions 'to entertain a guest' the basic meaning
must have been 'to offer, to hand over': e.g.Kir. aš tart-, tabaq t. 'to
offer, to hand over a dish, a plate', Kazakh 'to entertain a guest, to
keep sb for guest' (R III, 858.). Derivate: tartu: 'entertainment'. Kāšγ.:
tartïn 'Verproviantierung' (Brock. 197.) ; a figura etymologica: tartïn
tarttï 'he drew provisions' (Clauson, 534.). 'To deal cards' can have set
forth from a basic meaning 'to hand over' (Jud. 7o9.).

A further extension of this variety of meaning is 'to present
a gift, a tribute, peškeš, a "voluntary" gift to the feudal lord' is to
be found in all Turkic languages: tartïγ, tartïg, tartïq, tartï,tartu[28]
A figura etymologica: tartïγ tart- 'offrir des présents' (PdC, 197.).

The figurative sense 'to draw into the length' is an organic
evolution of the basic verb starting from the meaning of space, and naturally applied also to the space of time: uzaqqa tart- 'to last long' (R III,
858.), Kir. altïn-čïdan tartïp 'from 6 o'clock on' (Jud.7o9.).

Another expression for a person to move forward or backward,e.
g.Kir. jol tart- 'to head for, to go towards', tart beri! 'come hither!';
anï-yar tart! 'go towards him!' (R III, 859.).

To the group of meanings denoting 'to hold back' belongs the
chain of meanings 'comprehend, contain; contents, quantity ~ quality' in
Common Turkic tartïm, e.g. Kir. tartïmï jaxši 'of good quality'; Common
Turkic: tartïmlï, e.g.Kir. tartïmdū jigit 'a clever, intelligent youth'.

As basic meaning to tart- generally a forward movement is attributed, but there is a rather wide variety denoting the backward movement,
so e.g. Kazan Tatar, Kir. išten baš tartar 'to withdraw from labour'

XI

612

(R III,859.,Jud.7o9.), and a good number as seen above.

The most significant variety of this special meaning 'to withhold, to keep back, to pull back, to withdraw' is common usage in horseman
terminology; e.g.Kir. boǰu tart-, attïn bašïn tart- 'to keep the bridle
firm, to draw the reins', Alt. atïŋdï tart! 'ziehe die Zügel an!' (Jud.
7o9., R III, 859.). Osm. R. tartqï 'a gradual pulling in of the reins of
the horse' (R III, 866.).

Vámbéry's alert eye did notice that the same semantic element
'to withdraw, to hold back' was present in the reflexive derivates:tartïn-
Hung. tartózkodik in two disparate meanings, a) 'to withdraw from', and
b) 'to sojourn, stay somewhere' (R III, 861; Jud. 711.). The noun derivate: tartï 'Maaß in Worten, Überlegung' (R, III, 861.).

The same backward direction is indicated in the derivate adjectives: tartïnčaq, -ǰaq, -čay (Kazan Tatar, Tel, Shor, Bar,Kir., R III,
861-62.) 'eigensinnig, halsstarrig, stetig, widerspensig (especially horses), schüchtern'. The root is valid also in maritime terminology: Kir.
tartqïn 'ebb (the withdrawal of the flow)'.

4.2. And now let us subject the semantic varieties of the Hungarian verb tart- to a scrutiny. The Hungarian Nyelvtörténeti szótár [Dic-
tionary of old Hungarian Texts] enumerates the basic meanings under 14
headings,the New Hungarian Etymological Dictionary separates 43 shades of
meanings, the Hungarian Explanatory Dictionary classifies the meanings
under VII major categories, and subcategories.[29]

The comparision of the Hungarian and the Turkic verb tart-
shows contiguity in the following semantic realms: 2. sustineo, aufrecht
halten; 3. protendo, hinhalten; 4. contineo, complector, enthalten; 7.
asservo, custodio, bewahren, verwahren; 1o. duro, dauern; 11. nutricor,
nähren.[3o]

A number of semantic varieties are nowadays expressed by the
aid of prefixes in Hungarian. In the period of the Bulgaro-Turkic contact
(because the lack of prefixes) orientation in space (and time) could be
expressed only by the help of adverbs, the other solution was to adopt
special verbs indicating the direction (or the modalities) of the verb.
This was the case in Hungarian; there existed already verbs to denote
the action: ' to pull, to hold, to keep', but there was no special term
for 'to pull back, to hold back, to keep back', for horse-drilling.

One of the widest realms on the area of basic meaning of the
Hungarian verb tart- is the orientation pointing towards the rear: 'to

XI

hold back, to keep back, to withhold'. The importance of this direction
is clearly expressed in the varieties enumerated under cols. I, 1, 2, 3,
6, 8, 1o, 11, 12, 13, 14 in the Explicative Dictionary. I,1: to keep
back sb from changing place, to prevent sb from falling down, etc.; I,2:
to withhold sb from moving away; I, 3: to make, to compell sb (or: sth)
to keep his (its) state, position; I, 6: to detain, to impede, to retard,
etc. from leaving, from doing sth; I,8: to restrain, to check oneself;
I,1o: to keep within rules, etc.etc.[31]

The enumerated examples are in accordance with one item of the
basic meanings of the Turkic verb tart- 'to pull back, to hold back, to
keep back'.

The second next corresponding meaning of tart- (eltart-) corresponds to Turkic aš tart- 'to keep, to entertain (with food)', or the
derivate tartly 'provisions'.

The close contact of space and time concept is shown by the
denotation of duration in both languages, Turkic and Hungarian alike:
tart. (Idő) tartam is a newly applied word for 'space of time', but the
word tartalom 'contents' is to be met with in Turkic tartīm, and the adjective tartīmlī. The expression valamerre tart has its counterpart in
Turkic yol tart-, tart beri! (see above).

The Hungarian tart- has also many derivates both verbal and
nominal: tartózkodik valamitől: 'to restrain, to refrain from sth' - cf.
Turkic tartīnmaq.

The adjective tartózkodó 'restraining, refraining' is an exact counterpart of the Turkic tartīnčaq.

In enumerating all these semantic varieties I did not mean to
say, that all correspondencies should have been taken over from Turkish
into Hungarian, because the common mental creativity may have brought
about some of the coincidences in meanings by themselves.

But at the same time it should be a mistake to suppose that
only the widest, the most general, fundamental meaning could serve a
basis for loanword. Loanwords are taken over mostly together with the
objects unknown up to that time to the language community, of (though
more rarely) a special verb, a term for an action unfamiliar to them.

4.3. But the discrepancy between the basic meanings objected
by Budenz and Szinnyei is not so wide at all, even in the roots, as they
supposed, because there is no unbridgeable gap between the meaning of

XI

the Turkic and the Hungarian verb. The semantic area of a word-group
from the realm of Indoeuropean languages will suffice for a parallel of
general linguistics. Let us quote the Latin correspondences of the word
group denoting 'to extend, draw, stretch, etc.' and 'to hold, to keep,
etc.' both being derived from the Indoeuropean root ten- /tend-: teneo
'to hold, to keep', tendo 'to draw, to stretch'; tenor 'ununterbrochener
Lauf, Fortdauer', tenax 'festhalten, zäh' (cf. Turkic tartïnčaq), tempus
'Zeitspanne', tenus 'erstreckend bis ...' (exact counterparts of the verbs
tart- denoting duration both in Turkic and Hungarian); English: contents
(cf.Turkic tartïm, Hungarian tartalom/, attendo 'heading for' (cf. tart,
yol tart-), contendo, to fight' (cf. Turkic tartïš-)[32]

A similar semantic correspondency is reflected also in the
doublets of the Russian verbs dergat' 'to pull, etc.' and deržat' 'to
hold, keep'.[33]

5.1. Vámbéry in his above quoted treatize and books among his
equations emphasized the meaning relating to the time concept: tart 'to
last, to take time, etc.'. This seems to signify that he took this meaning as the basic one which might have served for the basis of adoption.
This hypothesis has a weighty supporting argument, as the term denoting
the time concept in Hungarian idő 'time' is a loanword from Turkic.
(Cf. Uighur, etc. öd 'time').[34]

The main reason which is counterindicating against this supposition is, that the meaning 'to last, etc.' is clearly a secondary one
even in Hungarian, as the main concept underlying as basis for the Hungarian verb must have been - according to the above analysis - also 'to
pull, stretch, pull back, hold tight'. So I should like to submit a more
likely, and more concrete version for the solution of the original motif
of the adoption of the verb.

5.2. By the middle of the first millenium there ensued a fundamental change in the social and economic life of the Hungarian tribes,
they have changed their dwelling places from the forest zone towards the
steppe zones, where the importance of the horse for transport, as saddle
animal, for breeding purposes was considerably enhanced. In my opinion
the development of horsemanship may have been instrumental in the adoption of the term tart- a drilling term for horsebreeding, and mounting
purposes; tart- in the meaning 'to pull back, to hold back, to keep back'.

The issue of Hungarian horsemanship is an old feud of Hungarian early history. Half a century after the subsiding of the storm of
the "Turkic-Ugric battle" of the 1870-80ies, at the turning of the 20th-

3oth years of the present century a passionate dispute arose around the
Ugrian or Turkic origin of Hungarian horsemanship.

It was a commonly accepted viewpoint among Hungarian linguists
that already at the period of the Ugrian unity Hungarians were acquainted
with the use of horse, used common terms for the grassing period (másodfű,
harmadfű ló 'two, three years old horse'), for the gear of the saddle
horse: nyereg 'saddle', ostor 'whip', (orr) fék 'muzzle halter'. The Finno-Ugrian,or Ugric etymologies of these terms had been accepted in linguistic literature ever since the acknowledgement of the Finno-Ugric origin of the Hungarian language.[35] Moreover major specialists dealing
with the Turkic impact on early Hungarian society took this viewpoint for
a decided fact.[36]

Even an eminent protagonist for the Turkic origin of the Hungarians (the alledged substitution of the Finno-Ugric idiom instead of
the Trukic vernacular maternal tongue), Stephen Zichy, did take the Finno-Ugric descendancy of the mentioned terms for granted.[37]

The vital issue in the debate was the role of the horse played
in the life of Hungarians before the impact exerted by the Bulgaro-Turks
on Hungarians in the 5th-9th centuries.

In Hungarian historical textbooks and in the general opinion
on early history the opposite viewpoint prevailed that Hungarians became
horseback archers, ("kriegerisches Reitervolk") by the Turkic impact.[38]

Against this view it was G.Mészöly, who in 1929/3o joined battle; the banner in his argumentation were the four terms as evidence of
the Ugric origin of Hungarian horse breeding.[39]

In the course of the debate Zichy (as mentioned) did not deny
the Ugric essence of the preliminary terms related to the use of horse,
the emphasis in his argumentation was laid on the Hungarian way of life,
and military organisation often stressed by medieval chroniclers; he
asserted that Hungarians became "horseman poeple" under Turkic impact.

A solution of this vital problem could not be met, because the
basic issue, the social-economic structure of the Hungarians in that period has not been elucidated. Moreover, the terms characterising the social status of early Hungarians were not equivocal. Mészöly himself in
his triggering article used the term "people riding horseback" in the
initiating paragraph, and "horseman people" in the concluding, which is
far from identical, the one meaning occasional use of the horse for riding purposes, the second a fundamental feature of life.[4o]

XI

The debate did not clarify the phases, stages of the acquaintance with the horse, its keeping, breeding, economic and military use. The sway of horse keeping cannot be decided solely on basis of the enumerated terms, but the terms as features characterising the social-economic development do give a reasonable answer.

If the primary requirements to the use of the horse for riding purposes did exist with the Ugric tribes, or peoples, even then the innuendo presumably came from Turkic neighbours, as the basic term, the name of the horse ló (as also the similar Vogul and Ostiak word for it) came from Turkic side, prior to the separation of the three components of the Uric unity.[41]

The elevation of horse breeding to a higher level with the Hungarians after their separation from the Ugric unity was evidently in connection with the advance towards the steppe land where geographic conditions favoured the more vigorous development of horse breeding.[42]

By the southward migration the increase of pasture land enhanced the extent of horse-breeding, and especially the increased use of the animals for saddle horse was a great implement in changing their way of life.

5.2.2. The development, or advancement of economic and military use of the horse is characterised by two Turkic loanwords, the gyeplő 'bridle' and kantár 'harness', both of which represented a higher stage of skill in horsemanship, than the former: muzzle halter (fék)[43]

The bridle and the rein have meant a great advance in the use of the horse both for hauling power and riding purpose, making the horse easier manageable. The different stages of horsemanship has been reached, of course, at different times by people on different level of social-economic evolution, and under different geographic conditions.[44]

5.2.3. It is interesting to note that there is a peculiar correspondence in some Indoeuropean languages between the term bridle and rein, and the action exerted by their help, which is adequately characterised by the verb in Turkish and Hungarian alike: tart- 'to pull back, to hold tight, etc.'

Bridle (Anglosaxon brigdel) is a derivate from the verb bregdan 'to pull (to pull back)', the same Middle-High-German term bridel has been taken over by the French as: bride. The modern German term for 'bridle' Zügel is a direct descendant of the verb ziehen 'to pull'.[45]

XI

The German term __Zaum__ 'bridle' (synonyms of which are: Zugrie-
men, Zugseil - derivates of __ziehen__ also) goes back to the German root
__tuh__ (__tug__) 'to pull'.[46]

The term __rein__, French __rein__ derives from Vulgar Latin ^__retina__,
a derivate of __retinere__[47] - the Turkic and Hungarian counterpart of which
is equally: __tart-__.

In my opinion the verb __tart-__ is the proper verbal term for the
handling of the horse by the aid of the bridle and the rein (Hung.__kantár__,
__gyeplő__), and it was taken over at the same epoch of the early Turkic impact (Bulgaro-Turkic epoch). The present form of __tart-__ in Chuwash __turt-__
must not lead us astray, as in Proto Chuwash it sounded also __tart-__.[48]

Footnotes

1) __Nyelvtudonányi Közlemények__ (NyK) VIII (187o), p.178.
2) __A magyarok eredete__, Budapest, 1882, pp.549-55o.
3) __A magyarság bölcsőjénél__, Budapest, 1914, p.212.
4) J.Budenz: __NyK__, X, p.72, 111; J.Szinnyei: __Egyetemes Philológiai__
   __Közlöny__, 1882, pp. 55-56.
5) __NyK__, X,111 (and also __NyK__ XVIII, 224, etc.); __MUSz__ No.2o3, p.184.
6) __Szófejtő Szótár__ (__SzófSz.__) p.3o3.
7) __A magyar nyelv történeti-etimológiai szótára__ (TESz) vol.III. in
   manuscript (to which by the courtesy of the Editor I had access in
   spring 1974.)
8) UAJb XXXI (1959), pp. 244-245.
9) See __Drevnetjurkskij Slovar'__, Leningrad 1969, pp.538-539; G.Clauson,
   An Etimological Dictionary of Pre-Thirteenth-Century Turkish, Oxford, 1972, pp. 534-535.
1o) New Redhouse Turkish-English Dictionary, Istanbul, 1968. p.1o99.
11) __Derleme Sözlüğü__, vol.IV, Ankara, 1969. pp.1373-1374.
12) E.R.Tenišev, __Tuvinsko-Russkij Slovar'__, Moscow, 1968. p.43o.
13) __Versuch eines Etymologischen Wörterbuches der Türksprachen__, Hel-
    sinki, p.465.
14) Ural-Altaische Wortforschungen, Studia Orientalia, XVII/3, p.46.;
    TESz, vol. III. (MS).
15) Kalmückisches Wörterbuch, Helsinki, p. 383-384. - Cf. Doerfer,
    Türkische und mongolische Elemente im Neupersischen, vol.II.,
    Wiesbaden, 1965, p.437.

618

16) Poppe, N., Vergleichende Grammatik der altaischen Sprachen, vol.I, p.87.
17) Kotwicz, W., Issledovanie po altajskim jazykam,Moscow,1962,pp.38-4o.
18) NyK, VIII, 178.
19) A magyarok eredete, p. 549-55o.
2o) A magyarság bölcsőjénél, p.212.
21) NyK, X, 72.
22) Egy. Phil. Közl. pp. 55-56.
23) Hajdu, P., A magyarság kialakulásának előzményei, Nyelvtudományi Értekezések, No.2. p.29.
24) Of course, besides loanwords adopted because of their euphemistic and atmospheric effect.
25) The word is widespread in all Turkic languages, it would have been superfluous to bring all similar examples, so the following major reference dictionaries have been quoted: Radloff, Wb., vol.III.; Clauson, Etym.Dict.; Drevnetjurkskij Slovar' (DTSl.). From modern dictionaries I quoted only the Kirghiz Dictionary of K.K. Judachin, Kirgizsko-russkij slovar', Moscow, 1965, pp.7o8-71o. (Jud.), P.de Courteille, Dictionnaire Turk-Oriental, Paris, 187o, (PdC) 195-196.
26) We can meet reverse cases also Persian expressions could be coined on Turkic model. The ferocious tug-of war for the possession of a goat-skin, (a beheaded carcass), filled with sand weighing approximately 35-4o kgs is called in Turkic: oylaq tart-, ulaq tart-, 'to fight for (to pull) the goatskin'. Among Afgani Turkomans in Persian surroundings it sounds: buz kaši a Persian calque of the same meaning. (A lively description of this fierce fight with artistic photos see: National Geographic Magazine, vol. 144, No.5. pp. 661-667.).
27) Clauson, op.cit. p.535.
28) Clauson, p.535; R III, 861; Doerfer, II, p.436.
29) Magyar Nyelvtörténeti Szótár (NySz), Budapest, 189o-1893, III. cols. 458-489; TESz. Vol.III; A magyar nyelv értelmező szótára (ÉrtSz) vol. VI, 1962, pp. 522-527.
3o) NySz, III, col. 458.
31) ÉrtSz., VI, pp. 522-524.
32) Pokorny, Indogerm. Etym. Wb., I, pp.1o64-1o66; Walde-Hofmann, Lat. Etym. Wb., vol.II, pp.662-664; 664-665; Ernoult-Meillet, Dict.etim. langue latine, p. 683.
33) Vasmer, Russ. Etym.Wb., I, p.341.

XI

34) Gombocz, Die bulgarisch-türkischen Lehnwörter in der ungarischen
Sprache (BTLw), 85-86; Ligeti: MNy LVI, 298; MNy LXII, 395.

35) Munkácsi, B.: Ethnográphia V. (1894) pp. 166-17o; same: Ethnográphia XVI (19o5), pp. 71-72; Ethnogr. XLII (1931), p.13;Szinnyei,
Die Herkunft der Ungarn, p 31.; Hajdu: Nyelvtud. Ért. No.2.,p.49.

36) Németh, Gy., A honfoglaló magyarság kialakulása, pp. 124-125.

37) Zichy, I., A magyarság őstörténete és műveltsége a honfoglalásig.
(A magyar nyelvtudomány kézikönyve, I/5.) p.5o; Later he reconsider-
ed this point of view; MNy, XXVII, (1931) p.13.

38) Cf. KSz, VI, p.194.

39) Mióta lovas nép a magyar ?: Népünk és Nyelvünk (NéNy) vol.I,2o6-212,
214.; Munkácsi: Ethnogr. XLII (1931), pp. 11-13.

4o) NéNy, I, 212, 214.

41) Vámbéry, A magyarság eredete, p.287.; A magyarság őstörténete,1934.
(Edited by: L.Ligeti), p. 59.; Ligeti: AOH XXIX/3, (1975),p.279.

42) Hajdu: Nyelvtud. Ért. No.2, p.5o.

43) Gombocz in 1912 (BTLw, p.78) was not convinced that kantár 'bridle'
belonged to the early layer of Turkic loanwords in Hungarian. But
his hesitation was mostly due to the late appearance of the word
in Hungarian sources (A.D.16o7), and because of the scarce evidence
in Turkic for his time. (But see: TESz, II, p.35o.)
Zichy in his earlier work (A magyarság őstörténete és műveltsége
a honfoglalásig,p. 5o.) did not find the etymology of gyeplő (<
Turkic iplik) convincing from the semantic view, saying that iplik
in Turkic languages meant only 'rope, string, thread'. Later on he
changed his mind MNy XXVII (1931) p.13., having acquired new evidence and having come to the conviction, that his former starting
point was erroneous, as loanwords were not always taken over in
their "basic meaning". (See TESz, I, 1127).

44) Cf. the same stages of evolution of the classical nomads of the
southern Eurasian steppeland: U. Kőhalmi, K., A steppék nomádja
lóháton, fegyverben. Budapest, 1972. pp.63-66.

45) Mayer-Lübke, Roman.Etym.Wb. p.117; Dauzat, Dict.Etym.p.113.;Klein,
E., Compreh.Etym.Dict.Engl.Lang. vol.I, p. 1ii.

46) Kluge, Etym.Wb. d.deutschen Spr. 11th ed. p.7o4.

47) Mayer-Lübke, op.cit. p. 6oo; Klein, Compreh.Dict.Engl.vol.II,p.1322;
Dauzat, Dict.Etym. p.623.

48) Gombocz, Z., Honfoglalás előtti bolgár-török jövevényszavaink, ed.
L. Ligeti, 196o, p.19.

XI

PART III

HISTORICAL STUDIES

Acta Orientalia Academiae Scientiarum Hungaricae, Tomus XXIX (2), pp. 133–186 (1975)

EINE ARMENISCHE CHRONIK VON KAFFA
AUS DER ERSTEN HÄLFTE DES 17. JAHRHUNDERTS

VON

E. SCHÜTZ

1. Über die Geschichte der Krim im ausgehenden Mittelalter sind wir schon gut unterrichtet. Als ausgiebige Quellen kommen in erster Linie die Annalen der osmanischen Geschichtsschreiber in Betracht, die in den Standardwerken von Hammer und Zinkeisen verwertet worden sind. Dazu kommen die in der Krim abgefaßten und von Hammer und Smirnow schon reichlich benützten einheimischen Chronika. Eine von A. Zajączkowski kürzlich herausgegebene Chronik vom Sohn des in Kaffa residierenden osmanischen Beglerbegs, Abdullah ibn Rizvan, ist ein interessantes Gegenstück zu unserer Chronik, da sie ebenso die wirrevollen Jahre der Krimchane Džanibek und Mehmed III Kerej ausführlich behandelt.

Außer den die Kriegsereignisse behandelnden Schriften sind jene von besonderem Belang, die uns mit den sozialen und wirtschaftlichen Verhältnissen des Krimchanats bekannt machen. Zu diesem Zwecke dienen als erstrangige Geschichtsquellen die Berichte der Botschafter und Gesandten. Im Zeitalter des 30jährigen Krieges gab es einen regen Verkehr von diplomatischen Missionen auch in der Krim, beide Koalitionen trachteten die Krimtataren für sich zu gewinnen. In den Archiven liegt viel unveröffentlichtes Material, um von den fernsten anzufangen, auch in den nordischen Ländern; die Veröffentlichung einer interessanten Aktensammlung aus den Instruktionsbüchern der Dänischen Kanzlei für Auswärtige Angelegenheiten ist bald zu erhoffen (J. Matuz). Noch viel unausgebeutetes Material befindet sich in den Archiven der Habsburger Koalition. Für die Kenntnis der sozial-wirtschaftlichen Lage des Krimchanats ist noch immer der Bericht des Gesandten des polnischen Königs und transsylvanischen Prinzen, St. Báthory, die *Tartariae Descriptio* (1578) des Martin Broniewski die wertvollste Quelle. Ein neuentdeckter interessanter Bericht aus derselben Periode von A. Taranowski (1569) ist unlängst erschienen (Tardy—Vásáry).

Ein besonders wertvolles Material ist außerdem aus den Archiven von Genua und Venedig zu erwarten und auch die Berichte der Missionäre des päpstlichen Stuhles bzw. der Congregatio de Propaganda Fide blieben noch unausgebeutet. Die Berichte des Dominikanerpräfekts von Kaffa, E. Dortelli

1

XII

d'Ascoli, dienen schon seit einem Jahrhundert als erstrangige Quelle für die Periode der Jahre 1620—1630.

Ein reiches Material bietet uns eben die «unparteische» Partei, Rußland, mit den Berichten der russischen Gesandten, die, um die Gunst des Räuberstaates zu gewinnen, die Krimchane regelmäßig mit «Geschenken» aufsuchten. Die Akten des Auswärtigen Amtes (Posol'skij Prikaz) sind zwar nur teilweise und nur in Regesten veröffentlicht (*ITUAK, ZOOID*), man besitzt jedoch eine mustergültige Bearbeitung des reichen Materials von A. A. Novoseljskij für die Jahre 1600—1650 (und in der Beilage auch für die Periode von 1558—1600).

Ein umfangreiches und wenig publiziertes Material bieten die Bittschriften der polnischen, ungarischen, russischen usw. Gefangenen, die in den Kasematen von Čufut-Kale schmachteten oder als Sklaven in der Landwirtschaft unter elenden Umständen dahinsiechten (vgl. 225, 39;228, 06).

Zu diesem Fragenkomplex wird in der Chronik des Xačatur Kafajeci ein wichtiger Beitrag geleistet.

2. Die Chronik des armenischen Priesters Xačatur von Kaffa (Kafajeci) umfaßt 25 Blätter einer im Jerewaner "Mesrop Maštoc" Archiv (Matenadaran) verwahrten Handschrift (No. 7709, Seiten 220/v—244/v).[1]

In der wissenschaftlichen Literatur ist die kurze Chronik zuerst von A. Abrahamian der Öffentlichkeit zugänglich gemacht worden,[2] die kritische Ausgabe derselben erschien in der von W. Hakobian herausgegebenen Sammlung «Kleiner Chronica der 13—18. Jahrhunderte».[3]

Die Chronik berichtet über die in Kaffa, dem Sitz des türkischen Beglerbegs, bzw. auf der Halbinsel Krim im Zeitabschnitt von 1615—1658 vorgegangenen Ereignisse. Doch mehrere Blätter der Handschrift sind abhandengekommen, so daß die Aufzeichnungen über die Zeitabschnitte 1633—36 (S. 221,38) und 1640—1646 (S. 223,08) fehlen.

Das aus 248 Blättern bestehende Notizbuch enthält außer der Chronik wertvolle literarische Texte. Eigentlich ist das Büchlein von dem 16jährigen Jüngling mit der Aufzeichnung von 35 Liedern (*tay*) namentlich bekannter Hymnendichter und mehr als 20 Volksliedern (*hayren*) begonnen worden.[4]

---

[1] Einige Notizen über die Regierungsjahre der Krimchane auf den Seiten 148/v, 149/r-v, 150/r werden hier in den Anmerkungen angeführt.

[2] Zeitschrift *Etschmiadsin*, Jg. 1944. No. 1. 39—51. S. *Manr. Žam.* 205.

[3] *Manr Žamanakagrut'junner* 13—18 dd. (Abkürzung: *Manr. Žam.*) Jerewan, Bd. I. 1951. 205—236. In der folgenden Übersetzung werden auch die Recto- und Versoseiten der Blätter der Handschrift angegeben; die Zeilenzahlen, 5, 10, 15 usw. werden nur nach der Ausgabe vermerkt.

[4] *C'uc'ak Dzeragrac'* [Handschriftenkatalog des Maštoc Archivs (Matenadaran)] (arm.) Bd. II. Jerewan, 1970. 591.

Da in den frühen handschriftlichen Liedersammlungen nur vier von diesen
Volksliedern erhalten geblieben sind, stellt also diese Handschrift die erste
einzigartige Sammlung armenischer Volkslieder dar.[5]

Der Verfasser der Chronik bzw. der Abschreiber oder Aufzeichner der
erwähnten Lieder war der Priester Xačatur aus Kaffa. Sein Name erscheint
in einigen Kolophonen (MS S. 66/r, 138/v) und wird auch in einem Krypto-
gramm verborgen (238/v — 222,32.)

Die Handschrift ist ein Autograph-Exemplar des Verfassers, in dem auch
außer den Angaben persönlicher Art, den ganzen Text hindurch die Anwesen-
heit, die persönliche Teilnahme des Verfassers fühlbar ist. Priester Xačatur
liefert genaue Daten über sich und seine Familie: Laut einer Bemerkung war
er 1656 64 Jahre alt, ist also 1592 geboren.[6]

Der Priester Xačatur, der vor seiner Weihe den Namen Xačgruz trug,
der «Unwürdige, Staub und Asche», schildert farbenreich seine Priesterweihe
(März 15, 1624) (212,01). Er schrieb auch kurze Notizen über seine ander-
weitige Tätigkeit; er fungierte 1645 als Geistlicher für fünf Monate in Baxči-
Saraj (222,03), und verbrachte 1649 ungefähr drei Monate in Istambul (222,06).

Die Aufzeichnungen brechen 1658 ab, aus diesem Umstand folgert
W. Hakobian, daß unser Chronist an der Jahreswende 1658—59 starb.

3. Der Zeitabschnitt der Chronik umfaßt die erste Hälfte des 17. Jahrhunderts. Diese Periode war das Zeitalter des 30jährigen Krieges, wo die Gegner
für und gegen die Reformation und unter dem Vorwand der Glaubensunter-
schiede für die europäische Hegemonie kämpften.

Durch den Sieg des niederländischen Freiheitskampfes und die entscheidende Niederlage der unbezwingbar geglaubten spanischen Armada sind
die österreichischen Habsburger ihrer unentbehrlichen Hilfe, des spanischen
Dynastiezweiges, beraubt worden. Aber auch die religiöse Verschiedenheit
hinderte Frankreich nicht daran, das protestantische Schweden zu unterstützen, und England und Holland boten natürlich all ihre materiellen Kräfte
auf, um die Gegner des österreichischen Kaisers zu unterstützen. An der Seite
der Habsburger stand, infolge ihrer dynastischen Verkettungen und der
jesuitischen Beeinflussung, nur das polnische Herrscherhaus.

[5] A. Mnacakanian, *Haykakan mijnadaryan žoyovrdakan erger* (Mittelalterliche
armenische Volkslieder) Jerewan, 10. S. W. Mikaelian, *Грими haykakan gayut'i patmut'yun*
(Geschichte der armenischen Diaspora auf der Krim), Jerewan 1964. 316—317.
[6] Geheiratet hat er am 24. August 1617, am Tage der Heiligen Anna (208,19),
seine Frau hieß Anna, sie starb am 9. September 1623, wahrscheinlich als Opfer einer
Fehlgeburt (208,25). Sein Sohn hieß Qutlubej, geboren am 6. Juni 1618 (208,21), die
Tochter Edirmelik, geboren am 7. September 1620 (208,22). — Was den Wohlstand der
Familie betrifft kaufte er das Haus des Restakes (Aristakes) für seine Tochter Edirmelik,
die am 1. Oktober 1637 heiratete (221,45).

1*

In Rußland hat zwar der Bolotnikow-Aufstand und die polnische Intervention am Anfangs des Jahrhunderts der im vorigen Jahrhundert eingeleiteten
Expansion (die Einverleibung der Kasaner und Astrachaner Khanate) vor-
übergehend Einhalt geboten, doch infolge der Gelähmtheit des Habsburger
Blocks, und da auch von anderer Seite keine Gefahr drohte, konnte die Anglie-
derung Sibiriens durch die Söldner der Kaufleutedynastien ungestört weiter
geführt werden.

Die Krimtataren wurden von den Russen durch einen Pelztribut
(Geschenk) beschwichtigt, und wenn von Zeit zu Zeit einige Mirzas den erkauf-
ten Frieden mit ihren Plünderungszügen störten, so sind davon lediglich die
an der Grenze des Wüstfelds (Dikoe Pole) liegende Ortschaften betroffen
worden.

Im Türkischen Reich gewann in dieser Zeit die verschärfte Krise immer
mehr Oberhand, die Janitscharenaufstände und die Haremintrigen unter-
wühlten die Kräfte des Golemreiches. Die Schwäche der einander gegenüber-
stehenden Lager der beiden (österreichischen und türkischen) Kaiser riefen
also einen Zustand des Gleichgewichts hervor, keiner der beiden wagte es und
vermochte den anderen bekriegen.

Dieser Waffenstillstand an der westlichen Grenze bot dem Sultan freie
Hand zum Aufhalten des persischen Druckes, der Feldzüge von Schah Abbas
und Schah Sefi (z. B. 1619: 209,16). Auch an diesem entlegenen Kriegsschau-
platz wurden die leichten Reitertruppen der Krimtataren eingezogen, es
bedeutete schon ein augenfälliges Merkmal der zunehmenden Schwäche, da
die Krimchane sich erdreisteten, dieser Vasallen-Verpflichtung nur zögernd
und teilweise Genüge zu leisten (z. B. 1631: 219,42). Eine andauernde Abwe-
senheit der Streitkräfte hätte die Halbinsel einer ernsten Gefahr seitens der
Kosaken ausgesetzt.

Das Hauptfeld für die ständigen Plünderungszüge der Krimtataren
bedeutete eben das naheliegende Grenzgebiet des polnischen Staates (*Korel.*
1621: 210,8/29; 1629: 216,11; 1631: 220,02; 1649: 225,12; 1650: 225,21) und
etwas seltener die angrenzenden Länder, die Moldau (*Boghdan*, 1650: 225,28)
und Transsylvanien (*tabur Madžarin* 'das ungarische Heer' 1657: 228,05).

Für die nördlichen Vorposten des türkischen Reiches und ihre Vasallen
stellten nur die Kosaken eine ernste Gefahr dar. In den türkisch-polnischen
Akten erschienen die Überfälle der Kosaken als ein ständiger Beschwerde-
punkt. Die unaufhörlichen Raubzüge der flinken, uneinholbaren leichten
Boote (*šajqa*, *qajïq*, *sandal*) bildeten eine ständige Plage für die Nordküste
Anatoliens, ganz bis zur Hauptstadt. Zu den Gegenmaßnahmen schien zwar
die Krim für die türkischen Seekräfte die geeignetste Stützbasis zu bieten,
doch diese Strafzüge gegen die Dneperfestungen scheinen nicht viel Erfolg
erzielt zu haben (1617: 208,26; 1627: 213,37). Eigentlich ist dem Vorposten
der Festung Azov (*Azaq*) die größte Aufmerksamkeit gewidmet worden, und

so gelang es den Donkosaken, sich der Festung nur für einige Jahren zu bemächtigen (Kriegsvorbereitungen 1640 222,38).

Die Krimtataren wagten es selten, einen Feldzug gegen ihre nächsten Nachbarn, die Kosaken, zu führen, obwohl jene jahraus-jahrein Überfälle gegen die Krim richteten. Als angegebener Grund für diese Angriffe galt, daß die Krim türkischer Vasallenstaat war. Die Kosaken verfolgten gegenüber den Tataren, ebenso wie auch gegenüber den Türken, die Taktik, Zusammenstöße zu vermeiden. Nur ausnahmsweise griffen sie die Schlüsselburg der Halbinsel an (Orkapu, Perekop, arm. Orinberan) (1623: 211,33), ihre leichten Schiffe, Kähne, Boote umgingen die gefährlichen Knotenpunkte und überfielen die Hafenstädte, wo wenig kampfkräftige Tataren und viel Beute zu erwarten war (die Saporoger Kosaken: 1616: 205,13; 1622: 211,13; 1629: 215,40; 1656: 227,14. Die Kosaken von Kašot: 1624: 212,14; 1628: 217,03; 1633: 221,27; 1655: 226,34).

Die zunehmende Schwäche des türkischen Reiches wird augenfällig auch durch das Verhalten der Chane zum Sultan gekennzeichnet. Dies ist besonders im Zeitalter des Krimchans Mehmed Kerej III. (1623–1627) und seines Qalghas, Šahin Kerej, bemerkbar, die sich 1624 den Verordnungen des Sultans mit Waffen widersetzten, den Absetzungsferman einfach unbeachtet ließen, so daß der Sultan sich am Ende genötigt fühlte, die vom Chan ‹ertrotzte› Macht mit Chalat und Ferman zu bestätigen (s. *GOR*, V, 36–37; Smirnov, 490.). Unsere Chronik schildert diese Periode besonders anschaulich (1624–25: 212,22–213,17). Aber auch die Chane Džanibek Kerej (1610–1623, 1627–1635), wie auch Inajet Kerej (1635–37) schalteten und walteten mit mehr oder weniger Selbständigkeit. Auch Islam Kerej (1644–54) führte eine ziemlich unabhängige Politik (s. *GOR*, V. 344; Novoseljskij, 396; Smirnov, 511).

Die türkische Pforte wußte doch die unbändigen Tataren in Zaum zu halten, sie reizte die Brüdergeschlechter, die Noghaier, gegen die Tataren auf. Unsere Chronik enthält Aufzeichnungen über die gegenseitigen Fehden, Blutrachen zwischen den Kerejs und der Mansur Sippe, den Noghaiern Qantemirs (1627: 213,17/31; 1628: 214.08; 1628: 215,25; 1637: 222.14).

Die ständigen Kriegsoperationen verlangten immer mehr Geld, und die Steuerschraube wurde auch in der Krim immer fester gezogen: Charadsch und Ispendsche wurden im Übermaß eingetrieben (*xaraǰ*: 1627: 213,26; 1630: 216,22; 1646: 223,42; 1657: 227,44; *ispenǰe* 1631: 216,42; 1649: 225,04; *hasil xaraǰ*: 1632: 221,13–27). Und die Steuereintreibung verschärfte sich noch durch die Korruption der Lokalverwaltung, es wurden sogar 4–5 (3–4) jährige Kinder in die Steuerbücher (*defter*) aufgenommen (1630: 216,26/35).

Dazu überbürdete man die Bevölkerung stets mit Fronarbeit (*jasaγ*): Fuhrwerkstellung, Arbeitsdienst, Proviant für die türkischen Stoßtruppen, die gegen die Dneperfestungen, gegen den von den Donkosaken besetzten Azov (1637–1641) ins Feld zogen (1627: 213,37; 1632: 220,05; 1640: 222,38).

XII

Die Staatswirtschaft des Krimchanats stand auf den unsicheren Füßen der extensiven Naturalwirtschaft. Die Luxusansprüche der Hofhaltungen der Chane und der Mirzas werden durch Raubzüge gedeckt, wo den wesentlichsten Ertragsartikel die Gefangenen darstellten (1621: 210,13; 1629: 216,03/12; 1628: 217,05; 1649: 225,13,32; 1655: 226,34). Die Sklavenmärkte, die Vermittleraktion der Kaufleute, die Unterhandlung um die Lösegelder gehörten zu den gewohnten Bildern in einigen Hauptmarktplätzen, Orkapu, Kaffa usw. (1650: 225,42; 1657: 228,05).

Einen wesentlichen Teil in der Chronik bildet die Beschreibung des alltäglichen Lebens, in erster Linie die Naturplagen: Erdbeben: 1615: 208,07; 1618: 209,03; 1619: 209,13/26; 1626: 213,23; 1640: 222,28; 1656: 227,05; Sturm, Überschwemmung: 1617: 208,15; 1618: 209,02/22; 1631: 219,15—40; 1633: 220,25; 1657: 228,01; Feuerbrunst: 1618: 209,02; 1633: 220,11; Epidemie, Hungersnot: 1618: 209,02; 1619: 209,25; 1621: 210,41; 1623: 211,19; 1628: 215,15; 1646: 223,19—40; 1655: 226,34; Wassernot: 1621: 210,05; 1623: 211,41; 1624: 212,35; 1628: 215,15; 1631: 219,40.

Im Mittelpunkt des Interesses eines Priesters steht natürlich das religiöse Leben der armenischen Kirchengemeinde, die Beziehung zum Mutterlande, aus dem vom armenischen Patriarchen (Katholikos) oft Legaten und Priester kommen, man bringt die nur aus Etschmiadzin beziehbare Mirrha, es kommen Priester zur Eintreibung der Kirchengebühren und Sammlung von Almosen. Die Geistlicher werden mit all ihren positiven und negativen Charakterzügen geschildert, es wird nicht verhehlt, daß auch unter ihnen manchmal korrupte Figuren zu finden sind.

4. Was den Zustand der Handschrift betrifft, ist sie ziemlich defekt. An manchen Stellen gibt es Lücken von mehreren Seiten, so daß Berichte über mehrere Jahre gänzlich fehlen (1633—36: 221,38; 1640—46: 223,08), die letzten. Seiten sind schwer beschädigt, die Ränder der Blätter abgerissen, nur der Vollständigkeit halber ist es versucht worden die letzten Seiten zu übersetzen. Dazu boten uns die vom Herausgeber, W. Hakobian, mit großer Sorgfalt und Sachkenntnis ausgeführten Textergänzungen eine wesentliche Hilfe. Die übernommenen Anmerkungen, und manche brieflichen Erläuterungen W. Hakobians sind mit dem Signum *W. H.* vermerkt worden. Georg Abgarian hatte die Liebenswürdigkeit die ganze Übersetzung zu prüfen. Er hat viele wertvolle Ratschläge zur Korrektion gegeben, wofür ich meinen aufrichtigen Dank auch hier aussage.

Die armenische Schrift widerspiegelt die westarmenische Aussprache der türkisch-tatarischen Wörter. Die Fremdwörter haben wir dem westarmernischen Lautwert gemäß umgeschrieben und in Klammern beigegeben. Die tatarischen Wörter sind allerdings in tatarischer und nicht in der gewohnten ottomanischen Form wiedergegeben, z. B. der Name der Dynastie der Krimchane:

Kerej und nicht *Girej*. Die zahlreichen Wörter des staatlichen Lebens sind ottomanisch-türkisch, was auch dadurch gekennzeichnet ist, daß der Sitz des türkischen Beglerbegs Kaffa war. Jedenfalls muß es in Betracht gezogen werden, daß das Armenische ein anderes Phonemsystem besitzt. Es gibt ursprünglich keine Zeichen (auch keinen Laut) für palatale Labiale: *nogar — nöger* 'Gefolgsmann'; besonders in nichterster Silbe steht *a* anstatt türk. *ä*: *čätän — čatan* 'Korb'; *x* entspricht dem *q*: *xabax — qabaq* 'Tor'.

Da die Übersetzung keine armenische linguistische Aufgabe zu lösen bezweckt, und die ostarmenischen Personen- und Ortsnamen im allgemeinen geläufiger sind, außerdem noch in der Erzählung viele aus dem Mutterlande gekommene Personen (manche mit gleichem Namen) erscheinen, habe ich die armenischen Personennamen und auch die (in Klammern vermerkten) armenischen Fachausdrücke in ostarmenischer (OA) Form wiedergegeben. Die entsprechenden westarmenischen Varianten (WA) werden in dem Namen- und Wortindex angegeben.

Im laufenden Text der Übersetzung — bei den allgemein gebräuchlichen türkisch-tatarischen Wörtern — bedienen wir uns der vulgären Umschreibung: Chan, Krim, Qalgha.

Chronik des Xačatur Kafajeci

208 5 220/v 1615, Zodiakzeichen: Zwillinge, Sonntagsbuchstabe (littera dominicalis) 7, numerus aureus 100, Epakta 21, Mondzahl (littera lunaris) 2. Dieses Jahr, am 26. Mai, Freitag, ist die Stadt Kaffa von einem Erdbeben erschüttert worden. Die Stadtmauer stürzte nieder, die Erde erbebte, die Häuser stürzten ein, der Boden geriet in Bewegung, die Geschöpfe sind in Schrecken gesetzt worden, **10** die Frauen jammerten, die Kinder weinten, das Meer erhob sich, schlug Wellen, dann zog es sich zurück. Es sei Lob dem Bewirker (all dieser) Wunder.

1616, am 20. Juli, am Samstag in der Nacht, kamen die Kosaken (*urus*) und bestürmten Kaffa, verwüsteten viele Stadtviertel, diese Stadt wird aber wieder erneuert.

15 1617, am 17. Juli kam ein (ausgiebiger) Regen auf die Stadt, die Flüsse traten aus ihrem Bett, (die Flut) schwemmte 10—20 Brücken weg, 20—30 Häuser stürzten ein, 5—6 Leute ertranken; viele Wunder geschahen wegen unserer Sünden, am Mittwoch.

221/r Im Monate August, am 24. Tage, am Sonntag der heiligen Anna **20** trat ich Sündiger in das weltliche Leben ein, veranstaltete eine Hochzeit.

Mein Sohn Qutlubej ist 1618, am 6. Juni, Samstag, geboren. Meine Tochter, Edirmelik ist 1620, am 7. September, Donnerstag, geboren.

1623 ist meine Frau Anna am 9. September an Schwangerschaft **25** in Gott verschieden.

1617 bestürmte Memi Pascha mit zehn Galeeren (*qadïrya*) die Kosaken
(*urus*). Memi war der Pascha unseres Kaffa, ein gutmütiger und wackerer
Mann, er war der Freund des Landes. Die Kosaken (*urus*) töteten ihn und
eroberten drei Galeeren, schleppten viele Leute in Gefangenschaft, metzelten
einige nieder, **30** andere wieder schlugen sie in die Flucht. Im August gab es
(also) eine große Trauer in der Stadt Kaffa, und alle (Leute) waren erschüttert.

1618 begab sich Sultan Ahmat zu Gott, **221/v** und Sultan Mustafa setzte
sich an seinen Platz, er herrschte **35** drei Monate. Wegen der Unhelligkeiten
der Zeit löste man ihn ab, und setzte Osman an seine Stelle, es geschahen **209**
viele Unhelligkeiten in der Stadt Istambul. Und hernach brach eine Feuersbrunst in der Stadt aus, sie entfachte Brände an vielen Orten, es brach eine
große Epidemie aus, dann kam ein heftiges Gewitter, und die Flüsse traten
aus ihrem Bett. Am 2. Juli, Donnerstag, erschütterte ein Erdbeben die Stadt
Kaffa. Dann ist ein Frauenzimmer **5** mit vier männlichen Sprößlingen (von
Gott) beschenkt worden, wir alle waren in Staunen versetzt, waren voll Ver-
wunderung und priesen Gott, den Schöpfer. Und dann an (jenem) Sonntag
verbrannte sich ein Frauenzimmer auf Versuchung des Satans. Sie heizte in den
Backofen ein, hieb die Spitze ab, sprang hinein, ihre Hausleute und ihre Söhne
waren nicht zuhause. **10** Als sie kamen, war sie schon verbrannt und das Haus
vom Feuer ergriffen. Alle beweinten sie. Ihr Gemahl war nicht da, zwei Tage
später kam er nach Hause und fand seine Frau nicht vor. Große Wunder
geschahen am 2. August. **222/r** Am 13. (August) gab es wieder Erdbeben.
Im Monate September, im zweiten Mondviertel, kam (wieder) ein Erdbeben.
Und danach ist ein Komet **15** erschaffen worden. Der Oktober gebar Säbel.
Der Dezember gebar einen Kometen.

Aus dem Lande der Perser (*Karmir Glux*) kamen traurige Gerüchte
(*xabar*), daß viele Soldaten (*asker*) niedergemetzelt worden sind, viele (vor-
nehme) Herren fielen und der Chan nur mit Mühe und Not entkam.

Am 15. April kehrte Džanibek Kerej (*Džanbekere*) von den Persern
(*Qïzïlbaš*) zurück. Am 27. **20** wurde eine Feier (*donanma*) in Kaffa veranstaltet.
Am 21. April verschied Priester Hovannes in Gott.

Am 26. August kam ein heftiger Schauer über unsere Stadt Kaffa. Drei
Teile der Bollwerke stürzten ein, zwei Arsenale (*tarsana*) und dazu der Turm
der Mädchen (*qïzlar qula*). Und darauf kam eine plötzliche **25** große Epidemie
und kein Haus blieb ohne Tränen. Am 10. September in der Nacht kam ein
Erdbeben, es dröhnte dermaßen, daß manche sagten, es sei ein Geschütz abgefeuert worden. All diese Wunder geschahen wegen unserer Sünden.

222/v 1620 ließ Džanibek Kerej Chan Silbermünzen prägen. Für **3**
Monate ist die Stadt verschlossen worden, Kauf und Verkauf hörten auf,
bis Juli **30** und August, dann haben sich (die Gemüter) allmählich beruhigt.
Wisset wohl meine Freunde, es sind schon zehn Jahre, daß er Chan geworden
ist, hiermit wird es zum vierten Male sein, daß er Münzen prägen ließ.

XII

Wir haben die Kirche des heiligen Thoros in Arbeit genommen, Gott segne das Volk. Sie haben die Kirche am 23. September weißgetüncht, ließen ein Altarbild **35** mit dem Bild der Gottesgebärerin, des heiligen Lusavorič, des heiligen Sargis, des Heerführers und seines Sohnes Martiros und Minas des Wundertäters malen. Und auch ein anderes Gemälde für den heiliger Altar, das die Heilige Mutter und ihren einziggeborenen Säugling, Jesus, darstellte. Sie ist eingeweiht worden am Samstag des Heiligen Jakob, des Bischofs von Nisibis, unter dem Erzbischoftum **40** des Ter Xačatur Wardapet und des Bischofs Ter Thoros, die geistliche Vorsteher von Kaffa sind. Am 30. November abends, am 15. Mondtag, entstand eine Mondfinsternis Mittwoch abend um 4 Uhr bis **223/r** 5 Uhr morgens. Donnerstag früh kam ein Donner und ein Gewitter.

Im Jahre 1621, zum Zodiakzeichen des Skorpion, **45** am 18. Dezember zu Beginn des Winters. Der Winter hat lange gedauert und war hart, wer könnte all die Widerwärtigkeiten erzählen, die uns wegen unserer Sünden trafen. **210** Solche wundersame (Ereignisse) hatten nicht einmal die 100jährigen Greise gesehen. Das Meer vor unserer Stadt Kaffa fror auf 3 Meilen ein, und zwar bildete sich eine derartige Eiskruste, daß das Wasser überhaupt nicht zum Vorschein kam und die Leute auf dem Eis herumspazierten. Einer ging so weit, bis er 1500 Schritte (*daban*) zählte, und für eine lange Zeit gab es keine Spur von ihm. **5** Die Brunnen versiegten, und es gab kein Brot und kein Holz zum Heizen. Viele arme Leute starben vor Kälte, die Füße und Hände sind ihnen abgefroren und sie wurden verkrüppelt. Devlet Kerej (*Dolvetkere*) Sultan führte einen Feldzug gegen Korel, verwüstete ihr Lager (*tabur*), verheerte viele Städte; viele Leute, **223/v** Männer und Frauen, **10** kleine Knaben führten sie in Gefangenschaft, und viele Säuglinge (oder: Bücher) nahmen sie mit und 50 Seelen aus unserem Volke des Erleuchters (Grigor); und aus ihrem Volke kamen unzählige und zahllose Gefangene, der Weg war von Schnee und Frost bedeckt, viele Gefangene und Soldaten (*asker*) starben auf dem Wege vor Kälte und Frost, viele Wagen und Pferde **15** blieben auf dem Wege, viele ließen ihre Kameraden dort, viele verließen ihre Diener, viele ließen Lebensmittel zurück, und viel Hab und Gut (*mal, xazina*) blieb auf dem Wege.

Die harte Kälte dauerte 3 Monate lang, Tag und Nacht, und ließ bis zum 15. März nicht nach, dann (erst) erblickten wir Sonne **20** und Strahlen. Dann wieder sagte man, daß in Istambul die Dardanellen (*Boghaz*) bis auf 18 Meilen eingefroren sind. Manche sagten, so etwas gab es nur im Jahre 647, zu Zeiten des Königs Konstantin. Es sei Lob dem Schöpfer der göttlichen Zeichen.

224/r Und da gab es wieder etwas Unerwartetes heute, am 9. April, **25** am Montag, da kam Schnee. Und am 7. Mai, da schneite es wieder, es wurde kalt und ein heftiger Wind wehte, am Montag wurden die Wiesen und Berge von Sulxat mit Schnee bedeckt, der Schnee stand eine Spanne hoch.

XII

Der König der Hagarier (Ottomanen), Sultan Osman, und der König der Magier (hier: der Tatarchan), Džanibek Kerej (*Džanbekere*) Chan, zogen mit Reiterscharen gegen Korel, im Monat Juli **30** mit vielen Truppen (*asker*), kehrten aber unverrichteterdinge zurück, da sie sie nicht bekämpfen konnten. Ein Mirza, namens Tamurxan (Qantemir) aus der Sippe der Noghaier, war viel siegreicher und kampflustiger als die Hagarier (Ottomanen), er verheerte und verbrannte viele Orte, machte viele Gefangene und schickte sie zum König der Hagarier (dem türkischen Sultan). Und jener **35** (Sultan Osman II.) hat ihn (Qantemir) sehr liebgewonnen, bezeugte ihm viel Ehre und Hochschätzung, er setzte ihn in die Würde eines Hofadeligen und Beglerbegs für Rumelien und der Stadt Silistra ein.

224/v Und der König (Sultan Osman) kehrte zurück in sein Land, da das erste (doch) das Königtum war, warum hat er überhaupt in den Krieg ziehen müssen, er war im Alter **40** eines Jünglings und hatte keinen gescheiten und klugen Mann zur Seite. Und nachher kam eine Hungersnot in unser Land, und viele Städte wurden von einer tödlichen Epidemie und viel Leiden überfallen.

Im Jahre 1622 wiederum wurden die Hagarier (Ottomanen) von Gott verflucht und bestraft. Die Landesherren **45** und Großherren beachteten die Vorschriften des Königs (türkischen Sultans) nicht und gehorchten seinem Befehl nicht, sie überschritten die göttlichen Gesetze. **211** Sie steinigten und töteten ihren Herrscher Sultan Osman; die Großherren befehdeten sich und metzelten einander nieder und schlugen sich auf Säbel und Degen; die Stadtleute befehdeten sich und schmiedeten Ränke gegeneinander. Viel Übel herrschte im Lande und große Trauer **5** in der Stadt Istambul. Es jammerte das Volk und alle Leute, da sie noch (niemals) ähnliches gesehen oder gehört hatten, daß Diener und Großherren **225/r** Janitscharen und Spahis zusammen eine Verschwörung anzettelten und den Herrscher töteten. Betrauernswert und beklagenswert war Sultan Osman, da er eben das Jünglingsalter erreichte und kaum reif zur Regierung war, vier Jahre bekleidete er das Königsamt und nicht mehr. **10** Eine Strafe für die Bestrafer, mit ihren Säbeln haben sie sich selber getötet. Sie setzten Sultan Mustafa auf den Thron. Ein Gelächter und eine Schande wurden sie vor allen Völkern. Am 10. Juni in der Nacht und am Montag früh kamen die Kosaken (*urus*) und drangen mit 33 Booten (*qajïq*) in die Bucht von Kaffa ein. Sie konnten aber keinen Schaden anrichten, **15** schimpflicherweise kehrten sie um und gingen davon, 5 Tage hielten sie sich im Hafen (*liman*) Xughri auf, verursachten viel Schaden, 5 Schiffe nahmen sie und verwüsteten und zerstörten die Obstgärten der Taten.

Im Jahre 1623 ließ Džanbek Kerej (*Džanbekere*) Chan Münzen prägen; unsere Stadt wurde durch tödliche Epidemie und Hungersnot heimgesucht. Es brach eine furchtbare Epidemie **20** und Hungersnot aus, ein Scheffel (*kila*) Weizen kostete 600 Silbermünzen (*stak*), wir haben es mit eigenen Augen

gesehen. Viele Leute begaben sich nach Taman, und dort erwarben sie Lebensmittel. Gott erboste sich aber nicht übermäßig, er zürnte wegen unserer Sünden,
erbarmte sich aber der Stadt Taman, **225/v** und damit sättigte er uns. Im
Dezember fing es an, ist aber auch zuendegegangen. **25** Am 9. Mai, Freitag,
wurde Mehmed Kerej (*Mehemedkeraj*) Chan und kam nach Kaffa, Džanibek
Kerej ergriff die Flucht. Devlet Kerej (*Dolvetkera* der Qalgha) Sultan und
Džanibek Kerej Chan sind betrauernswert und beklagenswert geworden. Da sie
der Herrscherwürde noch zu Lebenszeiten enthoben wurden, konnten sie sich
nur einen dürftigen Unterhalt besorgen und in Not begaben sie sich nach
Istambul. Es kam **30** Mehmed Kerej (*Mehemmedkere*) Chan, er setzte sich für
4 Jahre auf den Herrscherthron. Er sammelte seine Großherren und führte
einen Feldzug gegen Tamurxan (Qantemir) in Akkerman.

Im Monat September kamen die Kosaken (*urus*) gegen Orinberan
(Orkapu, Perekop), sie erstürmten die Stadt, steckten sie in Flammen und
verheerten sie, und die Christen metzelten sie nieder: 30 000 **35** Reitervolk
die Hälfte Fußvolk, auch viele Tataren brachten sie um und nahmen sie
gefangen. Viele Leute sind auf den Hund gekommen und fielen in Armut.

Im Oktober kam der Chan mit Tamurxan (Qantemir) und den Noghaiern.

Es erfolgte ein Wechsel in der Herrscherwürde, Sultan Mustafa ist abgesetzt worden **40** und Sultan Murad an seine Stelle gekommen.

226/r Es trat ein Mangel an Wasser ein, für lange Zeit fanden wir kein
Trinkwasser, alle Brunnen wurden bloßgelegt (aufgewühlt), daraus trank man,
niemand fragte, ob es süß ist oder bitter. Das Wasser in der Zisterne trocknete
aus und auch alle Schachtbrunnen und Quellen versiegten völlig.

45 Pfarrer (*kahana*) Avetik begab sich am 17. September zu Gott.

212 1624, am 15. März, am sechsten Tage des Fastens (*ayuhacʻkʻ*), am
Sonntag des Erleuchters (Grigor), bin ich der Unwürdige, Staub und Asche,
faul und träge, ein minderwertiger Diakon, der sündige Xačgruz, zum Priester
(*kahana*) geweiht worden, obwohl ich des Ranges und des Grades unwürdig
bin. **5** Gott erleuchte die Seele des Avetik und meines Subalternen, Priester
(*kahana*) Ter Xačatur, der sich für mich so viel geplagt hat, da er mein Schwiegersohn und Beichtvater war. Unter den Prälaten (*araǰnort*) XačaturWardapet
und den Bischöfen (*hajrapet*) Ter Thoros und Ter Movses Qrīmeci ist mir durch
ihre rechte Hand die Ehre der Weihung zuteilt geworden, als **10** ich nach
Ablauf des 40tägigen (Fastens), am Donnerstag, dem 29. April für den Unsterb-
lichen die Messe gelesen hatte, und es ist mir die Ehre des Heiligen Sakraments
des ewigen Segens, des makellosen Leibes und ehrenvollen Blutes unseres
Herren Jesu Christi zuteil geworden.

Am 11. April, Sonntag, drangen die Kosaken (*urus*) von Kašot ins obere
Stadtviertel von (Eski) Krim ein **15 226/v** nahmen Christen gefangen, nahmen
den Solz der Christen, das Heilge Kreuz mit sich, und stießen das Kloster
des Ter Movses in die Finsternis.

XII

144 E. SCHÜTZ

Am 3. Mai, Montag, kam Šahin Kerej Sultan (der Qalgha) aus Persien (*Karmir Glux—Qïzïlbaš*), und die Leute beglückwünschten einander wegen seiner Ankunft, **20** da er ein gerechter König (Qalgha) war und (man hofft) er wird uns Frieden bringen.

Und wieder kamen neue unerwartete, erstaunliche Ereignisse, es kamen Džanibek Kerej Chan und Devlet Kerej (*Dolvetkere* Qalgha Sultan) am 24. Mai (1624), Montag. Das wurde eine Erschütterung für jederman und eine Aufregung **25** für unsere große Stadt. Es gab überhaupt keine Lebensmittel, weder für Menschen noch für das Vieh, da alle Läden zugesperrt wurden, alle Fruchthandlungen, Fleischbänke und Brotladen, da die Verfluchten unsere Stadt in großen Scharen umzingelten. 75 Tage lang ankerten 40 Galeeren (*qadïrya*) (in der Bucht). Der gottlose Džanibek Kerej und **30** Devlet Kerej und andere Bösewichte blockierten uns. Alltäglich kämpften sie gegen Šahin Kerej und Mehmed Kerej (*Mehemedkera*), konnten sie aber nicht besiegen und kehrten beschämt um. Einige **227/r** ereilte der Tod, andere kamen halbtod zurück, viele mußten ihre Freunde und Brüder beweinen und die gefallenen Pferde beklagen. Das Getreide verdorrte, die Quellen **35** trockneten aus, es fehlte an Fuhrwerk, die Tiere winselten (jämmerlich), da sie kein Gras fanden, sie leckten den Boden, die Männer klagten, die Frauen jammerten, die Kinder weinten und die Väter trösteten sie, daß heute oder morgen (schon) Frieden kommen wird, die geschlossenen Türen wieder geöffnet werden, und bei uns wieder Freude herrschen wird. Man sagte einander tröstend «heute oder morgen» **40** bis dem Krieg ein Ende wurde. Und als der erste August zu Ende ging und der Sonntagmorgen lichthell erschien, ergriff Džanibek Kerej die Flucht, der (Qalgha) Sultan nahm die Fahne, und kaum ist es ihnen gelungen, sich auf das Schiff (*qadïrya*) zu retten. Viel Kriegsvolk ist niedergehauen worden, die am Sterben waren — starben, die Gesunden flohen, einige warfen sich ins Meer, andere (flüchteten) in die Berge und die Vororte (*mahala*), konnten sich aber kaum retten. 500—600 Langmützen (Soldaten) sind gefunden und gefangengenommen worden. **213** 900—700 wurden niedergemetzelt, viele Leichnahme lagen aufgestapelt an der Küste, zwei Wezire (*vazir*) sind gefallen, ein Großwezir wurde verletzt (*jaralï*), (die übrigen) bestiegen die Galeere (*qadïrya*) und entfernten sich. **227/v** Šahin Kerej war dort mit vielen Kriegsleuten (*asker*). Die Noghaier und Kosaken (*urus*) umgaben **5** alle Basteien im Stadtviertel (*mahala*), rissen viele Häuser nieder, raubten uns aus, zertrümmerten die Mühlen, verwüsteten die Klöster und richteten viel Unheil bei uns an.

Gott der Schöpfer sei gelobt, Gott war nicht allzu sehr gegen uns erzürnt, er erbarmte sich unser. Die gottlosen Hagarier (Ottomanen) konnten uns nicht überwinden und eilten beschämt von dannen. **10** Dem König der Könige, dem (lieben) Gott, danken wir für sein Erbarmen, daß er Šahin Kerej (Qalgha) Sultan und Mehmed Kerej Chan mit Kraft füllte, gottbegnadet war der Chan,

Acta Orient. Hung. XXIX. 1975

XII

begnadet war de (Qalgha) Sultan, der im Bezirk Sulxat und in der Stadt Kaffa regierte, es wurde Wohlstand und Frieden, Liebe und Versöhnung, 15 am 15. September (1624) veranstaltete man eine Feier (*donanma*) und es herrschte viel Jubel. Und nach diesen Ereignissen raffte sich Šahin Kerej auf und zog ins Feld, viele Noghaier verschleppte er und brachte sie mit ins Land. So geschah es.

Am 16. im Monat Dezember, am Donnerstag, nachts um 1 Uhr, erhob sich ein heftiger Wind, richtete viel Schaden an, stürzte Mauer und Häuser um, 20 zertrümmerte zwei Minarete (*minara*) und riß viele Bäume mit Laub und Wurzel in (Eski?) Krim aus.

228/r 1626 geschah wieder ein Wunder, im Monat Mai spaltete sich der Erdboden; Berge und Gipfel stürzten nieder und gegeneinander und stürzten in die Tiefe.

25 1626 im April ließ (der Chan) neue Münzen (*əstak*) prägen.

1627 geschahen viele Widerwärtigkeiten und eine schwere Steuer (*xarǰ*) wurde von den Christen eingetrieben. Der Chan raffte sich auf und führte einen Feldzug (*sefer*) gegen die Tscherkessen. Er bürdete der Stadt (Kaffa) eine große Steuer (*xarǰ*) auf. Einige gaben 5 Goldstücke, manch andere 4 Gold, andere wieder 30 3 Goldmünzen und etliche gaben 2 Gold.

Der Elende (*faqir fuqara*), Tamurxan (Qantemir) Pascha, kam mit bösem Vorhaben. Šahin Kerej überfiel ihn in der Nacht, zerstörte (seine Kräfte), ihn selber trieb er in die Flucht. Seine Frau und Kinder, alle Habe und Schätze (*mal u xazna*) blieben hier. Mahmud Agha sammelte (seine) Reiter, überfiel ihn, er trieb aber das Reitervolk auseinander, Mahmud Agha 35 entkam nur mit Not, entblößt und beschämt flüchtete er nach Akkerman.

228/v Und nach all diesem kam der Befehl vom König (vom türkischen Sultan), daß Ozun Burg gestürzt werden soll. Uns sind Männer nötig (lautete der Befehl), uns ist Geld für Karren (*araba*) nötig. Das Geld ist gesammelt worden, Silbermünzen, Gold, Gurusch (*xruš*) von Armeniern und Türken. Wir Christen gaben viele Männer, 40 mehrere Meister, mehrere Fuhrleute (*arabaǰi*), mehrere Arbeiter (*īryat*). Der Chan und der (Qalgha) Sultan machten sich mit vielem Kriegsvolk (*asker*) auf den Weg. Und danach kamen 12 Galeeren (*qadīrya*), um gegen Ozun zu ziehen. Zu diesem Zwecke waren 1500 *Qantar* Zwieback-Brot nötig (*baksimat*). Manches bucken wir, manches kauften wir und gaben es ihnen, damit sie gehen.

45 Es kam Wardapet Karapet und verbot 6 Priestern (*kahana*) (die Funktion), 214 aber nachher hob er das Verbot auf, die unerlaubten Ehen trennte er, ließ Almosenbehälter für Jerusalem in einer jeden Kirche aufstellen, und dann begab er sich nach Jerusalem. Er war ein wohlgebildeter und glaubenstüchtiger Wardapet mit zwei Schülern.

Das Volk restaurierte und schmückte die Quelle der sieben Quellen, das Wardewan Glux vom Heiligen Thoros. 5 Gott segne die Seelen der ersten Erbauer und der späteren Verzierer. Amen.

XII

229/r 1628 versammelte Šahin Kerej (Qalgha) Sultan wieder das Reitervolk, raffte sich auf und zog gegen Qantamur. 10 Mit vielen Kriegsleuten
(*asker*) setzte Šahin Kerej über die Donau (*Tuna*), aber danach folgte viel
Unheil: Qantamur vereinbarte sich mit Čïtaq, er schlug den (Qalgha) Sultan
und vernichtete all seine Truppen. Es fielen Großherren, es fielen Mirzas, nur
mit Not konnte sich der (Qalgha) Sultan über die Donau (*Tuna*) retten und
gelangte in die Hauptstadt (*taxt*). Danach kam Qantamur 15 ihm auf den Fer-
sen bis nach Baxča-Saraj, er umzingelte sie von vier Seiten und belagerte sie.
Bis zum Ende des Monats machte er sie so schwach (*zabun*), daß ihnen keine
Kraft mehr blieb, weder zu entfliehen noch zu kämpfen. Wenn er (Qantamur)
es noch zehn Tage fortgesetzt hätte, so hätten sie sich ergeben. Sie hatten weder
Lebensmittel für sich, noch Heu für ihre Pferde. Die verfluchten Noghaier
229/v verwüsteten die Gegend von allen vier Seiten, zertrümmerten die Häuser
und verheerten die Umgebung, 20 Schaf und Vieh (*davar*) verschleppten sie
und alle Pferde ließ man den Kriegsleuten aufessen. Sie richteten viel Böses an;
das wir weder aufzählen noch erzählen können (es wäre kaum möglich, alles
zu erzählen). Doch sandte Gott Licht, es kamen 12 000 Kosaken (hier steht:
haj) aus Korel, der Chan und das Kriegsvolk hatten keine Kunde (*xabar*), nur
der (Qalgha) Sultan wußte davon, er schickte heimlich einen Mann (zu ihnen).
Als sie ankamen, 25 ließen sie sich ins Gefecht mit den Noghaiern ein, sie kon-
solidierten die Lage des Chans und des (Qalgha) Sultans bis zu einem gewissen
Grade, sie bereiteten dem Kampf ein Ende. Viele Krieger (*asker*) blieben auf
dem Feld. Qantamur floh, er kam nach Kaffa mit seinen Noghaiern und mit
seinen Leuten (*xalq*), mit 1000 oder 500 Jurten (*odov*) und Gespann, Pferden
und Kamelen, Büffeln und Schafen, mit Frauen und Kindern, mit Sklaven
und Dienern und zog in Kaffa ein. Sie kamen und füllten 30 Kaffa, die Häuser, die Burggelände, die verheerten Vororte, die Hesar Peč 230/r Burgwälle
(*qandaq*), sie füllten alles am 22. Mai, dem Donnerstag der Himmelfahrt.
Und nach alldem flüchteten alle Armenier und Türken aus Toprakkala in die
Zitadelle, kein Mensch blieb draußen. Man dachte: vielleicht werden sie heute
kommen und uns überfallen, doch sie irrten sich, sie kamen nicht, 35 sie feierten
ihr Bajramfest, und dann kamen sie. Als sie ankamen, da zertrümmerten sie
viele Häuser und verheerten viele Dörfer, Schafe und Vieh (*davar*), außerdem
schleppten sie Stiere (*baqr*), Ochsen und Büffel mit; die Besitzer gingen (den
Tieren) weinend nach, einige fanden die Hälfte (von ihnen) vor, einige fanden
keine, und weinend kamen sie zurück. Verflucht sei sein Name und auch er
selber, Mehmed 40 Pascha, der der Haupt der Stadt war, und andere verfluchte (*bayi*) Großherren, sie alle kamen und verübten viel Unheil, sie ließen
230/v Graben (*qandaq*) graben; einer (sagte): in zehn Tagen, ein anderer, in
fünfzehn Tagen wird man den Chan herbeibrigen. Soviel Lüge schwatzte man,
einige (sagten), man wird ihn zu Lande bringen, manche (sagten) zu Meer;
es kamen falsche Zeugen, man feuerte Kanonen (*top*) ab, man setzte Fahnen

XII

(*bajraq*) auf, **45** Herolde (*tellal*) verkündeten, daß der Chan angekommen sei. Die falschen Gerüchte nahmen kein Ende. Der Chan (Mehmed Kerej) und (Šahin Kerej Qalgha) Sultan umzingelten mit vielen Kriegern, **215** mit den 12 000 Kosaken (*urus*) die Stadt, es entstand ein Gefecht. (Sie verlautbarten:) Kommt heraus, und bringt euren Chan, damit wir uns treffen. (Die Burgleute) verschlossen das Mauerwerk und kamen nicht heraus, jene feuerten Kanonen (*top*) und Gewehre (*tuvak*) ab, (aber) auch (die Gegner) schossen auf sie los. Sie verschleppten Schaf und Vieh (*davar*), **5** zertrümmerten die Häuser der Stadt, von Toprakkala; wo sie nur etwas fanden, nahmen sie es, sie stürzten die Mauer ein, gruben den Boden auf, drei Kirchen öffneten sie (mit Gewalt), zertraten, verheerten alles, **231/r** Kronleuchter und Weihrauchfässer nahmen sie mit, Eisengegenstände und Vorhänge nahmen sie, Bücher und Bibeln erbeuteten sie, was sie nur vorfanden, nahmen sie, und wo sie nichts fanden, da zertrümmerten und vernichteten sie alles, **10** sie nahmen das Eisen aus den Scheiben in den Kirchen und in den Häusern. Danach drangen sie in die Klöster ein, die Türe sprengten sie, den heiligen Tisch zerhieben sie. Sie drangen in die Mühlen ein, nahmen die Mühlenräder und die Eisenbestandteile, sie richteten viel Übel im Lande an, (und all dies) wegen unserer Sünden. Einen Monat, anderthalb Monate war die Stadt verschlossen, Kauf und Verkauf **15** hörte auf, Brot und Almosen blieben aus, es gab kein Heu und die Wasserversorgung ist abgebrochen. Die Tiere brüllten, die Leute seufzten, die Frauen weinten, die Kinder jammerten. Für zwei Gold (pro Qantar?) kaufte man Weizen von Schiffen. Wer was hatte, der aß, wer nichts hatte, jammerte und flehte zu Gott. Tag und Nacht, Armenier und Türken, Große und Kleine, alle kamen zur Zitadelle, **231/v 20** und man sagte, diese Nacht oder die nächste wird er (ihn) vernichten, man schrie und heulte, bis der Kampf doch ein Ende nahm. Der Chan (Džanibek Kerej) und (Devlet Kerej Qalgha) Sultan kamen mit 43 Galeeren (*qadīrya*). Als er ankam, wurde jener (Šahin Kerej Qalgha Sultan) vernichtet und floh nach Arabat, er begab sich in die Burg mit den 12000 Kosaken (hier: *haj*). Und jener (Džanibek Kerej) ging und setzte sich am 12. August auf den Thron. **25** Die Worte des verfluchten Noghaiers verwirklichten sich, der Chan gab Befehl, den Großherrn Azamat zu töten. Kaum kamen Qantamur und Šahsuvar mit einigen (Gefolgsleuten) am 24. August, am Sonntag der Heiligen Anna, herbei, enthauptete man den Mustafa Mirza mit einem seiner Gefolgsmänner (*nogar*). Das Haupt des Mirza nahmen sie mit, den Körper begruben sie an Ort und Stelle. **30** Xīdīr ist aus dem Hause entflohen, Bučana fand man zu Hause zur Kerzenzündung, es waren vier Männer (beisammen), zwei entflohen, den Mirza und den Gefolgsmann (*nogar*) töteten sie auf der Stelle.

232/r Und danach lebten Šahin Kerej und der Chan in Korel, bei dem Chan der Noghaier. Nach Verlauf eines Jahres kamen sie gegen die Krim **35** mit 40 000 Kosaken (hier: *haj*) und Noghaiern, Schmierköpfen (*majlībaš*) und

Lagerrüstung (*tabur*), kehrten aber beschämt zurück. Es war Gottes Fügung,
daß ihr Lager (*tabur*) von innen vertilgt wurde, jene kamen an, metzelten
10 000 Leute nieder, oder etwas weniger, die gebliebenen (*bayi*) kehrten um
und gingen von dannen.

40 1629 kamen die Kosaken (*urus*) einen Weg von zwei Tagen und
überfielen Qara-Su, Čarsu-Bazar, steckten die Häuser in Brand und verheerten
sie, einige Leute nahmen sie gefangen, andere metzelten sie nieder, danach
fielen sie Mangup an, drangen (in die Stadt) ein, nahmen Habe und Kleinod
(*mal u xazna*), dann gingen sie auf Sughda los, im Bezirk der Taten richteten
sie viele Verheerungen an, **45** um nur einiges zu erwähnen. Es waren schwere
Zeiten. **232/v** Und am 3. Juli bestürmten sie Otuz, **216** nahmen die Leute
gefangen, Männer und Frauen. Die Braut von Herrn Musli fiel in ihre Hände,
er hatte 1000 Gulden für sie zu zahlen, von den anderen (*bayi*) nicht zu sprechen, die in Gefangenschaft fielen und gefangen blieben, einige wurden losgekauft, andere nicht.

Und nach all diesen (Ereignissen) kamen 50 Boote (*šajxa*) von Fenerlïr
5 mit Lastbooten (?*sandïxt*) und fielen Gozlev (Gözleve) an und steckten die
Stadt in Brand. Sie brannten Čarsu Bazar nieder, und verheerten es. In vielen
Orten machten sie Gefangene und Beute, dann gingen sie davon. Danach über-
fielen sie die Stadt Akkermann und verheerten sie, den ganzen (*butun*) Sommer
richteten sie viele Verheerungen an. Zuerst stürmten sie Gazandib, acht kleinere
Dörfer steckten sie in Brand und **10** verwüsteten sie. Danach raffte sich der
(Qalgha) Sultan (Dolvat Kerej) mit vielem Kriegsvolk (*asker*) auf und führte
eine Razzia (*sefer*) gegen Korel, mußte aber ohne Erfolg zurückkehren. Viele
Leute brachten sie um, viele fielen in Gefangenschaft. 7000 ? brachten.
Es gäbe noch vieles, unzähliges, wer könnte (all dies) erzählen. Devlet Kerej
(*Dolvatkere*) Sultan ist entkommen, Qantamur **233/r 15** aber kam nicht. Salmaša
kam in die Krim, dann ging er weg, auch die Noghaier rief man zurück aus
diesem Land (*jurt*), Gülum bij kam und setzte sich an Qantamurs Platz.

1629, im Monat Dezember, kam eine Wärme, die Pflanzen lebten wieder
auf, im Januar schwollen und blühten sie auf, der Flieder **20** öffnete wieder
seine Knospen. Das war Gottes Fügung, wer konnte es wissen.

1630 nahm der verfluchte Hasan Agha Steuer (*xaraǰ*) in Kaffa ein,
er peinigte das Volk und die Geistlichen: 'schreibt das Volk von Kaffa zusammen und ihr Einkommen, die Bewohner von (Eski?) Krim **25** und die Dorf-
bewohner', alle ließ er in die Steuerbücher (*defter*) eintragen. Er ging in den
Bezirk der Taten, machte viel Aufruhr, 4—5jährige Knaben nahm er als steuer-
pflichtig (*xaraǰ*), von den (ehemaligen Glaubens-?) Verweigernden nahm er
Steuer (*xaraǰ*).

Der Pascha von Kaffa und der katholische Bischof verschieden am selben
Tage, den Bischof beerdigte man, den Leichnam des Pascha trug man nach
Istambul, **30** im Monat August, in der Fastenwoche der Gottgebärerin.

XII

Im September kam ein (anderer) Pascha, er war ein gutmütiger Mensch, ein Freund der Stadt. Fünf Monate bekleidete er sein Amt, man setzte ihn am 29. Januar ab, da ging er zum Chan. Heute, am Samstag bewarf man den Hasan Agha mit Steinen, er floh und entkam nur mit Mühe und Not, Gott nahm Rache **35** für die 3—4jährige Knaben.

Als wir ins Jahr 1631 eintraten, geschah auch ein anderes wundersames Ereignis: 33 Männer von den Dienern des abgesetzten (*manzul*) Paschas entschlüpften am hellichten Tage aus dem Gefängnis (*haps*), es gelang ihnen, ein Schiff zu besteigen, und sie entfernten sich, die Leute in der Stadt blieben verblüfft. Zwei Schiffe verfolgten sie, um sie zu erwischen, **40** aber ohne Erfolg kehrten sie zurück; es entstand ein Gefecht, einige starben, andere sind verletzt (*jaralï*) worden. Dann verfolgte sie der Pascha mit einer Galeere (*qadïrya*), konnte sie aber nicht erreichen, kehrte also zurück und trieb eine Sondersteuer (*ïspenje*) von der Stadt ein. Die Einwohner petitionierten, der Chan petitionierte (*arz*), daß er der Vorstand der Stadt bleibe, es wurde aber nicht so. Oh weh, laßt uns aus tausend Kehlen klagen (tausendmal oh weh!), daß in der Stadt kein gerechter Mensch lebte, er verließ die Stadt und ging weg. **45** Es kam ein verfluchter Pascha an seine Stelle, ein böser und ruchloser, ein Verschuldeter; das alles geschah wegen unserer Sünden. Kein Geistlicher, kein Laie ist verschont worden, immer wieder verlangte er neuen Charadsch; fungiert entweder für Pascha, oder Gouverneur (*amildar*), **217** oder Bevollmächtigter (*nazir*), was gesagt wird, was gemacht wird, geschieht durch ihn. wenn nur Gott dafür Rache nehmen wollte!

233/v 1628, am 20 April, am Sonntag, griffen die Kosaken (*urus*) von Kašot Kaffa, das Stadtviertel (*mahala*) der Kirche der Himmelfahrt an. Der Verfluchte, **5** der Sohn Tuman Beys, kam, machte Gefangene, einige raubte er aus, andere metzelte er nieder und richtete viel anderes Übel an. Sie nahmen Elemšahbegs Frau, nahmen Xubat, schleppten sie weg und noch einige andere. Den Preis setzten sie auf 500 Goldstücke fest, bis man aber (verspätet?) das Gold brachte, töteten sie alle. Man brachte den Leichnam der Frau von Elemšahbeg, **10** die Körper einiger anderer Christen blieben dort. Xubat ist mit Not losgekauft worden; es erhob sich eine große Trauer in der Stadt, als man die Leichname (*laš*) brachte, vor dem Georgischen Tor (*Guři qabaq*) weinten und jammerten Armenier und Türken gleicherweise. Da die Kosaken (*urus*) nur bis zu Teke kamen, gelobt sei Gott, ist unser Stadtviertel verschont geblieben. Vom Dach (*čardaq*) des Zekerja (Zacharias) **15** sind zwei Gewehre abgefeuert worden; jene (die Kosaken) sahen es, kehrten um und gingen weg. und wir sind befreit worden.

1631 schickte der Patriarch von Istambul einen Bischof zu uns zur Eintreibung der Kirchengebühren wegen der erlaubten und unerlaubten Ehen. Am Sonntag des Heiligen Jakob (18. Dezember) verlasen der Vater der Kirche des H. Sargis die Messe zelebrierende **20** Paronter Ter Andreas und der Diakon (*sarkavag*) Galust einen Brief, wir Priester waren alle zufrieden, sie bekannten uns ihre Sünden. Man kam mit Xodža Mīsir, zuvor gingen sie in die Kirche, und zwar die Johannes des Täufers, der Priester Ter Grigor, mit dem Beinamen Xrmadži (Dattelverkäufer).

25 Paronter Xačatur sandte eine Beschuldigung und Bann aus dem Kloster, dem Xodža Mīsir. Am 5. Januar, zur Lampenzündung brachte man den Bann. Am 16. Januar, Montag, ist in die Kirche der Heiligen Erzengel eine Versammlung der Priester und des Volkes einberufen worden und Paronter Andreas leitete eine Untersuchung (Prüfung) ein. Dem Priester Ter Maghake (Malakias) nahm man den Philon, 30 aus dem Grunde, daß er auf eigene Faust vorging, er brachte einen Pfarrer (*kahana*) nach Qara-Su und ließ ihn weihen, man brachte ihn herbei, und man warf ihn hinaus, deshalb entstand ein Lärm, auch dem Neugeweihten nahm man den Philon weg. (Auch) Nerses Abegha nahm man den Philon ab. Xodža Markare, Xodža Lačin, Lusbaron, Ter Minas gingen, 35 brachten den Paronter zur Stelle und stifteten Versöhnung.

234/r 1629, am Freitag des Warager Kreuzes, verschied Paronter Thoros in Gott. 15 Tage danach verschied auch der Priester (*kahana*) Ter Markare, er war ein Gastpfarrer (*musafir*), ein Wanderprediger (*γarib*) ohne Oberhaupt: es gab weder einen Bischof noch einen 40 Wardapet, die Beerdigung ist von Geistlichen (*kahana*) bewerkstelligt worden. Es kam Xačatur Wardapet mit dem lichtstrahlenden Mirrha von Etschmiadzin, er war ein neugeweihter Legat von Ter Movses Katholikos. Zwei Schüler hatte er, einen Einsiedler (*čignawor*) und einen Subdiakon (*kisasarkavag*).

45 1630, im Juni, kam unser Ter Xačatur Wardapet aus Polen. An jenem Samstag 218 kamen die zwei Wardapets zusammen, und es freuten sich Priester und Volk. Der Legat übernachtete in der Stadt, unser Wardapet suchte Unterkunft in seinem Kloster, der Übelverhindernden Gottgebärerin (*Čarxapan Astuacacin*), einige heißen ihn Beschützer (Sponsor) und andere *Besdegirman*.

5 Der Legat hat sein Urteil über die Priester gefällt, 4—5 Priester schloß er von der Messelesung aus, er nahm Strafgelder, Gold, Bücher, Kreuz, Becher im allgemeinen, das eine freiwillig, das andere wider Willen, auch das Volk bestrafte er, den Wardan, den Harutiwn und noch einige andere. Jede Kirche der Stadt besuchte er, was man gab, nahm er an, man gab einen Priesterstab, 10 man gab ihm Menologiebücher (*Hajsmawurkʻ*).

Ter Xačatur, der neu geweihte Bischof (*paronter*) kam im Juli aus Etschmiadzin, zwei Wardapete, ein Hajrapet kamen zusammen in die Kirche Heiligen (Gregors, des) Erleuchters. Alle drei empfing Ter Xačatur, den Legat mit Ehrfurcht, dem Paronter wusch er die Füße und erwies ihm Ehre. Der Legat 15 setzte den Paronter (in sein Amt) ein und den Ter Mekertič schickte er nach Gözleve, Baxča-Saraj, Qara-Su, in die Dörfer der ganzen Halbinsel Krim, sie gingen, übten ihre Legatenmission aus und empfingen (die Gaben).

XII

(Er) war ein Mann der gerne herumging, manchmal sagte er: «ich gehe nach Kaffa», manchmal: «ich gehe nach unserem Toprakkala» ... oder er sagte: «ich gehe», oder er sagte: **20** «ich gehe nicht, bringt mir das Geld». Wir waren gebunden, blieben, es gab keine Möglichkeit, das Geld zu sammeln. Dann wieder raffte er sich auf, und ging selber, übte seine Legatenaufgabe selber aus, dann kam er zurück und blieb in Qara-Su, er sandte den Kaffanensern Nachricht: «kommt und nehmt mich mit oder schickt mir Mirrha».

234/v Wir sandten die Mirrha, dann erboste er sich gegen uns Kaffanenser. **25** Dann gingen die Wohlhabenden zu ihm, und wir Priester gingen ähnlicherweise hin, da freute er sich, von drei Kirchen verlangte er 100 Gurusch, von zwei Kirchen nahm er 30 Gurusch, von unserer Kirche des Heiligen Thoros nahm er 30 Gurusch, dann schüttete er Mirrha in Qara-Su. Nach Aghuhack begab er sich am zweiten Donnerstag nach Balïqlï, um ein Schiff zu besteigen, **30** dort gab es keins, deshalb ging er nach Gezlov (Gözleve), auch dort gab es keins, also kehrte er zurück und ging nach Kaffa, Xodža Mïsïr bereitete für ihn ein Schiff, Gott segne ihn, er hielt sich ein Jahr, eine Zeit in Kaffa, Gezlov, Qara-Su und anderen Ortschaften auf, am meisten aber kam er in unsere Stadt.

1631, heute ist Samstag, der 30. April, **35** da kam er dieselbe Stunde, bestieg das Schiff und fuhr davon, Gott beschere ihm gute Reise.

Priester (*kahana*) Nerses verschied in Gott am 10. April, am Sonntag des heiligen Ostern, die Fackel des Heiligen Georgs (Kirche) erlosch. Dies versetzte uns in Kummer, er war ein guter Ordensbruder, er war unser Seelenbruder, Gott **40** erleuchte seine Seele und stelle ihn in denselben Rang und dieselbe Würde, wie die 24 Priester, Amen.

Und heute ereilte uns wieder eine große Trauer, (uns beide) Geistliche und Volk, da die Fackel unseres Landes erlosch, der Stolz der Christen ist verschwunden, das Auge Kaffas verdunkelte sich; **45** da unser Pastor verschied, ist er zum Haupt der Herde erhoben worden. Ter Xačatur Wardapet verschied heute aus dieser Welt, **219** er ging hinauf in den Himmel, am ersten Tag des Mai, am Sonntag. Wegen der Dürre haben wir viel gebetet (viele Kniefälle gemacht). Da waren 21 Priester (*kahana*), zwei auf Besuch (*musafir*), einer aus Gözleve, der andere aus Baberd, der eine war Mönch (*abeγa*), der andere dieser Wardapet seeligen Andenkens. **5** Wir haben eine Prozession veranstaltet, der Wardapet machte einen Schritt, dann einen zweiten, aber weiter ging es nicht, er ging und legte sich nieder, seine Zunge wurde gelähmt, ... wir hielten eine Messe, er empfahl seine Seele Gott. Es kam Xačatur Paronter aus (der Stadt) Krim, er kam heute zur Beerdigung des Pastors der Herde an. Betet mit, daß Gott seine Seele erleuchte. **10** Bereite Gott ihm denselben Stand, und dieselbe Krone wie den 24 Wardapeten. Amen. Geistlicher und Laien verkündet Klage aus tausend Kehlen. Er war ein guter Mensch und ein vollkommener Wardapet, sein Fehler (seine Sünde — *xalat*) war, daß er ein Liebhaber des

2*

XII

Weins und ein Trinker war, deshalb war er unbeliebt bei dem Volk, und man
hat ihm keine Ehre erwiesen.

235/r 15 Am 5. Juli Sonntagmorgen erboste sich Gott gegen die Stadt
Qara-Su wegen unserer Sünden. Es kam ein Regen, es kam ein Donnerwetter,
ein Blitzen, es kam eine Überschwemmung über die ganze Stadt, zertrümmerte
die Häuser, Kaufläden, die Brücken, die Obstgärten (*baxča*), die Villen (*saraj*),
die Dächer (*čardaq*), die Bäume und Laubkronen, die Lederwerkstätten (*tabaq
xana*) und **20** die Färberwerkstätten (*bojaxana*), die Freiküchen (*ašči*) und die
Kalbsfußladen (*pačaǰi*), die Leinwandläden (*bezzaz*) und die Seidenstoff-
händlerein (*xazaz*), die Brot- unf Fleischläden (*qasab*), die Bozastuben (*bozaǰi*)
und die Weinstuben (*mejxanaǰi*), alles zertrümmerte und verheerte die Überschwemmung und der Wasserstrom (*sel*). Tausend oder fünfhundert oder
noch mehr Leute ertranken, Armenier und Türken, Bewohner von Kaffa und
Qara-Su, Händler (*bazirgan*) und Reisende (*musafir*), **25** die Heimatlosen
(*ɣarib*), die Wanderer, die Bummler (Herrenlosen). Einigen riß der Flut die
Frau mit, der Mann blieb (am Leben), von anderen (Familien) nahm er den
Mann weg und die Frau blieb allein. Von einigen riß er Haus und Habe, Mann
und Frau, Kind und Lebensmittel riß alles mit und stürmte davon. Von einigen
(Familien) nahm er den Mann und zwei Söhne mit, bei anderen die Frau mit
drei oder vier Kindern. Es ähnelte der Sündflut Noahs. **30** Der Strom riß
die große Brücke des Minas Wardapet und Sultans ab, fegte Steine und
Holzblöcke weg, Nägel und Eisenbestandteile, so daß nicht einmal die Stelle
sichtbar blieb. Er fegte einen Teil (*paj*) der drei Teile der Stadt weg. Zaunwerk
(*čatan*) und die Stadtmauer stürzten ein, zwei Bäder gingen zugrunde, die Vor-
hallen (*ǰamekan*) sind vertilgt, 2 Moschees vernichtet worden, die Moscheeschule
(*medrese*) ist eingestürzt und **35** die Schüler (*soxta*) wurden totgeschlagen.
Und es sind viele andere wunderbare Ereignisse geschehen, unsere dem
Heiligen Auxentius gewidmete armenische Kirche ist verschont geblieben. Von
den nebenanstehenden Häusern sind einige eingestürzt, andere blieben unver-
sehrt. Die Wände einiger Häuser sind eingestürzt, der Dachboden anderer ist
eingesunken, von einigen nahm der Strom die Hälfte mit, die andere Hälfte
blieb, die Wasserleitungskanäle (*arx*) und Mühlen wurden vernichtet. Viele
Wunder geschahen. **40** Im Monat Juli kam viel Regen. In unserer Stadt Kaffa
verminderte sich das Wasser, gewiß werden wir Not leiden.

Die Kriegstruppen (*asker*), Tataren und Türken, begaben sich nach
Persien (*Qïzïlbaš*) (1631), im Dezember zogen die Spahis ab, die Tataren blieben.
235/v Devlet Kerej (*Dolvatkerej* Qalgha) Sultan ist in Gott verschieden, der
Bruder des Chans, der Nur ed-Din (*Noradin*) Sultan, **220** der Sohn des Salamat
Kerej Chan, setzte sich als *Qaghïlgha* an seine Stelle. Der Sohn des Chans, (Mu-
barek Kerej) Sultan führte im Monat Januar einen Feldzug (*sefer*) gegen Korel.

1632 gab es einen schweren Winter. Was die Stadt an Geld gehabt hätte,
ist vernichtet worden, Kauf und Verkauf haben aufgehört, der Chan **5** kündete

Frohnarbeit (*jasaɣ*) an, es gab keine Fuhrwerke (*araba*), man geriet in die Klemme. Dieses Jahr war ein Schaltjahr, in allen Dingen herrschte Mangel. Seit Sommer gab es kein Viehfutter. Auch der Winter blieb solcher Art: die Tiere vermagerten, auch das Geflügel alles, die Trappen (*duvadaq*) ließen sich mit (bloßer) Hand fangen, sie kamen hinein in die Dörfer und Städte. 10 Von den Feldtruppen (*seferli*) ist die Hälfte niedergemetzelt worden, die andere Hälfte kehrte mit Mühe und Not heim.

Am 15. Februar (1633) brach in Kaffa eine Feuersbrunst aus, vier-fünf Kaufläden sind abgebrannt, doch kaum gekommen, löschte man sie. Am Donnerstag am frühen Morgen, kamen zwei Schiffe des Abaza (Pascha). Sie brachten den gefallenen Sohn des Ali Pascha, man brachte (die Leiche) mit Tränen und Klagen vom Schiff, man führte sie von hinten in die Stadt. 15 Ja, Gott hat sich erzürnt, und jene Nacht erhob sich ein Wind, ein Sturm (*hurtuna*), die Mühlen sind losgerissen worden, von der Stadtmauer brach ein Stück herunter und stürzte auf drei Häuser nieder, viel Außergewöhnliches geschah, Ahmad Sofi, sagte man, ist mit Haus und Kegel, mit Sohn und Tochter zusammen, völlig vernichtet worden.

Am 17. Februar, am Freitag, ist das Volk zusammengerufen worden, 20 die Leute versammelten sich und wälzten die Steine weg, sechs Leichen entdeckte man, zwei Männer und Frauen, und noch zwei Kinder fanden den Tod unter den Steinen und Balken, und noch viele (andere) Menschen fielen dem Sturm zum Opfer. Der Mann Ahmad Sofi war ein Wucherer und hatte eine von Pferden getriebene Mühle; das Haus ist eingestürzt, die Mühle vernichtet worden, die Pfänder, die er aufbewahrte, blieben (verschont) unter den Trümmern, 25 einige Leute fanden (ihren Pfandgegenstand) und nahmen ihn, andere fanden nichts und blieben in Not.

In Istanbul geschahen viele Widerwärtigkeiten, den großen, gefürchteten Xosrow Pascha hat man hingerichtet, vor dem jeder vor Furcht wie Espenlaub zitterte. Wir Brüder sind in böse Zeiten geraten, Gott schütze uns vor den Versuchungen . . .30 . . . 236/r und viele andere Großherren sind getötet worden. Die Spahis metzelte man nieder, einige mit Dolch und Schwert, andere wieder sind erwürgt worden, manche ins Meer geworfen, und wieder andere waren geflüchtet. Wo man 5 Leute beisammen vorfand, wenn sich 10 Leute an derselben Stelle befanden, tötete man sie bei Tag und bei Nacht in ihrem Hause. 50—100 Häuser sind in Brand gesteckt worden, 35 viele Frauen wurden Witwen, viele Söhne ihres Vaters beraubt. Früher hat Abaza Pascha die Janitscharen getötet, jetzt tötete Murad die Spahis.

Džanibek Kerej (*Džanbekerej*) gab im Juni den Befehl, ein Bajram mit Hammelopfer zu veranstalten.

40 Der *Qaghilgha* Sultan (Azamat) kam, er ging zur Audienz zum Chan, dann begannen sie sich eine Weile zu streiten, dann begaben sie sich in (die Stadt) Anapa. Der Chan ging davon, der (Qalgha) Sultan blieb dort, es war

XII

Freitag, Segbans (*sejmen*) kamen (und sagten:), wir machen eine Feier (*šenlik*) und feuerten die Flinten (*tvak*) ab. Ein Verfluchter schoß mit der Flinte dem (Qalgha) Sultan in den Körper (*gošt*), das Blut füllte seinen Schoß **45** und auf der Stelle gab er seine Seele dem Schöpfer zurück. Er war ein gerechter (Qalgha) Sultan und gutgesinnt, es ist ein Jammer und schade um ihn, da es (nur) **5** Monate dauerte, daß er das Amt des *Qaghïlgha* bekleidete. **221** Er hatte zwei Brüder, jene ergriffen die Flucht Mehemet Kerej ist an seine (Azamats) Stelle für Sultan eingesetzt worden. Im Monat Juli kamen Schiffe aus Azaq, sie brachten Gesandte (*elči*) des Šahin Kerej, zwei Personen: der eine war ein Kaffanenser, der andere ein Mirza, sie hatten viel Schätze (*xazina*) mit, die sie dem Herrscher brachten. **5** Unsere Spahis von Kaffa versammelten sich, verhafteten die zwei Gesandten (*elči*) setzten sie in Haft (*haps*) in den Turm (*qula*) und machten Anstalten, in das Schiff einzudringen, um sich die Schätze (*xazna*) anzueignen. Jene waren alle Janitscharen und leisteten Widerstand, so kam es zu einem Gefecht. Sie konnten nicht ins Schiff eindringen und kehrten ohne Erfolg zurück. Die Janitscharen versammelten sich, die Spahis versammelten sich, sie ließen sich in einen Kampf ein, **10** die Tore der Burg wurden geschlossen. Nach zwei Tagen ist der Wunsch der Janitscharen erfüllt worden, die Gesandten wurden aus der Burg gewiesen, ins Schiff geführt und mit ihrem Schatze weggeschickt.

236/v Und hernach wurde ein Einkommensteuer an die Kaffanenser bemessen, die man *hasïl xarj* nennt, sowohl die Steuer wie ihre Benennung ist verhaßt, pro Kopf je 3 Goldstücke. **15** Die Christen weinten, jammerten und sagten: «wir haben keine Möglichkeit diese (Summe) zu bezahlen, die Vorschrift lautet auf 2 Gulden, also nehmt nur zwei, wenn nicht, dann besteigen wir ein Schiff und gehen zum König (zum türkischen Sultan), (also) erlaube es uns». Es gab einen Richter aus (dem Viertel?) Erdwall, dessen Name Musaoghli war oder wohl Sutčioghli (Sohn des Milchhändlers), dieser Verfluchte war der Richter, er gab einen Befehl nicht für 2, sondern für **20** 3 (Gulden), da er Bestechungsgeld erwartete, die Christen blieben also in ihrer mißlichen Lage. Sie sahen, daß es nicht ging, also schickten sie jemanden zur Pforte. Als unser Mann wegging, da gab ein frommer christlicher Ri(chter) den Befehl aus, es sollten 2 Goldstücke verlangt werden. Aber leider nahm man es nicht an, viele Christen beschwerten sich, **25** der Pascha der Stadt ist abgesetzt (*manzul*) worden. Es kam ein Vertreter (*kehja*) des neuen Paschas, er stand auf unserer Seite, (aber) der verfluchte Qadi nahm den Befehl nicht an. Da schickten wir wieder jemanden, (doch) wir wissen (noch) nicht, wie es sein wird. Und es geschah wieder etwas Seltsames: Es kamen 16 Galeeren (*qadïrya*) in Kaffa an und man sagte, daß 7 Boote (*qajïq*) an der Seite von Kerč sind. Diese 7 Boote (*qajïq*) **30** richteten viele Verheerungen an, jetzt kamen die 16 Galeeren (*qadïrya*) mit vielen Männern und gingen gegen sie los, aber sie konnten die leichten Boote (*sandal-qajïq*) nicht einholen. Sie töteten einander und alle fielen ins

XII

Meer. Im Meer gab es eine Seichte (Sandbank), alle blieben darin. Von 30 Männern kamen kaum 10 zurück, von 20 kaum 5, **35** der Rest (*bayi*) kehrte ohne Erfolg und beschämt zurück. Zwei Tage hielten sie noch aus, dann entfernten sie sich, sie sind vertrieben worden. Und was war der Gewinn davon? Außer (*bašqa*) dem Verlust an Ausrüstung 7 Karren Männer kamen nackt, barfuß, sie sind kaum entkommen. Sie waren nicht so viel, daß man auf sie geachtet hätte; sie (die Sieger) sind gegangen, (und) sie (die Besiegten) sind gekommen.

237/r 1637 sind die zwei Brüder des Inajet Kerej **40** von den Noghaiern, d. h. von Qantemir, getötet worden, (kaum) ein Jahr war es, daß Ibrahim Pascha, genannt Bičkidži, gekommen war, da tötete ihn der (Qalgha) Sultan. Im Verlauf eines Jahres starben sie, der betrauernswerte Inajet Kerej blieb. Er ging zum König (zum türkischen Sultan), der Herrscher schickte Bahadir (*Bader*) Kerej, ihn (Inajet Kerej) aber ließ er töten.

45 Durch Gottes Fügung kaufte ich das Haus des Restakes und gab es der Edirmelik. **222** Wir veranstalteten eine Hochzeit, (die Vermählten) sind verheiratet worden, am ersten Tage des Oktobers, am Montag des Warager Kreuzes.

1645 ging ich nach Baxča Saraj, und fünf Monate übte ich dort das Amt des Geistlichen aus. Das Jahres-Zodiakzeichen war Bock, **5** Ostern fiel auf den 6. April.

1649 ging ich im August nach Istanbul, im November kam ich (zurück), Ostern fiel auf den 25. April.

238/r Es war für Inajet Kerej Chan ein kummervolles Geschick (*hajiw*), das ihn traf. Die Erde erzitterte und das Land erbebte vor Leiden, man dichtete Klagelieder, weil **10** man eines so guten Herrschers beraubt worden war, eines gerechten (*adil*) Sultans, der «wie die Blumen zur Fühlingszeit aufblühten, und (bald wieder) vor den Augen der Menschen verschwanden».

1637, im Monat Mai, ist im Lande ein sehr trauriges Ereignis geschehen. Jetzt erwachte Bahadir (*Batïr*) Kerej Chan aus dem Traum und schwor ihnen (den Noghaiern) Blutrache, er tötete Salmaša Mirza **15** und andere verfluchte (*bayi*) Mirzas gleichwohl, ob kleine oder große, bis zum Wickelkind. Er rottete die Mansur-Sippe aus. Der gottlose Oraq Mirza trug auch Blutschuld, einige sagen, daß er für die Häupter von 18 Königssöhnen und Nachkommen verantwortlich ist, jetzt ist (seinem Leben) ein Ende bereitet worden, der Böse ist böse zugrundegegangen.

20 1639, am 3. Mai, rafften Noghaier, Čaghataier und Tataren sich auf und verließen die Krim, die drei gingen im gegenseitigen Einverständnis, dann hielten sie Rat (*kengäš*), der eine ging nach Hadži Tarchan, der andere nach Tscherkessien und der dritte kehrte um und kam zurück in die Krim.

1640, am Jahresanfang, begab sich Sultan Murad **25** zu Gott, da er ein gerechter Herrscher war und mächtig im Kriege, rief (sein Tod) im ganzen

XII

Lande große Trauer hervor. Als Herrscher ist an seiner statt sein Bruder
Sultan Ibrahim eingesetzt worden. So ist es.

Am 9. März, am Sonntag des Verwalters auf Montag früh, kam ein Erdbeben, das das Land erschütterte, und alle sind von Schrecken erfaßt worden.

238/v 30 Dies ist eine Geheimschrift (Monogramm), der Weise wird es
erkennen, der Unwissende wird erstaunen; Bruder erinnere dich meiner, des
Sünders.

Xačatur erec — Ter Philippos Katholikos — Kirakos — **35** Martiros
— Vardan, Nikoghos — Simeon.

Es war 1640, viele Krieger kamen nach Kaffa, mit dem Schiff, auf dem
Meer, mit Galeeren (*qadīrya*), mit Schiffen, mit Booten (*qajïq*), **40** aus dem
Sandschak Kastamuni, 900 *timari* Spahis, stellten 50—60 Zelte (*čadïr*) auf,
schlugen Lager vor der Burg (*qula*) Toprakkala auf. Dann requirierten sie
Pferde, beschlagnahmten Wagen (*araba*), und im Juni begaben sie sich nach
Azov (*Azaq*). Der Chan, der Pascha, und außerdem auch andere (*bayi*) Begler-
begs, die vornehmen Paschas, die gewichtigen Großherren, das Kriegsvolk von
Rumelien (*Urumeli asker*), die Truppen von der Moldau (*Boghdan*), **45** Tata-
ren, Noghaier, Čaghataier, Tscherkessen, es ist unmöglich sie alle aufzuzählen.
Die Feldtruppen der zwei Herrscher bestanden aus 72 Völkerschaften
(*millat*).

223 Sie begaben sich nach Azov (*Azaq*), richteten viel Meuterei an, sind
aber sehr getadelt worden, daß sie ohne Beute zurückkehrten. Azov konnten
sie nicht einnehmen, und so kehrten sie schimpflicherweise zurück. 40 000
Stoßtruppen fielen und auch noch andere. Wer könnte all das Unglück erzählen, das die Stadt Azov heimsuchte? Es herrschte eine große Not.

5 Man bohrte Minengänge (*layim*) aus der Burg in eine jede Richtung,
wo es ottomanische (*Osmanlï*) Truppen gab, öffnete man Gasse (*soqaq*) nach
Gasse. Die Sprengung eines jeden Minenganges (*layim*) schleuderte Tausende
von Seelen in den Himmel empor und es fielen ebensoviel Leichen (*leš*) herunter, einige Kopf nach unten und manche. . .

239/r 10 Sieben Monate kämpften sie, sie nahmen die Insel Kreta,
entweder ist dies wahr oder nicht.

Schändlicherweise zog die Höllenbrut der Großherren Širin und der
Mirzas, gegen den Chan, fünf Monate gab es eine Hölle im Lande, dann wurde
Frieden gestiftet.

15 Es kamen in unsere Stadt drei Wardapete, Sargis, Thoros, Arakel,
ein Legat, ein Abegha und ein geistlicher (*kahana*) Almosensammler. In unserem Lande herrschte (große) Not, Handel gab es keinen, die Chanen, die
Großherren Höllenbrut und das Volk zitterte, so sind wir zum letzten Elend
gekommen.

1646 war am 29. März Ostern **20** für uns Armenier, es herrschte schwere
Not, der Preis eines Viertels (Weizen) ist auf zwei Gurusch gestiegen, wer hat

XII

überhaupt Brot gesehen? Arme und Elende (*faqir fuqara*) waren in Not. Die Reichen überfielen ein Haus nach dem anderen, der Qadi, der Najib, wo sie nur Weizen aufspürten, nahmen sie ihn mit Gewalt weg. Wo es vier Viertel Weizen gab, gaben sie eins davon dem Eigentümer, und (das übrige) verteilten sie. Der Schiffsverkehr kam zum Stehen, die Warenzufuhr (*araba*) blieb aus, 25 die Stadt blieb verschlossen bis zur Mitte der großen Fastenzeit. Am 22. März kamen viele Fuhrwerke, so daß die Stadt gesättigt wurde, Gott sandte sie und bereitete sie, für das Volk ohne Lebensmittel und ohne Hoffnung, da wir weder *akn* noch *guman* hatten (als Wortspiel unübersetzbar). 23., heute ist Sonntag, es kamen zwei Wagenzüge mit Brot aus Qara-Su, so daß unsere Gegend gesättigt wurde. 30 Das Zodiakzeichen war Capricorn, Interkalation 22, Mondzahl 13, littera dominicalis 4, numerus aureus 8. Der Wezir, der nach Malta gegangen ist, ist im Gefecht getötet worden.

239/v Laßt uns zu unserem Land zurückkehren, d. h. in die Stadt Kaffa, die wir nördliche Gegend und Land der Hunnen nennen, in dem Milch und Honig fließt. 35 Es dauert aber schon sieben Jahre, daß Teuerung herrscht, jetzt hat Gott so verfügt, daß wir für die frühere Billigkeit bestraft (*qarar*) werden, Gott sei gelobt. Aber was können wir tun, Azov wurde unser Verhängnis, die Güter sollen dorthin gebracht werden. 5 Schiffe, 5 Barken (?) sind mit Proviant (*zaxira*) und allerlei anderen Gütern nach Azov gefahren. 40 Und danach kamen Janitscharen mit 6 Schiffen, manche Leute sagten es seien 500. 7 Schiffe Spahis erbitterten unsere Stadt. Sie verlangten 2000 Säcke (*čual*) und Körbe (*čatan*) und von Armeniern und Türken je 6 Gurusch Charadsch. Das Sammeln der Beute und das Verprügeln ist in 3—4 Tagen erledigt worden. Die vier Galeeren (*qadïrya*) und 13 Schiffe fuhren ab, und 500 Säcke (*čual*) 45 noch hernach. Am 16. August, am Sonntag der Heiligen Jungfrau (Mariä Himmelfahrt), 224 kam der Pascha von Trabzon mit 5—6 Schiffen mit vielen Soldaten (*asker*), alle Spahis kamen heraus aus der Burg (*qula*) und schlugen zahllose Zelte (*čadir*) auf.

1647 im Lande der Franken, das Malta genannt wird, ist es schon drei Jahre her, daß sie (die Malteser) mit den Hagariern (Ottomanen) kämpfen, jetzt 5 ist die Stadt Suta erobert worden.

Dem Chan ist ein Sohn geboren worden, die Tochter vermählte er mit Sultan Ibrahim, aus diesem Grunde sind am 12. Januar in allen Städten große Feiern (*donanma*) veranstaltet worden, so auch hier.

Der verfluchte Mufti hat gegen das Kloster Surb Nišan (vom Heiligen Kreuz) böse Pläne angezettelt, 10 er ging zu Islam Chan, belog ihn und sagte: «Herrscher, gib mir einen Platz, damit ich mich in deine Stadt Krim einsetze.» Des Herrschers Herz 240/r wurde verwirrt, er sagte: «Also soll es sein, wo du möchtest, das soll dir beschert werden.» Der Gottlose sagte: «Es gibt dort ein Kloster, unbewohnt, es gibt keinen Menschen darin.» Der andere erwiderte: «Wenn du es denkst, so gehe, und genieße es.»

XII

15 Oh weh, Schande (*keš*) auf dich, Gottloser und Sündiger, oh du böse Satansbrut, du hast den Herrscher (Islam Kerej Chan) belogen, daß es dort keinen Eigentümer gibt, davon haben die Christen keine Nachricht (*xabar*). Jener raffte sich auf und ging: «also ich gehe ins Kloster, ich werde eine Moschee daraus machen, ein Minaret (*minara*) werde ich erbauen». 20 Paronter Xačatur und Bischof Grigor waren ganz verwirrt, sie wußten nicht, was zu tun sei. Die Gläubigen versammelten sich aus der Stadt Krim, aus den Dörfern, Männer und Frauen, gelangten zum Tor des Klosters, sie gingen hinein und verriegelten das Tor. Als der Verfluchte kam, fand er keinen Eingang, also mußte er beschämt und unverrichteter Sache zurückkehren. Die Kaffanenser und die Bewohner von Qara-Su gingen zum Chan: 25 «Gib es (das Kloster) uns !» Viel Kleinod ging (auf Bestechung). Gott nehme Rache dafür.

1649 kam Aristakes Wardapet nach Kaffa, dann ging er zusammen mit Paronter Grigor nach Qara-Su, dort weihten sie einen Priester (*kahana*) und zwei Archidiakonen (*sarkavag*). Zum Fest der Geburt Christi fand die Weihe statt, sie blieben dort bis Aghuhackʻ. 30 Dann sollte er nach Gözleve gehen, nach Baxča-Saraj gehen, predigen und Belehrungen geben.

Es kam ein Gerücht aus Gözleve, daß die Mohammedaner mit der Erlaubnis des Chans Islam Kerej die Kirche wegnahmen. Die Gottlosen kamen, rissen die Kirche nieder, zerstörten sie, die Christen blieben erstarrt, am 16. März 35, Freitag, in der Woche der Marterung des Erleuchters, zum Eintritt (des Heiligen Gregors) in die Grube.

240/v Ostern fiel auf den 25. März, die Christen blieben ohne Seelsorge, die Priester weinten, es gab eine große Trauer. Oh weh, unserem armenischen Volke und der Stadt Gözleve. Und nachher 40 geschah ein unerwartetes Ereignis in unserer Stadt Kaffa. Der Wezir war ein Pascha, die Janitscharen von Azov (*Azaq*) empörten sich, und richteten viel Unheil in der Stadt an. Sie ermordeten 2—3 Leute des Pascha, einige verprügelten sie, manche erstachen sie mit dem Dolch. Aus diesem Grunde wurde eine Gerichtssitzung (*divan*) im Palast veranstaltet. (Plötzlich) brach ein Balken, und der Palast stürzte ein, 45 viele Leute stürzten in die Tiefe und starben, ungefähr 200 Leute mehr oder weniger wurden verkrüppelt, 225 einigen die Füße, einigen die Hände, anderen der Kopf und wieder anderen das Herz, am Freitag des Verrats und der Kreuzigung, es geschah also ein Wunder. Doch die Gottlosen haben sich nicht gebessert. Die Verordnungen (*emr*) hielten sie nicht ein, sie trieben die *Ispendže*-Steuer im Übermaß ein.

5 Und nachher, am 15. April, zelebrierte Paronter Grigor die Weihe, Ter Simeon wurde für Kašot geweiht, und Ter Zakarias für das Land bzw. Gözleve, drei Depirs, Hovhannes mein Schüler, Pastor der Kirche vom Heiligen Georg. Am Montag 10 gingen wir . . . die Stadtmauer, jene die zurückblieben, wurden verprügelt, sollten Strafgeld zahlen.

Und danach zog Islam Kerej Chan mit viel Kriegsvolk gegen Korel,

XII

viele Bezirke der Armenier wurden verwüstet, und er drang in die Stadt Bar
ein. Den Herren der Stadt, Potocki mit seinem 241/r Sohne 15 und mit seinem
Wezir, hat man mit anderen adeligen Herren gefangengenommen und als
Gefangene nach der Krim verschleppt, ins Gefängnis geworfen, in Eisenfesseln
geschlagen, in der Stadt Ghala, in der Burg der Juden; ihr Lösegeld wurde
für viele Dahekan festgelegt. Dann schickte der Chan neue Truppen nach den
ersten, diese zerstörten viel, verwüsteten viele Dörfer und Städte und führten
überhaupt 20 die ganze Bevölkerung in Gefangenschaft. Wer könnte all das
Übel erzählen, das sie traf; das Land Korel ist verwüstet worden.

Als wir in das Jahr 1650 eintraten, raffte sich Sultan Qrim Kerej auf
und zog mit seiner Reiterschar gegen Moskau. Er drang in die Moldau (*Boghdan*) ein und zog über das Land, aber jene waren miteinander im Einverständnis und sagten: «wir sind keine Empörer, wir sind die Untertanen der
Ottomanen (*Osmanli*) 25 und wollen uns euch nicht unterwerfen». Da wandte
sich der (Qalgha) Sultan Qrim Kerej mit seinen Truppen um, zog den Säbel
und es entstand ein derartiger Kampf, daß die Erde erzitterte, so etwas gab
es noch niemals. Er machte viele Gefangene, verwüstete viele Städte. Der Prinz
der Moldau (*Boghdan*) konnte (mit Not) entkommen, er flüchtete in die
Burgstadt (Lwow?). 30 Die Tataren verwüsteten das Land und Chmel(nickij)
drang bis in das Land Polen ein. Er rückte in Polen vor und machte unzählige
Gefangene; 300 Leute aus unserer Sippe des Erleuchters. Alle sind als
Gefangene in die Hände der Ungläubigen, Gottlosen gefallen. Und was ist
wieder die Ursache, daß der Ungläubige den gläubigen Christen in Gefangen-
schaft schleppt, nicht einen 35 nicht zwei, Sommer und Winter (hindurch)?
Mich dünkt es, daß die Leute die Bilder jedes Jahr austauschen, sich neue
Götter wählen, 241/v in ihrem Hause Bilder verehren, Weihrauch streuen und
Kerzen zünden, wiederholt die Knie beugen, aber Gott nicht verehren, nur
handerzeugte (Götzen), das ist die Ursache, daß sie in den Händen der Tataren und der Sippe der Bogenschützen im Tartarus verschmachten müssen. 40
Es kamen die Gefangenen, gelangten in unser Land, in (die Stadt) Krim
und Kaffa, Qara-Su und Baghča-Saraj, Gözleve und Orinberan (Orkapu —
Perekop), wo unsere Christen versammelt sind, man kaufte sie los und befreite
viele andere (*bayi*), wer könnte alle vorgefallene Geschehnisse erzählen, da
sie zahllos, unzählig waren.

45 Hovhannes Wardapet kam aus dem Land Polen, er hatte einen
Abegha, Ter Husik, der in Orinberan verschied, man brachte ihn 226 nach
Klein-Qara-Su und beerdigte ihn daselbst. Im Winter verbrachte der Wardapet
die Jahreszeit im (Kloster) des Heiligen Sargis. Es kam als Legat Gabriel,
Wardapet aus Etschmiadzin mit lichtstrahlendem Weihrauch ins (Kloster)
des Heiligen Sargis, Pastor der Herde und (der Kirche) der Erzengel. Dann
ging er nach Qara-Su, Baghča-Saraj, Gözleve, 5 in die Ortschaften der Krim.
Dann kam er in die Stadt (Kaffa) zum Anfang des allgemeinen Fastens

(*ayuhac'k'*) und er segnete alle (Leute) als Legat. Am heiligen Ostern übernahm er meine Messe in (der Kirche) des Heiligen Thoros und weihte den Abegha: Ter Sargis und zwei Diakone (*sarkavag*). Dann kam Hakob Wardapet ... ein unmoralischer, ein Vielfraß, ein Wassertringer und Verschwender, ein nachlässiger Schüler. **10** Er stellte sich (den Hörern) gegenüber und sprach ein Wirrwarr in Versform, das er selber zusammengeschmiedet und geschrieben hat, es ist schade um das weiße Papier, das er mehr beschmutzte als das Antlitz.

242/r Neuer Weizen ist gebracht worden, man verkaufte ihn für 110 Silbermünzen (*stak*), der menschenliebende Gott sei gelobt, wenn Gott etwas gibt, gibt er es reichlich. **15** Wer ist fähig, alle Gottestaten zu erkennen! Es verging kaum eine Stunde, man zahlte 60 Silber (dafür), noch ein Tag verging, man gab (nur noch) 40, und noch ein anderer Tag — da gab man ein Gold für ein Maß (*kapič*). Überhaupt hebt (Gott) den Bescheidenen empor und erniedrigt den Hochstehenden, (er bewerkstelligt), daß der Diener Herr werde, der Herr sich bücke. Ebenso ging es Derwisch Mohammed Pascha, der Wezir wurde, war er doch der Diener des Scheichs. **20** Die Kaffanenser hörten hiervon, man suchte ihn auf, einigen gab er Geschenke, dem Bittsteller (*čelub*) Aghawürde, jedoch er ist kurzlebig gewesen, er verschied, einige sagten, daß er ein guter Mensch war, er hätte für Kaffa viel getan, wenn er weiter gelebt hätte. Und dagegen der gottlose Ipšir, der viel Ungerechtes und viel Unfug (*jelalutiwn*) angerichtet hat, **25** Beglerbegs tötete, (viele) Güter und (Kleinodien) hamsterte ...

242/v 32 Im Juli ist jener stärker geworden, ging und nahm mit 34 Booten (*šajqa*) die Stadt Taman ein, setzte ein sehr hohes Lösegeld fest, einige sind losgekauft worden, andere blieben in Gefangenschaft und hilflos. Dann kam eine unerwartete Epidemie, **35** so daß kein Haus ohne Kummer blieb. Im September kam Kertaghač Pascha als Beglerbeg und Nazir in unsere Stadt Kaffa.

Aus dem (Patriarchen-) Stuhl des Erleuchters in Etschmiadzin ist Ter Philippos verschieden. Ter Hakob setzte sich auf seinen Stuhl des Themenvorstandes, er regierte von Osten bis Westen in der nördlichen Gegend, **40** d. h. in der Hauptstadt Kaffa und (im Bezirk) Krim, d. h. im Land der Hunnen. Ein Jahr peinigte er uns, es kamen in die Stadt ein Bischof (*hajrapet*) und fünf Wardapete, Gott Erlöser befreie und erlöse uns.

Wir traten in das Jahr 1656 ein, das Zodiakzeichen ist der Skorpion, das Land ist voller Güter, alle Früchte stammen von Gott, **45** der viele, unzählige Schiffe (zu uns) lenkt. Täglich 100, 200, 300, 400, 500 Wagenladungen (*araba*), manche sagen, daß 227 heute ein Schiff mit ... Wagenladung Weizen eintraf, ging ... das Land versorgte. Es sei Lob dem Gönner und Geschenkgeber, unserem Gott, wer könnte Gottes freigiebige, reichliche Gnade erzählen und loben ... **5** es gab ein Erdbeben, am Dienstag ... jener kam gegen ... konnte es aber nicht einnehmen, sie kämpften mit den Türken, dann kehrten sie

XII

zurück. Danach ging er nach Delibalt, gewann die Oberhand, metzelte die Leute nieder und nahm sie gefangen.

243/r David Wardapet kam als Legat zu uns aus Etschmiadzin vom neueingeweihten Katholikos, Ter Hakob, mit dem lichtstrahlenden Mirrha (Chrisma), 10 im Oktober ein Abegha mit einem Diakon (*sarkavag*). Im Winter erging es uns schlecht, mit tiefem Schnee, ein Verfall der Tiere, der Schafe, für drei Monate verfielen die Pferde, das Vieh, und die Schafe der Noghaier, so daß sie vor Hunger starben, auch das Futtertier hatte nichts zu fressen. Und nach alledem kamen noch zwei ... Die Kosaken (*urus*) überfielen sie alle und metzelten die armen Beklagenswerten nieder.

15 Im Jahre 1657, am 29. März, feierten wir Ostern. In diesem Jahre erschien auch ein anderes Übel ... da der König der Ottomanen (*Osmanli*) ... kam, verlangte er 5 (?) ... Handwerker (*iryat*), ... Eisenschmiede ... und von allen übrigen Handwerken, zehn Tage ... spät gegeben. Und nach alldem 20 erlegte man (Steuer) ... dem Land, den Armeniern, (Tataren), Griechen, Juden auf. Die Mohammedaner sagten, wir haben nichts zu geben. Unsere Armenier (gaben) sofort, der Tatar Pascha der Stadt sagte, ihr sollt geben; was sollen wir geben, ... sagten wir, der Chan ... verordnete, kommt rafft euch auf ... Am 21. März, am Palmsonntag, versammelten sich die Reichen (*dolvat*) und die 25 armen Leute (*faqir fuqara*) in der Kirche des Heiligen Thoros, 243/v also gehen wir, Gottes Fügung soll (erfüllt werden). Auf dem Wege kam ein Regen, ein Schneegestöber und heftiger Sturm (*boran*), so daß einige Leute auf dem Wege blieben, später kehrten sie zum Heiligen Thoros zurück; alle Leute gingen nach Hause, die Kirchen sind am Palmsonntag zugesperrt worden, in den Nacht fand die Zeremonie des «Türöffnens» nicht statt. 30 Am Montag, Dienstag, Mittwoch, Donnerstag kamen die Wohlhabenden mit Kerzen (*mom*), Zucker, Geschenken (*peškeš*), die übrigen Leute, das Volk feierten Ostern unter Furcht und Zittern, einige zogen keine (Fest)kleider an, färbten keine Eier, ... 44 1500 Gurusche (Charadsch), oder noch mehr, gab Kaffa.

244/r 45 Am 16. Juni abends verfinsterte sich der Mond. Am nächsten Abend kam ein Regen, so daß viele Häuser 228 einstürzten, (der Strom) riß viele Brücken weg, verschleppte eine Frau mit zwei Kindern, der Vater blieb in Verzweiflung zurück. Verschleppte einen Imam, die Frau und das Kind blieben verzweifelt zurück. So viel Unerwartetes ereignete sich, der Chan raffte sich auf mit vielem Reitervolk ... da keine Nachricht kam, unerwartet kam die Nachricht (*xabar*) 5, daß der Chan 60 Tabor ... von Ungarn ... mit frohem Herzen ... unsere Städtler freuten sich, veranstalteten deshalb eine Feier (*donanma*) ... der Chan in unsere Stadt noch nicht gekommen ist ... Osmanli ...ist eingeschlossen geblieben ... verschloß die Meerenge (*Boghaz*), wer kommt, kann nicht zurückkehren, ...wenn nur Gott ihn losläßt, zu jener Zeit gab es eine Festlichkeit (*donanma*) 10 am 6. Oktober, für drei Tage. Dann wieder ein Fest (*donanma*) der der Kreuzerhöhung (*Xačverkʿ*) ... drei Tage und drei Nächte fochten sie, bis die Europäer (Franken) umkehrten, der Weg ist frei geworden, so ist es. Da kamen drei Wardapets in unsere Stadt . . .

15 Ter Martiros . . .
    Ed[elstein] und Krone des Landes
    244/v und Legat von Jerusalem.
    Ein Schüler von Astuacatur Wardapet,
    Mitkämpfer von Eleazar Wardapet;
    [gebürtig] aus dem Lande der Hunnen,
    [Zögling] des Klosters des Heiligen Kreuzes,
    Stolz der Krim und Wardapet von Kaffa.
    Als Kind war er ein frommer Junge,
    Er verdient ein hohes Alter.

20 Bruder, der Preis des Brotes (Weizen) erhöhte sich wieder, man sagt 200 . . . Gott erbarme sich unser. . . diesen Winter. Im Sommer gebe Gott und. . . die Geschöpfe. An allen Dingen leiden wir Not. . . und an Geld ebenso.

    Im Jahre von einem Tausend,
    Hundert und dazu noch sieben [1658]
    Der Monat war (eben) **25** April,
    Wir erhielten da die Nachricht,
    Die traurig' und kummervolle,
    Bittren Tod unsres Paronters,
    Daß Ter Grigor sei verschieden
    Auf dem Weg von Jerusalem.
    Er konnte sie nicht erreichen.

Trauer erfaßte die Stadt, seinen erhabenen Kloster der Übeltilgende *(Čarxapan)* Mariae, der Gottgebärerin. **30** und wieder die Krim der Hunnen, . . . das glänzende Heilige Kreuz [Kloster], und des ganzen Landes, der Stadt . . . Krim, er war unser allgemeiner Vorstand . . . Gott gebe wieder. . .

Anmerkungen

208,01 Spätere Eintragungen auf der ersten Seite: (MS 220/r) «1583 Es kam Osman Pascha und richtete viele Verheerungen an.
    1584 (Die Kirche) Gottesgebärerin Goli ist genommen und (die Kirche) Heiliger Freitag verheert worden.»
    208,08 Vgl. dieselbe Nachricht bei Andreas Sarkavag «35 Türme (*yula*) stürzten ein» (*Manr. Žam.* I. 161,12). Über die Errichtung der Mauer berichtet

XII

dieselbe Chronik: «1467 am 16. November ist der Bau der neuen Mauer und der Festung beendet worden» (*Ibid.* I. 161,19).

208,13 Die Saporoger (und auch die Kašoter) Kosaken werden in unserer Chronik mit der lokalen tatarischen Benennung *urus* bezeichnet, die seit dem Kiewer Reich die südliche Bevölkerung schlechthin bezeichnete. Das Fürstentum Moskau und später das unter Moskau vereinigte Russische Reich ist von den Tataren ursprünglich *Moskov* genannt worden (vgl. 225,23 und auch die frühen Reiseberichte: Russia seu Moscovia). Die erweiterte Bedeutung des Völkernamens *urus* für das ganze Russische Reich ist bei den Tataren durch den regen diplomatischen Verkehr mit Moskau eingebürgert worden. So wird der russischer Zar auch in den tatarischen diplomatischen Schriften: *uluġ urusnung ve purusnung . . . padšahī* genannt (z. B. Veliaminov-Zernov, *Materialy*, 40 und passim).

In der oben zitierten zeitgenössischen armenischen Chronik (Matenadaran No. 1869) werden sie die *γazax*en von *urus* genannt. (*Manr. Žam.* I. 161,08. In der Übersetzung gebrauchen wir bedeutungsgemäß: Kosak (*urus*).)

208,33 Sultan Ahmed I 1603—1617, Mustafa I 1617, Osman II. 1618—1622, Mustafa I. (zum zweitenmal) 1622—1623.

209,15 Ein Komet in der Form eines gebogenen Säbels erschien auch über Istambul, was damals als Zeichen für einen neuen persischen Krieg usw. gedeutet wurde (*GOR* IV, 511).

209,17 Džanibek Kerej nahm an dem Feldzug der Ottomanen gegen Persien mit einem 30 000 Mann (nach Novoseljskij: 10 000) starken Heer teil. Seine Armee erlitt schwere Verluste (*GOR* IV, 499; Smirnov, 479—480; Novoselskij 99—100).

Armenisch *Karmir Glux* («Rotkopf») für *Qīzīlbaš* (209,19) = das (schiitische) Perserreich.

209,19 Džanibek Kerej Chans Regierungsjahre 1610—1623, 1627—1635. Die Dynastie der Krimchane heißt auf Tatarisch *Kerej, Keräj, Kirej*. In unserer Chronik kommen die Schreibarten: *Kerej, Keraj, Kere* vor. J. Németh leitet die Benennung der Dynastie von dem Namen des mongolischen Stammes der *Kereiten* ab (*UAJb* Bd. 36, 362—363). (Die türkische Form *Girej* tritt in Kafejecis Chronik nicht auf.)

209,28 Unter den Genuesern gab es ein lokales Münzamt für (Silber-) Münzen niedriger Währung, eben für den Handel mit den Tataren, auf der einen Seite mit dem Tamgha. Auch die Chane der Goldenen Horde ließen auf der Krim Münzen prägen (Smirnov, 142—143, 184—193; Spuler, 113). M. Broniewski (1578) sah selber ein Münzamt ein Solxat (Eski Krim), wo Kleinmünzen geprägt wurden (*ZOOID* VI, 359, 364. Schwandtner, III 268, 287. Jakobson, 106, 110). D'Ascoli berichtet, daß die Münzen innerhalb eines Jahrzehnts (1620—1630) viermal gewechselt wurden, was für den Chan einen großen Nutzen, für die Untertanen aber einen wesentlichen Verlust bedeutete (*ZOOID* XXIV/2. 115). Siehe hier noch 209,32; 211,18; 213,25.

209,33 Die Kirche des Heiligen (Surb) Thoros lag außerhalb der Mauer von Kaffa (Bžškian, 352).

209,35 Grigor Lusaworič — Gregor der Erleuchter, der legendäre Bekehrer der Armenier zum Christentum und erster Patriarch (nach der Überlieferung: A. D. 302—326). S. Chronik von Agathangelos (V. Langlois, *Collection des historiens anciens et modernes de l'Arménie*, I. Paris 1881. 122—134, 150—169 ff.).

209,36 Surb Sargis, Heerführer des armenischen Königs, Tiridat III. (A. D, 287/298—330). S. Ačarian, *Andznanunneri baťaran* (Personennamen-Lexikon), IV, Jerewan 1948. 402—404.

209,39 Feiertag des hl. Jakob von Nisibis (arm. Mcbin) am 16. Dezember 1620. (W. H.)

209,42 Marginalnote MS 222/v und 223/r: «1621, 13. April, am Karfreitag, ist Ter Xačatur Priester (*kahana*) und Sakristan (*lusarar*) der Kirche zum hl. Erzengel geweiht worden.

1628 am 6. April, am Palmsonntag, verschied Xačatur kahana in Gott.»

210,07 Devlet Kerej (*Dolvetkere*) Qalgha Sultan († 13. Nov. 1631).

Die ersten Kerej Chane gebrauchten den Titel *Sultan* auf ihren Münzen. Später ist der Ehrentitel *Sultan* auf die nichtregierenden Mitglieder — also den Qalgha und den Nureddin — der Dynastie übergegangen (so auch bei den Usbeken und Kasachen), *EI* II, 181—182.

210,08 *Korel.* In einem früheren Aufsatz (Könige und Eidechsen. Bemerkungen zum Fortleben des ungarischen Wortes *király* «König» in kiptschakischen Sprachen. In: *Proceedings of the IXth Meeting of the PIAC—Naples*, 1970. 259—267) versuchte ich das Wort etymologisch zu analysieren: Das Wort *Korel* müßte ursprünglich auf den ungarischen Terminus *keral* (*király*) «König» zurückgehen, eine Variante des im Slawischen als *kral* eingebürgerten Terminus. Das ungarische Wort entwickelte sich lautgesetzlich zu *köräl* im Krimtatarischen, was im (Slawischen und) Armenischen *korel* lautete (da hier die palatalen Labiale fehlen). Das Wort könnte also auf das Zeitalter der ungarischen Herrschaft in Halitsch zurückgehen, und so pflanzte sich der Ausdruck durch die litauische Oberherrschaft dieses Grenzgebietes bis zum polnischen Königtum fort.

Die Krimtataren bezeichneten den polnischen König schlechtweg als «König», z. B. *uluy qiral qardašïmïz* «unser Bruder, der Großkönig», oder einfach als *qïralïmïz* (Veliaminov-Zernov, 109—110).

Aufgrund dieser Angaben ist versucht worden, *Korel* mit Polen zu identifizieren (so bei Mikaelian, 140, Fußnote 75; Schütz, *PIAC IX Proceedings*, 264). Aber eben die Angaben der Chronik Xačatur Kafajecis machen darauf aufmerksam, daß es sich hier um ein begrenzteres Gebiet handelt. An einigen Stellen gibt die Chronik keine genauere Bestimmung des Gebietes: 1620 und auch 1629 führt der Qalgha Devlet Kerej und 1631 Mubarek Kerej eine Razzia gegen *Korel* (210,08; 216,11; 220,02) durch. Doch bei dem Feldzug von Islam Kerej (225,13) wird bemerkt, daß seine Truppen bis zur Stadt Bar vorrückten und sie das ganze Land *Korel* (*Korelac' tun*) verwüsteten. Wie aber auch aus anderen Quellen gut bekannt ist, sind diese Raids gegen das polnische Grenzgebiet Podolien gerichtet worden, also kann mit Recht gefolgert werden, daß es sich hier um die Woiwodschaft Podolien handelt. Auf Grund dieser Angaben behauptet schon W. Hakobian, daß hier *Korel* die Landschaft Südwest-Ukraina, das Gebiet Kamenets Podolsk—Žitomir—Berdičew, bedeutet (*Manr. Žam.* I. 230, Fußnote 12). Genau diesen Schauplatz bietet der Krieg bei Chotin (1621: 210,29).

Auf das Handelszentrum Lwow weist aber ein Schreiben von Mengli Girej an Iwan III (1509) hin, wo von einem Kaffanenser Kaufmann die Rede ist, der früher ins «königliche Land» ging, um Handel zu treiben (*Sbornik Russkago Istor. Obščestva*, Bd. 95. 76. apud Mikaelian, 149).

Einige andere Stellen in der Chronik scheinen auf ein noch weiteres Gebiet zu deuten: 1628 eilen 12 000 Kosaken aus *Korel* dem Šahin Kerej zur Hilfe (214,22) und der besiegte Qalgha findet für Jahre in *Korel* Unterkunft (215,34). Auf dasselbe Gebiet weisen Angaben in der Fortsetzung der Chronik von Andreas Evdokeci hin, wo 1616 die Kosaken aus *Korel* die Stadt Kaffa (*Manr. Žam.* I. 161,15) und 1614 die Kosaken von Urus Sinope in Brand setzen (161,08). Da hier genau die Saporoger Kosaken gemeint sind, ist es klar, daß *Korel* auch das einstmalige Litauisch-Podolien bezeichnen könnte.

Es gibt aber keinen Grund dafür, unter *Korel* schlechtweg das ganze Polen zu verstehen, da die Bezeichnung eine abgegrenztere Bedeutung hat. Als Bogdan Chmelnickij bis nach Polen vorrückte, ist dies mit *Lehac' erkir* ausgedrückt.

Also zusammenfassend sollte die ursprüngliche Bedeutung von *Korel* auf das polnisch-ukrainische Grenzgebiet bezogen werden, später auch auf das von den registrierten Kosaken bewachte Territorium und allmählich auf das ganze west-ukrainische Kosakengebiet erweitert werden. Die Fluktuation der Bedeutung des Ausdruckes widerspiegelt also die Veränderungen der politischen Situation.

210,09 Die große Beute und der Verlust tausender Gefangener wegen der furchtbaren Kälte wird ähnlich auch vom Chronisten Axent geschildert (Schütz, *An Armeno-Kipchak Chronicle*, 44—49. Vgl. Novoseljskij 100).

210,10 Arm. *girg* kann ein Schreibfehler, entweder für «Buch» oder für «Wickelkind» sein. (Die Tataren wußten wohl, wie hoch die Armenier die Bücher schätzen, und so erbeuteten sie überall auch Bücher, die sie dann für ein hohes Lösegeld den Armeniern wieder verkauften. (S. z. B. *AOH* XIX, 369).) W. Hakobian entscheidet sich hier für: Wickelkind.

210,26 Der Ortsname *Sulxay* ist mit Recht auf *Sulxat* emendiert worden

XII

(W. H.). Die Stadt (25 Km westlich von Kaffa) *Surxat, Solchat* (Schiltberger: *Sulchat*, J. Barbaro: *Sorgathi*) usw. war Zentrum der Steppenlandschaft, Residenz des Statthalters, (Al-Kalkašandi: «Die Hauptstadt der Krim Solgat.» Tiesenhausen, I. 413), von den Tataren einfach Krim (später Eski Krim) genannt, so auch in unserer Chronik (s. unter Krim). Die Benennung *Solxat* gilt hier mehr für den Bezirk (Keppen, 338—346; Smirnov, 73—88; Jakobson, 105—108; Kondaraki, XIV. 101, ff.; Bruun, II. 121—158).

210,28 Die Schlacht unter Chotin: *GOR* IV, 523. ff.; Zinkeisen, III. 737—742; Novoseljskij, 100; Schütz, *An Armeno-Kipchak Chronicle*, 40—85.

210,32 Tamurxan—Qantemir werden 6 Städte und die Beglerbegwürde, Paschalik von Očakow, für seine Tapferkeit verliehen. Er erhielt auch den Ehrentitel *emir ul-umerā* (*GOR* IV. 528—529; Smirnov, 491; Novoseljskij, 100—101; Schütz, 52—55).

211,01 Der Aufruhr in Istanbul und der Tod Sultan Osmans II (*GOR* IV. 540—545; Zinkeisen, III. 744—750).

211,15 Der wunderbare Hafen von Kaffa wurde schon von dem Reisenden Ibn Battuta (1334) beschrieben (Tiesenhausen I, 280).

211,16 Tatin tun—Land (Bezirk) der Taten. S. Minorski: *EI* IV, 755—757; Schaeder: *Festschrift Giese*, 1941, 1—12. Schütz, *The Tat People in the Crimea, AOH*, 1976. (Vortrag gehalten zur 100. Jahreswende des Arabischen Lehrstuhles der Universität Budapest, 8. Mai, 1974.)

211,19 Die Krim war früher der Speicher für Konstantinopel, mit den wichtigsten Waren Weizen und gesalzenem Fisch (Broniewski: *ZOOID* VI, 349. Schwandtner, III, 273; Heyd, II. 166, 177, 191. Jakobson, 110). (Vergleiche noch weitere Stellen über Hungersnot in der Krim. S. Einleitung).

211,30 Mehmed Kerej III Chan (1623—1627). Sein Qalgha: Šahin Kerej (Smirnov, 480; Novoseljskij, 108—109). Emendation der Regierungszeit «3 Monate» auf «4 Jahre». (W. H.)

211,33 Arm. Orinberan, Türkisch: Orkapu, Russisch: Perekop (*or-* 'Graben, Erdwall', *qapu* 'Tor'; Arm. *beran* 'Mund, Öffnung').

211,43 Die Wasserversorgung der großen Stadt bedeutete immer ein schweres Problem für Kaffa. Schon früh sind Stauanlagen zum Auffangen des Regenwassers errichtet worden, doch die wichtigsten Ausrüstungen waren die Dränageanlagen (*ariq*-System) und die Kondensatoren, aus denen das Wasser in die Fontäne floß. Um der Wassernot vorzubeugen, sind von den Genuesern mehrere Wasserreservoire, Zisternen erbaut worden (Jakobson, 114—115 usw.). — Was die Tätigkeit der Armenier in dieser Frage betrifft, ließ der armenische Bischof (laut dem Impositoi Officii Gasariae von 1316) schon vor der Ankunft der Genuesern eine Wasserleitung durch die Stadt führen. *Monumenta Historiae Patriae*, 380 (vgl. Mikaelian, 332—334). Für «Zisterne, Schöpfrad» wird hier das im Osmanischen übliche persisch-arabische Wort *dolab* gebraucht.

XII

212,14 Die Urusen von Kašot: Vielleicht lagerten diese Kosaken am Nebenfluß *Kočeti* des Kubans (Golobuckij, V. A., *Černomorskoje kazačestvo*, Kiev 1957. 239—240, 261, 366).

Eine andere Alternative: die Angreifer wären aus der Sippe der 1620—1630 aus der Dzungarei nach der Wolga übergesiedelten Kalmüken, der *Košot* (Pelliot: *Notes critiques d'histoire kalmouke*, Paris, 1960).

Es ist bekannt, daß die Wolga-Kalmüken unter der Regierung Mehmed Kerej Chans einen Angriff gegen die Krim planten (*GOR* V, 342—343). Im gegebenen Falle handelt es sich ausdrücklich um die Don-Kosaken, wie die Berichte der russischen Gesandten beweisen (S. Novoseljskij, 129).

Die angenommene Etymologie des Sippennamen *košot* ist der Plural von Mong. *košigun, košun* (Pelliot, 76), Türk. *qošun*, in kiptschakischen Sprachen *qoš* 'Militärabteilung' (Poln. *kosz* 'id.'), vgl. *koševoj* (hetman) 'Kosakenführer', doch kommt im Kiptschakischen ein -*t* Plural nicht vor.

Die am Wolgafluß erscheinenden Ortsnamen *Košutowka* (N von Astrachan) und *Košot* (W von Astrachan) sind wohl späteren Ursprungs und erhielten ihren Namen vielleicht als Lagerstätte der Kalmückenhorden.

212,14 Krim (var. Qrim, Xrim, Xīrīm, Ghrim, in arabischer Schrift: Qirim, Qiram; Cremum, seu ut a Tartaris Crimum dicitur, Broniewski, *ZOOID*, VI, 346; Schwandtner, III, 268; Keppen, 343, Smirnov, 59—74). Im Armenischen bleibt *i* und *ī* in der ersten Silbe in der Schrift gewöhnlich unbezeichnet; es kann also *Xrim* oder *Xīrim* gleichfalls gelesen werden: 225,16; 226,40; 228,18,30). Früherer Name: *Sulxat* (s. 210,26; 213,13).

Solxat—Qrim war der Sitz des jeweiligen Statthalters, und ursprünglich führte nur die Stadt den Namen, später ist er aber auf die ganze Halbinsel übertragen worden (Keppen, 338—346). Auch schon in unserer Chronik: 222,21,23.

212,18 Als Mehmed Kerej die Gunst des türkischen Sultans und seine Chanwürde 1610 verlor, flüchtete sein Bruder zu Schah Abbas nach Persien. Jetzt (1624) ist er aus Persien zurückgerufen und in die Qalghawürde wieder eingesetzt worden (Smirnov, 479—480; Novoseljskij, 108—109).

213,12 Der Qalgha, Šahin Kerej, wird in erster Linie erwähnt, da eigentlich *er* den Ruder führte (Novoseljskij, 107).

213,13 Sulxat—Qrim blieb auch unter der Goldenen Horde Regierungssitz des Statthalters (Tiesenhausen, I. 63, 192, 363; Barthold: *EI* II, 1162; Spuler, 313—314; Mikaelian, 84, 90, 102—103), und auch unter den ersten Kerejs blieb es Residenz der Chane. Als Hadži Kerej den Sitz der Krimchane nach der West-Krim verlegte, wurde (Eski)-Krim für eine Zeit das Lehen der Qalgha (Smirnov, 248). S. auch 210,26.

213,21 Marginalnote: 227/v. «Es kam der Dženkči ('der Kampflustige') genannte Hovhannes Vardapet 1616.»

213,28 Über den Feldzug gegen die Čerkessen vgl. Novoseljskij, 119.

213,31 *Vaxir fuxara* (— faqir fuqara) wahrscheinlich als Verspottung seines Ehrentitels *emir-ul-umerā* (Smirnov, 491, 495. S. auch Anmerkung zu 210,32).

213,32 Die Abrechnung mit der Sippe Qantemirs wird von Smirnov (491) ins Jahr 1626 verlegt, obwohl das Ereignis 1627 stattfand (Novoseljskij, 119, 121, Fußnote 84. — *GOR* V, 37. Vom Gesichtspunkt des Kaffaer Beglerbegs gesehen: Rizvan, 93—94).

213,37 Ozun, Özän (in den russischen Berichteten: Oza, Ozu, Uza, Uzu) — Dneper. Die Festungen werden bei den Tataren einfach mit dem Namen des Flußes benannt (Smirnov, 346). Die Hohe Pforte, die zu dieser Zeit allzu oft durch die Überfälle der Kosaken belästigt wurde, schickte einen Ferman nach dem anderen und rief die Krimchane auf, die Kosaken in Zaum zu halten (*ibid.* 481).

214,08 Die Beschreibung des wirrevollen Jahres 1628 wird meistens nur aufgrund der auf ottomanischen Quellen beruhenden Werke geschildert. Diese sollen durch die wertvolle Schilderung des Dortelli d'Ascoli (*ZOOID* XXIV) und die Berichte der russischen Gesandten ergänzt werden (vgl. Novoseljskij, 120—121).

214,22 Die Korrektion von Akkusativ-Lativ («nach Korel») in Ablativ-Elativ («aus Korel») von W. Hakobian ist unbedingt richtig.

Die aus Korel (s. Anmerkung zu 210,08) kommenden Hilfstruppen — 12 000 Mann — werden 214,22; 215,24 (und auch 215,35) *haj* genannt, was Armenisch 'Armenier' bedeuten würde. Aber auch aus anderen Quellen ist bekannt, daß es die Hilfstruppen der (Saporoger) Kosaken, 6000 oder 4000 Tausend Mann, unter der Leitung des Hetmans Dorošenko waren (Novoseljskij, 120; Evarickij, II, 214), auch in demselben Absatz unserer Chronik (215,01) *urus* also «Kosak» genannt. Šahin Kerej Qalgha schloß schon 1624 ein Bündnis mit den Kosaken (Novoseljskij, 118).

Haj kann als ergänzende Apposition für die Einheit «Mann» kaum stehen, da so das Substantiv fehlen würde. Als *hajn* 'jener' (s. 223,05) kann es wegen des Zahlwort-Adjektivs (12 000) nicht gelten. Vielleicht könnte es eine abgekürzte Form des ukrainischen Wortes *hajdamak* sein, was die Benennung der Saporoger Kosaken war (Hrinčenko, *Slovarj ukrainskago jazyka*. I, 265; F. Sławski, *Słownik etymologiczny języka polskiego*, I, 391—392). In jedem Falle steht das Wort für: Kosak.

214,30 Hesar—Frenghisar, der ursprüngliche Sitz, die Zitadelle der Genueser. *Pečan xandax* 'der Burggraben der Bollwerke', vgl. unten 225,10.

215,22 Laut anderen Quellen kam Džanibek Kerej, sein Qalgha Devlet Kerej und das türkische Heer mit 60 Galeeren und 20 Booten (Novoseljskij, 120).

215,23 Burg Arabat, 50 km nördlich von Kaffa an der Küste des Asower Meeres.

XII

215,25 Azamat Kerej ist 1631 anstelle des verstorbenen Qalghas, Devlet Kerej ernannt worden, doch nach 5 Monaten ließ ihn der Chan erschießen.

215,33 Der Chan, Mehmed Kerej, und der Qalgha, Šahin Kerej, sind zu den Saporoger Kosaken geflohen und mitsamt den kleinen Noghaiern führten sie einen Feldzug (40 000 Mann stark, Zinkeisen, IV, 503) gegen den neueingesetzten Krimchan. Der Feldzug ist jedoch ganz fehlgeschlagen. Es brach eine Zwietracht zwischen den Tataren, den Saporoger Kosaken und den Noghaiern aus (Novoseljskij, 135—137). Die Ereignisse der letzten 5 Jahre sind bei Smirnov (481—497) ganz verwirrt (Novoseljskij, 121, Fußnote 84).

215,35 *haj*, hier Kosak, s. oben 214,22.

215,38 *bayi* kann das arabisch-persische Wort *bāyi* 'ungerecht, ungehorsam, usw.' sein (W. H.) aber öfter steht es für *bāqī* 'übriger'.

215,40 und 216,04: 1629 kamen von der einen Seite die Don-Kosaken, 2000 Mann, und im Mai (216,04) von der anderen Seite die Saporoger Kosaken (Smirnov, 496—497; Novoseljskij, 136—137).

215,43 Mangup, alte Festung und Stadt in den Bergen der SW-Krim. D'Ascoli: die Stadt war ohnedies schon ganz verwüstet (*ZOOID*, XXIV, 113, 117, 121; Keppen, 261—290; Jakobson, 124—127; Vasiliev, 272, f.).

215,46 Otuz, Festung und Hafen zwischen Sudaq und Kaffa (Keppen, 101—106; Smirnov, 128).

216,04 *Fener(ler)* 'Lichtturm' genannte Promontorien (vgl. griechisch *Lampas*) gab es mehrere, auch in der Krim, an der Tarxankuter und auch an der Sebastopoler Landspitze, also wären diese Umschlagplätze der Kosaken gewesen. Allerdings war die Umkreisung der schwer bezwingbaren Landenge Orkapu (Perekop) die gewöhnliche Razzia-Angriffstaktik der Kosaken.

216,05 Im Text steht *sandīxtov*. W. Hakobian hält es neben Gezlov (Gözleve) für einen Ortsnamen. M. E. könnte es vielleicht eine Art Lastboot (*sandīq* 'Kasten, Truhe') darstellen (mit anorganischem -*t*). — Die erwähnten Städte waren nicht so befestigt, daß man auf 'Sturmleiter' (Arm. *sanduyk'*), oder 'Hakenleiter' denken konnte.

216,09 Gazandib — Bucht und Promontorium am Südufer des Asowschen Meeres, zwischen Arabat und Kertsch.

216,15 Salmaša Mirza war der Vetter von Qantemir, s. noch 222,14. (D'Ascoli, *ZOOID* XXIV, 164; Novoseljskij, 119.)

216,16 Gulim Diveev Mirza, Qantemirs Bruder und Nachfolger (Novoseljskij, 114, 119). Es gibt auch einen Ort Gülüm bij in der Krim (Kondaraki, I/1, 99).

216,18—21 Der nächste Absatz steht als Randbemerkung an den Seiten MS 233/r—v. (W. H.)

216,26 Über die Steuermaßnahmen s. Einleitung.

216,30 D. h. August, 10—13, 1629. (W. H.)

XII

216,35 Die Bemerkung über die 3—4jährigen Kinder bezieht sich auf Zeile 216,26.

216,36—217,02 Dieser Absatz ist (in gedrängter Schrift) nachträglich eingetragen worden.

216,45 Das Amt eines Paschas kostete viele Bestechungsgelder. Bis man diese hohe Stufe erreicht hat, ist man arg verschuldet (W. H.).

217,13 Vielleicht wäre es hier von einem Derwischkloster (*tekke*) die Rede.

217,17 In der Handschrift steht: *patuirak* 'Legat', anstatt *patriarkʿ*. (W. H.)

217,18 *čhaskʿ* — Die Blutverwandschaft bis zum siebenten Grade, die Verwandschaft bis zum vierten waren ausschließende Faktoren bei Eheschließung (Fr. Tournebize, *Histoire politique et réligieuse de l'Arménie*, 616).

217,19 Sonntag des hl. Jakob, 18. Dezember; s. noch 209,39.

217,23 Die Kirche Johannes des Täufers (Hovhan Mkrtič) wurde 1348 außerhalb der Zitadelle (im heutigen Bezirk: Karantäne) erbaut (*Vizantijskij Vremennik*, VIII, 181—185).

217,28 Die Kirche Surb Hreštakapet, die Kirche der Erzengel Michael und Gabriel (s. Bžškian, 350—351). Die armenisch-katholische Kirche ist 1408 in italienischem Stil erbaut worden (*Vizantijskij Vremennik* VIII, 185—191; Jakobson, 115. Über die katholischen Armenier in der Krim s. Tournebize, 326—327).

217,36 Das Fest des Warager Kreuzes fiel im Jahre 1629 auf den 27. September (W. H.). Das Warager Kreuz ist nach der Überlieferung ein Stück des Kreuzes Christi, das von den Märtyrern Gajane und Hripsime zur Zeit ihrer legendären Wallfahrt in der Provinz Waspurakan gelassen worden war, und an dessen Stelle (ungefähr 10 km vom Wan-See entfernt) man später ein Kloster erbaut hatte (M. Thierry, *Monastères arméniens de Vaspurakan*. *REArm* VI, 141—161).

217,40 Marginalnote: «Paronter Moses starb in Istanbul.» (W. H.)

217,43 Movses III. von Thatev, Katholikos der armenischen Kirche, 1629—1632.

217,45 Ter Xačatur, von Patriarch Movses entsandter Legat zu den armenischen Gemeinden der Diaspora und Gesandter zu Papst Urbanus VIII (*Revue des Études Arméniennes* VII (1927) 22, ff.).

218,03 Die Ruinen der alten Kirche und des Klosters der hl. Jungfrau Čarxapan ('Übelverhindernde') erwähnt von Bžškian, 323.

218,04 Vielleicht vom populären Gemeinwitz humoristisch «Leinenwalkerei» genannt (*bez* 'Leinen', *degirmän* 'Mühle') wo die beschmutzte seelische Wäsche Reinigung findet?

218,07 *aski* — *skih* — *skah* 'Becher' (G. Abgarian).

218,10 *Hajsmavurkʿ* — 'Menologie'.

218,13 Nach Dortelli d'Ascoli gab es 28 (1634), nach Beauplan (1650) 32, Pidou (1669) 24 und Peysonnel (1775) 24 armenische Kirchen in Kaffa (Kondaraki, XIV, 128; *Vizantijskij Vremennik*, VIII, 170; Mikaelian 323—327).

218,28 1629 dauerte die Fastzeit vom 16. Februar bis zum 27. März (W. H.). *Aghuhacʻkʻ* 'Salz und Brot' ist die armenische Benennung des 40tägigen Fastens.

218,29 *Balïklï* — Balaklawa, Stadt an der SW-Küste der Krim (Jakobson, 120—121).

218,38 Die alte, kleine, einfache Kirche und das Kloster von Surb Georg lagen außerhalb der Mauer, in der Richtung Kule kapusi, auch Wallfahrtsort (Bžškian, 351—352).

219,20 Es werden hier eben die charakteristischen armenischen Handwerke hervorgehoben (Jakobson, 110). Die meisten ausgeübten Handwerke spiegeln auch die Grabinschriften wider (L. Xačikian, *Kolophone armenischer Handschriften*, XIV. Jahrhundert (arm.), I, 359—367 usw. Mikaelian, 195).

219,40 Das armenische Viertel: Xaraghač (Bžškian, 244).

219,42 Der Sultan forderte Džanibek Kerej Chan auf, große Streitkräfte gegen den Schah schicken. Doch wegen des Waffenstillstandes, den sie auf Geheiß des Sultans 1630 mit Polen auf sieben Jahre schließen mußten, und da dieser Umstand das Mißtrauen des Zars hervorrief, benötigte sie auf der Hut zu sein, und so konnten sie nur eine 4000 Mann starke Division schicken (*GOR* V, 129—130; Smirnov, 506—507; Novoseljskij, 175—176).

219,44 Der Bruder des Chans, der Qalgha Devlet Kerej, ist am 13. November 1631 gestorben. An seiner statt setzte der Chan Džanibek Kerej Selamets Sohn, Azamat Kerej, ein. Unser Text läßt unerwähnt, daß der Chan Juni 1632 Azamat erschießen ließ und für Qalgha (im Text mit Schreibfehler: *Xayičxan*) seinen eigenen Bruder Mamet und für Nureddin seinen Sohn Mubarek einsetzte, der also den Feldzug (mit 15 000 Tataren und Noghaiern) gegen Podolien [Korel] führte (Novoseljskij, 194—195, 183).

Die Verwechslung bzw. Verwirrung im Texte ergibt sich daraus, daß sowohl der Sohn des Chans als auch des Selamets (1608—1610) beide Mubarek hießen.

Die Auseinandersetzung zwischen dem Chan und dem Qalgha, Azamat wird unter 220,40—221,02 ausführlich geschildert.

219,45 Qalgha (hier: *xayičxan*, recte mit -*l*-) Titel des Thronfolgers (Barthold: *EI* II, 742; Smirnov, 350—362), erscheint in den Dokumenten und Schriften der Krimchane als *qayïlya—qayalya—qaylïyai* (vgl. Matuz, *Qalgha. Turcica* Bd. 2. (Paris) 1970). So bei Rizvan *passim*, und auch in unserer Chronik: 220,40.

220,06 Der Satz ist von G. Abgarian zu: *xot čikʻar amaṙne* emendiert und demgemäß übersetzt worden.

220,10 Bezieht sich auf Feldzug unter 219,42.

Acta Orient. Hung. XXIX. 1975

220,23 Im regen Handelsleben Kaffas entwickelte sich auch eine Schicht der Wucherer (vgl. Jakobson, 111).

220,27 Als Opfer der Intrigen des Qaimakams Redžeb Pascha ist Xosrow Pascha der Großvezir im Februar 1632 hingerichtet worden. Für die entfachte Meuterei der Spahis nahm Sultan Murat IV 1633 blutige Rache (*GOR* V, 130—147; Novoseljskij, 174).

220,29 Hier scheint ein Blatt zu fehlen. (W. H.)

220,42 *Seymen* (*segban*), diese Söldner erhielten ihren Sold von der Pforte (Smirnov, 414). Džanibek Kerej ernannte Mametša Agha zum Kommandant der Segbans und 1628 nahm er dessen Tochter zur Frau (Novoseljskij, 184—185).

221,01 Eine Ergänzung des unklaren Satzes 219,44—45. Die Brüder des erschossenen Azamats flohen, Mubarek nach Perekop, Safat Kerej nach Kaffa (Novoseljskij, 195).

Die Aufeinanderfolge der Ereignisse: die Flucht der Brüder Azamat Kerejs und die Ankunft der Gesandten scheint darauf zu deuten, daß die Söhne Selamet Kerejs doch in irgendeiner Verbindung mit Šahin Kerej, dem früheren Qalgha, standen. Šahin ließ sich bei der Sippe Beslenej im Kaukasus nieder, und von dort versuchte er Džanibek Kerej zu stürzen, doch sind seine Gesandten ergriffen worden (Novoseljskij, 195, Fußnote 67).

221,18 Im MS *xew hoүaparisp* (*xew* '(Wall)graben', *hoүaparisp* 'Erdwall, Erdbastei') vielleicht ein armenischer Ausdruck für die türkische Benennung des Viertels: *Topraqkala* (auch W. Hakobian meint, es sei ein Viertel). (Nach G. Abgarian sollte die Grundbedeutung des Wortes *xev* 'toll' beibehalten werden.)

221,25 *kehja = kethüda.*

221,37 In (stylistisch nicht einwandfreien) Chroniken ist oft nur das persönliche Fürwort *na, nok'a* gebraucht, ohne das Subjekt genauer anzugeben. Diesen höchst lakonischen, rätselhaften Satz hat G. Abgarian trefflich gelöst.

221,38 Hier fehlen einige Blätter, die die Ereignisse der Jahre 1633—36 enthalten (W. H.).

221,39 Eine höchst gedrängte und ungenaue Zusammenfassung des letzten wirrevollen Regierungsjahres von Inajet Kerej. Das Ulus von Qantemir in Akkerman erlitt eine völlige Niederlage. Die Mirzas erkannten die Oberhoheit des Krimchans an, aber sobald sich eine Möglichkeit bot, überfielen sie die Krimtataren, und warfen auch den Qalgha, Husam Kerej, und den Nureddin Seadet (die Brüder des Chans) nieder, 30. April 1637.

Die Verweigerung des geforderten Kontingents (diesmal 60 000 Soldaten) im April 1636 für einen Feldzug gegen die Perser ist als Abtrünnigkeit gewertet worden. Um die Unabhängigkeit zu erringen, sollte das Zentrum der türkischen Herrschaft in der Krim, Kaffa, erobert werden. Kaffa ergab sich bald und lieferte den Pascha Bičkiči Ibrahim aus, der hingerichtet wurde (Zinkeisen, IV, 514; Novoseljskij, 246—247). — Inzwischen verlieh aber der türkische Sultan dem Batir Kerej (1637—1642) die Chanswürde, so daß Inajet Kerej

XII

nichts anderes übrig blieb, als sich zum Sultan zu begeben, wo er gerügt und erwürgt wurde (*GOR*, V, 226—227; Smirnov, 518—519; Novoseljskij, 249).

221,45—222,07 Diese Aufzeichnungen persönlichen Charakters sind später auf eine leere Seite eingetragen worden, und fügen sich nicht in die chronologische Reihenfolge ein.

221,45 Edirmelik, Tochter des Priesters Xačatur, s. 208,22.

222,02 1. Oktober, Feier des Warager Kreuzes, S. oben 217,36.

222,11 Zwei Zeilen aus einem Klageliede (G. Abgarian).

222,14 Diese Ereignisse sind Kettenglieder früherer Blutracheakte. Damals tötete Qantemirs Bruder, Salmaša Mirza, den Schwiegervater des Krimchans (Novoseljskij, 119). Eusam und Seadet Kerej sind am Vorabend der Ankunft Bahadur (Batïr) Kerejs getötet worden. (*Ibid.* 245 und hier: 221,39.) Als Vergeltung sind jetzt 25 Mirzas getötet worden. Die völlige Ausrottung der Familien von Qantemirs Gefolgsleuten ist mit denselben Worten («bis zum Wickelkind») auch in den Moskauer Gesandtenberichten charakterisiert. Salmaša Mirza gelang es zwar zuerst zu fliehen, er ist aber dann doch in die Hände der Krimtataren geraten. Die Chronologie dieser Vergeltungsakte steht keineswegs fest. Die Hinrichtung Uraq (Oraq) Mirzas und anderer Mirzas wird von den russischen Botschaftern unter dem 14. Mai 1639 berichtet (Smirnov, 512—513; Novoseljskij, 282—283).

222,16 Die Mansuren, die zweitgrößte tatarische Adelssippe, Kondaraki, X, 61—64.

222,19 Zitat aus der Bibel: Matthäus 21,41 (W. H.).

222,20 Höchstwahrscheinlich sind in diesem Bericht zweierlei Ereignisse verschmolzen. Ein Feldzug gegen die Asower Kosaken und der Auszug der verschiedenen Noghaier Sippen aus der Krim.

Bahadir Kerej übersiedelte die Mehrzahl der Kleinen und Großen Noghaier nach der Krim. Die dadurch hervorgerufene Entvölkerung der Steppe trug zur Eroberung der Burg Asow durch die Kosaken 1637 bei. Deshalb erließ der türkische Sultan mehrere Befehle, die Noghaier frei in die Steppe zurückkehren zu lassen. Die verschiedenen Mirzas hielten Rat mit ihren Gefolgsleuten, und es kam zu einem Massenauszug aus der Krim ungefähr 30 000 der Musa-Sippe, der Kasi-Sippe, der großen und kleinen Noghaier (Novoseljskij, 284—285).

222,27 Sultan Ibrahims Regierungszeit, 1640—1648.

222,28 Am 4. Sonntag der Fastenzeit wird das Gleichnis des ungetreuen Verwalters (Arm. *Tntes*) in der Messe gelesen (Lukas 16, 1—15).

222,30 Hier sind die Namen: Xačaturs, des Chronisten, und seiner Amtsvorgesetzten in Geheimschrift gegeben. Wir geben nur die Entzifferung nach W. Hakobian.

222,38 Die Belagerung der Burg Asow s. *GOR* V, 310—312; Novoseljskij, 286, ff,; Evarickij II, 228; Golobuckij, 191—192.

XII

222,40 Sandschak Kastamuni in NW Anatolien.

222,44 Boghdan = Moldau.

222,45 Der Ausdruck *čaɣataj* ist nach dem Zusammenbruch der Dynastie auf die Völkerschaft von West-Turkestan, für die Reiternomaden des Timuriden-Reiches, verallgemeinert worden, bezog sich allerdings nur auf die Militärkaste (Eckmann, *Chagatay Manual*, 2—3; Barthold, *12 Vorlesungen*, 219, 245).

223,03 Die verschiedenen Zahlangaben über die Kontingente der Türken und Tataren s. Novoseljskij, 286. Der Verlust der Türken war riesig groß, von einem Augenzeugen auf 18 000 geschätzt.

223,05 Das Wort *hajn* kommt auch an anderen Stellen vor (223,32). Es könnte eventuell eine archaisierende (oder pseudodialektale) Schreibart des armenischen Wortes *hèn* 'Feind' darstellen. Doch ist viel wahrscheinlicher zu vermuten, daß es das demonstrative Fürwort *ajn* 'jener, dieser' ist (vgl. 226,32), mit einer unetymologischen Aspiration (auch W. Hakobian vertritt diese Meinung).

223,09 Hier fehlen einige Blätter (W. H.).

223,10 Dieses ungenaue Gerücht vom 25 Jahre währenden Kriege um die Insel Kreta scheint sich auf die Einnahme der Hafenstadt Canea zu beziehen, 19. August 1645 (*GOR* V, 380—383; Zinkeisen, IV, 739).

223,12 Aller Wahrscheinlichkeit nach bezieht sich obige Stelle auf die bewaffnete Auseinandersetzung zwischen der tatarischen Aristokratie (eine der einflußreichsten unter ihnen die Širins) und den Mirzas, bald nach der Ankunft des neuen Chans, Islam III Kerej (1644—1654) (Smirnov, 527, ff.).

223,20—25 In den 40er Jahren herrschte auf der Krim eine starke und langwierige Krise in der Volkswirtschaft: Dürre, Mißernte, kein Viehfutter, keine Lebensmittel, schon ab 1641 und das setzte sich sechs und mehrere Jahre fort. Dazu war noch die türkische Flotte im Mittelländischen Meer beansprucht, so daß der Sultan verbot, die Schiffe zu Ausfuhrzwecken nach der Krim zu benützen. — Hierauf bat 1644 der Chan um die Genehmigung des Sultans, gegen Moskau einen Feldzug führen zu dürfen (Novoseljskij, 313, 342, 333).

223,25 Die Fastenzeit dauerte 1646 vom 9. Februar bis 19. März (W. H.).

223,27 *akn(kaluťiwn)* = 'Erwartung', *guman* = 'Hoffnung' (G. Abgarian).

223,28 Durch die Stadttore kamen täglich 500, 600 ja sogar 900 und 1000 Fuhrwerke mit Lebensmitteln und allerlei Waren beladen, bis zum Abend blieb ihnen nichts zu verkaufen übrig (D'Ascoli: *ZOOID* XXIV, 118; Jakobson, 139).

223,28 1646, 23, März, war Montag (W. H.).

223,31 Die Stelle bezieht sich wahrscheinlich auf Sultanzade Mohammed Pascha, der 12. Juli 1646 in Kreta am hitzigen Fieber starb (W. H.). *GOR*,

V. 401. — Über die Benennung des Krieges Malta anstatt Kreta s. unten 224,03.

223,32 *hajn* 'jener', s. 223,05.

223,35 Über die sieben Jahre während Teuerung s. oben 223,20.

223,38 In der Handschrift steht: *topaz*. Das Wort sollte zu Osm. *tombaz* 'Barke, flacher Kahn, Ponton' korrigiert werden. — Der Fachausdruck ist auch in den balkanischen Sprachen als Lehnwort verbreitet, und sogar im Ungarischen (17. Jh.). Vgl. S. Kakuk, *Recherches sur l'histoire de la langue osmanlie des XVIe et XVIIe siècles. Bibliotheca Orientalis Hungarica* XIX, 398.

223,41 Die Eintreibung von Sonderleistungen von der Bevölkerung verschärften sich vor einer jeden Kriegsoperation. So 1626 vor dem Feldzug gegen die Čerkessen (213,28), gegen die Burg Ozun (213, 37) (vgl. Mikaelian, 216—217).

223,43 *cec* 'Verprügeln' für *ecz*, Emendation von W. H.

223,45 16. August, Mariä Himmelfahrt.

224,03 Da eben vor der Ingangsetzung des Krieges gegen Kandia (Insel Kreta) ein türkisches Geschwader von Malthesern überfallen, und auch aus taktischen Gründen das Gerücht verbreitet wurde, daß der Krieg eigentlich gegen die Maltheser geführt wird (*GOR* V, 363, ff; Zinkeisen, IV. 569—579.). — Suda ist eine Stadt auf der Insel Kreta. — 'Franke' ist der allgemeine Ausdruck für «Europäer» (vgl. türk. *frengi*).

224,06 Ibrahim I., türkischer Sultan, 1640—1648.

224,06 Hammer gibt keine näheren Angaben über die neue Frau (*GOR* V, 413).

224,09 Surb Nišan — Surb Xač — Das hl. Kreuz. Das Kloster ist 1338 in der Berglandschaft 4—5 Km von Solxat (Eski Krim) erbaut worden (Bžškian 324—327). Kunsthistorische Beschreibung von Jakobson: *Vizantijskij Vremennik* VIII, 173—181.

224,10 Islam III. Kerej Chan, 1644—1654 (*GOR*, V, 342—345; Smirnov, 529).

224,29 Also verweilte Aristakes Wardapet vom 6. Januar bis zum Beginn des Fastens (*Aghuhac'k'*), 5. Februar 1649, in Qara-Su (W. H.).

224,32 Bei Bžškian ohne Zeitangabe erwähnt: Im armenischen Viertel ist die Kirche S. Nikolaus von den Tataren in Brand gesetzt worden (S. 287). Der Priester Johannes (Begleiter des russischen Gesandten), der 1634—1635 die Krim besuchte, berichtet über eine Kathedrale, die in eine Moschee umgewandelt worden ist (Kondaraki, XIV, 26).

224,35 16. März, Samstag, 34. Tag der Fastenzeit, Gedenktag des hl. Gregors «Eintritt in die Grube», als er in den tiefen Graben (Xor-Virap) geworfen wurde. S. oben 209,35.

225,02 Karfreitag.

225,07 Kašot — ein Stadtviertel der Armenier von Kaffa (Grigor Kamaxec'i, *Žamanakagrut'iwn* (Chronik), Jerusalem 1915. 60. Vgl. Mikaelian, 111, 286. S. noch 212,14).

225,10 Die im 14. Jahrhundert eingewanderten Armenier sind außerhalb der genuesischen Bollwerke der Zitadelle (Frenghisar) angesiedelt worden. Zur Verteidigung ihres Viertels errichteten sie eine äußere Stadtmauer. Von der 1 Meile langen Mauer blieb ein Teil neben der Quarantäne bis heute erhalten (Bžškian, 332. Mikaelian, 328—329. Vgl. oben 214,31). Vielleicht ist hier von Ausbesserungsarbeiten die Rede.

225,14 Nikolaus Potocki, Hetman der polnischen Armee und sein Sohn Stephan und andere Adelige sind am 25. Mai 1648 bei Korsun von den vereinigten Streitkräften der Tataren und Bogdan Chmelnickij gefangen genommen worden (*The Cambridge History of Poland*, 511; Smirnov, 545; Evarickij, II. 242.) Über die Teilnahme der Tataren: s. Novoseljskij, 395; Smirnov, 538—543, ff.

225,17 Ghala — Čufut Kala — Castellum Judeorum, heilige Stadt der Karaiten, Vorstadt von Baxči Saraj (Keppen, 308—318; Kondaraki, XV, 194—204; Bruun, II/2. 135; Jakobson, 128—129).

225,22 Qrïm Kerej Qalgha, Bruder des Chans Islam III. Kerej. S. oben 224,10.

225,23 Die Tataren veranlaßten hiermit Prinz Lupul, einen Vertrag mit Chmelnickij zu schließen (*Cambridge History of Poland*, 513). Das Gerücht der Ungehorsamkeit des Chans gelangte bald nach Istanbul (Smirnov, 544).

225,30 Bogdan Chmelnickij Kosakenhetman.

225,32 d. h. Armenier. Über Grigor, den Erleuchter der Armenier s. oben 209,35; 224,35.

225,39 Bezeichnung der tatarisch-türkischen Völker. (Vgl. *History of the Nation of the Archers. HJAS* vol. 12. (Dec. 1949), 384.)

225,40 Kaffa ist seit der genuesischen Periode einer der größten Sklavenmärkte geworden (Jakobson, 110). Der Sklavenhandel wird von den Genuesern nicht verboten, sondern eben gefördert, und in dem Officium Gasariae (1449) amtlich geregelt. Für das Ausmaß des Sklavenhandels sind folgende Zahlen bezeichnend: Zur Zeit der Einnahme Kaffas fanden die Türken dort 30.000 Gefangene vor (Ph. Bruun, *Krimskij poluostrov*, 6. Apud Mikaelian, 142). Allein von den Russen (mit denen die Tataren zu dieser Zeit in Frieden lebten!) entführten sie in der ersten Hälfte des 17. Jahrhunderts 150—200.000 Gefangene (Nach den Errechnungen von Novoseljskij, 436). Aus Polen (*Korel*) schleppten sie natürlich viel mehr Gefangene weg, laut Beauplan (17. Jh.) in 2 Wochen: 50.000 (Jakobson, 135).

Sie ließen durch die Gefangene die Felder bebauen, behandelten sie wie das Rindvieh (Broniewski, *ZOOID*, VI, 357; Schwandtner, III, 284) Für die Wohlhabenden verlangten sie hohe Lösegelder. Über die Unterhandlungen berichtet auch Broniewski (*ibid.* 363; Schwandtner, III, 294.)

226,01 Klein Qara-Su: s. Smirnov, 334.

226,01 Surb Sargis war die Mutterkirche der Armenier auf dem Hauptplatz der Stadt Kaffa, mit einem kleinen Kloster im Hofe (Bžškian, 349—350. Vgl. oben 209,36).

226,02 Die Besuche der Etschmiadziner Legaten auf der Krim, s. Mikaelian, 282, ff.

226,04 Die Ortschaften mit bedeutender armenischer Diaspora in der Krim, s. Bžškian, 242—356.

226,09 Pers. *čap rast* «trotziger Schüler» (W. H.).

226,12 Das Gleichnis scheint auf den tatarisch-türkischen Ausdruck *qara yüzlü* 'mit schwarzem Antlitz — beschämt' hinzuweisen.

226,16 *kapič* — ungefähr 2 Liter (Vgl. *REArm* V, 377—380).

226,19 Der frühere Kapudan-Pascha Derwisch Mehemmed verschied am 29. Oktober 1654. Die Amtszeit seines Nachfolgers, Ipšir Mustafa Pascha, dauerte kaum einige Monate. *GOR* V, 583, 607—631. (Der Scheich ist das Haupt des Derwischordens.)

226,26—31 In den schwer beschädigten Zeilen handelt es sich um die kurzfristige Wezirwürde Mehmeds und seine Erwürgung und den Antritt des neuen Wezirs, Murad Pascha.

226,36 *hajn* 'jener' = die Kosaken. S. auch oben 223,05.

226,37 Vielleicht identisch mit dem Čerkessen Ketɣač Ahmed Pascha, dem früheren grausamen Sandschakbeg von Syrien (*GOR* V, 396).

226,37 Die armenischen Patriarchen Philippos I. Aghbakeci, 1633—1655 und Hakob IV. Džughajeci, 1655—1680.

226,40 Nördliche Gegend, Land der Hunnen — historisierende traditionelle Benennung der (Ost)Krim.

227,17 Fronarbeit für die Türken (Mikaelian 214—218). S. Einleitung.

227,29 In der Nacht von Palmsonntag versammelten sich in den armenischen Gemeinden die Gläubiger vor der Kirchentür, und dann fand die Zeremonie des «Türöffnens» (*durnbac'ek'*) statt (G. Abgarian).

227,36—43 Die Zeilen sind schwer beschädigt, also weggelassen. Es handelt darin um die ungleiche Aufteilung der Charadschsteuer unter den Städten (Bezirken) der Krim, die die Bevölkerung gegeneinander aufhetzte.

228,05 Der lückenhafte Text behandelt wahrscheinlich das traurige Ereignis, als die aus dem polnischen Feldzug zurückkehrenden Feldscharen von Georg II. Rákóczy, Prinz von Transsylvanien, in die Gefangenschaft der Tataren gerieten. Der Heerführer Johann Kemény ist nach zwei Jahren gegen ein hohes Lösegeld losgekauft worden (Zinkeisen. IV. 873).

228,08,13 Vielleicht handelt es sich um die Dardanellensperre der Venetianer (Frank) in 1656 (Zinkeisen, IV. 849—855).

228,10 Fest der Kreuzerhöhung, 13. September 1657 (W. H.).

228,15 Martiros Krimeci (?—1683) gebürtig aus Kaffa, der seine elementare Erziehung in der Klosterschule von Surb Nišan (S. Xač S. 224,09) erhielt. 1645 wurde er Schüler des Patriarchen von Jerusalem, Astauacatur Taroneci. Martiros richtete sich lebhaft gegen die Bewegung des Eleazar von Aintab, den Gegenkatholikos von 1663. Martiros war aber nicht immer Gegner von Eleazar. In dem Jahrzehnt, als die griechischen Priester den Armeniern das S. Jakob-Kloster wegnehmen wollten (1657), kämpfte Martiros mit ihm Schulter an Schulter für die Rechte der Armenier. Martiros war zweimal für eine kurze Zeit (1659—1660 und 1682) Patriarch von Konstantinopel; 1661 ist er zum Bischof der armenischen Diozöse der Krim geweiht, und zum Legaten für Anatolien ernannt worden. Als Dichter schrieb er die Geschichte der Krim (bzw. der armenischen Diaspora) in Versen (310 Zeilen) (A. Martirosian, *Martiros Ghrimec'i* (arm.), Jerewan, 1958. 142—152). — Die Zeilen 15—20, 24—27 sind in gereimter Versform. (Vgl. *ibid*, 8—9.)

228,35 Nachträgliche Eintragungen der Regierungsjahre der Qrimchane: MS 148/v Qazi Kerej Chan starb in Qazikerman, Januar 1608. Ostern fiel auf den 27. März. So ist es.

Selamet Kerej (*Salamat*) Chan kam am 2. Mai aus Istambul nach Kaffa, am Montag. Er regierte 2 Jahre lang, da **40** kam Džanibek Kerej Chan und nahm seinen Platz ein.

1620 kam Džanibek Kerej Chan.

1623 kam Mehemmed Kerej Chan, am 9. Mai, Freitag. 1624 kam Šahin Kerej, am 3. Mai, Montag. Da kam wieder Džanibek Kerej, am 24. Mai, **45** Montag. Er verübte viel Übel im Land und **229** ging beschämt weg. Dann kam 1629 Džanbekej (sic!).

1635 kam Inajet Kerej (*Inajetkre*); Džanbekra ging nach Istanbul.

149/r 5 1637 kam Batirkeraj, der dritte Bruder. 1640 kam Mehemmed Keraj Chan.

149/v 1644, am 28. Juli, Montag. Wardawar **150/r** kam Islamkrej Chan mit 9 Galeeren. Mit Qrim Kerej Sultan 1654 begab er sich zu Gott **10** am ersten Tag im Juli.

Index hominum et locorum*

* Die Zahlangaben beziehen sich auf Seite/Zeile der Ausgabe (nicht MS!) (Zu den fetten Zahlen gehören Anmerkungen)

Abkürzungen:

A	— Anmerkung zu	AA	— Altarmenisch
ON	— Ortsname	OA	— Ostarmenisch
PN	— Personenname	WA	— Westarmenisch

XII

XII

XII

Kerč — ON in O-Krim 221,29
Kerej (Var. Keraj, Kere) — Dynastie der Krimchane (Osmanisch: Girej): passim. **209,19**
Keork, Kevork (OA Georg) s. Georg
Kertaghač Pascha **226,36**
Kirakos (AA Kirakos, WA Giragos) 222,34
Kīrīkor (OA Grigor) s. Grigor
Kizilbaš s. Qīzīlbaš und Karmir Glux
Konstantin — byzantinischer Kaiser 210,21
Korel — ON (208,13); **210,08,29**; 214,22; 215,34; 216,11; 220,02; 225,13,21
Kreta — Insel (Kretes) **223,10,31**; **(224,03)**
Krikor AA, OA Grigor — Gregor
Krim (Var. Xrīm, Ghrīm, Qrīm, Qīrīm) s. Qrim
Lačin Xodža — Bewohner von Kaffa 217,34
Leh(k'), Lehac tun — Polen 217,46; 225,30,45; Lehac erkir **210,08** 225,30
S. Lusavorič — Gregor der Erleuchter **209,35** 210,11, 212,02
S. Lusavorič — Kirche in Kaffa 218,13
(Lupul) — Prinz von Moldau (Boghdan) **225,23**
Madžar — Ungarn, die Ungarn **228,05**
Maghake kahana — Malakias 217,29
Mahmud Agha 213,33,34
Malta — Insel **223,31**; **224,03**
Mangup — Stadt in SW Krim **215,43**
Mansur Oghli — tatarische Sippe **222,16**
Mardiros — AA un OA Martiros
Margare (AA und OA Margare, WA Markare) kahana 217,37
Margare Xodža — Bewohner von Kaffa 217,33
Markare s. Margare
S. Martiros 209,36
Martiros (Krimeci) — Patriarch v. Konstantinopel, Legat (†1683) 222,35(?); **228,15**
Megerdič s. AA und OA Mekertič (Mkrtič)
Mehemed — Pascha von Kaffa 214,39
Mehemet (*Mehemetkere*) Qalgha Sultan 221,01
Mehemmed (Mehmed, Derviš) Pascha, Großvezir **226,19,28**
Mehmed III. Kerej *(Mehemedkeraj, Mehemmedkere)* Chan (1623—1627) 211,25,30; 212,31; 213,13,25; (214,46); A 228,42
Mehmed IV Kerej (*Mehemmedkeraj*) Chan (1641—1644) A 229,06
Mekertič (Məkərtič), kahana 218,15
S. Mekertič (AA, OA Məkərtič, WA Məgərdič), Kirche in Kaffa **217,23**
Memi Pascha 208,27
Mgrdič s. Mekertič

Minas Priester 217,34
Misïr Xodza — Bewohner von Kaffa 217,22,26; 218,31
Mkrtič s. Mekertič
Moldau s. Boghdan
Moskov — Moskau, Rußland 225,23 (s. Urus **208,13**)
Movses Paronter 217,40
Movses Qrimeci — Abt des Klosters S. Nišan 212,08; 212,17
Movses IV. Tatevaci — Katholikos (1629—1632) 217,43
Murad Pascha Großwezir **226,'26**),29
Murad IV. — türkischer Sultan (1623—1640) 211,40; 220,37; 222,24
Musaoghli Sutčioghli Richter 221,18
Musli PN 216,01
Mustafa Mirza 215,28
Mustafa I. — türkischer Sultan (1617, 1622—1623) 208,34; 211,11,39
Nerses Abegha 217,33; 218,37
(S. Nikolas)-Kirche in Gözleve (**224,32**)
Nikolos PN 222,38
S. Nišan — Kloster in (Eski) Krim s. (S.) Xač
Noradin Sultan (Nureddin) — hier: Sohn des Selamet Kerej 219,45
Oraq — Qantemirs Bruder 222,16; (**222,14**)
Orkapu — Arm. Orinberan, Russ. Perekop, Stadt in N-Krim **211,33**; 225,42,46
Osman II. — türkischer Sultan (1618—1622) 208,36; 210,28,(35),38; 211,
    01,08
Otuz — Stadt und Hafen in SO-Krim **215,46**
Ozun — Festung an der Dneper-Mündung **213,37**,42
Pascha von Kaffa 216,28,29,31,41,47 und passim
Perekop s. Orkapu
T. Philippos I. Aghbakeci — armenischer Patriarch (1633—1655) 222,33;
    226,37
Polen s. Leh(k')
Potocki Nikolas polnischer Hetman **225,14**
Q meistens mit X (manchmal mit Gh) geschrieben
Qala s. Ghala
Qantemir Mirza: *Tamurxan* **210,32**; 211,32,37; 213,31; *Xantamur*: 214,09,11;
    214,14,26; 215,26,(34); 216,14,16; *Xantemir*: 221,40
Qarasu (*Xarasu*) — Stadt in O-Krim 215,41; 217,31; 218,16,22,27,32; 219.15,24;
    223,29; 224,24,27; 225,41; 226,04
Klein Qarasu — Stadt in O-Krim 226,01
Qazi II Kerej Chan (*Ghazi, Xazi*) (1588—1596, 1596—1608) A 228,35
Qazi Kerman (*Xazikerman*) ON A 228,35
Qïzïlbaš (*X^izïlbaš*) — Persien 209,19; 219,42 s. auch Karmir Glux
Qïzlar qula (*X^izlar xula*) — Mädchenturm 209,24

XII

Qrīm (Krim, *Xrīm, Xïrīm, Ghrīm*) Stadt in O-Krim = Solxat, Eski Krim
  212,14; 213,20; 216,15,24; 219,07; 224,11; 225,16,41; 226,40; 228,18,30,31
Qrīm — Halbinsel 218,16; 222,21,23
Qrīm Kerej Sultan — Qalgha von Islam III. Kerej Chan 225,22; N 229,09
Qutlubej (*Xutlubej*) — Xačatur Kafajecis Sohn 208,21
Restakes (*ərəstakes*) Aristakes — Bewohner von Kaffa 221,45
Rumelien s. Urumeli
Salmaša Mirza — Bruder **216,15**; **222,14**
Salamat (Selamet) Kerej I. Krimchan (1608—1610) 221,01; A 228,38
Sandīxt — ON?? A **216,05**
Sargis (Aussprache WA und OA: Sarkis) Abegha 226,07
Sargis Wardapet 223,15
Sargis Zorawar — Feldherr, Märtyrer **209,36**
S. Sargis — Kloster in Kaffa **217,19**; **226,01**,03
Selamet s. Salamat
Simeon Priester 222,38; 225,07
Solxat s. Sulxat
Sughda — Sudaq Hafen und Festung in SO-Krim 215,44
Sulxat — (Eski) Qrim **210,26**; (**212,14**); 213,13
Surb Xač — Kloster in O-Krim s. Xač
Suta — Stadt in Kreta 224,05
Šahin Kerej Sultan — Qalgha von Mehmed III. Kerej Krimchan 212,18,31
  213,03,12,16,31; 214,08,10,(46); 215,33; A 228,43
Šahsuvar — PN 215,26
Širin — Mirza und Sippe **223,12**
Taman — Halbinsel 211,21, 23; 226,32
Tamurxan **210,32**; 211,32,37; 213,31 s. Qantemir
Tatin tun — Land der Taten **211,16**; 215,44; 216,25
Tavit (OA Davit) s. David
T. Thoros — Priester in Kaffa 209,40; 211,08; 223,15
Thoros Paronter 217,36
S. Thoros — Kirche in Kaffa **209,33**; 214,04; 218,27; 226,07; 227,25,28
Topraqkala (*Topraxala*) Stadtviertel in Kaffa 214,32; 215,05; 218,19; 222,41
  s. auch *Xew*
Trabizon — Trapezunt, Hafenstadt in NO-Anatolien 224,01
Tuman bej — Bewohner von Kaffa 217,05
Tuna — Donau 214,09,14
Urumeli asker — Truppen von Rumelien 222,44
Vardan (Aussprache OA und WA Wartan) Priester 218,08; 222,37
Warager Kreuz **217,36**; 222,02
T. Zakaria Priester 225,07
Zekerja — Bewohner von Kaffa 217,44

XII

Fachausdrücke* und Völkernamen

abegha (AA *abeła*, WA *apegha*) — Neupriester (unverheiratet)

aghuhac'k' (AA *ałuhac'k'*) — 40-tägige Fastenzeit **218,28** und *passim*

azg Lusaworči — Volk des Erleuchters der Armenier **225,32** und *passim*

baron (<Franz. *baron*) OA *paron* — Herr

baronder, OA *paronter* — Klostervorsteher, Bischof

čerkes — Land, Volk oder Kriegstruppe der Tscherkessen **222,45** s. auch
    Index locorum

čaghataj — Kriegstruppen aus dem Timuridenreich **222,45**

der (AA und OA *ter*) — s. *ter*

depir (AA, OA *dpir*, WA *tbir*) — geistl. Grad: Lektor, Chorsänger

erec (*jerec'*) — gr. Presbyteros — Priester

frank — Europäer (**224,03** Malthäser; **228,08** Venetianer)

Hagarier — Ottomanen **210,33,34,43**; **213,09**

haj — Armenier (hier irrtümlicherweise für 'Kosak' gebraucht) **214,22**;
    215,24,35

hajrapet, WA *hajrabed* — Bischof, (Patriarch)

xač — Kreuz

kahana (AA *kahanaj*) — Priester (verheiratet)

Kosak s. *urus*

nišan — ('Zeichen') Synonym für *xač* — Kreuz

noghaj — Noghaier **210,31**; **211,37**; **213,04,17**; **214,18, 25,27**; **215,25,34,35**;
    216,15; **221,40**; **222,20,45**; **227,11**

nureddin **219,45** sonst nur mit dem Titel *Sultan* erwähnt **210,07**

osmanlï — Ottomantürke **223,05**; **225,24**; **227,16**; **228,07**

paron s. WA *baron*

paronter, WA *baronder* (<*baron* + *der*) — Klostervorsteher, Bischof

qalgha — Thronfolger des Krimchans **219,45** und *passim* und s. *qaghïlgha*

qaghïlgha — Qalgha **219,45**; **220,40,46**

qïzïlbaš — Perser, s. *Index locorum*

S. — Abkürzung für: *Surb*

sarkavag (WA *sargavak*) — Diakon

Sultan — 1. Titel des Qalghas und des Nureddins *passim* **210,07**, 2. türki-
    scher Sultan, hier öfter «König» genannt

surb (WA *surp*) — heiliger

T. — Abkürzung für: *Ter*

tat — Volksname, s. *Index locorum*: Tatin tun

---

* Bei der Erklärung der kirchlichen Ausdrücke auf Deutsch war mir der Wiener
Mechitarist, Erzbischof G. Manian (Mányó) behilflich, wofür ich ihm auch hier meinen
aufrichtigen Dank aussage.

XII

tbir (OA *dpir*) — kirchl. Lektor, Chorsänger
ter (WA *der*) — Herr, Vater, Pater (vor Namen der Geistlicher)
urus — Kosak **208,13,**26,28; 211,13,33; **212,14**; 213,04; (**214,22**); 215,01,40;
217,04,13; 227,14
vardapet (AA *vardapet*, WA *vartabed*, OA *vartapet*) — doctor theologiae
Wardapet s. *vardapet*

Literatur

DORTELLI D'ASCOLI, E., *Opisanie Černogo morja i Tatarii: ZOOID* (*Zapiski Odesskago obščestva istorii i drevnostej*, Bd. XXIV/2.
BARTHOLD, W., — *Giray: EI* II, 181—182; *Krim, ibid.* II, 1162—1163; *Qalgha* II, 742.
BRONIEWSKI, MARTIN, *Opisanie Kryma: ZOOID*, Bd. VI. (1867)
BRONIEWSKI: J. G. SCHWANDTNER, *Scriptores rerum Hungaricarum veteres, ac genuini*, Tyrnaviae, 1765. Bd. III, 247—298: *Descriptio Tartariae*.
BRUN, F. (BRUUN, PH.), *Černomorje*, I—II, Odessa 1879—1880.
BŽŠKIAN (BŽŠKEAN), M., *Čanaparhorduťiwn i Lehastan* (Reise nach Polen). Venedig 1830.
EVARICKIJ, D., *Istorija, zaporožskich kozakov*. Bd. II., St. Pbg. 1895.
GOLOBUCKIJ, V. A., *Zaporožskoe kazačestvo*. Kiew 1957.
GOR s. Hammer, J.
HAKOBIAN (HAKOBJAN), W., *Manr Žamanakagruťjunner XIII—XVIII dd.* (Kleine Chroniken, 13—18 Jh.). Bd. I., Jerewan 1951.
HAMMER, J., *Geschichte des Osmanischen Reiches*. Bd. IV, V. Pest 1829.
HEYD, W., *Histoire du commerce du Levant au moyen-âge*, I—II. Leipzig, 1885—86.
JAKOBSON, A. L., *Srednevekovyj Krym*. Moskau—Leningrad 1964.
(Jakobson, A. L., *Armjanskaja srednevekovaja architektura v Krymu. Vizantijskij Vremennik* VIII (1956), 166—191.
KEPPEN (KÖPPEN), P., *Krymskij Sbornik*. St. Pbg. 1837.
KONDARAKI, V. CH., *Universaljnoe opisanie Kryma*. St. Pbg. 1875.
Manr Žam. s. Hakobian
MATUZ J., *Eine Beschreibung des Khanats der Krim aus dem Jahre 1669. Acta Orientalia* (*Havniae*) XXVIII (1964), 129—151.
MATUZ, J., *Qalgha: Turcica. Bd.* 2 (Paris 1970), 103—129.
MIKAELIAN, V., *Ťrimi hajkakan gaghuťi patmuťjun* (Geschichte der armenischen Diaspora in der Krim). Jerewan 1964.
NOVOSELJSKIJ, A. A., *Borjba Moskovskogo gosudarstva s tatarami v pervoj polovine XVII veka*. Moskau—Leningrad 1948.
REA — *Revue des Études Arméniennes*, 1920—1933.
REArm — *Revue des Études Arméniennes*, Neue Folge, 1964—
Rizvan — Abdullah ibn Rizvan, *La Chronique des Steppes Kiptchak, Tevārīh-i Dešt-i Qipčaq, du XVIIe siècle.* Edition critique par A. Zajączkowski. Warschau 1966.
SCHÜTZ, E., *An Armeno-Kipchak Chronicle on the Polish-Turkish Wars in 1620—1621.* Budapest 1968.
SMIRNOV, V. D., *Krymskoe chanstvo pod verchovenstvom Otomanskoj porty do načala XVIII veka.* St.Pbg 1887.
SPULER, B., *Die Goldene Horde. Die Mongolen in Russland, 1223—1502.* Leipzig 1943.
TARDY, L.—VÁSÁRY, I., *A. Taranowskis Bericht über seine Gesandtschaftsreise in der Tartarei* (1569), *AOH* XXVIII, f. 2.
TIESENHAUSEN (TIZENGAUZEN) V., *Sbornik materialov, otnosjaščichsja k istorii Zolotoj Ordy.* Bd. I. St. Pbg. 1884.
TOURNEBIZE, FR., *Histoire politique et réligieuse de l'Arménie.* Paris 1900.
VASILIEV, V. V., *The Goths in the Crimea*, Cambridge, Mass. 1936.
VELIAMINOV—ZERNOV, V. V., *Materialy dlja istorii Krymskago chanstva.* St. Pbg. 1864.
Vizantijskij Vremennik s. Jakobson
ZINKEISEN, J. W., *Geschichte des Osmanischen Reiches in Europa.* Bd. III, IV, Gotha, 1855, 1856.

XII

Acta Orientalia Academiae Scientiarum Hung. Tomus XXXI (1), pp. 77—106 (1977)

THE *TAT* PEOPLE IN THE CRIMEA

BY

EDMOND SCHÜTZ

1. The Russian steppes were the site of several successive waves of migrations in the course of history, nomad hordes from Central Asia followed one another in this region. The sedentary cultures of this region were wiped off by these hurricanes, but the tribes who transiently settled on the steppe-land were, on their turn, swept away by newer invaders. Those who were left from the former were incorporated in the new tribal confederations and were used as outpost in the subsequent raids, or were driven to the edges of the area of migrations, to the foothills of the Caucasus and to the Crimea.

The mighty Peninsula of the Black Sea did not belong to the central region of the nomad empires that developed in the southern steppes, nevertheless it was invaded in succession by the Huns, Khazars, Pechenegs, Comans, Mongols-Tatars and the Kipchak tribes, the latter being the main force of the Golden Horde.

The Goths who fled to the Peninsula from the Huns were driven into the mountains, while the southern coast was under Greek, Byzantine and Genoese rule in succession.

Thus the coastal region of the Crimea became a *reservoir* of various fragmentary peoples. Side by side with the great nations, or tribal confederations, in the description of medieval travellers, an ethnic group called *Tat* is mentioned in the Pontic region. This name stands for a people who have been found along the northern shore of the Sea of Azov speaking Greek, along the Caspian Sea coastline speaking Persian[1], and in the Roumanian and Bulgarian parts of Dobrudja speaking Tatar.

V. Minorsky gave a thorough analysis of the history and name of the Tats in his article in the *Enzyklopädie des Islam*, and the researches of H. H. Schaeder yielded a series of new data and solutions to complete the overall picture.[2]

[1] Minorsky, 757—59; recent works on the Persian Tats: B. V. Miller, *Taty, ich rasselenie i govory*, Baku 1929; A. L. Grjunberg, *Jazyk severoazerbajdžanskich tatov*, Leningrad 1963.

[2] S. Bibliography.

The word *tat* appears already in the early Turkic sources. The name was first mentioned in the Orkhon inscriptions, but the interpretation of this source entailed many problems. In the sentence *on oq oylïna tatïnga tägi* the word *tat* was first interpreted by Á. Vámbéry properly «Ansässiger, Untertan ; settler, subject». W. Thomsen gave a translation and explanation of standing validity : «bis zu den Söhnen der zehn Pfeile (der westlichen Türken) und ihren Tat (ihren Untertanen fremden Ursprungs)». In the new translation of T. Tekin this sentence appears as : « . . . up to the descendants and subjects of the On Oq».[3]

Kāšġarī in his *Dīvān* maintained that the term was applied to «Persians» by the Turks (I, 454; II, 280). The wide use of the word *tat* is shown by its repeated occurrence in Kāšġarī's work even in verbal derivatives. The expression *kāfir uyġuri* (I, 39, 16) he used in another passage was given more than one interpretation. H. H. Schaeder, who put forward the most probable one, maintained that here the author does not refer to pagan Uygurs, but to «pagans living in the country of the Uygurs». Summarizing the different shades of meaning Schaeder gave the following exhausting definition to the term *tat* : die nichttürkischen Untertanen des Uigurenstaates, «in der Hauptsache Iranier, sowohl Sogdier, wie Leute vom anderen Ufer des Amudarya.»[4]

Taking into account the importance of the Sogdians in Eastern and Western Turkestan, Kljaštornyj interpreted the ethnic name *Tat* as «Sogdian». This would seem to be an attractive theory since the Sogdians were the closest Iranian neighbours of the Turks. It is, however, contradicted by the separate occurrence of the name of Sogdia in the Orkhon inscriptions, moreover the name of the Sogdians, the main trading partners of the Turks was well known in the Eastern Turkic empires.[5] Kljaštornyj himself deals extensively with their history in the same work.

After that the name of the *Tat*s disappeared from the Turkish literature. It does not occur in the outstanding monuments of the Karakhanid period and is also missing from the classics of the Chagatay literature.[6] This, however, does not prove its extinction, it was only replaced in literary works with the word *tažik* (and *farsi*) the *tat* anyhow being a popular term of a somewhat

[3] A. Vámbéry, *Noten zu den alttürkischen Inschriften*: *MSFOu* XII (1899), 88 ; W. Thomsen, *Turcica*: *ZDMG* 78 (1924), pp. 143 sqq. ; Cf. also Schaeder, 5 ; T. Tekin, *A Grammar of Orkhon Turkic*, Indiana Univ. Publ., *Uralic & Altaic Series*, vol. 69, 1968 : *Bilge Kagan Inscriptions*: BK N 15 (and KT S 12), 281, 263 ; W. Barthold, *12 Vorlesungen über die Geschichte der Türken Mittelasiens*, Leipzig 1935, 91, 240.

[4] K. Brockelmann, *Mitteltürkischer Wortschatz*: *BOH* I, s.v. tat, tatyqmaq, tatlamaq, tatlaq, tatlašmaq, pp. 198—199 ; Minorsky, 756 ; Schaeder, 2—4, 3 ; C. Brockelmann, *Altturkestanische Volkspoesie*: *Festschrift Fr. Hirt*, 19 D.

[5] S. G. Kljaštornyj, *Drevnetjurkskie runičeskie pamjatniki*, Moscow 1964, 122—123.

[6] Excepted in the compound titulature : *tat tawġač* and the Chagatay dictionaries compiled at later date. Cf. Schaeder, 7—8, 14.

pejorative shade of meaning. It survived although in the vernacular, as shown by the Chagatay glossaries later compiled.

In the opinion of Klaproth the name was applied to all kind of subjected population, alien to the ruling Turko-Tatar tribes.[7]

In the literature it only occurs in the *Šejere-i Terākime*, Abū'l-Ġāzī's Turkman Genealogy, written intentionally in a popular style. Speaking of the times of the descendants of Oghuz Khan Abū'l-Ġāzī said that «in Iraq, Khorasan and the Maverannahr the rulers (*padišah*), soldiers (*sipah*), and *raya*s were all *Tat*s, there was nobody except *Tat*s». The region referred to was in fact inhabited mainly by Persians, but this would rather correspond to the state of affairs of the lifetime of Abū'l-Ġāzī himself, projecting later events and conditions back into the undefined era of Oghuz khan, the *heros eponymos*.[8]

Whereas in Central Asia the name *Tat* was replaced by the ethnic term *Tajik*, it survived in the language of the peoples of the Oghuz branch from the Seldjuk period throughout the Ottoman rule.[9]

Among the Chagatay and Ottoman-Turkish lexicographic data the meaning «Persian, Iranian» dominated. E.g. in the *Sanglax*: «*firqa-i tājik*», according to the *Lehçe-i Osmani* it was applied to the old Iranian and Kurdish populations of provinces absorbed into the Ottoman Empire[10] (Radl. III, 899).

The remark of Z. V. Togan, according to which centuries ago (14th cent.?) the entire population settled in Turkestan was called *Tat*, and the communication of Samojlovič (to Minorsky) that the inhabitants of Khiva were once (einstmals) also called by that name (perhaps as a memory of the old Iranian population of Khwarizm)[11] both may reflect a reminiscence of the Chagatay glossaries or Abū'l-Ġāzī's remark.

From the earliest sources on the second prevalent meaning was «settled people» as shown by the examples of the Chagatay dictionaries: «a class of serfs, who do not live in towns and, without being actual slaves (*kul*), are in the service of landed gentry (*akābir*)». In the Kipchak glossaries: «peasant» (*Idrāk*), «villager» (*Bulġat*), «fallah» (*Tuḥfat*).[12]

---

[7] Full particulars s. Schaeder, 16—33. — Klaproth: *Zap. Imp. AN* XXIV (1874), 51; cf. Brun, II, 241.

[8] Kononov, XLI, 56.

[9] Schaeder, 5—7.

[10] *Sanglax*, 152r; *Lehçe-i Osmani* > B. de Meynard: «surnom donné au population d'origin persan ou Kourde». The quotation in English from: Clauson, 449.

[11] Minorsky, 756; Schaeder, 9.

[12] Véliaminov-Zernov, 162; P. de Courteille, 194: «gens de bas étage qui n'habitent pas dans les villes; ceux qui s'attachent à la personne d'un grand, sans faire parti de ses esclaves». Clauson's translation, p. 449. — V. Izbudak, *El-Idrâk Haşiyesi*, Istanbul 1936, p. 46: *Tat* (19): «Türkçe bilmez, dilsiz; arap, farsi». — Zajączkowski, *Bulġat al-Muštaq*, I, tat «étranger»; Atalay, *Ettuḥfet*: tat «şehirli; yerli çiftçi». Above, Clauson's definitions, i.e., translations are quoted.

The terming «settled people» involves, to a certain extent, a derogatory meaning, triggered by the feeling of superiority of nomad Turks. The pejorative meaning was perpetuated, and in the course of time, even more stressed : e.g. in the Dictionary of Véliaminov-Zernov : «a class of unemployed roughs», or B. de Meynard «pauvre,. misérable, d'humble condition, etc.»[13]

The name *Tat*, both as an ethnic name and in the figurative sense, might be found in the language of the Armenians, the neighbours of the Caucasian Tats. The Tats were known as hard-working farmhands who hired themselves out for temporary agricultural jobs. The social inferiority of the Tats lended a pejorative shade of meaning to the word in this case, too. The Tats spoke a language not understood by the landlords, so it acquired also the meaning «dumb, (or even) mute». This interpretation may also be found in Turkish, e.g. *Idrāk* : «türkçe bilmez, dilsiz».[14] H. Ačarean compared this meaning with the word *nemec* meaning «German» in Slavonic languages and also used for someone whose tongue was not understood being a foreigner. The word *nemec* in these languages was derived from the word *nem* meaning «mute». Schaeder also pointed to this parallelism, the second meaning «barbaric, mute» of the ethnic term *Tat*.[15]

The use of the term *Tat* as an ethnic name is not the least equivocal. Besides meaning «Persian, Iranian» it has in the 19—20th centuries reported to denote people living in the Crimea and speaking a Turco-Tatar dialect. Several Russian Turcologists referred to these Tats ; according to Radloff : «von den Einwohnern im westlichen Teile der Krym habe ich die Tataren, die nördlich von Sydak wohnen, Tat nennen hören (sonst ist mir der Ausdruck *tat* in keinem Dialekte aufgestossen)». The personal communication of Samojlovič to Minorsky gives an even more detailed definition : «gegenwertig legen die Noghai-Tataren der nördlichen Krim den Spitznamen Tat allen Muslimen der Südküste der Halbinsel bei, die ein Gemisch von türkisierten Volksstämmen sind».[16]

Among the officials of the territory of the Crimean Khanate, there was a minister dealing with the affairs of the Tats of the southern coast (*tat-aǧasï*).[17] This indicates their importance in the region.

The Turco-Tatar language does not define at the same time their ethnic affiliation, original native tongue and origin. An interesting duality is mani-

---

[13] Véliaminov-Zernov—PdC—B. de Meynard—Radloff, III, 900. — Clauson 449.
[14] Izbudak, *El-Idrâk*, 46.
[15] H. Ačarean, *Hayeren gawaṙakan baṙaran*, 341 ; see also s.v. *zaza* 315. — Schaeder, 14—15. — Both words : *nemec* «German» and *nema* «dumb, mute» have been adopted separately from Slavic to Hungarian : *német, néma*, Kniezsa, *A magyar nyelv szláv jövevényszavai*, I/1, 354—355.
[16] Radloff, III, 899 ; Minorsky, 756.
[17] Kondaraki, X, 47.

fested by the population of the colony of Mariupol, where only the Greek people are called Tats, while the Turkish speaking part of the settlement area was called: *bazarian*.[18]

In the following it will be attempted to solve these contradictions by the analysis of data hitherto unattended to.

2. The Greek population living in Mariupol and the surrounding villages on the coast of the Sea of Azov had been known in the literature, but it was V. Grigorovič, professor in Odessa, who called attention to the archaic traits in the language of these settlers. In his paper «On the mixed Greek-Turkish population of Mariupol», Otto Blau, who was interested in Turkish linguistic monuments in Greek script originating from this area, included long passages translated into German from the book of V. Grigorovič published in Odessa in 1874, in which he analysed the language of the inhabitants of Mariupol and the surrounding 12—15 villages, called Tats.[19]

In compliance with her policy of integration of the Crimean peninsula, after the Treaty of Küčük Kainarji (1774) an ukase was issued by Empress Catherine ordering the transfer of 18 407 Greeks from the southern Crimean coastline into Mariupol and the surrounding villages.[20] The Tat settlers came from the area of the orthodox eparchy lying between Čufut-Kale (Kirker) and Sudaq. The centre of the new settlement was named Mariupol (Mariampol) after the valley and village called Marijnoe Selo (Marianopol), known of its Uspenskij Monastery (Dormitio Mariae), on the outskirts of the capital of the eparchy Bakhči Sarai, along the road leading to Čufut-Kale. The names of the villages surrounding Mariupol were derived from their former domiciles in the Crimea, in part after the villages of the area between Sebastopol and Tepe-Kermän, and in part after those around Sudaq.[21]

Data relating to the earlier history of the Greek speaking Tats are known from records deriving from the Genoese era. In these the famous vine-growing region of the Greeks around Sudaq are mentioned. When in 1365 the Genoese recaptured Sudaq from the Tatars, a special clause of the 1380—1381 treaty dealt with the eighteen villages near Sudaq: «Queli dixoto casay li quai eran sotemixi e redenti a Soldaya».[22] The name of the tax levied on vine-growing

[18] Grigorovič/Blau, 577.

[19] *Ibid.*, 576—580.

[20] From among the 31,386 displaced Crimean Christian citizens 12,598 Armenians had been settled down in Rostov on the Don river and in the neighbouring 10 villages. Barxudarian, 39. Cf. *Hungaro-Turcica*, 191.

[21] Grigorovič/Blau, 577; Keppen, 100, 75—78, 43; Kondaraki, I/1, 63—64; Gavriil: *ZOOID* I, 197—204; Vasiliev, 280.

[22] In the translation of Silvestre de Sacy: «les dix-huit villages qui étoient soumis et annexés à Soldaja». Keppen, 84—86; Brun, II, 144; Heyd, II, 204—205; Vasiliev, 177—178, 181.

6

(ambelopatico) also shows that viticulture had been introduced by the Greeks and that it was carried on under the Genoese rule as well.[23]

This land around Sudaq was given as an estate in feud to the Hoǰa Haǰi Bayram by Batu (Sayin) Khan. This *tarxan* privilege was renewed by the Khan of the Golden Horde, Timur Kutlug (1395—1400) for the descendants of the Hoǰa in H. 800/A.D. 1396. However, the inhabitants named Tat are not mentioned in this document.[24]

Vine-growing in the Crimea was not restricted to the region of Sudaq; rich vineyards were to be found everywhere on the slopes of the hillsides in the peninsula. Martin Broniewski, envoy of the Polish king Stephen Báthory, mentions the orchards and vineyards around Kaffa in 1578 with admiration : «vineas, pomaria et hortos fere infinitos illa (i.e. Caffa civitas) habet». His account on the vine-growing area extending for more than two miles next to Sudaq is even more enthusiastic : «vineas, pomaria, quae ad duo et amplius milliaria extenduntur, a Caphensibus, Judaeis et Christianis nunc etiam ibi coluntur. Nam universae Tauricae vinum optimum ibi nascitur». The area of the vine-district in later times extended as far as 40 kilometres, which means that it was practically contiguous to the gardens around Kaffa.[25]

The fame of Sudaq vineyards remained unmarred in the following centuries. Field-marshal Münnich in his «Tagebuch» opted for the superiority of the wine from Sudaq in respect of both colour and flavour.[26]

The «Tat» nationality of this vine-growing people is mentioned in a very early record. Hans Schiltberger, a Bavarian soldier who was taken prisoner in the battle of Nicopolis in 1396, visited several countries in the Near East in the service of different Turkish and Tatar lords, as a slave. He also travelled in the Crimea and a very precious account on the Tats is due to him : «Item ein stat haist Karkery und hatt ein guts landt und haist Sutti und die haiden heyssentz Thatt und sein Christen darinn in chrichischem glauben und hatt gut weinwachs . . .[27] [There is a town Kirkor and has a good land and is called Sutti and the pagans call it Thatt inhabited by Christians of Greek faith, and has good vineyards . . .]». The name *Sutti* had formerly been emended to *Cuthi*

[23] Heyd, II, 207.

[24] Vámbéry, *Uigurische Sprachmonumente*, 172—173; Radlov: ZVOIRAO III, 17—38; A. O. Hasan: *Türkiyat Mecmuası*, III, 207—228.

[25] Broniewski/Schwandtner, 270, 271; Broniewski: ZOOID VI, 348, 347; Keppen, 124; Brun, II, 155; Jakobson, *Sr. Krym*, 118.

[26] Brun, II, 156. It is worth mentioning that according to the evidence of Adam Evorka (Jávorka?) French consul of Hungarian origin the vineyards had been tilled with the hard labour of Hungarian captif-slaves. Brun, *ibid.*, Kondaraki, VI, 59; — On the vine production of the subsequent period see: Kondaraki, I, 230; V, 56. — Later in the Potemkin era in the valleys of the Sudaq region left behind by the Greek colonists Hungarian Tokai vines had been planted, Kondaraki, I, 232.

[27] Schiltberger, 63.

and Schiltberger's account was considered an important source relating to the Goths in the Crimea.[28] The conclusion was drawn by Brun that *Tat* was the Tatar word for «Gothia».[29] This explanation was refuted by H. H. Schaeder, who regarded *Sutti* as a form variant or distortion of Sudaq, Sogdaq, Sugda, Soldaia,[30] and so the name *Thatt* clearly reflect the wine-growing Christians of Greek faith in the vicinity of Sudaq.

The name *Tat* given to the Greek gardners living around Sudaq also survived later on, as shown by the Armenian source dating from two centuries later. A peculiar, seemingly territorial term : *Tat'in tun* occurs several times in the Chronicle of Kaffa written by an Armenian priest, Khachatur, reporting on the events of the period between 1615—1648.[31]

The basic meaning of *tun* in Armenian is «house, domus», but it also means «estate, manor». The word *tun* in combination with *Tat'*, apparently a proper name, at first glance I took for the term for an estate of a landlord named *Tat'*. Other passages, of the Chronicle, to be described below, did not contradict this interpretation, as M. Broniewski also accounted on vineyards owned by landlords of different nationalities around Kaffa. However, the word *tun* is frequently used also in a wider sense, in addition to «home» also «homeland» (cf. «Heim — Heimat»). The word *tun* also occurs with such a meaning in the above-mentioned Chronicle referring to larger areas, counties or even countries. For example : *Honac' tun* «the land of the Huns» (160, 41) ;[32] *Frankac' tun* «the land of the Franks» (Malta, in the given case, 224, 03) ; *Korelac' tun* «Korel — West-Ukraine». Beside the current name for Poland, *Lehastan*, the expression *Lehac' tun* meaning «the land of the Poles» is frequently used in Armenian. The word *Lehk'* (pl. nom.) may in Classical Armenian (Grabar) mean either «Poles», or «Poland». That the word *tun* in this case meant «land, region» is shown by the simultaneously used term *Lehac' erkir* «land of the Poles, Poland» (225, 30, 45).[33] The singular *tat* in the expression *Tat'in tun* may have been misleading, but it should not be forgotten that the names of people are frequently used in the singular in the Turkish-Tatar languages (singularia tantum).[34] The aspirated sound did not cause any difficulty in the interpretation, as generally this sound represents the common *t* of Turkish. So the

---

[28] W. Tomaschek, *Die Goten in Taurien*, 5 sq. ; Minorsky, 756 ; even Vasiliev, 193 ; Pelliot, 155.

[29] Brun, II, 236.

[30] Schaeder, 10.

[31] *Manr Žam.* I, 211, 16 ; 215, 44 ; 215, 25. See also the «Index hominum et locorum» in the German translation of same, *AOH* XXIX/2, 184.

[32] *Hungaro-Turcica*, 199.

[33] *AOH* XXIX/2, 184, 165.

[34] Schütz, *An Armeno-Kipchak Chronicle*, 104.

XIII

linguistic evidence corresponded to the historical fact that this region was inhabited by Tats, i.e. *Tat'in tun* meant «the land of Tats».

The «land of Tats» (*Tat'in tun*) is mentioned in the following loci of the Chronicle of the Kaffan priest, Khachatur. Locus 211,16 : after killing of the Turkish sultan Osman II and the succession of Mustafa I in 1622, the Cossacks raided the port of Kaffa with 33 ships (*qayïq*) and inflicted much damage in the surrounding region as well. «They also devastated the orchards (*baxče*) of the land of Tats». In 1629 the Cossacks again invaded several Crimean cities and also attacked Sughda (i.e. Sudaq) «causing much damage in the land of Tats» (215,44). The purpose of the Cossacks in ruining the Tats' gardens was to cause heavy losses to the Turks by depriving them of the rich agricultural and vine-growing regions under their direct rule, and first of all, make a rich booty.[35]

The third locus referring to the Tats is in a quite different context. It relates that in 1630 when the *defterdar* (the commissioner of finance of the province) Hasan Agha entered in the tax roll the population of Kaffa, Eski Krim (Solkhat) and the surrounding villages, he was especially fussy about the Tats (216,25—27) : *Tat'in tunn gənac' šat aymunk' araw, 4 taroy 5 taroy tyak'n xaraǰ grec' urac'oyac'n xaraǰ iaṫ.* In the German translation I interpreted this passage as follows : «He went to the land of the Tats, made much fuss, put boys of the age of 4—5 years on the tax roll, and took tax (kharaj) from the refusers».[36] It was usual in the practice of tax collection by the Turks, moreover the *defterdar*s preparing the tax rolls and levying the various services had an outright instruction, to record not only the heads of the families but also their grown-up sons. In this case the *defterdar* committed a severe encroachment in surpassing the age limit by far.

One is inclined to raise doubts: boys of 4 or 5 could hardly have been taxable, and the wicked Hasan Agha might have taken off the boys for (or instead of) kharaj.[37] The young age of the boys, under the taxable age, would in itself be insufficient reason to challenge the translation, but surely the first instance many of us would be liable to think of the institution of the *devşirme* (boy toll, Knabenlese). Still in the course of translation I discarded this idea, because the relation of Turks and Greeks seemed undisturbed at that time. But since then I changed my mind.

To augment the ranks of the Janissary corps from the beginning of the Ottoman rule, boys of minor age from the Christian population of subdued countries were carried off as a form of toll. Later this draft procedure became

---

[35] *Manr Žam.* 211, 16 ; 215, 44, and *AOH* XXIX/2, 142, 148, 166.

[36] Hakobian, *Manr Žam.* 216, 25—27 ; *AOH* XXIX, 148, 137. «Glaubens-verweigender» simply meant: Christians who refused to become converted to Mahometanism.

[37] My Polish colleague, Z. Abrahamowicz expressed similar doubts in a letter addressed to me.

a regular custom repeated every five years.[38] The institution of *devşirme* is wide-known from the historical sources. Let us now quote the description of this institution by Bartholomaeus Gyurgievits (taken captive in the battle of Mohács) from his eyewitness experience put down in his «Libellus . . . de afflictione captivorum». In the chapter «On the taxes collected from Christians» he wrote : «When the Christian has fulfilled all his obligations, the Turks still have the right to select from among his children the best one, to let him be circumcised, to take him away from his parents and make a soldier of him . . . There are no words to describe the tears, wailing and lament that go with the parting. The father be present to see his son, educated in the cult of Christ, to be carried off to the army of Satan, in order to fight against Christ. The boy is dragged off and has to leave his relatives, pals and friends dear to him for ever and will be drafted in future among those whom the Greeks call father- and motherless (orphans)».[39]

The possibility of similar events taking place in the land of the Tats made me reconsider the translation of the above cited sentence. I was induced to change my mind, and take the *devşirme* into account in this case, mainly because of the problem of interpretation not of the former sentence, but because of the problems of interpretation of a further passage of the Chronicle (216,34—35), to be explained below.

The expression *xaraĵ grel* could be interpreted in two ways : 1. «to put on the tax roll levied on Christians (*xaraĵ*)», 2. «to put on the forced recruiting list of the boys' toll, Knabenlese». Such interpretation could be reached also by a slight emendation of the text : *grel* might be a mistake for *gerel*. The Armenian verbal part of the construction *gerel* means «to take prisoner» with other expressions *geri aŕnel* «to take prisoner», or *geri varel* «to drag off into captivity». The mistake of spelling might have been inspired eventually by the initial syllable of a synonime *grawel* (< P *giraw*) «appropriate, confiscate, etc.».[40] The carrying off of children into captivity is also mentioned in the

---

[38] Papoulia, B. D., *Ursprung und Wesen der «Knabenlese» im Osmanischen Reich*: *Südosteuropäische Arbeiten* 59 (München 1963), 85.

[39] Jam cum omnia officia praestiterint, adhuc jus est Turcae, optimum quemque ex liberis deligere, quem circumcisum, submotumque a conspectu parentum in militum alit . . . Nemo verbis explicare potest, quibus lachrymis, gemitu, singultibusve, istiusmodi divulsio fiat. Pater filium, quem in cultum Christi educaverat, rapi videt ad militiam Satanae, ut Christum oppugnet : filius abstrahitur a parentibus, perpetuo inter alienissimos victurus : quicquid eum est sanguine, sodalitate gratum, familiaritate amicum, relicturus : postmodum in eorum numero futurus, quos Graeci *apatoras*, et *amétoras* vocare solent. (*Continuatio Peregrini de afflictione tam captivorum, quam sub tributo viventium Christianorum*. In : *Calendarium Tyrnaviense*, ad annum J. Chr. M.DCC.XLI, Tyrnaviae 1741, C 1/r. The rarissime copy received by the courtesy of Mr. L. Tardy.)

[40] Malxassianc, St., *Hayerèn bacatrakan baŕaran*, vol. I. Yerevan 1944, 430, 475 ; Hr. Ačaŕean, *Hayerèn armatakan baŕaran*, vol. I, Yerevan 1971, 543, 604.

XIII

Kaffan Chronicle: in 1621 the troops of the Crimean Tatar Kalgha Devlet
Kerei «took many people, men, women and small boys captive» *ayrk' ew kanayk'
mantr tyayk' geri arel èr* (210,10). Anyway, in the quoted case the captives were
taken in a plundering raid (*sefer*).

The sentence withstanding clear interpretation was: *astuac vrèž araw
3.4 taru tyayoc'n ahn či t'oy* (216,34—35), which in the German translation I interpreted: («on Sunday stones were thrown at Hasan Agha [the wicked defterdar], he fled and only got away with great trouble), God took revenge
for the 3—4 years old boys...». When making the translation I wondered why
in this passage boys of 3—4 years were mentioned, whereas earlier the Chronicler wrote about 4—5 year old boys. Moreover, the last three words of the
original Armenian sentence seemed not to fit into the context. Interpretation
of the text was made difficult by the lack of interpunctuation. If, however,
we put a semi-colon, or full stop after *araw*, and the words following it regard
as a co-ordinate clause, the following verbatim translation can be made:
«God took revenge[;] for the 3—4 years old boys no fear was left».[41] I.e. the
4—5 year old boys were carried off as *kharaĵ* (*devşirme*), but when the wicked
Defterdar was driven away, there was no fear that the same might happen
to the younger children. With this emendation both passages became clear,
furnishing further interesting evidence as to the fate of the Greeks around
Sudaq under Ottoman rule.

These Greek Tats coming from around Sudaq were then, after the Treaty
of Küčük-Kainarĵi (1774), transferred to villages on the northern coast of the
Sea of Azov. Since they were inhabitants of the province of Cherson and Sudaq
the old Byzantine ecclesiastical (and administrative) unit was preserved.

When in the middle of the eleventh century the Byzantine provinces in
the Crimea were endangered by the raids of the Polovtzian-Cuman tribes, the
gates of the castle and the citadel were fortified by the Strategos of Cherson
and Sugdaia, the Patrikios Leo Aliatés. The inscription dated 1059, carved
into a marble cornice testifies to the early existence of this administrative
unit of the Greeks of the coastland.

With the Tatar invasion the importance of Cherson diminished; moreover it was completely destroyed by Nogai's hordes in 1299.[42] Its people must
have fled to Byzantium, or rather to more secluded parts of the Peninsula.
The nomad Tatars did not invade the south-western part of the Crimea, neither
the mountain ranges nor the coastline. The south-western territory was handed

---

[41] *Manr Žam.* 216, 34—35; *AOH* XXIX, 149. This enigmatic sentence could be
solved by the change of the punctuation, similar to the Dodona oracle: *Ibis redibis
nunquam peribis in bello.*

[42] V. V. Latyšev, *Sbornik grečeskich nadpisej*, 15—17. Jakobson, *Sredn. Chersones*,
31. — Tizengauzen, I, 112.

out as fief by Nogai to the Beys of Yaslav (Suleshev) together with the fortress Kirkor, lying in the borderland of the steppe country.[43] This administrative unit persevered into the Tatar era, as shown by the document issued by Timur Kutlug in H. 800/A.D. 1396, confirming the land-ownership of the grandsons of Haji Bayram Hoja. The estate — to which Sudaq and its surroundings also belonged (*Sudaq atlïq käntning jivari*) — lay, according to this document, in the *tümän* of Qrim and Qirker (Qirq yer, Qirqor).[44]

This shows that the Byzantine administrative centres were shifted by some 25—50 kilometres, from the Byzantine sphere into the Tatar zone or its proximity. The devastated Cherson was replaced by Kirker (Čufut Kale); the later capital was built for a summer residence of the Khan by the end of the 15th century, next to Kirkor. The role of Sudaq was taken over by Eski Krim (Qrim, Solkhat) on the south-eastern nomadic marches. The Tatar counter-part for the administrative term 'province' is *tümän*.

The administrative pattern inherited from the Byzantine era was, at the same time the traditional pattern of church life : the ecclesiastical units coincided with the civil units of administration.[45]

In the ninth century the ecclesiastical units in the territory of Byzantine Gothia were raised from bishoprics to the rank of archbishoprics. They are mentioned as such in the appendix of the chronicle of Georgios Kodinos (Expositio officiorum Sanctae ac magnae Ecclesiae, juxta eorum ordinem) : No. 16. Cherson, No. 34. Gothia, No. 35. Sugdaia.[46] With the accession of Andronikos Palaiologos to the throne (1283) they were raised to the rank of metropoles, No. 83. Gothia, No. 96. Sugdaia.[47]

With the devastation of Cherson, i.e. in the Polovtzian-Cuman era Phyl-lai became the centre of the thema Cherson ; the town might be identical with Kirkor, or lay at least in the same area. Phyllai in the 12th century was united with the archbishopric of Sugdaia,[48] as indicated in the decree issued by Patriarch Lucas in 1158, in which the metropole is mentioned as : . . . τοῦ Σουγδοφούλλων. The act of unification is also shown by the *Explicatio* : Ἡ δὲ Σουγδαία καὶ αἱ Φοῦλλαι, in the Paris edition with the following explanation : Sugdaea et Phullae, duo erant Archiepiscopatus, sed conjunctae

---

[43] Jakobson, *Sredn. Chersones*, 37.
[44] See note 24. (In the sense of popular etymology misinterpreted by Vámbéry).
[45] Bertier-Delagarde : *ITUAK* No. 57, p. 65 ; Jakobson, *Sredn. Krym*, 82, 124 ; Vasiliev, 276 sqq.
[46] Keppen, 42—43, 131 ; Kondaraki, XVI, 48.
[47] Keppen, 68 ; cf. Jakobson, *Sredn. Chersones*, 32.
[48] Brun, II, 129 ; Keppen, 131, 179 (n. 272), 308 (The site of the town not being identified yet). The recent view of archeologists : *Ist. i arch. Kryma* 18, 45 (n. 13).

unam nunc Metropolim efficiunt, or in the Exposition of Emperor Andonikos : *Σουγδαία ἦν ὡς καὶ Φοῦλλα*.[49]

The *ex libris* found in the books brought from the old homeland and preserved at the parishes of Mariupol and some of the villages bears testimony to the original ecclesiastical administrative units to which these Tat people belonged : *τῆς μητροπόλεος Σουγδαίας καὶ Χερσῶνος*. A Gospel from Yenisala had, according to a note in it, originally belonged to the parish of Kaffa in the eparchy of Sugdaia and Cherson.[50]

This administrative form of eparchies survived and functioned with a validity for the Greeks of Mariupol and the surrounding villages gathered in a much smaller community. Ignatios, the patriarch leading the *exodus* from the Crimea in 1778, had the title of the Metropolitan of Gothia and Kaffa, which meant the conservation of the old ecclesiastical system. The term Gothia was used in order to stress ancientry, and the wide scope of their ecclesiastic jurisdiction.[51]

The expression *gothograikoi* (*γοτθογραίκοι*) frequently occurring in medieval Greek sources should not be regarded as referring to the ethnical composition of the population, it simply meant «Greeks living in the province of Gothia». The mixed population of Sudaq is known from Arab, Byzantine and Genoese sources, but the Tats from the surrounding region must have had Greek ancestors.[52]

In any case, part of the people living in the coastal region of the Crimean peninsula, got under a strong Tatar influence : they generally used Tatar as colloquial language, dressed in a Tatar fashion,[53] but still many, if not all, also knew Greek, although an archaic form which was hard to understand for someone speaking modern Greek, as reported by Archimandrite Gavriil in 1844.[54]

The Tatar tongue failed to supersede the Greek dialect. Hundred years after the *exodus* V. Grigorovič and O. Blau succeeded in recording this dialect as spoken by the great-grandchildren of the emigrants. Greek was not only used for ecclesiastical purposes, in the Greek schools of Mariupol this dialect must have been spoken besides being taught classical Greek.[55]

Summarising, it might be stated that the Tats of Mariupol were the descendants of Byzantine Greek settlers. However their distinction by the Turko-Tatars was based mainly not on their Greek language or special Tatar

[49] Keppen, 131. Cf. Vasiliev, 276.
[50] Grigorovič/Blau, 579.
[51] Keppen, 43 ; Jurgevič : *ZOOID* XIV, 5 ; Jakobson, *Sredn. Chersones*, 18.
[52] Vasiliev, 123.
[53] Kondaraki, I/1, 154 ; Heyd, II, 370 («l'élément grec fortement représenté»).
[54] Gavriil : *ZOOID* I, 203—204.
[55] *Ibid.*

dialect, but first of all on their ethnic and anthropological and social characteristics.

3. In the 19th century another group of the Tat people emigrated from
the Crimea. These emigrants, speaking exclusively a Tatar dialect, settled in
Dobrudja. To throw light on their origin, their past history must be scru-
tinized.

Extensive archaeological excavations have been sponsored by the Soviet
Government to continue the immense work started in the last century to
explore the Sarmatian and Alan cultures that existed in this region before the
ancient Greek and Byzantine settlements.

These ancient people merged with those who came after them in the next
thousand years, and thus must be distinguished from the Alans and Asses
mentioned by the travellers on the south-western part of the Crimea in the
13th to 15th centuries. Some of the Alan and Ass tribes joined several of the
successive nomad confederations of the age of migrations and got as far as
the westernmost parts of Europe, while others merged with the Huns and
Avars. Those left behind settled in the southern parts of present-day Russia
or were driven to the foothills of the Caucasus or to the Crimean peninsula.[56]

The latest wave of Alans and Asses must have been due to the defeat
they suffered from the hand of the Mongols in 1222. When Jebe and Sübötei
after having crossed the Straits of Derbend encountered united forces of the
Kipchaks and Alans, they succeeded treacherously to confront the allies, and
to defeat them one by one.[57] Some tribes after the defeat fled to the Crimea
through the isthmus of Perekop, or through the Cimmerian Strait. This fresh
wave might account for the frequent mention of the Alans and Asses in sources
relating to the southwestern Crimea in the 13th to 15th centuries.

Alans were sporadically mentioned in the eastern Crimea as well. When
Nogai burned Kaffa down, he also captured «Moslem, Alan and Frank» merchants.[58] The delegation sent by Baibars, the Mamluk Sultan to the Khan of
the Golden Horde found different peoples in Eski Krim (Solxat): Kipchaks,
Russians and Alans. Alans were continually present in Sudaq, the trading
centre of the Crimea up to the 13th century.[59] The Alans fighting in the army
of Nogai might have come from the Kipchak steppes under Nogai's rule, or
from among the Alans living in the Crimea [60]

---

[56] Marquart, *Streifzüge*, 361, 368; Czeglédy, K., *Nomád népek vándorlása Nap-
kelettől Napnyugatig* : Kőrösi Csoma Kiskönyvtár 8, pp. 33—39.

[57] Ibn al-Athir : Tizengauzen, I, 23—27; Rašid ed-Din : Tizengauzen, II, 32—33.
Cf. Jakobson, *Sredn. Chersones*, 28—29; Vasiliev, 162.

[58] Baibars : Tizengauzen, I, 112; cf. Spuler, 75.

[59] Ibn az-Zahir : Tizengauzen, I, 63.

[60] Pachymeres, V, 236, apud Brun, II, 137.

XIII

In the travellers' accounts of the 13th to 15th centuries a region in south-west Crimea was repeatedly mentioned as Alania. According to G. Barbaro, in the Crimea beyond Kaffa, there lies Gothia and then Alania (on the island) extending in the direction of Moncastro.[61] Naturally this description and the kind relying mostly on tradition and use of a customary geographic term also bearing the marks of the ever-changing political situation, cannot be taken for exact geographic definitions. But surely, Gothia stretched as far as Mangup and Eski Kermen, and then came Alania. The definition of Alania by Barbaro was misinterpreted by some historians and geographers because of his mention-ing Moncastro: «A poi la Alania, la qual va per la insula verso Moncastro.» But, of course, the region does not mean the *Dikoe pole*, as clearly shown by the adverbial phrase *per la insula* «along the island».[62]

In the list given by Marco Polo of the lands taken by Batu we find Alania, Gothia and Gazaria. This seems to correspond to the list of Barbaro, but the complete list points to a different region, as after Alania immediately Lac, Menjar, and Zic are mentioned in the enumeration, and only then follow Gothia and Gazaria.[63] In this list Alania is grouped among the regions of people living in the foot-hills of the Caucasus. *Lac*-s are found in the Daghestan even today; *Menjar* in all probability stands for the frequently mentioned town Majar, and the *Zic*-s are the descendants of Circassians. So surely in this list Alania denotes the Caucasian territory of the Alans.

The vague geographical term Alania given by Isidorus approximately to the region extending from the Don to the Danube reflects the dominant role of the Alans in the early first milleneum.[64]

The Alania mentioned by G. Barbaro clearly refers to the land of Alans in the Crimea. Barbaro knew the classical authors well, he mentions them in his preface (3rd paragraph), and he also knew the accounts of Marco Polo and the other travellers of the Tatar era. He did not draw up the topography of this region to show off his knowledge of literature or to prove how well in-formed he was. He lived in Tana for 15 years as the trade and diplomatic commissioner of Venice and also knew Caucasian Alania, as he travelled through it during his trip to Persia.

Data on Alania in the Crimea are known from other sources as well. In a list enumerating the bishoprics in 1384, we find the eparchy of Alania

---

[61] Barbaro, § 51, p. 131, 157. *Alania, la qual va per la insula verso Moncastro*, in the misinterpreted translation of Vasiliev: «Alania, which runs parallel with the island towards Moncastro», p. 219.

[62] Cf. Brun, II, 137.

[63] According to Bratianu the *lac*-s could mean *lesg*-s, *Recherches sur le commerce génois*, 299; in the opinion of Vasiliev the *Menjar* may stay for 'Mingrelians', 168.

[64] Isidorus Hispalensis: *Patrologia Latina*, LXXXII, col. 504.

besides those of Cherson and Gothia.[65] Among the earlier sources we might mention more precisely the geographical location of the land of the Alans-Asses in the Crimea : «Kerker . . . is situated in the country of the Asses.»[66] In the 13th century Kerker and its region came under the rule of the Tatar emirs of Yaslav (Suleshev), fief-holders of Nogai.

Mention of the Alans in the Crimea is often made in the later Turkish historical literature as well. For instance, Ali efendi writes : «*Qïrqer Sarï Kermän şimalisinda balad Asdan bir qɔl'adïr.* [Kirker is a castle of the Ass country north of Sari-kermän.]»[67]

An authentic account on the Alans around Kirker was given by Theodore, Bishop of Alania (ordained bishop around 1240). His bishoprics also included not only the territory of the Alans in the Caucasus, but also of those in the Crimea. He gave a precise description of the whereabouts of the Alans in the Crimea, moreover of their way of life. According to this account, the Alans had lived around Cherson, and originally been the mercenary defenders of the city and fortress, but by the time of Theodore they had moved to the mountains where they lived scattered in deserted places, in cave dwellings, under primitive conditions ; they had neither cattle folds nor huts.[68]

The Alan-Ass troops hired to defend the Byzantine province of Cherson against the successive waves of nomad assaults lost their importance with the end of the Byzantine rule in the Crimea. The caves they inhabited and in which they kept animals, belonged to the numerous «cave cities (*peščernye goroda*)»,[69] Kirkor and around it. These caves were remnants of localities of the fortresses in the south-western foot-hills erected in the Sarmatian period and later during Gothic and Byzantine rule. As time passed, the superstructure of the buildings and the localities carved in rock — serving military, economic and later, ecclesiastic purposes — have been demolished by the enemy and erosion and so they looked very soon a series of caves.[70]

When making inferences to the numerical ratio of an Alan-Ass population in this area, it must not be forgotten that Nogai had considerable Alan-Ass contingents, and the lords of the district succeeding him (Nogai died A.D. 1300), the beys of Yaslav, were fief-holders of Nogai.[71]

---

[65] *Acta Patr. Const.* II, Nr. 3€7 apud Brun, II, 137.

[66] The Arabic Text of Abu'l Feda, 214 ; *Géographie d'Aboulféda*, traduite par M. Reinaud, II, 319. apud Vasiliev, 166. Cf. Jakobson, *Sredn. Chersones*, 31.

[67] Smirnov, 104.

[68] *Patr. Graeca*, CXL, col: 393 ; Brun, II, 136 ; Jakobson, *Sredn. Chersones*, 31 ; Vasiliev, 167—168.

[69] Jakobson, *Sredn. Chersones*, 19—20. — Pallas, II, 72 ; Keppen, 247.

[70] Vejmarn : *Ist. i arch. Krymɔ*, 48, 52—54. Cf. also Jakobson, *Sredn. Krym*, 50—51, 100, et passim.

[71] Smirnov, 102 ; Tizengauzen I, 112 ; Jakobson, *Sredn. Krym*, 128.

Based on the above mentioned sources there has been a tendency in the historical-philological literature to overestimate the role of the Alans in this area, which was most probably due to the automatical linking of the Sarmatan-Alan period with the later Alan-Ass settlers. It must not be forgotten, however, that Crimean Alania, i.e. the territory inhabited also by Alans, bordered upon or rather partly coincided with the western part of *Gothia montana* and that Phyllai, i.e. Kirker (mentioned in connection with the Alans living in the mountains), also belonged to Gothia.

The background of the geographic term Gothia goes back as far as the Hun times. The Goths being defeated by the Huns partly fled to the Crimea. After the death of Attila and the fall of the Hun empire the returning Huns withdrew also into the steppes of the Crimea, and so the Goths took refuge in the mountain region. The exact location of the Goths, later vassals, and mercenaries of the Byzantine empire, as well as the place called Doros, the centre of Gothia montana, is still debated.[72] Doros in all probability might be identified with Mangup or some other fortress in the vicinity, but it was by all means in this region. The term Gothia, the Life of John, Bishop of Gothia, and the local succession of the principality of Doros-Theodoro[73] made some researchers think that the Goths continued to live in this territory up to the Turkish invasion (1475) and even thereafter.[74]

The survival of the language would be the most important evidence of their continuous presence. This was thought to be proved by remarks found in the descriptions of travellers, e.g. Rubruk from the 13th century: «Gothi quorum idioma est teutonicum».[75] In virtue of the verb standing in *praesens historicus*, the statement was interpreted as referring to the times of Rubruk (1253). A. A. Vasiliev translated this sentence as follows: «Goths, who spoke the Teutonic tongue».[76] In the anthology of Chr. Dawson of the accounts of travellers of the Tatar period the translation of *Teutonicus* was modernised to «German»: «among them were many Goths, who speak German».[77] The translation I suggest to eliminate the ambiguity: «Gothia, the native tongue (vernacular) of the inhabitants of which was Teutonic» would reflect the non-committal standpoint as to the age. The account of Rubruk was not based on first-hand experience, because he only sailed along the southern coast of

[72] Vasiliev, 47, sqq. See one of the major sources: the «Life of John of Gothia» (*Acta Sanctorum*, Jun. VII).

[73] Bănescu, *Contribution à l'histoire de la seigneurie de Théodoro-Mangoup en Crimée: Byz. Zschr.* XXXV, 24; Vasiliev, 40.

[74] Tomaschek, *Die Goten in Taurien*, Wien 1881; and others. Against the theory: Jakobson, *Rannesredn. Chersones*, 43, sqq; Id., *Sredn. Chersones*, 18.

[75] Rubruk/Wyngaert, I, 170.

[76] Vasiliev, 165.

[77] Rubruk/Dawson, 93.

the Peninsula (*navigantes coram ea*) and landed in Sudaq, i.e on the eastern end.[78]

Nevertheless Rubruk, the learned Franciscan friar, gave credit to his informers, having, himself, carefully prepared for the journey by studying the works of classic authors and the reports of missionaries and travellers concerning the geography and ethnography of the region. Thus the name Gothia to him automatically might have suggested the survival of the Gothic people.

Schiltberger's *Reisebuch*, already referred to, is an especially interesting source concerning the Goths and at the same time the Tats.[79] In the second relevant passage the variants *Kuthia/Ruthia* were interpreted to refer to the Goths, and *Sutti* in the first passage was also emended to *Kuthi*.[80] On this basis Ph. Brun identified the Tats with the Goths (*Kuthi*).[81] Even A. A. Vasiliev accepted the Kuthia variant. Based on these data Tomaschek and others tried to prove the survival of the Goths in the Crimea up to modern times.[82]

Text analysis, however, disproved these constrained arguments. The *Kuthia/Ruthia* variants turned out to stand for *Churin* (Nuremberg MS), the name of a people in the Caucasus and it was shown that the place name *Sutti* cannot be emended to Kuthi, but should be read *Sugdi* ($>$ *Sukti*), variants of the name of the city Sugdaq, Sugda, etc.[83]

The continuous use of the term «Gothia» perpetuated the belief in the survival of the Goths. Even G. Barbaro fell for the rumor. He tells us that his servant spoke with Goths: «The Goths speak German. I know this because I had a German servant with me; they spoke with each other and understood each other completely, like someone from Friuli understands a person from Florence».[84] It is known, that G. Barbaro had never been in the Crimean Gothia. The case of his servant may be explained in different ways. The most plausible of these is that in Tana, where merchants from many different nationalities came together, the servant might have met some Germans (ev. merchants) from the Crimea.[85]

The report of A. G. Busbecq on the Crimean Goths was highly misleading. He based his account on information obtained from two Crimean envoys in

---

[78] Rubruk/Wyngaert, I, 165.

[79] Schiltberger/Langmantel, 63.

[80] *Ibid.*, 97, 140.

[81] Brun, II, 241.

[82] Tomaschek: see above, note 74; Pelliot, 155; Vasiliev, 193.

[83] Schaeder, 10—11.

[84] *Gothi parlano in todesco; so questo perchè, havendo un fameglio todesco, con mi, parlavano insieme et intendevansi assai rasonevolemente, cusì como se intenderia un furlano con un fiorentino.* Barbaro, p. 131, 157. Cf. Brun, II, 236.

[85] Barbaro, § 51, pp. 131, 181; Vasiliev, 219—220.

XIII

Constantinople in 1554, and listed mostly modern vocables.[86] Scientists of the 19th century have already refuted these arguments for the survival of the Gothic tongue in the 16th century. P. S. Pallas criticized the data of Busbecq as early as in 1793—94.[87]

These and similar accounts failed to prove the survival of the Gothic language. No direct or indirect traces of this language is found in the tongue of the Crimean people, either in that of the Greeks who emigrated to Mariupol, or of the Tatars (Tats) or Turks who settled in the southern regions of the Crimea.

The various ethnic groups merged in this area, from the Tauric aborigines, through the Sarmatians-Alans, Greeks, Goths and Byzantines down to the succeeding tribes of Tatars and Turks. This merging of the population was observed already by Pachymeres in the period of Mihail Palaiologos in the second half of the 13th century : «the Alans, Zikhs, Goths, Russians and other different neighbouring peoples, mixed with them the Tatars ; they adopted their customs, assumed their tongue and clothes».[88] The view of the natural mixing of the peoples is upheld by modern critical historiography. A. A. Vasiliev in his book on the history of the Goths in the Crimea also stated : «the Goths did not survive during the Middle Ages . . . they gradually lost their nationality and their Germanic tongue and were first hellenized and later tartarized».[89]

From the point of view of the ethnic groups of earlier times it is remarkable that Goths and Alans are mentioned side by side in the sources. In a letter written in 1334 by Mario Sanudo to Philip VI, «Gothi et aliqui Alani» are reported to live under the Tatar rule.[90]

That the Goths might have merged with the Alans defending the border of the Byzantine empire and later living on the feudal estate of the beys of Yaslav is shown by the tradition perpetuated by G. Barbaro, who maintained that in the region of «Crimean Alania» «the first inhabitants were Alans, then came the Goths who invaded the country and the issues of this merger of the two tribes call themselves Gothalans».[91] Based on his readings, Barbaro identified the Alans of this conglomeration with those of the Sarmatian-Alan period. This is a good example how historians in the Middle Ages tried to explain contemporary information in the light of classical sources in order to lend

---

[86] A. G. Busbequii, *Legationis Turcicae Epistolae*, IV ; Kondaraki, VIII, 26 ; Vasiliev, 269—271.

[87] Pallas, II, 318 ; Brun, *Černomorskie goty i sledy dolgogo ich prebyvanija v Južnoj Rossii* : *Zapiski Imp. AN* XXIV, 51 ; Id., II, 237—241 ; Vasiliev, 269—271.

[88] *Pachymeris Historiae de Michaele Palaeologo*, V, 4. apud Vasiliev, 172.

[89] Vasiliev, p. V, 220, 275.

[90] Brun, II, 137.

[91] Barbaro, § 51, p. 157.

historical credit to their statements. Other examples might be found in Plano Carpini, Rubruk and others, who tried to compare contemporary geographical, ethnic and other information with those obtained from their readings. Nevertheless the hearsay of the day under the historical disguise can be readily identified in these chronicles.

There are facts behind the perseverence of this tradition, in addition to the conservativism of the historical-geographical terminology, which deserve attention.

There are no data to prove the survival of this geographical (Alania— Gothia) and ethnographic (Alans—Goths) tradition among the people living in the Crimea at present, but its continuity might be, interestingly, discovered when studying certain characteristics of the Tat people originating from the regions of the Crimea that were contiguous to Gothia, who migrated to the Roumanian and Bulgarian sides of Dobrudja.

The Tatars and Tats have come to Dobrudja relatively late ; the majority settled there after the Crimean War (1854) and live side by side — and even mixed — in Roumania (approximately 21 .000 .) and Bulgaria (approx. 5—6 .000 .[92]

The language, ethnography and other features of the Tatars of this region have been studied fairly extensively, while the Tats have been neglected by researchers, because of their numerical inferiority. There is only one thorough study dealing with the language of the Tats by Vl. Drimba, who carried on linguistic research in the Roumanian Dobrudja in 1956—57.

As a result of the migrations, mixing and the strong Ottoman-Turkish influence, it is rather difficult to classify the Crimean Tatar dialects as to the details. However, the language of the Tatars inhabiting the steppes (*čöl*), can be in main lines distinguished from that of the Tatars living in the mountainous region or on the coast, by some of its phonetic peculiarities.[93]

The largest group of the Tats living in the Roumanian part of the Dobrudja are those found in the Hîrşova and Medgidia districts ; they call themselves *Baidar Tats*. They came from the Baidar valley (Bajdarskaja dolina) in the Crimea, from 12 villages in the narrow basin of the Yayla mountain, and settled in the following villages of the Hîrşova district: Roumanian *Haydar* (Tatar *Aydar*), *Dulgheru* (T. *Dülger*), *Rahman* (T. *Raxman*), *Horia* (T. *Müslübey*), *Crişan* (T. *Müslüy*), *Băltăgeşti* (T. *Baltaÿï*) and *Tichileşti* (T. *Tekeli*) as well as in the Medgidia district in the villages of *Siliştea* and *Dunărea* (T. *Boyaşšïq*).[94]

[92] J. Blaskovics, *Dobruca Tatarlarının halk türküleri* : *Németh Armağanı*, Ankara 1962, 69—70 ; Mándoki, *Devinettes tatares de Bulgarie* : *AOH* XXI, 369—370.

[93] *PhTF*, I, 369, sqq.

[94] Drimba, 68—69 with a map-sketch.

XIII

These Tats left the Crimea when in the course of the Crimean War the English and French army invaded the Peninsula and having captured Balaklava stationed their troops in the twelve villages of the valley.[95]

Another group of Tats came from the region of Içel on the southern coast of the Crimea. These Içel-Tats settled in the village *Capidava* (T. *Qalaköy*) in the Hîrşova district.[96]

The language of the Dobrudjan Tats differs slightly from that of the Dobrudjan Tatars, and the latter because of these (mostly phonetic) peculiarties ridicule the speech of the Tats.

According to the information from St. Mándoki Kongur, one of the best experts of the Tatar dialects of Bulgarian Dobrudja, the slow, higher pitched and thinner intonation of the Tats differs from the dynamic speach of the Tatars characterised by a strong logical stress. The Tats have a sing-song intonation. According to Kondaraki, also the Crimean Içel-Tats «speak with a specific singing tone that cannot be heard elsewhere in the Crimea».[97]

The anthropological and ethnic difference between the Tatars and Tats is conspicuous. The Tatars are typically round-faced, short and dark, among the Tats prevail two types : the most characteristic feature of many of them is their high stature, fair hair and blue eyes.[98] The Nordic appearance of these people made Mándoki to liken them to the Swedes. The other type frequently found among the Tats does not resemble the Tatar type either : these have a thin face, sharp nose, less fair complexion, so that the overall impression is Iranian.

The conspicuous Nordic character suggests that the ancestors of this group might have been the Goths. But certainly not the ones who settled in Lesser Scythia in the middle of the first thousand years A.D. The Gothic language of those survived in Lesser Scythia for a long time ; Ulfila, who translated the Bible into Gothic also lived here. The latest report about these Goths is due to Walafrid Strabo, a Frankish poet of the 9th century, who mentioned that there remained a small number of Goths in this area, who spoke the Gothic tongue, and as late as his time used the Gothic translation of the Bible.[99]

After the ninth century ethnical stability or continuity in this area of stormy historical upheavals is improbable. The Goths must have become gradually slavonised, merged in the continuous flow of nomad Turkic tribes if they preserved in this area of constantly changing population at all. From

---

[95] Kondaraki, I/1, 125—128 ; XIII, 143.
[96] Drimba, 68.
[97] Drimba, 71 ; Kondaraki, I/1, 149.
[98] Drimba, 68.
[99] *Patrologia Latina* CXIV, col. 927 (apud Vasiliev, 38).

XIII

the 15th century on this coastal area was the main route of expansion of the Ottoman Turks towards Poland and the Crimea.

The possibility of local continuity of the ancestors of the Tats is also contradicted by the circumstance that the Tats adopted a distinct and specific dialect and not the language of the Tatars who lived in their close vicinity.

The other main argument against the local continuity of Tats is the tradition living among them as regards their origin with an exact location of their old country in the Baidar valley and the southern Içel coast in the Crimea.[100]

The facts behind their specific anthropological character which sharply distinguishes them from the Tatar people should be looked for in their earlier history in the Crimea. In the light of the historical and geographical findings described so far the Baidar and Içel Tats may be classified an ethnical mixture of the ancient Gothic and Alan population who had adopted the language of the ruling class of the local Tatar tribe. This conclusion would solve the problem of the Nordic and Iranian traits of the Tats. The abundant literature dealing with the survival of the Goths (and Alans) in the Crimea, somehow ignored this anthropologic peculiarity of the Tat people living in the Dobrudja.

The Dobrudjan Tats are also strongly distinguished from the Tatars of this region by their occupation. According to the personal communication of St. Mándoki Kongur, the Tats are mostly merchants, craftsmen or farmers as opposed to the Tatars whose most typical occupation is animal husbandry. The Tats willingly take up hired work in the towns, the Tatars not.

The personal character of the Tats is also different: they are more earnest, even morose, and labour hard from morning till night.

All these anthropological and ethnical peculiarities are apparent at first glance not only to the scientific observer (linguist, ethnographer, anthropologist), but is felt also by the Tatars and the Tats themselves.

Although looked down upon the Tatar majority, the Tats are a self-conscious people. They willingly mix and intermarry with the Tatars, and thus the difference between them may disappear or at least become less conspicuous after a few generations.

4. The common noun or ethnic name *Tat* had different shades of meaning during its long history as shown by the early sources and up to modern times.

Two tendencies in the change of the meaning of the word might be postulated. One is an extension: Iranian ethnic element > neighbouring, subdued people (in general) and the other is a restriction from the general to the particular: neighbouring, subdued people > the actual neighbour.

[100] Kondaraki, I/1, 149.

With ethnic names the etymological deliberations may fail to reveal the origin, or the original meaning because many peoples adopted foreign names due to the intermingling of the tribes. The studies of V. Minorsky and H. H. Schaeder and the data described above suggest that there may have occurred an extension of meaning after all, issuing from the denotation of a special Iranian neighbour and resulting in an ethnic name denoting different peoples or ethnic groups alien to the Turko-Tatars as also shown by the case of the two different groups of the Crimean Tats.

5. The appearance of the apposition *tat birlä tavġač* among the titles of the Crimean Khans is unexpected.[101] The word *tavġač* had been a frequent element of the titles of the Karakhanid khans. According to Barthold it signified the devotion towards the Chinese «state idea».[102]

The ethnic name *tavġač* can hardly be expected to have preserved its original meaning during the thousand years of the history of the different Turkic peoples. The name of the Tavġač people who founded a state in North China as members of the Hsien-pi tribal confederation,[103] after their disappearance i.e. absorption into the local population, became to be attached to their conquered homeland.

The term *tavġač xan* in the Karakhanid titulature and further on did neither reflect the nomad origin, nor the Chinese affiliation, it only referred to the Central Asian homeland or empire,[104] intentionally implying the grand past and ancientry.

A counterpart to this concentration of meaning to denote the empire notion might be found also in Indian and Persian (> Armenian) in the case of the coupled term *Čin-Mačin*, and in Arabic *Şin-Māşin*,[105] referring to the empire of China and the adjacent subjected countries ruled by nomad chieftains, who have been soon absorbed into the Chinese commonwealth.

Two explanations might be offered to this late reappearance of this title (1627),[106] one historical, the other diplomatic.

The use of the title *tat birlä tavġač* by the Crimean khans was all the more peculiar since the southern coastline of the Peninsula, where the Tats lived, was under direct Ottoman rule, under the administration of the Beglerbey of Kaffa.

---

[101] Kāšġarī, II, 224 ; III, 378 ; Kāšġarī/Atalay, I, 463. — Budagov, I, 329 ; Radloff, III, 899 ; Clauson, 449 ; — Minorsky, 756 ; Schaeder, 13 ; Pelliot, 155.

[102] Barthold, 98.

[103] Ligeti, L., *Le tabgatch, un dialecte de la langue sien-pi* : *Mongolian Studies* (*BOH* XIV), 265, sqq.

[104] Schaeder, 13—14; Pritsak, O., *Die Karachaniden* : *Der Islam* XXXI, 20.

[105] Kāšġarī, III, 378 ; Schaeder, 14 ; Clauson, 438.

[106] Véliaminov-Zernov, 31.

The virtual extension of the authority of the Kereis to the southern coast, or at least the stressing of the unity of the Tatar rule in the Crimea, was only possible in the period when the Crimean Khan was powerful enough for such a demonstration of his authority or when he was allowed to do so by the balance between his land and the Ottoman sultans.

The power of the Ottoman empire was weakened at the beginning of the seventeenth century by several decades of war with the Persians (under Shah Abbas) mostly on Armenian territory. The signs of decline may be detected in the relation of the sultans with the Crimean khans. Muhammad Kerei III. (1623—27) khan rose in revolt against the sultan. (However the main role in this upheaval must be attributed to Šahin Kerei Qalgha, the actual ruler who had stood for several years in the service of the Persian Shah, so the incentive might have been fostered also by an outside party.) The toppling of the balance to the Khan's side was shown by the issue of the events: in spite of the dethroning fermar the Sultan ultimately was forced to confirm Muhammad Kerei in his khan's authority.[107] The pursuit of independence was even stronger under the khans who followed: Džanibek Kerei (1610—23, 1627—35), and Inayet Kerei (1635—37).[108]

Accordingly, the title *tat bïrlä tavġač* first appeared in a document of Džanibek Kerei (1627). The title reflecting the aspirations for power of the Crimean khans became a standard formula in diplomatic and chancery practice: *Uluġ orda (ve) uluġ yurtnïŋ ve Dešt-i Qïpčaqnïŋ ve taxt-i Qïrïmnïŋ ve sansïz köp tatarnïŋ ve sagïšsïz noġaynïŋ ve taġ ara čerkesning ve tat bilä tavġačning uluġ padšahi ve hem uluġ sultani* . . . [The great padishah and great sultan of the Great Horde, the Great Yurt, the Dešt-i Qipčaq and the country of the Qrim, innumerable Tatars, countless Nogais, and Cherkesses in the mountains and Tats and Tavġač]. These titles were used as a cliché for centuries with only slight variations.[109]

The perpetuation of this voluminous *'unvān* might also be due to the development of chancery, and the practice of written records in the administration as a result of the personal contacts of Šahin Kerei with Persia as well as the cultural, diplomatic and trade connections with the Timurid, later Khwarezmian, empires. The intermingling of the Karakhanid with the Chingisid tradition and with the Timurid revival of the latter ought to be studied in depth.[110]

---

[107] *GOR*, 36—37; Smirnov, 490. A vivid description of his reign by Khachatur the Armenian priest, s. Schütz, *Armenische Chronik: AOH* XXIX, 137, 144.

[108] Smirnov, 490 sqq., 511.

[109] Véliaminov-Zernov, No. 12, 13, 15, 16, 17 (A.D. 1628—1630), pp. 26, 31, 34, 41, 51, 62, 65; Nos. 47—57 (A.D. 1639, 1640); No. 148 (A.D. 1651), No. 231 (1670), etc.

[110] Pritsak, *Die Karachaniden*, 20, 48, 52—55, etc.; Schaeder, 13—14; Broniewski: *ZOOID* VI, 353; Rizvan, 83.

The appearance of the attribute *tat birlä tavġač* at the end of the list of the titles of the khans[111] might raise doubts as to its importance in the demonstration of power. Anyway, this position might be attributed to the actual geographic situation : Tatars — Nogais — Cherkesses — Tats — Tavġač,[112] the last representing the ancient homeland. May be, they have been only included to make the list longer and thus more impressive.

As regards the semantic structure of the expression H. H. Schaeder called attention to the preference for alliteration, e.g. in the ethnic confederation Türk — Türgiš, and others.[113] It might be added that such kind of alliterations for the sake of intensification are frequent in adjectives (*kap-kara* «pitch dark», *kïp-kïrmïzï* «glaring red»). The use of doublets to suggest intensification of the meaning might be a feasible suggestion.

It should be noted that a similar pairing of words was popular when honouring other monarchs, for instance, in the same document the Tsar of all Russians was called : . . . *uluġ urusnîng ve purusnîng uluġ padšahï* . . . «the great emperor of the great Russians and Prussians . . .».[114] The juxtaposition similar to *Tat — Tavġač* might be met with other Altaic peoples in a subordinated or coordinated relation to one another. The example of *tatabï qïtai* might be quoted, in which the transformation of meaning *qïtai* was similar to that of the word *tavġač*. The sequence of the ethnic names in these combinations did not indicate their relative importance, in some cases the name of the auxiliary tribe came first, just as in practice, the vanguard advanced first. It must be decided in each case individually what the points of view in coupling the names actually were, whether political, military or linguistic prevailed.

6. Popular etymological interpretations of different geographical names are frequently found in chronicles and travellers' accounts. These are not always the learned conjectures of the author, but often witty explanations they heard from the local population based on rhyming analogies or on superstitions.

There are few places in the Crimea which would have so many popular etymological explanation of their names as Kirker, later called Čufut-Kale. This may be attributed to the many spellings and pronunciations the name of the town had. The variants occurring in the travellers' accounts have been listed by Keppen : Kirker, Kerkri, Cherchiar(de), Chercher, Kirkyer, Kirkor.[115]

---

[111] Fekete, L., *Einführung in die osmanisch-türkische Diplomatik*, Budapest 1926, LV ; Reychman, J. — Zajączkowski, A., *Handbook of the Ottoman-Turkish Diplomatics*, 153, 158 ; Ivanics, M., *Formal and Linguistic Peculiarities of 17th Century Crimean Tatar Letters addressed to Princes of Transylvania* : *AOH* XXIX, 215—221; Matuz, 4.

[112] See the enumeration of the people under the scepter of the Khan, above p. 99.

[113] Schaeder, 13.

[114] Véliaminov-Zernov, No. 10 (p. 26) ; 11 (p. 31).

[115] Keppen, 308—318 ; Smirnov, 102.

Speaking about Kirker in the land of Asses Abu'l-Feda (1321) noted that the name meant «forty men». Brun maintained that Abu'l-Feda was wrong in interpreting Kirker for «forty men». According to Vasiliev, it was Reinaud, Abu'l-Feda's French translator, who committed the error by his interpretation «quarante hommes».[116] But this latter view cannot be accepted, because in the translation of Jacobus Reiske the same expression might be found : «Kerkri vox Turcica quadraginta viros notans, est arx munitissima».[117] This explanation was then accepted and transmitted in the literature. For instance, Said Muhammad Riza repeated it in his work «The History of the Crimea» with reference to Abu'l-Feda.[118]

Although it may appear a pseudo-scientific conjecture, this etymology should rather be regarded as a popular tradition because it was widely known among the people, offering an easy solution to popular linguistic common-sense, *qïrq* meaning in Turkish «forty» and *er* «man».

Different popular legends may also be taken in consideration with this explanation. On the flatland towards Kerch, near the Russian village Zuya, there is a cave called *Xïrx aziz* meaning «forty Moslem martyrs». According to the legend, the forty martyrs were killed by giaours surprising them at prayer. Christians living in the vicinity maintain, however, that the cave used to be a sanctuary of forty Christian martyrs.

The mingling of legend and toponyms is at hand in the following case : the previous name of the Tatar village lying between *Aziz* and Aq-Čoqur was *Kirk(y)er*.[119]

The Karaims living in Čufut Kale seem to have adopted this common story enjoying wide popularity, and fabricated a legend of their own : the coat of arms over the main gate of the bastion was believed to commemorate the victory of forty Karaim families under Mengli Kerei.[120]

Another popular etymological explanation of the city's name appears to be even more frequent and more ancient. This starts from another spelling, *Kirk-yer*, which is interpreted in Turkish as «forty places».[121] Almost all medieval travellers mention this variety.

It is remarkable that Abu'l Feda himself mentions this version in another passage explaining the name Qirim: «The Crimea (Alkirim) is the name of a coun-

---

[116] Abu'l Feda, 214 ; Abu'l Feda/Reinaud, 319 ; cf. Keppen, 309 (note 447) ; Brun, II, 135 ; Jakobson, *Sredn. Krym*, 81 ; Vasiliev, 166 (note 2).

[117] *Abulfedae opus geographicum*. Ex Arabico Latinum fecit J. J. Reiske, apud Keppen, 309 (note 447).

[118] Apud Smirnov, 104.

[119] Kondaraki, I/1, 25 ; *ibid.*, 66 (note).

[120] *Ibid.*, 65—66.

[121] Abu'l Feda, 200 ; Abu'l Feda/Reinaud, 282. Cf. Vasiliev, 166 (note 4).

try having forty cities». Rubruk also relates that there are «forty castles between Soldaia and Cherson».[122]

But in most of the accounts the expression «forty villages, places» is mostly understood to refer to the city Kirker alone, the later Čufut Kale. G. Barbaro in his valuable account reported that the Tatars had two places (surrounded with ramparts) in the Crimea, Solxat and Cherchiarde, the latter meaning «forty places» (*quaranta luoghi*) in their tongue.[123]

This toponym lending itself for such an easy popular etymological interpretation must have misled A. Vámbéry in his translation of the 1396 document of Timur Kutlug in Turkish: *Bu kündin ilgerü qīrīm birlä qīrq-yernīng tümenide sudaq atlīq kentning jevairindä*[124] as «Vom heutigen Tage angefangen (sollen seine Söhne Ilki Hadschi Mehemmed und Mahmud) in der Krim, im Bezirke der Vierzig Orte in der Umgebung des Ortes namens Sudaq ... unabhängige Terchane sein». The words referring to Kirker ought to have been translated as «in the Tümen of Krim (here: Eski Krim, i.e. Solxat) and Kirker». This definition would have corresponded to the old Byzantine civil and ecclesiastical administrative district.

The interpretation of the chronicles is not unequivocal in the modern literature either. Based on the accounts of Abu'l Feda and Rubruk, W. Heyd maintains that the popular etymology of the name of Kirker and the forty Crimean places (*yer* «luogho, pl. luoghi») or forts (*castellum*) are two different things.[125] A partly similar view is held by A. L. Jakobson, who made use of the account of Rubruk when reconstructing the history of the Crimea. From the 13th century onwards the Tauric Peninsula became devided into feudal estates, so Jakobson ventures the remark whether the forty castles (*quadraginta castella*) might not have been the mountain top residences of the feudal landlords, wherefrom they could dominate the people of the lowlands.[126]

H. H. Schaeder tried to solve the contradiction arising from the name of a single city and the meaning of forty castles by postulating that it, in fact, referred to forty places originally, the best known being Solgat, Sudaq and Kaffa, but later on the meaning became restricted to a single city.[127]

Already in 1880 Ph. Brun in his study «Notices sur la Gazarie» asserted that the *quadraginta castella* in Rubruk referred to Kirker.[128] This was all the more acceptable because Rubruk himself had never travelled through the

[122] Rubruk/Wyngaert, I, 170; Dawson, 93 (lines 1—2) «forty small towns».
[123] Barbaro, 129, 154 (§ 46).
[124] Vámbéry, *Uig. Sprachmon.*, 172—173. Cf. Radlov: *ZVOIRAO* 3 (1888), 19—21.
[125] Heyd, II, 209 (note 1).
[126] Jakobson, *Sredn. Krym*, 81; Idem, *Sredn. Chersones*, 31.
[127] Schaeder, 11.
[128] Apud Brun, II, 135 (note 53). Cf. Rubruk/Wyngaert, I, 170.

XIII

Peninsula, he only sailed along the southern coast and identified readily the popular etymology with the castles and ramparts he saw on the shore. Vasiliev also accepted this explanation, although — being historian not a linguist — he did not exclude the alternative that the name was restricted to denote Kirker only later on, and originally it meant the coastal region from Cherson to Sudaq.[129]

It is not only the inaccuracy of the sources which justifies the indecision in the interpretation, but also a parallel lends itself for the changed meaning of a place name in the area, and the name of the Peninsula itself. The name *Krim* was originally used to mean a town, Solxat; later when the name was transferred to the denotation of the entire Peninsula, the town was called «Eski Krim» to distinguish the two notions. The original state of affairs is represented in the travel accounts of Martin Broniewski relating to 1578 :«Cremum: Tartari ab eo loco Crimenses vulgo nunc appellantur [Krim, by the name of this place the Tartars now are called Crimeans]».[130]

When scrutinizing these main sources, it appears that neither Rubruk nor Barbaro did in fact travel widely in the Peninsula. Rubruk had seen only the city of Sudaq, and the northern steppe-region, while Barbaro secretly visited Kaffa (lying in the eastern end) on one occasion. Thus their accounts were based on the reports of Turkish informers who retold these popular etymologies to the travellers. So *yer* is commented as «place» by Barbaro, and «castle» (*castellum*) by Rubruk.

Other explanations of the name Kirker were also prevailing among the people. The variant *Kirkor* gave rise to the most frequent of these. In the reports of the Russian envoys only the velar variant was used. The second half of the word, *or* could mean «hole, pit, ditch» in the Turko-Tatar languages. Thus the name Kirkor was interpreted as meaning «forty caves».[131]

This popular etymology might have been supported by the Nogai name of the Strait of Perekop, *Or* (*Orqapu* in Ottoman Turkish). In his «Crimean Chronicle» Riza offered the following explanation : *lisan-i tatar üzre xandaq ma'nasïnda olan or* «*Or* which means *xandaq* (= pit, ditch) in the Tartar tongue».[132]

The name of the village Kirker, in the vicinity of Aziz and Aq-Čoqur, might have contributed to the deriving of *Kirkor* from *Or*, the word *čoqur* being a synonym of *or* «ditch».[133]

[129] Vasiliev, 166.
[130] Smirnov, 59 sqq.; Keppen, 338—346; Broniewski/Schwandtner, 268.
[131] Smirnov, 109—115, 334, 338; R I, 1046—1048; *Pamjatniki diplomat. snošenij*, 354, 379, 417, 419, etc.
[132] Smirnov, 338, n. 5.
[133] Kondaraki, I/1, 66.

The abundance of cave-like forts carved in rock in the old Greek or even more ancient cities in the southwestern Crimea (Eski Kermen, Mangup, etc.) may have encouraged these conjectures. The origin and purpose of these caves have been subject to much debate. The expression «cave cities (peščernye goroda)» is common in literature and daily use. The subterranean part of the buildings in the fortifications carved into rock were originally used for military purposes, storage and later also for cult. The superstructures were demolished by the enemy and the erosion finished the job of destruction and in the end they in fact looked like caves. The Asses, Alans in Byzantine service, after the collapse of the rule of the Empire in the Crimea made use of these caves for dwelling purposes and even for sheep folds, and later the caves were taken in use by the sect of Karaites settled down in this town.[134]

All the popular etymologies agree in interpreting the first half of the name of Kirker as «forty», but the word *qïrq* also had a wide meaning of general use «many, numerous». Examples of this meaning are : *qïrq ayaq* «centipede», or the place name *Qïrq bulaq* which did not mean «forty springs» but «many», etc.

The multiples of forty, e.g. forty thousand, were frequently used in the description of army troops, where it evidently meant not the actual number but a multitude of threatening strength.[135]

The origin of Kirker, Kirkor is most probably something what was suggested by Keppen: it probably has been derived from a Greek term : *Kirkos*. There are, however, no sources to prove this theory.[136]

Kirker by this name was first mentioned as the estate of the beys of Yaslav. It became a district centre proper during the reign of the Kereis (Gireis). In the 15th century Mengli Girei moved his residence from Solxat to Kirker, Baxči Sarai only served as a summer residence of the Khan, the important diplomatic conferences were held in Kirker, where in the casemates the most precious prisoners (for whom the highest ransom could be stipulated) were also kept. This is where János Kemény, who was later to become the Prince of Transylvania, languished in prison and wrote in 1657 his «devout prayer» among «prisoners taken by the Tatar khan, who kept them in dreadful captivity in his residence in the land of Crimea, in the fort Čufut Kale built on a rock above the city of Bakčesarai.»[137]

[134] Pallas, II, 72 ; Keppen, 247 ; Kondaraki I/1, 67 ; *Ist. i arx. Kryma*, 48, 52, 54.
[135] Keppen, 312 (note 454) ; *Hungaro-Turcica*, 188.
[136] Keppen, *ibid.*
[137] Kemény J., *Önéletírása és levelei* [Autobiography and letters], Budapest 1959, 391 ; Nagy, R., *A krími tatár rabok történetéből* [Hungarians in Crimean Tatar captivity], Losoncz 1918.

XIII

Bibliography

Barbaro i Kontarini o Rossii, K istorii italo-russkich svjazej v XV v. Podg. E. Č. Skržinskaja, Leningrad 1971.

Barthold, W., *12 Vorlesungen über die Geschichte der Türken Mittelasiens*, Berlin 1935.

Broniewski, Martin, *Opisanie Kryma ZOOID* VI (1867).

Broniewski: Schwandtner, J. G., *Scriptores rerum Hungaricarum veteres, ac genuini*, Tyrnaviae 1765. vol. III, 247—298 : *Descriptio Tartariae.*

Brun, F. (Bruun, Ph.), *Černomorje,* I—II. Odessa 1879—1880.

Clauson, G., *An Etymological Dictionary of Pre-Thirteenth-Century Turkish,* Oxford 1972.

Drimba, Vl., *Dialectul tat din Dobrogea : Foneticǎ şi Dialectologie,* vol. III. Bucarest.

Gavriil, A. Ch. i T., *Pereselenie Grekov iz Kryma v Azovskuju guberniju i osnovanie Gotijskoj i Kafijskoj eparchii :* ZOOID I, 1844, 197—204.

Grigorovič/Blau : O. Blau, *Über die griechisch-türkische Mischbevölkerung um Mariupol.* Nach W. Grigorowitsch's Bemerkungen über die Sprache der Taten : *ZDMG* XXVIII, 576—583.

Heyd, W., *Histoire du commerce du Levant au moyen-âge,* I—II, Leipzig 1885—86.

Hungaro-Turcica. Studies in Honour of Julius Németh. Ed. Gy. Káldy-Nagy. L. Eötvös University. Budapest 1976.

Istorija i archeologija srednevekovogo Kryma, Red. A. P. Smirnov, Izd-vo AN SSSR, Moscow 1958.

Jakobson, A. L., *Rannesrednevekovyj Chersones : MIA* No. 63., Moscow—Leningrad 1959.

Jakobson, A. L., *Srednevekovyj Chersones, XII—XIV vv.: MIA* No. 17., Moscow—Leningrad 1950.

Jakobson, A. L., *Srednevekovyj Kryа,* Moscow—Leningrad 1964.

Kāšġarī : Maḥmūd al-Kāšġarī, *Dīwān Luġat at-Turk* (transl. B. Atalay), I—III, Ankara 1939—1941, *Dizin,* 1943.

Kāšġarī/Brock.: *Mitteltürkischer Wortschatz,* bearbeitet von C. Brockelmann : *BOH* I, Budapest 1928.

Keppen (Köppen), P., *Krymskij Sbornik,* SPbg 1837.

Kondaraki, V. Ch., *Universaljnoje opisanie Kryma,* SPbg 1895.

Kononov, A. N., *Rodoslovnaja turkmen, Sočinenie Abu-l-Gazi chana chivinskogo,* Moscow—Leningrad 1958.

Manr Žam. : Hakobian, V., *Manr Žamanakagrut'yunner XIII—XVIII dd.* [Chronica minora saec. XIII—XVIII.], vol. I., Erevan 1951.

Matuz, J., *Krimtatarische Urkunden im Reichsarchiv zu Kopenhagen (Islamkundliche Untersuchungen* Bd. 37.) Freiburg 1976.

Minorsky, V., *Tāt : EI* IV, 755—755.

Pallas, P. S., *Bemerkungen auf einer Reise in die südlichen Statthalterschaften des Russischen Reichs in den Jahren 1793 und 1794,* II. Leipzig 1803.

Pelliot, P., *Notes sur l'histoire de la Horde d'Or.* Paris 1949.

Radlov, V., *Jarlyki Toktamyša i Temir-Kutluga :* ZVOIRAO III, 1888, 1—40.

Rubruk/Wyngaert : *Sinica Franciscana. Itinera et relationes Fratrum Minorum saeculi XIII et XIV.,* I. Quaracchi—Firenze 1929.

Rubruk/Dawson: *Mission to Asia. Narratives and Letters of the Franciscan Missionaries to Mongolia and China in the 13th and 14th centuries,* Ed. Chr. Dawson, New York 1966.

Schaeder, H. H., *Türkische Namen der Iranier :* Festschrift Giese (*Die Welt des Islams,* Sonderband), Leipzig 1941, 1—34.

Hans Schiltbergers Reisebuch. Herausg. V. Langmantel, Tübingen 1885.

XIII

Schütz, E., *Eine armenische Chronik von Kaffa aus der ersten Hälfte des 17. Jahrhunderts* : *AOH* XXIX/2.

Schütz, E., *Tatok a Krim félszigeten* [Tat people in the Crimea]. Paper read on the occasion of the 100th anniversary of the Chair of Arabic Studies of the University of Budapest, May 8, 1974.

Smirnov, V. D., *Krymskoe chanstvo pod verchovenstvom Otomanskoj porty do načala XVIII veka*, SPb 1887.

Spuler, G., *Die Goldene Horde. Die Mongolen in Russland, 1223—1502*. Leipzig 1943.

Tizengauzen, V. G., *Sbornik materialov otnosjaščichsja k istorii Zolotoj Ordy*, vol. I. SPb 1884, vol. II. Moscow—Leningrad 1941.

Vámbéry, H., *Uigurische Sprachmonumente*, Innsbruck 1870.

Vasiliev, A. A., *The Goths in the Crimea*, Cambridge Mass. 1936.

XIII

TETAL IN CHAPTER 50
OF THE CHRONICLE OF SEBEOS[1]

by

Edmond Schütz
(Budapest)

Beginning with the 7th century, the rich flow
of Byzantine chronicles came to a standstill for
one and a half centuries. As Middle Persian historical sources of this age were also lost, the
history of the northern border of the Sassanian
Empire can be reconstructed only from the fragments preserved by Arab and Persian historians
living and writing some centuries later.[2]

For this reason Armenian sources of the 7th and
8th centuries gain an exceptional value. These
sources are all the more important in the study
of the history of the nomad tribal federations of
Inner Asia because they contain first-hand information. The reason for this was that the church
center coincided with the residence of the Sassanian governor (*marzpan*) and the best-educated
clergymen lived here. The chronicler could easily
have been the court priest of one of the first
magnate dynasties. After the loss of Armenian
state independence, in 387 or 428, the greatest
families, the Bagratuni or Mamikonian princes,
played a leading role in the local government,
as well as in the body of the staff-officers of
Armenian detachments integrated into the Sassanian or Byzantine armies. In this position a
court priest could get direct political or military information.

The Armenian troops were sent by the two powers
sharing the Armenian soil to military expeditions
on their farthest borders. This device, besides
being a direct military strategy, was also aimed
at eliminating possible centers of resistance.
This deliberate minority policy is properly
characterized by the letter to the Shahinshah
Khosrow Aparvez attributed to the emperor
Maurice. The emperor tells the Shah how he had

XIV

sent Armenians on military service to Thrace in
order to get rid of these turbulent elements, and
urges the Shah to do the same with his Armenian
subjects by sending them to the East.[3]

This background gives us a clue to the problem
of how the chroniclers, in our case Sebeos,[4]
could have acquired first-hand information from
the Armenian troops, in some cases even from one
of the Bagratunis themselves. Through this channel
he could have obtained detailed information about
the military exploits of Sembat Bagratuni, the
governor of the Province Hyrkania (585-605), of
the campaigns against the rebellious Kushans in
the northwest area and the Hephtalites, perhaps
even from Veraztiroc, son of Sembat, mentioned
several times in the Chronicle.[5]

The value of the Chronicle as a source of information for the history of the northern neighbors of the Sassanian Empire was recognized rather
early by J. Markwart, but at the end of the last
century a considerable part of the Armenian sources was not accessible to him, and some of his
basic ideas, as, for example, his explanation of
the ethnic name *Tetal*, were erroneous.[6]

Of great help in the explanation of the deteriorated or missing passages were the borrowings of
the later chroniclers.[7] This fact was also recognized later by J.Markwart, but he had no access to
much of the valuable material which would have
allowed him to reassess his former conclusions.[8]

The final identification of the nomads, named
Tetal by Sebeos, and the historical-philological
analysis of the relevant passages, has been done by
K. Czeglédy, who came to the conclusion that
Sebeos consistently applied the term *Tetal* to the
Western Turks,[9] solving thereby an intricate prob-
lem concerning these northern nomads.

Considerable progress in Armenian philological
analysis of the Sebeos Chronicle was made by the
monograph of G. Abgarian. He solved the "enigma"
of the provenience of the "Initial Chronicle"
(i.e., the four introductory chapters) by showing
that this part did not originally belong to the
Chronicle, but that it was attached to it quite by
chance. Even in the 13th century, the Chronicle
was known without this annexed part. Through precise philological analysis and a series of astute
collations with parallel passages, Abgarian was
able to date the origin of the "Initial Chronicle"
to the 11th century. At the end of the 16th cen-

tury, fragments of this Chronicle, since lost, were
attached by mistake to the present text of Sebeos.

But because the northern nomads, or *Tetal*, play
an active role in only the later chapters, Abgarian's findings have no bearing on our present problem, the *Tetal*- "Western Turk" terminology.[10]

In the following notes I wish to touch upon
only two minor questions connected with the term
Tetal: first, to clarify the structure of Chapter
50 (38) of the Sebeos chronicle, and second, to
try to find a special explanation for the inconsistent use of the term in this chapter.

* * *

After the murder of the Caliph Omar (644), a
rivalry began between the two sons-in-law of the
Prophet and three of his intimate companions. From
the resultant struggle, which cost Caliph Osman
his life in 656, the Egyptian faction emerged as
the strongest. The conflict ended only in 661, when
Mauviya seized power. The dissolution of the Arabs,
their splitting into four factions between 656 and
661, is described by Sebeos in Chapter 50 (38):
"And God has sent turbulence into the camps of
Ismael and their unanimity was split, they got
into a quarrel, and were divided into four factions.
One was the part from the side of India, the other
part which held Asorestan (Syria) and the regions
of the *Tetal* (*t'etalac'ik*), and another part in
the land of the Arabs (*tačik*) and the place called
Askaron."[11]

The wording of this passage is rather obscure,
and this might be the reason why J. Markwart left
it out of his analysis. Neither M. I. Artamonov
nor D. M. Dunlop took heed of it. It was only K.
Czeglédy who turned his attention to the passage,
gave an analysis of the turbulent historical situation of the strife between the Arabic factions,
and elucidated the historical background which led
to the dissolution of the Arabs. He explained the
alliance of the Egyptian faction with the *Tetal*
as a consequence of the historical background:
that from the second revolutionary center, Iraq,
troops had been sent out to conquer the northern
regions,and therefore Sebeos was justified in joining the troops from Iraq stationed in the *Tetal*
garrison with the Egyptian revolutionary party.

K. Czeglédy came to the conclusion that *Tetal*
in this case also referred to the "Western Turks,"
that is, to peoples not in Tokharistan or Trans-
oxiana, but in Khazaria under the sway of the
Western Turks.[12]

XIV

This localization seems to be corroborated by the circumstance that in the former instances the *Tetal* were mentioned only in this context: the troops of the *Tetal* (*zawrk' t'etalac'*) or the king of the *Tetal* (*t'agawor t'etalac'*) have the Kushan under their rule. It is only in the preceding Chapter 49 (37) that the *Tetal* region (land, country: *kolmank' t'etalac'*) is mentioned for the first time.[13]

In Chapter 49 (37) Sebeos relates that the Arab troops, unable to subdue the rebellious Medic tribes,[14] turned toward the North and, having defeated the guard of the Čor Gate, looted the regions beyond. But auxiliary troops from the *Tetal* region soon arrived and smashed the Arab troops, so that only a few remnants escaped destruction.

The country devastated by the Arabs was the land of the Causasian Huns, north of which lay Khazaria,[15] which was ruled by the Western Turks in the years 630-650. In this case, as demonstrated by K. Czeglédy, the term *Tetal* signifies Western Turks garrisoned on Khazarian territory.[16] Similarly, the land of the *Tetal* is mentioned in Chapter 50 (38), which seems to show that the two episodes which occurred relatively close in time took place in a similar historical-geographical area. Another possibility is that the wording of Chapter 49 (37) might have influenced the passage of the following Chapter 50 (38).

* * *

Chapter 50 (38) also presents textological problems. This chapter deals with the final establishment of Arab rule over Armenia, and can be divided into three major parts. There is disagreement among philologists about the sequence of the last paragraphs. In the present state of the text, the narration of the events (A-1) preceding the struggle of the Arab factions in 656, and of the events (A-2) leading to the election of Mauviya in 661, are interrupted by a paragraph (B) containing quotations from the Old Testament.[17]

Paragraph B begins with a quotation from the Book of Jeremiah (XV,14): "for a fire is kindled in mine anger, which shall burn upon you," which refers to the Arab Conquest as a disaster that has descended on the Armenians as a punishment from Heaven. The next quotation refers to the administration of social justice: "and they are going to be consumed by fire, and the depths of their mountains will waste away." Since the Chronicler

XIV

was aware of the ambiguity of the passage, he
provided the gloss: "that is, the violence of the
lords." He also clarified the passage concerning
the cloud of arrows raining down on them: "like-
wise will they (that is, the Arabs) from the
desert *Sin* rush down on the sinful people, causing
famine, brandishing daggers, and bringing disaster."
To complete the simile concerning the desert beast,
he adds a quotation from Daniel's prophecy (VI,7):
"and behold the fourth beast, terrible and powerful, and exceedingly strong; and it has great iron
teeth; it devours and breaks into pieces, and
stamps the remainder with its feet." The escala-
tion of celestial judgment ends with the punishment of the scourges of God (that is, the Arabs).
Again, a sentence from Jeremiah is cited (XLVI,
21): "the day of their calamity is come upon them,
the time of their visitation." The Chronicler adds
his own prophecy to this: "which will follow in
due course."[18]

Paragraph B intersects the continuous flow of
the narrative. This feature of the structure of
the text attracted the attention of a number of
philologists. N. Akinean was of the opinion that
the order of the last pages must have been mixed
up, and that, in fact, this paragraph containing
biblical quotations must originally have stood at
the end of the chapter.[19]

Up to a point, this argument seems to be valid,
since, in several instances, pages are missing or
misplaced in the Chronicle. It might be worth mentioning that such misplacements of pages or paragraphs of the text could easily have been caused
by the similarity of the words which begin or end
successive lines.[20] In the present case, the paragraph of biblical quotations and that of the text
relating the division of the Arabs into four
factions both begin: *ard*, "now, presently." (Sebeos favors the use of *ard* at the head of paragraphs).

As only a single manuscript[21] has come down to
us, comparison of variants and reconstruction of
the deteriorated parts is not possible. Only philological and historical argumentation can remedy
this deficiency.[22]

G. Abgarian concurs with N. Akinean's view on
the displaced pages and brings weighty arguments
in support of this interpretation. The close connection between the narrative parts A-1 and A-2 is
evident in the phrases which refer to one another.

XIV

160

For example, the phrase "and this same year Armenians defected from the Ismaelites (that is, the Arabs)" is found at the beginning of A-2, and the date exactly corresponds to that of the last event mentioned in part A-1, namely, the return of Katholikos Nerses to his patriarchate.[23]

There are other correspondences which link the two parts. The demonstrative pronouns in part B point to facts or persons encountered only in part A-2. The "fourth beast" in Daniel's prophecy refers to Muaviya, the victor in the rivalry between the four factions. Only part A-2 mentions Muaviya and the division of the Arab world into four factions. On the basis of this evidence, G. Abgarian draws the conclusion that pages had been displaced and that paragraph B had originally concluded the Chronicle.

G. Abgarian finds the weightiest argument in the initial sentence of paragraph B, which gives rise to many philological and thematic problems. This sentence contained, according to the quite convincing interpretation of Abgarian, an apology by the Chronicler for inadvertently not putting this paragraph in its proper place.[24]

That paragraph B concluded the Chronicle could also be substantiated by the argument that part A-2 could have been composed by another author or scribe writing a continuation of the Chronicle of Sebeos, and thereby appending A-2.[25]

Such an argument, however, has the weakness that it does not account for the cross-references between parts B and A-2. Of course, demonstrative pronouns which refer forward in the narrative have no conclusive weight in this argument, since a later author might have attempted to link up his continuation with the preceding part. But it is hardly credible that the same chronicler would have taken the trouble to insert such demonstratives in order to efface traces of his own authorship.

In a certain sense, a supposed separate authorship of A-2 would also seem to be supported by the vague use of the ethnic term *Tetal*. The term is used consistently throughout the Chronicle,[26] but in the last Chapter 50 (38) one has the impression that it is not the appropriate term, or that it is perhaps even used by mistake.

Still, in my opinion, the above arguments do not indisputably testify to the supposed inversion of the paragraphs of the last chapter.

XIV

Of course, it is scarcely defensible that
paragraph B should have been drawn up earlier
than A-2; the presence of demonstrative pronouns
referring to A-2 are not conclusive evidence to
this effect. Events were not always jotted down in
the chronicles day by day, but were summarized by
months, even by years. The final texts were established only after the direct impact of events had
subsided. Even those chronicles drawn up at the
time of the occurrence of events suffer from omissions, later insertions, inversions, and mixing up
of paragraphs, all the more because the importance
of daily events does not lie exclusively in their
chronological sequence but also in their thematic
correspondences.

In my opinion, paragraph B was drawn up later
than the events, or part of the events, recorded
in part A-2. Presumably, the author composed the
paragraph under the impression of A-2, but if he
had intended to place B at the end of Chapter 50
(38), nothing prevented him from doing so. In
that case, how should we understand the author's
apology: "Now though talking in vain, I leave the
thing of the sequence of events, according to the
defective contemplation of my mind, and not according to the worthy divine grace of knowledge...
and I shall corroborate it with the words of the
Prophet, who uttered them as the Lord commanded
him."[27] The sentence is rather obscure and admits
different interpretations, each without conclusive proof.

The decisive factor or issue, in my view, is
precisely the deliberate adoption of this sequence
of paragraphs by the author. If Sebeos had appended the biblical sentences to the very end of
Chapter 50 (38), the Chronicle would have gained
an impressive finale, but the quotations would
have been degraded to a merely illustrative
character. It was a technique popular with medieval
authors, however, to attribute accomplished facts
and events to celestial predestination, or at
least to impute such a character to them. The
Bible contains prophecies applicable to nearly
every sort of situation and historical occurrence.
The quotations enumerated in B comprise a list of
celestial judgments in hierarchial order: the
sins of the people in general precedes the sins of
the lords, and the consequence for both is the
punishment (in our case, the Arabs) rushing forth
from the *Sin* desert. From among the beasts, it is

XIV

the "fourth" which stamps down all others and remains victorious in the battlefield; here, the
"fourth" corresponds to Muaviya, the founder of
the Omayyad dynasty.

But Sebeos was not entirely consistent in his
quotation of prophecies, since the subjugation of
Armenia was already an accomplished fact, related
previously in the Chronicle. The subsequent prophecy quoted from Daniel referred to events to
come whose outcome, of course, was already known
to Sebeos--thus, in reality, it was a *vaticinatio
ex eventu*. The author's apology was meant to excuse his interrupting the narration of the events
to interject biblical quotations, partly to casti-
gate for sins committed, partly to foretell the
future.

In short, I think that the original sequence
of the concluding paragraphs of Chapter 50 (38)
must have been similar to the present text:
A-1--B--A-2.

* * *

Returning to the other topic, the territorial
division of the Arab factions, the passage connect-
ing the *Tetal* and the Arabs in Egypt remains a
problematic issue.

After Osman's murder in 656 and the subsequent
internal struggle, the Arabs emerged as the strongest faction in Egypt.[28] The passage mentioning
the *Tetal* as the allies of the Egyptians remains
inexplicable even if the meaning Tokharistan, or
Transoxania, is attributed to "*Tetal* land," because Tokharistan was conquered by Qutaybah only
in 705, and it was a decade later before he could
penetrate Ferghana.[29] It was mainly for this reason
that Czeglédy identified the *Tetal* of this passage
with the *Tetal* of another territory, the *Tetal*
ruling over Khazaria.[30]

Below I will try to present a different explanation of this problem.

Medieval chroniclers, even while giving us accurate accounts of contemporary events, often
adopt an argument of celestial predestination as
an explanation of history. This is understandable
because the medieval author is almost exclusively
imbued with ecclesiastic literature, the Bible as
well as the writings of the Church fathers. In most
cases it is not the essence of the topic which
counts, but the literal interpretation.[31]

The application of biblical quotations to accounts of contemporary events often arises from

XIV

superficial similarities between them, both in
content and in wording. As to the application of
the sense of the quotations, a good example is
given by the prophecies enumerated above, but when
it comes to words, a simple phonetic accord would
suffice, e.g., in the case of the substitution
Heftal - *Hep^ctal* - *Tetal*, adopted by the medieval
author.

Most philologists are of the opinion that the
term *Tetal* taken from the Armenian Anonymous Chronicle has become the equivalent of *Hep^ctal* (Hephta-
lite) by mere consonance,[32] and later by the identification of the geographic site of the nomadic
tribes in the northeastern borderland of the Sassanian Empire. Consequently, the term was applied to
the "Western Turks."

I am of the opinion that the appearance of *Tetal*
in the passage about the Arab factions could be derived from a similar phonetic identification. In
our case, we would expect the allies of the Arabs
in Egypt to be not the *Tetal*, but the Kushites,
i.e., the Ethiopians, neighbors of the Egyptians.
The Chronicler equated the *Kusit* with the *Kusan* because of the phonetic resemblance of the
names.

In his early years Sebeos was fairly well informed about contemporary events on the northern
frontier, but his knowledge of the Arab world was
rather deficient and his accounts thereof less
detailed, perhaps because he was an old man by the
time he composed his Chronicle. This might have
been the reason for the obscurity of the passage
about the Arab factions.

His predilection for biblical names applied to
peoples, however, was not a result of old age.
Even in his younger years, he did not refer to
the Western Turks by their proper name, but by the
term *Tetal* borrowed from the Anonymous Chronicle.
He erroneously called the Arabs "Ismaelites" and
the Ethiopians "Kushans", and equated the latter
with the *Tetal*.

As was the case with other chroniclers, his
daily reading was the Bible, as well as other
church literature, including the anonymous
Chronicle. In the latter chronicle, *Kus*, the
biblical eponym of the Ethiopians, often appears
in the *Liber generationis*: "*Kus* and from him derives the generation of the Aithiops."[33] This
identification was most probably supported by a
passage where *Kusan* was written instead of *Kusit*:

XIV

"*Kušahs*, i.e. Aithops."[34] The passage in the An-
nex of the Hippolytus Chronicle in the translation of J. Markwart reads: "157. und die Völker,
deren Sprachen von einander unterschieden werden,
sind diese... (15) Inder, (16) Khušankh, welche
sind Ethiopier, (17) Egipter." Concerning this
passage, Markwart comments as follows: "Kušankh
ist die Bezeichnung der Khušan in Tochāristān,
die der Übersetzer hier wegen der Ähnlichkeit mit
dem Namen der Khusiten-Athiopier einführt."[35]

Another, although weaker, link must not be left
out of our considerations. In the enumeration of
peoples after the *Kušan* (13), the "first Arabs"
(14) were mentioned.[36] To show how much consonance
counted in the substitution of ethnic names,
another example can be quoted from the Anonymous
Chronicle, where κοσσαῖοι were translated by
Khušankh.[37]

Not only with ethnic names but also with topographical terminology the chronicler must have
been under the influence of the Anonymous Chronicle. In the quoted passage, the site of the first
Arab faction was "from the side of India."[38] This
reminds me of the enumeration of people in the
Anonymous Chronicle, where just before *Kušan*
(here, Aithiops), Indians (*Hndikk^c*) were mentioned.

The enumeration of the *Kuš* descendancy could
also have been a cause for topographical misinter-
pretation: "Egypt, Ethiopia, which faces toward
India, and still another Ethiopia, whence flows
the river of the Kushites (*Kušac'ik'*)."[39]

The region lying beyond Scythia remained a
terra incognita in the landscape of Ptolemy, as
in the Armenian adaptation of it. In the topographical view of Sebeos, the river Phison, which
unites seven tributaries, was similar to the
Vehrot,[40] which was identified with the Ganges and
Indus rivers, both flowing into the Indian Bay.[41]
This distorted topographical view was common to
all Armenians, and was derived from the Armenian
Geography (*Ašxarhac'oyc'*):[42] "The river Phison
originates in Turkestan and compasseth the whole
land of Havilath (*qui circumit omnem terram
Hevilath*)."[43] And in the Eden of Genesis (2,11),
the second river was the Gihon: "which compasseth
the whole land of Cush (*qui circumit omnem terram
Aithiopiae* [Gen. 2,13])."

At that time, the Arab Conquest had not reached
the Oxus, but the name of the big river (*Jaihuin*)[44]
must have been known to the Arab troops pursuing

Yezdegerd as far as the northeastern frontier of
the Sassanian Empire--the land of the *Tetal* (Western Turks)--and must have figured in the strategic
plans of Arab warfare.

There are other similarities that might have
played a role in the identification of the region
mentioned in our passage, the site of which was
deprived of an exact topography. There was a passage in Ptolemy, as also in the Armenian Geography,
according to which the "fisheating Ethiopians"
(*jknaker Etiopacik*-- ἰχθυοφαγοι Αἰθίοπες)
originated from the *Sinai* land (Σίναι),
or the region of the *Sinón thesis* (Σινῶν θέσις)
situated toward the Indian Ocean.[45]

A similar phonetic consonance might have been
instrumental in the identification of these regions of Scythia, the *Sinai* and *Sinón thesis*, and
the *Sin* desert, the territory from which the Arabs
emerged.

In my opinion, Sebeos was influenced neither by
specific knowledge nor by explicit information in
his identifications of peoples of the Barbarian
World. Rather, his identifications were often the
result of confusion of ethnic names with Biblical
names due to their phonetic resemblance.

Notes

1. Abbreviations:
Seb/Malx.: *Sebeosi episkoposi Patmut'iwn*(Published
   by St. Malxaseanc, Yerevan, 1939).
Seb/Tifl.: *Patmut'iwn Sebeosi i Herakln* (Bishop
   Sebeos: The History of Herakleios), (Tiflis,
   1913). A defective reprint of the St. Petersburg
   edition was published by K. Patkanian in 1879.
   Neither the SPb. edition, nor its Russian
   translation (*Istorija imperatora Irakla.
   Sočinenija Sebeosa pisatelja VII veka*, Trans-
   lated by K. Patkanian, SPb. 1862), was accessible
   to me.
Seb/Macl.: *Histoire d'Héraclius par l'évèque Sebèos*,
   Traduit de l'arménien et annoté par Fr. Macler
   (Paris, 1904).
Markwart, *WZKM* XII: J. Markwart, Historische Glos-
   sen zu den altürkischen Inschriften, *WZKM* XII,
   1898, pp. 157-200.
Czeglédy, Korai: K. Czeglédy, A korai kazár
   történelem forrásainak kritikájához (*Remarks on*

XIV

the *Critical Analysis of the Sources of Early Khazar History*), *MTAOK* XV/1-2, 1959, pp. 107--128; the English translation is to appear in *Acta Antiqua Hung.*, 1975.

Czeglédy, Bahrām Čōbīn: K. Czeglédy, Bahrām Čōbīn and the Persian Apocalyptic Literature, *Acta Orient. Hung.* VIII, 1958, pp. 21-43.

Soukry: *Géographie de Moise de Corène d'après Ptolemée*, Traduit par A. Soukry, Venice: S. Lazzaro, 1881.

Hippolytus: *Hippolytus Werke, Bd. IV. Die Chronik*, hergestellt von A. Bauer, Nebst einem Beitrag von J. Markwart, Leipzig 1929, pp. 393-558: Anhang. Übersetzung aus Moses Kaɫankajtvac'i und der armenischen Chronik vom Jahre 686/7 bis zum Ende der Kaiserliste. Herausgegeben von J. Markwart und A. Bauer.

Ananun: *Ananun Žamanakagrut'iwn* (Anonymous Chronicle, or the Chronicle of the 7th c. Anonymous), Published by B. Sargisean, Venice: S. Lazzaro, 1904.

Trever, *SA* XXI: K. V. Trever, Kušany, xionity i eftality po armjanskim istočnikam IV-VII vv. (K istorii narodov Srednej Azii), *Sovjetskaja Arxeologija* XXI, 1954, pp. 131-147.

Abgarian: G. Abgarian, *"Sebeosi Patmut yune ew Ananuni are'c'vac'* (The "Chronicle of Sebeos" and the Enigma of the Anonymous Chronicler), (Yerevan, 1965).

Krikorean: M. K. Krikorean, *Ditoɫut'iwnner ew srbagrut'iwnner Sebiosi patmagroc' bnagrin veray* (Remarks and Corrections to the Text of the Sebeos Chronicle), Wien: Mechitaristen--Druckerei, 1973.

2. Fragments of Middle Persian literature also rarely occur in Armenian chronicles: e.g., in Sebeos' Chronicle, there appear fragments of the epic romance of Bahrām Čōbīn interwoven with the history of Bistām. See Czeglédy, Bahrām Čōbīn, pp.22ff.

3. *Seb/Malx.*, p. 49; *Seb/Tifl.*, pp.75; *Seb/Macl.*, pp. 30-31.

4. As to the Chronicler himself, an article has recently been published by G. Abgarian, who views the issue from a new angle:"Ditoɫut'yunner Sebeosi Patmut'yan masin"(Remarks on the History of Sebeos), *Banber Matenadarani*, Yerevan 1958, Nr. 4, pp. 61-72; id., Remarques sur l'histoire de Sébeos, *Revue des Études Arméniennes, N.S.* I, 1964, pp. 203-215. I shall return to the problem of the author on another occasion.

XIV

5. *Seb/Malx.* XXII-XXVII, p. 61-69; *Seb/Tifl.*
XIV-XIX, pp. 94-109; *Seb/Macl.* XIV-XIX, pp. 42-
52.
6. Czeglédy, Korai, p. 109.
7. The importance of these borrowings for the
evaluation of the Chronicle was already recognized by Armenologists of the last century. The
corresponding passages taken over by the Chroniclers Thomas Arcruni, Stepannos Asolik, Vardan
Arevelci and Hovhannes Katholikos were appended,
in extenso, to the Tiflis edition of the Patkanov
edition, pp. 249-320.
8. Czeglédy, Korai, p. 115, n.18.
9. Czeglédy, Korai, provides a detailed list of
sources. But the range of meaning of ethnic names,
especially with nomad tribal federations of loose
composition,is subject to constant change due to
changes in their historical-geographical situation. The change in the signification of "Northern
people" (*hiwsisayin azger*) in the age of Sebeos
was characterized by Czeglédy, Herakleios török
szövetségesei (The Turkic Allies of Herakleios),
Magyar Nyelv XLIX, 1953, pp. 322-323. (See the
same article in English translation in the present
volume.)
10. I wish to return to the subject of the *Tetal*
mentioned in Chapter 2, "The Uprising of the Par-
thians," on another occasion.
11. *Seb/Malx.*, pp. 155, 27-156, 1; *Seb/Tifl.*,
p. 247, 12-20; *Seb/Macl.*, pp. 148, 27-149, 3. The
Armenian gives *kołmn* "side," *kołmank* "region, land,
country."
12. Czeglédy, Korai, pp. 126-127.
13. *Seb/Malx.*, p. 151, 19; *Seb/Tifl.*, p. 241, 1;
Seb/Macl., p. 144.
14. An important emendation to the list of peoples
living in the Median Mountains was made by G.
Abgarian, who added the ethnic group, the "Gels."
See: *op. cit.*, pp. 199-202.
15. Soukry, p. 27; Czeglédy, Korai, p. 125.
16. Czeglédy, Korai, pp. 121-125, 127.
17. To facilitate references, we shall refer to
the three separate parts of Chapter 50 (38) by
the letters A-1, B, and A-2.
18. *Seb/Malx.*, p. 154, 6-31; *Seb/Tifl.*, pp. 244-
246; *Seb/Macl.*, p. 147.
19. *Matenagrakan hetazotut'iwnner* (Untersuchungen
zur Geschichte der armenischen Literatur), vol. II,
Wien: Mechitaristen- Druckerei 1924, p. 35; id.,
Handes Amsorya, 1923, p. 224.

XIV

20. Instructive examples of such omissions, caused by external motives, are given by G. Abgarian, *op. cit.*, pp. 67-69.

21. The MS No.2639, copied in 1672 in the Amerdol Monastery (in the region of Lake Van) and kept at present in the Matenadaran State Archives in Yerevan, contains the best copies of some of the most important chronicles.

22. Better manuscripts used by some later chroniclers, but since lost, enabled philologists from K. Patkanian to G. Abgarian and M. Krikorian to reconstruct some deteriorated passages of MS Nr.2639. However, no variant text of Chapter 50 (38) exists.

23. Abgarian, p. 203.

24. *Ibid.*, pp. 204-205.

25. Such continuations are also found in Armenian chronicles, e.g., in those of Samuel of Ani, Michael Syrus (Asori), etc.

26. Czeglédy, Korai, pp. 115, 118, 119, 120, 125.

27. The beginning lines of paragraph B.

28. C. Brockelmann, *History of the Islamic Peoples*, New York: Capricorn Books, 1960, pp. 63-67; cf. Czeglédy, Korai, p. 126.

29. Philip K. Hitti, *History of the Arabs,* New York: MacMillan, 1963, p. 209.

30. See above, note 12.

31. A rare exception to this attitude in the same period is presented by the 7th c. geography, attributed to Moses of Khoren and, from 1877 on, also to Ananias of Shirak. See the introductory sentences in Soukry, p. 5, French translation, p. 1.

32. The Middle Persian name of the Hephtalites, *Heftal*, became *Hep'tal* with the Armenians as a result of sound substitution. Because of their phonetic similarity, Sebeos identified this ethnic name with *Tetal*, taken from *Diamerismos*; cf. Czeglédy, Heftaliták, hunok, avarok, onogurok (Hephtalites, Huns, Avars, Onogurs), *Magyar Nyelv* L, 1954, p. 145; id., "Bemerkungen zur Geschichte der Chazaren", *Acta Orient. Hung.* XIII, 1961, p. 246, n.4.; id., Bahrām Čōbīn, p. 23, n.10. Markwart's theory, according to which *Tetal* should be the ethnic name *Heftal* augmented by a Caucasian t- prefix (*Eranšahr*, p. 59; *Streifzüge*, p. 56) is not accepted by modern philology; cf. Czeglédy, Korai, pp. 109-110. Concerning the Hellenistic culture in Transcaucasia and the origin of the Thessalian descendancy of Iberians and Alvans, see Czeglédy, "Kaukázusi hunok, kaukázusi avarok"

XIV

(Caucasian Huns, Caucasian Avars), *Antik Tanul-mányok* II, 1954, p. 131, n.57.

33. *Ananun*, pp. 6, 26; 5, 4; 29, 31.

34. *Ibid.*, p. 9, 29.

35. Hippolytus, pp. 482-483. Even scholars of later ages mixed up the two ethnic names; thus, e.g., in 1864 N. O. Emin identified the Kushans with Kushites in the Achaimenid Inscriptions; *apud*: Trever, *SA* XXI, p. 132.

36. Hippolytus, p. 480.

37. *Ibid.; Ananun*, p. 9, 9. See the remark of J. Markwart: " κοσσαῖοι ist durch die Ubersetzung auf die Kušan in Tochāristān bezogen."

38. The translation of Macler. for whom the first faction of the Arabs "est dans l'Inde," is erroneous; cf. *Seb/Macl.*, p. 148, ult.

39. Hippolytus, p. 474, 103/2; *Ananun*, 7, pp. 35-36.

40. *Seb/Malx.*, p. 67; *Seb/Tifl.*, p. 105; *Seb/Macl.*, p. 49.

41. St. Malxaseanc took this identification for a mistake and a later interpolation; see Seb/Malx., p. 67, 186; cf. Krikorean, p. 47.

42. Soukry, pp. 42-43.

43. M. Krikorean emended this passage and analyzed the identifications of the rivers Phison, Ganges, and Indus; *op. cit.*, pp. 46-51.

44. *Encyclopédie de l'Islam*, vol. I, p. 467: Amu Darya.

45. Soukry, p. 46: *Siwnikia, Siwnec'ik'*; in the short version of the 7th c. Geography: *Sineac'ik'*; cf. *Movsesi Xorenac'woj Matenagrut'iwnk'*, Venice 1865, p. 616.

XIV

EDMOND SCHÜTZ

THE STAGES OF ARMENIAN SETTLEMENTS
IN THE CRIMEA*

For a whole century a dispute has been going on as to the date of the earliest appearance of Armenians in the area north of the Black Sea. There are two contradictory concepts in circulation, the one relating the role of the Armenians to the period of Genovese rule over the southern maritime coastline of the Crimea, the other to the 11th century as a consequence of mass emigration from their homeland triggered by the invasion of the Seljuq tribes. The partisans of the latter point of view generally deal with the 11th-13th centuries almost as a unity, extending the chronical evidence of the period of Tatar invasions of the 13th century equivocally to earlier times. The outcome of nomad warfare, of devastations and depredation might well have been similar, non the less, we must delineate the chronology of the mass emigrations following the Seljuq and Tatar invasions, separated by two centuries.

We have in this case — as in historical literature everywhere — lengthy relations about the immediate consequences of incursions of the enemy troops, the devastation of the country, the whole-sale massacre of the population, the dragging away of thousands of captives. The chronicles contemporary to the Seljuq and Tatar invasions are full of jeremiads bewailing these lamentable events [1].

---

* Standard literature on the central topic in Armenian: M. Bežiškian (Bžškean), *Canaparhordut'iwn i Lehastan*, Venice, 1830; H. Ter-Abrahamian, *Patmut'iwn Xrimu*, Teodosia, 1865; V. Mikaelian, *Ghrimu haykakan gałut'i patmut'yun*, Yerevan, 1964; A.G. Abrahamian, *Hamařot urvagic hay gałt'avayreri patmut'yan*, Yerevan, I, 1964. (Crimea: pp. 157-196; Poland: 197-233); H. Manandian, *K'nnakan tesut'yun hay žołovrdi patmut'yan*, Yerevan, III, 1952; X.A. Porkšeyan, «Erb è katarvel hayeri mutk'ə Ghrim» *Patma-banasirakan Handes*, 1962, No. 2, pp. 105-117.

[1] *Patmut'iwn Aristakisi Lastivertc'woy*, published by K.N. Yuzbašian, Yerevan, 1963; *Povestvovanie vardapeta Aristakesa Lastivertci*, transl. by K.N. Yuzbašian, Moscow, 1968, cap. XVI, XXIV; Kirakos Gandzakec'i, *Patmut'iwn Hayoc*, publ. by K.A. Melik-Ohanjanian, Yer., 1961; French translations: by M. Brosset, *Deux historiens arméniens*, SPb, 1871 and by Ed. Dulaurier, «Les Mongols d'après les historiens arméniens» *Journal Asiatique*, série V, tome XI; Russian translation: *Istorija Armenii*, translated by L.A. Xanlarian, Moscow, 1976. (Abbreviations: a) Kirakos; b) Kir/Bros; c) Kir/Dul; d) Kir/Xan).

116

XV

But there is no mention of the fugitives leaving their homeland for good. Of course, the population does not want to leave his home and personal effects, they bewail the dead and they hide in cellars and mountain recesses. In any case, there are some thousands who flee at the first rumour of the approach of the enemy, because in the case of both the Seljuqs and the Tatars the sedentary population had its previous experience from earlier inroads. The Seljuqs made incursions in 1048, 1054, 1062 preceding the final blow, the seizure of Ani, the Armenian capital in 1064. The Tatars arrived twenty years prior (1221) to their ultimate conquest of the Transcaucasus [2]. Still it happened, that in districts, lying further away from the marchroute of military operations, the population was in the delusion that probably « the devil might not be so black, as depicted » [3], so people of a village headed by their priest, bearing aloft the cross, marched in procession cordially to receive the Tatars, but learnt a deplorable lesson at their own cost, they got exterminated [4].

The immediate repercussion of the population in the war-march areas was, they fled where they could [5], but this meant, in the first instance, their immediate neighbourhood, hiding places in the surrounding countryside. The direction of their flight, the goal of emigration to a foreign land was related only later by the local historian, at the time when considerable masses accumulated in a region, a foreign country or district. On the experience of the pioneers subsequent thousands followed, but this might have happened decades or one or more hundred years later.

The local chronography's attention was focused on the local events of atrocities, and, in the case of the Seljuq devastations we have been informed only by outside sources, in the first instance by Matthew of Edesse, about the outcome of the continuous onslaughts (at about the 1070-ies): « And many districts became desolate, and the Eastern provinces devastated, the country of Rum stood in ruins, and nowhere the pople found bread to eat, and place to repose and have a rest, only in Edessa and in her region. And in Antioch and all the country of Cilicia and as far as Tarsos and all the region of Marash, and Tluk and all their area people could not find a rest, and all human beings fled together and came into this land in innumerable masses, thousands after thousands, and tenthousands after tenthousands floated all around in the country. » [6]

---

[2] Not to mention the devastations of the Khwârazm-Shâh Jalâl ad-Dîn in 1225-1228: *The Cambridge History of Iran*, vol. 5. *The Saljuq and Mongol Periods*, ed. by J.A. Boyle, Cambridge, 1968, pp. 327-330. (Abbr.: *CHI*, V); Kirakos, pp. 224-228; Kir/Dul. 203-209; Kir/Xan. 149-150.

[3] Not to mention the wide-spread legend about Prester John in Inner Asia expected to come to rescue the Christians oppressed by the Mahometans; e.g. L. Olschki, *Marco Polo's Asia*, Calif. Univ. Press, 1960, pp. 387.ff.

[4] Kirakos, p. 202; Kir/Dul. 199; Kir/Xan. 138.

[5] H. Manandian, *K'nnakan patmut'iwn*, p. 62.ff.

[6] Matthiew of Edesse: *Patmut'iwn Matt'eosi Urhayec'woy*, Jerusalem, 1869, pp. 261-262; same, Vagharšapat, 1898, p. 217.

XV

In this case the historical background is quite clear, the Seljuq incursions were preceded by the premeditated displacement policy of the Byzantine court, who in 1021 for strategic considerations moved the whole Arcruni principality, 14.000 men with kith and kin from their homesite in the northern Van Lake region to Cappadocia. And so did the other Armenian principalities fare: the kingdom of Ani in 1045, and the prince of Kars in 1064. The Armenian population of the Eastern borderland was shifted inside the Eastern Byzantine themes.

So after the Seljuq inroads the most natural direction to flee to were the already established Armenian principalities in Cappadocia, and when the Seljuq incursions were reiterated during the following decades, from Cappadocia they moved further to the South, finally to Cilicia, the area hidden by the Tauros ranges.

There is no mention in the sources, the chronicles of a possible flow of Armenian fugitives towards the North, and no wonder, beside the alluring proximity of the newly established Armenian settlements in the South, the steppes north of the Caucasus, and also the Crimea, just a decade previously (from 1050 on) were conquered by another branch of Inner-Asiatic nomads, the Kipchak-Comans.

And now let us cast a cursory glance at the possible evidences relating to the earliest appearance of Armenians in the regions north of the Caucasus and the Black Sea. As a matter of fact Armenians, as international traders, might have shown up pretty early far North. As to the testimony of a reliable Travel account of the 10th century, Ibn Faḍlân, the Khalif's envoy A.D. 921 to the Volga-Bulgarians, entering the Khan's tent at first sight became aware of precious Armenian carpets, by which the tent was bolstered[7].

Though this remark is no direct proof of the presence of Armenians at this time in the Volga-Kama region, the carpets might have had the trade label « Armenian », and imported by the very activ Volga-Bulgarian agents. But, in any case, the appearance of single Armenian merchants or rather caravans cannot be denied. It must be considered, that after the fall of the Bulgarian Khanate, in the 14th century there existed a dense Armenian settlement in this region[8].

The most reliable evidence of the presence of Armenians in the Northern Black Sea area the testimony of the tombstones (xačkᶜars) must be considered, if only the worn-off slabs could be deciphered equivocally. Dates, figures are indicated by capital letters or riddlesome ligatures, which

---

[7] Z.V. Togan, « Ibn Fadlâns Reisebericht » *Abh. f. Kunde d. Morgenl.* vol. 4, No. 3, p. 64; A.P. Kovalevskij, *Kniga Axmeda Ibn Fadlana i ego putešestvie na Volgu v 921-922 gg.* Xarkov, 1956, p. 137; Ibn Fadlan, *Putešestvie na Volgu.* Ed. Kračkovskij, Moscow-Leningrad, 1939, p. 73.

[8] B.V. Miller, « Ob armjanskix nadpısjax v Bolgarax i Kazani » *Izv. Ross. Akad. ist. mat. kult.,* vol. IV, 1925, pp. 65-80.

XV

have always provided ample occasion to disputes. Xr. Kučuk-Ioannesow, reader of the Lazarev Institute in Moscow, during the 1895-1896 years discovered, collected 150 Armenian tombstones of Armenians in this region. For the earliest he dated two *xačk'ars*: one, preserved in the Museum of Theodosia, to A.D. 1027 (Arm. Cal. 476 + 551), and the other in the Church S. Sargis to 1047 (496 + 551). But his reading of the worn-off characters has not been endorsed by successive research, the one being dated A.D. 1327, the other to 1557[9]. The rest of the tombstones were from the period following the Tatar conquest.

The presence of Armenians in the Crimea was attested by documentary evidence, several notarial acts dating from the decade 1280-1290 connected with trade deals between Armenian and Genovese merchants[10]. Armenians because of their trading experience all around the Near East were surely welcome partners in commercial enterprises towards the Eastern countries mostly via Trapezunt to Iran and further on, or towards the South to Egypt.

But such documents do not furnish a definite proof as to their citizenship, these Armenians might have been single settlers, or simple partners in the deals of Genovese factors.

The most important port on the coastline preceding the upswing of Caffa, had been Sudaq. A fairly important Armenian settlement must have existed there by the end of the 13th century, as — according to the testimony of a marginal comment in the Sudaq Synaxarion a heated dispute was going on between the local Armenian and Greek clergy in 1292 about the exact dating of the Easter-day[11].

But in the research of early settlements also the territories North and Northeast of the Crimea might be taken into consideration, because the transit route towards these regions must have led rather via the Crimean seaports, than the one through the Caucasus mountains, and following the steppe zone and marsh-land around the Azov Sea, risking the danger to be attacked and looted by steppe nomads.

There are evidences — though of unequal authenticity — of the existence of an Armenian settlement in Kiev, the whole series of which has recently been subjected again to a careful philological analysis by Y.

[9] Xr. Kučuk-Ioannesow, « Starinnye armjanskie nadpisi i starinnye rukopisi v predelax jugo-zapadnoj Rusi i v Krymu », *Drevnosti vostočnye, Trudy Vost. Komissii Mosk. Arxeol. Obšč.* vol. II, No. 3, Moscow, 1903, pp. 70, 67; I.I. Babkov, « Očerki po istoričeskoj i kul'turnoj geografii Kryma. II. Drevnejšaja armjanskaja nadpis' Feodosijskogo muzeja; k voprosu o vremeni pojavlenja armjan v Tavride », *Izv. Gos. Geogr. Obšč.*, vol. 71, No. 9, 1939, p. 1985; I.A. Orbeli, « Dva serebrjannyx kovša XVI veka s armjanskoj i grečeskoj nadpisjami ». *Izbrannye trudy*, Yerevan, 1963, p. 214.
[10] G.I. Brătianu, *Actes des notaires génois de Péra et de Caffa de la fin du treizième siècle* (1281-1290), Bucarest, 1927, pp. 173, 244, 271.
[11] *Zapiski Odesskogo Obščestva Istorii i Drevnostej*, V., p. 609.; F. Brun (Ph. Bruun), *Černomor'e. Sbornik izsledovanij po istoričeskoj geografii Južnoj Rossii*, part II, Odessa, 1880, pp. 139-140.

119

XV

Daškevič [12]. A documentary evidence pointing back beyond the Tatar conquest period, is the Biography of Saint Agapitos, who cured and revived invalids. An Armenian phisician, being an eyewitness of the miracles of the Saint became a convert. From the context of the relation of the Saint's Life — the original of which can be presumably dated to the 1080-90-ies — we learn, that there was an Armenian community in Kiev at that time [13].

Another conclusive document from the neighbouring area is the privilege dated March 31, 1243, granted by the Hungarian king, Bela IV, to the Armenians settled down in the suburb of the ancient Hungarian capital Esztergom (Latin: Strigonium), after the Tatar conquest the see of the Archbishop [14]. The document states that units of the Armenian community have arrived to the country during the reign of Bela IV. (1235-1270) and his predecessors [15], but as we do not find any previous mention of them, so we must suppose that the bulk arrived after their flight from the Armenian mother-land in 1236 and the following years. The privilege granted to them free trade all over the country, and they must have made use of it, as after one generation they disappeared, though the territory, called « terra Armeniorum » preserved their memory up to 1290 [16].

There is no likelihood that Armenians should have immigrated in the foregoing centuries in considerable masses to Hungary [17], as we have ample documentary material about traders of different nationalities: Mahometans (Ismaelites) and Jews from the early period of the Arpad dynasty [18], but none of Armenians. The Chronicle of Simeon of Kéza enumerated also Armenians among the nationalities accompanying the Hungarians at the time of their conquest of the territory of Hungary around A.D. 896 [19], but this statement is of no conclusive value, the Chronicler used the topos-technique telescoping the state of affairs of the second half of the 13rd century back to the Conquest period.

Twenty years ago I tried to take another possibility of explanation

[12] Ya. Dachkévytch, « Les arméniens à Kiev (jusqu'à 1240) » *REArm*, X, pp. 305-358. and XI, pp. 323-375.

[13] *Paterik kievo-pečerskogo monastyrja*, izd. Arxeografičeskoj komissii, SPb, 1911, pp. 93-95.; *REArm*, XI, pp. 323-330.

[14] *Monumenta Ecclesiae Strigoniensis*. Ed. Fr. Knauz. I, Strigonii, (Esztergom), 1874. pp. 345-346.

[15] « cum Armeni, praedecessorum ipsius Domini Regis et suo temporibus in Strigonium ad hospitandum congregati » *ibid.*

[16] *Monumenta Ecclesiae Strigoniensis*, II, pp. 142, 248, 274-75, 271, (A.D. 1315: p. 707.?). Cf. K. Schünemann, *Die Entstehung des Städtewesens in Südosteuropa*, Südostaeuropäische Bibliothek I, Breslau, 1929, pp. 56, 67.

[17] At most, single or a few individuals from among the Armenians, displaced by the Byzantine nationality policy to the Balkans. Cf. E. Schütz, « Ungarisch *katapan*, armenisch *katapan* », *Handes Amsorya*, 1961, No. 11-12, cols. 515-520.

[18] K. Czeglédy, « Az Árpád-kori mohammedánokról és neveikről » *Nyelvtudományi Értekezések*, No. 70, pp. 254-259; Gy. Pauler, *A magyar nemzet története az Árpádházi királyok alatt*, II. Budapest, 1899, pp. 191-194.

[19] *Scriptores Rerum Hungaricarum, tempore ducum regumque stirpis Arpadianae gestarum*. Ed. E. Szentpétery, Budapest, 1937, p. 192.

120

XV

into account, supposing that the Armenian community might have come from the Cilician Armenian kingdom. Andrew II., king of Hungary, on his return from a Crusade warfare from the Holy Land via Cilicia, in 1217, betrothed his son to the daughter of the Armenian king, Levon II (1198-1219), maturing the idea of building up an empire in the Southeast of Europe. First I cherished the thought, Armenian mercants and knights might have accompanied him to Hungary. But because the linguistic analysis of some loanwords, borrowed from Armenian into Hungarian at that age, contradicted to this supposition, so I abandoned the idea of a possible Cilician origin of the Armenian settlement of Esztergom [20].

To sum up our findings, we lack narrative and documentary sources to prove the existence of Armenian settlements in the northern and northwestern regions prior to the Mongol conquest. The Hungarian and the Polish documents, privileges testifying the presence of Armenians, are of a later date. Still one should not dismiss the idea that Armenians showed up sporadically in the North. There must have been Armenian traders also in the preceding centuries, and a more momentous community in the state of the Kievan Russ [21].

Still in dealing with the Armenian mass emigrations, the consequences of the Seljuq and Tatar disasters are generally taken comprehensively, saying that after the Seljuq and Tatar invasions Armenians fled to the North and to the South. But where did this generally recurring comprehensive statement take its origin?

If we try to trace back this assertion, disseminated by the Armenian clerical authors of the last century, we come to the conclusion that directly or indirectly Minas Bežiškian's very popular « Travel Accounts to Poland » [22] served for the major literary source. However, we have to remark that Bežiškian was not the pioneer, who investigated the old documents and inscriptions of the Armenian communities, but some other erudite clergymen before him (St. Roszka, H. Zohrabian, etc.), and many more after him.

Minas Bežiškian, after having been named vicar of Tauria (the Crimea) started in 1820 on a long journey to visit all centers belonging to his diocese, and on the way he visited all important Armenian communities in Galicia, Novo-Rossia, and the Crimea. Before starting on his journey, he made thorough studies as to the past and present state of these areas. The first result was a book on the history of the Black Sea area « Patmut'iwn Pontosi » (1819). He could make good use of the information furnished by H. Zohrabian, whose thorough researches in the 1790-ies in the Lwow episcopate and other archives had been incorporated into the encyclopedic compendium of historical geography compiled by the Venice Mekhitarists [23].

---

[20] *Magyar Nyelv* LIV, 1958, pp. 450-460. Armenian summary of same by N. Fogolyán, *Pazmaveb*, 1961, No. 6-8. pp. 151-154. - *Magyar Nyelv* LV, 1959, pp. 125-126.

[21] *REArm*, XI, 323. ff.

[22] M. Bežiškian, *Canaparhordut'iwn i Lehastan*, Venice, 1830.

[23] <u>Gh</u>. *Inǰiǰian, Ašxarhagrut'iwn čoric' masanc' ašxarhi*, I-XI, Venice, 1802-1805.

121

XV

Bežiškian in his book comprising accounts on his findings in the different Armenian communities, tried to give a summary of the past connected with their motherland, *expressis verbis* with the town Ani, and gave a survey of the contemporary state of each community. Concerning the beginning and the establishment of the first Armenian settlements he presented different solutions contradicting to each other.

A comprehensive summary we find in the first paragraph (§. 130.) of the chapter on « The dispersion of the inhabitants of Ani » (*Crumn Anecʿwocʿ*) where he described the subsequent waves of emigrant groups as following: « And in the year of the Lord 1060, when Ani passed into the hands of aliens, a large number of the inhabitants of Ani... in concert with their fellow-countrymen living in the surrounding area took leave from Armenia, and started on a route toward Poland and Moldavia. And in the year of the Lord 1064 — when the Persians (i.e. the Seljuqs) seized and looted Ani, the majority of the inhabitants set forth and followed upon the tracks of their forefathers winding their way towards Moldavia, and from these to Poland. But at the time of the sixth seizure (of Ani), in the year of the Lord 1239 the leaders of the remainder of the population left for Tataristan and settled down in the district of Ažderkhan (Astrakhan) in Aq-Sarai, and others dispersed to different places, to Sis, Džulfa and Van. » [24]

In another chapter we find an erroneous date for the seizure of Ani, which does not correspond to the historical truth. The invasion of Alp Arslan into Armenia was qualified by him the motif triggering the exodus of the Armenians, but the seizure of Ani dated to 1062 instead of 1064. Here he repeated the assertion that the Armenian settlers of Poland took their origin from the emigrants of the Seljuqid era [25].

In the continuation of the chapter « The dispersion... » we find the clew for this distortion of the date, the much discussed document of the Lwow Episcopalian Archive with the wording: « Theodor great prince, son of Demetr to the Armenians of Našoxačʿ(ean). Who wish to come here, they should come to help me, and I am going to grant them freedom for three years. And when you should be with me, you might freely go wherever it pleases you. In the year 1062 » [26].

So, this was the date, which induced Bežiškian to make the former correction from 1064 to 1062. Bežiškian said that the text of the document was a translation from Ruthenian into Armenian, but, in fact, the Ruthenian original did not bear any date. Furthermore, the Ruthenian original, published by F.X. Zacharyasiewicz differed from the Latin translation, or better to say, was a somewhat amplified version of it [27].

---

[24] Bežiškian, p. 83., §. 130.
[25] Bežiškian, p. 54., §. 81.
[26] Bežiškian, p. 85., §. 134.
[27] Ya. Dachkévitch, « Les arméniens à Kiev », *REArm.* X, p. 342. ff.

122

XV

It is rather doubtful, if Bežiškian had seen the Ruthenian version at all, because his Armenian version squares verbally with the Latin version, even the date 1062 has been appended. Furthermore, the term « dux » in the Armenian text required a Latin original for basic text, and not a Ruthenian, where the title of the Prince « kniaz » would rather have been translated as « išxan » in the Armenian text.

Bežiškian used the document also in reference to the Armenian inhabitants of Kamenets Podolsk: « In the year 1062 Dux Theodor invited the people of Ani (Anec'ik') to come and settle down in Podolia, in the capital Kamenic »[28]. Though this sentence is not put in quotation marks, but the wording reflects the text of the above cited document, only the explicit mentioning of the town Kamenic is absent from the original.

A further circumstance which makes it rather questionable that Bežiškian would have seen the original, is, that the historian P. Köppen, visiting Lwow in 1822 could not see the document either[29].

A somewhat different version was presented by A.M. Pidou, the theatin monk, an emissary of the Congregatio de Propaganda Fide in his « Breve relatione » in 1669[30], and a similar text in the « Compendiosa relatio » by an anonymous author in 1676. The only essential difference between the two was the place of origin of the Armenians to whom the invitation was addressed: « Armenians of Tataristan » in the former, and « Armenians of Xerson » (i.e. the Crimea) in the latter[31].

Pidou's « Relation » in Latin did not exert an influence on historical thoughet, because it has never been published in its original language, but in Polish translation in 1876 and later in Armenian in 1884.

The « original » document has been used by the Armenian Episcopate of Lwow to prove the ancestral rights of the community, and confirmed in 1641 by the Polish king, Wladyslaw IV, the previous Hungarian prince of Transylvania. The disputes of church authorities about the rights of the Armenian church in Poland though composed in Latin, remained in ecclesiastic circles, preserved in archives. The historical explanations and archeographic disputes about the authenticity of the document in the 18-19th centuries were published in Polish and Russian, and so disregarded by western historiography[33].

---

[28] Bežiškian, p. 135, §. 214.
[29] REArm, X., 345.
[30] Břni miut'iwn Hayoc' Lehastani, SPb, 1884, p. 11.
[31] Břni miut'iwn, p. 152.
[32] F. Bischoff, Das alte Recht der Armenier in Lemberg, Wien, 1862. F. Bischoff, « Das alte Recht der Armenier in Poland » Oesterreichische Blätter für Literatur und Kunst (Beilage zur Oesterreichisch-Kaiserlichen Wiener Zeitung), 1857, No. 28. 217-219; No. 33, pp. 257-260.
[33] Ya. Daškevič, « Gramota Fedora Dmitroviča 1062 roku » Naukovoinformacijnij Bjuleten' Arxivnogo Upravlinnja URSR, Kiev, 1962, No. 4, pp. 9-20; Ya. Dachkévitch, « Les arméniens » REArm, X, pp. 341-349; Ya. Daškevič, Armjanskie kolonii na Ukraine v istočnikax i literature XV-XIX vekov, Erevan, 1962.

123

XV

The historical problems of the Armenian communities in Galicia and the documentation were introduced into western historiography, at first, by Ferdinand Bischoff, professor of history of Law for ten years (1855-1865) at the university of Lwow, and then for thirty years in Graz (1865-96)[34].

At any rate, the Armenian line of researchers had a wider influence on historical and public thought. Of Roszka's « Annals of the Armenian Church » only a part had been published in the last century (1896) and the entire text only recently (1964)[35]. H. Zohrabian's researches never came out separately, only incorporated into Akontz's geographic encyclopedia[36].

But both of this sources have been used by M. Bežiškian. From the §§. 130 and 134. it is obvious that he had Roszka's « Annals » in his hand. In his interpretation he simply amalgamated Roszka's information with the current version: In 1060 Demetrios had been prince of Galicia, and in 1062 his son Theodor invited the Armenians to serve for auxiliary troops for him[37]. He omitted, however, to mention, that the rebellious subjects against whom he needed the help, were the Poles. This, of course, did not fit into the context of a privilege of an Armenian community on a soil, the Lwow district, which later has been annexed by Poland.

So the date indicated by Roszka was the third one introduced by Bežiškian into his narrative. In his effort to bring these differring variants into harmony, he mixed up the component parts of the different informations. Beside the three versions of the date there were even more variants for the place of origin of the Armenian immigrants: Tataristan (Pidou), Xerson (Comp. relatio), the people of Aniand, the two versions in the document: *Nošoxač(ean)* or *Kosoxackie*. The atribute indicating the place of origin « kosoxackie » had been interpreted with an emendation tentatively already by A. Petruševič (1853) and recently in his thorough critical study accepted by Y. Daškiewič as « ko-so(l) xackim » ʿSolxacensibus Armenisʾ i.e. « the Armenians of Solxat »[38]. Even if the document was not authentic, but the memory upheld by it might go back to tradition: a considerable mass of the Armenian community of Lwow and the neighbouring district, Kamenets Podolsk might have come from the region of Solxat in the Crimea[29].

---

[34] F. Bischoff, *Urkunden zur Geschichte der Armenier in Lemberg*, Wien, 1864; see also footnote No. 32.

[35] Gh. Ališan, *Kamenicʿ, taregirkʿ hayocʿ Lehastani ew Ṙumenioy* », Venice, 1896, pp. 131-146; St. Roškay, *Žamanakagruťiwn kam tarekankʿ ekełecʿakankʿ*, Vienna, 1964. (p. 112).

[36] See footnote No. 23.

[37] Bežiškian, pp. 83-84.

[38] *REArm*, X, pp. 342, 343, 354. - The conjecture of A. Petruševič accepted also by I. Lynnyčenko, *Čerty iz istorii soslovij v Jugozapadnoj (Galickoj) Rusi XIV-XV vv.*, Moscow, 1894, p. 113.

[39] See below.

XV

The most essential point in the enumeration of the historical interpretations of the northern emigration of the Armenians for the 11th century was, that it must have been just this alleged document of Lwow, which induced earlier historians, and first of all, Minas Bežiškian and the Armenian authors in his wake [40] to proclaim the earliest Armenian settlers of Lwow and Kamenets Podolsk emigrants of the inset of the Seljuqid era, leaving their homeland after the conquest of Ani: 1064.

Bežiškian and his followers have totally left out of sight the historical fact, the accumulation of a dense Armenian population of Cappadocia, and later of Cilicia after the conquest of the Bagratid Kingdom, the principality of Kars by the Seljuqs [41].

That Bežiškian was aware of his neglect, is shown by the sentence he appended about the dispersion of the Armenians after the Tatar conquest 1236 (1239): « the leaders of the remainder of the population went... to Aq-Sarai, and others dispersed to different places, to Sis, Džulfa, and Van. » [42] The last clause was verbally taken over from the Nesvita Chronicle [43], only the sequence of the settlements was changed into chronological order, Sis was put first.

Previous research has already proved that the document on which the hypothesis of the northern and north-western direction of mass emigration was mainly based was not authentic [44], and above, I have tried to demonstrate the major literary propagator of this version, Minas Bežiškian, whose popular work contributed much to the dissemination of the idea of the northern route of Armenian mass emigration after the seizure of Ani.

But Bežiškian's work, at the same time, contained the most essential narrative source, the colophon in a Crimean *Haysmavurk^c* (Menologie), the s.c. Nesvita Chronicle, the relation of the « History of Caffa » [45]. The Chronicle was compiled by scribe David in 1690 in Caffa, but the story was not the invention of the scribe, it was (partly) taken over from an earlier source about the northern route of flight after the Tatar invasion, to Aq-Sarai and later to Caffa.

Essentials of the relation were present in the « History of Ani » written by Abraham Katholikos (1734-37) [46], which story was represented also in the cherished literary manual of Ghazar Džahkeci (1737-1751) « The coveted Paradise » [47]. But the two venerable authors linked up the mass

[40] Ter-Abrahamian (see No. p. 116); K. Kušnerian, *Patmut'iwn gałt'akanut'iwn Xrimu hayoc*, Venice, 1895, and others.
[41] Matthiew of Edesse (see footnote No. 6.)
[42] Bežiškian, p. 83, §. 130.
[43] Bežiškian, p. 337.
[44] See above No. 33.
[45] Matenadaran MS, No. 7442. - Bežiškian, pp. 335-342.
[46] In the Appendix of his « Patmutiwn », Vagharšapat, 1870, pp. 101-109; Translation: « Histoire d'Ani » *Collection d'historiens arméniens*, traduits par M. Brosset, SPb, 1876, pp. 330-335.
[47] *Girk' astuacabanakan or koči Draxt c'ankali*, Constantinople 1735, 629-634.

125

XV

flight of the inhabitants of Ani with an earthquake (A.D. 1319), destroying the sinful city, because of the debauched life of the people.

Neither was the story an invention of the erudite clerics, we possess an even earlier versified version of the narrative by Martiros Xrimeci, according to whom the mass emigration of the Armenians was a consequence of the Tatar conquest [48].

A variety of this later context was represented by the Nesvita Chronicle, and the preceding paragraph literally copied from the chapter of Kirakos Gandzakeci on « The seizure of Ani » [49].

This mass emigration following the Tatar conquest is generally also connected with a fixed date; 1236 (1239). We should like to emphasize that this emigrations was not a single event at a single date, but a gradual sequence of waves of emigrants, a continuous dwindling of the population, starting with the shock of the sudden attack, and continuing for a whole century as a consecutive decadence of the productive forces.

For all the history of the Tatar invasion to Transcaucasia we have ample narrative sources, heart-rendering description of the wholesale slaughter, the devastation of the country. Most of the people sought refuge in fortified places, but « neither did the earth hide the squatters, nor the rocks and caves cover up the people who sought for a shelter, neither the massive walls of forts, nor the deep valley coombs. » [50]

In the Chronicle of Kirakos — an eye-witness of the events — we have a vivid description of this process, how the people of the villages, the peasants from the fields fled to the surrounding mountains. When Vanakan Vardapet, the great teacher, after the destruction of his monastery led his pupils to a cave south of the fort Tavuš, a group of village people joined them. But soon the Tatar troops arrived and many of them, the chronicler himself, were taken captive [51].

But there is no relation or even a direct hint in any of the contemporary Armenian chronicles of their mass flight to foreign countries [52].

According to the Nesvita Chronicle the Armenians fled at first (in 1299 - sic!) to Aq-Sarai, the residence of the Tatar Khan of the Ulus Juči.

---

[48] A.A. Martirosian, *Martiros Ghrimec'i*, Yerevan, 1956, pp. 142-152.
[49] Kirakos, pp. 258-59; Kir/Bros, 127-28; Kir/Dul, 237-38; Kir/Xan, 165-66.
[50] Kirakos, pp. 238-39; Kir/Bros, 118; Kir/Dul, 217; Kir/Xan, 155-56.
[51] Kirakos, p. 243; Kir/Bros, 120; Kir/Dul, 223; Kir/Xan, 158.
[52] Vanakan vardapet and Kirakos were direct eyewitnesses of the events, Vardan Arevelci gave only a succint summary of the inset of the occupation period, taken from the chronicles of Vanakan vdp. and Kirakos. See H. Oskian, *Hovhannes vanakan ew iwr dproc'ə*, Vienna, 1922. Grigor Akanci's attention was focused mainly on the history of the Cilician Armenian Kingdom at the later Ilkhanid era. R.P. Blake and R.N. Frye, « History of the nation of the archers (the Mongols) by Grigor of Akanc' », *Harvard Journal of Asiatic Studies,* vol. 12, (1949), 269-283. V.A. Hakobyan, *Manr žamanakagruť yunner XIII-XVIII dd.,* Yerevan, I-II, 1951-1956, vol. I, 17-101; II, 1-172. Russian translation of latter: A.G. Galstian, *Armjanskie istočniki o mongolax,* Moscow, 1962.

126

Although this date does not square with the date of the Tatar invasion to the Transcaucasus, but the memory of events by the lapse of time, during centuries gets entangled. I should venture to suggest a supposition for the intrusion of this date into this contaminated information. The year 1299 was marked by a momentous event, the death of Noghai, major-domo of the Golden Horde, by his office, a supreme authority, a co-ruler, a king-maker in fact. This date must have got deeply inprinted in the memory of the people of Caffa, because some months prior to his defeat and death, he led a campaign against Caffa in order to take revenge for the murder of his grandson, who on his tax-collecting campaign had been killed in Caffa [53].

There is no reason for us to doubt the verisimilitude of the information of the Nesvita Chronicle, that the first gaol of the fleeing Armenians might have been Aq-Sarai, the residence of Batu Khan. Though the Transcaucasus was administered by special military leaders: Čormaghan, Baiju, but the overlord was the head of Juči Ulus, at this time Batu Khan. So the subject nationalities — having suffered abuse from local authorities — took refuge with him. Surely many people turned to him after the invasion, but this layer must have consisted of the noble classes: « Kings, princes, feudal lords, traders applied to him (Batu), all who have suffered injustice and been deprived of their family estate. And he dispensed justice... » [54]

The supremacy of the Golden Horde over the Transcaucasus was maintained even after the death of Batu (1256), however, after the establishment of the Ilkhanid rule in Persia (1258) their right was challenged by the Ilkhanids and Transcaucasia became a battle-field between the two branch-lines.

The mass emigration of the Armenian population was not a single act triggered by the atrocities of the Tatar troops, but a continuous streaming of fugitives elicited by the sharp decline of the economic situation.

Of course the first fatal blow to Armenian economy was dealt at the inset, the Tatar troops had not the slightest sense of protection of the agriculture.

In 1236 they arrived « just at harvest season, when the crop has not yet been reaped, and garnered into the barn, they let their camels and horses granze up all the grain and trample down the rest. » [55] They rooted out the vineyards [56], used the fruit trees, the vines for fuel [57]. When the Tatars

[53] V.G. Tizengauzen, *Sbornik materialov otnosjaščixsja k istorii Zolotoj ordy*, vol. I. SPb, 1884, 111-112. B. Spuler, *Die Goldene Horde, Die Mongolen in Russland, 1223-1502*, Leipzig, 1943, pp. 75-76

[54] Kirakos, p. 358; Kir/Dul, 453-59; Kir/Bros, 172; Kir/Xan, 218.

[55] Kirakos, p. 261, 238; Kir/Bros, 129, 118; Kir/Dul, 240, 216; Kir/Xan 167, 155.

[56] Kirakos, p. 236; Kir/Bros, 117; Kir/Dul, 214; Kir/Xan, 154.

[57] In Transcaucasia it was a great sin to cut out fruittrees even at war. Mxitar Goš, *Girk' Datastani*, ed. by X. Thorossian, Yerevan, 1975, p. 302. Russian transl.: *Armjanskij Sudebnik Mxitara Goša*, ed. B.M. Arutjunjan, Yerevan, 1954, p. 144. Cf. Manandian, *K'nnakan tesut'yun*, vol. III, 196.

XV

withdrew to their winter quarters to the Mughân steppe area, the surviving peasants had nothing to eat, had no grain for sowing, no cattle to till the land [58].

The Tatars destroyed the means and instruments of production, so the situation could hardly have ameliorated. The « peace-era » brought about the customary nomad administration system.

One of the head administrators, the vilest, called Bugha sent tax-collectors out; the Mathometans, Persians were the wickedest in exaction and extortion [59].

The state of affairs did not change under the subsequent rulers. During the reign of the great khan Manghu a general recensement was ordered in the subjected areas. Registers of the taxable population were drawn up, including even the boys from 10 years on. The peasants were deprived of the remainder of their resources. The ones, who tried to escape and hided, were mercilessly whipped or even killed; of the miserables, who had nothing to give, the sons were seized and taken away [60].

The state of economy was equally deplorable through all the Ilkhanid rule, the tax-press became no less tight with the distance of the government center, but it grew even worse, as local tax-collectors extorted higher taxes for their own benefit without impunity.

The constant exactions were instrumental even for the labouring masses to leave their country. Arable land was left behind, no labour hand available. The state of affairs is reflected in the votive inscription A.D. 1283 of a rich merchant, who « bought Hovk^c village for four thousand gold ducats during hard times, when land was cheap, and gold dear, (and gave it as a gift to the church of... Getik ») [61]. This inscription of Gošavank is an eloquent example of the serious consequences of nomad devastation and exploitation.

The situation was the same in all the Ilkhanid Empire, as clearly announced by the *yarlik* of Ghazan Khan (1295-1304): « Because of the abuses and pillages most part of the population in the countryside left their motherland and settled down in foreign countries, the towns and villages were left void ». Ghazan Khan and his councillor, Rashîd ad-Dîn were aware of the disastrous consequences of merciless exploitation and tried to withhold local authorities from excessive extortions [62].

---

[58] Still by the Lord's mercy and their own labor they could carry on. See note No. 55.

[59] Kirakos, pp. 312-13; Kir/Bros, 155; Kir/Dul, 447-48; Kir/Xan, 193-94.

[60] Kirakos, p. 363; Kir/Bros, 175; Kir/Dul, 461; Kir/Xan, 221. - Grigor Akanci, *HJAS* vol. 12, 1949, pp. 324-25.

[61] K. Kostanianc, *Vimakan taregira*, SPb, 1913, pp. 124-25; H.A. Manandian, *The Trade and Cities of Armenia in Relation to Ancient World Trade*, transl. by N.G. Garsoian, Lisbon, 1965, p. 186.

[62] Rašid-ad-Din, *Sbornik letopisej*, transl. by A.K. Arends, vol. III, p. 251; *CHI*, V. 493, ff.

128

XV

The culmination point of this process of depopulation of Armenia becomes obvious in a *yarlïk* of Abû Saʿîd, the last Ilkhanid. The *yarlïk* datable to the decade 1319-1335 was preserved in a Persian inscription on the wall of the Manuche mosque in the town Ani: « Beside *tamgha* and the justified tributes no other tax should be raised from anybody under the cover of *kalân, nemeri, tarx* and other kind of taxes as formerly it was in use in the town Ani and other parts of Georgia... unlawful levies had been collected... and violance applied. The places became desolate, the common people dispersed, the mayors of the towns and districts left their movables and immovable estates and gone away... » [63] These historical sources all testify to the effect, that the mass emigration of the people, the depopulation of Armenia has been a gradual process, consequence of the plundering, of the merciless extortions, in brief, of the nomad view of life of the occupants.

And now let us return to the other end of the route, the goal of these emigrants. The Nesvita Chronicle relates: « the Armenians in Aq-Sarai having been constantly harrassed by the Tatars sent an envoy to the Genovese authorities to Caffa »... concluded an agreement with them and settled down there in 1330 [64].

The date for the establishment of the Armenian settlement in Caffa (1330) coincides with the date of the inscription of the Manuche mosque. Even if we do not take this coincidence of the figures literally, this detail of information in the Nesvita Chronicle may have preserved the memory of the arrival of a considerable group of immigrants. Even if it did not indicate the beginning of the Armenian settlement, but rather a certain state of repletion of the community.

Another source of population supply is often neglected, the layer of emigrants of Cilician Armenia. The small kingdom was a « pet vassal » of the Ilkhanids, but had to share the peripeties of the decline and decay of the Empire. The process started after the defeat of ʿAin Jalut (1260). Cilician Armenia, the vassal duty of which was to furnish auxiliary troops for the Mongol warfares, became a victim of incessant inroads of the Mamluks for the following century (A.D. 1266, 1270, 1275, 1277, 1279, 1298, 1321, 1335, etc.) [65]. The defenceless Kingdom succumbed to the joint attacks of the Mamluks and the Sultan of Iconium in 1360. The whole shoreline was seized by them and in 1375 the capital Sis fell. The Cilician Armenian Kingdom ceased to exist and a considerable part of the

[63] V.V. Barthold, « Persidskaja nadpis' na stene anijskoj mečeti Manuče » *Sočinenija*, vol. IV, pp. 318; Cf. Manandian, *Trade and Cities*, p. 178.
[64] Bežiškian, p. 338, §. 504.
[65] S. Der-Nersessian, « The Kingdom of Cilician Armenia », *A History of the Crusades*. Ed. K.M. Setton, II. Univ. of Pennsylvania Press, 1962, pp. 654-55; G.G. Mikaelian, *Istorija Kilikijskogo armjanskogo gosudarstva*, Yerevan, 1952, pp. 336, 345, 408-9, 411, 426, 447, 457, aso.

XV

population sought refuge in the countries north and northwest, where Armenian settlements had already been established.

The Crimea became a reservoir for a sequence of groups of Armenian immigrants deserting their homeland because of the nomad Tatar rule to avoid extermination and the continuous economic deterioration depriving them of the prime necessities of life.

The continuous development and growth of the Armenian community is testified by a series of contemporary local documents.

Already from the end of the 13th century notary acts have been preserved bearing evidence to the active participation of Armenians in their trading operations [63]. By the beginning of the 14th century Armenians in Caffa had their special quarters *extra muros,* adjacent to the inner city walls, several Armenian churches were erected. Special orders issued, prior to 1316, by the Genovese authorities to secure the protection of the water supply system installed by the Armenian bishop, attest the creative participation of the Armenian community in the common matters of the town [67].

The areas to which the Armenians immigrated at the turn of the 13th-14th centuries are enumerated in the Nesvita Chronicle: « ...they settled down in Theodosia (i.e. Caffa), Ghazarat and Surxat » (Solxat, later: Eski Krim) [68].

Caffa became one of the foremost trading transit centers toward the northern ports of Asia Minor, Trapezunt and Sinope, and first of all of Constantinople. The Crimea was the leading caterer of Constantinople with victuals (wheat, salt, salted fish, etc.), mediator of slaves, of Russian fur, skins [69]. The Armenians took part in their trading activities towards the Near and Middle East, the Genovese could make good use of their trading experience.

In the above enumeration the only enigmatic topographic site is Ghazarat. According to tradition related by the Chronicle the site, lying on the river called by the Tatars « *Mughal özen* » (i.e. ʿMongolian riverʾ) had been the headquarters of « the garrison stationed there by the order of Širin, prince of the Genovese » [70].

As I explained elsewhere some items involved in this information were erroneous: Širin was no Genovese prince, but one of the leading clans in the Crimean Tatar hierarchy, overlords of the Eastern provinces [71]. Ghazarat

---

[66] See footnote No. 10.
[67] « Impositio Officii Gazariae », *Monumenta Historiae Patriae* vol. II, 1838, 408, 380. Cf. W. Heyd, *Histoire du commerce du Levant au moyen-âge,* II, Leipzig, 1886, p. 172.
[68] Bežiškian, p. 338.
[69] W. Heyd, *Histoire du commerce,* I, 498, II, 166, 177, 191.
[70] Bežiškian, p. 328.
[71] E. Schütz, « Armeno-kiptschakisch und die Krim » *Hungaro-Turcica, Studies in honour of J. Németh,* (Abbr.: J. Németh Mem. Vol.) Budapest, 1976, 198-99.

130

was not a separate town [72], the term « Gazaria » used all through the middle ages was applied to the administrative center of the Crimea (but very often also — as *pars pro toto* — to the whole peninsula) administered by the governor of the tribal confederations of the successive nomad hordes from the Khazars up to the Comans and (Crimean) Tatars. The term « Gazaria, Ghazarat » preserved, perpetuated the memory of the earliest Turkic overlords, the Khazars.

Solxat [73] (Surxat, Eski Krim) was the residence of the governor installed by the Golden Horde, lying on the frontier of contact between the two territories: the Genovese administered the coastline south of the Taurid mountain range, whereto the nomads never penetrated; the northern steppe region remained the pasture field of the nomads.

At the time of their immigration a good number of Armenians settled down in Solxat, a frontier barter center, and the settlement flourished for more than a century. Armenians by the middle of the 14th century had a special quarter for themselves, 9 churches and a superb monastery in the vicinity, the Surb Xač ('Holy Cross'), a cultural and educational center of the Crimean Armenians [74].

With the establishment of the Girei (Kerei) dynasty asserting in 1449 its independence towards the suzerainty of the Golden Horde·overlords, the old residence was given up, and the capital moved to the center of the peninsula: Kirkor and Baxči Sarai.

By all means, the former lustre of Solxat was reflected even in her ruins, the sight of which elicited admiration from the Polish envoy, Martin Broniewski, in 1578 [75]. The relics of the town described in 1820 by Minas Bežiškian were impressive even after 400 years of dereliction [76].

With the shift of the residential center the Armenian settlement must have dwindled. But the major incentive to the shift might have been the sharpening hostilities between the Tatars and the Genovese, by the middle of the 15th century, which must have induced the (presumably Kipchak speaking) Armenians partly to move over to Caffa, partly to leave for Poland.

All the time from their arrival to the peninsula up to the Turkish conquest in 1475 we are informed with approximative figures about the

[72] Already P. Köppen could not trace it down anywhere, see *Krimskij Sbornik*, SPb, 1837, 344. S. Siestrzencewicz de Bohusz (*Histoire du royaume de la Chersonèse Taurique* SPb, 1824, p. 320.) took it identical with Solxat, based on the information of the Archbishop I. Argutinskij. Cf. *J. Németh Mem. Vol.*, p. 199. See also Brun, *Cernomor'e*, II, 138.

[73] P. Köppen, *Krimskij Sbornik*, p. 3-4-45.

[74] A.L. Jakobson, « Armjanskaja srednevekovaja arxitektura v Krymu » *Vizantijskij Vremennik*, VIII, 1956, pp. 173-181.

[75] « Martini Broniovii de Biezdzfedea, Stephani I. Poloniae Regis nomine bis in Tartariam Legati Descriptio Tartariae. Ad primam Editionem Coloniensem Anni MDXCV. denuo recognita & emendata », *Scriptores rerum Hungaricarum veteres, ac genuini* (ed. J.G. Schwandtner), III, 268.

[76] Bežiškian, pp. 321-22.

131

XV

number of the Armenians by the Genovese documents. The concern of the Genovese administration was focused only on the inhabitants under their scepter, i.e. Caffa; for Solxat they do not contain any figures.

As to the inhabitants of Caffa, from the Genovese Statutes of 1439 we learn that the number of Armenians must have been approximately 30.000, but at the time of the Turkish conquest the estimate, again based on Genovese sources, signals their number to cca 46.000 - 2/3-s of the total population amounting to 70.000, at the same time the Genovese administrative layer being altogether 1 1/2% [77]. May this sharp increase of about 50%-s of the Armenian population of Caffa — in course of one generation — be due to the hostilities getting more and more acute between the Girei dynasty and Caffa and to a shift of Armenians from Solxat to Caffa?

But the Ottoman Turkish conquest (1475) brought about a decisive decline first of all of the Armenian and Greek population. Only a fraction of them remained in Caffa, the town got into a deplorable state, as it has been characterised by Broniewski a century after the conquest, in 1578: « Civitas pristinum splendorem maxima parte amisit; templa Christianorum Romana demolita, aedes dirutae, muri et turres... collapsa jacent... templa tantum catholica duo, et Armenica itidem integra supersunt... Turcis, Armenis, Judaeis, Italis et Graecis Christianis paucissimis habitatoribus... » [78]

The sharp decrease of the population was explained in different ways by historians, already by contemporary informants. The fist impression was the wholesale massacre. The Nesvita Chronicle amplified these atrocities with an afore planned murder of the leaders of the Armenian community, who refused to become renegades and adopt the Mahometan creed [79].

According another version introduced into literary circulation 40.000 of the inhabitants of the peninsula were taken captive and shipped to Constantinople. This version served for a basis of a theory for Hr. Ačarian, saying that these 40.000 people — a majority of whom must have been Armenians — constituted the core of the Armenian community of Constantinople. But neither the documentary sources corroborate this assertion, nor the figures of the contemporary census [80].

The majority of historians and linguists generally ascribe the shrinkage of the Armenian population of the Crimea to their mass emigration to Poland, where they joined their compatriotes, earlier settlers. The prepon-

---

[77] *Atti della Società Ligure di Storia Patria,* Genova, V. 415; VII/2, pp. 343, 480, 482.

[78] *Scriptores Rerum Hungaricarum,* III.: Broniewski « Tartariae Descriptio », p. 271.

[79] Bežiškian, pp. 339-340.

[80] H. Ačarian, *K'nnut'yun Polsahay barbari,* Yerevan, 1941, pp. 8; The figure of captives taken from: J.v. Hammer, *Geschichte des Osmanischen Reiches,* Pesth, 1834. p. 524. - H. Berberian, *Niwt'er K. Polsoy hayoc' patmut'ean hamar,* Vienna, 1965. pp. 50-52; R. Mantran, *Istanbul dans la seconde moitié du XVII' siècle,* Paris, 1962, 44-53.

XV

derance of this new wave of immigrants to the two provinces on the Polish borderline (wojewodstwo Russkoe and w. Podolskoe) is confirmed by their special Coman-Kipchak idiom. Although we do not possess any written document from the Crimea in this language in Armenian letters, but all linguistic peculiarities point towards the Crimea as source of origin [81]. The exchange of the Armenian vernacular for the Kipchak-Coman idiom was so complete that Armenians in the new settlements, in the Lwow and Kamenets Podolsk area used this idiom for all kind of purposes: common language, official use, literary composition, and even ecclesiastical needs [82]. Such a thorough change could have taken its origin in the Crimea, in a dense Kipchak-Coman environment. The forerunner of this idiom had not been the language of the Crimean Tatars of the 16th century, but a dialect surviving from the earlier Comanic type of Turkic languages. The area of such surroundings seems to have been the contact zone between the steppe-land and the Genovese colony, the residence of the Tatar governor, Solxat [83]. The localisation of the origin of Armeno-Kipchak seems to be confirmed by Troki karaim tradition, which holds Solxat for the birth area of the Karaim, the sister idiom of Armeno-Kipchak.

The void space remaining after the mass departure of the Armenian population of Caffa has never again been replaced, though from the inset of the 17th century in Caffa a certain revival can be noticed [84].

A new phase of the Armenian settlement began by the turn of the 16th-17th centuries [85]. A wave of Armenian fugitives arrived from East-Anatolia, from the area infested by incessant internal warfare, to avoid the onslaughts of the troops of the Jelâlî movement. The fugitive intellectuals, many of whom bore the name of their native twon Tokat for their personal name: Tokateci — enumerate the areas of refuge of the masses fleeing after the destruction of Tokat by the Jelâlîs in 1600:

---

[81] E. Schütz, « On the Transcription of Armeno-Kipchak », *Acta Orientalia Hungarica,* 1961, p. 140.
[82] PhTF, I, p. 82; PhTF, II, pp. 801-805.
[83] P. Köppen, *Krimskij Sbornik,* pp. 338-346; A.L. Jakobson, *Srednevekovyj Krym,* Moscow-Leningrad, 1964, 105-108; J. Németh Mem. Vol. pp. 200-203.
[84] The diminution of the Armenian population after 1475 is documented also by the abatement of literary activity. The mecenates to give commission for copying dwindled, the Mss copied in this period show a sharp decline: from the 23 copies in the 15th century to 10 in the 16th. The 17th century brought about a steep upswing to 103 Mss. (preserved in the Matenadaran, see *C̆uc̆ak dzeragrac̆ Mastoc̆i anvan Matenadarani,* vol. I, 1965, cols. 160-161.) - The three periods are clearly discernible also in the achievement of the miniaturists: in the 14-15th centuries Nader and his sons represented a high level of art (pp. 27. ff.), the 16th cent. meant a low tide (p. 72.), and the 17th cent. a revival (72. ff.) E.M. Korxmazian, *Armjanskaja miniatura Kryma (XIV-XVII vv.),* Yerevan, 1978.
[85] Documented also by the Chronicle of Xac̆atur of Caffa, see E. Schütz, « Eine armenische Chronik von Kaffa aus der ersten Hälfte des 17. Jahrhunderts », *Acta. Orient. Hung.,* XXIX, 1975, 133-186 Cf. G. Abgarian's article in the *Lraber* (1977, No. 6.) of the Acad. Sciences of the Armenian SSR.

133

XV

« They were dispersed just like dust,
All of them departed to different places;
Some went to Istanbul,
Some to Bursa, Adrana
Many of them to Urumeli (= Rumelia)
To the land of Franks, to Boghdan (= Moldavia), to Leh
(= Poland). » [86]

Comparatively a lesser mass chose the Crimea as their place of refuge. Generally emigrants headed for lands, provinces where there existed an Armenian settlement before, and so they could expect help and support from their compatriots to begin a new life.   The affluence of the new settlers in Caffa during the subsequent centuries was far inferior compared to the past. The main reason was the complete change in international trade. The flourishing trade between the East and the Crimea ceased, the East-West international transit route, which led via the Lwow region further to Western Europe lost its importance.   The eyes of Western trade became focused on the perspective of the New World. Moreover, the power in the trading centers of the East, have been concentrated in the hands of other potentates, who had their own routes to lead their commercial activities. The trade of spices, jewels, and delicacies of the Indies got into the hands of the English and Dutch India companies, and the Persian Safavide Empire also preferred the southern routes, via the Syrian and Turkish ports.

So the Crimea nominally under Tatar domination, but in reality under Ottoman-Turkish rule, remained though the granary of Istanbul, but lost its role of important link in the chain of international trade, and carried on a modest life of a Levantine province. Sir John Chardin, on his journey to Persia in 1673 noted down rather modest figures according to the Christian population of Caffa: altogether 800 Greek and Armenian families [87]. The Armenians of this era were engaged partly in local trade, but most of them as craftsmen, and kitchen-gardeners growing orchards and cultivating vineyards. Their number did not change considerably during the subsequent century.

When the Russian army defeated the Turks, in virtue of the treaty of Kučuk-Kainarji in 1774, the Crimea got under Russian domination. The Tzarist regime wanted to consolidate its rule over the southern region — the northern coastline of the Black Sea — once a pasture land of the Noghai Tatars, and for this purpose intended to repopulate this area by sedentary Christian elements. The Christians were moved out from the Crimea, the Greeks to Ekaterinoslav, the Armenians to a newly created and

[86] Gh. Ališan, *Hayapatum*, vol. III, Venice, 1901, p. 315; N. Akinian, *Hing panduxt tałasac̄ner*, Vienna, 1921, p. 120.
[87] *Voyages du Chevalier Chardin en Perse, et autres lieux de l'Orient*. Ed. L. Langlès, Paris, vol. I, 1811, pp. 125-26.

XV

designed town Nor-Nakhichevan, next to the site of the present day Rostov on the Don and 8 neighbouring villages. For the time of their expatriation we have exact figures of the population from the table drawn up by general A.V. Suvorov for the government: the number of Armenians was 12.600 from which 5.500 of Caffa, 2.800 of Qarasubazar (later immigrants from Caffa), etc. [88].

In the 19th century there again appear Armenians in the beautiful peninsula, cca 5-6.000 altogether, new settlers and repatriates from the Nor-Nakhichevan region.

* * *

Because of the treatment of the origins and stages necessarily at an unequal length a summing up of our findings might seem desirable.

The hardest problem argued about for a century has been the time of the arrival of the earliest settlers in the Crimea and to the Northwest. The strained formula which in this respect treated the 11th-13th centuries as a compact entity and indiscriminately connected the Seljuq and Tatar invasions, left out of account the historical fact, that in the Seljuqid era Cappadocia, Cilicia and North-Syria were replenished by a dense Armenian population, and none of the sources make any mention to the northern route.

The theory of a mass flight of Armenians towards the North in the Seljuqid era has essentially been based on the single document of the Lwow Archive (dated 1062) the authenticity of which had long ago been refuted. Armenian tradition because of the proximity of the dates of the alleged document (1062) and the seizure of Ani (1064) connected the two, and established the theory of the early northern route. The dissemniation of it was mainly due to Bežiškian's « Travel Accounts », the popularity of which was greatly enhanced by the exposition of the direct Ani lineage of the settlements, reflected also by the apocryph subtitle under which it has been advertised ever since: « The History of Ani or Journey to Poland. » [89]

Once the starting point clarified the stages of the settlements have got into a clear light: the mass flight after the Tatar invasion (1236), the flight to espace the Jelâlîs (1600), the displacement to Novo-Rossia (1778). Of course, neither flight has been a single-time event, but a process entailed by the atrocities and the deterioration of the economic situation.

A sharp dividing line between the stages was drawn by the Turkish conquest (1475), when the majority of the Armenian population left the Crimea for Podolia and Moldavia. Even if there was no total cessation in the continuity of the settlements with the emigration after 1475, but the newcomers of the Jelâlî era found only a rather thin layer of the early Armenian community centers in the Crimea.

---

[88] V.B. Barxudarian, *Nor Naxičevani haykakan gałut'i patmut'yun* (1779-1861 tt.), Yerevan, 1967, 39; Mikaelian, (No. 1), p. 369.

[89] *Catalogo delle pubblicazioni*, Casa editrice armena dei patri mechitaristi, San Lazzaro - Venezia 1960, p. 32.

135

XV

Acta Orientalia Academiae Scientiarum Hung. Tomus XLV (1), 3—22 (1991)

THE DECISIVE MOTIVES OF TATAR FAILURE IN THE ILKHANID—MAMLUK FIGHTS IN THE HOLY LAND

EDMOND SCHÜTZ

After his succession to the throne of the Great Khan, Möngke sent his brother Hülegü to the Near East, to take over and extend the realm carved out by the *noyons* Chormaghan, Baiju and Eljigedei in Persia and the Trans-caucasus.[1] Hülegü made great conquests in 1258—1259, in a single year he took the Baghdad Kaliphate and the impregnable fortresses of the *assassins* ("ha-shish-eaters").[2]

Further territories of the Near East seemed to be easy prey, such as the area under the Ayyubid prince ings of the Saladdin progeny, but from 1250 on, this region came under the tutelage of the Mamluks, who soon proved to be very tough adversaries. The same year, Hülegü set out with a huge army of about 6 *tümens* and in the period of one month he took the Northern emirates, Edessa, Harran, and Aleppo one after the other, and with the rumour of the impending *blitzkrieg*, Hama, Homs and Damascus quickly surrendered.

The kings of Lesser Armenia — who in 1244 "voluntarily" accepted the vassalage of the Tatars — were compelled to participate in the Tatar war-fare.[3] Thus, Hethum I, the Cilician king and Bohemond, the prince of Antiochia (Hethum's son-in-law) were present, as auxiliaries, in the military opera-tions, but cherished the hope, that with the help of the Tatars, the Holy Land could be freed from under the Mahometan yoke.[4]

At this juncture an unexpected event occurred. Hülegü received a message informing him of the death of his brother Möngke, the Great Khan. As it was the rule in the Mongol Empire on such occasions for the kinsmen of

---

[1] Rashid/Russ., III. 24; Rashid/Engl., 246.

[2] Kirakos/Fr. 114, sqq, 139—141; Kirakos/Russ. 152, sqq, 176—78; Haithon, 163—65/296—97.

[3] Kirakos/Fr. 183—86; Kirakos/Russ. 228—31; Akantsi, 298—303; Haithon, 168—70/300—301; Smbat, 101—2; Meyvaert, 255—56; Grousset: *Croisades*, III. 567—73; Grousset: *Empire*, 351—56; Boyle: *CHP* V, 342—49.

[4] Kirakos/Fr. 189—190; Kirakos/Russ. 230—31; Vardan/Russ. 13; Smbat, 104—6; Akantsi, 333. sqq; Grousset: *Croisades*, III. 576—91; Grousset: *Empire*, 350—51; Runci-man, III. 305—11; Haithon, 168—71; Smith, *HJAS* 44, 310.

Acta Orient. Hung. XLV, 1991
Akadémiai Kiadó, Budapest

the rulers of the apanage-*ulus*-es to convene for the election of the next emperor, without delay Ilkhan Hülegü set out to return home.[5] There could have
been several reasons for his speedy return home: the first — the most pal-
pable—must have been to rush to his father's *yurt* and participate at the
funeral ceremonies and the *qurultay* of the new election. Moreover, because
of his very close attachment to Qubilai (at least the Persian Rashid ad-Din
repeatedly stressed the importance of this kinship connection)[6] Hülegü
obviously thought he needed to be present, all the more so as his younger
Ariq Böke, seemed to have the covert and soon overt aim of acquiring brother,
the Khaghan's dignity for himself.

As Hülegü intended to pursue the warfare in Syria at a later date,
he left a garrison detachment in Syria, under the leadership of his valiant
commander Kitbugha, who acquired an excellent reputation in the battle of
Baghdad. It could also have been foresight to leave the commander Kitbugha
on-the-spot, who — being of Nestorian faith — may have had closer
contact with the local Christians. (The deputy was Baidar *noyon*, the governor
of Damascus.)[7]

Immediately upon hearing the news that Hülegü had departed, the
Mamluk Sultan Qutuz set out from his camp: first he crushed the reconnais-
sance troops who had pushed forward, and Kitbugha's detachment rushed to
their rescue in vain. The information provided by the sources is questionable,
but the commander of the vanguard must have been Baidar.[8]

However, this military move of the Mamluks could be achieved only with
the active cooperation or rather foul play of the crusaders, who gave them free
passage below Acre.[9] This unexpected opening gave Qutuz the opportunity to
attack Kitbugha from the flank. The battle under Mount Thabor, at ʿAyn
Jālūt ("Goliath Spring") ended with the crushing defeat of the Tatar detachment. Kitbugha was captured and beheaded on the Sultan's order.[10]

As a rule, the Syrian campaign has generally been dealt with by enumerating the simple facts of an almost unhindered march of the Tatar conquerors,
but, soon the battle of ʿAyn Jālūt, fanfared as a tremendous sensation, a fatal
and ultimate catastrophe. For the Egyptians, the victory was truly an unex-

[5] Rashid/Russ., 50; Boyle: *CHP* V, 351; Grousset: *Empire*, 363.

[6] Rashid/Russ., 50; Rashid/Engl. 255.

[7] Rashid/Russ., 51—52;

[8] Grousset: *Croisades*, III. 600; Grousset: *Empire*, 364; Boyle: *CHP* V, 351; Smith: *HJAS* 44, 326.

[9] Akantsi, 348—49; *RHC, Doc. Arm.* II: *Chiprois*, 753; Boyle: *CHP* V, 351; Thorau: *Baibars*, 92.

[10] Rashid/Russ., III. 53—53; Rashid/Engl., 305; Vardan/Russ., 14; Haithon, 173—74/304—5; otherwise: Smbat, 106—7; Grousset: *Croisades*, III. 603—4; Grousset: *Empire*, 364—65; Boyle: *CHP* V, 351—52; Spuler: *Iran*, 57; Runciman, III. 312—13; Morgan, 155—57; Smith: *HJAS* 44, 307, sqq; Thorau: *ʿAyn Jālūt*, 236—41.

pected surprise, at least common belief would not have expected a victory over the notoriously invincible Tatars. But there was no such thought on the Tatar side. At the time, for Hülegü this battle meant only a skirmish of detachments.

Often historical literature conveys the impression that the battle of ʿAyn Jālūt signified an irretrievable turn in the history of the Tatar Ilkhanids, moreover, of the entire Mongol Empire, and from time to time there are estimates, re-examinations and reappraisals, basically of a similar nature.

As in the case of military events, researchers generally first of all made a comparison between the strength of the belligerent parties. This method seems to be all the more justified, as the battle was fought by armies of similar type, basically mounted cavalry.

The assessment of the Tatar forces is comparatively easy, as two basic figures are available: according to the Chronicle of Kirakos of Gandsak: 20,000 fighters, and Haithon's Chronicle: 1 *tümen*.[11] In historical literature generally the 2 *tümens* figure is accepted, the unit under Baidar's command being estimated to be 1,000—2,000. Anyhow *tümen* was a comprehensive term, and did not always have an exactly defined effective figure.

The Mamluk strength was not easy to define. There is no precise contemporary figure for the force. As a rule, the figure 12,000 of the late Nuvairi (†1332) is taken as a basis, and in modern historiography, also by J. A. Smith jr. An approximately similar figure (10,000) was already fixed by contemporaries as suitable for the campaign led by Saladin against Palestine. A more detailed estimate (Poliak, Ayalor) was derived from the number of military districts: 24 districts — each of a strength of 1,000 — which would make 24,000 in all. Comparatively even this figure seems to be acceptable, if one presumes that part of the army was relegated as a rear-guard in the home garrison.

During his assessment, J. M. Smith jr. agreed with the thesis that more than 6,000 soldiers should be added, the *halqa*, the strength of the local tribal units.[12] In this decision, a parity with the Tatar forces must probably have played a part. In his re-examination, P. Thorau pondered about the strengths, starting from the 10,000 men of the Saladin age, up to the total of Baibars' heydays numbering up to 40.000. This latter figure is contemplated by Thorau for the peak of Baibars' career; for the "turbulent" decade of 1250—60 he gave an estimate of 15,000—20,000.[13] Here again — it seems — the comparative

---

[11] Kirakos/Fr., 189 erroneously: (2000); Kirakos/Russ., 230; Haithon, 173/303; Grousset: *Empire*, 364; Boyle: *CHI* V, 351; Smith: *HJAS* 44, 309—10; Thorau: ʿAyn Jālūt, 236—37;

[12] Smith: *HJAS* 44, 312 (complete analysis).

[13] Thorau: ʿAyn Jālūt, 237.

assessment is in question. The principle of balance also came to the fore in Thorau's Baibars monography ("annähernd zahlenmässiger Ebenbürtigkeit"). But neither with J. M. Smith jr., nor with P. Thorau does it become clear what strength they assigned for the units of the rear-guards.[14]

In contrast to this concept, earlier handbooks generally take the Mamluk superiority for granted. In the year following the victory of Baibars at 'Ayn Jālūt, he succeeded Qutuz (whom he mercilessly stabbed).[15] Taking into account the fact that the main body of the Mamluk force was under the command of Baibars, a numerical superiority cannot be ruled out, however, it has to be admitted that the peak expansion might have been reached in the next decade.

In most comparisons of the two forces, a vital issue is omitted and overlooked. On one side, the Egyptian Mamluks consisted of a complete army, while for the Tatars, the unit under Kitbugha's command was a detachment, a garrison unit. Thus the belligerent parties cannot be described as being equivalent, not to mention the foregoing decade, which for the Tatars meant incessant warfare and marches, so the army arriving in Syria must have been in a rather fatigued state.

The most important components were primarily the quite unexpected circumstances. The Tatars certainly counted on the fact that the Crusaders would by no means interfere or give any assistance to the Mamluks. The second factor, which decisively contributed to the fatal issue of the battle, was the conduct of the North Syrian Ayyubid units, incorporated into the Tatar frontline on both wings. The Syrians engaged in premeditated deception, soon after the clash of the frontlines, they defected and thus left gaps open for Mamluk intrusion.

Such a role was played by the Emir of Homs, al-Malik al-Ashraf, who when placed in a critical position decided to desert. Soon after the Mamluk victory he received his reward and was reinstated to his emirate. The Melik of Aleppo was also accused of having betrayed the Tatar army, but he was left on the Tatar side, and the wrath of Hülegü overtook him, he was executed together with his 300 men.[16]

A similar story was related on Sarim ad-Din Üzbek by an Arab Chronicler, Qirtay: after the fall of Homs, having been captured, he (Sarim ad-Din) joined the Tatars, but secretly informed the Mamluk Sultan about the Tatar forces and even offered that after the clash of the two lines, he would defect to their side together with his troops and thus through the gap they could penetrate the Tatar lines.[17]

---

[14] Thorau: *Baibars*, 94.

[15] Grousset: *Croisades*, III. 600; Grousset: *Empire*, 364; Boyle, V, 351; Thorau: *Baibars*, 98—99.

[16] Rashid/Russ., III. 53; Spuler; *Iran*, 57; Thorau: *Baibars*, 96.

[17] Qirtay, *Tarix*, in: Thorau, *Baibars*, 97; Thorau: *'Ayn Jālūt*, 238—39.

So ultimately it becomes quite clear that in 1260 Kitbugha simply walked into a trap, because of the free passage granted by the Crusaders to the Mamluk forces and the desertion of several Ayyubid Syriac units (Rashid/Russ. III. 52).

However, victory is a victory regardless of the trick with which it was won, and so it is comprehensible that the Mahometan sources recount the entire episode as a total victory. And in next year, after his succession to the throne, a memorial pillar has been erected by Baibars on the site of the battle, as a token of his own decisive role in the victory.

In his Baibars monography, P. Thorau rather contractedly described the ʿAyn Jālūt battle as a clever tactical manoeuvre ("durch geschickte taktische Manöver vernichtend geschlagen '), but with objectivity he added that the victory had been won by the complete Egyptian army and stressed the point that the Mamluks destroyed only *one* army, and not *the* Mongol forces. The event was described by D. Morgan, approximately in a similar style, remarking that ʿAyn Jālūt "marked the putting of a term to Mongol expansion . . . but it would be going too far to say that that single battle in any real sense halted the Mongol advance."[18]

*

But now let us turn back to the home march of the main Ilkhanid army. J. M. Smith jr. blames Ilkhan Hülegü for his move, in his mind it was a "strategic miscalculation" to withdraw his whole army neither for participation at the *qurultay* nor eventually against the Golden Horde.[19] The answer to this problem is not so decided.

The triggering effect of the subsequent events was surely the death of the Great Khan Möngke. The fundamental provision of the *yasa* at the Great Khan's death was that all senior scions of the Jingisid clan should assemble for the election of the new Great Khan. For Hülegü it was probably a major embarrassment that he received the message of the death with such a considerable delay. This was all the more unprecedented, as he was one of the major senior family members who should have been alerted first by the youngest brother, Ariq böke being present in the home *yurt*. Möngke died on August 11, 1259, and the message reached him March 1260, with a seven month delay. This delay is all the more strange, as allegedly — at least according to Rashid ad-Din — Hülegü was in close contact with Ariq böke.[20] There was no plausible reason for the delay. It could not have been casual negligence, but a deliberate offence of dynastic rules. For the purpose of messages, routes for messengers

[18] Thorau, *Baibars*, 94, cf. 120. Morgan, 156.
[19] Smith: *HJAS* 44, 328.
[20] Rashid/Engl., 255.

had been established and ensured from the Ögödei regime, and in the neighbouring countries under the ruling generals of the Ilkhanids the military and trading routes represented a fine network of mutual contact, and every 25—30 miles messengers were awaited by a complete set of relay horses.[21]

What was the real background to the late delivery of the message? The youngest brother might have resorted to the fraudulent tactic, that as both of his brothers had their own home *yurt:* one in China, one in Persia, and both of them were waging war and fairly far away,[22] eventually the basic provisions of the *yasa* could be applied (which in the literal sense had never been implemented) that the youngest brother, the son presiding in the family *yurt,* the *otcigin* should retain the home-*yurt* for imperial apanage.[23]

In this respect, Ariq böke must have felt all the more strengthened, as Qaidu the senior of the Ögödei clan, and the Chaghataid Alghu accepted this solution, and Ariq enjoyed firm support on the Western border from Berke, the Khan of the Golden Horde. With such patrons backing him, Ariq böke adopted the title of Great Khan.[24] But Qublai, the brother next following Möngke in seniority, also aspired to be the Great Khan. He set out for the central *yurt,* and his army and his partisans proclaimed him the Great Khan on June 4, 1260,[25] i.e. exactly the same date, when Hülegü back from Syria arrived at Akhlat (a town on the northern coast of the Van Sea).[26] The battles between Ariq and Qublai in the following years definitely decided the matter in favour of Qublai.[27]

Hülegü sided with Qublai, so it could be expected that he would quickly set out to go to Qublai's support. At any rate Hülegü made preparations — according to Kirakos of Gandsak — he set out to confront Berke, and sent his son, Abagha with 3 tüments to Khorassan. According to Haithon, he positioned his son in Tabriz and then set out to march to the East; according to Rashid ad-Din to the borderline of Khorassan.[28]

Being aware of the prospective outcome of the fight, Hülegü served the cause of Qublai with his presence on the Khorassan border, keeping Alghu the unstable neighbour of Ariq in check. He then launched an assault against Qaidu and Kutuktu.[29]

[21] Rubruck (Dawson), 146; Morgan, 103—7, etc.
[22] Rashid/Engl., 230; Grousset: *Empire*, 285; Boyle: *CHP* V, 351.
[23] Rashid/Engl., 163, 202; Spuler: *Iran*, 372, 388.
[24] Rashid/Russ., III. 50; Rashid/Engl. 230, 251; Spuler: *Iran*, 61—63; Smith: *HJAS* 44, 328.
[25] Rashid/Engl., 252.
[26] Rashid/Russ., 50.
[27] Rashid/Engl., 252—60.
[28] Kirakos/Fr., 193; Kirakos/Russ. 237; Haithon, 172; Rashid/Russ. 50; Boyle: *CHP* V, 351.
[29] Rashid/Engl., 255, 261—2.

XVI

However, Hülegü not only had to move towards the north-east, but also towards the north-west. J. M. Smith jr. is of the opinion that Hülegü should not have needed to concentrate his army in Iran against the Golden Horde, as Khan Berke mobilized his forces only in 1262 against him.[30] But this argumentation — in my opinion — is not sufficient to refute the motivation for an earlier alert. Berke Khan had concluded an alliance with the Sultan the previous year, and so Berke and the other Khans, the other allies of Ariq böke, already represented potential adversaries in 1260.[31] But Berke also had other motives for his hostile attitude to Hülegü. He professed the Muslim creed with neophyte zeal, and was utterly infuriated when he received news of the sacking of Baghdad, and the killing of the Kaliph, and Hülegü's subsequent moves against the Muslims.[32] These motives naturally gained a special echo in the Arab sources, though in Western and Armenian sources one also finds ample information, of course, here as victory news.

In addition, a grave family slight was involved: at the start of the Persian warfare, several nephews of Berke together with their detachments had been assigned as auxiliary troops to Hülegü's army, but the Jochid princes were later convicted of (alleged) criminal offences and executed in the Ilkhanid camp.[33]

Open hostilities between Berke and Hülegü broke out in 1262, it was Khan Noghai, who led the troops intruding through the Caucasus, and the hostilities continued up to their lives' end (Hülegü † 1265, Berke † 1266). Even Hülegü's successor, Khan Abagha continued the warfare, he had palisades (Mongol *Sibe*) erected along the Kura river.[34]

All these motives would have been sufficient to foster a feud between the Jochid and Hülegid family branches, but a basic seed of discord had been sown by the differing concept regarding the territorial boundaries between the clan *yurts* established by the *yasa*. Originally, the territorial boundaries had not been exactly delineated, so the Jochid branch claimed propriety rights over the Caucasus.[35] This claim had not been established before the Ilkhanid period, as the previous regents of the Caucasian region were only subaltern generals and regents.[36]

---

[30] Rashdi/Russ., III, 59; Smith: *HJAS* 44, 328.

[31] Grousset: *Croisades*, III. 613; *Grousset:* Empire, 397; Boyle: *CHP* V, 351; Spuler: *Iran*, 63; Morgan, 157.

[32] Akantsi, 332–33; Grousset: *Empire*, 354–56; Morgan, 144.

[33] Juvaini, II. 608; Rashid/Engl., 123; Rashid/Russ., III. 54, 59–60; Kirakos/Fr. 192; Kirakos/Russ., 236; Akantsi, 338–41; Grousset: *Empire*, 398; Boyle: *CHP* V, 353.

[34] Rashid/Russ., III. 58–60, 68; Kirakos/Fr., 193; Kirakos/Russ., 238; Vardan/Russ., 27; Grousset: *Empire*, 366; Boyle: *CHP* V. 353–54.

[35] Rashid/Engl., 307–8; Juvaini, I. 42–43; Morgan, 144, etc.

[36] Kirakos/Fr., 116, sqq, 140, 156, sqq. Kirakos/Russ., 152, sqq., 177. sqq.

But Hülegü, by virtue of the mandate bestowed upon him by the Great Khan Möngke, claimed supremacy over the entire Near East, including the Transcaucasus.[37]

It has been common case in Mongol chancellery practice that each sovereign or prince adopting a vassal state had to make an appearance in the Court of the Great Khan, in Qaraqorum. This was also the case with the Georgian and Armenian kings, who were directed to the Great Khan. By way of Sarai-Batu they set out: Avag atabeg in 1239, and the Georgian kings, then Simbat the Armenian army commander (1248), and later the king of Lesser Armenia, Hethum I (1254).[38]

That this principle survived even later on is indicated by the step of Khan Tokhta (1291—1312), who wanted to revive this claim half a century later.[39]

But apart from the possible threats coming from the north-east and the north-west flank, probably there may have been another motive, which prevented Hülegü from instantaneously sending auxiliary troops to the east in July 1260. The other reasoning that might have been instrumental in halting his hand was that both by age and authority he was more senior than Ariq böke or comparatively attained the same dignity level as Qublai, so eventually he might also have coveted the imperial throne. His hesitance might have had another meaning: probably he waited for the rivalry to come to an end. This possible version has not been suggested by historical literature,[40] most possibly because of the close fraternal attachment to Qublai, (at least emphasised by Rashid-ad-Din,) though it must be taken into account that a sharp-eyed contemporary witness, chronicler Haithon suggested another version: "the barons awaited his [Hülegü's] return as they wanted to put him on the throne".[41]

*

To summarize the results attained by Ilkhan Hülegü in Syria: in the course of a single month, Hülegü took a fair number of centres of the Syrian emirates, while the others preferred to declare their submission, so his warfare directed against the Syrian field at the turn of the 1250—60 years can be considered a brilliant victory.

---

[37] Rashid/Engl., 255—56: Rashid/Russ. III. 23—24; Mikaelian, 317.
[38] Kirakos/Fr., 129—31, 156—58, 176—81; Kirakos/Russ., 167—69, 194—96, 222—26; Akantsi, 324—27; Smbat, 98; *REA, Doc. arm.* II, p. 164. *Letter of Smbat,* 90; Mikaelian, 301, 314—17.
[39] Juvaini, I. 42; Rashid/Russ., III. 23; Boyle: *CHP* V, 352; Morgan, 144.
[40] Just the opposite: "did not offer himself as candidate": Grousset: *Empire,* 363.
[41] Haithon, 172/303; Boyle: *CHP* V, 351.

XVI

In the opposite direction, historical attention is focused on the ʿAyn Jālūt defeat, and proclaimed it a fatal fiasco, and estimates and re-examinations appeared putting this failure into the limelight, effacing all the other positive achievements.

In historical literature, evaluating the battles of the Tatars and Mamluks, and the role of the Crusaders, two different versions appear, which — of course — had been conditioned by the sources deriving from the different parties.

Arab sources were prejudiced in favour of the Ayyubid emirates and the succeeding Mamluks, the Syrian and Armenian chronicles on the contrary, sympathised with and felt compassion for the Tatars, for on several occasions the latter acted in cooperation with the Christians to promote their cause.

R. Grousset was of the conviction that the Crusaders should have closely cooperated with the Tatars before and after the battle of ʿAyn Jālūt. And so he blamed the Crusaders for having given free passage for the Mamluk army on the coastal strip, which enabled the Mamluks to attack the Tatars in the flank and thus bring about their defeat, and herewith provoke their own cataclysm. R. Grousset was certainly aware that the Crusaders did not act of their own choice, but because the centre of the Persian Ilkhanids, Tabriz, was far away, and the Mamluks were encamped in the neighbourhood.

If they could have acted on their own free will, they surely would have chosen the Tatar side, because the Tatars generally behaved indifferently toward the profession of creed. Moreover, from the beginning, the Christians had sympathy with the Tatars, because before their appearance on the scene positive rumours had spread all over the Near East about the country of priest Johannes,[42] the major component of which news was that there were Mongol tribes (kereits, naimans), which adopted the Christian (Nestorian) faith. The same news had also been given by the Armenian constable Simbat in 1248. This expectance had also been increased by the Western missionary-envoys, who reported about the tolerant attitude of the Tatars toward the Christians.

The enthusiastic estimate of the Ilkhanids was increased by the fact that the wife of Khan Hülegü, Doquz Khatun, and Hülegü's army commander, Kitbugha both professed the Nestorian creed.[43] Even the successors of Ilkhan Hülegü were on good terms with the Christians living in the Near East, and the Tatar envoys sent to the West sought for close contact and alliance with the Western powers.

The good reputation of the Tatars was also enhanced by the information provided by the Armenian chroniclers. After the arrival of Ilkhan Hülegü on the Near Eastern front, King Hethum I, the monarch of Lesser Armenia,

[42] Zarnke, Fr.: *Der Priester Johannes, Abh. kgl. Sächs. Ges. Wiss. Phil-hist. Klasse.* VII. VIII. vol. 1879—1896. Yule-Cordier, 2. vol., 231—37; Rubruck (Dawson), 122—23.
[43] Haithon, 169—70; Akantsi, 340—41.

participated in the Syrian campaign with an army amounting to 1 *tümen*, jointly with his son-in-law Bohemund VI, prince of Antioch.[44] Already at the outset of the campaign, Hülegü promised King Hethum that after the reconquest of the Crusader fortresses he would return them to them. He also put down this promise in his letter addressed to the French King, Louis IX.[45]

But negative intermezzos came in between, when by chance one of the Crusader barons, Count Julien of Sidon's patrol clashed with Kitbugha's advance forces and the nephew of Kitbugha was killed in the encounter. The consequence was that the enraged Tatars sacked Sidon and burnt it down.[46] This unfortunate intermezzo has often been cited by the propagators of the negative essence of Christian-Tatar relations.

On basis of some documentary evidence from the Holy Land, P. Jackson demonstrated that prior to 1261, the Ilkhans in the Holy Land "did not lavish particular benevolence on the Christians" at the time of the occupation of the north-Syrian region. Their friendly posture . . . after 1262—63 . . . distorted an accurate appreciation of the situation in 1260." To a certain degree, J. Richard shared this opinion, and D. Morgan professed a similar view. P. Thorau warns historians of coming under the influence of the pro-Tatar attitude. He quotes the remarks of several Christian chroniclers about the demeanour of the Tatars; of course, Tatars were hard warriors, and had little sense of Western chivalry.[47]

Of course, it is obvious that for an accidental onlooker, who by chance found himself in the middle of the Tatar military operations, the main experience must have been horror and revulsion. For this reason, in the courts of the European kings and the Pope's residence, the judgement of the Tatars remained a negative one even later on. The experience of the Tatar invasion in the European neighbourhood two decades earlier and the letters of the Great Khans inviting the Western courts to declare their submission could hardly have elicited a more favourable estimate. A range of opinions of a similar type form the bulk of the contemporary repercussions, gathered into a collection by Gian A. Bezzola, reflecting the dominant picture of the Tatars in the European mind up to 1270.[48]

It is comprehensible that at the time of the intrusion of the Crusaders, fierce hatred flared up in the Muslim emirates against the Christians, but as

[44] Haithon, 170/304; Akantsi, 344—45; Vardan/Russ., 13; Grousset: *Empire*, 361.

[45] Meyvaert, 257—58, lines 70—93.

[46] Haithon, 174/304—5; Grousset; *Croisades*, III. 594; Grousset: *Empire*, 363—64.

[47] Jackson, P.: *The Crisis of the Holy Land in 1260: English Historical Review*, 95 (1980), pp. 481—513.; Richard, J., *The Mongols and the Franks: Journal of Asian History*, 3 (1969); pp. 51—52.; Morgan, 155. Thorau, *Baibars*, 89.

[48] Bezzola, G. A.; *Die Mongolen in abendländischer Sicht (1220—1270)*. Bern—München 1974.

XVI

they came into closer contact during the next century, their relations underwent a certain change: a sort of peaceful co-existence and mutual commercial relations.

After the battle, of ʿAyn Jālūt, following the accession of Baibars to power, relations between the Mamluks and Crusaders radically altered. During the military alert and almost five years long fighting between the Golden Horde and the Ilkhanids, Baibars gained a free hand to keep the Syrian emirates undisturbed in his hands. Having no competitor-adversary he started to take one Crusader fortress after the other: in 1263 the Krak des Chevaliers, the impregnable stronghold of the Hospitalers, then Toron, in 1266 the Templar Safad, and Kaisareia and in the same year invaded Armenian Cilicia.[49] Being aware of the imminent danger, King Hethum personally hastened to Ilkhan Abagha (1265–81) in order to ask for auxiliary troops to ward off the Mamluks. But at that exact time Baibars appeared with unequalled rapidity and defeated the altercating Armenian lords, and dragged the elder son of Hethum into captivity.[50]

Then in the next year (1267–8) Baibars continued his conquests. The Crusader fortresses perched on the Amanus mountains fell into his hands without resistance. After taking Jaffa and Tripoli, he then marched forward to Antioch. Not a single inland fortress was left in Crusader hands, only a few strongholds on the shore of the Mediterranean.

As a matter of fact, Baibars was a cautious strategist. When rumours came of Louis the Saint's preparations for a second Crusade and the English prince Edward would join in the venture, Baibars withdrew his troops. This was a temporary respite for the Templar Tartus, and the Hospitaler al-Markab.

S. Louis ultimately directed his new venture not against the Mamluks, but towards Tunis, so Prince Edward was left alone. However he landed at Acre in May 1271, but his troops alone were not sufficient for a successful military operation, so after his futile venture he returned home. Unfortunately, just about this time, Khan Abagha being harrassed on the north-west and north-east fronts by his brother-neighbours, could not start a co-ordinated action.

Khan Abagha succeeded in driving back the attack of the Golden Horde, but had hardly finished, when he was placed under pressure by the next brother-*ulus*, the Chaghataid branch, when in 1269–70 Khan Barak made an advance on Khorassan. The agressor was driven back, but he still had to lead a punitive expedition against Barak in order to forestall a new assault.[51]

---

[49] Grousset; *Croisades*, III. 622–31.; Thorau: *Baibars*, 161, sqq.

[50] Akantsi, 356–73; *Crusades* (Setton) II, 653–54; Grousset: *Croisades*, III. 634–35; Runciman, III. 322.

[51] Rashid/Russ., 69–88; Grousset: *Empire*, 369; Boyle: *CHP* V. 360.

Thus it is obvious that the balance of military opportunities and endeavours of the Mamluks and Ilkhanids was radically unequal. The good nephews all along the north-west and north-east frontiers were always ready to utilize any opportunity to attack their southern brother, so the Ilkhans could not take advantage of any opportunity to enter into an alliance with any Crusader army landing on the seashore, and so to proceed with a joint venture against the Mamluk Sultan, who on his part was always free to act.

When Khan Abagha received the news of Edward's arrival, all he could do was to send a detachment of 1 *tümen*, but this detachment was of no avail, since Baibars' *hinterland* was always free and clear, so he could withdraw instantaneously before any counterattack appeared.

To counterbalance the northern frontier engagements, which prevented him from proceeding on the Syrian front, Abagha sent several envoys over the years to the Pope (1273—74), and to the French and the English kings (1276—77) to urge the Western monarchs to enter an alliance and joint expeditions. But the kings had their own grave or sometimes trifling problems, so they sent the envoys back with obliging and courteous promises, and so Abagha's repeated endeavours against the Mamluks were in vain.

In the years after Baibars' death (July 1, 1277), when political instability in Egypt prevailed, Abagha could not take advantage of this opportunity, because he was again threatened by the northern neighbours. As soon as Abagha gained some scope for action, he set his forces into action on the route trodden formerly by Hülegü. He did not guess that instead of the two puppet sultans, who had easily been wiped out by Qalavun (1279—90), he would be confronted by a forceful and cunning adversary. In order to ensure safety on his flanks, Qalavun concluded a truce with the neighbouring Crusader orders. Abagha marched at the head of his army towards the region of Hama—Homs. The allied Georgian and Armenian troops drove one flank of the Sultan back. But at this juncture — the main enemy again appeared — the Chaghataid brothers made inroads from the north-east, which obliged Abagha to rush back to Khorassan, and this was the decisive factor.

Although at this time, Abagha was almost certain of total victory, and his army-divisions, left in charge of his valiant commander Mengü Temür, were winning, at Homs the commander was wounded, the army lost stability and withdrew across the Euphrates. This again turned the scales in favour of the Sultan — but the next year, with firm decision Abagha again made preparations to set out against Qalavun. However, death (April 1, 1282) prevented him from starting his new campaign.[52]

Based on the experience of his predecessors, the next Ilkhan Arghun (1284—1291) thought the prospects of success could be secured with a campaign

[52] Rashid/Russ., III. 96—97; Haithon, 182—83/310—11; *Chiprois*, 786; Grousset: *Croisades*, III. 699—700; Grousset: *Empire*, 371; Boyle: *CHP* V, 363; Spuler: *Iran*, 75.

previously co-ordinated with the European Crusaders and for this purpose he sent four envoys to the Pope in 1285—1287, to the French King Philip the Fair in 1289—1290, and to the English King Edward, who some years earlier (1271) as a prince had led a Crusade to the Holy Land.[53]

The initiation of an anti-Mamluk action was prevented by internal strife in the Ilkhanid camp, the rebellion of the Ilkhan's brother-in-law Nauruz, the omnipotent military governor of Khorassan, which smouldered for four years (1289—94) in the frontier zone of the Chaghataids — and in 1289 in addition the Golden Horde also rushed forward at Derbent. Arghun stricken with disease for two years could not move, and died 1291, so all the plans and hopes were frustrated.[54]

Under such circumstances, it was not surprising that during Arghun's reign at the end of the 1280s, all the ultimate fortresses of the Crusaders fell one after the other: Latakiyya in 1287, Tripoli 1289 and Acre in 1291, the last triumph of the Holy Land. And the domino-principle came into motion, all the last forts on the Mediterranean shore — Sidon, Beirut and four more fortresses did not even offer resistance. In this way, the Crusader presence in the Holy Land was liquidated.

Also R. Grousset stated that after 1291, with the fall of Acre, from the Christian point of view there was no longer a possibility and necessity for any Tatar progress against the Mamluk power, as the Holy Land had factually been lost for Christianity.[55] This assertion is a simple reflection of the future in the cognition of the historical result.

In the contemplation of the contemporaries, the idea of the possibility of a reiterated liberation of the Holy Land did not cease. This thought was represented by a number of projects elaborated by contemporary thinkers, and several versions analyzed the motives, which entailed the loss of the Holy Land and gave hints and advice on the strategy to retrieve it. The earliest, and the most careful plan was elaborated by the Cilician Armenian Count Haithon, who in 1307, handed it over to the Pope.[56]

The European great powers did not abandon the idea of starting new Crusades, and it was only the political constellation which prevented them from putting the initiative into motion. The Ilkhans, throughout their reign, also represented the idea of a joint venture together with the Western powers or even alone and they repeatedly made efforts to accomplish the plan.

The years following Arghun's death by no means favoured the start of such an action. This occurred only in 1295, when Ghazan Khan, an extra-

---

[53] *Crusades* (Setton), III. 531—34.

[54] Rashid/Russ., III. 119—25.

[55] Grousset: *Croisades*, III. 734, sqq., 752—63; Runciman, III. 412—423.

[56] Haithon: *RHC, Doc. arm.* II; Schütz—Sinor (French text transl. by Mickel): *Haython, the Chronicler.* Indiana University (in press)

ordinary personality, both by the calibre of his military and political genius, stepped on the throne (1295—1304).

It would be futile to ponder on the question of to what degree Ghazan's campaign set in motion in 1299 corresponded to the strategy of Hülegü, because it was the geographical site that primarily determined the march-route, and the details of elaborating the plan. Ilkhan Ghazan occupied Aleppo, he vanquished the Mamluk main army below Homs in December 1299 and in January 1300 he marched into glorious Damascus.[57]

After this victorious progress, one would justifiably have expected that the possession of Syria was decided in favour of the Tatars. But this time again the northern neighbours, the nephew clans intervened. Taking advantage of the Ilkhan's absence, they directed an assault against the Ilkhanid ulus. The feudal lord, Kutlugh Khoja, of the domains of Afghanistan bordering on Persia, made an advance into the South-Persian provinces, and scorched the regions of Sistan, Kerman and Kars. Ghazan had no other choice than to return to his domain from his Syrian campaign. And what followed next, was the same result as after the withdrawal of Ilkhan Hülegü. Immediately afterwards the Mamluk forces arrived and took possession of Syria.

But Ghazan did not accept the loss of Syria, in 1302 he again sent a full army under the command of Kutlugh-Shah. But it was routed, not only by the superior forces and the adroit tactics of the Mamluks, but also by the cunning tactic of the Damascus inhabitants, who opened up the sluices, so that the Tatar army encamped on the fields, became completely flooded, and only a fraction of the army could get home with the utmost struggle. The battle was vividly described by a clear-sighted eyewitness, Haithon, the nephew of the Cilician Armenian king, the ally of the Ilkhan.[58]

The forty years of rivalry between the Tatars and the Mamluks is easy to assess: two excelling Ilkhans with special abilities: Hülegü in 1260 and Ilkhan Ghazan in 1300, gained an overwhelming victory in the Syrian region, but could not crown their campaign with the seizure of the territory of Egypt, the heartland of the Mamluk regime, and the complete crushing of the Mamluk forces, so immediately after the departure of the main army Syria was retaken by the Mamluks. The military operations started without the participation of the Ilkhans, by commanders with a minor detachment, and became a failure: during the reign of Abagha in 1281, and that sent by Ghazan in 1303, etc. In these latter cases, the numerical superiority of the Mamluks could also have played an important role.

---

[57] Rashid/Russ., III. 195—96; Haithon, 194—99/317—21.

[58] Rashid/Russ., III. 195—96; Haithon, 199—203/321—24; Grousset: *Empire*, 382—83; Boyle: *CHP* V, 393; Spuler; *Iran*, 102.

The Tatars also directed a score of raids of units of 1,000 to 2,000 men against the North-Syrian area, but these attacks were only intended to devastate the region, and frighten the enemy.

Historical handbooks on the description of the Tatar—Mamluk wars generally give a detailed story of the Tatar victories and defeats in Syria, and mostly attribute the final outcome of the battles to the supremacy of firearms or the numerical superiority of the forces. Attention is mainly concentrated on the outcome of a single battle of ʿAyn Jālūt, without giving a survey of the sequence of the variegated circumstances of the military situation of the more than half a century of Tatar—Mamluk opposition and the different qualities of the — peaceful or hostile — hinterlands of the confronting parties.

Such a basic stance is also taken by the recently published, most detailed and thorough investigation of this topic, the voluminous essay of J. M. Smith jr. "ʿAyn Jālūt: Mamluk Success or Mongol Failure?" — as revealed by the title. The essay subjected the different clashes of the Tatars and Mamluks to a microscopic examination, but all this minute work was carried out to deduce conclusions to explain the ʿAyn Jālūt defeat. The strategy of Ilkhan Hülegü was "defective", the author states,[59] but the background, the circumstances, and decisive motives were omitted. Certainly there are often similarities between the warfare in several details and particularities, and equations can be drawn in several particularities, but certain decisive motives are again unmentioned.

In his analysis of the battles, J. M. Smith jr., imputes the primary importance to the inferiority to the "material" components, the superior qualification of the Mamluk soldiers, and the inferior quality of the arrows and the horses of the Tatars.

First let us take the main element, the superior technical quality of the arrows.[60] Concerning the archery techniques of the nomads, there are a number of handbooks covering the different ages, but based on such description one can hardly make an exact differentiations between the Tatars and the Mamluks.

In order to form a judgement in this matter, I will quote the example of the clash of Ilkhan Ghazan with the Mamluk Sultan in 1299, who hurried in all haste with all his men to surprise the weary and fatigued soldiers of the Tatar Khan, of whom only a minor portion had arrived in the area after a long march. Ghazan Ilkhan was aware of the dangerous situation, and he would have liked to avoid the battle, because he knew that his soldiers, who "were spread over the field, would not be able to reach him and ordered all who were with him to dismount. The Tatars placed their horses around them, streched their bows and arrows, and waited until the enemy was near to them. Then

[59] Smith: *HJAS* 44, pp. 328—31, note 52.
[60] *Ibid.*, 314—26.

they fired their arrows all at one time . . . The first [Mamluks] stumbled and those who came after tripped over them . . . and thus one fell over the other and the Tatars, well trained in the art of archery, fired frequently and rapidly, so that few of the Saracens escaped being either killed or wounded." When the Sultan became aware of the situation he withdrew.[61]

J. M. Smith jr. also came across this military accident and hinted to it in a footnote. Still he attributed the Tatar victory in this case to be eventually won by a superior number of forces,[62] although this case clearly showed, that the victory has been won by the ingenious realization of the unexpected situation, by a quick maneouvre, and successful tactical move.

Nomad warfare — or rather warfare in general — always used different means to achieve the desired end, either one or the other means, or a well applied complexity of them. The main clue was to instantaneously react to the unforeseen.

Foremost experts of nomad warfare have always analyzed the role of horses, an other decisive factor.[63] Tatar horses were a well fed breed, and had ample grazing fields. Thus in Persia, in the NW area — Maragha, Tebriz, on the steppes of the Arax riverside, on the slopes of the Ala-dagh, and in the NE on the grazing fields of Khorassan, the mounts and spare reserve horses were in good condition before each campaign. In the Syrian area, especially south of Damascus, there was less area for grazing, so the stock of Tatar horses had to be withdrawn in turns to northern areas for amelioration. In contrast to this, the horses of the Mamluks were better acclimatized to the desert climate, and fed on less, but more nutritive fodder.

Because of the great distances and the different terrain characteristics, the Tatars had to take more reserve-horses with them, 4—5 per soldier, either relay horses, or as pack animals. This extra number of horses represented a considerable surplus, and increased the difficulties of advancing forward. With such a large amount of luggage, the armies moved at a considerably slow, rather moderate space, and this was certainly an incomparable drawback. An adversary could gain exhaustive intelligence news well in advance.

Regarding the personal factor: what constituted the power balance ratio between the two warfares, the first in 1241—42 waged as far as Poland and Hungary, and the great campaign in the south-west to Persia and the Transcaucasus, prepared in the late 1230s and developed 20 years later by the Ilkhanids to take the Baghdad Caliphate and Syria?

The military tactical system — the lightning cavalry attack, the surrounding of enemy troops and encircling manoeuvres, major and minor tricks,

[61] Haithon, 191—93/316—18. Schütz—Sinor, *Haithon, the Chronicler*

[62] Smith: *HJAS*, vol. 44, p. 324, note 53; Boyle: *CHP* V, 388.

[63] E. g., Sinor: *Horse and Pasture*, ; Smith: *HJAS*, 44, 331—40, 345; Meyvaert, p. 258, lines 95—96; Morgan, 156.

ambushes, and the master-art archery — were basically the same or similar in most Mongol campaigns, which brought them victory and fame. But concerning the enemies, it must not be forgotten that in feudal Europe and in Russia the Tatars met only single separated petty Russian principalities; while in Poland and Hungary the armies were totally unaccustomed to nomad tactics, and mainly consisted of cumbersome heavy cavalry under clumsy feudal management. In Syria — on the contrary — they were encountered by Mamluk armies mostly similar to the Tatar type of military system, the forces having been recruited via Crimea of Kipchak and Circassian slaves, but trained and accustomed to desert fighting terrain.

In my opinion, the lack of attainment of Tatar success was primarily due to the geopolitical situation of the Ilkhanid Khanate, the hostile attitude of the Northern brother-*uluses* and the distance between the site of the battle-field and their *ulus*.

During its existence, the Persian Ilkhanate had always been threatened from the north-west by the Golden Horde, and from the north-east by the Chaghatai *ulus*. As soon as the Persian Tatars set out on a raid or a campaign against the Mamluks, each time the booty-motivated uncle or nephew arrived from the north of the Caucasus or from the north-east region, Khorassan, and so the Ilkhans were compelled to return to their bases in Persia without fulfilling their assignment.

In the meantime, the Mamluk Empire was in an undisturbed state from its northern or southern neighbours. Each time the Tatars had to withdraw, having been menaced by their northern kins, the Mamluks hastened back and recaptured the territories in North Syria or often proceeded as far as Cappadocia and Cilician Armenia, devastating cities and the countryside.[64] So the northern kins of the Tatars were on each occasion one of the principal decisive factors of the Ilkhanid misfortune.

The next negative factor was the distance between the battlefield and the garrison. The Tatar army had to proceed 1,000—1,200 km in order to get from Tebriz to Aleppo, the first outpost of the Syrian battle-zone and 1,500 km to Damascus — at the same time, for the Mamluk army the distance from their Cairo garrison to Damascus was less than half the distance: only 650 km each time with no menace in the back neither from the Lybian desert, nor from Nubia.

When comparing the logistics, one must not only take the distance in a linear sense into account, but also the additional burdens of warfare: the Tatar forces had to get through rather strenuous, difficult, mostly mountainous regions with all their loads, pack-animals, and spare-horses, and so the disadvantages were multiplied many times over. At the same time, the Mamluk

---

[64] *Crusades* (Setton), II. 654, sqq; Mikaelian, 334, sqq, 366, sqq, 408, sqq.

army moved over a rather well known region, where they were acquainted with all the hiding places suitable for ambush. Moreover, the Arab population accepted the Mamluks without resistance partly because of their Muslim creed.

In addition, another most important factor must be taken into consideration, on only two occasions could the Tatar army seize Syria, and only for a couple of months, each time they had to withdraw from the territory because of northern onslaughts. And just before the battle of 'Ayn Jālūt, the whole Tatar army was compelled to withdraw, because Ilkhan Hülegü had to hasten back to take part at the Great Khan's election. Under such conditions, it is comprehensible that during their repeated inroads they could by no means count on the support of the local Syrian population, who encountered them unwillingly or confronted them as enemies.

And there was still another decisive factor in favour of the Mamluks. The majority of the crusader castles, situated all along the Syrian coastline had been taken during the reign of two outstanding Sultans, Baibars (1260—1277) and Qalavun (1279—1290). The majority of the historians mainly impute these victories to the extraordinary military talent of these two warlords. But one must take into consideration the fact that the capture of the crusader castles took place during the absence of the Tatar forces or immediately after their departure to encounter their northern enemies. The great victories were won by some clever tactic or ruse. In 1260 the victory at 'Ayn Jālūt was due to the free passage the Mamluks received from the Crusaders of Acre, in 1300 again it ensued because of the sudden withdrawal of the Ilkhan to meet the northern intruders, in 1303 because the inhabitants of Damascus opened the sluices and flooded the area of the prospective encounter of the adversaries. This is not to say that cunning planning during the military operations and careful implementation did not represent special military talent. But the decisive factor was the geopolitical position of the two parties, which was completely different. The Mamluks had not been menaced from the south or from the western deserts in Egypt by any adversary. Thus with Mamluk victory the fortune of the parties seemed to be definitively decided.

However, the Tatar offensive endeavours sustained the hope in the European powers or in some optimistic thinkers that with the help of the Tatars, the Holy Land could probably be reconquered by the Crusaders for the Christians and there were quite a number of clerics who elaborated plans for the Pope, and especially for the French kings, to initiate new crusades, in which they circumstantially described the debility of the Mamluk Empire. One of the earliest of such projects was drawn up by Haithon, Count of Coricos, the nephew of Hethum II, king of Lesser Armenia, and in 1307 handed over to the Pope residing transitorily in Poitiers.[65]

[65] See note 56. above

XVI

There could be several weighty reasons why this thorough and carefully elaborated essay on the state of the Mamluk Empire, and the military execution of a successful crusade against it, could not be realised: e.g. the death of Ilkhan Abu Said in 1335, completely undermined the Tatar presence in the region and led to a completely changed power balance.

But there were also several other reasons of universal significance: rivalry, competition between the Western powers, the outbreak of the French — English 100 year war, and the plague of the Black Death that swept over the whole Mediterranean area in the 1330 decades.

However, Mamluk supremacy did not prove to be permanent either. The most successful Sultan of Ottoman expansion, Selim I. Yavuz, put an end to Mamluk supremacy in the Near East, and incorporated the Mamluk Empire into his extended domain. Henceforth, the s.c. Later Crusades were directed against the Ottoman Empire.[66]

Abbreviations

Akantsi — Grigor of Akants, History of the Nation of the Archers (the Mongols). *HJAS* 12, 1949.

Atiya, A. S., *The Crusade of the Later Middle Ages.* London 1938.

Boyle, J. A., *The Cambridge History of Iran*, vol. 5.: *The Saljuq and Mongol Periods.* Cambridge 1968.

CHP — *The Cambridge History of Iran* — See Boyle

Chiprois — see *RHC*

Crusades (Setton) — *A History of the Crusades*, ed. K. M. Setton. The University of Wisconsin Press. vol. II (1962) and III.

Der-Nersessian, S., The Kingdom of Cilician Armenia In: *Crusades*, vol. II. chap. XVIII.

Grousset, R., *Histoire des Croisades*, III. vol. Paris 1936.

Grousset, R., *The Empire of the Steppes. A History of Central Asia.* New Brunswick, N. J., 1970.

Haithon — Hayton, La Flor des Estoires de la Terre d'Orient. — Historia Tartarorum. In: *RHC, Doc. arm.* II.

Haython — Schütz, E., Sinor, D., (Transl. by Mickel, E.), *Haython, the Chronicler.* Indiana University (in press).

Hitti, Ph. K., *History of the Arabs.* New York 1977. 10th ed.

HJAS — *Harvard Journal of Asiatic Studies*, 12th vol.: Akantsi; 44th vol.: Smith.

Juvaini — ʿAta-Malik Juvaini, *The History of the World Conqueror.* Transl. by J. A. Boyle. vol. I—II. Manchester Univ. Press 1958.

Kirakos/Fr. — *Deux historiens arméniens, Kirakos de Gantzac, Histoire d'Arménie . . .* St. Petersbourg, 1871.

Kirakos/Russ. — Kirakos Gandsakeci, *Istorija Armenii.* Transl. L. A. Hanlarian. Moscow 1976. *(Pamjatniki Pismennosti Vostoka* LIII).

[66] Atiya, A. S., *The Crusade in the Later Middle Ages.* London 1938. pp. 379—397, 435—62, 463—79.

INDEX

1

2

4

Mahmud: II, 254
Maku region: II, 267
Mamluks, Mamluk forces: XVI, 3, 5, 6, 7, 11, 13, 14, 16, 17, 18, 19, 20, 21
Manghu, khan: XV, 128; see also Möngke
Mangup: XIII, 92, 104
Mans, Rafael du: II, 261
Maragha: XVI, 18
Marand: II, 268
Mariupol: XIII, 81, 88, 94
Markar, Khoja: II, 283
Martelli, nuncio: II, 315
Martiros: XII, 177, 178
Marutha dpir: III, 124
Matthew of Edesse: XV, 117
Maurice, emperor: XIV, 155
Mazanderan: II, 261, 264
Mechitarists of Trieste and Vienna: IX, 307, 309
Mecmua-I Ahbar: IX, 307
Mecopa monastery: VIII, 107
Mediterranean (White) Sea: II, 255
Mekhitar Gosh (Mechitar Gos): I, 140; V, 101
Mekhitarists of Venice: XV, 121
Melanawor, Nikolos: VII, 193
melik (provincial lord): II, 259
Melkisedek, katholicos (Melkisedek Garnetsi): II, 248, 268, 269, 270, 271, 272, 273, 273, 274, 275, 276, 277, 278, 280, 285, 286, 287, 288, 289, 290, 291, 292
Memi, pasha: XII, 140
Mezőkeresztes (Haçova): II, 249
Mezopotamia: II, 249, 257
Mikolajowicz, Simon: II, 303
military expressions, Ottoman Turkish: V,104
Minas: see Tokateci, Minas
mirliva: II, 250
Mkrtič: VIII, 107
Mokk: II, 256
Moldavia (Moldau): II, 258, 291, 316; V, 104, 107, 108, 114, 115; VII, 190; X, 284; XV, 122, 135
Möngke, khan: XVI, 3, 7; see also Manghu
Mongol invasion: II, 315
Movses, katholicos (Movses Vardapet): II, 269, 272, 273, 274, 278, 286, 287, 288, 291, 292, 293; XII, 143 (Ter Movses Qrïmeci)
Muaviya: XIV, 160, 162

Mughal: VII, 198
Mughal özen: VII, 198, 199; XV, 130
Mughân steppe: XV, 128
muqata, tax: II, 273
Murad IV, sultan: II, 275
Murat (Murad), sultan: XII, 143, 153, 155, 172
Muš (Much): IX, 311, 324
Mustafa, sultan: XII, 140, 142, 143, 163; XIII, 84

Nader, Codex illuminator: VII, 200
Nakhichevan: II, 259, 261, 272, 279, 280
Nerses, katholicos: XIV, 160
Nerses, Priester: VII, 187
Nesvita Chronicle: II, 256; XV, 125, 126, 127, 129, 130, 132
Neswiater Chronik von Kaffa: VII, 185, 187, 194, 195, 198, 199
New Julfa: II, 260, 262, 263, 264, 270, 280, 282, 283, 284
New-Julfan Armenian colony: II, 269
Nicholas, archbishop: see Torosowicz, Nikol
Nikol: see Torosowicz, Nikol
Nikoleanc, Oxentios: V, 106
Nogai (Noghai): X, 261; XIII, 89, 91; XV, 126; XVI, 9
Noghaier: VII, 195
Northern Mesopotamia (Asorestan): II, 256
Novo-Rossia: XV, 135
Nur ed-Din, sultan: XII, 152
Nuwairi: X, 261, 262
nvirak (legate): II, 268

obedience (hnazandut'iwn): II, 276
Ögödei regime: XVI, 8
Omar, caliph: XIV, 157
Omayyad dynasty: XIV, 162
Orinberan: XII, 159
Orkapu: XII, 138
Ormanian: II, 270
orthography, Armenian: I, 143, 146, 148, 149, 150
osadey: V, 108
Oshakan: II, 257
Osman, sultan: II, 253
Osman II., sultan: X, 263, 264; XII, 142, 163, 166; XIII, 84

8

12

www.ingramcontent.com/pod-product-compliance
Lightning Source LLC
Chambersburg PA
CBHW021544260326

41914CB00001B/164